THE ENCYCLOPEDIA
of the
DEMOCRATIC PARTY

Volume Four

Edited by

GEORGE THOMAS KURIAN

JEFFREY D. SCHULTZ
Associate Editor

Sharpe Reference

An imprint of M.E. Sharpe, INC.

CONTENTS

Volume 4

Bill Clinton at the Democratic National Convention, New York, 1992. *Source:* Associated Press.

CONVENTIONS

— 1832 —

The Democratic Party held its first Presidential Nominating Convention in May 1832 in Baltimore. The decision to hold a national convention grew out of a call from New Hampshire Jacksonian Democrats. These individuals viewed the convention as a forum in which to concentrate the opinions of the people, not as a method to supplant the people's choices for president and vice president.

The convention's first order of business was to establish voting mechanisms. Each state was given a number of delegates equal to its electoral votes. This method of voting was used in all future Democratic Conventions until 1940, when Democratic voting strength was taken into consideration. One member of each delegation was responsible for reporting the state's votes. In order to receive the nomination, a candidate had to garner two-thirds of the votes. This two-thirds majority was changed in 1936 to a simple majority.

Andrew Jackson and his selection for vice presidential candidate, Martin Van Buren, had no difficulty in being chosen by the delegates on the first ballot. Rather than draft a national platform, state delegations were instructed to go home and develop one specific to their state's needs.

— 1836 —

The second Democratic Presidential Nominating Convention met in Baltimore in May 1835. President Andrew Jackson chose this early date to help ensure the selection of Martin Van Buren, his personal choice for the nomination. The convention, while easily selecting Van Buren, had several voting and seating issues to resolve.

The two-thirds-majority rule that had been established at the first convention was initially overturned on a vote of delegates (231–210); however, the move failed on a voice vote. In addition, the question was raised whether "two-thirds" meant two-thirds of those present or two-thirds of all possible delegates. With Alabama, Illinois and South Carolina unrepresented because they had not sent delegations, the decision was that the two-thirds rule applied only to those delegates in attendance.

In addition to the voting problems, issues of both over- and underrepresentation were raised. On the one extreme, Maryland's delegation ballooned to 188 delegates to cast its 10 votes. On the other extreme, Tennessee's 15 votes were all wielded by one businessman. Perhaps most disturbing was the arrival of two Pennsylvania delegations. Unable to determine which delegation to seat, the other delegates seated both groups and had them share the state's votes.

Martin Van Buren won the presidential nomination unanimously. Richard M. Johnson of Kentucky received the two-thirds votes necessary on the first vice presidential ballot, despite concerns over his personal life. The alleged slayer of Tecumseh, Johnson had once lived with a mulatto mistress, by whom he had two daughters.

Once again the convention dispersed without writing a national platform, although an address was published in the party's newspaper, the *Washington Globe*.

— 1840 —

For the third consecutive time, the Democrats held their convention in Baltimore, in May 1840. Martin Van Buren was easily nominated by acclamation as the party's standard-bearer. However, the convention appointed a committee to recommend individuals for the post of vice president in order to avoid a bitter floor fight. The personal life of Richard M. Johnson continued to be a source of embarrassment for the party. In the end, the special committee decided that each state would choose the vice presidential candidate to appear on its ballot.

For the first time in American history, a platform defining the national goals of the party was written. The document, though shorter than 1,000 words, clearly identified the party's belief in strict construction of the Constitution and states' rights.

— 1844 —

As delegates from every state except South Carolina—though several prominent South Carolina political leaders were in attendance—convened in Baltimore in May 1844, President Martin Van Buren's chance for renomination began to fade, in large part because of his statement against the annexation of Texas, given on the eve of the convention. Though he received a simple majority on the first ballot, on succeeding ballots Lewis Cass of Michigan gained votes and eventually surpassed Van Buren. The convention was deadlocked, as neither candidate could muster the two-thirds majority necessary to win the nomination.

On the ninth ballot a dark-horse, compromise candidate, James K. Polk, was selected. Polk was the former speaker of the House and governor of Tennessee. Senator Silas Wright of New York, a friend of Van Buren, was unanimously nominated for the vice presidency on the first ballot. However, Wright telegraphed the convention to decline the post. George M. Dallas of Pennsylvania was selected on the third ballot to be Polk's running mate.

As a precursor to a formal national committee, the convention appointed a central committee to run the nationwide party organization. Unlike the 1840 convention, the 1844 convention did not write a formal party platform but did appoint a committee to draft resolutions. The resolutions mirrored many of the themes of 1840 with several additional ones, the most important being the recommendation to annex both Oregon and Texas.

— 1848 —

In May 1848 delegates gathered in Baltimore for the fifth consecutive time. Every state sent a delegation. New York, in fact, sent two, representing the two major factions of the state's party. The more conservative wing, known as the Hunkers, and the more liberal wing, labeled the Barnburners, were both seated by the convention and instructed to split the votes between the two delegations. This arrangement did not satisfy either faction. The Barnburners left the convention, and the Hunkers refused to participate.

Senator Lewis Cass of Michigan was the front-runner for the nomination. Although a northerner, his stance on the issue of slavery—that the inhabitants of the territories should determine whether their territory would be slave or free—was acceptable to southern delegates. On the fourth ballot, Cass received the two-thirds vote necessary for the nomination. Two-thirds, however, was determined by discounting those votes allotted to New York because of its delegations' refusal to participate. The vice presidential nomination went to General William O. Butler of Kentucky on the second ballot.

For the first time, convention delegates formed a national committee, comprised of one member from each state, that would handle party affairs until the next convention.

The party's platform continued to stress the theme of a limited federal government. In addition, the convention adopted a plank stating that Congress did not have the power to interfere with slavery in the states.

— 1852 —

As the Democratic Convention delegates gathered in Baltimore in June 1852, the growing controversy over slavery was the central concern of all those in attendance. For the first time, the delegates were called to order by their national chair, Benjamin F. Hallet of Massachusetts. In his first official act, he limited each state's delegation to the number of electoral votes the state held. Excess delegates were permitted to stay but had to move to the rear of the convention hall.

With the two-thirds rule in place, the delegates began the arduous task of selecting a nominee. There were four major contenders: Senator Lewis Cass of Michigan, the party's standard-bearer in 1848, Senator James Buchanan of Pennsylvania, Senator William L. Marcy of New York, and the young rising senator from Illinois, Stephen A. Douglas. At various points throughout the balloting, each of these men led; however, none was able to muster the two-thirds majority necessary to capture the nomination.

Amid a growing deadlock, the Virginia delegation entered a new name, Franklin Pierce of New Hampshire, on the 35th ballot. Pierce had served in both houses of Congress but was relatively unknown and not identified with any party faction. Pierce received 15 votes on that 35th ballot but gradually gained strength as the compromise candidate. On the 49th ballot, Pierce was nominated with 279 of the 288 votes cast.

With the presidential nomination set, attention turned to the number-two position. The Maine delegation suggested that a southerner, Senator William R. King of Alabama, be nominated. On the second ballot, King was nominated by a roll call, receiving 277 of the 288 votes cast.

The party platform continued with many of the same nine resolutions that had been part of earlier platforms. The most significant addition was a plank supporting the Compromise of 1850.

— 1856 —

Delegates from all 31 states gathered in Cincinnati, Ohio, in June 1856, for the Democratic Party's seventh convention—the first one held outside of Baltimore. Once again, New York had two contending delegations. The convention voted to seat both of them and divide the votes between them.

The three main contenders for the nomination were President Franklin Pierce of New Hampshire, James Buchanan of Pennsylvania, and Stephen A. Douglas of Illinois. On the first ballot, Buchanan led, with Pierce a close second. However, as the balloting continued, Pierce lost ground to both Buchanan and Douglas. After the 16th roll call, Douglas withdrew from consideration. This move enabled the delegates to select the former ambassador to Great Britain, James Buchanan, unanimously on the 17th ballot.

Votes for 11 different candidates for vice president were cast on the first ballot. However, the New England delegations quickly united behind Representative John C. Breckinridge of Kentucky, resulting in his nearly unanimous selection as the vice presidential nominee.

The party platform was divided into two sections. The first section dealt with domestic issues, the chief one being slavery. The party adopted the stance that slavery was not to be interfered with by Congress in the states and territories or in the District of Columbia. The second section, on foreign affairs, was dramatically nationalistic and expansionist.

— 1860 —

The Democratic Convention that assembled in Charleston, South Carolina, in April 1860 was one of the most contentious conventions in American history. Threatening the division of the party, the issue of slavery had grown in the years since the last convention to become the most important political question of the day.

Democratic National Convention in Cincinnati, Ohio, June 14, 1856. *Source:* Library of Congress.

From the outset, a bitter dispute between the northern and southern delegates arose over the wording of the party's slavery plank. Two reports on the issue were submitted to the convention, both calling for the reaffirmation of the 1856 party plank. The majority report—the one backed by the South—favored adding that no government could interfere with slavery in the territories. The minority report, taking a more moderate approach, favored letting the issue be settled by the Supreme Court. After intense debate, both reports were recommitted to the platform committee. The new reports by the committee varied little from the original ones. A motion by Benjamin F. Butler of Massachusetts to endorse only the original language of the 1856 platform was defeated. In a sectional vote, the minority plank was adopted by a vote of 165 to 138.

Angered by the slavery plank, 45 delegates from nine states left the convention. The chair of the convention, Caleb Cushing of Massachusetts, breaking with precedent, decided to require two-thirds of the total votes instead of the votes of two-thirds of those present. This rule made it almost impossible for any candidate to achieve the required votes.

Despite his large lead over his closest competitor, Stephen A. Douglas of Illinois was unable to garner the two-thirds majority necessary to secure the nomination. In addition, his support from southern Democrats diminished because of his continued support of popular sovereignty. After three days and 57 presidential ballots, the delegates voted to recess for six weeks and reconvene in Baltimore. This vote marked the first and only time in American history that a major party adjourned a convention and moved it to another city.

When the convention regrouped in Baltimore in June, the first issue that had to be settled was whether to seat the delegates who had bolted from the Charleston convention. Once again, two reports were sent to the convention. The majority report recommended that all delegates be seated except those from Alabama and Louisiana. The minority report recommended that a larger portion be seated. The minority report was defeated on the first ballot. Continued haggling, however, led to another walkout. This time, the majority of delegates from Virginia, North Carolina, Tennessee, Maryland, Kentucky, Missouri, Arkansas, California, and Oregon, as well as the anti-Douglas Massachusetts delegates, bolted. This walkout left fewer than two-thirds of the total number of delegates present.

Douglas continued to hold his large lead in the presidential balloting, but it was impossible for him to win the necessary two-thirds majority. On a voice vote, the delegates moved on the second ballot to declare

Douglas the candidate. The selection of the vice presidential candidate was left to the remaining southern delegates, who selected Senator Benjamin Fitzpatrick of Alabama. However, shortly after the convention adjourned, Fitzpatrick declined the nomination. For the first time, the national committee selected the vice presidential nominee, Hershel V. Johnson, the former governor of Georgia.

— 1864 —

As the shattered remnants of the Democratic Party gathered in Chicago in late August 1864, another dispute over the continuation of the war once again threatened to divide the party. Three factions, each with its own views of the war, arose at the convention. The largest group, the Copperheads, favored a quick negotiated peace with the South. The second faction supported the war but was highly critical of President Abraham Lincoln's administration. The third and smallest faction supported Lincoln's prosecution of the war and defected to the Republican Party.

Although deeply divided, the Democratic Party believed that its chances for electoral victory were great because of the protracted war with the South. General George B. McClellan of New Jersey, a Copperhead and former commander of the Union Army, won on the first ballot. Clement Vallandigham, the leader of the Copperheads, moved to have McClellan's nomination made unanimous. Another Copperhead, Representative George H. Pendleton of Ohio, was unanimously selected as the vice presidential candidate after shifts by Illinois, Kentucky and New York created a bandwagon.

The platform adopted by the convention reflected its strong Copperhead influence. It was highly critical of the Lincoln administration and its use of martial law. The party called for an immediate end to hostilities and a negotiated peace.

— 1868 —

The reunited Democratic Party convened for its first postwar convention on July 4, 1868, in New York City's Tammany Hall. The chair of the national committee opened the convention with harsh criticism of the Republican Party's Reconstruction plans.

The decision was made to maintain the two-thirds-majority-of-all-votes rule that had been adopted in Charleston in 1860. While the party's 1864 vice presidential candidate, George H. Pendleton, led the balloting in the early stages, his peak of $156\frac{1}{2}$ votes on the

View of the Tent in Which the Democratic National Convention of 1864 Was Held, Chicago, Illinois. *Source:* Library of Congress.

The Democratic National Convention. The Delegates Assembled in the Grand Hall of the Tammany Building Cheering on the Name of George H. Pendleton, 1868. *Source:* Library of Congress.

eighth ballot was well short of the 212 needed to secure the nomination. President Andrew Johnson received modest support from the delegates.

After the collapse of the Pendleton tide, a movement began for General Winfield Scott Hancock of Pennsylvania. As Hancock gained in strength, delegates opposed to him moved for adjournment after the 16th ballot. While the measure was defeated, Hancock was only able to garner $144\frac{1}{2}$ votes on the 18th ballot.

Senator Thomas A. Hendricks of Indiana became the new front-runner until, on the 22nd ballot, the Ohio delegation cast all of its votes for the permanent chair of the convention, Horatio Seymour, former governor of New York. While Seymour discouraged the growing movement for his candidacy, he was unanimously selected to be the party's standard-bearer.

General Francis P. Blair Jr. of Missouri, a former Republican, was unanimously selected as the vice presidential nominee on the first ballot.

The party's platform was adopted without debate by a voice vote. Its major planks declared that the issues of slavery and secession had been settled by the Civil War, that the radical Republican plan of

Reconstruction was too severe and that President Johnson had been unfairly treated. For the first time, the issue of money was addressed in the platform, with the Democrats favoring the inflationary plan of printing more greenbacks.

— 1872 —

The Democratic Convention of July 1872 showed the underlying weakness in the post–Civil War party. In a Baltimore convention that lasted only six hours, the Democrats endorsed the candidates selected a month earlier by the newly formed Liberal Republicans. On the first vote, Horace Greeley, editor of the *New York Tribune* and frequent critic of the Democratic Party, was selected by 686 of the 732 delegates. The Liberal Republican vice presidential nominee, B. Gratz Brown, governor of Missouri, garnered 713 votes. With only one hour of debate, the party adopted the platform drafted by the Liberal Republicans, which called for amnesty for southerners, the end of Reconstruction, and civil service reform. It also advo-

The Democratic National Convention in Session at Ford's Opera House, Baltimore, Maryland, July 20, 1872. *Source:* Library of Congress.

The Democratic National Convention, Exchange Hall, St. Louis, Missouri, June 1876. *Source:* Library of Congress.

cated a hard-money policy, a reversal of the 1868 party platform.

— 1876 —

Recognizing the growing importance of the West, the Democratic Party held its convention in St. Louis, Missouri, in late June 1876. The issue of the two-thirds-majority rule was once again revisited, with the proposal that it be abolished in the 1880 convention.

The two leading candidates for the nomination were both governors, Samuel J. Tilden of New York and Thomas A. Hendricks of Indiana. Tilden's most substantial opposition was from the New York delegation's Tammany faction, which disliked Tilden's reforming activities aimed at limiting the influence of the Tammany machine. Tilden, however, had little difficulty in securing the nomination on the second ballot, and Hendricks was the nearly unanimous choice for vice president.

At the heart of the Democratic platform, which took on the unusual format of written paragraphs rather than numbered planks, was the theme of reform. Many of the paragraphs opened with the language

"Reform is necessary . . ." Chief among the party's targets for reform were civil service, immigration and tariff levels.

— 1880 —

The Democratic Party met in Cincinnati, Ohio, in June 1880 for its 13th nominating convention. At the outset, there was a controversy, as New York had two competing delegations. The one led by the powerful Tammany Hall machine sought to capture 20 of New York's 70 votes. However, the convention voted not to seat any of the machine's delegates.

Despite Samuel J. Tilden's indecision over notifying his supporters that he did not wish to seek renomination, several other candidates moved into the spotlight. General Winfield Scott Hancock of Pennsylvania, as well as Senator Thomas F. Bayard of Delaware and Representative Henry G. Payne of Ohio were the leading candidates.

After Tilden made clear his decision not to run, the Tilden forces voted for House Speaker Samuel J. Randall of Pennsylvania. Nevertheless, the convention delegates began to rally around Hancock, and by the

The Democratic National Convention, June 23, 1880. The Break for Hancock. *Source:* Library of Congress.

end of the second ballot he captured 705 of the 738 votes. The vice presidential nomination went to William H. English, former representative from Indiana, the only candidate for the position.

The party platform was accepted without debate or opposition. Its planks continued the themes that were central to the 1876 platform, though the style consisted of short, sharp phrases rather than the more flowery language of its immediate predecessor. Of particular note, the platform attacked the results of the 1876 election as a great fraud on the American people. The election of 1876 was determined by a special committee in Congress that ruled the disputed election returns in favor of Republican candidate Rutherford B. Hayes. Hayes won the electoral college count 185 to 184, even though Tilden won the popular vote. The Democrats conceded the election results but gained the end of Reconstruction in the process.

— 1884 —

The July 1884 Democratic Convention in Chicago marked the first time that territories and the District of Columbia were permitted to send voting delegates.

The initial activity of the convention focused on procedural matters. The Tammany Hall faction of the New York delegation unsuccessfully sought the repeal of the unit rule, which dictated that the entire New York delegation had to vote together. As in previous conventions, the two-thirds rule came under pressure, although the roll call on its repeal was suspended when it became apparent that the rule would remain in effect.

New York Governor Grover Cleveland was the front-runner for the nomination from the first ballot. However, Senator Thomas A. Hendricks of Indiana, who had placed former Senator Joseph E. McDonald's name on the initial ballot, became a strong contender on the second ballot. The New York governor secured the nomination when the North Carolina delegation switched its votes to him.

Hendricks was chosen as the vice presidential nominee, though his delegation from Indiana was upset that he had not been selected for the top spot.

The party's platform was one of the longest produced during the nineteenth century. Nearly one-third of its 3,000 words were devoted to attacks on the Republican Party's rule. The increasingly important issue of the tariff was addressed by a plank supporting it for both revenue and protectionist purposes.

— 1888 —

The Democratic Convention met in St. Louis, Missouri, in June 1888. For the first time since the Civil War, the party was in control of the White House. While the renomination of Grover Cleveland was not contested, the number-two spot was vacant because of the death of Vice President Thomas A. Hendricks in 1885. When former Ohio Senator Allen G. Thurman easily won the nomination on the first ballot, red bandannas were hung up all around the hall, a Thurman political symbol tied to his public snuff habit.

The party platform in 1888 was essentially the same document produced in 1884. Instead of attacking the Republicans, however, it praised the enlightened policies of President Cleveland and the Democrats.

— 1892 —

While the stormy Chicago weather of June 1892 frequently interrupted the proceedings of the Democratic Convention, as rain came through the roof, the Tammany Hall machine orchestrated a storm of an-other type by trying to sabotage the renomination of Grover Cleveland in favor of David B. Hill, the current governor of New York.

Despite not having the support of his home state's delegation, Cleveland easily garnered enough votes to win the nomination. The contest then shifted to the vice presidential nomination, for which four men contended. After a series of switched votes at the end of the initial roll call, Adlai E. Stevenson of Illinois, former representative and assistant postmaster in the first Cleveland administration, was selected.

The central platform issue of 1892 was the tariff. The platform's original noncommittal phrasing on this issue was easily replaced by an amendment from the floor urging the tariff's use only for revenue purposes. In addition to the tariff issue, the party supported the equal coinage of gold and silver and the construction of a canal in Nicaragua.

— 1896 —

When the Democrats convened in Chicago in July 1896, the political landscape was dominated by one issue, currency. The party was split into its eastern dele-

The Democratic National Convention in Chicago. View of the Exposition Hall Interior During a Session of the Convention, 1884. *Source:* Library of Congress.

The Democratic National Convention, St. Louis, Missouri, 1888. Interior View of the Convention Hall, Exposition Building. *Source:* Library of Congress.

The Democratic National Convention, Chicago, 1896. Delegates Crowding Their Way into the Hall. *Source:* Library of Congress.

gations, which favored the hard-money policies of the gold standard, and the southern and western delegations, which favored soft money and the unlimited coinage of silver.

The prosilver delegates scored their first victory when they defeated the election of David B. Hill, governor of New York, as temporary chair, substituting Senator John W. Daniel of Virginia. Two additional prosilver developments dramatically shaped the convention. The first was the seating of the Nebraska delegation, whose leader was the ardently prosilver William Jennings Bryan. The second was the successful fight not to seat the hard-money Michigan delegates.

While the gold forces declined to offer a candidate for the presidency, the silver forces were slow to unite behind one candidate. Fourteen different individuals received votes on the first ballot. The leading figure, Representative Richard P. "Silver Dick" Bland of Missouri, and the electrifying young Nebraskan, Bryan, whose "Cross of Gold" speech catapulted him into contention, were the two front-runners. The Bryan movement continued to pick up support until the fifth ballot, when Bryan received enough votes to win the nomination. While Bryan had garnered almost all of the 768 silver votes, none of the 162 gold delegates participated in the balloting.

A tight race for the vice presidential nomination ensued as Bryan did not indicate a preference. The vote went to Maine shipbuilder Arthur Sewell on the fifth ballot.

The party platform's major plank advocated the unlimited coinage of silver. While the gold forces tried to delay the proposal by linking it to an international silver agreement, the well-orchestrated silver forces carried the day, with a plank supporting the immediate coining of silver at a 16-to-1 ratio.

— 1900 —

The Democratic Convention that gathered on July 4, 1900, in Kansas City, Missouri, showed renewed party unity, as the issue of currency had subsided in the years since the preceding convention. David B. Hill, the New York governor who had been prevented from being elected the temporary chair four years earlier by the silver forces, gave the seconding speech on behalf of the party's unanimous choice as standard-bearer, William Jennings Bryan.

The selection of a vice presidential candidate took only one ballot and several vote switches. Adlai E. Stevenson of Illinois, vice president under Grover Cleveland, was the unanimous choice.

The party platform was adopted without debate. It stressed a growing anti-imperialist sentiment. The Democrats criticized the McKinley administration's expansionist policies in the Spanish-American War. In addition, the Democrats attacked the formation of monopolies, calling for a comprehensive antitrust legislative agenda. The party also included a call for the unlimited coinage of silver, in order to prevent the withdrawal of Bryan as the party's nominee.

— 1904 —

While not a candidate for the presidency at the July 1904 Democratic Convention in St. Louis, Missouri, William Jennings Bryan played several important roles, leading the unsuccessful debate to seat a pro-Bryan delegation from Illinois and seconding the nomination of Senator Francis M. Cockrell of Missouri as a candidate for president. Cockrell was one of eight candidates and was a distant third after the first roll call.

The leading candidates for the position were Alton B. Parker, chief justice of the New York Court of Appeals, and Representative William Randolph Hearst. Despite Hearst's progressive record, Bryan did not support him for fear of losing control of the progressive wing of the party. As a result, the more conservative Parker was nominated.

Parker, after hearing of his nomination, sent a telegram to the convention announcing his support for the gold standard and indicating that the party should select a new candidate if it did not like his position. Supporters believed that currency was not an issue, and it was not mentioned in the party platform. A sick Bryan rose from his bed to lead the opposition on the floor. In the end, the convention delegates voted 794–191 with the Parker supporters.

The delegation then chose Senator Henry G. Davis of West Virginia as the vice presidential nominee. Davis, at the age of eighty, was the oldest candidate ever nominated by a convention. The delegates hoped that he would use his vast personal wealth to subsidize the campaign.

The 1904 Democratic Party platform was adopted without debate by a voice vote. It touched upon nearly two dozen topics with almost equal emphasis. The themes of anti-imperialism and antimonopoly continued, and there was an increased emphasis on domestic issues.

— 1908 —

The Democratic Convention in Denver, Colorado, in July 1908 was the first to be held in a western state. From the outset, the convention was dominated by William Jennings Bryan and his forces. A credentials dispute in the Pennsylvania delegation led to the seating of a pro-Bryan delegation because of alleged voting irregularities in five Philadelphia districts.

Bryan's nomination was little more than a formality. He received nearly 90% of the votes on the first ballot. The choice of a vice presidential candidate was left to the delegates, who chose former Indiana gubernatorial candidate John W. Kern.

The first part of the Democratic platform condemned the link between Republican forces and big business, especially large campaign contributions. In addition, the platform adopted most of the minority platforms that had been rejected at the Republican convention three weeks earlier, including the creation of the Department of Labor, the direct election of senators, and the eight-hour workday for government employees. To these planks were added ones supporting an income tax, lower tariffs, and increased power for the Interstate Commerce Commission.

— 1912 —

In June 1912, the Democrats returned to Baltimore, for the first time since 1872. The tensions between the conservative elements of the party and the more progressive ones continued to shape the convention activities. William Jennings Bryan—the party's candidate in 1896, 1900 and 1908—opposed the nomination of the more conservative Alton B. Parker, the party's standard-bearer in 1904, as temporary chair. Instead, Bryan nominated his running mate in the 1908 election, John W. Kern of Indiana. Kern declined the post, hoping to encourage Parker to do the same. When Parker refused, Kern nominated Bryan. The resulting roll-call vote found the conservative forces to be in the majority.

The selection of Parker as chair led to tens of thousands of telegrams' being sent to Baltimore in support of Bryan. These telegrams undoubtedly influenced the final selection of a candidate. The two leading candidates were House Speaker Champ Clark of Missouri and the more progressive governor of New Jersey, Woodrow Wilson.

The Wilson forces scored two early and important victories. The first was the abolishment of the Ohio delegation's unit rule. The unit rule eliminated the state

Democratic National Convention Hall (*interior*), 1908. *Source:* National Archives.

convention's binding instructions, which required all delegates, even those elected to support Wilson, to vote for favorite son candidate Governor Judson Harmon. The second was the convention's seating of a pro-Wilson delegation from South Dakota, contrary to the credentials committee recommendation.

After nine ballots, the convention saw little movement in the selection process. Wilson maintained a lead over Clark, though not the two-thirds majority needed. On the tenth ballot, New York shifted its votes to Clark, putting the Speaker in the lead. However, this tenth ballot would mark the peak for Clark's support. During the 14th ballot, Bryan addressed the delegates, urging them not to be controlled by the Tammany delegation. His Nebraska delegation shifted its votes to Wilson. The slow trend toward Wilson continued. After 42 ballots, the convention adjourned for the night.

The next day, on the 48th ballot, Representative Oscar W. Underwood of Alabama and the former front-runner, Clark, withdrew from the race. Wilson's defeat of Clark marked the first time since 1844 that a candidate who initially had a simple majority did not receive the two-thirds majority.

While Wilson preferred Underwood as his running mate, the Alabama representative did not want the post. Instead, the nomination went to Governor Thomas R. Marshall of Indiana.

The party's platform was accepted without debate. Most of the planks were similar to those passed by the 1908 convention.

— 1916 —

The Democrats' choice for presidential candidate as they convened in June 1916 in St. Louis, Missouri, was clear. President Woodrow Wilson was renominated by a vote of 1,092 to 1. A delegate from Illinois voted against Wilson, not because he did not wish to see the president run again, but because he objected to a motion to renominate by acclamation. Wilson's vice president, Thomas R. Marshall, was renominated by acclamation.

The most important issue of the day was war. Europe was embroiled in yet another conflict that the party wanted to avoid. William Jennings Bryan, who was defeated in his attempt to be seated as a delegate from Nebraska, was nevertheless invited to address the convention. The theme of his speech was that America must stay out of the war in Europe. The overwhelming antiwar sentiment of the convention concerned Wilson, who instead chose to stress national unity.

A mild platform debate occurred over the wording of Wilson's national unity plank, which some dele-

gates believed would offend German Americans. The platform also contained a plank on woman suffrage. The convention adopted the position that the vote should be extended to all women rather than leaving the decision to the individual states. The rest of the platform reflected many of the progressive themes that had shaped the Wilson administration and the 1912 platform, with two notable exceptions. Gone were the planks advocating a single-term presidency and defending states' rights.

— 1920 —

As the Democratic Convention opened in June 1920 in San Francisco, there was no recognized leader of the Democratic Party. President Woodrow Wilson's health and sinking popularity made a third term unlikely. However, he did not endorse any other candidate.

On the first roll call, 24 different men received votes. Though none of the candidates had received even a simple majority, the race was clearly among three candidates. William Gibbs McAdoo, Wilson's son-in-law and former treasury secretary, led after the first roll call with 266 votes. McAdoo had withdrawn from the race several days earlier, but his supporters were undeterred. Attorney General A. Mitchell Palmer, famous for his role in the "Red scare," was in second place with 254 votes. In third place was Governor James M. Cox of Ohio. On the second and last ballot of the evening, the candidates remained in the same positions with relatively the same number of votes.

On the second day of balloting, Cox started to gain on his two chief rivals. Supporters of McAdoo and Palmer successfully called for a recess after the 16th ballot. However, by that time, Cox had gained a substantial lead over the other two candidates. After the recess, Cox's lead narrowed but was not overcome.

On the third day of balloting, McAdoo was able to surpass Cox on the 30th ballot. McAdoo's lead was three votes, but he was still well short of the required two-thirds vote. A motion to remove the losing candidate on each successive vote was defeated. A long, drawn-out battle for the nomination continued until the 39th ballot, when the Indiana delegation switched from McAdoo to Cox. However, it was not until the 44th ballot that victory for the Cox forces was clear. After the balloting in that roll call, the convention adopted a motion to declare Governor James M. Cox the unanimous nominee.

Cox's handpicked vice presidential candidate, the 38-year-old governor of New York, Franklin Delano Roosevelt, was nominated by acclamation.

The party platform's main function was to praise the Wilson administration's accomplishments. The document did support the United States' entry into the League of Nations, and it was sympathetic to the Irish struggle for independence without recognizing an independent Ireland.

— 1924 —

The 1924 Democratic National Convention, which assembled on June 24 in New York City's Madison Square Garden, was the longest convention in American political history. When the convention ended on July 17, a record 103 ballots for the presidential nominee had been cast.

The two leading candidates for the nomination reflected an intense rural-versus-urban split. The urban forces were led by Alfred E. Smith, governor of New York. Smith, of Irish ancestry, was a Roman Catholic and an ardent opponent of Prohibition and the Ku Klux Klan. On the other side, William Gibbs McAdoo of California, leader of the rural forces, was a Protestant, a strong proponent of Prohibition and tolerant of the Klan. With these striking contrasts as well as the two-thirds rule in effect, it is little wonder that deadlock marked this convention.

During the 38th ballot, William Jennings Bryan, a delegate from Florida, was given permission to address the convention on his opposition to Smith. The venerable Democrat was harshly booed by the urban forces.

After the 66th ballot, a number of proposals to end the deadlock were considered. The first recommendation was that the convention meet in executive session and listen to each of the candidates; the second was to invite Smith alone to address the convention. Both of these measures fell short of the necessary two-thirds majority.

After the 73rd ballot, it was recommended that the lowest vote getter be dropped. This measure went down to defeat, $589\frac{1}{2}$ to 496. The most drastic proposal was heard and defeated after the 75th ballot. The motion would have adjourned the convention for two weeks to be reconvened in Kansas City, Missouri.

When voting resumed after a weekend recess, delegates voted to release themselves from their commitments. After the 93rd ballot, Franklin Delano Roosevelt announced that Smith would pull out of the race if McAdoo would do the same. McAdoo refused. However, after the 99th ballot, he released his delegates as he knew victory was beyond reach.

With McAdoo's delegates freed, John W. Davis of New York gained in strength. Smith's delegates shifted

Democratic National Convention, June 1924. Ohio Delegation Cheering on Cox. *Source:* National Archives.

to Alabama's Senator Oscar W. Underwood. However, after the 103rd ballot, Davis's lead was dramatic, though not yet near two-thirds. Before the 104th roll-call vote could be taken, Iowa switched its votes to Davis, causing other delegations to do the same. After nine days of balloting, the Democrats had finally selected a candidate.

While Tennessee labor leader George L. Berry led on the first ballot for vice president, the nomination went to Governor Charles W. Bryan of Nebraska, the younger brother of William Jennings Bryan.

The heated and drawn-out selection of the presidential nominee was also reflected in the work of the platform committee. The 1924 platform supported entry into the League of Nations based upon a popular national referendum. The platform included a plank that was intended to secure religious liberty for all groups. While the plank adopted did not specifically condemn the actions of the Ku Klux Klan, the defeated minority plank had. The Democrats once again praised the Wilson administration and criticized the corruption of the Republicans. A states' rights plank missing from the platforms of 1916 and 1920 was returned. However, this must be contrasted with the platform's call for increased regulation of business and campaigns.

— 1928 —

As the Democratic delegates convened in Houston in June 1928, they wanted to avoid another fiasco like the 1924 convention. Governor Alfred E. Smith, leader of the urban forces at the 1924 convention, was the party's front-runner. William Gibbs McAdoo, leader of the rural forces in New York in 1924, was not a candidate for the nomination as he feared his participation would lead to another deadlocked convention that would destroy party unity.

For the first time, a nonpolitician, Claude G. Bowers of Indiana, a historian and editorial writer for the *New York World*, was selected to serve as temporary chair of the convention.

Franklin Delano Roosevelt rose once again to place the name of Smith, whom he had dubbed the Happy Warrior in the previous convention, into nomination. On the initial roll call, Smith was ten votes shy of the two-thirds necessary to be the nominee. The Ohio delegation switched 44 of its votes to put Smith over the top.

There was little opposition to the nomination of Senate Minority Leader Joseph T. Robinson of Arkansas as the vice presidential candidate. Robinson, a "dry" Protestant, was the first southerner nominated by either party since the Civil War.

Some delegates were disappointed in the party's nominee over the issue of Prohibition. The party platform called for the enforcement of the 18th Amendment, while the nominee thought the policy should be changed. Agriculture was another issue of great importance. The Democrats favored a system of loans for cooperatives and the creation of a federal farm board while opposing farmer subsidies. Once again, the Democratic platform specifically mentioned states' rights, especially in the area of education, as an important distinction between the Democrats and the Republicans.

— 1932 —

As the Democratic delegates assembled in Chicago in June 1932, they knew that the Great Depression gave them their best chance of regaining the White House in more than two decades.

The two leading candidates for the nomination were Governor Franklin Delano Roosevelt of New York and the man he had three times nominated, Alfred E. Smith, former governor of New York.

Several prenomination roll calls indicated that Roosevelt's forces would prevail at the convention. In two credentials disputes, the pro-Roosevelt delegates were seated. The first involved the delegation from Louisiana, headed by Senator Huey P. Long. The second involved the delegation from Minnesota. In addition to these credentials victories, Roosevelt delegates succeeded in having their preferred permanent chair, Senator Thomas J. Walsh of Montana, appointed.

After an all-night session of roll calls, the delegates adjourned at 9:15 A.M. after the third ballot, with Roosevelt well in the lead but short of the two-thirds majority necessary to secure the nomination.

When the delegates reconvened the next evening, William Gibbs McAdoo of California announced his delegation's support for Roosevelt. Other states soon followed, and Roosevelt secured the nomination on the fourth ballot. Breaking with tradition, Roosevelt flew to Chicago to accept the nomination in person, pledging a "New Deal" for the American people.

House Speaker John Nance Garner of Texas was unanimously selected as the vice presidential nominee.

The 1932 Democratic platform was highly critical of Republican policies, which it blamed for the depression. However, the document did not offer many proposals to solve the situation. The party did call for unemployment relief and a balanced budget. The most exciting vote took place when the "dry" forces were defeated and the party called for the repeal of Prohibition.

Democratic National Convention, Chicago, 1940. *Source:* National Archives.

— 1936 —

The Democratic Convention held in Philadelphia in June 1936 did not have a single roll-call vote. The only issue that faced the convention was the elimination of the two-thirds rule, which had been in effect and controversial since the party's first convention in 1832. The rule was repealed, and concessions on delegate allocations were made to southern delegations to ensure their continued strength in future conventions.

President Franklin Delano Roosevelt and Vice President John Nance Garner were renominated by acclamation after an entire day of seconding speeches. Roosevelt, once again, took the stage to accept the nomination and give a rousing speech in which he condemned Republicans as "economic royalists" and spoke of the destiny of the generation.

The 1932 platform continued to call for a balanced budget and the extensive programs of the Roosevelt administration. In addition, the states' rights plank was removed as the Democrats reevaluated the role of the federal government. The platform also called for the United States to remain neutral and avoid being drawn into the growing hostilities in Europe.

— 1940 —

As Democrats convened in Chicago in July 1940, the party faced a dilemma. On the second night of the convention, a message was read from President Franklin Delano Roosevelt stating that he did not wish to seek a third term and that the delegates should choose whomever they saw fit. The delegations, led by a Chicago city official, broke into an hour-long pro-Roosevelt rally.

The next day, Roosevelt easily won the nomination, and the draft-Roosevelt movement achieved its goal on the first ballot. Roosevelt handpicked Agriculture Secretary Henry A. Wallace of Iowa as his preferred running mate. However, conservative forces opposed the former Republican and liberal Wallace. Eleanor Roosevelt appeared at the convention to warn of her husband's withdrawal if Wallace were not accepted. In a heavily divided vote, Wallace was able to obtain a majority and the nomination, though he was asked not to address the convention.

The platform, which was adopted without a roll call, was divided into three major parts. The first detailed American military preparedness and the party's foreign policy. The second addressed the benefits the New Deal had brought to specific segments of the economy. The third section outlined the New Deal's welfare policies.

— 1944 —

Unlike the convention four years earlier, Franklin Delano Roosevelt made it known to the delegates assembled in Chicago in July 1944 that he would accept the nomination for a fourth term. There was little doubt that Roosevelt would win the nomination, though there were other candidates, namely Harry F. Byrd of Virginia, whose supporters were opposed to the New Deal's domestic agenda, and former Postmaster General James A. Farley. Roosevelt accepted the nomination via a radio address from the San Diego Naval Base.

The real choice for delegates was whom to select as the vice presidential nominee. In an uninspiring letter, Roosevelt indicated to the delegates that they should vote for whomever they thought best but that, if he were a delegate, he would vote for Vice President Henry A. Wallace. However, privately Roosevelt was more interested in either Senator Harry S. Truman of Missouri or Supreme Court Justice William O. Douglas as his running mate. The party leadership preferred Truman to the more liberal Douglas. After the first roll call, Wallace led over the senator from Missouri. After the second roll call, in which Truman passed Wallace, Alabama began a bandwagon of switchers to Truman.

The party platform was a short one, only 1,360 words. Much of the verbiage was used to praise Roosevelt's accomplishments and argue for the creation of an international organization with American participation that could ensure peace. In addition, the platform favored the creation of an independent Jewish state in Palestine.

— 1948 —

When the Democrats gathered in Philadelphia in July 1948, their domination of the political landscape looked in jeopardy. The Republicans had regained control of the Congress in 1946, and southern Democrats and conservatives were not enamored with the party.

The southern delegates had two chief complaints. The first reason for their dissatisfaction was that the redistribution of delegates that had been promised to southern delegations in return for the repeal of the two-thirds rule had netted the South a miserly two additional votes for each state that went for Franklin Delano Roosevelt in 1944. The South's second concern was the growing issue of civil rights. Mississippi's delegation members had instructions that they were to bolt the convention if a states' rights plank were not reinserted into the platform. The delegation was also denied power to support any candidate who favored Harry S. Truman's civil rights program. A minority committee report was introduced that recommended the delegation not be seated. The report was defeated on a voice vote.

Texas, in conjunction with several other states, sought unsuccessfully to have the two-thirds rule reinstated. This proposal was also defeated by a voice vote.

During the initial balloting for the presidential nomination, the Mississippi delegation and 13 members of the Alabama delegation left the convention in protest of the party's stance on civil rights. Nevertheless, Truman easily won the balloting on the first roll call.

The convention's keynote speaker, Senator Alben W. Barkley of Kentucky, was nominated by acclamation as the party's vice presidential candidate.

The civil rights plank of the platform was a source of controversy. However, the broadly written statement of the committee was adopted after several more restrictive and more liberal alternatives were defeated. Much of the remainder of the platform praised Truman's leadership in domestic and foreign affairs and criticized the Republican "do-nothing" 80th Congress for its failure to address pressing issues while passing destructive legislation like the Taft–Hartley Act.

— 1952 —

The Democrats convened in Chicago in July 1952 hoping to heal the split experienced in 1948. To that end, no delegation was seated unless it would pledge to have the Democratic national ticket placed on its respective state's ballot under the party's heading. Several southern states had placed the Dixiecrat ticket of Thurmond–Wright on the state ballot under the heading "Democratic Party." Three state delegations—Virginia, Louisiana, and South Carolina—refused to take the pledge, arguing that state law already covered the issue. After much debate and confusion, the three delegations were seated without taking the pledge.

Governor Adlai E. Stevenson of Illinois, the grandson of the Adlai E. Stevenson who was the Democratic nominee for vice president in 1892 and 1900 and who served as vice president from 1893 to 1897,

Democratic National Convention, Chicago, July 1952. Adlai Stevenson Addressing the Delegates. *Source:* National Archives.

was the front-runner for the party's nomination. Stevenson, however, was not interested in the nomination, but a draft-Stevenson movement quickly developed. After the first ballot Senator Estes Kefauver of Tennessee was the leader, but by the third ballot the Illinois governor had the necessary majority to win the nomination.

Senator John H. Sparkman of Alabama was chosen by Stevenson to be his running mate. The delegation confirmed Sparkman by acclamation.

The platform adopted by the 1952 convention was very similar to that of 1948, including the civil rights plank. It was adopted by a voice vote, although Georgia and Mississippi asked to be recorded in opposition.

— 1956 —

The nominating speeches at the Democratic Convention of August 1956 in Chicago featured an all-star cast of nominators. Future president John F. Kennedy rose

to nominate the 1952 standard-bearer, Adlai E. Stevenson. Former President Harry S. Truman, who openly criticized Stevenson, seconded the nomination of W. Averell Harriman, governor of New York. Eleanor Roosevelt addressed the convention in support of Stevenson.

In reality, the issue of who would be the 1956 standard-bearer had been decided much earlier, as Stevenson had defeated his chief rival, Senator Estes Kefauver of Tennessee, in the primaries. On the first ballot, Stevenson easily secured the party's nomination.

Stevenson stunned the convention by not selecting a running mate personally. Instead, the delegates were left to select whomever they wanted. The early leader, Senator Kennedy of Massachusetts, was eventually beaten out by Senator Kefauver when Senator Albert A. Gore of Tennessee withdrew and threw his support to his fellow Tennessean. Kennedy quickly moved to have Kefauver's nomination made unanimous.

The platform was a lengthy document of nearly 12,000 words. It was divided into 11 sections. The first section, dealing with foreign policy and defense, criticized Eisenhower for spending too much money on defense. The remaining ten planks dealt with domestic issues, the chief one being the civil rights plank, which sought to extend the enforcement of Supreme Court decisions in that area as well as the passage of an equal rights amendment. A modest states' rights plank was inserted, which identified education as the primary responsibility of the states.

— 1960 —

As Democrats gathered in Los Angeles in July 1960, the vote-allocation system had been changed by the Democratic National Committee to a population-based system rather than the Democratic-voting-strength method previously used. Once again, the issue of a loyalty pledge was raised. On a voice vote, delegates adopted the 1956 measure that expected delegates to work in the best interests of the party.

Going into the convention, Senator John F. Kennedy of Massachusetts held a commanding lead over his next closest primary rival, Senate Majority Leader Lyndon B. Johnson of Texas. Despite the nomination of nine men, Kennedy was able to secure the simple majority necessary on the first ballot.

In a move that surprised many at the convention, Kennedy chose his chief rival, Johnson, as his running mate. Johnson was nominated by acclamation.

Kennedy's acceptance speech, delivered to a capacity crowd at the Los Angeles Coliseum, emphasized the challenges that lay ahead for the nation "on the edge of a new frontier."

The platform was adopted by voice vote, though the civil rights and government-spending planks were openly debated on the floor. The platform, of approximately 20,000 words, was the longest one written by

Democratic National Convention, Chicago, 1956. A General View of the Convention Floor. Former President Truman (*right*) Is Speaking from His Box in the Spectator Section of the Amphitheater, Urging the Democratic National Committee to Accept the Report of the Platform Committee, Including the Controversial Civil Rights Plank. *Source:* United Press International.

Senator Kennedy at the Los Angeles Coliseum for the 1960 Democratic National Convention. Mrs. Kennedy and Johnson Are Behind Him. *Source:* Wide World.

either party to date. In addition to the civil rights and government-spending planks, the platform contained planks on tax reform, foreign aid, disarmament, immigration and a minimum wage.

— 1964 —

The Democratic Convention that gathered in Atlantic City, New Jersey, in August 1964 was the largest one to date in American political history, with 5,260 delegates and alternates present to cast the 2,316 votes. A new vote-allocation formula based upon population and voter support for the Kennedy–Johnson ticket increased the number of delegates from the 1960 total of 1,521.

A credentials challenge involving Mississippi's two delegations reflected the growing issue of race in

America. The Mississippi Freedom Democratic Party sent an integrated delegation, while the state committee sent an all-white delegation. Senator Hubert H. Humphrey of Minnesota negotiated a settlement that included seating the state committee's delegation on the condition that it support the national ticket. The compromise, which was approved by the convention, was not acceptable to either party. All but four members of the state's regular delegation refused to sign the pledge supporting the national ticket and left the proceedings.

The convention also required the Alabama delegation to sign personal loyalty oaths because the state party had placed unpledged electors on the ballot. Forty-two of the state's 53 delegates and alternates refused to sign and left the convention.

President Lyndon B. Johnson was nominated by ac-

Democratic National Convention, 1964. Johnson and Humphrey in Front. *Source:* Associated Press.

clamation to be the party's standard-bearer. For the first time, a presidential nominee addressed the convention to announce his choice for the vice presidential nominee. Johnson told the convention that he wanted Humphrey. The Minnesota senator was nominated by acclamation.

Attorney General Robert F. Kennedy addressed the convention, introducing a film about the presidency of his late brother.

The party's ever-growing platform was approved by a voice vote. The nearly 22,000-word document attempted to do several things. First, it highlighted the accomplishments of the Kennedy and Johnson administrations. This portion of the document was nearly three-quarters of the entire platform. The remaining portions addressed issues from national defense and peace to civil rights and extremism. Unlike its Republican counterpart, the tone of the document was subdued. This milder tone, the party hoped, would further emphasize the difference between its candidates and the Republicans' staunchly conservative Goldwater–Miller ticket.

— 1968 —

With the area around the Democratic Convention in Chicago looking more like a war zone than a party convention, Democrats gathered from August 26 to 29, 1968, to nominate Vice President Hubert H. Humphrey of Minnesota for the party's top post. In addition, the party used the opportunity to support the Vietnam policies of the Johnson–Humphrey administration.

Nearly 32,000 law enforcement officers, army regulars, Illinois National Guard troops, FBI and Secret Service agents were employed to keep the Vietnam War protesters away from the various sites where party regulars were meeting and staying. While the amphithe-

Democratic National Convention in Chicago, 1968. *Source:* Roger Malloch/Magnum.

ater where the convention was meeting was quiet because of a security ring of barbed wire and armed guards stretching for several blocks, demonstrations were dispersed with the use of tear gas near downtown hotels housing delegates. The police arrested 589 protesters during the convention, and more than 200 police officers and demonstrators were injured.

The convention itself had an unprecedented number of credentials disputes. The majority of the cases involved the issue of racial imbalance in the state's delegation. By a voice vote, the convention voted to seat an integrated Democratic faction from Mississippi in place of the traditionally segregated party regulars. Most of the remainder of the cases were settled by the credentials committee in favor of the regular state delegations. However, three cases went to a roll-call vote.

In the first case, an overwhelming majority voted to seat the Texas regular delegation led by Governor John B. Connally.

The second case involved Georgia. The credentials committee recommended that both delegations be seated and that the vote be divided between them. Minority reports in favor of the Loyal National Democrats, led by state Representative Julian Bond, and of the party regulars, led by Governor Lester G. Maddox, were both defeated. In the end, the credentials committee report was approved by a voice vote.

The third case, involving Alabama, had three factions vying for the state's votes: the party regulars, the largely black National Democratic Party of Alabama, and the integrated Alabama Independent Democratic Party. The credentials committee recommended seating all the regulars who would sign the loyalty pledge, with alternates being drawn from the Alabama Independent Democratic Party. Once again, by a voice vote, the convention approved the committee's plan.

The delegates voted to abolish the unit rule for the convention as well as for all levels of party activity, including the 1972 Presidential Nominating Convention. In addition, the convention adopted the minority report's requirement that delegates to the 1972 convention should be selected publicly and in the same year as the convention.

As the presidential balloting began, the worst violence inside and outside of the convention ensued. Outside, the police were dealing with the worst of the demonstrations. Inside, security guards were physically ejecting party workers of Chicago Mayor Richard J. Daley because they did not have the proper credentials. Convention chair, House Majority Leader Carl Albert of Oklahoma, refused to entertain motions to adjourn the convention and reconvene two weeks hence.

Vice President Humphrey easily secured the presidential nomination on the first ballot, outdistancing Senator Eugene J. McCarthy of Minnesota and Senator George McGovern of South Dakota, both of whom represented the liberal, antiwar factions.

Before the vice presidential balloting began, a filmed tribute to the late Senator Robert F. Kennedy of New York was aired.

Humphrey chose Senator Edmund S. Muskie of Maine to be his running mate. As the first roll-call vote was in progress, Mayor Daley was recognized by the chair. Daley moved that Muskie be nominated by acclamation.

Much of the 18,000-word platform addressed the issue of Vietnam. The platform continued to support strong American involvement in the war but specified conditions for an end to the hostilities. In addition to the war, the Democrats responded to issues ranging from crime to the reform of the electoral college.

— 1972 —

Prior to the July 10–13, 1972, Democratic Convention in Miami Beach, dramatic changes were instituted to organize the party's convention rules, structure, and delegate selection.

To this end, two special commissions were formed. The first was the Commission on Rules, chaired by Representative James O'Hara of Michigan. This commission created the first set of rules to govern convention procedure. Among the proposals that were accepted by the Democratic National Committee were: (1) a new vote-allocation formula based upon electoral college strength and past Democratic voting strength in presidential elections, (2) a ban on floor demonstrations for candidates, (3) a random-order roll call determined by lot rather than the traditional alphabetical roll, (4) a requirement that minority reports be released prior to the convention to allow review, and (5) an equality of representation for men and women on committees and among convention officers.

The second group, the Commission on Party Structure and Delegate Selection, was originally chaired by Senator George McGovern of South Dakota. His replacement, Representative Donald M. Fraser of Minnesota, and the commission made 18 specific recommendations to the national committee. These changes would have to be adopted by all state party committees if their delegates were to be seated at the 1972 convention. Among the changes made by the commission were: (1) the elimination of the unit rule, (2) the limitation that no more than 10% of the delegation could be appointed by the state committee, and (3) the stipulation that the entire delegate selection process had to be done publicly in easily accessible locations in the same calendar year as the convention.

With all the new changes, there were a record 82 credentials challenges. The credentials committee started its work two weeks before the convention opened, as the 82 cases involved nearly 40% of the delegates. The two most controversial cases involved the Illinois and California delegations.

Fifty-nine delegates from Illinois, including Mayor Richard J. Daley, were unseated on grounds that the selection process had violated five of the new guidelines. The convention voted to seat a group that favored McGovern led by Chicago Alderman William Singer and black activist Jesse Jackson.

In the California case, the credentials committee overruled the California winner-take-all primary rule, taking 151 delegates away from McGovern. These seats were distributed to the other candidates, most notably Senator Hubert H. Humphrey of Minnesota, according to the votes received in the primary.

As a result of the numerous credentials challenges that went in favor of front-runner McGovern, the party's other two leading candidates, Senator Humphrey and Senator Edmund S. Muskie of Maine, withdrew from the race. On the first roll call, McGovern easily garnered enough votes to win the party's nomination.

McGovern's first choice as running mate, Senator Edward M. Kennedy of Massachusetts, refused consideration. His second choice, Senator Thomas F. Eagleton of Missouri, won a protracted roll-call vote that saw 70 other candidates receive votes.

In his early-morning acceptance speech to the convention, McGovern stressed his antiwar theme and encouraged the nation to "come home" to its founding ideals.

The 1972 Democratic platform was the most liberal party statement penned. Most of the proposals were written by separate committees that did not attempt to coordinate their work. The nearly 25,000-word document dealt extensively with domestic issues, including planks endorsing income redistribution and guaranteed annual incomes. Its foreign policy sections were in stark contrast to the party's previous platforms. Rather than speak of the dangers of communism, the planks advocated peace in Indochina and improved relations with the communist countries. On Vietnam the platform was clear: the first thing the new administration would do would be to completely withdraw all American forces from Indochina.

A minority platform offered by the wheelchair-bound Governor George C. Wallace of Alabama that sought constitutional amendments banning busing and permitting school prayer, reinstatement of the death penalty, and the reconfirmation of Supreme Court justices by the Senate was rejected by voice votes. However, two minority planks offered by other delegates were added since McGovern did not object to them. The first was a pro-Israel plank. The second was a proposal to allocate surplus federal lands to American Indians.

After the convention closed, McGovern's running mate, Senator Eagleton, disclosed that he had been voluntarily committed to a hospital three times between 1960 and 1966 for nervous exhaustion. At first, McGovern stuck by his choice. However, as time went on, it became clear that Eagleton would have to resign the nomination, a first in American history. McGovern announced that his choice to replace Eagleton was Ambassador to France R. Sargent Shriver of Maryland. Shriver had formerly directed the Peace Corps and the Office of Economic Opportunity. The Democratic National Committee formally nominated Shriver at its Washington, D.C., meeting on August 8, 1972.

— 1976 —

The Democratic Convention of July 1976 was a show of party unity after two consecutive divisive conventions. The delegates who gathered in New York City had chosen as the party's presidential nominee in the primaries and caucuses an outsider, Governor James E. "Jimmy" Carter of Georgia.

While the convention did not see any credentials challenges come to the floor for voting, the rules committee report did lead to controversy. The Democratic National Committee had adopted new rules for delegate selection because of the controversies of the previous conventions. In addition, the committee raised the required minority challenge from 10% of the credentials committee to 25%.

Carter supporters beat back an effort by more liberal members of the convention to have extended debates on platform issues. The pro-Carter forces thought that this would needlessly lengthen the proceedings. However, the liberal forces were able to bring to a vote the issue of loophole primaries—a delegate selection method that allows a winner-take-all basis within a congressional district. While Carter and Democratic National Committee Chair Robert S. Strauss favored the minority report, which advocated simply reviewing these primaries at a later date, the liberal forces had the majority report, which advocated eliminating loophole primaries, adopted by a voice vote.

The issue of equal representation of women and men was another controversial issue. Carter favored the majority report, which merely encouraged the equal representation of men and women in state delegations but did not require it. In a meeting with representatives of the party's women's caucus, a compromise was reached that strengthened the language of Carter's position, although it stopped short of requiring equal representation.

While three other names were placed in nomination, Carter easily won as his two chief rivals, Governor Edmund G. Brown Jr. of California and Representative Morris K. Udall of Arizona, appeared before the convention prior to the beginning of the first roll call to announce their support for Carter. By the time the first roll call was completed and all the switches were made, a motion for the unanimous nomination of Carter was entertained and passed on a voice vote.

Admitting that he had changed his mind three times in the last month, Carter announced his choice of Senator Walter F. Mondale of Minnesota as his running mate. Mondale's nomination was a landslide victory on the first ballot. In his acceptance speech, Mondale criticized former President Richard M. Nixon for Watergate and President Gerald R. Ford for pardoning Nixon. The attack brought the delegates to their feet.

Carter, trying to be a candidate of all Democrats, offered something to everyone in his acceptance speech. To the right, he offered a balanced budget, among other things. To the left, he championed universal health care. His speech included agendas and statements that would appeal to almost all the elements of the party.

The 1976 platform had also been largely controlled by Carter. Rather than create a specific agenda for the party, the platform spoke in broad language of the generic goals of the party. The only minority plank entered and passed was one calling for the repeal of the 1939 Hatch Act, which prohibited federal employees from running for office and participating in partisan campaigns. Among the remaining planks of the platform were statements of support for the gradual implementation of national health care, the reduction of unemployment, pardons for Vietnam War resisters and deserters, a strategic arms limitation treaty with the Soviet Union, and the reform of the tax system.

— 1980 —

The August 1980 Democratic Convention in New York City was a deeply divided meeting. The first term of President Jimmy Carter had not gone well. The economy was slipping into a deeper recession, and the Iranian hostage crisis loomed large. The convention hall was filled with the chanting of "We want Ted," a reference to Carter's chief rival, Senator Edward M. Kennedy of Massachusetts.

Despite these problems, Carter had done well in the primaries and caucuses. He had enough delegates to win the nomination easily. However, Kennedy had a chance to win the nomination if he could have the party's binding rule repealed. The binding rule required that delegates vote on the first ballot for the candidate whom they had been sent to support.

The two sides had agreed to a one-hour debate on the rule scheduled for the first night of the convention. The televised debate featured the proponents of the rule change arguing that political conditions had drastically changed since the primaries. Influential Washington lawyer Edward Bennet Williams encouraged the delegates not "to vote themselves into bondage to a candidate." Carter forces countered that the rule was fair and had been adopted at the 1978 rules meeting. They insisted that the complaint from Kennedy was poor sportsmanship as he only objected to the rule when he realized Carter was going to win. In the end, the convention voted against a change in rules by a margin of 58% to 42%. With the outcome settled, Kennedy withdrew his name from consideration for the presidential nomination.

When it came to shaping the party platform, the Kennedy forces had more success. Kennedy won two roll-call votes on his proposals that jobs be the number-one priority and that Medicaid fund abortions. In addition, Carter lost a key vote on the minority report to withhold campaign funds from candidates who did not support the Equal Rights Amendment.

The 40,000-word document also contained much of Kennedy's economic plan for the country. The Carter forces, overwhelmed by the support that the senator had generated for his proposals, conceded much of the language though objecting to many of the specifics. In the end, Carter accepted the platform as a way to forge party unity.

Kennedy, for his part, publicly endorsed Carter and the party's platform. With this, Carter was easily renominated as the party's standard-bearer. In his acceptance speech, Carter called on Kennedy to work with him in the future.

The vice presidential nomination easily went to the incumbent, Walter F. Mondale. Mondale's acceptance speech praised Carter at length and rallied the delegates into chanting "Not Ronald Reagan."

— 1984 —

Despite fears that radical and homosexual protesters would turn the July 1984 San Francisco Democratic Convention into a repeat of the 1968 Chicago disaster, the conflicts between protesters and police were minor and nonviolent. More important, the party was able to heal some of the political wounds from previous conventions with a rousing show of unity.

The source of this unity was anger toward Republican President Ronald Reagan. Governor Mario M. Cuomo of New York set the stage with a fiery condemnation of Reagan's "shining city on a hill." Also addressing the delegates was the charismatic civil rights activist Jesse Jackson. The party selected Senator Edward M. Kennedy to introduce the presidential nominee, former Carter Vice President Walter F. Mondale of Minnesota. Kennedy, in his introduction, called the Republican Party of Reagan a "cold citadel of privilege."

Mondale selected Representative Geraldine Ferraro of New York as his running mate. For the first time in American history, a woman was on the national ticket of a major party. Ferraro's nomination was made by acclamation.

The platform reflected the diverse influences of the party's chief candidates for the 1984 election—Mondale, Jackson and Senator Gary Hart of Colorado. At its core, the platform was an attack on the Reagan administration and the Republican Party. The platform's planks were more liberal in their support for homosexuals and abortion, while more conservative in their economic policies. However, the party maintained its traditional support for unions, women, blacks, environmentalists and the disadvantaged.

The platform successfully united the three presidential contenders and produced a united party going into the 1984 presidential election.

— 1988 —

The Democrats held their July 1988 convention in Atlanta. For the first time in several decades, the party truly came together in order to forge a unified force for the White House. The only threat to internal peace was the runner-up in the Democratic primaries, civil rights activist Jesse Jackson.

The front-runner, Governor Michael S. Dukakis of Massachusetts, had enough votes going into the convention to ensure his nomination. Nevertheless, Jackson forces had threatened to stage boycotts and a

walkout. The convention could have gotten out of hand when Dukakis bypassed Jackson for Senator Lloyd Bentsen of Texas as his running mate. However, a lengthy meeting among the three men and their appearance on the stage together helped prevent a protest by Jackson supporters.

The theme for the convention was unity. Unlike previous conventions, credentials disputes and rules reports were agreed to in advance by both the Dukakis and Jackson camps. State Treasurer Ann Richards of Texas gave a keynote address that attacked George Bush, the Republican nominee, as well as set an agenda for the party's future. The enthusiasm generated by Richards, however, was marred by an extended speech by former President Jimmy Carter.

Despite the unified front, several platform issues showed the differences between Jackson's more liberal following and the Dukakis moderates. Jackson, with the support of Manhattan Borough President David Dinkins, argued that taxes had to be raised on the wealthy and corporations in order to balance the budget. Others argued that adoption of the plank would confirm the Republican image of the Democrats as the "tax and spend" party. The minority plank was defeated.

The second issue of distinction was the minority proposal to ban the first use of nuclear weapons. Dukakis opposed this plank because it would potentially limit his ability as commander in chief and his negotiating position with the Soviet Union. Once again, the issue was resolved in favor of the moderate Dukakis forces.

Jackson was successful, however, in having nine amendments incorporated into the platform. These dealt with issues ranging from the denunciation of military aid to Central America to increased spending on education. These concessions to Jackson were more symbolic than substantive as the overall platform was clearly shaped by Dukakis forces.

The presidential nominating balloting followed an evening dedicated to a series of speeches by the party's liberal wing. Senator Edward M. Kennedy of Massachusetts and Jackson roused the crowded Omni center with tributes to the party's liberal heritage. On a reconciliatory note, Jackson called on the liberal and conservative wings of the party to find a common agenda in order to secure electoral victory.

On the next night, Dukakis's name was placed into nomination by his friend Governor Bill Clinton of Arkansas. On the first ballot, Dukakis easily won the nomination. When the roll call finished, Willie Brown Jr., speaker of the California House and national campaign manager for Jackson, asked that Dukakis's nomination be made by acclamation.

Following a series of speeches praising Bentsen's work, the senator from Texas was nominated by acclamation for the party's second spot. In his speech, Bentsen tried to unify the party by praising Jackson and attacking the Reagan administration.

Dukakis's acceptance speech followed a series of pump-priming flourishes, including a commissioned musical piece by the Boston Pops. Dukakis ensured the success of his speech by addressing only issues about which the party was unified and avoiding those like abortion and taxes about which there were still large differences. The delegates ended the convention as the most unified Democratic Party since 1976.

— 1992 —

The Democratic Convention of July 1992 in New York City's Madison Square Garden strongly showed the new, more centrist political party. The party nominee, Governor William Jefferson "Bill" Clinton of Arkansas, and the platform reflected the ideas of the moderate Democratic Leadership Council and its think tank, the Progressive Policy Institute. The move to a more moderate and centrist party that marked the 1988 convention was now well established.

Unlike previous conventions, there were relatively few concessions to the liberal wing, led by civil rights activist Jesse Jackson and former Governor Edmund G. Brown Jr. of California. In the end, Jackson endorsed the Arkansas governor while Brown and his followers withheld their support. The convention's one moment of controversy involved whether or not Brown would be permitted to address the convention in prime time. Clinton and Democratic National Committee Chair Ron Brown required an endorsement of Clinton as the price for the time slot. Many Governor Brown supporters jeered other speakers and placed tape over their mouths in protest.

The convention featured a special opening program to highlight the six Democratic women vying for the Senate. In addition, the delegates heard three keynote addresses, from Senator Bill Bradley of New Jersey, Governor Zell Miller of Georgia, and former Representative Barbara Jordan of Texas. These three speakers stressed the changes in the party and criticized the Bush administration.

The 1992 platform was a more moderate document than its immediate precursors. Gone were the more liberal planks, and in their place were ones supporting law and order and the death penalty and others limiting welfare benefits to two years. However, the platform continued its support for abortion rights and civil rights for homosexuals. Four minority planks offered by presidential contender and former Senator Paul E. Tsongas of Massachusetts were defeated.

While former President Jimmy Carter vouched for Clinton's character, Governor Mario M. Cuomo of New York formally nominated the Arkansas governor. After the roll call, in which Clinton easily outdistanced his opponents, his nomination was made by acclamation.

Clinton's selection of Senator Albert Gore of Tennessee as his vice presidential running mate made the Democratic ticket the youngest in the twentieth century.

Clinton's 54-minute acceptance speech touched on many of the issues addressed in the party platform. In addition, he made repeated references to himself as the "comeback kid," a nickname he adopted after rumors of his philandering ways and his avoidance of the Vietnam War draft failed to derail his candidacy. In the tradition of the New Deal and the New Frontier, Clinton offered the country a "New Covenant."

PLATFORMS

— 1840 —

1. *Resolved*, That the federal government is one of limited powers, derived solely from the constitution, and the grants of power shown therein, ought to be strictly construed by all the departments and agents of the government, and that it is inexpedient and dangerous to exercise doubtful constitutional powers.

2. *Resolved*, That the constitution does not confer upon the general government the power to commence and carry on, a general system of internal improvements.

3. *Resolved*, That the constitution does not confer authority upon the federal government, directly or indirectly, to assume the debts of the several states, contracted for local internal improvements, or other state purposes; nor would such assumption be just or expedient.

4. *Resolved*, That justice and sound policy forbid the federal government to foster one branch of industry to the detriment of another, or to cherish the interests of one portion to the injury of another portion of our common country—that every citizen and every section of the country, has a right to demand and insist upon an equality of rights and privileges, and to complete and ample protection of person and property from domestic violence, or foreign aggression.

5. *Resolved*, That it is the duty of every branch of the government, to enforce and practice the most rigid economy, in conducting our public affairs, and that no more revenue ought to be raised, than is required to defray the necessary expenses of the government.

6. *Resolved*, That congress has no power to charter a national bank; that we believe such an institution one of deadly hostility to the best interests of the country, dangerous to our republican institutions and the liberties of the people, and calculated to place the business of the country within the control of a concentrated money power, and above the laws and the will of the people.

7. *Resolved*, That congress has no power, under the constitution, to interfere with or control the domestic institutions of the several states, and that such states are the sole and proper judges of everything appertaining to their own affairs, not prohibited by the constitution; that all efforts by abolitionists or others, made to induce congress to interfere with questions of slavery, or to take incipient steps in relation thereto, are calculated to lead to the most alarming and dangerous consequences, and that all such efforts have an inevitable tendency to diminish the happiness of the people, and endanger the stability and permanency of the union, and ought not to be countenanced by any friend to our political institutions.

8. *Resolved*, That the separation of the moneys of the government from banking institutions, is indispensable for the safety of the funds of the government, and the rights of the people.

9. *Resolved*, That the liberal principles embodied by Jefferson in the Declaration of Independence, and sanctioned in the constitution, which makes ours the land of liberty, and the asylum of the oppressed of every nation, have ever been cardinal principles in the democratic faith; and every attempt to abridge the present privilege of becoming citizens, and the owners of soil among us, ought to be resisted with the same spirit which swept the alien and sedition laws from our statute-book.

— 1844 —

1. *Resolved*, That the American Democracy place their trust, not in factitious symbols, not in displays and appeals insulting to the judgment and subversive of the intellect of the people, but in a clear reliance upon the intelligence, patriotism, and the discriminating justice of the American masses.

Resolved, That we regard this as a distinctive feature of our political creed, which we are proud to maintain before the world, as the great moral element in a form of government springing from and upheld by the popular will; and we contrast it with the creed and practice of Federalism, under whatever name or form, which seeks to palsy the will of the constituent, and which conceives no imposture too monstrous for the popular credulity.

Resolved, therefore, That, entertaining these views, the Democratic party of this Union, through their delegates assembled in general convention of the States, coming together in a spirit of concord, of devotion to the doctrines and faith of a free representative government, and appealing to their fellow-citizens for the rectitude of their intentions, renew and reassert before the American people the declaration of principles avowed by them on a former occasion, when, in general convention, they presented their candidates for the popular suffrages.

1. That the Federal Government is one of limited powers, derived solely from the Constitution, and the grants of powers shown therein ought to be strictly construed by all the departments and that it is inexpedient and dangerous to exercise doubtful constitutional powers.

2. That the Constitution does not confer upon the General Government the power to commence or carry on a general system of internal improvements.

3. That the Constitution does not confer authority upon the Federal Government, directly or indirectly, to assume the debts of the several States, contracted for local internal improvements or other State purposes; nor would such assumption be just or expedient.

4. That justice and sound policy forbid the Federal Government to foster one branch of industry to the detriment of another, or to cherish the interests of one portion to the injury of another portion of our common country—that every citizen and every section of the country has a right to demand and insist upon an equality of rights and privileges, and to complete and ample protection of person and property from domestic violence or foreign aggression.

5. That it is the duty of every branch of the government to enforce and practice the most rigid economy in conducting our public affairs, and that no more revenue ought to be raised than is required to defray the necessary expenses of the government.

6. That Congress has no power to charter a United States Bank, that we believe such an institution one of deadly hostility to the best interests of the country, dangerous to our republican institutions and the liberties of the people, and calculated to place the business of the country within the control of a concentrated money power, and above the laws and the will of the people.

7. That Congress has no power, under the Constitution, to interfere with or control the domestic institutions of the several States; and that such States are the sole and proper judges of everything pertaining to their own affairs, not prohibited by the Constitution; that all efforts, by abolitionist or others, made to induce Congress to interfere with questions of slavery, or to take incipient steps in relation thereto, are calculated to lead to the most alarming and dangerous consequences, and that all such efforts have an inevitable tendency to diminish the happiness of the people and endanger the stability and permanency of the Union, and ought not to be countenanced by any friend to our Political Institutions.

8. That the separation of the money of the government from banking institutions is indispensable for the safety of the funds of the government and the rights of the people.

9. That the liberal principles embodied by Jefferson in the Declaration of Independence, and sanctioned in the Constitution, which makes ours the land of liberty and the asylum of the oppressed of every nation, have ever been cardinal principles in the Democratic faith; and every attempt to abridge the present privilege of becoming citizens, and the owners of soil among us, ought to be resisted with the same spirit which swept the alien and sedition laws from our statutebook.

Resolved, That the proceeds of the Public Lands ought to be sacredly applied to the national objects specified in the Constitution, and that we are opposed to the laws lately adopted, and to any law for the distribution of such proceeds among the States, as alike inexpedient in policy and repugnant to the Constitution.

Resolved, That we are decidedly opposed to taking from the President the qualified veto power by which he is enabled, under restrictions and responsibilities amply sufficient to guard the public interests, to suspend the passage of a bill, whose merits cannot secure the approval of two-thirds of the Senate and House of Representatives, until the judgments of the people can be obtained thereon, and which has thrice saved the American People from the corrupt and tyrannical domination of the Bank of the United States.

Resolved, That our title to the whole of the Territory of Oregon is clear and unquestionable; that no portion of the same ought to be ceded to England or any other power, and that the reoccupation of Oregon and the reannexation of Texas at the earliest practicable period are great American measures, which this Convention recommends to the cordial support of the Democracy of the Union.

— 1848 —

Resolved, That the American Democracy place their trust in the intelligence, the patriotism, and the discriminating justice of the American people.

Resolved, That we regard this as a distinctive feature of our political creed, which we are proud to maintain before the world as the great moral element in a form of government springing from and upheld by the popular will; and we contrast it with the creed and practice of Federalism, under whatever name or form, which seeks to palsy the will of the constituent, and which conceives no imposture too monstrous for the popular credulity.

Resolved, therefore, That, entertaining these views, the Democratic party of this Union, through their Delegates assembled in general convention of the States, coming together in a spirit of concord, of devotion to the doctrines and faith of a free representative government, and appealing to their fellow-citizens for the rectitude of their intentions, renew and reassert before the American people the declaration of principles avowed by them when, on a former occasion, in general convention, they presented their candidates for the popular suffrage.

1. That the Federal Government is one of limited powers, derived solely from the Constitution; and the grants of power shown therein ought to be strictly construed by all the departments and agents of the Government; and that it is inexpedient and dangerous to exercise doubtful constitutional powers.

2. That the Constitution does not confer upon the General Government the power to commence and carry on a general system of internal improvements.

3. That the Constitution does not confer authority upon the Federal Government, directly or indirectly, to assume the debts of the several States, contracted for local internal improvements, or other State purposes; nor would such assumption be just or expedient.

4. That justice and sound policy forbid the Federal Government to foster one branch of industry to the detriment of another, or to cherish the interests of one portion to the injury of another portion of our common country; that every citizen, and every section of the country, has a right to demand and insist upon an equality of rights and privileges, and to complete and ample protection of person and property from domestic violence or foreign aggression.

5. That it is the duty of every branch of the Government to enforce and practice the most rigid economy in conducting our public affairs, and that no more revenue ought to be raised than is required to defray the necessary expenses of the Government, and for the gradual but certain extinction of the debt created by the prosecution of a just and necessary war, after peaceful relations shall have been restored.

6. That Congress has no power to charter a national bank; that we believe such an institution one of deadly hostility to the best interests of the country, dangerous to our republican institutions and the liberties of the people, and calculated to place the business of the country within the control of a concentrated money power, and above the laws and the will of the people; and that the results of Democratic legislation, in this and all other financial measures upon which issues have been made between the two political parties of the country, have demonstrated to candid and practical men of all parties, their soundness, safety, and utility in all business pursuits.

7. That Congress has no power under the Constitution to interfere with or control the domestic institutions of the several States, and that such States are the sole and proper judges of everything appertaining to their own affairs, not prohibited by the Constitution; that all efforts of the Abolitionists or others made to induce Congress to interfere with questions of slavery, or to take incipient steps in relation thereto, are calculated to lead to the most alarming and dangerous consequences; and that all such efforts have an inevitable tendency to diminish the happiness of the people, and endanger the stability and permanence of the Union, and ought not to be countenanced by any friend to our political institutions.

8. That the separation of the moneys of the Government from banking institutions is indispensable for the safety of the funds of the Government and the rights of the people.

9. That the liberal principles embodied by Jefferson in the Declaration of Independence, and sanctioned in the Constitution, which makes ours the land of liberty, and the asylum of the oppressed of every nation, have ever been cardinal principles in the Democratic faith, and every attempt to abridge the present privilege of becoming citizens and the owners of soil among us, ought to be resisted with the same spirit which swept the alien and sedition laws from our statutebook.

Resolved, That the proceeds of the public lands ought to be sacredly applied to the national objects specified in the Constitution; and that we are opposed to any law for the distribution of such proceeds among the States, as alike inexpedient in policy and repugnant to the Constitution.

Resolved, That we are decidedly opposed to taking from the President the qualified veto power, by which he is enabled, under restrictions and responsibilities amply sufficient to guard the public interests, to suspend the passage of a bill whose merits cannot secure the approval of two thirds of the Senate and House of Representatives, until the judgment of the people can be obtained thereon, and which has saved the American people from the corrupt and tyrannical domination of the Bank of the United States, and from a corrupting system of general internal improvements.

Resolved, That the war with Mexico, provoked on her part by years of insult and injury, was commenced by her army crossing the Rio Grande, attacking the American troops, and invading our sister State of Texas; and that, upon all the principles of patriotism and laws of nations, it is a just and necessary war on our part, in which every American citizen should have shown himself on the side of his country, and neither morally nor physically, by word or by deed, have given "aid and comfort to the enemy."

Resolved, That we would be rejoiced at the assurance of peace with Mexico founded on the just principles of indemnity for the past and security for the future; but that, while the ratification of the liberal treaty offered to Mexico remains in doubt, it is the duty of the country to sustain the administration in every measure to provide for the vigorous prosecution of the war, should that treaty be rejected.

Resolved, That the officers and soldiers who have carried the arms of their country into Mexico, have crowned it with imperishable glory. Their unconquerable courage, their daring enterprise, their unfaltering perseverance and fortitude when assailed on all sides by innumerable foes, and that more formidable enemy, the diseases of the climate, exalt their devoted patriotism into the highest heroism, and give them a right to the profound gratitude of their country, and the admiration of the world.

Resolved, That the Democratic National Convention of the thirty States composing the American Republic, tender their fraternal congratulations to the National Convention of the Republic of France, now assembled as the free-suffrage representatives of the sovereignty of thirty-five millions of republicans, to establish government on those eternal principles of equal rights for which their Lafayette and our Washington fought side by side in the struggle for our own national independence; and we would especially convey to them, and to the whole people of France, our earnest wishes for the consolidation of their liberties, through the wisdom that shall guide their counsels, on the basis of a democratic constitution, not derived from grants or concessions of kings or parliaments, but originating from the only true source of political power recognized in the States of this Union—the inherent and inalienable right of the people, in their sovereign capacity, to make and to amend their forms of government in such manner as the welfare of the community may require.

Resolved, That in view of the recent development of the grand political truth of the sovereignty of the people, and their capacity and power for self-government, which is prostrating thrones and erecting republics on the ruins of despotism in the Old World, we feel that a high and sacred duty is devolved, with increased responsibility, upon the Democratic party of this country, as the party of the people, to sustain and advance among us constitutional "liberty, and fraternity," by continuing to resist all monopolies and exclusive legislation for the benefit of the few at the expense of the many, and by a vigilant and constant adherence to those principles and compromises of the Constitution which are broad enough and strong enough to embrace and uphold the Union as it was, the Union as it is, and the Union as it shall be, in the full expansion of the energies and capacity of this great and progressive people.

Voted, That a copy of these resolutions be forwarded, through the American Minister at Paris, to the National Convention of the Republic of France.

Resolved, That the fruits of the great political triumph of 1844, which elected James K. Polk and George M. Dallas President and Vice-President of the United States, have fulfilled the hopes of the Democracy of the Union—in defeating the declared purposes of their opponents to create a national bank; in preventing the corrupt and unconstitutional distribution of the land proceeds, from the common treasury of the Union, for local purposes; in protecting the currency and the labor of the country from ruinous fluctuations, and guarding the money of the people for the use of the people, by the establishment of the constitutional treasury; in the noble impulse given to the cause of free trade, by the repeal of the tariff of 1842 and the creation of the more equal, honest, and productive tariff of 1846; and that, in our opinion, it would be a fatal error to weaken the bands of political organization by which these great reforms have been achieved, and risk them in the hands of their known adversaries, with whatever delusive appeals they may solicit our surrender of that vigilance, which is the only safeguard of liberty.

Resolved, That the confidence of the Democracy of the Union in the principles, capacity, firmness, and integrity of James K. Polk, manifested by his nomination and election in 1844, has been signally justified by the strictness of his adherence to sound Democratic doctrines, by the purity of purpose, the energy and ability which have characterized his administration in all our affairs at home and abroad; that we tender to him our cordial congratulations upon the brilliant success which has hitherto crowned his patriotic efforts, and assure him, that at the expiration of his Presidential term, he will carry with him to his retirement the esteem, respect, and admiration of a grateful country.

Resolved, That this Convention hereby present to the people of the United States, Lewis Cass, of Michigan, as the candidate of the Democratic party for the office of Vice-President of the United States.

— 1852 —

Resolved, That the American democracy place their trust in the intelligence, the patriotism, and the discriminating justice of the American people.

Resolved, That we regard this as a distinctive feature of our political creed, which we are proud to maintain before the world as the great moral element in a form of government springing from and upheld by the popular will; and we contrast it with the creed and practice of federalism, under whatever name or form, which seeks to palsy the will of the constituent, and which conceives no imposture too monstrous for the popular credulity.

Resolved, therefore, that, entertaining these views, the democratic party of this Union, through their delegates assembled in a general convention, coming together in a spirit of concord, of devotion to the doctrines and faith of a free representative government, and appealing to their fellow-citizens for the rectitude of their intentions, renew and reassert before the American people the declaration of principles avowed by them when on former occasions, in general convention, they have presented their candidates for the popular suffrages.

1. That the federal government is one of limited powers, derived solely from the constitution, and the grants of power made therein ought to be strictly construed by all the departments and agents of the government; and that it is inexpedient and dangerous to exercise doubtful constitutional powers.

2. That the constitution does not confer upon the general government the power to commence and carry on a general system of internal improvements.

3. That the constitution does not confer authority upon the federal government, directly or indirectly, to assume the debts of the several States, contracted for local and internal improvements or other State purposes; nor would such assumption be just or expedient.

4. That justice and sound policy forbid the federal government to foster one branch of industry to the detriment of any other, or to cherish the interests of one portion to the injury of another portion of our common country; that every citizen, and every section of the country, had a right to demand and insist upon an equality of rights and privileges, and to complete and ample protection of person and property from domestic violence or foreign aggression.

5. That it is the duty of every branch of the government to enforce and practice the most rigid economy in conducting our public affairs, and that no more revenue ought to be raised than is required to defray the necessary expenses of the government, and for the gradual but certain extinction of the public debt.

6. That Congress has no power to charter a national bank; that we believe such an institution one of deadly hostility to the best interests of the country, dangerous to our republican institutions and the liberties of the people, and calculated to place the business of the country within the control of a concentrated money power, and above the laws and the will of the people; and that the results of democratic legislation in this and all other financial measures upon which issues have been made between the two political parties of the country, have demonstrated, to candid and practical men of all parties, their soundness, safety, and utility in all business pursuits.

7. That the separation of the moneys of the government from banking institutions is indispensable for the safety of the funds of the government and the rights of the people.

8. That the liberal principles embodied by Jefferson in the Declaration of Independence, and sanctioned in the constitution, which make ours the land of liberty and the asylum of the oppressed of every nation, have ever been cardinal principles in the democratic faith; and every attempt to abridge the privilege of becoming citizens and the owners of the soil among us ought to be resisted with the same spirit that swept the alien and sedition laws from our statute-books.

9. That Congress has no power under the constitution to interfere with or control the domestic institutions of the several States, and that such States are the sole and proper judges of everything appertaining to their own affairs not prohibited by the constitution; that all efforts of the abolitionists or others made to induce Congress to interfere with questions of slavery, or to take incipient steps in relation thereto, are calculated to lead to the most alarming and dangerous consequences; and that all such efforts have an inevitable tendency to diminish the happiness of the people and endanger the stability and permanency of the Union,

and ought not to be countenanced by any friend of our political institutions.

Resolved, That the foregoing proposition covers, and was intended to embrace, the whole subject of slavery agitation in Congress; and therefore the democratic party of the Union, standing on this national platform, will abide by and adhere to faithful execution of the acts known as the compromise measures settled by the last Congress—"the act for reclaiming fugitives from service or labor" included; which act, being designed to carry out an express provision of the constitution, cannot, with fidelity thereto be repealed nor so changed as to destroy or impair its efficiency.

Resolved, That the democratic party will resist all attempts at renewing, in Congress or out of it, the agitation of the slavery question, under whatever shape or color the attempt may be made.

Resolved, That the proceeds of the public lands ought to be sacredly applied to the national objects specified in the constitution; and that we are opposed to any law for the distribution of such proceeds among the States, as alike inexpedient in policy and repugnant to the constitution.

Resolved, That we are decidedly opposed to taking from the President the qualified veto power, by which he is enabled, under restrictions and responsibilities amply sufficient to guard the public interests, to suspend the passage of a bill whose merits cannot secure the approval of two-thirds of the Senate and House of Representatives, until the judgment of the people can be obtained thereon, and which has saved the American people from the corrupt and tyrannical domination of the Bank of the United States, and from a corrupting system of general internal improvements.

Resolved, That the democratic party will faithfully abide by and uphold the principles laid down in the Kentucky and Virginia resolutions of 1798, and the report of Mr. Madison to the Virginia legislature in 1799; that it adopts those principles as constituting one of the main foundations of its political creed, and is resolved to carry them out in their obvious meaning and import.

Resolved, That the war with Mexico, upon all the principles of patriotism and the laws of nations, was a just and necessary war on our part, in which every American citizen should have shown himself on the side of his country, and neither morally nor physically, by word or deed, have given "aid and comfort to the enemy."

Resolved, That we rejoice at the restoration of friendly relations with our sister republic of Mexico, and earnestly desire for her all the blessings and prosperity which we enjoy under republican institutions; and we congratulate the American people on the results of that war, which have so manifestly justified the policy and conduct of the Democratic Party, and insured to the United States, "indemnity for the past and security for the future."

Resolved, That, in view of the condition of popular institutions in the Old World, a high and sacred duty is devolved, with increased responsibility upon the democratic party of this country, as the party of the people, to uphold and maintain the rights of every State, and thereby the Union of the States, and to sustain and advance among us constitutional liberty, by continuing to resist all monopolies and exclusive legislation for the benefit of the few at the expense of the many, and by a vigilant and constant adherence to those principles and compromises of the constitution, which are broad enough and strong enough to embrace and uphold the Union as it was, the Union as it is, and the Union as it shall be, in the full expansion of the energies and capacity of this great and progressive people.

— 1856 —

Resolved, That the American Democracy place their trust in the intelligence, the patriotism, and the discriminating justice of the American people.

Resolved, That we regard this as a distinctive feature of our political creed, which we are proud to maintain before the world as the great moral element in a form of government springing from and upheld by the popular will; and we contrast it with the creed and practice of Federalism, under whatever name or form, which seeks to palsy the will of the constituent, and which conceives no imposture too monstrous for the popular credulity.

Resolved, therefore, That, entertaining these views, the Democratic party of this Union, through their Delegates assembled in a general Convention, coming together in a spirit of concord, of devotion to the doctrines and faith of a free representative Government, and appealing to their fellow-citizens for the rectitude of their intentions, renew and reassert before the American people, the declarations of principles avowed by them when, on former occasions in general Convention, they have presented their candidates for the popular suffrage.

1. That the Federal Government is one of limited power, derived solely from the Constitution; and the grants of power made therein ought to be strictly construed by all the departments and agents of the government; and that it is inexpedient and dangerous to exercise doubtful constitutional powers.

2. That the Constitution does not confer upon the General Government the power to commence and carry on a general system of internal improvements.

3. That the Constitution does not confer authority upon the Federal Government, directly or indirectly, to assume the debts of the several States, contracted for local and internal improvements, or other State purposes; nor would such assumption be just or expedient.

4. That justice and sound policy forbid the Federal Government to foster one branch of industry to the detriment of any other, or to cherish the interests of one portion to the injury of another portion of our common country; that every citizen and every section of the country has a right to demand and insist upon an equality of rights and privileges, and to complete and ample protection of person and property from domestic violence or foreign aggression.

5. That it is the duty of every branch of the Government to enforce and practice the most rigid economy in conducting our public affairs, and that no more revenue ought to be raised than is required to defray the necessary expenses of the Government, and the gradual but certain extinction of the public debt.

6. That the proceeds of the public lands ought to be sacredly applied to the national objects specified in the Constitution; and that we are opposed to any law for the distribution of such proceeds among the States, as alike inexpedient in policy and repugnant to the Constitution.

7. That Congress has no power to charter a national bank; that we believe such an institution one of deadly hostility to the best interests of the country, dangerous to our republican institutions and the liberties of the people, and calculated to place the business of the country within the control of a concentrated money power, and above the laws and the will of the people; and that the results of Democratic legislation in this and all other financial measures upon which issues have been made between the two political parties of the country, have demonstrated to candid and practical men of all parties, their soundness, safety, and utility, in all business pursuits.

8. That the separation of the moneys of the Government from banking institutions is indispensable for the safety of the funds of the Government and the rights of the people.

9. That we are decidedly opposed to taking from the President the qualified veto power, by which he is enabled, under restrictions and responsibilities amply sufficient to guard the public interests, to suspend the passage of a bill whose merits cannot secure the approval of two-thirds of the Senate and House of Representatives, until the judgment of the people can

be obtained thereon, and which has saved the American people from the corrupt and tyrannical domination of the Bank of the United States, and from a corrupting system of general internal improvements.

10. That the liberal principles embodied by Jefferson in the Declaration of Independence, and sanctioned by the Constitution, which makes ours the land of liberty and the asylum of the oppressed of every nation, have ever been cardinal principles in the Democratic faith, and every attempt to abridge the privilege of becoming citizens and the owners of soil among us, ought to be resisted with the same spirit which swept the alien and sedition laws from our statute-books.

And Whereas, Since the foregoing declaration was uniformly adopted by our predecessors in National Conventions, an adverse political and religious test has been secretly organized by a party claiming to be exclusively American, it is proper that the American Democracy should clearly define its relation thereto, and declare its determined opposition to all secret political societies, by whatever name they may be called.

Resolved, That the foundation of this union of States having been laid in, and its prosperity, expansion, and pre-eminent example in free government, built upon entire freedom in matters of religious concernments, and no respect of person in regard to rank or place of birth; no party can justly be deemed national, constitutional, or in accordance with American principles, which bases its exclusive organization upon religious opinions and accidental birth-place. And hence a political crusade in the nineteenth century, and in the United States of America, against Catholic and foreign-born is neither justified by the past history or the future prospects of the country, nor in unison with the spirit of toleration and enlarged freedom which peculiarly distinguishes the American system of popular government.

Resolved, That we reiterate with renewed energy of purpose the well considered declarations of former Conventions upon the sectional issue of Domestic slavery, and concerning the reserved rights of the States.

1. That Congress has no power under the Constitution, to interfere with or control the domestic institutions of the several States, and that such States are the sole and proper judges of everything appertaining to their own affairs, not prohibited by the Constitution; that all efforts of the abolitionists, or others, made to induce Congress to interfere with questions of slavery, or to take incipient steps in relation thereto, are calculated to lead to the most alarming and

dangerous consequences; and that all such efforts have an inevitable tendency to diminish the happiness of the people and endanger the stability and permanency of the Union, and ought not to be countenanced by any friend of our political institutions.

2. That the foregoing proposition covers, and was intended to embrace the whole subject of slavery agitation in Congress; and therefore, the Democratic party of the Union, standing on this national platform, will abide by and adhere to a faithful execution of the acts known as the compromise measures, settled by the Congress of 1850; "the act for reclaiming fugitives from service or labor," included; which act being designed to carry out an expressed provision of the Constitution, cannot, with fidelity thereto, be repealed, or so changed as to destroy or impair its efficiency.

3. That the Democratic party will resist all attempts at renewing, in Congress or out of it, the agitation of the slavery question under whatever shape or color the attempt may be made.

4. That the Democratic party will faithfully abide by and uphold the principles laid down in the Kentucky and Virginia resolutions of 1798, and in the report of Mr. Madison to the Virginia Legislature in 1799; that it adopts those principles as constituting one of the main foundations of its political creed, and is resolved to carry them out in their obvious meaning and import.

And that we may more distinctly meet the issue on which a sectional party, subsisting exclusively on slavery agitation, now relies to test the fidelity of the people, North and South, to the Constitution and the Union—

1. *Resolved*, That claiming fellowship with, and desiring the co-operation of all who regard the preservation of the Union under the Constitution as the paramount issue—and repudiating all sectional parties and platforms concerning domestic slavery, which seek to embroil the States and incite to treason and armed resistance to law in the Territories; and whose avowed purposes, if consummated, must end in civil war and disunion, the American Democracy recognize and adopt the principles contained in the organic laws establishing the Territories of Kansas and Nebraska as embodying the only sound and safe solution of the "slavery question" upon which the great national idea of the people of this whole country can repose in its determined conservatism of the Union—Non-interference by Congress with slavery in State and Territory, or in the District of Columbia.

2. That this was the basis of the compromises of 1850—confirmed by both the Democratic and Whig parties in national Conventions—ratified by the peo-ple in the elections of 1852, and rightly applied to the organization of Territories in 1854.

3. That by the uniform application of this Democratic principle to the organization of Territories, and to the admission of new States, with or without domestic slavery, as they may elect—the equal rights, of all the States will be preserved intact—the original compacts of the Constitution maintained inviolate—and the perpetuity and expansion of this Union insured to its utmost capacity of embracing, in peace and harmony, every future American State that may be constituted or annexed, with a republican form of government.

Resolved, That we recognize the right of the people of all the Territories, including Kansas and Nebraska, acting through the legally and fairly expressed will of a majority of actual residents, and whenever the number of their inhabitants justifies it, to form a Constitution, with or without domestic slavery, and be admitted into the Union upon terms of perfect equality with the other States.

Resolved, finally, That in view of the condition of popular institutions in the Old World (and the dangerous tendencies of sectional agitation, combined with the attempt to enforce civil and religious disabilities against the rights of acquiring and enjoying citizenship, in our own land)—a high and sacred duty is devolved with increased responsibility upon the Democratic party of this country, as the party of the Union, to uphold and maintain the rights of every State, and thereby the Union of the States; and to sustain and advance among us constitutional liberty, by continuing to resist all monopolies and exclusive legislation for the benefit of the few, at the expense of the many, and by a vigilant and constant adherence to those principles and compromises of the Constitution, which are broad enough and strong enough to embrace and uphold the Union as it was, the Union as it is, and the Union as it shall be, in the full expansion of the energies and capacity of this great and progressive people.

1. *Resolved*, That there are questions connected with the foreign policy of this country, which are inferior to no domestic question whatever. The time has come for the people of the United States to declare themselves in favor of free seas and progressive free trade throughout the world, and, by solemn manifestations, to place their moral influence at the side of their successful example.

2. *Resolved*, That our geographical and political position with reference to the other States of this continent, no less than the interest of our commerce and the

development of our growing power, requires that we should hold as sacred the principles involved in the Monroe Doctrine: their bearing and import admit of no misconstruction; they should be applied with unbending rigidity.

3. *Resolved*, That the great highway which nature, as well as the assent of the States most immediately interested in its maintenance, has marked out for a free communication between the Atlantic and the Pacific oceans, constitutes one of the most important achievements realized by the spirit of modern times and the unconquerable energy of our people. That result should be secured by a timely and efficient exertion of the control which we have the right to claim over it, and no power on earth should be suffered to impede or clog its progress by any interference with the relations it may suit our policy to establish between our Government and the Governments of the States within whose dominions it lies. We can, under no circumstances, surrender our preponderance in the adjustment of all questions arising out of it.

4. *Resolved*, That, in view of so commanding an interest, the people of the United States cannot but sympathize with the efforts which are being made by the people of Central America to regenerate that portion of the continent which covers the passage across the Interoceanic Isthmus.

5. *Resolved*, That the Democratic party will expect of the next Administration that every proper effort be made to insure our ascendancy in the Gulf of Mexico, and to maintain a permanent protection to the great outlets through which are emptied into its waters the products raised out of the soil and the commodities created by the industry of the people of our Western valleys and the Union at large.

Resolved, That the Democratic party recognizes the great importance, in a political and commercial point of view, of a safe and speedy communication, by military and postal roads, through our own territory, between the Atlantic and Pacific coasts of this Union, and that it is the duty of the Federal Government to exercise promptly all its constitutional power to the attainment of that object, thereby binding the Union of these States in indissoluble bonds, and opening to the rich commerce of Asia an overland transit from the Pacific to the Mississippi River, and the great lakes of the North.

Resolved, That the Administration of Franklin Pierce has been true to the great interests of the country. In the face of the most determined opposition it has maintained the laws, enforced economy, fostered progress, and infused integrity and vigor into every department of the Government at home. It has signally improved our treaty relations, extended the field of commercial enterprise, and vindicated the rights of American citizens abroad. It has asserted with eminent impartiality the just claims of every section, and has at all times been faithful to the Constitution. We therefore proclaim our unqualified approbation of its measures and its policy.

— 1860 —

1. *Resolved*, That we, the Democracy of the Union in Convention assembled, hereby declare our affirmance of the resolutions unanimously adopted and declared as a platform of principles by the Democratic Convention at Cincinnati, in the year 1856, believing that Democratic principles are unchangeable in their nature, when applied to the same subject matters; and we recommend, as the only further resolutions, the following:

2. Inasmuch as differences of opinion exist in the Democratic party as to the nature and extent of the powers of a Territorial Legislature, and as to the powers and duties of Congress, under the Constitution of the United States, over the institution of slavery within the Territories,

Resolved, That the Democratic party will abide by the decision of the Supreme Court of the United States upon these questions of Constitutional law.

3. *Resolved*, That it is the duty of the United States to afford ample and complete protection to all its citizens, whether at home or abroad, and whether native or foreign born.

4. *Resolved*, That one of the necessities of the age, in a military, commercial, and postal point of view, is speedy communication between the Atlantic and Pacific States; and the Democratic party pledge such Constitutional Government aid as will insure the construction of a Railroad to the Pacific coast, at the earliest practicable period.

5. *Resolved*, That the Democratic party are in favor of the acquisition of the Island of Cuba on such terms as shall be honorable to ourselves and just to Spain.

6. *Resolved*, That the enactments of the State Legislatures to defeat the faithful execution of the Fugitive Slave Law, are hostile in character, subversive of the Constitution, and revolutionary in their effect.

7. *Resolved*, That it is in accordance with the interpretation of the Cincinnati platform, that during the existence of the Territorial Governments the measures

of restriction, whatever it may be, imposed by the Federal Constitution on the power of the Territorial Legislature over the subject of the domestic relations, as the same has been, or shall hereafter be finally determined by the Supreme Court of the United States, should be respected by all good citizens, and enforced with promptness and fidelity by every branch of the general government.

— 1864 —

Resolved, That in the future, as in the past, we will adhere with unswerving fidelity to the Union under the Constitution as the only solid foundation of our strength, security, and happiness as a people, and as a framework of government equally conducive to the welfare and prosperity of all the States, both Northern and Southern.

Resolved, That this convention does explicitly declare, as the sense of the American people, that after four years of failure to restore the Union by the experiment of war, during which, under the pretence of a military necessity of war-power higher than the Constitution, the Constitution itself has been disregarded in every part, and public liberty and private right alike trodden down, and the material prosperity of the country essentially impaired, justice, humanity, liberty, and the public welfare demand that immediate efforts be made for a cessation of hostilities, with a view of an ultimate convention of the States, or other peaceable means, to the end that, at the earliest practicable moment, peace may be restored on the basis of the Federal Union of the States.

Resolved, That the direct interference of the military authorities of the United States in the recent elections held in Kentucky, Maryland, Missouri, and Delaware was a shameful violation of the Constitution, and a repetition of such acts in the approaching election will be held as revolutionary, and resisted with all the means and power under our control.

Resolved, That the aim and object of the Democratic party is to preserve the Federal Union and rights of the States unimpaired, and they hereby declare that they consider that the administrative usurpation of extraordinary and dangerous powers not granted by the Constitution—the subversion of the civil by military law in States not in insurrection, the arbitrary military arrest, imprisonment, trial, and sentence of American citizens in States where civil law exists in full force; the suppression of freedom of speech and of the press; the denial of the right of asylum; the open and avowed disregard of State rights; the employment of unusual test-oaths; and the interference with and denial of the right of the people to bear arms in their defense is calculated to prevent a restoration of the Union and the perpetuation of a Government deriving its just powers from the consent of the governed.

Resolved, That the shameful disregard of the Administration to its duty in respect to our fellow citizens who now are and long have been prisoners of war and in a suffering condition, deserves the severest reprobation on the score alike of public policy and common humanity.

Resolved, That the sympathy of the Democratic party is heartily and earnestly extended to the soldiery of our army and sailors of our navy, who are and have been in the field and on the sea under the flag of our country, and, in the event of its attaining power, they will receive all the care, protection, and regard that the brave soldiers and sailors of the republic have so nobly earned.

— 1868 —

The Democratic party in National Convention assembled, reposing its trust in the intelligence, patriotism, and discriminating justice of the people; standing upon the Constitution as the foundation and limitation of the powers of the government, and the guarantee of the citizen; and recognizing the questions of slavery and secession as having been settled for all time to come by the war, or the voluntary action of the Southern States in Constitutional Conventions assembled, and never to be renewed or reagitated; does, with the return of peace, demand,

First. Immediate restoration of all the States to their rights in the Union, under the Constitution, and of civil government to the American people.

Second. Amnesty for all past political offenses, and the regulation of the elective franchise in the States by their citizens.

Third. Payment of the public debt of the United States as rapidly as practicable. All moneys drawn from the people by taxation, except so much as is requisite for the necessities of the government, economically administered, being honestly applied to such payment, and where the obligations of the government do not expressly state upon their face, or the law under which they were issued does not provide, that they shall be paid in coin, they ought, in right and in justice, to be paid in the lawful money of the United States.

Fourth. Equal taxation of every species of property, according to its real value, including government bonds and other public securities.

Fifth. One currency for the government and the people, the laborer, and the office-holder, the pensioner and the soldier, the producer and the bond-holder.

Sixth. Economy in the administration of the government, the reduction of the standing army and navy; the abolition of the Freedmen's Bureau; and all political instrumentalities designed to secure negro supremacy; simplification of the system and discontinuance of inquisitorial modes of assessing and collecting internal revenue, so that the burden of taxation may be equalized and lessened, the credit of the government and the currency made good; the repeal of all enactments for enrolling the State militia into national forces in time of peace; and a tariff for revenue upon foreign imports, such as will afford incidental protection to domestic manufactures, and as will, without impairing the revenue, impose the least burden upon, and best promote and encourage the great industrial interests of the country.

Seventh. Reform of abuses in the administration; the expulsion of corrupt men from office; the abrogation of useless offices; the restoration of rightful authority to, and the independence of the executive and judicial departments of, the government; the subordination of the military to the civil power, to the end that the usurpations of Congress and the despotism of the sword may cease.

Eighth. Equal rights and protection for naturalized and native-born citizens at home and abroad; the assertion of American nationality, which shall command the respect of foreign powers, and furnish an example and encouragement to people struggling for national integrity, constitutional liberty, and individual rights, and the maintenance of the rights of naturalized citizens against the absolute doctrine of immutable allegiance and the claims of foreign powers to punish them for alleged crimes committed beyond their jurisdiction.

In demanding these measures and reforms we arraign the Radical party for its disregard of right, and the unparalleled oppression and tyranny which have marked its career.

After the most solemn and unanimous pledge of both Houses of Congress to prosecute the war exclusively for the maintenance of the government and the preservation of the Union under the Constitution, it has repeatedly violated that most sacred pledge, under which alone was rallied that noble volunteer army which carried our flag to victory.

Instead of restoring the Union, it has, so far as in its power, dissolved it, and subjected ten States, in time of profound peace, to military despotism and negro supremacy.

It has nullified there the right of trial by jury; it has abolished the habeas corpus, that most sacred writ of liberty; it has overthrown the freedom of speech and of the press; it has substituted arbitrary seizures and arrests, and military trials and secret star-chamber inquisitions, for the constitutional tribunals; it has disregarded in time of peace the right of the people to be free from searches and seizures; it has entered the post and telegraph offices, and even the private rooms of individuals, and seized their private papers and letters without any specific charge or notice of affidavit, as required by the organic law; it has converted the American capitol into a Bastille; it has established a system of spies and official espionage to which no constitutional monarchy of Europe would now dare to resort; it has abolished the right of appeal, on important constitutional questions, to the Supreme Judicial tribunal, and threatens to curtail, or destroy, its original jurisdiction, which is irrevocably vested by the Constitution; while the learned Chief Justice has been subjected to the most atrocious calumnies, merely because he would not prostitute his high office to the support of the false and partisan charges preferred against the President. Its corruption and extravagance have exceeded anything known in history, and by its frauds and monopolies it has nearly doubled the burden of the debt created by the war; it has stripped the President of his constitutional power of appointment, even of his own Cabinet. Under its repeated assaults the pillars of the government are rocking on their base, and should it succeed in November next and inaugurate its President, we will meet, as a subjected and conquered people, amid the ruins of liberty and the scattered fragments of the Constitution.

And we do declare and resolve, That ever since the people of the United States threw off all subjection to the British crown, the privilege and trust of suffrage have belonged to the several States, and have been granted, regulated, and controlled exclusively by the political power of each State respectively, and that any attempt by Congress, on any pretext whatever, to deprive any State of this right, or interfere with its exercise, is a flagrant usurpation of power, which can find no warrant in the Constitution; and if sanctioned by the people will subvert our form of government, and can only end in a single centralized and consolidated government, in which the separate existence of the States will be entirely absorbed, and an unqualified despotism be established in place of a federal union of co-equal States; and that we regard the reconstruction acts so-called, of Congress, as such an usurpation, and unconstitutional, revolutionary, and void.

That our soldiers and sailors, who carried the flag of our country to victory against a most gallant and determined foe, must ever be gratefully remembered, and all the guarantees given in their favor must be faithfully carried into execution.

That the public lands should be distributed as widely as possible among the people, and should be disposed of either under the pre-emption or homestead laws, or sold in reasonable quantities, and to none but actual occupants, at the minimum price established by the government. When grants of the public lands may be deemed necessary for the encouragement of important public improvements, the proceeds of the sale of such lands, and not the lands themselves, should be so applied.

That the President of the United States, Andrew Johnson, in exercising the power of his high office in resisting the aggressions of Congress upon the constitutional rights of the States and the people, is entitled to the gratitude of the whole American people; and in behalf of the Democratic party, we tender him our thanks for his patriotic efforts in that regard.

Upon this platform the Democratic party appeals to every patriot, including all the Conservative element, and all who desire to support the Constitution and restore the Union, forgetting all past differences of opinion, to unite with us in the present great struggle for the liberties of the people; and that to all such, to whatever party they may have heretofore belonged, we extend the right hand of fellowship, and hail all such cooperating with us as friends and brethren.

Resolved, That this Convention sympathize cordially with the workingmen of the United States in their efforts to protect the rights and interests of the laboring classes of the country.

Resolved, That the thanks of the Convention are tendered to Chief Justice Salmon P. Chase for the justice, dignity, and impartiality with which he presided over the court of impeachment in the trial of President Andrew Johnson.

— 1872 —

We, the Democratic Electors of the United States in Convention assembled, do present the following principles, already adopted at Cincinnati, as essential to just government.

1. We recognize the equality of all before the law, and hold that it is the duty of the Government in its dealings with the people to mete out equal and exact justice to all, of whatever nativity, race, color or persuasion, religion or politics.

2. We pledge ourselves to maintain the union of these States, emancipation and enfranchisement; and

to oppose any reopening of the questions settled by the thirteenth, fourteenth and fifteenth amendments of the Constitution.

3. We demand the immediate and absolute removal of all disabilities imposed on account of the rebellion which was finally subdued seven years ago, believing that universal amnesty will result in complete pacification in all sections of the country.

4. Local self-government, with impartial suffrage, will guard the rights of all citizens more securely than any centralized power. The public welfare requires the supremacy of the civil over the military authority, and the freedom of person under the protection of the *habeas corpus*. We demand for the individual the largest liberty consistent with public order; for the State, self-government, and for the Nation a return to the methods of peace and the constitutional limitations of power.

5. The Civil Service of the Government has become a mere instrument of partisan tyranny and personal ambition, and an object of selfish greed. It is a scandal and reproach upon free institutions, and it breeds a demoralization dangerous to the perpetuity of Republican Government.

6. We therefore regard a thorough reform of the Civil Service as one of the most pressing necessities of the hour; that honesty, capacity, and fidelity constitute the only valid claim to public employment; that the offices of the Government cease to be a matter of arbitrary favoritism and patronage, and that public station shall become again a place of honor. To this end it is imperatively required that no President shall be a candidate for re-election.

7. We demand a system of Federal taxation which shall not unnecessarily interfere with the industry of the people and which shall provide the means necessary to pay the expenses of the Government, economically administered, the pensions, the interest on the public debt, and a moderate annual reduction of the principal thereof; and recognizing that there are in our midst honest but irreconcilable differences of opinion with regard to the respective systems of protection and free trade, we remit the discussion of the subject to the people in their Congressional Districts, and the decision of the Congress thereon, wholly free from Executive interference or dictation.

8. The public credit must be sacredly maintained, and we denounce repudiation in every form and guise.

9. A speedy return to specie payment is demanded alike by the highest considerations of commercial morality and honest government.

10. We remember with gratitude the heroism and

sacrifices of the soldiers and sailors of the Republic, and no act of ours shall ever detract from their justly earned fame or the reward of their patriotism.

11. We are opposed to all further grants of lands to railroads or other corporations. The public domain should be held sacred to actual settlers.

12. We hold that it is the duty of the Government, in its intercourse with foreign nations, to cultivate the friendships of peace by treating with all on fair and equal terms, regarding it alike dishonorable either to demand what is not right or to submit to what is wrong.

13. For the promotion and success of these vital principles, and the support of the candidates nominated by this Convention, we invite and cordially welcome the co-operation of all patriotic citizens without regard to previous political affiliations.

— 1876 —

We, the delegates of the Democratic party of the United States, in National Convention assembled, do hereby declare the administration of the Federal Government to be in great need of immediate reform; do hereby enjoin upon the nominees of this Convention, and of the Democratic party in each State, a zealous effort and co-operation to this end, and do here appeal to our fellow-citizens of every former political connection to undertake with us this first and most pressing patriotic duty for the Democracy of the whole country. We do here reaffirm our faith in the permanence of the Federal Union, our devotion to the Constitution of the United States, with its amendments universally accepted as a final settlement of the controversies that engendered civil war, and do here record our steadfast confidence in the perpetuity of republican self-government; in absolute acquiescence in the will of the majority, the vital principle of republic; in the supremacy of the civil over the military; in the two-fold separation of church and state, for the sake alike of civil and religious freedom; in the equality of all citizens before just laws of their own enactment; in the liberty of individual conduct unvexed by sumptuary laws; in the faithful education of the rising generation, that they may preserve, enjoy and transmit these best conditions of human happiness and hope. We behold the noblest products of a hundred years of changeful history. But while upholding the bond of our Union and great charter of these our rights, it behooves a free people to practice also that eternal vigilance which is the price of liberty.

Reform is necessary to rebuild and establish in the hearts of the whole people the Union eleven years ago happily rescued from the danger of the secession of States, but now to be saved from a corrupt centralism which, after inflicting upon ten States the rapacity of carpet-bag tyrannies, has honeycombed the offices of the Federal Government itself with incapacity, waste and fraud; infected States and municipalities with the contagion of misrule, and locked fast the prosperity of an industrious people in the paralysis of hard times. Reform is necessary to establish a sound currency, restore the public credit and maintain the national honor.

We denounce the failure for all these eleven years to make good the promise of the legal tender notes, which are a changing standard of value in the hands of the people, and the non-payment of which is a disregard of the plighted faith of the nation.

We denounce the improvidence which, in eleven years of peace, has taken from the people in Federal taxes thirteen times the whole amount of the legal-tender notes and squandered four times their sum in useless expense, without accumulating any reserve for their redemption. We denounce the financial imbecility and immorality of that party, which, during eleven years of peace, has made no advance toward resumption, no preparation for resumption, but instead has obstructed resumption by wasting our resources and exhausting all our surplus income, and while annually professing to intend a speedy return to specie payment, has annually enacted fresh hindrances thereto. As such hindrance we denounce the resumption clause of the act of 1875 and we here demand its repeal. We demand a judicious system of preparation by official retrenchments, and by wise finance, which shall enable the nation soon to assure the whole world of its perfect ability and its perfect readiness to meet any of its promises at the call of the creditor entitled to payment

We believe such a system, well-advised, and, above all, intrusted to competent hands for execution, creating at no time an artificial scarcity of currency, and at no time alarming the public mind into a withdrawal of that vast machinery of credit by which ninety-five per cent of our business transactions are performed—a system open and public and inspiring general confidence—would from the day of its adoption bring healing on its wings to all our harassed industries, set in motion the wheels of commerce, manufactures and the mechanic arts, restore employment to labor, and renew in all its natural sources the prosperity of the people.

Reform is necessary in the sum and mould of Federal taxation, to the end that capital may be set free from distrust, and labor lightly burdened.

We denounce the present tariff levied upon nearly

four thousand articles as a masterpiece of injustice, inequality and false pretense, which yields a dwindling and not a yearly rising revenue, has impoverished many industries to subsidize a few.

It prohibits imports that might purchase the products of American labor; it has degraded American commerce from the first to an inferior rank upon the high seas; it has cut down the values of American manufactures at home and abroad; it has depleted the returns of American agriculture, an industry followed by half our people; it costs the people five times more than it produces to the treasury, obstructs the process of production and wastes the fruits of labor; it promotes fraud, fosters smuggling, enriches dishonest officials, and bankrupts honest merchants. We demand that all custom-house taxation shall be only for revenue. Reform is necessary in the scale of public expense, Federal, State and municipal. Our Federal taxation has swollen from sixty millions gold in 1860 to four hundred and fifty millions currency in 1870; our aggregate taxation from one hundred and fifty-four millions gold in 1860 to seven hundred and thirty millions currency in 1870, all in one decade; from less than five dollars per head to more than eighteen dollars per head. Since the peace the people have paid to their tax-gatherers more than thrice the sum of the national debt, and more than twice the sum for the Federal Government alone. We demand a rigorous frugality in every department and from every officer of the Government.

Reform is necessary to put a stop to the profligate waste of public lands and their diversion from actual settlers by the party in power, which has squandered two hundred millions of acres upon railroads alone, and out of more than thrice that aggregate has disposed of less than a sixth directly to the tillers of the soil.

Reform is necessary to correct the omissions of a Republican Congress and the errors of our treaties and our diplomacy, which has stripped our fellow-citizens of foreign birth and kindred race, re-erasing [re-crossing] the Atlantic from the shield of American citizenship, and has exposed our brethren of the Pacific coast to the incursions of a race not sprung from the same great parent stock, and in fact now by law denied citizenship through naturalization as being unaccustomed to the traditions of a progressive civilization, one exercise in liberty under equal laws; and we denounce the policy which thus discards the liberty-loving German and tolerates the revival of the coolie-trade in Mongolian women for immoral purposes, and Mongolian men held to perform servile labor contracts, and demand such modification of the treaty with the Chinese Empire, or such legislation within constitutional limitations, as shall prevent further importation or immigration of the Mongolian race.

Reform is necessary and can never be effected but by making it the controlling issue of the election and lifting it above the two issues with which the office-holding classes and the party in power seek to smother it:

First—The false issue with which they would enkindle sectarian strife in respect to the public schools, of which the establishment and support belong exclusively to the several States, and which the Democratic party has cherished from their foundation, and is resolved to maintain without partiality or preference for any class, sect or creed, and without contributions from the treasury to any.

Second—The false issue by which they seek to light anew the dying embers of sectional hate between kindred peoples once unnaturally estranged but now reunited in one indivisible republic, and a common destiny.

Reform is necessary in the civil service. Experience proves that efficient economical conduct of the Government is not possible if its civil service be subject to change at every election, be a prize fought for at the ballot-box, be an approved reward of party zeal instead of posts of honor assigned for proved competency and held for fidelity in the public employ; that the dispensing of patronage should neither be a tax upon the time of our public men nor an instrument of their ambition. Here again, profession falsified in the performance attest that the party in power can work out no practical or salutary reform. Reform is necessary even more in the higher grades of the public service. President, Vice-President, judges, senators, representatives, cabinet officers—these and all others in authority are the people's servants. Their offices are not a private perquisite; they are a public trust. When the annals of this Republic show disgrace and censure of a Vice-President; a late Speaker of the House of Representatives marketing his rulings as a presiding officer; three Senators profiting secretly by their votes as law-makers; five chairmen of the leading committees of the late House of Representatives exposed in jobbery; a late Secretary of the Treasury forcing balances in the public accounts; a late Attorney-General misappropriating public funds; a Secretary of the Navy enriched and enriching friends by a percentage levied off the profits of contractors with his department; an Ambassador to England censured in a dishonorable speculation; the President's Private Secretary barely escaping convictions upon trial for guilty complicity in frauds upon the revenue; a Secretary of War impeached for high crimes and misdemeanors—

the demonstration is complete, that the first step in reform must be the people's choice of honest men from another party, lest the disease of one political organization infect the body politic, and lest by making no change of men or parties, we get no change of measures and no real reform.

All these abuses, wrongs, and crimes, the product of sixteen years' ascendancy of the Republican party, create a necessity for reform, confessed by Republicans themselves; but their reformers are voted down in Convention and displaced from the cabinet. The party's mass of honest voters is powerless to resist the eighty thousand office-holders, its leaders and guides. Reforms can only be had by a peaceful civic revolution. We demand a change of system, a change of administration, a change of parties, that we may have a change of measures and of men.

Resolved, That this Convention, representing the Democratic party of the States, do cordially indorse the action of the present House of Representatives in reducing and curtailing the expenses of the Federal Government, in cutting down enormous salaries, extravagant appropriations, and in abolishing useless offices and places not required by the public necessities, and we shall trust to the firmness of the Democratic members of the House that no committee or conference and no misinterpretation of rules will be allowed to defeat these wholesome measures of economy demanded by the country.

Resolved, That the soldiers and sailors of the Republic, and the widows and orphans of those who have fallen in battle, have a just claim upon the care, protection and gratitude of their fellow citizens.

— 1880 —

The Democrats of the United States, in Convention assembled, declare:

1. We pledge ourselves anew to the constitutional doctrines and traditions of the Democratic party as illustrated by the teaching and example of a long line of Democratic statesmen and patriots, and embodied in the last National Convention of the party.

2. Opposition to centralization and to that dangerous spirit of encroachment which tends to consolidate the powers of all the departments in one, and thus to create whatever be the form of government, a real despotism. No sumptuary laws; separation of Church and State, for the good of each; common schools fostered and protected.

3. Home rule; honest money, consisting of gold and silver, and paper convertible into coin on demand; the strict maintenance of the public faith, State and National, and a tariff for revenue only.

4. The subordination of the military to the civil power, and a general and thorough reform of the civil service.

5. The right to a free ballot is the right preservative of all rights, and must and shall be maintained in every part of the United States.

6. The existing administration is the representative of conspiracy only, and its claim of right to surround the ballot-boxes with troops and deputy marshals, to intimidate and obstruct the election, and the unprecedented use of the veto to maintain its corrupt and despotic powers, insult the people and imperil their institutions.

7. We execrate the course of this administration in making places in the civil service a reward for political crime, and demand a reform by statute which shall make it forever impossible for a defeated candidate to bribe his way to the seat of the usurper by billeting villains upon the people.

8. The great fraud of 1876–77, by which, upon a false count of the electoral votes of two States, the candidate defeated at the polls was declared to be President, and for the first time in American history, the will of the people was set aside under a threat of military violence, struck a deadly blow at our system of representative government. The Democratic party, to preserve the country from the horrors of a civil war, submitted for the time in firm and patriotic faith that people would punish this crime in 1880. This issue precedes and dwarfs every other. It imposes a more sacred duty upon the people of the Union than ever addressed the conscience of a nation of free men.

9. The resolution of Samuel J. Tilden not again to be a candidate for the exalted place to which he was elected by a majority of his country men, and from which he was excluded by the leaders of the Republican party, is received by the Democrats of the United States with deep sensibility, and they declare their confidence in his wisdom, patriotism, and integrity, unshaken by the assaults of a common enemy, and they further assure him that he is followed into the retirement he has chosen for himself by the sympathy and respect of his fellow-citizens, who regard him as one who, by elevating the standards of public morality, merits the lasting gratitude of his country and his party.

10. Free ships and a living chance for American commerce on the seas, and on the land no discrimination in favor of transportation lines, corporations, or monopolies.

11. Amendment of the Burlingame Treaty. No more Chinese immigration, except for travel, education, and foreign commerce, and that even carefully guarded.

12. Public money and public credit for public purposes solely, and public land for actual settlers.

13. The Democratic party is the friend of labor and the laboring man, and pledges itself to protect him alike against the cormorant and the commune.

14. We congratulate the country upon the honesty and thrift of a Democratic Congress which has reduced the public expenditure $40,000,000 a year; upon the continuation of prosperity at home, and the national honor abroad, and, above all, upon the promise of such a change in the administration of the government as shall insure us genuine and lasting reform in every department of the public service.

— 1884 —

The Democratic party of the Union, through its representatives in National Convention assembled, recognizes that, as the nation grows older, new issues are born of time and progress, and old issues perish. But the fundamental principles of the Democracy, approved by the united voice of the people, remain, as the best and only security for the continuance of free government. The preservation of personal rights; the equality of all citizens before the law; the reserved rights of States; and the supremacy of the Federal Government within the limits of the Constitution, will ever form the true basis of our liberties, and can never be surrendered without destroying that balance of rights and powers which enables a continent to be developed in peace, and social order to be maintained by means of local self-government.

But it is indispensable for the practical application and enforcement of these fundamental principles, that the Government should not always be controlled by one political party. Frequent change of administration is as necessary as constant recurrence to the popular will. Otherwise abuses grow, and the Government, instead of being carried on for the general welfare, becomes an instrumentality for imposing heavy burdens on the many who are governed, for the benefit of the few who govern. Public servants thus become arbitrary rulers.

This is now the condition of the country. Hence a change is demanded. The Republican party, so far as principle is concerned, is a reminiscence; in practice, it is an organization for enriching those who control its machinery. The frauds and jobbery which have been brought to light in every department of the Government, are sufficient to have called for reform within the Republican party; yet those in authority, made reckless by the long possession of power, have succumbed to its corrupting influence, and have placed in nomination a ticket against which the independent portion of the party are in open revolt.

Therefore a change is demanded. Such a change was alike necessary in 1876, but the will of the people was then defeated by a fraud which can never be forgot, nor condoned. Again, in 1880, the change demanded by the people was defeated by the lavish use of money contributed by unscrupulous contractors and shameless jobbers who had bargained for unlawful profits, or for high office.

The Republican party during its legal, its stolen, and its bought tenure of power, has steadily decayed in moral character and political capacity.

Its platform promises are now a list of its past failures.

It demands the restoration of our Navy. It has squandered hundreds of millions to create a navy that does not exist.

It calls upon Congress to remove the burdens under which American shipping has been depressed. It imposed and has continued those burdens.

It professes a policy of reserving the public lands for small holdings by actual settlers. It has given away the people's heritage till now a few railroads, and non-resident aliens, individual and corporate, possess a larger area than that of all our farms between the two seas.

It professes a preference for free institutions.

It organized and tried to legalize a control of State elections by Federal troops.

It professes a desire to elevate labor. It has subjected American workingmen to the competition of convict and imported contract labor.

It professes gratitude to all who were disabled, or died in the war, leaving widows and orphans.

It left to a Democratic House of Representatives the first effort to equalize both bounties and pensions.

It proffers a pledge to correct the irregularities of our tariff. It created and has continued them. Its own Tariff Commission confessed the need of more than twenty per cent reduction. Its Congress gave a reduction of less than four per cent.

It professes the protection of American manufactures. It has subjected them to an increasing flood of foreign manufactured goods, and a hopeless competition with manufacturing nations, not one of which taxes raw materials.

It professes to protect all American industries.

It has impoverished many to subsidize a few.

It professes the protection of American labor.

It has depleted the returns of American agriculture—an industry followed by half of our people.

It professes the quality of all men before the law. Attempting to fix the status of colored citizens, the acts of its Congress were overset by the decision of its Courts.

It "accepts anew the duty of leading in the work of progress and reform." Its caught criminals are permitted to escape through contrived delays or actual connivance in the prosecution. Honeycombed with corruption, outbreaking exposures no longer shock its moral sense. Its honest members, its independent journals, no longer maintain a successful contest for authority in its councils or a veto upon bad nominations.

That change is necessary is proved by an existing surplus of more than $100,000,000, which has yearly been collected from a suffering people.

Unnecessary taxation is unjust taxation. We denounce the Republican party for having failed to relieve the people from crushing war taxes which have paralyzed business, crippled industry, and deprived labor of employment and of just reward.

The Democracy pledges itself to purify the Administration from corruption, to restore economy, to revive respect for law, and to reduce taxation to the lowest limit consistent with due regard to the preservation of the faith of the Nation to its creditors and pensioners.

Knowing full well, however, that legislation affecting the operations of the people should be cautious and conservative in method, not in advance of public opinion, but responsive to its demands, the Democratic party is pledged to revise the tariff in a spirit of fairness to all interests.

But in making reduction in taxes, it is not proposed to injure any domestic industries, but rather to promote their healthy growth. From the foundation of this Government, taxes collected at the Custom House have been the chief source of Federal Revenue. Such they must continue to be. Moreover, many industries have come to rely upon legislation for successful continuance, so that any change of law must be at every step regardful of the labor and capital thus involved. The process of reform must be subject in the execution to this plain dictate of justice.

All taxation shall be limited to the requirements of economical government. The necessary reduction and taxation can and must be effected without depriving American labor of the ability to compete successfully with foreign labor, and without imposing lower rates of duty than will be ample to cover any increased cost of production which may exist in consequence of the higher rate of wages prevailing in this country.

Sufficient revenue to pay all the expenses of the Federal Government, economically administered, including pensions, interest, and principal on the public debt, can be got, under our present system of taxation, from the custom house taxes on fewer imported articles, bearing heaviest on articles of luxury, and bearing lightest on articles of necessity.

We, therefore, denounce the abuses of the existing tariff; and, subject to the preceding limitations, we demand that Federal taxation shall be exclusively for public purposes and shall not exceed the needs of the Government economically administered.

The system of direct taxation known as the "Internal Revenue," is a war tax, and so long as the law continues, the money derived therefrom should be sacredly devoted to the relief of the people from the remaining burdens of the war, and be made a fund to defray the expenses of the care and comfort of worthy soldiers disabled in line of duty in the wars of the Republic and for the payment of such pensions as Congress may from time to time grant to such soldiers, a like fund for the sailors having been already provided; and any surplus should be paid into the Treasury.

We favor an American continental policy based upon more intimate commercial and political relations with the fifteen sister Republics of North, Central, and South America, but entangling alliances with none.

We believe in honest money, the gold and silver coinage of the Constitution, and a circulating medium convertible into such money without loss.

Asserting the equality of all men before the law, we hold that it is the duty of the Government, in its dealings with the people, to mete out equal and exact justice to all citizens of whatever nativity, race, color, or persuasion—religious or political.

We believe in a free ballot and a fair count; and we recall to the memory of the people the noble struggle of the Democrats in the Forty-fifth and Forty-sixth Congresses, by which a reluctant Republican opposition was compelled to assent to legislation making everywhere illegal the presence of troops at the polls, as the conclusive proof that a Democratic administration will preserve liberty with order.

The selection of Federal officers for the Territories should be restricted to citizens previously resident therein.

We oppose sumptuary laws which vex the citizen and interfere with individual liberty; we favor honest Civil Service reform, and the compensation of all United States officers by fixed salaries; the separation of Church and State; and the diffusion of free education by common schools, so that every child in the land may be taught the rights and duties of citizenship.

While we favor all legislation which will tend to the equitable distribution of property, to the prevention of monopoly, and to the strict enforcement of individual rights against corporate abuses, we hold that the welfare of society depends upon a scrupulous regard for the rights of property as defined by law.

We believe that labor is best rewarded where it is freest and most enlightened. It should therefore be fostered and cherished. We favor the repeal of all laws restricting the free action of labor, and the enactment of laws by which labor organizations may be incorporated, and of all such legislation as will tend to enlighten the people as to the true relations of capital and labor.

We believe that the public lands ought, as far as possible, to be kept as homesteads for actual settlers; that all unearned lands heretofore improvidently granted to railroad corporations by the action of the Republican party should be restored to the public domain; and that no more grants of land shall be made to corporations, or be allowed to fall into the ownership of alien absentees.

We are opposed to all propositions which upon any pretext would convert the General Government into a machine for collecting taxes to be distributed among the States, or the citizens thereof.

In reaffirming the declaration of the Democratic platform of 1856, that, "the liberal principles embodied by Jefferson in the Declaration of Independence, and sanctioned in the Constitution, which make ours the land of liberty and the asylum of the oppressed of every Nation, have ever been cardinal principles in the Democratic faith," we nevertheless do not sanction the importation of foreign labor, or the admission of servile races, unfitted by habits, training, religion, or kindred, for absorption into the great body of our people, or for the citizenship which our laws confer. American civilization demands that against the immigration or importation of Mongolians to these shores our gates be closed.

The Democratic party insists that it is the duty of the Government to protect, with equal fidelity and vigilance, the rights of its citizens, native and naturalized, at home and abroad, and to the end that this protection may be assured, United States papers of naturalization, issued by courts of competent jurisdiction, must be respected by the Executive and Legislative departments of our own Government, and by all foreign powers.

It is an imperative duty of this Government to efficiently protect all the rights of person and property of every American citizen in foreign lands, and demand and enforce full reparation for any invasion thereof.

An American citizen is only responsible to his own Government for any act done in his own country, or under her flag, and can only be tried therefor on her own soil and according to her laws; and no power exists in this Government to expatriate an American citizen to be tried in any foreign land for any such act.

This country has never had a well-defined and executed foreign policy save under Democratic administration; that policy has ever been, in regard to foreign nations, so long as they do not act detrimental to the interest of the country or hurtful to our citizens, to let them alone; that as a result of this policy we call the acquisition of Louisiana, Florida, California, and of the adjacent Mexican territory by purchase alone, and contrast these grand acquisitions of Democratic statesmanship with the purchase of Alaska, the sole fruit of a Republican administration of nearly a quarter of a century.

The Federal Government should care for and improve the Mississippi River and other great waterways of the Republic, so as to secure for the interior States easy and cheap transportation to tide water.

Under a long period of Democratic rule and policy, our merchant marine was fast overtaking and on the point of outstripping that of Great Britain.

Under twenty years of Republican rule and policy, our commerce has been left to British bottoms, and almost has the American flag been swept off the high seas.

Instead of the Republican party's British policy, we demand for the people of the United States an American policy.

Under Democratic rule and policy our merchants and sailors, flying the stars and stripes in every port, successfully searched out a market for the varied products of American industry.

Under a quarter of a century of Republican rule and policy, despite our manifest advantage of all other nations in high-paid labor, favorable climate and teeming soils; despite freedom of trade among all these United States; despite their population by the foremost races of men and an annual immigration of the young, thrifty and adventurous of all nations, despite our freedom here from the inherited burdens of life and industry in the old-world monarchies—their costly war navies, their vast tax-consuming, non-producing standing armies; despite twenty years of peace—that Republican rule and policy have managed to surrender to Great Britain, along with our commerce, the control of the markets of the world.

Instead of the Republican party's British policy, we demand on behalf of the American Democracy, an American policy.

Instead of the Republican party's discredited scheme and false pretense of friendship for American labor, expressed by imposing taxes, we demand on behalf of the Democracy, freedom for American labor by reducing taxes, to the end that these United States may compete with unhindered powers for the primacy among nations in all the arts of peace and fruits of liberty. With profound regret we have been apprised by the venerable statesman through whose person was struck that blow at the vital principle of republics (acquiescence in the will of the majority), that he cannot permit us again to place in his hands the leadership of the Democratic hosts, for the reason that the achievement of reform in the administration of the Federal Government is an undertaking now too heavy for his age and failing strength.

Rejoicing that his life has been prolonged until the general judgment of our fellow-countrymen is united in the wish that that wrong were righted in his person, for the Democracy of the United States we offer to him in his withdrawal from public cares not only our respectful sympathy and esteem, but also that best homage of freemen, the pledge of our devotion to the principles and the cause now inseparable in the history of this Republic from the labors and the name of Samuel J. Tilden.

With this statement of the hopes, principles and purposes of the Democratic party, the great issue of reform and change in administration is submitted to the people in calm confidence that the popular voice will pronounce in favor of new men, and new and more favorable conditions for the growth of industry, the extension of trade, the employment and the due reward of labor and of capital, and the general welfare of the whole country.

— 1888 —

The Democratic party of the United States, in National Convention assembled, renews the pledge of its fidelity to Democratic faith and reaffirms the platform adopted by its representatives in the Convention of 1884, and endorses the views expressed by President Cleveland in his last annual message to Congress as the correct interpretation of that platform upon the question of Tariff reduction; and also endorses the efforts of our Democratic Representatives in Congress to secure a reduction of excessive taxation.

Chief among its principles of party faith are the maintenance of an indissoluble Union of free and indestructible States, now about to enter upon its second century of unexampled progress and renown, devotion to a plan of government regulated by a written Constitution, strictly specifying every granted power and expressly reserving to the States or people the entire ungranted residue of power; the encouragement of a jealous popular vigilance directed to all who have been chosen for brief terms to enact and execute the laws, and are charged with the duty of preserving peace, insuring equality and establishing justice.

The Democratic party welcomes an exacting scrutiny of the administration of the Executive power which four years ago was committed to its trust in the election of Grover Cleveland as President of the United States; and it challenges the most searching inquiry concerning its fidelity and devotion to the pledges which then invited the suffrages of the people.

During a most critical period of our financial affairs, resulting from over taxation, the anomalous condition of our currency, and a public debt unmatured, it has by the adoption of a wise and conservative course, not only averted disaster, but greatly promoted the prosperity of the people.

It has reversed the improvident and unwise policy of the Republican party touching the public domain, and has reclaimed from corporations and syndicates, alien and domestic, and restored to the people, nearly one hundred millions of acres of valuable land to be sacredly held as homesteads for our citizens.

While carefully guarding the interests of the taxpayers and conforming strictly to the principles of justice and equity, it has paid out more for pensions and bounties to the soldiers and sailors of the Republic than was ever paid before during an equal period.

By intelligent management and a judicious and economical expenditure of the public money it has set on foot the reconstruction of the American Navy upon a system which forbids the recurrence of scandal and insures successful results.

It has adopted and consistently pursued a firm and prudent foreign policy, preserving peace with all nations while scrupulously maintaining all the rights and interests of our Government and people at home and abroad.

The exclusion from our shores of Chinese laborers has been effectually secured under the provisions of treaty, the operation of which has been postponed by the action of a Republican majority in the Senate.

Honest reform in the Civil Service has been inaugurated and maintained by President Cleveland, and he has brought the public service to the highest standard of efficiency, not only by rule and precept, but by the example of his own uniting and unselfish administration of public affairs.

In every branch and department of the Government under Democratic control, the rights and welfare of all the people have been guarded and defended; every public interest has been protected, and the equality of all our citizens before the law, without regard to race or section, has been steadfastly maintained.

Upon its record, thus exhibited, and upon the pledge of a continuance to the people of these benefits of good government, the National Democracy invokes a renewal of popular trust by the reelection of a Chief Magistrate who has been faithful, able and prudent.

They invoke in addition to that trust, the transfer also to the Democracy of the entire legislative power.

The Republican party, controlling the Senate and resisting in both Houses of Congress a reformation of unjust and unequal tax laws, which have outlasted the necessities of war and are now undermining the abundance of a long peace, deny to the people equality before the law and the fairness and the justice which are their right.

Thus the cry of American labor for a better share in the rewards of industry is stifled with false pretenses, enterprise is fettered and bound down to home markets; capital is discouraged with doubt, and unequal, unjust laws can neither be properly amended nor repealed.

The Democratic party will continue, with all the power confided to it, the struggle to reform these laws in accordance with the pledges of its last platform endorsed at the ballot-box by the suffrages of the people.

Of all the industrious freemen of our land, an immense majority, including every tiller of the soil, gain no advantage from excessive tax laws; but the price of nearly everything they buy is increased by the favoritism of an unequal system of tax legislation.

All unnecessary taxation is unjust taxation.

It is repugnant to the creed of Democracy, that by such taxation the costs of the necessaries of life should be unjustifiably increased to all our people.

Judged by Democratic principles, the interests of the people are betrayed, when, by unnecessary taxation, trusts and combinations are permitted and fostered, which, while unduly enriching the few that combine, rob the body of our citizens by depriving them of the benefits of natural competition. Every Democratic rule of governmental action is violated when through unnecessary taxation a vast sum of money, far beyond the needs of an economical administration, is drawn from the people and the channels of trade, and accumulated as a demoralizing surplus in the National Treasury.

The money now lying idle in the Federal Treasury, resulting from superfluous taxation amounts to more than $125,000,000, and the surplus collected is reaching the sum of more than $60,000,000 annually.

Debauched by this immense temptation the remedy of the Republican party is to meet and exhaust by ex-travagant appropriations and expenses, whether constitutional or not, the accumulation of extravagant taxation.

The Democratic remedy is to enforce frugality in public expense and abolish needless taxation.

Our established domestic industries and enterprises should not, and need not, be endangered by a reduction and correction of the burdens of taxation. On the contrary, a fair and careful revision of our tax laws, with due allowance for the difference between the wages of American and foreign labor, must promote and encourage every branch of such industries and enterprises by giving them assurance of an extended market and steady and continuous operations.

In the interest of American labor, which should in no event be neglected, the revision of our tax laws contemplated by the Democratic party would promote the advantage of such labor by cheapening the cost of necessaries of life in the home of every workingman and at the same time securing to him steady and remunerative employment.

Upon this great issue of tariff reform, so closely concerning every phase of our national life, and upon every question involved in the problem of good government, the Democratic party submits its principles and professions to the intelligent suffrages of the American people.

Resolution Presented by Mr. Scott, of Pennsylvania:

Resolved, That this convention hereby endorses and recommends the early passage of the bill for the reduction of the revenue now pending in the House of Representatives.

Resolution Presented by Mr. Lehmann, of Iowa:

Resolved, That a just and liberal policy should by pursued in reference to the Territories; that the right of self-government is inherent in the people and guaranteed under the Constitution; that the Territories of Washington, Dakota, Montana and New Mexico are, by virtue of population and development, entitled to admission into the Union as States, and we unqualifiedly condemn the course of the Republican party in refusing Statehood and self-government to their people.

Resolution Presented by ex-Governor Leon Abbott, of New Jersey:

Resolved, That we express our cordial sympathy with the struggling people of all nations in their effort to secure for themselves the inestimable blessings of self-government and civil and religious liberty. And we especially declare our sympathy with the efforts of those noble patriots who, led by Gladstone and Parnell, have conducted their grand and peaceful contest for home rule in Ireland.

— 1892 —

The representatives of the Democratic party of the United States, in National Convention assembled, do reaffirm their allegiance to the principles of the party, as formulated by Jefferson and exemplified by the long and illustrious line of his successors in Democratic leadership, from Madison to Cleveland; we believe the public welfare demands that these principles be applied to the conduct of the Federal Government, through the accession to power of the party that advocates them; and we solemnly declare that the need of a return to these fundamental principles of free popular government, based on home rule and individual liberty, was never more urgent than now, when the tendency to centralize all power at the Federal capital has become a menace to the reserved rights of the States that strikes at the very roots of our Government under the Constitution as framed by the fathers of the Republic.

We warn the people of our common country, jealous for the preservation of their free institutions, that the policy of Federal control of elections, to which the Republican party has committed itself, is fraught with the gravest dangers, scarcely less momentous than would result from a revolution practically establishing monarchy on the ruins of the Republic. It strikes at the North as well as at the South, and injures the colored citizen even more than the white, it means a horde of deputy marshals at every polling place, armed with Federal power; returning boards appointed and controlled by Federal authority, the outrage of the electoral rights of the people in the several States, the subjugation of the colored people to the control of the party in power, and the reviving of race antagonisms, now happily abated, of the utmost peril to the safety and happiness of all; a measure deliberately and justly described by a leading Republican Senator as "the most infamous bill that ever crossed the threshold of the Senate." Such a policy, if sanctioned by law, would mean the dominance of a self-perpetuating oligarchy of office-holders, and the party first intrusted with its machinery could be dislodged from power only by an appeal to the reserved right of the people to resist oppression, which is inherent in all self-governing communities. Two years ago this revolutionary policy was emphatically condemned by the people at the polls, but in contempt of that verdict the Republican party has defiantly declared in its latest authoritative utterance that its success in the coming elections will mean the enactment of the Force Bill and the usurpation of despotic control over elections in all the States.

Believing that the preservation of Republican government in the United States is dependent upon the defeat of this policy of legalized force and fraud, we invite the support of all citizens who desire to see the Constitution maintained in its integrity with the laws pursuant thereto, which have given our country a hundred years of unexampled prosperity; and we pledge the Democratic party, if it be intrusted with power, not only to the defeat of the Force Bill, but also to relentless opposition to the Republican policy of profligate expenditure, which, in the short space of two years, has squandered an enormous surplus and emptied an overflowing Treasury, after piling new burdens of taxation upon the already overtaxed labor of the country.

We denounce Republican protection as a fraud, a robbery of the great majority of the American people for the benefit of the few. We declare it to be a fundamental principle of the Democratic party that the Federal Government has no constitutional power to impose and collect tariff duties, except for the purpose of revenue only, and we demand that the collection of such taxes shall be limited to the necessities of the Government when honestly and economically administered.

We denounce the McKinley tariff law enacted by the Fifty-first Congress as the culminating atrocity of class legislation; we indorse the efforts made by the Democrats of the present Congress to modify its most oppressive features in the direction of free raw materials and cheaper manufactured goods that enter into general consumption; and we promise its repeal as one of the beneficent results that will follow the action of the people in intrusting power to the Democratic party. Since the McKinley tariff went into operation there have been ten reductions of the wages of the laboring man to one increase. We deny that there has been any increase of prosperity to the country since that tariff went into operation, and we point to the fullness and distress, the wage reductions and strikes in the iron trade, as the best possible evidence that no such prosperity has resulted from the McKinley Act.

We call the attention of thoughtful Americans to the fact that after thirty years of restrictive taxes against the importation of foreign wealth, in exchange for our agricultural surplus, the homes and farms of the country have become burdened with a real estate mortgage debt of over $2,500,000,000, exclusive of all other forms of indebtedness; that in one of the chief agricultural States of the West there appears a real estate mortgage debt averaging $165 per capita of the total population, and that similar conditions and tendencies are shown to exist in other agricultural-exporting States. We denounce a policy which fosters no industry so much as it does that of the Sheriff.

Trade interchange, on the basis of reciprocal advantages to the countries participating, is a time-honored doctrine of the Democratic faith, but we denounce the sham reciprocity which juggles with the people's desire for enlarged foreign markets and freer exchanges by pretending to establish closer trade relations for a country whose articles of export are almost exclusively agricultural products with other countries that are also agricultural, while erecting a custom-house barrier of prohibitive tariff taxes against the richest countries of the world, that stand ready to take our entire surplus of products, and to exchange therefor commodities which are necessaries and comforts of life among our own people.

We recognize in the Trusts and Combinations, which are designed to enable capital to secure more than its just share of the joint product of Capital and Labor, a natural consequence of the prohibitive taxes, which prevent the free competition, which is the life of honest trade, but believe their worst evils can be abated by law, and we demand the rigid enforcement of the laws made to prevent and control them, together with such further legislation in restraint of their abuses as experience may show to be necessary.

The Republican party, while professing a policy of reserving the public land for small holdings by actual settlers, has given away the people's heritage, till now a few railroads and non-resident aliens, individuals and corporate, possess a larger area than that of all our farms between the two seas. The last Democratic administration reversed the improvident and unwise policy of the Republican party touching the public domain, and reclaimed from corporations and syndicates, alien and domestic, and restored to the people nearly one hundred million (100,000,000) acres of valuable land, to be sacredly held as homesteads for our citizens, and we pledge ourselves to continue this policy until every acre of land so unlawfully held shall be reclaimed and restored to the people.

We denounce the Republican legislation known as the Sherman Act of 1890 as a cowardly makeshift, fraught with possibilities of danger in the future, which should make all of its supporters, as well as its author, anxious for its speedy repeal. We hold to the use of both gold and silver as the standard money of the country, and to the coinage of both gold and silver without discriminating against either metal or charge for mintage, but the dollar unit of coinage of both metals must be of equal intrinsic and exchangeable value, or be adjusted through international agreement or by such safeguards of legislation as shall insure the maintenance of the parity of the two metals and the equal power of every dollar at all times in the markets and in the payment of debts; and we demand that all paper currency shall be kept at par with and redeemable in such coin. We insist upon this policy as especially nec-

essary for the protection of the farmers and laboring classes, the first and most defenseless victims of unstable money and a fluctuating currency.

We recommend that the prohibitory 10 per cent tax on State bank issues be repealed.

Public office is a public trust. We reaffirm the declaration of the Democratic National Convention of 1876 for the reform of the civil service, and we call for the honest enforcement of all laws regulating the same. The nomination of a President, as in the recent Republican Convention, by delegations composed largely of his appointees, holding office at his pleasure, is a scandalous satire upon free popular institutions and a startling illustration of the methods by which a President may gratify his ambition. We denounce a policy under which the Federal office-holders usurp control of party conventions in the States, and we pledge the Democratic party to reform these and all other abuses which threaten individual liberty and local self-government.

The Democratic party is the only party that has ever given the country a foreign policy consistent and vigorous, compelling respect abroad and inspiring confidence at home. While avoiding entangling alliances, it has aimed to cultivate friendly relations with other nations, and especially with our neighbors on the American Continent, whose destiny is closely linked with our own, and we view with alarm the tendency to a policy of irritation and bluster which is liable at any time to confront us with the alternatives of humiliation or war. We favor the maintenance of a navy strong enough for all purposes of national defense, and to properly maintain the honor and dignity of the country abroad.

This country has always been the refuge of the oppressed from every land—exiles for conscience's sake—and in the spirit of the founders of our Government we condemn the oppression practiced by the Russian Government upon its Lutheran and Jewish subjects, and we call upon our National Government, in the interest of justice and humanity, by all just and proper means, to use its prompt and best efforts to bring about a cessation of these cruel persecutions in the dominions of the Czar and to secure to the oppressed equal rights.

We tender our profound and earnest sympathy to those lovers of freedom who are struggling for home rule and the great cause of local self-government in Ireland.

We heartily approve all legitimate efforts to prevent the United States from being used as the dumping ground for the known criminals and professional paupers of Europe; and we demand the rigid enforcement of the laws against Chinese immigration and the importation of foreign workmen under contract, to degrade American labor and lessen its wages; but we condemn and denounce any and all attempts to restrict the immigration of the industrious and worthy of foreign lands.

This Convention hereby renews the expression of appreciation of the patriotism of the soldiers and sailors of the Union in the war for its preservation, and we favor just and liberal pensions for all disabled Union soldiers, their widows and dependents, but we demand that the work of the Pension Office shall be done industriously, impartially and honestly. We denounce the present administration of that office as incompetent, corrupt, disgraceful and dishonest.

The Federal Government should care for and improve the Mississippi River and other great waterways of the Republic, so as to secure for the interior States easy and cheap transportation to tide water. When any waterway of the Republic is of sufficient importance to demand the aid of the Government, such aid should be extended upon a definite plan of continuous work, until permanent improvement is secured.

For purposes of national defense and the promotion of commerce between the States, we recognize the early construction of the Nicaragua Canal and its protection against foreign control as of great importance to the United States.

Recognizing the World's Columbian Exposition as a national undertaking of vast importance, in which the General Government has invited the cooperation of all the powers of the world, and appreciating the acceptance by many of such powers of the invitation so extended, and the broad and liberal efforts being made by them to contribute to the grandeur of the undertaking, we are of opinion that Congress should make such necessary financial provision as shall be requisite to the maintenance of the national honor and public faith.

Popular education being the only safe basis of popular suffrage, we recommend to the several States most liberal appropriations for the public schools. Free common schools are the nursery of good government, and they have always received the fostering care of the Democratic party, which favors every means of increasing intelligence. Freedom of education, being an essential of civil and religious liberty, as well as a necessity for the development of intelligence, must not be interfered with under any pretext whatever. We are opposed to State interference with parental rights and rights of conscience in the education of children as an infringement of the fundamental Democratic doctrine that the largest individual liberty consistent with the rights of others insures the highest type of American citizenship and the best government.

We approve the action of the present House of Representatives in passing bills for admitting into the Union as States of the Territories of New Mexico and Arizona, and we favor the early admission of all the Territories having the necessary population and resources to entitle them to Statehood, and while they remain Territories we hold that the officials to administer the government of any Territory, together with the Districts of Columbia and Alaska, should be *bona-fide* residents of the Territory or district in which their duties are to be performed. The Democratic party believes in home rule and the control of their own affairs by the people of the vicinage.

We favor legislation by Congress and State Legislatures to protect the lives and limbs of railway employees and those of other hazardous transportation companies, and denounce the inactivity of the Republican party, and particularly the Republican Senate, for causing the defeat of measures beneficial and protective to this class of wage workers.

We are in favor of the enactment by the States of laws for abolishing the notorious sweating system, for abolishing contract convict labor, and for prohibiting the employment in factories of children under 15 years of age.

We are opposed to all sumptuary laws, as an interference with the individual rights of the citizen.

Upon this statement of principles and policies, the Democratic party asks the intelligent judgment of the American people. It asks a change of administration and a change of party, in order that there may be a change of system and a change of methods, thus assuring the maintenance unimpaired of institutions under which the Republic has grown great and powerful.

— 1896 —

We, the Democrats of the United States in National Convention assembled, do reaffirm our allegiance to those great essential principles of justice and liberty, upon which our institutions are founded, and which the Democratic Party has advocated from Jefferson's time to our own—freedom of speech, freedom of the press, freedom of conscience, the preservation of personal rights, the equality of all citizens before the law, and the faithful observance of constitutional limitations.

During all these years the Democratic Party has resisted the tendency of selfish interests to the centralization of governmental power, and steadfastly maintained the integrity of the dual scheme of government established by the founders of this Republic of republics. Under its guidance and teaching the great principle of local self-government has found its best expression in the maintenance of the rights of the

States and in its assertion of the necessity of confining the general government to the exercise of the powers granted by the Constitution of the United States.

The Constitution of the United States guarantees to every citizen the rights of civil and religious liberty. The Democratic Party has always been the exponent of political liberty and religious freedom, and it renews its obligations and reaffirms its devotion to these fundamental principles of the Constitution.

THE MONEY PLANK

Recognizing that the money question is paramount to all others at this time, we invite attention to the fact that the Federal Constitution named silver and gold together as the money metals of the United States, and that the first coinage law passed by Congress under the Constitution made the silver dollar the monetary unit and admitted gold to free coinage at a ratio based upon the silver-dollar unit.

We declare that the act of 1873 demonetizing silver without the knowledge or approval of the American people has resulted in the appreciation of gold and a corresponding fall in the prices of commodities produced by the people; a heavy increase in the burdens of taxation and of all debts, public and private; the enrichment of the money-lending class at home and abroad; the prostration of industry and impoverishment of the people.

We are unalterably opposed to monometallism which has locked fast the prosperity of an industrial people in the paralysis of hard times. Gold monometallism is a British policy, and its adoption has brought other nations into financial servitude to London. It is not only un-American but anti-American, and it can be fastened on the United States only by the stifling of that spirit and love of liberty which proclaimed our political independence in 1776 and won it in the War of the Revolution.

We demand the free and unlimited coinage of both silver and gold at the present legal ratio of 16 to 1 without waiting for the aid or consent of any other nation. We demand that the standard silver dollar shall be a full legal tender, equally with gold, for all debts, public and private, and we favor such legislation as will prevent for the future the demonetization of any kind of legal tender money by private contract.

We are opposed to the policy and practice of surrendering to the holders of the obligations of the United States the option reserved by law to the Government of redeeming such obligations in either silver coin or gold coin.

INTEREST-BEARING BONDS

We are opposed to the issuing of interest-bearing bonds of the United States in time of peace and condemn the trafficking with banking syndicates, which, in exchange for bonds and at an enormous profit to themselves, supply the Federal Treasury with gold to maintain the policy of gold monometallism.

AGAINST NATIONAL BANKS

Congress alone has the power to coin and issue money, and President Jackson declared that this power could not be delegated to corporations or individuals. We therefore denounce the issuance of notes intended to circulate as money by National banks as in derogation of the Constitution, and we demand that all paper which is made a legal tender for public and private debts, or which is receivable for dues to the United States, shall be issued by the Government of the United States and shall be redeemable in coin.

TARIFF RESOLUTION

We hold that tariff duties should be levied for purposes of revenue, such duties to be so adjusted as to operate equally throughout the country, and not discriminate between class or section, and that taxation should be limited by the needs of the Government, honestly and economically administered. We denounce as disturbing to business the Republican threat to restore the McKinley law, which has twice been condemned by the people in National elections and which, enacted under the false plea of protection to home industry, proved a prolific breeder of trusts and monopolies, enriched the few at the expense of the many, restricted trade and deprived the producers of the great American staples of access to their natural markets.

Until the money question is settled we are opposed to any agitation for further changes in our tariff laws, except such as are necessary to meet the deficit in revenue caused by the adverse decision of the Supreme Court on the income tax.

But for this decision by the Supreme Court, there would be no deficit in the revenue under the law passed by the Democratic Congress in strict pursuance of the uniform decisions of that court for nearly 100 years, that court having in that decision sustained constitutional objections to its enactment which had previously been over-ruled by the ablest Judges who have ever sat on the bench. We declare that it is the duty of Congress to use all the constitutional power which remains after that decision, or which may come from its reversal by the court as it may hereafter be constituted, so that the burdens of taxation may be equally and impartially laid, to the end that wealth may bear its due proportion of the expense of the Government.

IMMIGRATION AND ARBITRATION

We hold that the most efficient way of protecting American labor is to prevent the importation of foreign pauper labor to compete with it in the home market, and that the value of the home market to our American farmers and artisans is greatly reduced by a vicious monetary system which depresses the prices of their products below the cost of production, and thus deprives them of the means of purchasing the products of our home manufactories; and as labor creates the wealth of the country, we demand the passage of such laws as may be necessary to protect it in all its rights.

We are in favor of the arbitration of differences between employers engaged in interstate commerce and their employees, and recommend such legislation as is necessary to carry out this principle.

TRUSTS AND POOLS

The absorption of wealth by the few, the consolidation of our leading railroad system, and the formation of trusts and pools require a stricter control by the Federal Government of those arteries of commerce. We demand the enlargement of the powers of the Interstate Commerce Commission and such restriction and guarantees in the control of railroads as will protect the people from robbery and oppression.

DECLARE FOR ECONOMY

We denounce the profligate waste of the money wrung from the people by oppressive taxation and the lavish appropriations of recent Republican Congresses, which have kept taxes high, while the labor that pays them is unemployed and the products of the people's toil are depressed in price till they no longer repay the cost of production. We demand a return to that simplicity and economy which befits a Democratic Government, and a reduction in the number of useless offices, the salaries of which drain the substance of the people.

FEDERAL INTERFERENCE IN LOCAL AFFAIRS

We denounce arbitrary interference by Federal authorities in local affairs as a violation of the Constitution of the United States, and a crime against free institutions, and we especially object to government by injunction as a new and highly dangerous form of oppression by which Federal Judges, in contempt of the laws of the States and rights of citizens, become at once legislators, judges and executioners; and we approve the bill passed at the last session of the United States Senate, and now pending in the House of Representatives, relative to contempts in Federal courts and providing for trials by jury in certain cases of contempt.

PACIFIC RAILROAD

No discrimination should be indulged in by the Government of the United States in favor of any of its debtors. We approve of the refusal of the Fifty-third Congress to pass the Pacific Railroad Funding Bill and denounce the effort of the present Republican Congress to enact a similar measure.

PENSIONS

Recognizing the just claims of deserving Union soldiers, we heartily indorse the rule of the present Commissioner of Pensions, that no names shall be arbitrarily dropped from the pension roll; and the fact of enlistment and service should be deemed conclusive evidence against disease and disability before enlistment.

ADMISSION OF TERRITORIES

We favor the admission of the Territories of New Mexico, Arizona and Oklahoma into the Union as States, and we favor the early admission of all Territories, having the necessary population and resources to entitle them to Statehood, and, while they remain Territories, we hold that the officials appointed to administer the government of any Territory, together with the District of Columbia and Alaska, should be *bona-fide* residents of the Territory or District in which their duties are to be performed. The Democratic Party believes in home rule and that all public lands of the United States should be appropriated to the establishment of free homes for American citizens.

We recommend that the Territory of Alaska be granted a delegate in Congress and that the general land and timber laws of the United States be extended to said Territory.

SYMPATHY FOR CUBA

The Monroe Doctrine, as originally declared, and as interpreted by succeeding Presidents, is a permanent part of the foreign policy of the United States, and must at all times be maintained.

We extend our sympathy to the people of Cuba in their heroic struggle for liberty and independence.

CIVIL-SERVICE LAWS

We are opposed to life tenure in the public service, except as provided in the Constitution. We favor appointments based on merit, fixed terms of office, and such an administration of the civil-service laws as will afford equal opportunities to all citizens of ascertained fitness.

THIRD-TERM RESOLUTION

We declare it to be the unwritten law of this Republic, established by custom and usage of 100 years, and sanctioned by the examples of the greatest and wisest of those who founded and have maintained our Government that no man should be eligible for a third term of the Presidential office.

IMPROVEMENT OF WATERWAYS

The Federal Government should care for and improve the Mississippi River and other great waterways of the Republic, so as to secure for the interior States easy and cheap transportation to tidewater. When any waterway of the Republic is of sufficient importance to demand aid of the Government such aid should be extended upon a definite plan of continuous work until permanent improvement is secured.

CONCLUSION

Confiding in the justice of our cause and the necessity of its success at the polls, we submit the foregoing declaration of principles and purposes to the considerate judgment of the American people. We invite the support of all citizens who approve them and who desire to have them made effective through legislation, for the relief of the people and the restoration of the country's prosperity.

— 1900 —

We, the representatives of the Democratic party of the United States assembled in National Convention, on the Anniversary of the adoption of the Declaration of Independence, do reaffirm our faith in that immortal proclamation of the inalienable rights of man, and our allegiance to the Constitution framed in harmony therewith by the fathers of the Republic. We hold with the United States Supreme Court that the Declaration of Independence is the spirit of our government, of which the Constitution is the form and letter.

We declare again that all governments instituted among men derive their just powers from the consent of the governed; not based upon the consent of the governed is a tyranny; and that to impose upon any people a government of force is to substitute the methods of imperialism for those of a republic. We hold that the Constitution follows the flag, and denounce the doctrine that an Executive or Congress deriving their existence and their powers from the Constitution can exercise lawful authority beyond it or in violation of it. We assert that no nation can long endure half republic and half empire, and we warn the American people that imperialism abroad will lead quickly and inevitably to despotism at home.

Believing in these fundamental principles, we denounce the Puerto Rican* law, enacted by a Republican Congress against the protest and opposition of the Democratic minority, as a bold and open violation of the nation's organic law and a flagrant breach of the national good faith. It imposes upon the people of Puerto Rico a government without their consent and taxation without representation. It dishonors the American people by repudiating a solemn pledge made in their behalf by the Commanding General of our Army, which the Puerto Ricans welcomed to a peaceful and unresisted occupation of their land. It dooms to poverty and distress a people whose helplessness appeals with peculiar force to our justice and magnanimity. In this, the first act of its imperialistic

*Please note that to avoid confusion, the editors have changed the original spelling of Puerto Rico (Porto Rico) to its current form.

programme, the Republican party seeks to commit the United States to a colonial policy, inconsistent with republican institutions and condemned by the Supreme Court in numerous decisions.

We demand the prompt and honest fulfillment of our pledge to the Cuban people and the world that the United States has no disposition nor intention to exercise sovereignty, jurisdiction, or control over the Island of Cuba, except for its pacification. The war ended nearly two years ago, profound peace reigns over all the island, and still the administration keeps the government of the island from its people, while Republican carpet-bag officials plunder its revenues and exploit the colonial theory, to the disgrace of the American people.

We condemn and denounce the Philippine policy of the present administration. It has involved the Republic in an unnecessary war, sacrificed the lives of many of our noblest sons, and placed the United States, previously known and applauded throughout the world as the champion of freedom, in the false and un-American position of crushing with military force the efforts of out former allies to achieve liberty and self-government. The Filipinos cannot be citizens without endangering our civilization; they cannot be subjects without imperiling our form of government; and as we are not willing to surrender our civilization nor to convert the Republic into an empire, we favor an immediate declaration of the nation's purpose to give the Filipinos, first, a stable form of government; second, independence; and third protection from outside interference, such as has been given for nearly a century to the republics of Central and South America.

The greedy commercialism which dictated the Philippine policy of the Republican administration attempts to justify it with the plea that it will pay; but even this sordid and unworthy plea fails when brought to the test of facts. The war of "criminal aggression" against the Filipinos, entailing an annual expense of many millions, has already cost more than any possible profit that could accrue from the entire Philippine trade for years to come. Furthermore, when trade is extended at the expense of liberty, the price is always too high.

We are not opposed to territorial expansion when it takes in desirable territory which can be erected into States in the Union, and whose people are willing and fit to become American citizens. We favor trade expansion by every peaceful and legitimate means. But we are unalterably opposed to seizing or purchasing distant islands to be governed outside the Constitution, and whose people can never become citizens.

We are in favor of extending the Republic's influence among the nations, but we believe that influence should be extended not by force and violence, but through the persuasive power of a high and honorable example.

The importance of other questions, now pending before the American people is no wise diminished and the Democratic party takes no backward step from its position on them, but the burning issue of imperialism growing out of the Spanish war involves the very existence of the Republic and the destruction of our free institutions. We regard it as the paramount issue of the campaign.

The declaration in the Republican platform adopted at the Philadelphia Convention, held in June, 1900, that the Republican party "steadfastly adheres to the policy announced in the Monroe Doctrine" is manifestly insincere and deceptive. This profession is contradicted by the avowed policy of that party in opposition to the spirit of the Monroe Doctrine to acquire and hold sovereignty over large areas of territory and large numbers of people in the Eastern Hemisphere. We insist on the strict maintenance of the Monroe Doctrine in all its integrity, both in letter and in spirit, as necessary to prevent the extension of European authority on this Continent and as essential to our supremacy in American affairs. At the same time we declare that no American people shall ever be held by force in unwilling subjection to European authority. We oppose militarism. It means conquest abroad and intimidation and oppression at home. It means the strong arm which has ever been fatal to free institutions. It is what millions of our citizens have fled from in Europe. It will impose upon our peace loving people a large standing army and unnecessary burden of taxation, and will be a constant menace to their liberties. A small standing army and a well-disciplined state militia are amply sufficient in time of peace. This republic has no place for a vast military establishment, a sure forerunner of compulsory military service and conscription. When the nation is in danger the volunteer soldier is his country's best defender. The National Guard of the United States should ever be cherished in the patriotic hearts of a free people. Such organizations are ever an element of strength and safety. For the first time in our history, and coeval with the Philippine conquest, has there been a wholesale departure from our time-honored and approved system of volunteer organization. We denounce it as un-American, un-Democratic, and un-Republican, and as a subversion of the ancient and fixed principles of a free people.

Private monopolies are indefensible and intolerable. They destroy competition, control the price of all material, and of the finished product, thus robbing both producer and consumer. They lessen the employment of labor, and arbitrarily fix the terms and conditions thereof; and deprive individual energy and small capital of their opportunity of betterment.

They are the most efficient means yet devised for appropriating the fruits of industry to the benefit of the few at the expense of the many, and unless their insatiate greed is checked, all wealth will be aggregated in a few hands and the Republic destroyed. The dishonest paltering with the trust evil by the Republican party in State and national platforms is conclusive proof of the truth of the charge that trusts are the legitimate product of Republican policies, that they are fostered by Republican laws, and that they are protected by the Republican administration, in return for campaign subscriptions and political support.

We pledge the Democratic party to an unceasing warfare in nation, State and city against private monopoly in every form. Existing laws against trusts must be enforced and more stringent ones must be enacted providing for publicity as to the affairs of corporations engaged in inter-State commerce, requiring all corporations to show, before doing business outside the State of their origin, that they have no water in their stock, and that they have not attempted, and are not attempting, to monopolize any branch of business or the production of any articles of merchandise; and the whole constitutional power of Congress over inter-State commerce, the mails and all modes of inter-State communication, shall be exercised by the enactment of comprehensive laws upon the subject of trusts. Tariff laws should be amended by putting the products of trusts upon the free list, to prevent monopoly under the plea of protection. The failure of the present Republican administration, with an absolute control over all the branches of the national government, to enact any legislation designed to prevent or even curtail the absorbing power of trusts and illegal combinations, or to enforce the anti-trust laws already on the statute-books proves that insincerity of the high-sounding phrases of the Republican platform.

Corporations should be protected in all their rights and their legitimate interests should be respected, but any attempt by corporations to interfere with the public affairs of the people or to control the sovereignty which creates them, should be forbidden under such penalties as will make such attempts impossible.

We condemn the Dingley tariff law as a trust-breeding measure, skillfully devised to give the few favors which they do not deserve, and to place upon the many burdens which they should not bear.

We favor such an enlargement of the scope of the inter-State commerce law as will enable the commission to protect individuals and communities from discrimination, and the public from unjust and unfair transportation rates.

We reaffirm and indorse the principles of the National Democratic Platform adopted at Chicago in 1896, and we reiterate the demand of that platform for an American financial system made by the American people for themselves, and which shall restore and maintain a bi-metallic price level, and as part of such system the immediate restoration of the free and unlimited coinage of silver and gold at the present legal ratio of 16 to 1, without waiting for the aid or consent of any other nation.

We denounce the currency bill enacted at the last session of Congress as a step forward in the Republican policy which aims to discredit the sovereign right of the national government to issue all money, whether coin or paper, and to bestow upon national banks the power to issue and control the volume of paper money for their own benefit. A permanent national bank currency secured by government bonds, must have a permanent debt to rest upon, and, if the bank currency is to increase with population and business, the debt must also increase. The Republican currency scheme is, therefore, a scheme for fastening upon the taxpayers a perpetual and growing debt for the benefit of the banks. We are opposed to this private corporation paper circulated as money, but without legal tender qualities, and demand the retirement of national bank notes as fast as government paper or silver certificates can be substituted for them. We favor an amendment to the Federal Constitution, providing for the election of United States Senators by direct vote of the people, and we favor direct legislation wherever practicable.

We are opposed to government by injunction; we denounce the blacklist, and favor arbitration as a means of settling disputes between corporations and their employees.

In the interest of American labor and the uplifting of the workingman, as the cornerstone of the prosperity of our country, we recommend that Congress create a Department of Labor, in charge of a secretary, with a seat in the Cabinet, believing that the elevation of the American laborer will bring with it increased production and increased prosperity to our country at home and to our commerce abroad.

We are proud of the courage and fidelity of the American soldiers and sailors in all our wars; we favor liberal pensions to them and their dependents, and we reiterate the position taken in the Chicago platform of 1896, that the fact of enlistment and service shall be deemed conclusive evidence against disease and disability before enlistment.

We favor the immediate construction, ownership and control of the Nicaraguan Canal by the United States, and we denounce the insincerity of the plank in the Republican National Platform for an Isthmian Canal in face of the failure of the Republican majority to pass the bill pending in Congress.

We condemn the Hay–Pauncefote treaty as a surrender of American rights and interests not to be tolerated by the American people.

We denounce the failure of the Republican party to carry out its pledges to grant statehood to the territories of Arizona, New Mexico and Oklahoma, and we promise the people of those territories immediate statehood and home rule during their condition as territories, and we favor home rule and a territorial form of government for Alaska and Puerto Rico.

We favor an intelligent system of improving the arid lands of the West, storing the waters for the purpose of irrigation, and the holding of such lands for actual settlers.

We favor the continuance and strict enforcement of the Chinese exclusion law, and its application to the same classes of all Asiatic races.

Jefferson said: "Peace, commerce and honest friendship with all nations; entangling alliance with none." We approve this wholesome doctrine, and earnestly protest against the Republican departure which has involved us in so-called world politics, including the diplomacy of Europe and the intrigue and land-grabbing of Asia, and we especially condemn the ill-concealed Republican alliance with England, which must mean discrimination against other friendly nations, and which has already stifled the nation's voice while liberty is being strangled in Africa.

Believing in the principles of self-government and rejecting, as did our forefathers, the claim of monarchy, we view with indignation the purpose of England to overwhelm with force the South African Republics. Speaking, as we believe, for the entire American nation, except its Republican office-holders and for all freemen everywhere, we extend our sympathies to the heroic burghers in their unequal struggle to maintain their liberty and independence.

We denounce the lavish appropriations of recent Republican Congresses, which have kept taxes high and which threaten the perpetuation of the oppressive war levies. We oppose the accumulation of a surplus to be squandered in such barefaced frauds upon the taxpayers as the shipping subsidy bill, which, under the false pretense of prospering American shipbuilding, would put unearned millions into the pockets of favorite contributors to the Republican campaign fund. We favor the reduction and speedy repeal of the war taxes, and a return to the time-honored Democratic policy of strict economy in governmental expenditures.

Believing that our most cherished institutions are in great peril, that the very existence of our constitutional republic is at stake, and that the decision now to be rendered will determine whether or not our children are to enjoy these blessed privileges of free government, which have made the United States great, prosperous and honored, we earnestly ask for the foregoing declaration of principles, the hearty support of the liberty-loving American people, regardless of previous party affiliations.

— 1904 —

The Democratic party of the United States, in National Convention assembled, declares its devotion to the essential principles of the Democratic faith which bring us together in party communion.

Under these principles local self-government and National unity and prosperity were alike established. They underlaid our independence, the structure of our free Republic, and every Democratic expansion from Louisiana to California, and Texas to Oregon, which preserved faithfully in all the States the tie between taxation and representation. They yet inspirit the masses of our people, guarding jealously their rights and liberties, and cherishing their fraternity, peace and orderly development. They remind us of our duties and responsibilities as citizens and impress upon us, particularly at this time, the necessity of reform and the rescue of the administration of Government from the headstrong, arbitrary and spasmodic methods which distract business by uncertainty, and pervade the public mind with dread, distrust and perturbation.

FUNDAMENTAL PRINCIPLES

The application of these fundamental principles to the living issues of the day constitutes the first step toward the assured peace, safety and progress of our Nation. Freedom of the press, of conscience, and of speech; equality before the law of all citizens; right of trial by jury; freedom of the person defended by the Writ of Habeas Corpus; liberty of personal contract untrammeled by sumptuary laws; supremacy of the civil over military authority; a well-disciplined militia; separation of Church and State; economy in expenditures; low taxes, that labor may be lightly burdened; prompt and sacred fulfillment of public and private obligations; fidelity to treaties; peace and friendship with all nations, entangling alliances with none; absolute acquiescence in the will of the majority, the vital principle of Republics—these are doctrines which Democracy has established as proverbs of the Nation, and they should be constantly invoked, and enforced.

ECONOMY OF ADMINISTRATION

Large reductions can easily be made in the annual expenditures of the Government without impairing the efficiency of any branch of the public service, and we shall insist upon the strictest economy and frugality compatible with vigorous and efficient civil, military and naval administration as a right of the people, too clear to be denied or withheld.

HONESTY IN THE PUBLIC SERVICE

We favor the enforcement of honesty in the public service, and to that end a thorough legislative investigation of those executive departments of the Government already known to teem with corruption, as well as other departments suspected of harboring corruption, and the punishment of ascertained corruptionists without fear or favor or regard to persons. The persistent and deliberate refusal of both the Senate and House of Representatives to permit such investigation to be made demonstrates that only by a change in the executive and in the legislative departments can complete exposure, punishment and correction be obtained.

FEDERAL GOVERNMENT CONTRACTS WITH TRUST

We condemn the action of the Republican party in Congress in refusing to prohibit an executive department from entering into contracts with convicted trusts or unlawful combinations in restraint of inter-State trade. We believe that one of the best methods of procuring economy and honesty in the public service is to have public officials, from the occupant of the White House down to the lowest of them, return, as nearly as may be, to Jeffersonian simplicity of living.

EXECUTIVE USURPATION

We favor the nomination and election of a President imbued with the principles of the Constitution, who will set his face sternly against executive usurpation of legislative and judicial functions, whether that usurpation be veiled under the guise of executive construction of existing laws, or whether it take refuge in the tyrant's plea of necessity or superior wisdom.

IMPERIALISM

We favor the preservation, so far as we can, of an open door for the world's commerce in the Orient without unnecessary entanglement in Oriental and European affairs, and without arbitrary, unlimited, irresponsible and absolute government anywhere within our jurisdiction. We oppose, as fervently as did George Washington, an indefinite, irresponsible, discretionary and vague absolutism and a policy of colonial exploitation, no matter where or by whom invoked or exercised. We believe with Thomas Jefferson and John Adams, that no Government has a right to make one set of laws for those "at home" and another and a different set of laws, absolute in their character, for those "in the colonies." All men under the American flag are entitled to the protection of the institutions whose emblem the flag is; if they are inherently unfit for those institutions, then they are inherently unfit to be members of the American body politic. Wherever there may exist a people incapable of being governed under American laws, in consonance with the American Constitution, the territory of that people ought not to be part of the American domain.

We insist that we ought to do for the Filipinos what we have done already for the Cubans, and it is our duty to make that promise now, and upon suitable guarantees of protection to citizens of our own and other countries resident there at the time of our withdrawal to set the Filipino people upon their feet, and independent, to work out their own destiny.

The endeavor of the Secretary of War, by pledging the Government's endorsement for "promoters" in the Philippine Islands to make the United States a partner in speculative exploitation of the archipelago, which was only temporarily held up by the opposition of Democratic Senators in the last session, will, if successful, lead to entanglements from which it will be difficult to escape.

TARIFF

The Democratic party has been, and will continue to be, the consistent opponent of that class of tariff legislation by which certain interests have been permitted, through Congressional favor, to draw a heavy tribute from the American people. This monstrous perversion of those equal opportunities which our political institutions were established to secure, has caused what may once have been infant industries to become the greatest combinations of capital that the world has ever known. These special favorites of the Government have, through trust methods, been converted into monopolies, thus bringing to an end domestic competition, which was the only alleged check upon the extravagant profits made possible by the protective system. These industrial combinations, by the financial assistance they can give, now control the policy of the Republican party.

We denounce protectionism as a robbery of the many to enrich the few, and we favor a tariff limited to the needs of the Government economically, effectively and constitutionally administered and so levied as not to discriminate against any industry, class or section, to the end that the burdens of taxation shall be distributed as equally as possible.

We favor a revision and a gradual reduction of the tariff by the friends of the masses and for the common weal, and not by the friends of its abuses, its extortions and its discriminations, keeping in view the ultimate end of "equality of burdens and equality of opportunities," and the constitutional purpose of raising a revenue by taxation, to wit: the support of the Federal Government in all its integrity and virility, but in simplicity.

TRUSTS AND UNLAWFUL COMBINATIONS

We recognize that the gigantic trusts and combinations designed to enable capital to secure more than its just share of the joint product of capital and labor, and which have been fostered and promoted under Republican rule, are a menace to beneficial competition and an obstacle to permanent business prosperity.

A private monopoly is indefensible and intolerable.

Individual equality of opportunity and free competition are essential to a healthy and permanent commercial prosperity; and any trust, combination or monopoly tending to destroy these by controlling production, restricting competition or fixing prices and wages, should be prohibited and punished by law. We especially denounce rebates and discriminations by transportation companies as the most potent agency in promoting and strengthening these unlawful conspiracies against trade.

We demand an enlargement of the powers of the Interstate Commerce Commission, to the end that the traveling public and shippers of this country may have prompt and adequate relief from the abuses to which they are subjected in the matter of transportation. We demand a strict enforcement of existing civil and criminal statutes against all such trusts, combinations and monopolies; and we demand the enactment of such further legislation as may be necessary effectually to suppress them.

Any trust or unlawful combination engaged in inter-State commerce which is monopolizing any branch of business or production, should not be permitted to transact business outside of the State of its origin, whenever it shall be established in any court of competent jurisdiction that such monopolization exists. Such prohibition should be enforced through comprehensive laws to be enacted on the subject.

CAPITAL AND LABOR

We favor the enactment and administration of laws giving labor and capital impartially their just rights. Capital and labor ought not to be enemies. Each is necessary to the other. Each has its rights, but the rights of labor are certainly no less "vested," no less "sacred" and no less "inalienable" than the rights of capital.

We favor arbitration of differences between corporate employers and their employees and a strict enforcement of the eight-hour law on all Government work.

We approve the measure which passed the United States Senate in 1896, but which a Republican Congress has ever since refused to enact, relating to contempt in Federal courts and providing for trial by jury in cases of indirect contempt.

CONSTITUTIONAL GUARANTIES

Constitutional guaranties are violated whenever any citizen is denied the right to labor, acquire and enjoy property or reside where interest or inclination may determine. Any denial thereof by individuals, organizations or governments should be summarily rebuked and punished.

We deny the right of any executive to disregard or suspend any constitutional privilege or limitation. Obedience to the laws and respect for their requirements are alike the supreme duty of the citizen and the official.

The military should be used only to support and maintain the law. We unqualifiedly condemn its employment for the summary banishment of citizens without trial, or for the control of elections.

WATERWAYS

We favor liberal appropriations for the care and improvement of the waterways of the country. When any waterway like the Mississippi River is of sufficient importance to demand the special aid of the Government, such aid should be extended with a definite plan of continuous work until permanent improvement is secured.

We oppose the Republican policy of starving home development in order to feed the greed for conquest and the appetite for national "prestige" and display of strength.

RECLAMATION OF ARID LANDS AND DOMESTIC DEVELOPMENT

We congratulate our Western citizens upon the passage of the measure known as the Newlands Irrigation Act for the irrigation and reclamation of the arid lands of the West—a measure framed by a Democrat, passed in the Senate by a nonpartisan vote, and passed in the House against the opposition of almost all the Republican leaders by a vote the majority of which was Democratic. We call attention to this great Democratic measure, broad and comprehensive as it is, working automatically throughout all time without further action of Congress, until the reclamation of all the lands in the arid West capable of reclamation, is accomplished, reserving the lands reclaimed for home-seekers in small tracts and rigidly guarding against land monopoly, as an evidence of the policy of domestic development contemplated by the Democratic party, should it be placed in power.

THE ISTHMIAN CANAL

The Democracy when entrusted with power will construct the Panama Canal speedily, honestly and economically, thereby giving to our people what Democrats have always contended for—a great inter-oceanic canal, furnishing shorter and cheaper lines of transportation, and broader and less trammeled trade relations with the other peoples of the world.

AMERICAN CITIZENSHIP

We pledge ourselves to insist upon the just and lawful protection of our citizens at home and abroad, and to use all proper measures to secure for them, whether native born or naturalized, and without distinction of race or creed, the equal protection of laws and the enjoyment of all rights and privileges open to them under the covenants of our treaties of friendship and commerce; and if under existing treaties the right of travel and sojourn is denied to American citizens or recognition is withheld from American passports by any countries on the ground of race or creed, we favor the beginning of negotiations with the governments of such countries to secure by new treaties the removal of these unjust discriminations.

We demand that all over the world a duly authenticated passport issued by the Government of the United States to an American citizen shall be proof of the fact that he is an American citizen and shall entitle him to the treatment due him as such.

ELECTION OF SENATORS BY THE PEOPLE

We favor the election of United States Senators by direct vote of the people.

STATEHOOD FOR TERRITORIES

We favor the admission of the Territory of Oklahoma and the Indian Territory. We also favor the immediate admission of Arizona and New Mexico, as separate States, and territorial governments for Alaska and Puerto Rico.

We hold that the officials appointed to administer the government of any Territory, as well as the District of Alaska, should be *bona-fide* residents at the time of their appointment of the Territory or district in which their duties are to be performed.

CONDEMNATION OF POLYGAMY

We demand the extermination of polygamy within the jurisdiction of the United States, and the complete separation of Church and State in political affairs.

MERCHANT MARINE

We denounce the ship subsidy bill recently passed by the United States Senate as an iniquitous appropriation of public funds for private purposes and a wasteful, illogical and useless attempt to overcome by subsidy the obstructions raised by Republican legislation to the growth and development of American commerce on the sea.

We favor the upbuilding of a merchant marine without new or additional burdens upon the people and without bounties from the public treasury.

RECIPROCITY

We favor liberal trade arrangements with Canada, and with peoples of other countries where they can be entered into with benefit to American agriculture, manufactures, mining or commerce.

MONROE DOCTRINE

We favor the maintenance of the Monroe Doctrine in its full integrity.

ARMY

We favor the reduction of the Army and of Army expenditures to the point historically demonstrated to be safe and sufficient.

PENSIONS FOR OUR SOLDIERS AND SAILORS

The Democracy would secure to the surviving soldiers and sailors and their dependents generous pensions, not by a arbitrary executive order, but by legislation which a grateful people stand ready to enact.

Our soldiers and sailors who defend with their lives the Constitution and the laws have a sacred interest in their just administration. They must, therefore, share with us the humiliation with which we have witnessed the exaltation of court favorites, without distinguished service, over the scarred heroes of many battles, or aggrandizement by executive appropriations out of the treasuries of prostrate peoples in violation of the act of Congress which fixes the compensation of allowance of the military officers.

CIVIL SERVICE

The Democratic party stands committed to the principles of civil service reform, and we demand their honest, just and impartial enforcement.

We denounce the Republican party for its continuous and sinister encroachments upon the spirit and operation of civil service rules, whereby it has arbitrarily dispensed with examinations for office in the interest of favorites, and employed all manner of devices to overreach and set aside the principles upon which the Civil Service is based.

SECTIONAL AND RACE AGITATION

The race question has brought countless woes to this country. The calm wisdom of the American people should see to it that it brings no more.

To revive the dead and hateful race and sectional animosities in any part of our common country means confusion, distraction of business, and the reopening of wounds now happily healed. North, South, East and West have but recently stood together in line of battle from the walls of Peking to the hills of Santiago, and as sharers of a common glory and a common destiny, we should share fraternally the common burdens.

We therefore deprecate and condemn the Bourbon-like selfish and narrow spirit of the recent Republican Convention at Chicago which sought to kindle anew the embers of racial and sectional strife, and we appeal from it to the sober common sense and patriotic spirit of the American people.

THE REPUBLICAN ADMINISTRATION

The existing Republican administration has been spasmodic, erratic, sensational, spectacular and arbitrary. It has made itself a satire upon the Congress, courts, and upon the settled practices and usages of national and international law.

It summoned the Congress in hasty and futile extra session and virtually adjourned it, leaving behind in its flight from Washington uncalled calendars and unaccomplished tasks.

It made war, which is the sole power of Congress, without its authority, thereby usurping one of its fundamental prerogatives. It violated a plain statute of the United States as well as plain treaty obligations, international usages and constitutional law; and has done so under pretense of executing a great public policy which could have been more easily effected lawfully, constitutionally and with honor.

It forced strained and unnatural constructions upon statutes, usurping judicial interpretation, and substituting for congressional enactment executive decree.

It withdrew from the Congress its customary duties of investigation which have heretofore made the representatives of the people and the States the terror of evildoers.

It conducted a secretive investigation of its own, and boasting of a few sample convicts, it threw a broad coverlet over the bureaus which had been their chosen field of operative abuses, and kept in power the superior officers under whose administration the crimes had been committed.

It ordered assault upon some monopolies, but paralyzed by a first victory, it flung out the flag of truce and cried out that it would not "run amuck"; leaving its future purposes beclouded by its vacillations.

APPEAL TO THE PEOPLE

Conducting the campaign upon this declaration of our principles and purposes, we invoke for our candidates the support not only of our great and time-honored organization, but also the active assistance of all of our fellow citizens who, disregarding past differences, desire the perpetuation of our constitutional Government as framed and established by the fathers of the Republic.

— 1908 —

We, the representatives of the Democracy of the United States, in National Convention assembled, reaffirm our belief in, and pledge our loyalty to, the principles of the party.

We rejoice at the increasing signs of an awakening throughout the country. The various investigations have traced graft and political corruption to the representatives of the predatory wealth, and laid bare the unscrupulous methods by which they have debauched elections and preyed upon a defenseless public through the subservient officials whom they have raised to place and power.

The conscience of the nation is now aroused to free the Government from the grip of those who have made it a business asset of the favor-seeking corporations. It must become again a people's government, and be administered in all its departments according to the Jeffersonian maxim, "equal rights to all; special privileges to none."

"Shall the people rule?" is the overshadowing issue which manifests itself in all the questions now under discussion.

INCREASE OF OFFICE-HOLDERS

Coincident with the enormous increase in expenditures is a like addition to the number of office-holders. During the past year 23,784 were added, costing $16,156,000, and in the past six years of Republican administration the total number of new offices created, aside from many commissions, has been 99,319, entailing an additional expenditure of nearly $70,000,000 as against only 10,279 new offices created under the Cleveland and McKinley administrations, which involved an expenditure of only $6,000,000. We denounce this great and growing increase in the number of office-holders as not only unnecessary and wasteful, but also as clearly indicating a deliberate purpose on the part of the Administration to keep the Republican party in power at public expense by thus increasing the number of its retainers and dependents. Such procedure we declare to be no less dangerous and corrupt than the open purchase of votes at the polls.

ECONOMY IN ADMINISTRATION

The Republican Congress in the session just ended made appropriations amounting to $1,008,000,000, exceeding the total expenditures of the past fiscal year by $90,000,000 and leaving a deficit of more than $60,000,000 for the fiscal year just ended. We denounce the heedless waste of the people's money which has resulted in this appalling increase as a shameful violation of all prudent considerations of government and as no less than a crime against the millions of working men and women, from whose earnings the great proportion of these colossal sums must be extorted through excessive tariff exactions and other indirect methods. It is not surprising that in the face of this shocking record the Republican platform contains no reference to economical administration or promise thereof in the future. We demand that a stop be put to this frightful extravagance, and insist upon the strictest economy in every department compatible with frugal and efficient administration.

ARBITRARY POWER—THE SPEAKER

The House of Representatives was designed by the fathers of the Constitution to be the popular branch of our Government, responsive to the public will.

The House of Representatives, as controlled in recent years by the Republican party, has ceased to be a deliberative and legislative body, responsive to the will of a majority of its members, but has come under the absolute domination of the Speaker, who has entire control of its deliberations and powers of legislation.

We have observed with amazement the popular branch of our Federal Government helpless to obtain either the consideration or enactment of measures desired by a majority of its members.

Legislative control becomes a failure when one member in the person of the Speaker is more powerful than the entire body.

We demand that the House of Representatives shall again become a deliberative body, controlled by a majority of the people's representatives, and not by the Speaker; and we pledge ourselves to adopt such rules and regulations to govern the House of Representatives as will enable a majority of its members to direct its deliberations and control legislation.

MISUSE OF PATRONAGE

We condemn as a violation of the spirit of our institutions the action of the present Chief Executive in using the patronage of his high office to secure the nomination for the Presidency of one of his Cabinet officers. A forced succession to the Presidency is scarcely less repugnant to public sentiment than is life tenure in that office. No good intention on the part of the

Executive, and no virtue in the one selected, can justify the establishment of a dynsty. The right of the people freely to select their officials is inalienable and cannot be delegated.

PUBLICITY OF CAMPAIGN CONTRIBUTIONS

We demand Federal legislation forever terminating the partnership which has existed between corporations of the country and the Republican party under the expressed or implied agreement that in return for the contribution of great sums of money wherewith to purchase elections, they should be allowed to continue substantially unmolested in their efforts to encroach upon the rights of the people.

Any reasonable doubt as to the existence of this relation has been forever dispelled by the sworn testimony of witnesses examined in the insurance investigation in New York, and the open admission of a single individual—unchallenged by the Republican National Committee—that he himself at the personal request of the Republican candidate for the Presidency raised over a quarter of a million dollars to be used in a single State during the closing hours of the last campaign. In order that this practice shall be stopped for all time, we demand the passage of a statute punishing by imprisonment any officer of a corporation who shall either contribute on behalf of, or consent to the contribution by, a corporation, of any money or thing of value to be used in furthering the election of a President or Vice-President of the United States or of any member of the Congress thereof.

We denounce the Republican party, having complete control of the Federal Government, for their failure to pass the bill, introduced in the last Congress, to compel the publication of the names of contributors and the amounts contributed toward campaign funds, and point to the evidence of their insincerity when they sought by an absolutely irrelevant and impossible amendment to defeat the passage of the bill. As a further evidence of their intention to conduct their campaign in the coming contest with vast sums of money wrested from favor-seeking corporations, we call attention to the fact that the recent Republican National Convention at Chicago refused, when the issue was presented to it, to declare against such practices.

We pledge the Democratic party to the enactment of a law prohibiting any corporation from contributing to a campaign fund and any individual from contributing an amount above a reasonable maximum, and providing for the publication before election of all such contributions.

THE RIGHTS OF THE STATES

Believing, with Jefferson, in "the support of the State governments in all their rights as the most competent administrations for our domestic concerns, and the surest bulwarks against anti-republican tendencies," and in "the preservation of the General Government in its whole constitutional vigor, as the sheet anchor of our peace at home and safety abroad," we are opposed to the centralization implied in the suggestion, now frequently made, that the powers of the General Government should be extended by judicial construction. There is no twilight zone between the Nation and the State in which exploiting interests can take refuge from both; and it is as necessary that the Federal Government shall exercise the powers delegated to it as it is that the State governments shall use the authority reserved to them; but we insist that Federal remedies for the regulation of interstate commerce and for the prevention of private monopoly shall be added to, not substituted for, State remedies.

TARIFF

We welcome the belated promise of tariff reform now offered by the Republican party in tardy recognition of the righteousness of the Democratic position on this question; but the people cannot safely entrust the execution of this important work to a party which is so deeply obligated to the highly protected interests as is the Republican party. We call attention to the significant fact that the promised relief is postponed until after the coming election—an election to succeed in which the Republican party must have that same support from the beneficiaries of the high protective tariff as it has always heretofore received from them; and to the further fact that during years of uninterrupted power no action whatever has been taken by the Republican Congress to correct the admittedly existing tariff iniquities.

We favor immediate revision of the tariff by the reduction of import duties. Articles entering into competition with trust-controlled products should be placed upon the free list, and material reductions should be made in the tariff upon the necessaries of life, especially upon articles competing with such American manufactures as are sold abroad more cheaply than at home; and gradual reductions should be made in such other schedules as may be necessary to restore the tariff to a revenue basis.

Existing duties have given to the manufacturers of paper a shelter behind which they have organized combinations to raise the price of pulp and of paper, thus imposing a tax upon the spread of knowledge. We demand the immediate repeal of the tariff on wood pulp, print paper, lumber, timber and logs, and that these articles be placed upon the free list.

TRUSTS

A private monopoly is indefensible and intolerable. We therefore favor the vigorous enforcement of the criminal law against guilty trust magnates and officials, and demand the enactment of such additional legislation as may be necessary to make it impossible for a private monopoly to exist in the United States. Among the additional remedies we specify three: First, a law preventing a duplication of directors among competing corporations; second, a license system which will, without abridging the right of each State to create corporations, or its right to regulate as it will foreign corporations doing business within its limits, make it necessary for a manufacturing or trading corporation engaged in interstate commerce to take out a Federal license before it shall be permitted to control as much as twenty-five per cent of the product in which it deals, the license to protect the public from watered stock and to prohibit the control by such corporation of more than fifty per cent of the total amount of any product consumed in the United States; and, third, a law compelling such licensed corporations to sell to all purchasers in all parts of the country on the same terms, after making due allowance for cost of transportation.

RAILROAD REGULATION

We assert the right of Congress to exercise complete control over interstate commerce and the right of each State to exercise like control over commerce within its borders.

We demand such enlargement of the powers of the Interstate Commerce Commission as may be necessary to enable it to compel railroads to perform their duties as common carriers and prevent discrimination and extortion.

We favor the efficient supervision and rate regulation of railroads engaged in interstate commerce. To this end we recommend the valuation of railroads by the Interstate Commerce Commission, such valuation to take into consideration the physical value of the property, the original cost of production, and all elements of value that will render the valuation fair and just.

We favor such legislation as will prohibit the rail-roads from engaging in business which brings them into competition with their shippers; also legislation which will assure such reduction in transportation rates as conditions will permit, care being taken to avoid reduction that would compel a reduction of wages, prevent adequate service, or do injustice to legitimate investments.

We heartily approve the laws prohibiting the pass and the rebate, and we favor any further necessary legislation to restrain, correct and prevent such abuses.

We favor such legislation as will increase the power of the Interstate Commerce Commission, giving to it the initiative with reference to rates and transportation charges put into effect by the railroad companies, and permitting the Interstate Commerce Commission, on its own initiative, to declare a rate illegal and as being more than should be charged for such service. The present law relating thereto is inadequate, by reason of the fact that the Interstate Commerce Commission is without power to fix or investigate a rate until complaint has been made to it by the shipper.

We further declare in favor of a law providing that all agreements of traffic or other associations of railway agents affecting interstate rates, service or classification, shall be unlawful, unless filed with and approved by the Interstate Commerce Commission.

We favor the enactment of a law giving to the Interstate Commerce Commission the power to inspect proposed railroad tariff rates or schedules before they shall take effect, and, if they be found to be unreasonable, to initiate an adjustment thereof.

BANKING

The panic of 1907, coming without any legitimate excuse, when the Republican party had for a decade been in complete control of the Federal Government, furnishes additional proof that it is either unwilling or incompetent to protect the interests of the general public. It has so linked the country to Wall Street that the sins of the speculators are visited upon the whole people. While refusing to rescue the wealth producers from spoliation at the hands of the stock gamblers and speculators in farm products, it has deposited Treasury funds, without interest and without competition, in favorite banks. It has used an emergency for which it is largely responsible to force through Congress a bill changing the basis of bank currency and inviting market manipulation, and has failed to give to the 15,000,000 depositors of the country protection in their savings.

We believe that in so far as the needs of commerce

require an emergency currency, such currency should be issued and controlled by the Federal Government, and loaned on adequate security to national and State banks. We pledge ourselves to legislation under which the national banks shall be required to establish a guarantee fund for the prompt payment of the depositors of any insolvent national bank, under an equitable system which shall be available to all State banking institutions wishing to use it.

We favor a postal savings bank if the guaranteed bank can not be secured, and that it be constituted so as to keep the deposited money in the communities where it is established. But we condemn the policy of the Republican party in providing postal savings banks under a plan of conduct by which they will aggregate the deposits of the rural communities and redeposit the same while trader Government charge in the banks of Wall Street, thus depleting the circulating medium of the producing regions and unjustly favoring the speculative markets.

INCOME TAX

We favor an income tax as part of our revenue system, and we urge the submission of a constitutional amendment specifically authorizing Congress to levy and collect a tax upon individual and corporate incomes, to the end that wealth may bear its proportionate share of the burdens of the Federal Government.

LABOR AND INJUNCTIONS

The courts of justice are the bulwark of our liberties, and we yield to none in our purpose to maintain their dignity. Our party has given to the bench a long line of distinguished judges, who have added to the respect and confidence in which this department must be jealously maintained. We resent the attempt of the Republican party to raise a false issue respecting the judiciary. It is an unjust reflection upon a great body of our citizens to assume that they lack respect for the courts.

It is the function of the courts to interpret the laws which the people create, and if the laws appear to work economic, social or political injustice, it is our duty to change them. The only basis upon which the integrity of our courts can stand is that of unswerving justice and protection of life, personal liberty and property. If judicial processes may be abused, we should guard them against abuse.

Experience has proved the necessity of a modification of the present law relating to injunctions, and we

reiterate the pledge of our national platforms of 1896 and 1904 in favor of the measure which passed the United States Senate in 1896, but which a Republican Congress has ever since refused to enact, relating to contempt in Federal courts and providing for trial by jury in cases of indirect contempt.

Questions of judicial practice have arisen especially in connection with industrial disputes. We deem that the parties to all judicial proceedings should be treated with rigid impartiality, and that injunctions should not be issued in any cases in which injunctions would not issue if no industrial dispute were involved.

The expanding organization of industry makes it essential that there should be no abridgement of the right of wage earners and producers to organize for the protection of wages and the improvement of labor conditions, to the end that such labor organizations and their members should not be regarded as illegal combinations in restraint of trade.

We favor the eight-hour day on all Government work.

We pledge the Democratic party to the enactment of a law by Congress, as far as the Federal jurisdiction extends, for a general employer's liability act covering injury to body or loss of life of employees.

We pledge the Democratic party to the enactment of a law creating a Department of Labor, represented separately in the President's Cabinet, in which Department shall be included the subject of mines and mining.

MERCHANT MARINE

We believe in the upbuilding of the American merchant marine without new or additional burdens upon the people and without bounties from the public treasury.

THE NAVY

The constitutional provision that a navy shall be provided and maintained means an adequate navy, and we believe that the interests of this country would be best served by having a navy sufficient to defend the coasts of this country and protect American citizens wherever their rights may be in jeopardy.

PROTECTION OF AMERICAN CITIZENS

We pledge ourselves to insist upon the just and lawful protection of our citizens at home and abroad, and to use all proper methods to secure for them, whether native born or naturalized, and without distinction of race or creed, the equal protection of the law and the enjoyment of all rights and privileges open to them under our treaties; and if, under existing treaties, the right of travel and sojourn is denied to American citizens, or recognition is withheld from American passports by any countries on the ground of race or creed, we favor prompt negotiations with the governments of such countries to secure the removal of these unjust discriminations.

We demand that all over the world a duly authenticated passport issued by the Government of the United States to an American citizen, shall be proof of the fact that he is an American citizen and shall entitle him to the treatment due him as such.

CIVIL SERVICE

The laws pertaining to the civil service should be honestly and rigidly enforced, to the end that merit and ability shall be the standard of appointment and promotion rather than services rendered to a political party.

PENSIONS

We favor a generous pension policy, both as a matter of justice to the surviving veterans and their dependents, and because it tends to relieve the country of the necessity of maintaining a large standing army.

HEALTH BUREAU

We advocate the organization of all existing national public health agencies into a national bureau of public health with such power over sanitary conditions connected with factories, mines, tenements, child labor and other such subjects as are properly within the jurisdiction of the Federal Government and do not interfere with the power of the States controlling public health agencies.

AGRICULTURAL AND MECHANICAL EDUCATION

The Democratic party favors the extension of agricultural, mechanical and industrial education. We therefore favor the establishment of district agricultural experiment stations and secondary agricultural and mechanical colleges in the several States.

POPULAR ELECTION OF SENATORS

We favor the election of United States Senators by direct vote of the people, and regard this reform as the gateway to other national reforms.

OKLAHOMA

We welcome Oklahoma to the sisterhood of States and heartily congratulate her upon the auspicious beginning of a great career.

PANAMA CANAL

We believe that the Panama Canal will prove of great value to our country, and favor its speedy completion.

ARIZONA AND NEW MEXICO

The National Democratic party has for the last sixteen years labored for the admission of Arizona and New Mexico as separate States of the Federal Union, and recognizing that each possesses every qualification successfully to maintain separate State governments, we favor the immediate admission of these territories as separate States.

GRAZING LANDS

The establishment of rules and regulations, if any such are necessary, in relation to free grazing upon the public lands outside of forest or other reservations, until the same shall eventually be disposed of, should be left to the people of the States respectively in which such lands may be situated.

WATERWAYS

Water furnishes the cheaper means of transportation, and the National Government, having the control of navigable waters, should improve them to their fullest capacity. We earnestly favor the immediate adoption of a liberal and comprehensive plan for improving every water course in the Union which is justified by the needs of commerce; and, to secure that end, we favor, when practicable, the connection of the Great Lakes with the navigable rivers and with the Gulf through the Mississippi River, and the navigable rivers with each other, and the rivers, bays and sounds of our coasts with each other, by artificial canals, with a view of perfecting a system of inland waterways to be navigated by vessels of standard draught.

We favor the coordination of the various services of the Government connected with waterways in one service, for the purpose of aiding in the completion of such a system of inland waterways; and we favor the creation of a fund ample for continuous work, which shall be conducted under the direction of a commission of experts to be authorized by law.

POST ROADS

We favor Federal aid to State and local authorities in the construction and maintenance of post roads.

TELEGRAPH AND TELEPHONE

We pledge the Democratic party to the enactment of a law to regulate, under the jurisdiction of the Interstate Commerce Commission, the rates and services of telegraph and telephone companies engaged in the transmission of messages between the States.

NATURAL RESOURCES

We repeat the demand for internal development and for the conservation of our natural resources contained in previous platforms, the enforcement of which Mr. Roosevelt has vainly sought from a reluctant party; and to that end we insist upon the preservation, protection and replacement of needed forests, the preservation of the public domain for home seekers, the protection of the national resources in timber, coal, iron and oil against monopolistic control, the development of our waterways for navigation and every other useful purpose, including the irrigation of arid lands, the reclamation of swamp lands, the clarification of streams, the development of water power, and the preservation of electric power, generated by this natural force, from the control of monopoly; and to such end we urge the exercise of all powers, national, State and municipal, both separately and in cooperation.

We insist upon a policy of administration of our forest reserves which shall relieve it of the abuses which have arisen thereunder, and which shall, as far as practicable, conform to the police regulations of the several States wherein the reserves are located, which shall enable homesteaders as of right to occupy and acquire title to all portions thereof which are especially adapted

to agriculture, and which shall furnish a system of timber sales available as well to the private citizen as to the larger manufacturer and consumer.

HAWAII

We favor the application of the principles of the land laws of the United States to our newly acquired territory, Hawaii, to the end that the public lands of that territory may be held and utilized for the benefit of bona-fide homesteaders.

THE PHILIPPINES

We condemn the experiment in imperialism as an inexcusable blunder which has involved us in enormous expense, brought us weakness instead of strength, and laid our nation open to the charge of abandoning a fundamental doctrine of self-government. We favor an immediate declaration of the nation's purpose to recognize the independence of the Philippine Islands as soon as a stable government can be established, such independence to be guaranteed by us as we guarantee the independence of Cuba, until the neutralization of the islands can be secured by treaty with other powers. In recognizing the independence of the Philippines our Government should retain such land as may be necessary for coaling stations and naval bases.

ALASKA AND PUERTO RICO

We demand for the people of Alaska and Puerto Rico the full enjoyment of the rights and privileges of a territorial form of government, and that the officials appointed to administer the government of all our territories and the District of Columbia should be thoroughly qualified by previous bona-fide residence.

PAN-AMERICAN RELATIONS

The Democratic party recognizes the importance and advantage of developing closer ties of Pan-American friendship and commerce between the United States and her sister nations of Latin America, and favors the taking of such steps, consistent with Democratic policies, for better acquaintance, greater mutual confidence, and larger exchange of trade as will bring lasting benefit not only to the United States, but to this group of American Republics, having constitutions, forms of government, ambitions and interests akin to our own.

ASIATIC IMMIGRATION

We favor full protection, by both National and State governments within their respective spheres, of all foreigners residing in the United States under treaty, but we are opposed to the admission of Asiatic immigrants who cannot be amalgamated with our population, or whose presence among us would raise a race issue and involve us in diplomatic controversies with Oriental powers.

FOREIGN PATENTS

We believe that where an American citizen holding a patent in a foreign country is compelled to manufacture under his patent within a certain time, similar restrictions should be applied in this country to the citizens or subjects of such a country.

CONCLUSION

The Democratic party stands for Democracy; the Republican party has drawn to itself all that is aristocratic and plutocratic.

The Democratic party is the champion of equal rights and opportunities for all; the Republican party is the party of privilege and private monopoly. The Democratic party listens to the voice of the whole people and gauges progress by the prosperity and advancement of the average man; the Republican party is subservient to the comparatively few who are the beneficiaries of governmental favoritism. We invite the cooperation of all, regardless of previous political affiliation or past differences, who desire to preserve a government of the people, by the people and for the people and who favor such an administration of the Government as will insure, as far as human wisdom can, that each citizen shall draw from society a reward commensurate with his contribution to the welfare of society.

— 1912 —

We, the representatives of the Democratic party of the United States, in national convention assembled, reaffirm our devotion to the principles of Democratic government formulated by Thomas Jefferson and enforced by a long and illustrious line of Democratic Presidents.

TARIFF REFORM

We declare it to be a fundamental principle of the Democratic party that the Federal government, under the Constitution, has no right or power to impose or collect tariff duties, except for the purpose of revenue, and we demand that the collection of such taxes shall be limited to the necessities of government honestly and economically administered.

The high Republican tariff is the principal cause of the unequal distribution of wealth; it is a system of taxation which makes the rich richer and the poor poorer; under its operations the American farmer and laboring man are the chief sufferers; it raises the cost of the necessaries of life to them, but does not protect their products or wages. The farmer sells largely in free markets and buys almost entirely in the protected markets. In the most highly protected industries, such as cotton and wool, steel and iron, the wages of the laborers are the lowest paid in any of our industries. We denounce the Republican pretence on that subject and assert that American wages are established by competitive conditions, and not by the tariff.

We favor the immediate downward revision of the existing high and in many cases prohibitive tariff duties, insisting that material reductions be speedily made upon the necessaries of life. Articles entering into competition with trust-controlled products and articles of American manufacture which are sold abroad more cheaply than at home should be put upon the free list.

We recognize that our system of tariff taxation is intimately connected with the business of the country, and we favor the ultimate attainment of the principles we advocate by legislation that will not injure or destroy legitimate industry.

We denounce the action of President Taft in vetoing the bills to reduce the tariff in the cotton, woolen, metals, and chemical schedules and the Farmers' free bill, all of which were designed to give immediate relief to the masses from the exactions of the trusts.

The Republican party, while promising tariff revision, has shown by its tariff legislation that such revision is not to be in the people's interest, and having been faithless to its pledges of 1908, it should no longer enjoy the confidence of the nation. We appeal to the American people to support us in our demand for a tariff for revenue only.

HIGH COST OF LIVING

The high cost of living is a serious problem in every American home. The Republican party, in its platform, attempts to escape from responsibility for present conditions by denying that they are due to a protective tariff. We take issue with them on this subject, and charge that excessive prices result in a large measure from the high tariff laws enacted and maintained by the Republican party and from trusts and commercial conspiracies fostered and encouraged by such laws, and we assert that no substantial relief can be secured for the people until import duties on the necessities of life are materially reduced and these criminal conspiracies broken up.

ANTI-TRUST LAW

A private monopoly is indefensible and intolerable. We therefore favor the vigorous enforcement of the criminal as well as the civil law against trusts and trust officials, and demand the enactment of such additional legislation as be necessary to make it impossible for a private monopoly to exist in the United States.

We favor the declaration by the law of the conditions upon which corporations shall be permitted to engage in interstate trade, including, among others, the prevention of holding companies, of interlocking directors, of stock watering, of discrimination in price, and the control by any one corporation of so large a proportion of any industry as to make it a menace to competitive conditions.

We condemn the action of the Republican administration in compromising with the Standard Oil Company and the tobacco trust and its failure to invoke the criminal provisions of the anti-trust law against the officers of those corporations after the court had declared that from the undisputed facts in the record they had violated the criminal provisions of the law.

We regret that the Sherman anti-trust law has received a judicial construction depriving it of much of its efficiency and we favor the enactment of legislation which will restore to the statute the strength of which it has been deprived by such interpretation.

RIGHTS OF THE STATES

We believe in the preservation and maintenance in their full strength and integrity of the three co-ordinate branches of the Federal government, the executive, the legislative, and the judicial, each keeping within its own bounds and not encroaching upon the just powers of either of the others.

Believing that the most efficient results under our system of government are to be attained by the full exercise by the States of their reserved sovereign powers, we denounce as usurpation the efforts of our opponents to deprive the States of any of the rights reserved to them, and to enlarge and magnify by indirection the powers of the Federal government.

We insist upon the full exercise of all the powers of the government, both State and national, to protect the people from injustice at the hands of those who seek to make the government a private asset in business. There is no twilight zone between the nation and the State in which exploiting interests can take refuge from both. It is as necessary that the Federal government shall exercise the powers delegated to it as it is that the States shall exercise the powers reserved to them, but we insist that Federal remedies for the regulation of interstate commerce and for the prevention of private monopoly, shall be added to, and not substituted for State remedies.

INCOME TAX AND POPULAR ELECTION OF SENATORS

We congratulate the country upon the triumph of two important reforms demanded in the last national platform, namely, the amendment of the Federal Constitution authorizing an income tax, and the amendment providing for the popular election of senators, and we call upon the people of all the States to rally to the support of the pending propositions and secure their ratification.

We note with gratification the unanimous sentiment in favor of publicity, before the election, of campaign contributions—a measure demanded in our national platform of 1908, and at that time opposed by the Republican party—and we commend the Democratic House of Representatives for extending the doctrine of publicity to recommendations, verbal and written, upon which presidential appointments are made, to the ownership and control of newspapers, and to the expenditures made by and in behalf of those who aspire to presidential nominations, and we point for additional justification for this legislation to the enormous expenditures of money in behalf of the President and his predecessor in the recent contest for the Republican nomination for President.

PRESIDENTIAL PRIMARY

The movement toward more popular government should be promoted through legislation in each State which will permit the expression of the preference of the electors for national candidates at Presidential primaries.

We direct that the National Committee incorporate in the call for the next nominating convention a requirement that all expressions of preference for Presidential candidates shall be given and the selection of delegates and alternates made through a primary election conducted by the party organization in each State where such expression and election are not provided for by State law. Committeemen who are hereafter to constitute the membership of the Democratic National Committee, and whose election is not provided for by law, shall be chosen in each State at such primary elections, and the service and authority of committeemen, however chosen, shall begin immediately upon the receipt of their credentials, respectively.

CAMPAIGN CONTRIBUTIONS

We pledge the Democratic party to the enactment of a law prohibiting any corporation from contributing to a campaign fund and any individual from contributing any amount above a reasonable maximum.

TERM OF PRESIDENT

We favor a single Presidential term, and to that end urge the adoption of an amendment to the Constitution making the President of the United States ineligible to re-election, and we pledge the candidates of this Convention to this principle.

DEMOCRATIC CONGRESS

At this time, when the Republican party, after a generation of unlimited power in its control of the Federal government, is rent into factions, it is opportune to point to the record of accomplishment of the Democratic House of Representatives in the Sixty-second Congress. We indorse its action and we challenge comparison of its record with that of any Congress which has been controlled by our opponents.

We call the attention of the patriotic citizens of our country to its record of efficiency, economy and constructive legislation.

It has, among other achievements, revised the rules of the House of Representatives so as to give to the Representatives of the American people freedom of speech and of action in advocating, proposing and perfecting remedial legislation.

It his passed bills for the relief of the people and the development of our country; it has endeavored to revise the tariff taxes downward in the interest of the consuming masses and thus to reduce the high cost of living.

It has proposed an amendment to the Federal Constitution providing for the election of United States Senators by the direct vote of the people.

It has secured the admission of Arizona and New Mexico as two sovereign States.

It has required the publicity of campaign expenses both before and after elections and fixed a limit upon the election expenses of United States Senators and Representatives.

It has passed a bill to prevent the abuse of the writ of injunction.

It has passed a law establishing an eight-hour day for workmen on all national public work.

It has passed a resolution which forced the President to take immediate steps to abrogate the Russian treaty.

And it has passed the great supply bills which lessen waste and extravagance, and which reduce the annual expenses of the government by many millions of dollars.

We approve the measure reported by the Democratic leaders in the House of Representatives for the creation of a council of National Defense, which will determine a definite naval program with a view to increased efficiency and economy.

The party that proclaimed and has always enforced the Monroe Doctrine, and was sponsor for the new navy, will continue faithfully to observe the constitutional requirements to provide and maintain an adequate and well-proportioned navy sufficient to defend American policies, protect our citizens and uphold the honor and dignity of the nation.

REPUBLICAN EXTRAVAGANCE

We denounce the profligate waste of the money wrung from the people by oppressive taxation through the lavish appropriations of recent Republican Congresses, which have kept taxes high and reduced the purchasing power of the people's toil. We demand a return to that simplicity and economy which befits a Democratic government and a reduction in the number of useless offices, the salaries of which drain the substance of the people.

RAILROADS, EXPRESS COMPANIES, TELEGRAPH AND TELEPHONE LINES

We favor the efficient supervision and rate regulation of railroads, express companies, telegraph and telephone lines engaged in interstate commerce. To this end we recommend the valuation of railroads, express companies, telegraph and telephone lines by the Interstate Commerce Commission, such valuation to take into consideration the physical value of the property, the original cost, the cost of reproduction, and any element of value that will render the valuation fair and just.

We favor such legislation as will effectually prohibit the railroads and express, telegraph and telephone companies from engaging in business which brings them into competition with their shippers or patrons; also legislation preventing the overissue of stocks and bonds by interstate railroads, express companies, telegraph and telephone lines, and legislation which will assure such reduction in transportation rates as conditions will permit, care being taken to avoid reduction that would compel a reduction of wages, prevent adequate service, or do injustice to legitimate investments.

BANKING LEGISLATION

We oppose the so-called Aldrich bill or the establishment of a central bank; and we believe our country will be largely freed from panics and consequent unemployment and business depression by such a systematic revision of our banking laws as will render temporary relief in localities where such relief is needed, with protection from control of dominion by what is known as the money trust.

Banks exist for the accommodation of the public, and not for the control of business. All legislation on the subject of banking and currency should have for its purpose the securing of these accommodations on terms of absolute security to the public and of complete protection from the misuse of the power that wealth gives to those who possess it.

We condemn the present methods of depositing government funds in a few favored banks, largely situated in or controlled by Wall Street, in return for political favors, and we pledge our party to provide by law for their deposit by competitive bidding in the banking institutions of the country, national and State, without discrimination as to locality, upon approved securities and subject to call by the government.

RURAL CREDITS

Of equal importance with the question of currency reform is the question of rural credits or agricultural finance. Therefore, we recommend that an investigation of agricultural credit societies in foreign countries be made, so that it may be ascertained whether a system of rural credits may be devised suitable to conditions in the United States; and we also favor legislation permitting national banks to loan a reasonable proportion of their funds on real estate security.

We recognize the value of vocational education, and urge Federal appropriations for such training and extension teaching in agriculture in co-operation with the several States.

WATERWAYS

We renew the declaration in our last platform relating to the conservation of our natural resources and the development of our waterways. The present devastation of the Lower Mississippi Valley accentuates the movement for the regulation of river flow by additional bank and levee protection below, and the diversion, storage and control of the flood waters above, their utilization for beneficial purposes in the reclamation of arid and swamp lands and the development of water power, instead of permitting the floods to continue, as heretofore, agents of destruction.

We hold that the control of the Mississippi River is a national problem. The preservation of the depth of its waters for the purpose of navigation, the building of levees to maintain the integrity of its channel and the prevention of the overflow of the land and its consequent devastation, resulting in the interruption of interstate commerce, the disorganization of the mail service, and the enormous loss of life and property impose an obligation which alone can be discharged by the general government.

To maintain an adequate depth of water the entire year, and thereby encourage water transportation, is a consummation worthy of legislative attention, and presents an issue national in its character. It calls for prompt action on the part of Congress, and the Democratic party pledges itself to the enactment of legislation leading to that end.

We favor the co-operation of the United States and the respective States in plans for the comprehensive treatment of all waterways with a view of coordinating plans for channel improvement, with plans for drainage of swamp and overflowed lands, and to this end we favor the appropriation by the Federal government of sufficient funds to make surveys of such lands, to develop plans for draining of the same, and to supervise the work of construction.

We favor the adoption of a liberal and comprehensive plan for the development and improvement of our inland waterways, with economy and efficiency, so as to permit their navigation by vessels of standard draft.

POST ROADS

We favor national aid to State and local authorities in the construction and maintenance of post roads.

RIGHTS OF LABOR

We repeat our declarations of the platform of 1908, as follows:

"The courts of justice are the bulwarks of our liberties, and we yield to none in our purpose to maintain their dignity. Our party has given to the bench a long line of distinguished justices who have added to the respect and confidence in which this department must be jealously maintained. We resent the attempt of the Republican party to raise a false issue respecting the judiciary. It is an unjust reflection upon a great body of our citizens to assume that they lack respect for the courts.

"It is the function of the courts to interpret the laws which the people enact, and if the laws appear to work economic, social or political injustice, it is our duty to change them. The only basis upon which the integrity of our courts can stand is that of unswerving justice and protection of life, personal liberty, and property. As judicial processes may be abused, we should guard them against abuse.

"Experience has proved the necessity of a modification of the present law relating to injunction, and we reiterate the pledges of our platforms of 1896 and 1904 in favor of a measure which passed the United States Senate in 1898, relating to contempt in Federal Courts, and providing for trial by jury in cases of indirect contempt.

"Questions of judicial practice have arisen especially in connection with industrial disputes. We believe that the parties to all judicial proceedings should be treated with rigid impartiality, and that injunctions should not be issued in any case in which an injunction would not issue if no industrial dispute were involved.

"The expanding organization of industry makes it essential that there should be no abridgement of the right of the wage earners and producers to organize for the protection of wages and the improvement of labor conditions, to the end that such labor organizations and their members should not be regarded as illegal combinations in restraint of trade.

"We pledge the Democratic party to the enactment of a law creating a department of labor, represented separately in the President's Cabinet, in which department shall be included the subject of mines and mining."

We pledge the Democratic party, so far as the Federal jurisdiction extends, to an employees' compensation law providing adequate indemnity for injury to body or loss of life.

CONSERVATION

We believe in the conservation and the development, for the use of all the people, of the natural resources of the country. Our forests, our sources of water supply, our arable and our mineral lands, our navigable streams, and all the other material resources with which our country has been so lavishly endowed, constitute the foundation of our national wealth. Such additional legislation as may be necessary to prevent their being wasted or absorbed by special or privileged interests, should be enacted and the policy of their conservation should be rigidly adhered to.

The public domain should be administered and disposed of with due regard to the general welfare. Reservations should be limited to the purposes which they purport to serve and not extended to include land wholly unsuited therefor. The unnecessary withdrawal from sale and settlement of enormous tracts of public land, upon which tree growth never existed and cannot be promoted, tends only to retard development, create discontent, and bring reproach upon the policy of conservation.

The public land laws should be administered in a spirit of the broadest liberality toward the settler exhibiting a *bona-fide* purpose to comply therewith, to the end that the invitation of this government to the landless should be as attractive as possible, and the plain provisions of the forest reserve act permitting homestead entries to be made within the national forests should not be nullified by administrative regulations which amount to a withdrawal of great areas of the same from settlement.

Immediate action should be taken by Congress to make available the vast and valuable coal deposits of Alaska under conditions that will be a perfect guarantee against their falling into the hands of monopolizing corporations, associations or interests.

We rejoice in the inheritance of mineral resources unequalled in extent, variety, or value, and in the development of a mining industry unequalled in its magnitude and importance. We honor the men who, in their hazardous toil underground, daily risk their lives in extracting and preparing for our use the products of the mine, so essential to the industries, the commerce, and the comfort of the people of this country. And we pledge ourselves to the extension of the work of the bureau of mines in every way appropriate for national legislation with a view to safeguarding the lives of the miners, lessening the waste of essential resources, and promoting the economic development of mining, which, along with agriculture, must in the future, even more than in the past, serve as the very foundation of our national prosperity and welfare, and our international commerce.

AGRICULTURE

We believe in encouraging the development of a modern system of agriculture and a systematic effort to improve the conditions of trade in farm products so as to benefit both consumer and producer. And as an efficient means to this end we favor the enactment by Congress of legislation that will suppress the pernicious practice of gambling in agricultural products by organized exchanges or others.

MERCHANT MARINE

We believe in fostering, by constitutional regulation of commerce, the growth of a merchant marine, which shall develop and strengthen the commercial ties which bind us to our sister republics of the south, but without imposing additional burdens upon the people and without bounties or subsidies from the public treasury.

We urge upon Congress the speedy enactment of laws for the greater security of life and property at sea; and we favor the repeal of all laws, and the abrogation of so much of our treaties with other nations, as provide for the arrest and imprisonment of seamen charged with desertion, or with violation of their contract of service.

Such laws and treaties are un-American, and violate the spirit, if not the letter, of the Constitution of the United States.

We favor the exemption from tolls of American ships engaged in coastwise trade passing through the Panama Canal.

We also favor legislation forbidding the use of the Panama Canal by ships owned or controlled by railroad carriers engaged in transportation competitive with the canal.

PURE FOOD AND PUBLIC HEALTH

We reaffirm our previous declarations advocating the union and strengthening of the various governmental agencies relating to pure foods, quarantine, vital statistics and human health. Thus united, and administered without partiality to or discrimination against any school of medicine or system of healing, they would constitute a single health service, not subordinated to any commercial or financial interests, but devoted exclusively to the conservation of human life and efficiency. Moreover, this health service should co-operate with the health agencies of our various States and cities, without interference with their prerogatives, or with the freedom of individuals to employ such medical or hygienic aid as they may see fit.

CIVIL SERVICE LAW

The law pertaining to the civil service should be honestly and rigidly enforced, to the end that merit and ability shall be the standard of appointment and promotion, rather than service rendered to a political party; and we favor a reorganization of the civil service, with adequate compensation commensurate with the class of work performed for all officers and employees; and also favor the extension to all classes of civil service employees of the benefits of the provisions of the employers' liability law. We also recognize the right of direct petition to Congress by employees for the redress of grievances.

LAW REFORM

We recognize the urgent need of reform in the administration of civil and criminal law in the United States, and we recommend the enactment of such legislation and the promotion of such measures as will rid the present legal system of the delays, expense, and uncertainties incident to the system as now administered.

THE PHILIPPINES

We reaffirm the position thrice announced by the Democracy in national convention assembled against a policy of imperialism and colonial exploitation in the Philippines or elsewhere. We condemn the experiment in imperialism as an inexcusable blunder, which has involved us in enormous expense, brought us weakness instead of strength, and laid our nation open to the charge of abandonment of the fundamental doctrine of self-government. We favor an immediate declaration of the nation's purpose to recognize the independence of the Philippine Islands as soon as a stable government can be established, such independence to be guaranteed by us until the neutralization of the islands can be secured by treaty with other Powers.

In recognizing the independence of the Philippines, our government should retain such land as may be necessary for coaling stations and naval bases.

ARIZONA AND NEW MEXICO

We welcome Arizona and New Mexico to the sisterhood of States, and heartily congratulate them upon their auspicious beginnings of great and glorious careers.

ALASKA

We demand for the people of Alaska full enjoyment of the rights and privileges of a Territorial form of government, and we believe that the officials appointed to administer the government of all our Territories and the District of Columbia should be qualified by previous bona-fide residence.

THE RUSSIAN TREATY

We commend the patriotism of the Democratic members of the Senate and House of Representatives which compelled the termination of the Russian treaty of 1832, and we pledge ourselves anew to preserve the sacred rights of American citizenship at home and abroad. No treaty should receive the sanction of our government which does not recognize the equality of all of our citizens, irrespective of race or creed, and which does not expressly guarantee the fundamental right of expatriation.

The constitutional rights of American citizens should protect them on our borders and go with them throughout the world, and every American citizen residing or having property in any foreign country is entitled to and must be given the full protection of the United States government, both for himself and his property.

PARCELS POST AND RURAL DELIVERY

We favor the establishment of a parcels post or postal express, and also the extension of the rural delivery system as rapidly as practicable.

PANAMA CANAL EXPOSITION

We hereby express our deep interest in the great Panama Canal Exposition to be held in San Francisco in 1915, and favor such encouragement as can be properly given.

PROTECTION OF NATIONAL UNIFORM

We commend to the several States the adoption of a law making it an offense for the proprietors of places of public amusement and entertainment to discriminate against the uniform of the United States, similar to the law passed by Congress applicable to the District of Columbia and the Territories in 1911.

PENSIONS

We renew the declaration of our last platform relating to a generous pension policy.

RULE OF THE PEOPLE

We direct attention to the fact that the Democratic party's demand for a return to the rule of the people expressed in the national platform four years ago, has now become the accepted doctrine of a large majority of the electors. We again remind the country that only by a larger exercise of the reserved power of the people can they protect themselves from the misuse of delegated power and the usurpation of government instrumentalities by special interests. For this reason the National Convention insisted on the overthrow of Cannonism and the inauguration of a system by which United States Senators could be elected by direct vote. The Democratic party offers itself to the country as an agency through which the complete overthrow and extirpation of corruption, fraud, and machine rule in American politics can be effected.

CONCLUSION

Our platform is one of principles which we believe to be essential to our national welfare. Our pledges are made to be kept when in office, as well as relied upon during the campaign, and we invite the co-operation of all citizens, regardless of party, who believe in maintaining unimpaired the institutions and traditions of our country.

— 1916 —

The Democratic Party, in National Convention assembled, adopts the following declaration to the end that the people of the United States may both realize the achievements wrought by four years of Democratic administration and be apprised of the policies to which the party is committed for the further conduct of National affairs.

I. RECORD OF ACHIEVEMENT

We endorse the administration of Woodrow Wilson. It speaks for itself. It is the best exposition of sound Democratic policy at home and abroad.

We challenge comparison of our record, our keeping of pledges and our constructive legislation, with those of any party of any time.

We found our country hampered by special privilege, a vicious tariff, obsolete banking laws and an inelastic currency. Our foreign affairs were dominated by commercial interests for their selfish ends. The Republican Party, despite repeated pledges, was impotent to correct abuses which it had fostered. Under our administration, under a leadership which has never faltered, these abuses have been corrected, and our people have been freed therefrom.

Our archaic banking and currency system, prolific of panic and disaster under Republican administrations—along the refuge of the money trust—has been supplanted by the Federal Reserve Act, a true democracy of credit under government control, already proved a financial bulwark in a world crisis, mobilizing our resources, placing abundant credit at the disposal of legitimate industry and making a currency panic impossible.

We have created a Federal Trade Commission to accommodate perplexing questions arising under the anti-trust laws, so that monopoly may be strangled at its birth and legitimate industry encouraged. Fair competition in business is now assured.

We have effected an adjustment of the tariff, adequate for revenue under peace conditions, and fair to the consumer and to the producer. We have adjusted the burdens of taxation so that swollen incomes bear their equitable share. Our revenues have been sufficient in times of world stress, and will largely exceed the expenditures for the current fiscal year.

We have lifted human labor from the category of commodities and have secured to the workingman the right of voluntary association for his protection and welfare. We have protected the rights of the laborer against the unwarranted issuance of writs of injunc-

tion, and have guaranteed to him the right of trial by jury in cases of alleged contempt committed outside the presence of the court.

We have advanced the parcel post to genuine efficiency, enlarged the postal savings system, added ten thousand rural delivery routes and extensions, thus reaching two and one-half millions additional people, improved the postal service in every branch, and for the first time in our history, placed the post-office system on a self-supporting basis, with actual surplus in 1913, 1914 and 1916.

II. ECONOMIC FREEDOM

The reforms which were most obviously needed to clear away special privilege, prevent unfair discrimination and release the energies of men of all ranks and advantages, have been effected by recent legislation. We must now remove, as far as possible, every remaining element of unrest and uncertainty from the path of the business men of America, and secure for them a continued period of quiet, assured and confident prosperity.

III. TARIFF

We reaffirm our belief in the doctrine of a tariff for the purpose of providing sufficient revenue for the operation of the government economically administered, and unreservedly endorse the Underwood Tariff Law as truly exemplifying that doctrine. We recognize that tariff rates are necessarily subject to change to meet changing conditions in the world's production and trade. The events of the last two years have brought about many momentous changes. In some respects their effects are yet conjectural and wait to be disclosed, particularly in regard to our foreign trade. Two years of a war which has directly involved most of the chief industrial nations in the world, and which has indirectly affected the life and industry of all nations are bringing about economic changes more varied and far-reaching than the world has ever before experienced. In order to ascertain just what those changes may be, the Democratic Congress is providing for a non-partisan tariff commission to make impartial and thorough study of every economic fact that may throw light either upon our past or upon our future fiscal policy with regard to the imposition of taxes on imports or with regard to the changed and changing conditions under which our trade is carried on. We cordially endorse this timely proposal and declare ourselves in sympathy with the principle and purpose of shaping legislation within that field in accordance with clearly established facts rather than in accordance with the demands of selfish interests or upon information provided largely, if not exclusively, by them.

IV. AMERICANISM

The part that the United States will play in the new day of international relationships that is now upon us will depend upon our preparation and our character. The Democratic Party, therefore, recognizes the assertion and triumphant demonstration of the indivisibility and coherent strength of the Nation as the supreme issue of this day in which the whole world faces the crisis of manifold change. It summons all men of whatever origin or creed who would count themselves Americans, to join in making clear to all the world the unity and consequent power of America. This is an issue of patriotism. To taint it with partisanship would be to defile it. In this day of test, America must show itself not a nation of partisans but a nation of patriots. There is gathered here in America the best of the blood, the industry and the genius of the whole world, the elements of a great race and a magnificent society to be welded into a mighty and splendid Nation. Whoever, actuated by the purpose to promote the interest of a foreign power, in disregard of our own country's welfare or to injure this Government in its foreign relations or cripple or destroy its industries at home, and whoever by arousing prejudices of a racial, religious or other nature creates discord and strife among our people so as to obstruct the wholesome process of unification, is faithless to the trust which the privileges of citizenship repose in him and is disloyal to his country. We therefore condemn as subversive to this Nation's unity and integrity, and as destructive of its welfare, the activities and designs of every group or organization, political or otherwise, that has for its object the advancement of the interest of a foreign power, whether such object is promoted by intimidating the government, a political party, or representatives of the people, or which is calculated and tends to divide our people into antagonistic groups and thus to destroy that complete agreement and solidarity of the people and that unity of sentiment and purpose so essential to the perpetuity of the Nation and its free institutions. We condemn all alliances and combinations of individuals in this country, of whatever nationality or descent, who agree and conspire together for the purpose of embarrassing or weakening our government or of improperly influencing or coercing our public representatives in dealing or negotiating with any foreign power. We charge that such conspiracies among a lim-

ited number exist and have been instigated for the purpose of advancing the interests of foreign countries to the prejudice and detriment of our own country. We condemn any political party which, in view of the activity of such conspirators, surrenders its integrity or modifies its policy.

V. PREPAREDNESS

Along with the proof of our character as a Nation must go the proof of our power to play the part that legitimately belongs to us. The people of the United States love peace. They respect the rights and covet the friendship of all other nations. They desire neither any additional territory nor any advantage which cannot be peacefully gained by their skill, their industry, or their enterprise; but they insist upon having absolute freedom of National life and policy, and feel that they owe it to themselves and to the role of spirited independence which it is their sole ambition to play that they should render themselves secure against the hazard of interference from any quarter, and should be able to protect their rights upon the seas or in any part of the world. We therefore favor the maintenance of an army fully adequate to the requirements of order, of safety, and of the protection of the Nation's rights, the fullest development of modern methods of seacoast defense and the maintenance of an adequate reserve of citizens trained to arms and prepared to safeguard the people and territory of the United States against any danger of hostile action which may unexpectedly arise; and a fixed policy for the continuous development of a navy worthy to support the great naval traditions of the United States and fully equal to the international tasks which this Nation hopes and expects to take a part in performing. The plans and enactments of the present Congress afford substantial proof of our purpose in this exigent matter.

VI. INTERNATIONAL RELATIONS

The Democratic administration has throughout the present war scrupulously and successfully held to the old paths of neutrality and to the peaceful pursuit of the legitimate objects of our National life which statesmen of all parties and creeds have prescribed for themselves in America since the beginning of our history. But the circumstances of the last two years have revealed necessities of international action which no former generation can have foreseen. We hold that it is the duty of the United States to use its power, not only to make itself safe at home, but also to make secure its just interests throughout the world, and, both for this end and in the interest of humanity, to assist the world in securing settled peace and justice. We believe that every people has the right to choose the sovereignty under which it shall live; that the small states of the world have a right to enjoy from other nations the same respect for their sovereignty and for their territorial integrity that great and powerful nations expect and insist upon; and that the world has a right to be free from every disturbance of its peace that has its origin in aggression or disregard of the rights of people and nations; and we believe that the time has come when it is the duty of the United States to join the other nations of the world in any feasible association that will effectively serve those principles, to maintain inviolate the complete security of the highway of the seas for the common and unhindered use of all nations.

The present administration has consistently sought to act upon and realize in its conduct of the foreign affairs of the Nation the principle that should be the object of any association of the nations formed to secure the peace of the world and the maintenance of national and individual rights. It has followed the highest American traditions. It has preferred respect for the fundamental rights of smaller states even to property interests, and has secured the friendship of the people of these States for the United States by refusing to make a more material interest an excuse for the assertion of our superior power against the dignity of their sovereign independence. It has regarded the lives of its citizens and the claims of humanity as of greater moment than material rights, and peace as the best basis for the just settlement of commercial claims. It has made the honor and ideals of the United States its standard alike in negotiation and action.

VII. PAN-AMERICAN CONCORD

We recognize now, as we have always recognized, a definite and common interest between the United States and the other peoples and republics of the Western Hemisphere in all matters of National independence and free political development. We favor the establishment and maintenance of the closest relations of amity and mutual helpfulness between the United States and the other republics of the American continents for the support of peace and the promotion of a common prosperity. To that end we favor all measures which may be necessary to facilitate intimate intercourse and promote commerce between the United States and her neighbors to the south of us, and such international understandings as may be practicable and suitable to accomplish these ends.

We commend the action of the Democratic administration in holding the Pan-American Financial Conference at Washington in May, 1915, and organizing the International High Commission, which represented the United States in the recent meeting of representatives of the Latin-American Republics at Buenos Aires, April, 1916, which have so greatly promoted the friendly relations between the people of the Western Hemisphere.

VIII. MEXICO

The Monroe Doctrine is reasserted as a principle of Democratic faith. That doctrine guarantees the independent republics of the two Americas against aggression from another continent. It implies, as well, the most scrupulous regard upon our part for the sovereignty of each of them. We court their good will. We seek not to despoil them. The want of a stable, responsible government in Mexico, capable of repressing and punishing marauders and bandit bands, who have not only taken the lives and seized and destroyed the property of American citizens in that country, but have insolently invaded our soil, made war upon and murdered our people thereon, has rendered it necessary temporarily to occupy, by our armed forces, a portion of the territory of that friendly state. Until, by the restoration of law and order therein, a repetition of such incursions is improbable, the necessity for their remaining will continue. Intervention, implying as it does, military subjugation, is revolting to the people of the United States, notwithstanding the provocation to that course has been great and should be resorted to, if at all, only as a last recourse. The stubborn resistance of the President and his advisers to every demand and suggestion to enter upon it, is creditable alike to them and to the people in whose name he speaks.

IX. MERCHANT MARINE

Immediate provision should be made for the development of the carrying trade of the United States. Our foreign commerce has in the past been subject to many unnecessary and vexatious obstacles in the way of legislation of Republican Congresses. Until the recent Democratic tariff legislation, it was hampered by unreasonable burdens of taxation. Until the recent banking legislation, it had at its disposal few of the necessary instrumentalities of international credit and exchange. Until the formulation of the pending act to promote the construction of a merchant marine, it lacked even the prospect of adequate carriage by sea.

We heartily endorse the purposes and policy of the pending shipping bill and favor all such additional measures of constructive or remedial legislation as may be necessary to restore our flag to the seas and to provide further facilities for our foreign commerce, particularly such laws as may be requisite to remove unfair conditions of competition in the dealings of American merchants and producers with competitors in foreign markets.

X. CONSERVATION

For the safeguarding and quickening of the life of our own people, we favor the conservation and development of the natural resources of the country through a policy which shall be positive rather than negative, a policy which shall not withhold such resources from development but which, while permitting and encouraging their use, shall prevent both waste and monopoly in their exploitation, and we earnestly favor the passage of acts which will accomplish these objects, reaffirming the declaration of the platform of 1912 on this subject.

The policy of reclaiming our arid lands should be steadily adhered to.

XI. THE ADMINISTRATION AND THE FARMER

We favor the vigorous prosecution of investigations and plans to render agriculture more profitable and country life more healthful, comfortable and attractive, and we believe that this should be a dominant aim of the Nation as well as of the States. With all its recent improvement, farming still lags behind other occupations in development as a business, and the advantages of an advancing civilization have not accrued to rural communities in a fair proportion. Much has been accomplished in this field under the present administration, far more than under any previous administration. In the Federal Reserve Act of the last Congress, and the Rural Credits Act of the present Congress, the machinery has been created which will make credit available to the farmer constantly and readily, placing him at last upon a footing of equality with the merchant and the manufacturer in securing the capital necessary to carry on his enterprises. Grades and standards necessary to the intelligent and successful conduct of the business of agriculture have also been established or are in the course of establishment by law. The long-needed Cotton Futures Act,

passed by the Sixty-Third Congress, has now been in successful operation for nearly two years. A Grain Grades Bill, long needed, and a permissive Warehouse Bill, intended to provide better storage facilities and to enable the farmer to obtain certificates upon which he may secure advances of money have been passed by the House of Representatives, have been favorably reported to the Senate, and will probably become law during the present session of the Congress. Both Houses have passed a good-roads measure, which will be of far-reaching benefit to all agricultural communities. Above all, the most extraordinary and significant progress has been made, under the direction of the Department of Agriculture, in extending and perfecting practical farm demonstration work which is so rapidly substituting scientific for empirical farming. But it is also necessary that rural activities should be better directed through co-operation and organization, that unfair methods of competition should be eliminated and the conditions requisite for the just, orderly and economical marketing of farm products created. We approve the Democratic administration for having emphatically directed attention for the first time to the essential interests of agriculture involved in farm marketing and finance, for creating the Office of Markets and Rural Organization in connection with the Department of Agriculture, and for extending the co-operative machinery necessary for conveying information to farmers by means of demonstration. We favor continued liberal provision, not only for the benefit of production, but also for the study and solution of problems of farm marketing and finance and for the extension of existing agencies for improving country life.

XII. GOOD ROADS

The happiness, comfort and prosperity of rural life, and the development of the city, are alike conserved by the construction of public highways. We, therefore, favor national aid in the construction of post roads and roads for like purposes.

XIII. GOVERNMENT EMPLOYMENT

We hold that the life, health and strength of the men, women and children of the Nation are its greatest asset and that in the conservation of these the Federal Government, wherever it acts as the employer of labor, should both on its own account and as an example, put into effect the following principles of just employment:

1. A living wage for all employees.
2. A working day not to exceed eight hours, with one day of rest in seven.
3. The adoption of safety appliances and the establishment of thoroughly sanitary conditions of labor.
4. Adequate compensation for industrial accidents.
5. The standards of the "Uniform Child Labor Law," wherever minors are employed.
6. Such provisions for decency, comfort and health in the employment of women as should be accorded the mothers of the race.
7. An equitable retirement law providing for the retirement of superannuated and disabled employees of the civil service, to the end that a higher standard of efficiency may be maintained.

We believe also that the adoption of similar principles should be urged and applied in the legislation of the States with regard to labor within their borders and that through every possible agency the life and health of the people of the Nation should be conserved.

XIV. LABOR

We declare our faith in the Seamen's Act, passed by the Democratic Congress, and we promise our earnest continuance of its enforcement.

We favor the speedy enactment of an effective Federal Child Labor Law and the regulation of the shipment of prison-made goods in interstate commerce.

We favor the creation of a Federal Bureau of Safety in the Department of Labor, to gather facts concerning industrial hazards, and to recommend legislation to prevent the maiming and killing of human beings.

We favor the extension of the powers and functions of the Federal Bureau of Mines.

We favor the development upon a systematic scale of the means already begun under the present administration, to assist laborers throughout the Nation to seek and obtain employment, and the extension of the Federal Government of the same assistance and encouragement as is now given to agricultural training.

We heartily commend our newly established Department of Labor for its fine record in settling strikes by personal advice and through conciliating agents.

XV. PUBLIC HEALTH

We favor a thorough reconsideration of the means and methods by which the Federal Government handles questions of public health to the end that human life

may be conserved by the elimination of loathsome disease, the improvement of sanitation and the diffusion of a knowledge of disease prevention.

We favor the establishment by the Federal Government of tuberculosis sanitariums for needy tubercular patients.

XVI. SENATE RULES

We favor such alteration of the rules of procedure of the Senate of the United States as will permit the prompt transaction of the Nation's legislative business.

XVII. ECONOMY AND THE BUDGET

We demand careful economy in all expenditures for the support of the Government, and to that end favor a return by the House of Representatives to its former practice of initiating and preparing all appropriation bills through a single committee chosen from its membership, in order that responsibility may be central, expenditures standardized and made uniform, and waste and duplication in the public service as much as possible avoided. We favor this as a practicable first step towards a budget system.

XVIII. CIVIL SERVICE

We reaffirm our declarations for the rigid enforcement of the civil service laws.

XIX. PHILIPPINE ISLANDS

We heartily endorse the provisions of the bill, recently passed by the House of Representatives, further promoting self-government in the Philippine Islands as being in fulfillment of the policy declared by the Democratic Party in its last national platform, and we reiterate our endorsement of the purpose of ultimate independence for the Philippine Islands, expressed in the preamble of that measure.

XX. WOMAN SUFFRAGE

We recommend the extension of the franchise to the women of the country by the States upon the same terms as to men.

XXI. PROTECTION OF CITIZENS

We again declare the policy that the sacred rights of American citizenship must be preserved at home and abroad, and that no treaty shall receive the sanction of our Government which does not expressly recognize the absolute equality of all our citizens irrespective of race, creed or previous nationality, and which does not recognize the right of expatriation. The American Government should protect American citizens in their rights, not only at home but abroad, and any country having a government should be held to strict accountability for any wrongs done them, either to person or property. At the earliest practical opportunity our country should strive earnestly for peace among the warring nations of Europe and seek to bring about the adoption of the fundamental principle of justice and humanity, that all men shall enjoy equality of right and freedom from discrimination in the lands wherein they dwell.

XXII. PRISON REFORM

We demand that the modern principles of prison reform be applied in our Federal Penal System. We favor such work for prisoners as shall give them training in remunerative occupations so that they may make an honest living when released from prison; the setting apart of the net wages of the prisoner to be paid to his dependent family or to be reserved for his own use upon his release; the liberal extension of the principles of the Federal Parole Law, with due regard both to the welfare of the prisoner and the interests of society; the adoption of the Probation System especially in the case of first offenders not convicted of serious crimes.

XXIII. PENSIONS

We renew the declarations of recent Democratic platforms relating to generous pensions for soldiers and their widows, and call attention to our record of performance in this particular.

XXIV. WATERWAYS AND FLOOD CONTROL

We renew the declaration in our last two platforms relating to the development of our waterways. The recent devastation of the lower Mississippi Valley and several other sections by floods accentuates the move-ment for the regulation of river flow by additional bank and levee protection below, and diversion, storage and control of the flood waters above, and their utilization for beneficial purposes in the reclamation of arid and swamp lands and development of water-power, instead of permitting the floods to continue as heretofore agents of destruction. We hold that the control of the Mississippi River is a National problem. The preservation of the depth of its waters for purposes of navigation, the building of levees and works of bank protection to maintain the integrity of its channel and prevent the overflow of its valley resulting in the interruption of interstate commerce, the disorganization of the mail service, and the enormous loss of life and property, impose an obligation which alone can be discharged by the National Government.

We favor the adoption of a liberal and comprehensive plan for the development and improvement of our harbors and inland waterways with economy and efficiency so as to permit their navigation by vessels of standard draft.

XXV. ALASKA

It has been and will be the policy of the Democratic Party to enact all laws necessary for the speedy development of Alaska and its great natural resources.

XXVI. TERRITORIES

We favor granting to the people of Alaska, Hawaii and Puerto Rico the traditional territorial government accorded to the territories of the United States since the beginning of our Government, and we believe that the officials appointed to administer the government of those several territories should be qualified by previous bonafide residence.

XXVII. CANDIDATES

We unreservedly endorse our President and Vice-President, Woodrow Wilson of New Jersey, and Thomas Riley Marshall of Indiana, who have performed the functions of their great offices faithfully and impartially and with distinguished ability.

In particular, we commend to the American people the splendid diplomatic victories of our great President, who has preserved the vital interests of our Government and its citizens, and kept us out of war.

Woodrow Wilson stands to-day the greatest American of his generation.

XXVIII. CONCLUSION

This is a critical hour in the history of America, a critical hour in the history of the world. Upon the record above set forth, which shows great constructive achievement in following out a consistent policy for our domestic and internal development; upon the record of the Democratic administration, which has maintained the honor, the dignity and the interests of the United States, and, at the same time, retained the respect and friendship of all the nations of the world; and upon the great policies for the future strengthening of the life of our country, the enlargement of our National vision and the ennobling of our international relations, as set forth above, we appeal with confidence to the voters of the country.

— 1920 —

The Democratic Party, in its National Convention now assembled, sends greetings to the President of the United States, Woodrow Wilson, and hails with patriotic pride the great achievements for country and the world wrought by a Democratic administration under his leadership.

It salutes the mighty people of this great republic, emerging with imperishable honor from the severe tests and grievous strains of the most tragic war in history, having earned the plaudits and the gratitude of all free nations.

It declares its adherence to the fundamental progressive principles of social, economic and industrial justice and advance, and purposes to resume the great work of translating these principles into effective laws, begun and carried far by the Democratic administration and interrupted only when the war claimed all the national energies for the single task of victory.

LEAGUE OF NATIONS

The Democratic Party favors the League of Nations as the surest, if not the only, practicable means of maintaining the permanent peace of the world and terminating the insufferable burden of great military and naval establishments. It was for this that America broke away from traditional isolation and spent her blood and treasure to crush a colossal scheme of conquest. It was upon this basis that the President of the United States, in prearrangement with our allies, consented to a suspension of hostilities against the Imperial German Government; the Armistice was granted and a Treaty of Peace negotiated upon the definite assurance to Germany, as well as to the powers pitted against Germany, that "a general association of nations must be formed, under specific covenants, for the purpose of affording mutual guarantees of political independence and territorial integrity to great and small states alike." Hence, we not only congratulate the President on the vision manifested and the vigor exhibited in the prosecution of the war; but we felicitate him and his associates on the exceptional achievement at Paris involved in the adoption of a league and treaty so near akin to previously expressed American ideals and so intimately related to the aspirations of civilized peoples everywhere.

We commend the President for his courage and his high conception of good faith in steadfastly standing for the covenant agreed to by all the associated and allied nations at war with Germany, and we condemn the Republican Senate for its refusal to ratify the treaty merely because it was the product of Democratic statesmanship, thus interposing partisan envy and personal hatred in the way of the peace and renewed prosperity of the world.

By every accepted standard of international morality the President is justified in asserting that the honor of the country is involved in this business; and we point to the accusing fact that, before it was determined to initiate political antagonism to the treaty, the now Republican chairman of the Senate Foreign Relations Committee himself publicly proclaimed that any proposition for a separate peace with Germany, such as he and his party associates thereafter reported to the Senate, would make us "guilty of the blackest crime."

On May 15 last the Knox substitute for the Versailles Treaty was passed by the Republican Senate; and this Convention can contrive no more fitting characterization of its obloquy than that made in the *Forum* magazine of December, 1918, by Henry Cabot Lodge, when he said:

"If we send our armies and young men abroad to be killed and wounded in northern France and Flanders with no result but this, our entrance into war with such an intention was a crime which nothing can justify. The intent of Congress and the intent of the President was that there could be no peace until we could create a situation where no such war as this could recur.

"We cannot make peace except in company with our allies.

"It would brand us with everlasting dishonor and bring ruin to us also if we undertook to make a separate peace."

Thus, to that which Mr. Lodge, in saner moments, considered "the blackest crime" he and his party in madness sought to give the sanctity of law; that which eighteen months ago was of "everlasting dishonor," the Republican Party and its candidates to-day accept as the essence of faith.

We endorse the President's view of our international obligations and his firm stand against reservations designed to cut to pieces the vital provisions of the Versailles Treaty and we commend the Democrats in Congress for voting against resolutions for a separate peace which would disgrace the nation.

We advocate the immediate ratification of the treaty without reservations which would impair its essential integrity; but do not oppose the acceptance of any reservations making clearer or more specific the obligations of the United States to the league associates. Only by doing this may we retrieve the reputation of this nation among the powers of the earth and recover the moral leadership which President Wilson won and which Republican politicians at Washington sacrificed. Only by doing this may we hope to aid effectively in the restoration of order throughout the world and to take the place which we should assume in the front rank of spiritual, commercial and industrial advancement.

We reject as utterly vain, if not vicious, the Republican assumption that ratification of the treaty and membership in the League of Nations would in any wise impair the integrity or independence of our country. The fact that the covenant has been entered into by twenty-nine nations, all as jealous of their independence as we of ours, is a sufficient refutation of such a charge. The President repeatedly has declared, and this Convention reaffirms, that all our duties and obligations as a member of the league must be fulfilled in strict conformity with the Constitution of the United States, embodied in which is the fundamental requirement of declaratory action by the Congress before this nation may become a participant in any war.

SENATE RULES

We favor such alteration of the rules of procedure of the Senate of the United States as will permit the prompt transaction of the nation's legislative business.

CONDUCT OF THE WAR

During the war President Wilson exhibited the very broadest conception of liberal Americanism. In his conduct of the war, as in the general administration of his high office, there was no semblance of partisan bias. He invited to Washington as his councilors and coadjutors hundreds of the most prominent and pronounced Republicans in the country. To these he committed responsibilities of the gravest import and most confidential nature. Many of them had charge of vital activities of the government.

And yet, with the war successfully prosecuted and gloriously ended, the Republican Party in Congress, far from applauding the masterly leadership of the President and felicitating the country on the amazing achievements of the American government, has meanly requited the considerate course of the chief magistrate by savagely defaming the Commander-in-Chief of the Army and Navy and by assailing nearly every public officer of every branch of the service intimately concerned in winning the war abroad and preserving the security of the government at home.

We express something that the Republican Convention omitted to express—we express to the soldiers and sailors of America the admiration of their fellow countrymen. Guided by the genius of such commanders as General John J. Pershing, the armed forces of America constituted a decisive factor in the victory and brought new lustre to the flag.

We commend the patriotic men and women, who sustained the efforts of their government in the crucial hours of the war, and contributed to the brilliant administrative success, achieved under the broad-visioned leadership of the President.

FINANCIAL ACHIEVEMENTS

A review of the record of the Democratic Party during the administration of Woodrow Wilson presents a chapter of substantial achievements unsurpassed in the history of the republic. For fifty years before the advent of this administration periodical convulsions had impeded the industrial progress of the American people and caused unestimatable loss and distress. By the enactment of the Federal Reserve Act the old system, which bred panics, was replaced by a new system, which insured confidence. It was an indispensable factor in winning the war, and to-day it is the hope and inspiration of business. Indeed, one vital danger against which the American people should keep constantly on guard, is the commitment of this system to partisan enemies who struggled against its adoption and vainly attempted to retain in the hands of speculative bankers a monopoly of the currency and credits of the nation. Already there are well-defined indications of an assault upon the vital principles of the system in the event of Republican success at the elections in November.

Under Democratic leadership the American people successfully financed their stupendous part in the greatest war of all time. The Treasury wisely insisted during the war upon meeting an adequate portion of the war expenditure from current taxes and the bulk of the balance from popular loans, and, during the first full fiscal year after fighting stopped, upon meeting current expenditures from current receipts notwithstanding the new and unnecessary burdens thrown upon the Treasury by the delay, obstruction and extravagance of a Republican Congress.

The non-partisan Federal Reserve authorities have been wholly free of political interference or motive; and, in their own time and their own way, have used courageously, though cautiously, the instruments at their disposal to prevent undue expansion of credit in the country. As a result of these sound Treasury and Federal Reserve policies, the inevitable war inflation has been held down to a minimum, and the cost of living has been prevented from increasing in this country in proportion to the increase in other belligerent countries and in neutral countries which are in close contact with the world's commerce and exchanges.

After a year and a half of fighting in Europe, and despite another year and a half of Republican obstruction at home, the credit of the Government of the United States stands unimpaired, the Federal Reserve note is the unit of value throughout all the world; and the United States is the one great country in the world which maintains a free gold market.

We condemn the attempt of the Republican party to deprive the American people of their legitimate pride in the financing of the war—an achievement without parallel in the financial history of this or any other country, in this or any other war. And in particular we condemn the pernicious attempt of the Republican Party to create discontent among the holders of the bonds of the Government of the United States and to drag our public finance and our banking and currency system back into the arena of party politics.

TAX REVISION

We condemn the failure of the present Congress to respond to the oft-repeated demand of the President and the Secretary of the Treasury to revise the existing tax laws. The continuance in force in peace times of taxes devised under pressure of imperative necessity to produce a revenue for war purposes is indefensible and can only result in lasting injury to the people. The Republican Congress persistently failed, through sheer political cowardice, to make a single move to-

ward a readjustment of tax laws which it denounced before the last election and was afraid to revise before the next election.

We advocate reform and a searching revision of the War Revenue Acts to fit peace conditions so that the wealth of the nation may not be withdrawn from productive enterprise and diverted to wasteful or nonproductive expenditure.

We demand prompt action by the next Congress for a complete survey of existing taxes and their modification and simplification with a view to secure greater equity and justice in the tax burden and improvement in administration.

PUBLIC ECONOMY

Claiming to have effected great economies in government expenditures, the Republican Party cannot show the reduction of one dollar in taxation as a corollary of this false pretense. In contrast, the last Democratic Congress enacted legislation reducing taxes from eight billions, designed to be raised, to six billions for the first year after the Armistice, and to four billions thereafter; and there the total is left undiminished by our political adversaries. Two years after Armistice Day a Republican Congress provided for expanding the stupendous sum of $5,403,390,327.30, and wouldn't even lop off the thirty cents.

Affecting great paper economies by reducing departmental estimates of sums which would not have been spent in any event, and by reducing formal appropriations, the Republican statement of expenditures omits the pregnant fact that the Congress authorized the use of one and a half billion dollars in the hands of various departments and bureaus, which otherwise would have been covered back into the Treasury, and which should be added to the Republican total of expenditures.

HIGH COST OF LIVING

The high cost of living and the depreciation of bond values in this country are primarily due to the war itself, to the necessary governmental expenditures for the destructive purposes of war, to private extravagance, to the world shortage of capital, to the inflation of foreign currencies and credits, and, in large degree, to conscienceless profiteering.

The Republican Party is responsible for the failure to restore peace and peace conditions in Europe, which is a principal cause of post-armistice inflation the world over. It has denied the demand of the President for necessary legislation to deal with secondary and local causes. The sound policies pursued by the Treasury and the Federal Reserve system have limited in this country, though they could not prevent, the inflation which was worldwide. Elected upon specific promises to curtail public expenditures and to bring the country back to a status of effective economy, the Republican Party in Congress wasted time and energy for more than a year in vain and extravagant investigations, costing the tax-payers great sums of money, while revealing nothing beyond the incapacity of Republican politicians to cope with the problems. Demanding that the President, from his place at the Peace Table, call the Congress into extraordinary session for imperative purposes of readjustment, the Congress when convened spent thirteen months in partisan pursuits, failing to repeal a single war statute which harassed business or to initiate a single constructive measure to help business. It busied itself making a pre-election record of pretended thrift, having not one particle of substantial existence in fact. It raged against profiteers and the high cost of living without enacting a single statute to make the former afraid or doing a single act to bring the latter within limitations.

The simple truth is that the high cost of living can only be remedied by increased production, strict governmental economy and a relentless pursuit of those who take advantage of post-war conditions and are demanding and receiving outrageous profits.

We pledge the Democratic Party to a policy of strict economy in government expenditures, and to the enactment and enforcement of such legislation as may be required to bring profiteers before the bar of criminal justice.

THE TARIFF

We reaffirm the traditional policy of the Democratic Party in favor of a tariff for revenue only and confirm the policy of basing tariff revisions upon the intelligent research of a non-partisan commission, rather than upon the demands of selfish interests, temporarily held in abeyance.

BUDGET

In the interest of economy and good administration, we favor the creation of an effective budget system,

that will function in accord with the principles of the Constitution. The reform should reach both the executive and legislative aspects of the question. The supervision and preparation of the budget should be vested in the Secretary of the Treasury as the representative of the President. The budget, as such, should not be increased by the Congress except by a two-thirds vote, each House, however, being free to exercise its constitutional privilege of making appropriations through independent bills. The appropriation bills should be considered by single Committees of the House and Senate. The audit system should be consolidated and its powers expanded so as to pass upon the wisdom of, as well as the authority for, expenditures.

A budget bill was passed in the closing days of the second session of the Sixty-sixth Congress which, invalidated by plain constitutional defects and defaced by considerations of patronage, the President was obliged to veto. The House amended the bill to meet the Executive objection. We condemn the Republican Senate for adjourning without passing the amended measure, when by devoting an hour or two more to this urgent public business a budget system could have been provided.

AGRICULTURAL INTERESTS

To the great agricultural interests of the country, the Democratic Party does not find it necessary to make promises. It already is rich in its record of things actually accomplished. For nearly half a century of Republican rule not a sentence was written into the Federal Statutes affording one dollar of bank credits to the farming interests of America. In the first term of this Democratic administration the National Bank Act was so altered as to authorize loans of five years' maturity on improved farm lands. Later was established a system of farm loan banks, from which the borrowings already exceed three hundred millions of dollars; and under which the interest rate to farmers has been so materially reduced as to drive out of business the farm loan sharks who formerly subsisted by extortion upon the great agricultural interests of the country.

Thus it was a Democratic Congress in the administration of a Democratic President which enabled the farmers of America for the first time to obtain credit upon reasonable terms and insured their opportunity for the future development of the nation's agricultural resources. Tied up in Supreme Court proceedings, in a suit by hostile interests, the Federal Farm Loan system, originally opposed by the Republican candidate for the Presidency, appealed in vain to a Republican

Congress for adequate financial assistance to tide over the interim between the beginning and the ending of the current year, awaiting a final decision of the highest court on the validity of the contested act. We pledge prompt consistent support of sound and effective measures to sustain, to amplify and to perfect the rural Credits Statutes and thus to check and reduce the growth and course of farm tenancy.

Not only did the Democratic Party put into effect a great Farm Loan system of land mortgage banks, but it passed the Smith–Lever Agricultural Extension Act, carrying to every farmer in every section of the country, through the medium of trained experts and by demonstration farms, the practical knowledge acquired by the Federal Agricultural Department in all things relating to agriculture, horticulture and animal life; it established the Bureau of Markets, the Bureau of Farm Management, and passed the Cotton Futures Act, the Grain Grades Bill, the Co-operative Farm Administration Act, and the Federal Warehouse Act.

The Democratic Party has vastly improved the rural mail system and has built up the parcel post system to such an extent as to render its activities and its practical service indispensable to the farming community. It was this wise encouragement and this effective concern of the Democratic Party for the farmers of the United States that enabled this great interest to render such essential service in feeding the armies of America and the allied nations of the war and succoring starving populations since Armistice Day.

Meanwhile the Republican leaders at Washington have failed utterly to propose one single measure to make rural life more tolerable. They have signalized their fifteen months of Congressional power by urging schemes which would strip the farms of labor; by assailing the principles of the Farm Loan system and seeking to impair its efficiency; by Covertly attempting to destroy the great nitrogen plant at Muscle Shoals upon which the government has expended $70,000,000 to supply American farmers with fertilizers at reasonable cost; by ruthlessly crippling nearly every branch of agricultural endeavor, literally starving the productive mediums through which the people must be fed.

We favor such legislation as will confirm to the primary producers of the nation the right of collective bargaining, and the right of co-operative handling and marketing of the products of the workshop and the farm and such legislation as will facilitate the exportation of our farm products.

We favor comprehensive studies of farm production costs and the uncensored publication of facts found in such studies.

LABOR AND INDUSTRY

The Democratic Party is now, as ever, the firm friend of honest labor and the promoter of progressive industry. It established the Department of Labor at Washington and a Democratic President called to his official council board the first practical workingman who ever held a cabinet portfolio. Under this administration have been established employment bureaus to bring the man and the job together; have been peaceably determined many bitter disputes between capital and labor; were passed the Child-Labor Act, the Workingman's Compensation Act (the extension of which we advocate so as to include laborers engaged in loading and unloading ships and in interstate commerce), the Eight-Hour Law, the act for Vocational Training, and a code of other wholesome laws affecting the liberties and bettering the conditions of the laboring classes. In the Department of Labor the Democratic administration established a Woman's Bureau, which a Republican Congress destroyed by withholding appropriations.

Labor is not a commodity; it is human. Those who labor have rights, and the national security and safety depend upon a just recognition of those rights and the conservation of the strength of the workers and their familes in the interest of sound-hearted and sound-headed men, women and children. Laws regulating hours of labor and conditions under which labor is performed, when passed in recognition of the conditions under which life must be lived to attain the highest development and happiness, are just assertions of the national interest in the welfare of the people.

At the same time, the nation depends upon the products of labor; a cessation of production means loss and, if long continued, means disaster. The whole people, therefore, have a right to insist that justice shall be done to those who work, and in turn that those whose labor creates the necessities upon which the life of the nation depends must recognize the reciprocal obligation between the worker and the state.

They should participate in the formulation of sound laws and regulations governing the conditions under which labor is performed, recognize and obey the laws so formulated, and seek their amendment when necessary by the processes ordinarily addressed to the laws and regulations affecting the other relations of life.

Labor, as well as capital, is entitled to adequate compensation. Each has the indefeasible right of organization, of collective bargaining and of speaking through representatives of their own selection. Neither class, however, should at any time nor in any circumstances take action that will put in jeopardy the public welfare. Resort to strikes and lockouts which endanger the health or lives of the people is an unsatisfactory device for determining disputes, and the Democratic Party pledges itself to contrive, if possible, and put into effective operation a fair and comprehensive method of composing differences of this nature.

In private industrial disputes, we are opposed to compulsory arbitration as a method plausible in theory, but a failure in fact. With respect to government service, we hold distinctly that the rights of the people are paramount to the right to strike. However, we profess scrupulous regard for the conditions of public employment and pledge the Democratic Party to instant inquiry into the pay of government employees and equally speedy regulations designed to bring salaries to a just and proper level.

WOMAN'S SUFFRAGE

We endorse the proposed 19th Amendment of the Constitution of the United States granting equal suffrage to women. We congratulate the legislatures of the thirty-five states which have already ratified said amendment and we urge the Democratic Governors and Legislatures of Tennessee, North Carolina and Florida and such states as have not yet ratified the Federal Suffrage Amendment to unite in an effort to complete the process of ratification and secure the thirty-sixth state in time for all the women of the United States to participate in the fall election.

We commend the effective advocacy of the measure by President Wilson.

WELFARE OF WOMEN AND CHILDREN

We urge co-operation with the states for the protection of child life through infancy and maternity care; in the prohibition of child labor and by adequate appropriations for the Children's Bureau and the Woman's Bureau in the Department of Labor.

EDUCATION

Co-operative Federal assistance to the states is immediately required for the removal of illiteracy, for the increase of teachers' salaries and instruction in citizenship for both native and foreign born; increased appropriation for vocational training in home economics; re-establishment of joint Federal and state employment service with women's departments under the direction of technically qualified women.

WOMEN IN INDUSTRY

We advocate full representation of women on all commissions dealing with women's work or women's interests and a reclassification of the Federal Civil Service free from discrimination on the ground of sex; a continuance of appropriations for education in sex hygiene; Federal legislation which shall insure that American women resident in the United States, but married to aliens, shall retain their American citizenship, and that the same process of naturalization shall be required for women as for men.

DISABLED SOLDIERS

The Federal government should treat with the utmost consideration every disabled soldier, sailor, and marine of the world war, whether his disability be due to wounds received in line of action or to health impaired in service; and for the dependants of the brave men who died in line of duty the government's tenderest concern and richest bounty should be their requital. The fine patriotism exhibited, the heroic conduct displayed, by American soldiers, sailors and marines at home and abroad, constitute a sacred heritage of posterity, the worth of which can never be recompensed from the Treasury and the glory of which must not be diminished by any such expedients.

The Democratic administration wisely established a War Risk Insurance Bureau, giving four and a half millions of enlisted men insurance at unprecedentedly low rates and through the medium of which compensation of men and women injured in service is readily adjusted, and hospital facilities for those whose health is impaired are abundantly afforded.

The Federal Board for Vocational Education should be made a part of the War Risk Insurance Bureau, in order that the task may be treated as a whole, and this machinery of protection and assistance must receive every aid of law and appropriation necessary to full and effective operation.

We believe that no higher or more valued priviledge can be afforded to an American citizen than to become a freeholder of the soil of the United States, and to that end we pledge our party to the enactment of soldier settlements and home aid legislation which will afford to the men who fought for America the opportunity to become land and home owners under conditions affording genuine government assistance unencumbered by needless difficulties of red tape or advance financial investment.

THE RAILROADS

The railroads were subjected to Federal control as a war measure, without any other idea than the swift transport of troops, munitions and supplies. When human life and national hopes were at stake profits could not be considered and were not. Federal operation, however, was marked by an intelligence and efficiency that minimized loss and resulted in many and marked reforms. The equipment taken over was not only grossly inadequate but shamefully outworn. Unification practices overcame these initial handicaps and provided additions, betterments and improvements. Economies enabled operation without the rate raises that private control would have found necessary, and labor was treated with an exact justice that secured the enthusiastic co-operation that victory demanded. The fundamental purpose of Federal control was achieved fully and splendidly, and at far less cost to the taxpayer than would have been the case under private operation. Investments in railroad properties were not only saved by government operation, but government management returned these properties vastly improved in every physical and executive detail. A great task was greatly discharged.

The President's recommendation of return to private ownership gave the Republican majority a full year in which to enact the necessary legislation. The House took six months to formulate its ideas, and another six months was consumed by the Republican Senate in equally vague debate. As a consequence, the Esch–Cummins Bill went to the President in the closing hours of Congress, and he was forced to a choice between the chaos of a veto and acquiescence in the measure submitted, however grave may have been his objections to it.

There should be a fair and complete test of the law until careful and mature action by Congress may cure its defects and insure a thoroughly effective transportation system under private ownership without government subsidy at the expense of the taxpayers of the country.

IMPROVED HIGHWAYS

Improved roads are of vital importance not only to commerce and industry but also to agriculture and rural life. The Federal Road Act of 1916, enacted by a Democratic Congress, represented the first systematic effort of the government to insure the building of an adequate system of roads in this country. The act, as amended, has resulted in placing the movement for improved highways on a progressive and substantial basis in every state in the Union and in bringing under actual construction more than 13,000 miles of roads suited to the traffic needs of the communities in which they are located.

We favor a continuance of the present Federal aid plan under existing Federal and state agencies, amended so as to include as one of the elements in determining the ratio in which the several states shall be entitled to share in the fund, the area of any public lands therein.

Inasmuch is the postal service has been extended by the Democratic Party to the door of practically every producer and every consumer in the country (rural free delivery alone having been provided for 6,000,000 additional patrons within the past eight years without materially added cost), we declare that this instrumentality can and will be used to the maximum of its capacity to improve the efficiency of distribution and reduce the cost of living to consumers while increasing the profitable operations of producers.

We strongly favor the increased use of the motor vehicle in the transportation of the mails and urge the removal of the restrictions imposed by the Republican Congress on the use of motor devices in mail transportation in rural territories.

THE POSTAL SERVICE

The efficiency of the Post Office Department has been vindicated against a malicious and designing assault, by the efficiency of its operation. Its record refutes its assailants. Their voices are silenced and their charges have collapsed.

We commend the work of the joint Commission on the reclassification of salaries of postal employees, recently concluded, which commission was created by a Democratic administration. The Democratic Party has always favored and will continue to favor the fair and just treatment of all government employees.

FREE SPEECH AND PRESS

We resent the unfounded reproaches directed against the Democratic administration for alleged interference with the freedom of the press and freedom of speech.

No utterance from any quarter has been assailed, and no publication has been repressed, which has not been animated by treasonable purposes, and directed against the nation's peace, order and security in time of war.

We reaffirm our respect for the great principles of free speech and a free press, but assert as an indisputable proposition that they afford no toleration of enemy propaganda or the advocacy of the overthrow of the government of the state or nation by force or violence.

INLAND WATERWAYS

We call attention to the failure of the Republican National Convention to recognize in any way the rapid development of barge transportation on our inland waterways, which development is the result of the constructive policies of the Democratic administration. And we pledge ourselves to the further development of adequate transportation facilities on our rivers and to the further improvement of our inland waterways, and we recognize the importance of connecting the Great Lakes with the sea by way of the Mississippi River and its tributaries, as well as by the St. Lawrence River. We favor an enterprising foreign trade policy with all nations, and in this connection we favor the full utilization of all Atlantic, Pacific, and Gulf ports, and an equitable distribution of shipping facilities between the various ports.

Transportation remains an increasingly vital problem in the continued development and prosperity of the nation.

Our present facilities for distribution by rail are inadequate and the promotion of transportation by water is imperative.

We therefore favor a liberal and comprehensive policy for the development and utilization of our harbors and interior waterways.

MERCHANT MARINE

We desire to congratulate the American people upon the rebirth of our Merchant Marine which once more maintains its former place in the world. It was under a Democratic administration that this was accomplished after seventy years of indifference and neglect, thirteen million tons having been constructed since the act was passed in 1916. We pledge the policy of our party to the continued growth of our Merchant Marine under proper legislation so that American products will be carried to all ports of the world by vessels built in American yards, flying the American flag.

RECLAMATION OF ARID LANDS

By wise legislation and progressive administration, we have transformed the government reclamation projects, representing an investment of $100,000,000, from a condition of impending failure and loss of confidence in the ability of the government to carry through such large enterprises, to a condition of demonstrated success, whereby formerly arid and wholly unproductive lands now sustain 40,000 prosperous families and have an annual crop production of over $70,000,000, not including the crops grown on a million acres outside the projects supplied with storage water from government works.

We favor ample appropriations for the continuation and extension of this great work of home-building and internal improvement along the same general lines, to the end that all practical projects shall be built, and waters now running to waste shall be made to provide homes and add to the food supply, power resources, and taxable property, with the government ultimately reimbursed for the entire outlay.

FLOOD CONTROL

We commend the Democratic Congress for the redemption of the pledge contained in our last platform by the passage of the Flood Control Act of March 1st, 1917, and point to the successful control of the floods of the Mississippi River and the Sacramento River, California, under the policy of that law, for its complete justification. We favor the extension of this policy to other flood control problems wherever the Federal interest involved justified the expenditure required.

THE TRADE COMMISSION

The Democratic Party heartily endorses the creation and work of the Federal Trade Commission in establishing a fair field for competitive business, free from restraints of trade and monopoly and recommends amplification of the statutes governing its activities so as to grant it authority to prevent the unfair use of patents in restraint of trade.

LIVE STOCK MARKETS

For the purpose of insuring just and fair treatment in the great interstate live stock market, and thus instilling confidence in growers through which production will be stimulated and the price of meats to consumers be ultimately reduced, we favor the enactment of legislation for the supervision of such markets by the national government.

PORT FACILITIES

The urgent demands of the war for adequate transportation of war material as well as for domestic need, revealed the fact that our port facilities and rate adjustments were such as to seriously affect the whole country in times of peace as well as war.

We pledge our party to stand for equality of rates, both import and export, for the ports of the country, to the end that there may be adequate and fair facilities and rates for the mobilization of the products of the country offered for shipment.

PETROLEUM

The Democratic Party recognizes the importance of the acquisition by Americans of additional sources of supply of petroleum and other minerals and declares that such acquisition both at home and abroad should be fostered and encouraged. We urge such action, legislative and executive, as may secure to American citizens the same rights in the acquirement of mining rights in foreign countries as are enjoyed by the citizens or subjects of any other nation.

MEXICO

The United States is the neighbor and friend of the nations of the three Americas. In a very special sense, our international relations in this hemisphere should be characterized by good will and free from any possible suspicion as to our national purpose.

The administration, remembering always that Mexico is an independent nation and that permanent stability in her government and her institutions could come only from the consent of her own people to a government of their own making, has been unwilling either to profit by the misfortunes of the people of Mexico or to enfeeble their future by imposing from the outside a rule upon their temporarily distracted councils. As a consequence, order is gradually reappearing in Mexico; at no time in many years have American lives and interests been so safe as they are now; peace reigns along the border and industry is resuming.

When the new government of Mexico shall have given ample proof of its ability permanently to maintain law and order, signified its willingness to meet its international obligations and written upon its statute books just laws under which foreign investors shall have rights as well as duties, that government should receive our recognition and sympathetic assistance. Until these proper expectations have been met, Mexico must realize the propriety of a policy that asserts the right of the United States to demand full protection for its citizens.

IRELAND

The great principle of national self-determination has received constant reiteration as one of the chief objectives for which this country entered the war and victory established this principle.

Within the limitations of international comity and usage, this Convention repeats the several previous expressions of the sympathy of the Democratic Party of the United States for the aspirations of Ireland for self-government.

ARMENIA

We express our deep and earnest sympathy for the unfortunate people of Armenia, and we believe that our government, consistent with its Constitution and principles, should render every possible and proper aid to them in their efforts to establish and maintain a government of their own.

PUERTO RICO

We favor granting to the people of Puerto Rico the traditional territorial form of government, with a view to ultimate statehood, accorded to all territories of the United States since the beginning of our government, and we believe that the officials appointed to administer the government of such territories should be qualified by previous bona-fide residence therein.

ALASKA

We commend the Democratic administration for inaugurating a new policy as to Alaska, as evidenced by the construction of the Alaska railroad and opening of the coal and oil fields.

We declare for the modification of the existing coal land law, to promote development without disturbing the features intended to prevent monopoly.

For such changes in the policy of forestry control as will permit the immediate initiation of the paper pulp industry.

For relieving the territory from the evils of long-distance government by arbitrary and interlocking bureaucratic regulation, and to that end we urge the speedy passage of a law containing the essential features of the Land–Curry Bill now pending, co-ordinating and consolidating all Federal control of natural resources under one department to be administered by a non-partisan board permanently resident in the territory.

For the fullest measure of territorial self-government with the view of ultimate statehood, with jurisdiction over all matters not of purely Federal concern, including fisheries and game, and for an intelligent administration of Federal control we believe that all officials appointed should be qualified by previous bona-fide residence in the territory.

For a comprehensive system of road construction with increased appropriations and the full extension of the Federal Road Aid Act to Alaska.

For the extension to Alaska of the Federal Farm Loan Act.

THE PHILIPPINES

We favor the granting of independence without unnecessary delay to the 10,500,000 inhabitants of the Philippine Islands.

HAWAII

We favor a liberal policy of homesteading public lands in Hawaii to promote a larger middle-class citizen population, with equal rights to all citizens.

The importance of Hawaii as an outpost on the western frontier of the United States, demands adequate appropriations by Congress for the development of our harbors and highways there.

NEW NATIONS

The Democratic Party expresses its active sympathy with the people of China, Czecho-Slovakia, Finland, Poland, Persia, Jugo-Slavia and others who have recently established representative governments and who are striving to develop the institutions of true Democracy.

ASIATIC IMMIGRANTS

The policy of the United States with reference to the non-admission of Asiatic immigrants is a true expression of the judgment of our people, and to the several states, whose geographical situation or internal conditions make this policy, and the enforcement of the laws enacted pursuant thereto, of particular concern, we pledge our support.

REPUBLICAN CORRUPTION

The shocking disclosure of the lavish use of money by aspirants for the Republican nomination for the highest office in the gift of the people, has created a painful impression throughout the country. Viewed in connection with the recent conviction of a Republican Senator from the State of Michigan for the criminal transgression of the law limiting expenditures on behalf of a candidate for the United States Senate, it indicates the re-entry, under Republican auspices, of money as an influential factor in elections, thus nullifying the letter and flaunting the spirit of numerous laws, enacted by the people, to protect the ballot from the contamination of corrupt practices. We deplore these delinquencies and invoke their stern popular rebuke, pledging our earnest efforts to a strengthening of the present statutes against corrupt practices, and their rigorous enforcement.

We remind the people that it was only by the return of a Republican Senator in Michigan, who is now under conviction and sentence for the criminal misuse of money in his election, that the present organization of the Senate with a Republican majority was made possible.

CONCLUSION

Believing that we have kept the Democratic faith, and resting our claims to the confidence of the people not upon grandiose promises, but upon the solid performances of our party, we submit our record to the nation's consideration and ask that the pledges of this platform be appraised in the light of that record.

— 1924 —

We, the representatives of the Democratic Party, in National Convention assembled, pay our profound homage to the memory of Woodrow Wilson. Our hearts are filled with gratitude that American democracy should have produced this man, whose spirit and influence will live on through the ages; and that it was our privilege to have co-operated with him in the advancement of ideals of government which will serve as an example and inspiration for this and future generations. We affirm our abiding faith in those ideals and pledge ourselves to take up the standard which he bore and to strive for the full triumph of the principles of democracy to which he dedicated his life.

DEMOCRATIC PRINCIPLES

The Democratic party believes in equal rights to all and special privilege to none. The Republican party holds that special privileges are essential to national prosperity. It believes that national prosperity must originate with the special interests and seep down through the channels of trade to the less favored industries to the wage earners and small salaried employees. It has accordingly enthroned privilege and nurtured selfishness.

The Republican party is concerned chiefly with material things; the Democratic party is concerned chiefly with human rights. The masses, burdened by discriminating laws and unjust administration, are demanding relief. The favored special interests, represented by the Republican party, contented with their unjust privileges, are demanding that no change be made. The Democratic party stands for remedial legislation and progress. The Republican party stands still.

COMPARISON OF PARTIES

We urge the American people to compare the record of eight unsullied years of Democratic administration with that of the Republican administration. In the former there was no corruption. The party pledges were faithfully fulfilled and a Democratic Congress enacted an extraordinary number of constructive and remedial laws. The economic life of the nation was quickened.

Tariff taxes were reduced. A Federal Trade Commission was created. A federal farm loan system was established. Child labor legislation was enacted. A good-roads bill was passed. Eight-hour laws were adopted. A secretary of labor was given a seat in the cabinet of the President. The Clayton Amendment to the Sherman Anti-Trust Act was passed, freeing American labor and taking it from the category of commodities. By the Smith–Lever bill improvement of

agricultural conditions was effected. A corrupt practice act was adopted. A well-considered warehouse act was passed. Federal employment bureaus were created, farm loan banks were organized and the federal reserve system was established. Privilege was uprooted. A corrupt lobby was driven from the national capital. A higher sense of individual and national duty was aroused. America enjoyed an unprecedented period of social and material progress.

During the time which intervened between the inauguration of a Democratic administration on March 4, 1913, and our entrance into the world war, we placed upon the statute-books of our country more effective constructive and remedial legislation than the Republican party had placed there in a generation.

During the great struggle which followed we had a leadership that carried America to greater heights of honor and power and glory than she had ever known before in her entire history.

Transition from this period of exalted Democratic leadership to the sordid record of the last three and a half years makes the nation ashamed. It marks the contrast between a high conception of public service and an avid purpose to distribute spoils.

G.O.P. CORRUPTION

Never before in our history has the government been so tainted by corruption and never has an administration so utterly failed. The nation has been appalled by the revelations of political depravity which have characterized the conduct of public affairs. We arraign the Republican party for attempting to limit inquiry into official delinquencies and to impede if not to frustrate the investigations to which in the beginning the Republican party leaders assented, but which later they regarded with dismay.

These investigations sent the former secretary of the interior to Three Rivers in disgrace and dishonor. These investigations revealed the incapacity and indifference to public obligation of the secretary of the navy, compelling him by force of public opinion to quit the cabinet. These investigations confirmed the general impression as to the unfitness of the attorney general by exposing an official situation and personal contacts which shocked the conscience of the nation and compelled his dismissal from the cabinet.

These investigations disclosed the appalling conditions of the Veterans Bureau with its fraud upon the government and its cruel neglect of the sick and disabled soldiers of the world war. These investigations revealed the criminal and fraudulent nature of the oil leases which caused the Congress, despite the indifference of the Executive, to direct recovery of the public domain and the prosecution of the criminal.

Such are the exigencies of partisan politics that Republican leaders are teaching the strange doctrine that public censure should be directed against those who expose crime rather than against criminals who have committed the offenses. If only three cabinet officers out of ten are disgraced, the country is asked to marvel at how many are free from taint. Long boastful that it was the only party "fit to govern," the Republican party has proven its inability to govern even itself. It is at war with itself. As an agency of government it has ceased to function.

This nation cannot afford to entrust its welfare to a political organization that cannot master itself, or to an Executive whose policies have been rejected by his own party. To retain in power an administration of this character would inevitably result in four years more of continued disorder, internal dissension and governmental inefficiency. A vote for Coolidge is a vote for chaos.

ISSUES

The dominant issues of the campaign are created by existing conditions. Dishonesty, discrimination, extravagances and inefficiency exist in government. The burdens of taxation have become unbearable. Distress and bankruptcy in agriculture, the basic industry of our country, is affecting the happiness and prosperity of the whole people. The cost of living is causing hardship and unrest.

The slowing down of industry is adding to the general distress. The tariff, the destruction of our foreign markets and the high cost of transportation are taking the profit out of agriculture, mining and other raw material industries. Large standing armies and the cost of preparing for war still cast their burdens upon humanity. These conditions the existing Republican administration has proven itself unwilling or unable to redress.

The Democratic party pledges itself to the following program:

Honest government.

We pledge the Democratic party to drive from public places all which make barter of our national power, its resources or the administration of its laws; to punish those guilty of these offenses.

To put none but the honest in public office; to practice economy in the expenditure of public money; to reverence and respect the rights of all under the constitution.

To condemn and destroy government by the spy and blackmailer which was by this Republican administration both encouraged and practiced.

TARIFF AND TAXATION

The Fordney–McCumber Tariff Act is the most unjust, unscientific and dishonest tariff tax measure ever enacted in our history. It is class legislation which defrauds the people for the benefit of a few, it heavily increases the cost of living, penalizes agriculture, corrupts the government, fosters paternalism and, in the long run, does not benefit the very interests for which it was intended.

We denounce the Republican tariff laws which are written, in great part, in aid of monopolies and thus prevent that reasonable exchange of commodities which would enable foreign countries to buy our surplus agricultural and manufactured products with resultant profit to the toilers and producers of America.

Trade interchange, on the basis of reciprocal advantages to the countries participating, is a time-honored doctrine of democratic faith. We declare our party's position to be in favor of a tax on commodities entering the customs house that will promote effective competition, protect against monopoly and at the same time produce a fair revenue to support the government.

The greatest contributing factor in the increase and unbalancing of prices is unscientific taxation. After having increased taxation and the cost of living by $2,000,000,000 under the Fordney–McCumber Tariff, all that the Republican party could suggest in the way of relief was a cut of $300,000,000 in direct taxes; and that was to be given principally to those with the largest incomes.

Although there was no evidence of a lack of capital for investment to meet the present requirements of all legitimate industrial enterprises and although the farmers and general consumers were bearing the brunt of tariff favors already granted to special interests, the administration was unable to devise any plan except one to grant further aid to the few. Fortunately this plan of the administration failed and under Democratic leadership, aided by progressive Republicans, a more equitable one was adopted, which reduces direct taxes by about $450,000,000.

The issue between the President and the Democratic party is not one of tax reduction or of the conservation of capital. It is an issue of relative burden of taxation and of the distribution of capital as affected by the taxation of income. The President still stands on the so-called Mellon Plan, which his party has just refused to indorse or mention in its platform.

The income tax was intended as a tax upon wealth. It was not intended to take from the poor any part of the necessities of life. We hold that the fairest tax with which to raise revenue for the federal government is the income tax. We favor a graduated tax upon incomes, so adjusted as to lay the burdens of government upon the taxpayers in proportion to the benefits they enjoy and their ability to pay.

We oppose the so-called nuisance taxes, sales taxes and all other forms of taxation that unfairly shift to the consumer the burdens of taxation. We refer to the Democratic revenue measure passed by the last Congress as distinguished from the Mellon Tax Plan as an illustration of the policy of the Democratic party. We first made a flat reduction of 25 per cent upon the tax of all incomes payable this year and then we so changed the proposed Mellon Plan as to eliminate taxes upon the poor, reducing them upon moderate incomes and, in a lesser degree, upon the incomes of multi-millionaires. We hold that all taxes are unnecessarily high and pledge ourselves to further reductions.

We denounce the Mellon Plan as a device to relieve multi-millionaires at the expense of other taxpayers, and we accept the issue of taxation tendered by President Coolidge.

AGRICULTURE

During the four years of Republican government the economic condition of the American farmer has changed from comfort to bankruptcy, with all its attendant miseries. The chief causes for this are:

(a) The Republican party policy of isolation in international affairs has prevented Europe from getting back to its normal balance, and, by leaving unsolved the economic problems abroad, has driven the European city population from industrial activities to the soil in large numbers in order to earn the mere necessaries of life. This has deprived the American farmer of his normal export trade.

(b) The Republican policy of a prohibitive tariff, exemplified in the Fordney–McCumber Law, which has forced the American farmer, with his export market debilitated, to buy manufactured goods at sustained high domestic levels, thereby making him the victim of the profiteer.

(c) The Republican policy of high transportation rates, both rail and water, which has made it impossible for the farmer to ship his produce to market at even a living profit.

To offset these policies and their disastrous results, and to restore the farmer again to economic equality with other industrialists, we pledge ourselves:

(a) To adopt an international policy of such co-operation by direct official, instead of indirect and evasive unofficial, means, as will re-establish the farmers' export market by restoring the industrial balance in Europe and the normal flow of international trade with the settlement of Europe's economic problems.

(b) To adjust the tariff so that the farmer and all other classes can buy again in a competitive manufacturers' market.

(c) To readjust and lower rail and water rates which will make our markets, both for the buyer and the seller, national and international instead of regional and local.

(d) To bring about the early completion of international waterway systems for transportation and to develop our water powers for cheaper fertilizer and use on our farms.

(e) To stimulate by every proper governmental activity the progress of the co-operative marketing movement and the establishment of an export marketing corporation or commission in order that the exportable surplus may not establish the price of the whole crop.

(f) To secure for the farmer credits suitable for his needs.

(g) By the establishment of these policies and others naturally supplementary thereto, to reduce the margin between what the producer receives for his products and the consumer has to pay for his supplies, to the end that we secure an equality for agriculture.

RAILROADS

The sponsors for the Esch–Cummins Transportation Act of 1920, at the time of its presentation to Congress, stated that it had for its purposes the reduction of the cost of transportation, the improvement of service, the bettering of labor conditions, the promotion of peaceful co-operation between employer and employee, and at the same time the assurance of a fair and just return to the railroads upon their investment.

We are in accord with these announced purposes, but contend that the act has failed to accomplish them. It has failed to reduce the cost of transportation. The promised improvement in service has not been realized. The labor provisions of the act have proven unsatisfactory in settling differences between employer and employee. The so-called recapture clause has worked out to the advantage of the strong and has been of no benefit to the weak. The pronouncement in the act for the development of both rail and water transportation has proved futile. Water transportation upon our inland waterways has not been encouraged, the limitation of our coastwise trade is threatened by the administration of the act. It has unnecessarily interfered with the power of the states to regulate purely intrastate transportation. It must therefore be so rewritten that the high purpose which the public welfare demands may be accomplished.

Railroad freight rates should be so readjusted as to give the bulky basic, low-priced raw commodities, such as agricultural products, coal and ores the lowest rates, placing the higher rates upon more valuable and less bulky manufactured products.

MUSCLE SHOALS

We reaffirm and pledge the fulfillment of the policy, with reference to Muscle Shoals, as declared and passed by the Democratic majority of the Sixty-fourth Congress in the National Defense Act of 1916, "for the production of nitrates or other products needed for munitions of war and useful in the manufacture of fertilizers."

We hold that the production of cheaper and high-grade fertilizers is essential to agricultural prosperity. We demand prompt action by Congress for the operation of the Muscle Shoals plants to maximum capacity in the production, distribution and sale of commercial fertilizers to the farmers of the country and we oppose any legislation that limits the production of fertilizers at Muscle Shoals by limiting the amount of power to be used in their manufacture.

CREDIT AND CURRENCY

We denounce the recent cruel and unjust contraction of legitimate and necessary credit and currency, which was directly due to the so-called deflation policy of the Republican party, as declared in its national platform of June, 1920, and in the speech of acceptance of its candidate for the presidency. Within eighteen months after the election of 1920 this policy resulted in withdrawing bank loans by over $5,000,000,000 and in contracting our currency by over $1,500,000,000.

The contraction bankrupted hundreds of thousands of farmers and stock growers in America and resulted in widespread industrial depression and unemployment. We demand that the Federal Reserve System be so administered as to give stability to industry, commerce and finance, as was intended by the Democratic party, which gave the Federal Reserve System to the nation.

RECLAMATION

The Democratic party was foremost in urging reclamation for the immediate arid and semiarid lands of the west. The lands are located in the public land states, and, therefore, it is due to the government to utilize their resources by reclamation. Homestead entrymen under reclamation projects have suffered from the extravagant inefficiencies and mistakes of the federal government.

The Reclamation Act of 1924, recommended by the fact-finding commission and added as an amendment to the second deficiency appropriation bill at the last session of Congress, was eliminated from that bill by the Republican conferees in the report they presented to Congress one hour before adjournment. The Democratic party pledges itself actively, efficiently and economically to carry on the reclamation projects, and to make equitable adjustment for the mistakes the government has made.

CONSERVATION

We pledge recovery of the navy's oil reserves, and all other parts of the public domain which have been fraudulently or illegally leased or otherwise wrongfully transferred to the control of private interests; vigorous prosecution of all public officials, private citizens and corporations that participated in these transactions; revision of the Water Power Act, the general leasing act and all other legislation relating to public domain, that may be essential to its conservation and honest and efficient use on behalf of the people of the country.

We believe that the nation should retain title to its water power and we favor the expeditious creation and development of our water power. We favor strict public control and conservation of all the nation's natural resources, such as coal, iron, oil and timber, and their use in such manner as may be to the best interest of our citizens.

The conservation of migratory birds, the establishment of game preserves, and the protection and conservation of wild life is of importance to agriculturists as well as sportsmen. Our disappearing national natural resources of timber calls for a national policy of reforestation.

IMPROVED HIGHWAYS

Improved roads are of vital importance, not only to commerce and industry, but also to agriculture and natural life. We call attention to the record of the Democratic party in this matter and favor continuance of federal aid under existing federal and state agencies.

MINING

Mining is one of the basic industries of this country. We produce more coal, iron, copper and silver than any other country. The value of our mineral production is second only to agriculture. Mining has suffered like agriculture and from the same causes. It is the duty of our government to foster this industry and to remove the restrictions that destroy its prosperity.

MERCHANT MARINE

The Democratic party condemns the vacillating policy of the Republican administration in the failure to develop an American flag shipping policy. There has been a marked decrease in the volume of American commerce carried in American vessels as compared to the record under a Democratic administration.

We oppose as illogical and unsound all efforts to overcome by subsidy the handicap to American shipping and commerce imposed by Republican policies.

We condemn the practice of certain American railroads in favoring foreign ships, and pledge ourselves to correct such discriminations. We declare for an American-owned merchant marine, American-built and manned by American crews, which is essential for naval security in war and is a protection to the American farmer and manufacturer against excessive ocean freight charges on products of farm and factory.

We declare that the government should own and operate such merchant ships as will insure the accomplishment of these purposes and to continue such operation so long as it may be necessary without obstructing the development and growth of privately owned American flag shipping.

NECESSITIES OF LIFE

We pledge the Democratic party to regulate by governmental agencies the anthracite coal industry and all other corporations controlling the necessaries of life where public welfare has been subordinated to private interests.

EDUCATION

We believe with Thomas Jefferson and founders of the republic that ignorance is the enemy of freedom and that each state, being responsible for the intellectual and moral qualifications of its citizens and for the expenditure of the moneys collected by taxation for the support of its schools, shall use its sovereign right in all matters pertaining to education. The federal government should offer to the states such counsel, advice and aid as may be made available through the federal agencies for the general improvement of our schools in view of our national needs.

CIVIL SERVICE

We denounce the action of the Republican administration in its violations of the principles of civil service by its partisan removals and manipulation of the eligible lists in the post office department and other governmental departments; by its packing the civil service commission so that commission became the servile instrument of the administration in its wish to deny to the former service men their preferential rights under the law; and the evasion of the requirements of the law with reference to appointments in the department.

We pledge the Democratic party faithfully to comply with the spirit as well as the regulation of civil service; to extend its provisions to internal revenue officers and to other employees of the government not in executive positions, and to secure to former service men preference in such appointments.

POSTAL EMPLOYEES

We declare in favor of adequate salaries to provide decent living conditions for postal employees.

POPULAR ELECTIONS

We pledge the Democratic party to a policy which will prevent members of either house who fail of re-election from participating in the subsequent sessions of Congress. This can be accomplished by fixing the days for convening the Congress immediately after the biennial national election; and to this end we favor granting the right to the people of the several states to vote on proposed constitutional amendments on this subject.

PROBATION

We favor the extension of the probation principle to the courts of the United States.

ACTIVITIES OF WOMEN

We welcome the women of the nation to their rightful place by the side of men in the control of the government whose burdens they have always shared.

The Democratic party congratulates them upon the essential part which they have taken in the progress of our country, and the zeal with which they are using their political power to aid the enactment of beneficial laws and the exaction of fidelity in the public service.

VETERANS OF WARS

We favor generous appropriations, honest management and sympathetic care and assistance in the hospitalization, rehabilitation and compensation of the veterans of all wars and their dependents. The humanizing of the veterans bureau is imperatively required.

CONTRIBUTIONS

The nation now knows that the predatory interests have, by supplying Republican campaign funds, systematically purchased legislative favors and administrative immunity. The practice must stop; our nation must return to honesty and decency in politics.

Elections are public affairs conducted for the sole purpose of ascertaining the will of the sovereign voters. Therefore, we demand that national elections shall hereafter be kept free from the poison of excessive private contributions. To this end, we favor reasonable means of publicity, at public expense, so that candidates, properly before the people for federal offices, may present their claims at a minimum of cost. Such publicity should precede the primary and the election.

We favor the prohibition of individual contributions, direct and indirect, to the campaign funds of congressmen, senators or presidential candidates, beyond a reasonable sum to be fixed in the law, for both individual contributions and total expenditures, with requirements for full publicity. We advocate a com-

plete revision of the corrupt practices act to prevent Newberryism and the election evils disclosed by recent investigations.

NARCOTICS

Recognizing in narcotic addiction, especially the spreading of heroin addiction among the youth, a grave peril to America and to the human race, we pledge ourselves vigorously to take against it all legitimate and proper measures for education, for control and for suppression at home and abroad.

PROHIBITION LAW

The Republican administration has failed to enforce the prohibition law; is guilty of trafficking in liquor permits, and has become the protector of violators of this law.

The Democratic party pledges itself to respect and enforce the Constitution and all laws.

RIGHTS OF STATES

We demand that the states of the Union shall be preserved in all their vigor and power. They constitute a bulwark against the centralizing and destructive tendencies of the Republican party.

We condemn the efforts of the Republican party to nationalize the functions and duties of the states.

We oppose the extension of bureaucracy, the creation of unnecessary bureaus and federal agencies and the multiplication of offices and office-holders.

We demand a revival of the spirit of local self-government essential to the preservation of the free institutions of our republic.

ASIATIC IMMIGRATION

We pledge ourselves to maintain our established position in favor of the exclusion of Asiatic immigration.

PHILIPPINES

The Filipino people have succeeded in maintaining a stable government and have thus fulfilled the only condition laid down by congress as a prerequisite to the granting of independence. We declare that it is now our liberty and our duty to keep our promise to these people by granting them immediately the independence which they so honorably covet.

ALASKA

The maladministration of affairs in Alaska is a matter of concern to all our people. Under the Republican administration, development has ceased and the fishing industry has been seriously impaired. We pledge ourselves to correct the evils which have grown up in the administration of that rich domain.

An adequate form of local self-government for Alaska must be provided and to that end we favor the establishment of a full territorial form of government for that territory similar to that enjoyed by all the territories except Alaska during the last century of American history.

HAWAII

We believe in a policy for continuing the improvements of the national parks, the harbors and breakwaters, and the federal roads of the territory of Hawaii.

VIRGIN ISLANDS

We recommend legislation for the welfare of the inhabitants of the Virgin Islands.

LAUSANNE TREATY

We condemn the Lausanne Treaty. It barters legitimate American rights and betrays Armenia, for the Chester oil concessions.

We favor the protection of American rights in Turkey and the fulfillment of President Wilson's arbitral award respecting Armenia.

DISARMAMENT

We demand a strict and sweeping reduction of armaments by land and sea, so that there shall be no competitive military program or naval building. Until international agreements to this end have been made we advocate an army and navy adequate for our national safety.

Our government should secure a joint agreement with all nations for world disarmament and also for a referendum on war, except in case of actual or threatened attack.

Those who must furnish the blood and bear the burdens imposed by war should, whenever possible, be consulted before this supreme sacrifice is required of them.

GREECE

We welcome to the sisterhood of republics the ancient land of Greece which gave to our party its priceless name. We extend to her government and people our cordial good wishes.

WAR

War is a relic of barbarism and it is justifiable only as a measure of defense.

In the event of war in which the manpower of the nation is drafted, all other resources should likewise be drafted. This will tend to discourage war by depriving it of its profits.

PERSONAL FREEDOM

The Democratic party reaffirms its adherence and devotion to those cardinal principles contained in the Constitution and the precepts upon which our government is founded, that Congress shall make no laws respecting the establishment of religion, or prohibiting the free exercises thereof, or abridging the freedom of speech or of the press or of the right of the people peaceably to assemble and to petition the government for a redress of grievances, that the church and the state shall be and remain separate, and that no religious test shall ever be required as a qualification to any office of public trust under the United States. These principles, we pledge ourselves ever to defend and maintain. We insist at all times upon obedience to the orderly processes of the law and deplore and condemn any effort to arouse religious or racial dissension.

LEAGUE OF NATIONS

The Democratic party pledges all its energies to the outlawing of the whole war system. We refuse to believe that the wholesale slaughter of human beings on the battlefield is any more necessary to man's highest development than is killing by individuals.

The only hope for world peace and for economic recovery lies in the organized efforts of sovereign nations cooperating to remove the causes of war and to substitute law and order for violence.

Under Democratic leadership a practical plan was devised under which fifty-four nations are now operating, and which has for its fundamental purpose the free co-operation of all nations in the work of peace.

The government of the United States for the last four years has had no foreign policy, and consequently it has delayed the restoration of the political and economic agencies of the world. It has impaired our self-respect at home and injured our prestige abroad. It has curtailed our foreign markets and ruined our agricultural prices.

It is of supreme importance to civilization and to mankind that America be placed and kept on the right side of the greatest moral question of all time, and therefore the Democratic party renews its declarations of confidence in the idea of world peace, the League of Nations and the world court of justice as together constituting the supreme effort of the statesmanship and religious conviction of our time to organize the world for peace.

Further, the Democratic party declares that it will be the purpose of the next administration to do all in its power to secure for our country that moral leadership in the family of nations which, in the providence of God, has been so clearly marked out for it. There is no substitute for the League of Nations as an agency working for peace, therefore, we believe, that, in the interest of permanent peace, and in the lifting of the great burdens of war from the backs of the people, and in order to establish a permanent foreign policy on these supreme questions, not subject to change with change of party administration, it is desirable, wise and necessary to lift this question out of party politics and to that end to take the sense of the American people at a referendum election, advisory to the government, to be held officially, under act of Congress, free from all other questions and candidacies, after ample time for full consideration and discussion throughout the country, upon the question, in substance, as follows:

"Shall the United States become a member of the League of Nations upon such reservations or amendments to the covenant of the League as the President and the Senate of the United States may agree upon?"

Immediately upon an affirmative vote we will carry out such mandate.

WATERWAYS

We favor and will promote deep waterways from the Great Lakes to the Gulf and to the Atlantic Ocean.

FLOOD CONTROL

We favor a policy for the fostering and building of inland waterways and the removal of discrimination against water transportation. Flood control and the lowering of flood levels is essential to the safety of life and property, the productivity of our lands, the navigability of our streams and the reclaiming of our wet and overflowed lands and the creation of hydroelectric power. We favor the expeditious construction of flood relief works on the Mississippi and Colorado rivers and also such reclamation and irrigation projects upon the Colorado River as may be found to be feasible and practical.

We favor liberal appropriations for prompt coordinated surveys by the United States to determine the possibilities of general navigation improvements and water power development on navigable streams and their tributaries, to secure reliable information as to the most economical navigation improvement, in combination with the most efficient and complete development of water power.

We favor suspension of the granting of federal water power licenses by the federal water power committee until Congress has received reports from the water power commission with regard to applications for such licenses.

PRIVATE MONOPOLIES

The Federal Trade Commission has submitted to the Republican administration numerous reports showing the existence of monopolies and combinations in restraint of trade, and has recommended proceedings against these violators of the law. The few prosecutions which have resulted from this abundant evidence furnished by this agency created by the Democratic party, while proving the indifference of the administration to the violations of law by trusts and monopolies and its friendship for them, nevertheless demonstrate the value of the federal trade commission.

We declare that a private monopoly is indefensible and intolerable, and pledge the Democratic party to vigorous enforcement of existing laws against monopoly and illegal combinations, and to the enactment of such further measures as may be necessary.

FRAUDULENT STOCK SALE

We favor the immediate passage of such legislation as may be necessary to enable the states efficiently to enforce their laws relating to the gradual financial strangling of innocent investors, workers and consumers, caused by the indiscriminate promotion, refinancing and reorganizing of corporations on an inflated and over-capitalized basis, resulting already in the undermining and collapse of many railroads, public service and industrial corporations, manifesting itself in unemployment, irreparable loss and waste and which constitute a serious menace to the stability of our economic system.

AVIATION

We favor a sustained development of aviation by both the government and commercially.

LABOR, CHILD WELFARE

Labor is not a commodity. It is human. We favor collective bargaining and laws regulating hours of labor and conditions under which labor is performed. We favor the enactment of legislation providing that the products of convict labor shipped from one state to another shall be subject to the laws of the latter state exactly as though they had been produced therein. In order to mitigate unemployment attending business depression, we urge the enactment of legislation authorizing the construction and repair of public works be initiated in periods of acute unemployment.

We pledge the party to co-operate with the state governments for the welfare, education and protection of child life and all necessary safeguards against exhaustive debilitating employment conditions for women.

Without the votes of Democratic members of Congress the child labor amendment would not have been submitted for ratification.

LATIN-AMERICA

From the day of their birth, friendly relations have existed between the Latin-American republics and the United States. That friendship grows stronger as our relations become more intimate. The Democratic party sends to these republics its cordial greeting; God has made us neighbors—justice shall keep us friends.

— 1928 —

We, the Democratic Party in convention assembled, pause to pay our tribute of love and respect to the memory of him who in his life and in his official ac-

tions voiced the hopes and aspirations of all good men and women of every race and clime, the former President of the United States, Woodrow Wilson. His spirit moves on and his example and deeds will exalt those who come after us as they have inspired us.

We are grateful that we were privileged to work with him and again pay tribute to his high ideals and accomplishments.

We reaffirm our devotion to the principles of Democratic government formulated by Jefferson and enforced by a long and illustrious line of Democratic Presidents.

We hold that government must function not to centralize our wealth but to preserve equal opportunity so that all may share in our priceless resources; and not confine prosperity to a favored few. We, therefore, pledge the Democratic Party to encourage business, small and great alike; to conserve human happiness and liberty; to break the shackles of monopoly and free the business of the nation; to respond to the popular will.

The function of a national platform is to declare general principles and party policies. We do not, therefore, assume to bind our party respecting local issues or details of legislation.

We, therefore, declare the policy of the Democratic Party with regard to the following dominant national issues:

THE RIGHTS OF THE STATES

We demand that the constitutional rights and powers of the states shall be preserved in their full vigor and virtue. These constitute a bulwark against centralization and the destructive tendencies of the Republican Party.

We oppose bureaucracy and the multiplication of offices and officeholders.

We demand a revival of the spirit of local self-government, without which free institutions cannot be preserved.

REPUBLICAN CORRUPTION

Unblushingly the Republican Party offers as its record agriculture prostrate, industry depressed, American shipping destroyed, workmen without employment; everywhere disgust and suspicion, and corruption unpunished and unafraid.

Never in the entire history of the country has there occurred in any given period of time or, indeed, in all time put together, such a spectacle of sordid corruption and unabashed rascality as that which has characterized the administration of federal affairs under eight blighting years of Republican rule. Not the revels of reconstruction, nor all the compounded frauds succeeding that evil era, have approached in sheer audacity the shocking thieveries and startling depravities of officials high and low in the public service at Washington. From cabinet ministers, with their treasonable crimes, to the cheap vendors of official patronage, from the purchasers of seats in the United States Senate to the vulgar grafters upon alien trust funds, and upon the hospital resources of the disabled veterans of the World War; from the givers and receivers of stolen funds for Republican campaign purposes to the public men who sat by silently consenting and never revealing a fact or uttering a word in condemnation, the whole official organization under Republican rule has become saturated with dishonesty, defiant of public opinion and actuated only by a partisan desire to perpetuate its control of the government.

As in the time of Samuel J. Tilden, from whom the presidency was stolen, the watchword of the day should be: "Turn the rascals out." This is the appeal of the Democratic Party to the people of the country. To this fixed purpose should be devoted every effort and applied every resource of the party; to this end every minor difference on non-essential issues should be put aside and a determined and a united fight be made to rescue the government from those who have betrayed their trust by disgracing it.

ECONOMY AND REORGANIZATION

The Democratic Party stands for efficiency and economy in the administration of public affairs and we pledge:

(a) Business-like reorganization of all the departments of the government.
(b) Elimination of duplication, waste and overlapping.
(c) Substitution of modern business-like methods for existing obsolete and antiquated conditions.

No economy resulted from Republican Party rule. The savings they claim take no account of the elimination of expenditures following the end of the World War, the large sums realized from the sale of war materials, nor its failure to supply sufficient funds for the efficient conduct of many important governmental activities.

FINANCING AND TAXATION

(a) The Federal Reserve system, created and inaugurated under Democratic auspices, is the greatest legislative contribution to constructive business ever adopted. The administration of the system for the advantage of stock market speculators should cease. It must be administered for the benefit of farmers, wage earners, merchants, manufacturers and others engaged in constructive business.
(b) The taxing function of governments, free or despotic, has for centuries been regarded as the power above all others which requires vigilant scrutiny to the end that it be not exercised for purposes of favor or oppression.

Three times since the World War the Democrats in Congress have favored a reduction of the tax burdens of the people in face of stubborn opposition from a Republican administration; and each time these reductions have largely been made for the relief of those least able to endure the exactions of a Republican fiscal policy. The tax bill of the session recently ended was delayed by Republican tactics and juggled by partisan considerations so as to make impossible a full measure of relief to the greater body of taxpayers. The moderate reductions afforded were grudgingly conceded and the whole proceeding in Congress, dictated as far as possible from the White House and the treasury, denoted the proverbial desire of the Republican Party always to discriminate against the masses in favor of privileged classes.

The Democratic Party avows its belief in the fiscal policy inaugurated by the last Democratic administration, which provided a sinking fund sufficient to extinguish the nation's indebtedness within a reasonable period of time, without harassing the present and next succeeding generations with tax burdens which, if not unendurable, do in fact check initiative in enterprise and progress in business. Taxes levied beyond the actual requirements of the legally established sinking fund are but an added burden upon the American people, and the surplus thus accumulated in the federal treasury is an incentive to the increasingly extravagant expenditures which have characterized Republican administrations. We, therefore, favor a further reduction of the internal taxes of the people.

TARIFF

The Democratic tariff legislation will be based on the following policies:

(a) The maintenance of legitimate business and a high standard of wages for American labor.
(b) Increasing the purchasing power of wages and income by the reduction of those monopolistic and

extortionate tariff rates bestowed in payment of political debts.

(c) Abolition of log-rolling and restoration of the Wilson conception of a fact-finding tariff commission, quasi-judicial and free from the executive domination which has destroyed the usefulness of the present commission.

(d) Duties that will permit effective competition, insure against monopoly and at the same time produce a fair revenue for the support of government. Actual difference between the cost of production at home and abroad, with adequate safeguard for the wage of the American laborer must be the extreme measure of every tariff rate.

(e) Safeguarding the public against monopoly created by special tariff favors.

(f) Equitable distribution of the benefits and burdens of the tariff among all.

Wage-earner, farmer, stockman, producer and legitimate business in general have everything to gain from a Democratic tariff based on justice to all.

CIVIL SERVICE

Grover Cleveland made the extension of the merit system a tenet of our political faith. We shall preserve and maintain the civil service.

AGRICULTURE

Deception upon the farmer and stock raiser has been practiced by the Republican Party through false and delusive promises for more than fifty years. Specially favored industries have been artificially aided by Republican legislation. Comparatively little has been done for agriculture and stock raising, upon which national prosperity rests. Unsympathetic inaction with regard to this problem must cease. Virulent hostility of the Republican administration to the advocates of farm relief and denial of the right of farm organizations to lead in the development of farm policy must yield to Democratic sympathy and friendliness.

Four years ago the Republican Party, forced to acknowledge the critical situation, pledged itself to take all steps necessary to bring back a balanced condition between agriculture and other industries and labor. Today it faces the country not only with that pledge unredeemed but broken by the acts of a Republican President, who is primarily responsible for the failure to offer a constructive program to restore equality to agriculture.

While he has had no constructive and adequate program to offer in its stead, he has twice vetoed farm relief legislation and has sought to justify his disapproval of agricultural legislation partly on grounds wholly inconsistent with his acts, making industrial monopolies the beneficiaries of government favor; and in endorsing the agricultural policy of the present administration the Republican Party, in its recent convention, served notice upon the farmer that the so-called protective system is not meant for him; that while it offers protection to the privileged few, it promises continued world prices to the producers of the chief cash crops of agriculture.

We condemn the policy of the Republican Party which promises relief to agriculture only through a reduction of American farm production to the needs of the domestic market. Such a program means the continued deflation of agriculture, the forcing of additional millions from the farms, and the perpetuation of agricultural distress for years to come, with continued bad effects on business and labor throughout the United States.

The Democratic Party recognizes that the problems of production differ as between agriculture and industry. Industrial production is largely under human control, while agricultural production, because of lack of co-ordination among the 6,500,000 individual farm units, and because of the influence of weather, pests and other causes, is largely beyond human control. The result is that a large crop frequently is produced on a small acreage and a small crop on a large acreage; and, measured in money value, it frequently happens that a large crop brings less than a small crop.

Producers of crops whose total volume exceeds the needs of the domestic market must continue at a disadvantage until the government shall intervene as seriously and as effectively in behalf of the farmer as it has intervened in behalf of labor and industry. There is a need of supplemental legislation for the control and orderly handling of agricultural surpluses, in order that the price of the surplus may not determine the price of the whole crop. Labor has benefited by collective bargaining and some industries by tariff. Agriculture must be as effectively aided.

The Democratic Party in its 1924 platform pledged its support to such legislation. It now reaffirms that stand and pledges the united efforts of the legislative and executive branches of government, as far as may be controlled by the party, to the immediate enactment of such legislation, and to such other steps as are necessary to establish and maintain the purchasing power of farm products and the complete economic equality of agriculture.

The Democratic Party has always stood against special privilege and for common equality under the law. It is a fundamental principle of the party that such tariffs as are levied must not discriminate against any industry, class or section. Therefore, we pledge that in its tariff policy the Democratic Party will insist upon equality of treatment between agriculture and other industries.

Farm relief must rest on the basis of an economic equality of agriculture with other industries. To give this equality, a remedy must be found which will include among other things:

(a) Credit aid by loans to co-operatives on at least as favorable a basis as the government aid to the merchant marine.

(b) Creation of a federal farm board to assist the farmer and stock raiser in the marketing of their products, as the Federal Reserve Board has done for the banker and business man. When our archaic banking and currency system was revised after its record of disaster and panic under Republican administrations, it was a Democratic Congress in the administration of a Democratic President that accomplished its stabilization through the Federal Reserve Act creating the Federal Reserve Board, with powers adequate to its purpose. Now, in the hour of agriculture's need, the Democratic Party pledges the establishment of a new agricultural policy fitted to present conditions, under the direction of a farm board vested with all the powers necessary to accomplish for agriculture what the Federal Reserve Board has been able to accomplish for finance, in full recognition of the fact that the banks of the country, through voluntary co-operation, were never able to stabilize the financial system of the country until the government powers were invoked to help them.

(c) Reduction through proper government agencies of the spread between what the farmer and stock raiser gets and the ultimate consumer pays, with consequent benefits to both.

(d) Consideration of the condition of agriculture in the formulation of government financial and tax measures.

We pledge the party to foster and develop co-operative marketing associations through appropriate governmental aid. We recognize that experience has demonstrated that members of such associations alone can not successfully assume the full responsibility for a program that benefits all producers alike. We pledge the party to an earnest endeavor to solve this problem of the distribution of the cost of dealing with crop surpluses over the marketed units of the crop whose producers are benefited by such assistance. The solution of this problem would avoid government subsidy, to which the Democratic Party has always been opposed. The solution of this problem will be a prime and immediate concern of a Democratic administration.

We direct attention to the fact that it was a Democratic Congress, in the administration of a Democratic President, which established the federal loan system and laid the foundation for the entire rural credits structure, which has aided agriculture to sustain in part the shock of the policies of two Republican administrations; and we promise thoroughgoing administration of our rural credits laws, so that the farmers in all sections may secure the maximum benefits intended under these acts.

MINING

Mining is one of the basic industries of this country. We produce more coal, iron and copper than any other country. The value of our mineral production is second only to agriculture. Mining has suffered like agriculture, and from similar causes. It is the duty of our government to foster this industry and to remove the restrictions that destroy its prosperity.

FOREIGN POLICY

The Republican administration has no foreign policy; it has drifted without plan. This great nation can not afford to play a minor role in world politics. It must have a sound and positive foreign policy, not a negative one. We declare for a constructive foreign policy based on these principles:

(a) Outlawry of war and an abhorrence of militarism, conquest and imperialism.

(b) Freedom from entangling political alliances with foreign nations.

(c) Protection of American lives and rights.

(d) Non-interference with the elections or other internal political affairs of any foreign nation. This principle of non-interference extends to Mexico, Nicaragua and all other Latin-American nations. Interference in the purely internal affairs of Latin-American countries must cease.

(e) Rescue of our country from its present impaired world standing and restoration to its former position as a leader in the movement for international arbitration, conciliation, conference and limitation of armament by international agreement.

(f) International agreements for reduction of all armaments and the end of competitive war preparations, and, in the meantime, the maintenance of an army and navy adequate for national defense.

(g) Full, free and open co-operation with all other nations for the promotion of peace and justice throughout the world.

(h) In our foreign relations this country should stand as a unit, and, to be successful, foreign policies must have the approval and the support of the American people.

(i) Abolition of the practice of the President of entering into and carrying out agreements with a foreign government, either de facto or de jure, for the protection of such government against revolution or foreign attack, or for the supervision of its internal affairs, when such agreements have not been advised and consented to by the Senate, as provided in the Constitution of the United States, and we condemn the administration for carrying out such an unratified agreement that requires us to use our armed forces in Nicaragua.

(j) Recognition that the Monroe Doctrine is a cardinal principle of this government promulgated for the protection of ourselves and our Latin-American neighbors. We shall seek their friendly co-operation in the maintenance of this doctrine.

(k) We condemn the Republican administration for lack of statesmanship and efficiency in negotiating the 1921 treaty for the limitation of armaments, which limited only the construction of battleships and ships of over ten thousand tons. Merely a gesture towards peace, it accomplished no limitation of armaments, because it simply substituted one weapon of destruction for another. While it resulted in the destruction of our battleships and the blueprints of battleships of other nations, it placed no limitation upon construction of aircraft, submarines, cruisers, warships under ten thousand tons, poisonous gases or other weapons of destruction. No agreement was ratified with regard to submarines and poisonous gases. The attempt of the President to remedy the failure of 1921 by the Geneva Conference of 1928 was characterized by the same lack of statesmanship and efficiency and resulted in entire failure.

In consequence, the race between nations in the building of unlimited weapons of destruction still goes on and the peoples of the world are still threatened with war and burdened with taxation for additional armaments.

WATERPOWER, WATERWAYS AND FLOOD CONTROL

The federal government and state governments, respectively, now have absolute and exclusive sovereignty and control over enormous waterpowers, which constitute one of the greatest assets of the nation. This sovereign title and control must be preserved respectively in the state and federal governments, to the end that the people may be protected against exploitation of this great resource and that waterpowers may be expeditiously developed under such regulations as will inspire to the people reasonable rates and equitable distribution.

We favor and will promote deep waterways from the Great Lakes to the Gulf and to the Atlantic Ocean.

We favor the fostering and building up of water transportation through improvement of inland waterways and removal of discrimination against water transportation. Flood control and the lowering of flood levels are essential to the safety of life and property, and the productivity of our lands, the navigability of our streams, the reclaiming of our wet and overflowed lands. We favor expeditious construction of flood relief works on the Mississippi and Colorado rivers and such reclamation and irrigation projects upon the Colorado River as may be found feasible.

We favor appropriations for prompt co-ordinated surveys by the United States to determine the possibilities of general navigation improvements and waterpower development on navigable streams and their tributaries and to secure reliable information as to the most economical navigation improvement, in combination with the most efficient and complete development of waterpower.

We favor the strict enforcement of the Federal Waterpower Act, a Democratic act, and insist that the public interest in waterpower sites, ignored by two Republican administrations, be protected.

Being deeply impressed by the terrible disasters from floods in the Mississippi Valley during 1927, we heartily endorse the Flood Control Act of last May, which recognizes that the flood waters of the Mississippi River and its tributaries constitute a national problem of the gravest character and makes provision for their speedy and effective control. This measure is a continuation and expansion of the policy established by a Democratic Congress in 1917 in the act of that year for controlling floods on the Mississippi and Sacramento rivers. It is a great piece of constructive legislation, and we pledge our party to its vigorous and early enforcement.

CONSERVATION AND RECLAMATION

We shall conserve the natural resources of our country for the benefit of the people and to protect them against waste and monopolization. Our disappearing resources of timber call for a national policy of reforestation. The federal government should improve and develop its public lands so that they may go into private ownership and become subjected to taxation for the support of the states wherein they exist. The Democratic administration will actively, efficiently and economically carry on reclamation projects and make equitable adjustments with the homestead entrymen for the mistakes the government has made, and extend all practical aid to refinance reclamation and drainage projects.

TRANSPORTATION

Efficient and economical transportation is essential to the prosperity of every industry. The cost of transportation controls the income of every human being and materially affects the cost of living. We must, therefore, promote every form of transportation to a state of highest efficiency. Recognizing the prime importance of air transportation, we shall encourage its development by every possible means. Improved roads are of vital importance not only to commerce and industry, but also to agriculture and rural life. The federal government should construct and maintain at its own expense roads upon its public lands. We reaffirm our approval of the Federal Roads Law, enacted by a Democratic administration. Common carriers, whether by land, water or rail, must be protected in an equal opportunity to compete, so that governmental regulations against exorbitant rates and inefficiency will be aided by competition.

LABOR

(a) We favor the principle of collective bargaining, and the Democratic principle that organized labor should choose its own representatives without coercion or interference.

(b) Labor is not a commodity. Human rights must be safeguarded. Labor should be exempt from the operation of anti-trust laws.

(c) We recognize that legislative and other investi-

gations have shown the existence of grave abuse in the issuance of injunctions in labor disputes. No injunctions should be granted in labor disputes except upon proof of threatened irreparable injury and after notice and hearing and the injunction should be confined to those acts which do directly threaten irreparable injury. The expressed purpose of representatives of capital, labor and the bar to devise a plan for the elimination of the present evils with respect to injunctions must be supported and legislation designed to accomplish these ends formulated and passed.

(d) We favor legislation providing that products of convict labor shipped from one state to another shall be subject to laws of the latter state, as though they had been produced therein.

UNEMPLOYMENT

Unemployment is present, widespread and increasing. Unemployment is almost as destructive to the happiness, comfort, and well-being of human beings as war. We expend vast sums of money to protect our people against the evils of war, but no governmental program is anticipated to prevent the awful suffering and economic losses of unemployment. It threatens the well being of millions of our people and endangers the prosperity of the nation. We favor the adoption by the government, after a study of this subject, of a scientific plan whereby during periods of unemployment appropriations shall be made available for the construction of necessary public works and the lessening, as far as consistent with public interests, of government construction work when labor is generally and satisfactorily employed in private enterprise.

Study should also be made of modern methods of industry and a constructive solution found to absorb and utilize the surplus human labor released by the increasing use of machinery.

ACCIDENT COMPENSATION TO GOVERNMENT EMPLOYEES

We favor legislation making fair and liberal compensation to government employees who are injured in accident or by occupational disease and to the dependents of such workers as may die as a result thereof.

FEDERAL EMPLOYEES

Federal employees should receive a living wage based upon American standards of decent living. Present wages are, in many instances, far below that standard.

We favor a fair and liberal retirement law for government employees in the classified service.

VETERANS

Through Democratic votes, and in spite of two Republican Presidents' opposition, the Congress has maintained America's traditional policy to generously care for the veterans of the World War. In extending them free hospitalization, a statutory award for tuberculosis, a program of progressive hospital construction, and provisions for compensation for the disabled, the widows and orphans, America has surpassed the record of any nation in the history of the world. We pledge the veterans that none of the benefits heretofore accorded by the Wilson administration and the votes of Democrat members of Congress shall be withdrawn; that these will be added to more in accordance with the veterans' and their dependents' actual needs. Generous appropriations, honest management, the removal of vexatious administration delays, and sympathetic assistance for the veterans of all wars, is what the Democratic Party demands and promises.

WOMEN AND CHILDREN

We declare for equality of women with men in all political and governmental matters.

Children are the chief asset of the nation. Therefore their protection through infancy and childhood against exploitation is an important national duty.

The Democratic Party has always opposed the exploitation of women in industry and has stood for such conditions of work as will preserve their health and safety.

We favor an equal wage for equal service; and likewise favor adequate appropriations for the women's and children's bureau.

IMMIGRATION

Laws which limit immigration must be preserved in full force and effect, but the provisions contained in these laws that separate husbands from wives and parents from infant children are inhuman and not essential to the purpose or the efficacy of such laws.

RADIO

Government supervision must secure to all the people the advantage of radio communication and likewise guarantee the right of free speech. Official control in contravention of this guarantee should not be tolerated. Governmental control must prevent monopolistic use of radio communication and guarantee equitable distribution and enjoyment thereof.

COAL

Bituminous coal is not only the common base of manufacture, but it is a vital agency in our interstate transportation. The demoralization of this industry, its labor conflicts and distress, its waste of a national resource and disordered public service, demand constructive legislation that will allow capital and labor a fair share of prosperity, with adequate protection to the consuming public.

CONGRESSIONAL ELECTION REFORM

We favor legislation to prevent defeated members of both houses of Congress from participating in the sessions of Congress by fixing the date for convening the Congress immediately after the biennial national election.

LAW ENFORCEMENT

The Republican Party, for eight years in complete control of the government at Washington, presents the remarkable spectacle of feeling compelled in its national platform to promise obedience to a provision of the federal Constitution, which it has flagrantly disregarded, and to apologize to the country for its failure to enforce laws enacted by the Congress of the United States. Speaking for the national Democracy, this convention pledges the party and its nominees to an honest effort to enforce the eighteenth amendment and all other provisions of the federal Constitution and all laws enacted pursuant thereto.

CAMPAIGN EXPENDITURES

We condemn the improper and excessive use of money in elections as a danger threatening the very existence of democratic institutions. Republican expenditures in senatorial primaries and elections have been so exorbitant as to constitute a national scandal. We favor publicity in all matters affecting campaign contributions and expenditures. We shall, beginning not later than August 1, 1928, and every thirty days thereafter, the last publication and filing being not later than five days before the election, publish in the press and file with the appropriate committees of the House and Senate a complete account of all contributions, the names of the contributors, the amounts expended and the purposes for which the expenditures are made, and will, at all times, hold open for public inspection the books and records relating to such matters. In the event that any financial obligations are contracted and not paid, our National Committee will similarly report and publish, at least five days before the election, all details respecting such obligations.

We agree to keep and maintain a permanent record of all campaign contributions and expenditures and to insist that contributions by the citizens of one state to the campaign committees of other states shall have immediate publicity.

MERCHANT MARINE

We reaffirm our support of an efficient, dependable American merchant marine for the carriage of the greater portion of our commerce and for the national defense.

The Democratic Party has consistently and vigorously supported the shipping services maintained by the regional United States Shipping Board in the interest of all ports and all sections of our country, and has successfully opposed the discontinuance of any of these lines. We favor the transfer of these lines gradually to the local private American companies, when such companies can show their ability to take over and permanently maintain the lines. Lines that can not now be transferred to private enterprise should continue to be operated as at present and should be kept in an efficient state by remodeling of some vessels and replacement of others.

We are unalterably opposed to a monopoly in American shipping and are opposed to the operation of any of our services in a manner that would retard the development of any ports or section of our country.

We oppose such sacrifices and favoritism as exhibited in the past in the matter of alleged sales, and insist that the primary purpose of legislation upon this subject be the establishment and maintenance of an adequate American merchant marine.

ARMENIA

We favor the most earnest efforts on the part of the United States to secure the fulfillment of the promises and engagements made during and following the World War by the United States and the allied powers to Armenia and her people.

EDUCATION

We believe with Jefferson and other founders of the Republic that ignorance is the enemy of freedom and that each state, being responsible for the intellectual and moral qualifications of its citizens and for the expenditure of the moneys collected by taxation for the support of its schools, shall use its sovereign right in all matters pertaining to education.

The federal government should offer to the states such counsel, advice, results of research and aid as may be made available through the federal agencies for the general improvement of our schools in view of our national needs.

MONOPOLIES AND ANTI-TRUST LAWS

During the last seven years, under Republican rule, the anti-trust laws have been thwarted, ignored and violated so that the country is rapidly becoming controlled by trusts and sinister monopolies formed for the purpose of wringing from the necessaries of life an unrighteous profit. These combinations are formed and conducted in violation of law, encouraged, aided and abetted in their activities by the Republican administration and are driving all small tradespeople and small industrialists out of business. Competition is one of the most sacred, cherished and economic rights of the American people. We demand the strict enforcement of the anti-trust laws and the enactment of other laws, if necessary, to control this great menace to trade and commerce, and thus to preserve the right of the small merchant and manufacturer to earn a legitimate profit from his business.

Dishonest business should be treated without influence at the national capital. Honest business, no matter its size, need have no fears of a Democratic administration. The Democratic Party will ever oppose illegitimate and dishonest business. It will foster, promote, and encourage all legitimate enterprises.

CANAL ZONE

We favor the employment of American citizens in the operation and maintenance of the Panama Canal in all positions above the grade of messenger and favor as liberal wages and conditions of employment as prevailed under previous Democratic administrations.

ALASKA—HAWAII

We favor the development of Alaska and Hawaii in the traditional American way, through self-government. We favor the appointment of only bona fide residents to office in the territories. We favor the extension and improvement of the mail, air mail, telegraph and radio, agricultural experimenting, highway construction, and other necessary federal activities in the territories.

PUERTO RICO

We favor granting to Puerto Rico such territorial form of government as would meet the present economic conditions of the island, and provide for the aspirations of her people, with the view to ultimate statehood accorded to all territories of the United States since the beginning of our government, and we believe any officials appointed to administer the government of such territories should be qualified by previous bona fide residence therein.

PHILIPPINES

The Filipino people have succeeded in maintaining a stable government and have thus fulfilled the only condition laid down by the Congress as a prerequisite to the granting of independence. We declare that it is now our duty to keep our promise to these people by granting them immediately the independence which they so honorably covet.

PUBLIC HEALTH

The Democratic Party recognizes that not only the productive wealth of the nation but its contentment and happiness depends upon the health of its citizens. It, therefore, pledges itself to enlarge the existing Bureau of Public Health and to do all things possible to stamp out communicable and contagious diseases, and to ascertain preventive means and remedies for these diseases, such as cancer, infantile paralysis and others which heretofore have largely defied the skill of physicians.

We pledge our party to spare no means to lift the apprehension of diseases from the minds of our people, and to appropriate all moneys necessary to carry out this pledge.

CONCLUSION

Affirming our faith in these principles, we submit our cause to the people.

— 1932 —

In this time of unprecedented economic and social distress the Democratic Party declares its conviction that the chief causes of this condition were the disastrous policies pursued by our government since the World War, of economic isolation, fostering the merger of competitive businesses into monopolies and encouraging the indefensible expansion and contraction of credit for private profit at the expense of the public.

Those who were responsible for these policies have abandoned the ideals on which the war was won and thrown away the fruits of victory, thus rejecting the greatest opportunity in history to bring peace, prosperity, and happiness to our people and to the world.

They have ruined our foreign trade; destroyed the values of our commodities and products, crippled our banking system, robbed millions of our people of their life savings, and thrown millions more out of work, produced wide-spread poverty and brought the government to a state of financial distress unprecedented in time of peace.

The only hope for improving present conditions, restoring employment, affording permanent relief to the people, and bringing the nation back to the proud position of domestic happiness and of financial, industrial, agricultural and commercial leadership in the world lies in a drastic change in economic governmental policies.

We believe that a party platform is a covenant with the people to be faithfully kept by the party when entrusted with power, and that the people are entitled to know in plain words the terms of the contract to which they are asked to subscribe. We hereby declare this to be the platform of the Democratic Party:

The Democratic Party solemnly promises by appropriate action to put into effect the principles, policies, and reforms herein advocated, and to eradicate the policies, methods, and practices condemned. We advocate an immediate and drastic reduction of governmental expenditures by abolishing useless commissions and offices, consolidating departments and bureaus, and eliminating extravagance to accomplish a saving of not less than twenty-five per cent in the cost of the Federal Government. And we call upon the Democratic Party in the states to make a zealous effort to achieve a proportionate result.

We favor maintenance of the national credit by a federal budget annually balanced on the basis of accurate executive estimates within revenues, raised by a system of taxation levied on the principle of ability to pay.

We advocate a sound currency to be preserved at all hazards and an international monetary conference called on the invitation of our government to consider the rehabilitation of silver and related questions.

We advocate a competitive tariff for revenue with a fact-finding tariff commission free from executive interference, reciprocal tariff agreements with other nations, and an international economic conference designed to restore international trade and facilitate exchange.

We advocate the extension of federal credit to the states to provide unemployment relief wherever the diminishing resources of the states makes it impossible for them to provide for the needy; expansion of the federal program of necessary and useful construction effected [sic] with a public interest, such as adequate flood control and waterways.

We advocate the spread of employment by a substantial reduction in the hours of labor, the encouragement of the shorter week by applying that principle in government service; we advocate advance planning of public works.

We advocate unemployment and old-age insurance under state laws.

We favor the restoration of agriculture, the nation's basic industry; better financing of farm mortgages through recognized farm bank agencies at low rates of interest on an amortization plan, giving preference to credits for the redemption of farms and homes sold under foreclosure.

Extension and development of the Farm Cooperative movement and effective control of crop surpluses so that our farmers may have the full benefit of the domestic market.

The enactment of every constitutional measure that will aid the farmers to receive for their basic farm commodities prices in excess of cost.

We advocate a Navy and an Army adequate for national defense, based on a survey of all facts affecting the existing establishments, that the people in time of peace may not be burdened by an expenditure fast approaching a billion dollars annually.

We advocate strengthening and impartial enforcement of the anti-trust laws, to prevent monopoly and unfair trade practices, and revision thereof for the better protection of labor and the small producer and distributor.

The conservation, development, and use of the nation's water power in the public interest.

The removal of government from all fields of private enterprise except where necessary to develop public works and natural resources in the common interest.

We advocate protection of the investing public by requiring to be filed with the government and carried in advertisements of all offerings of foreign and domestic stocks and bonds true information as to bonuses, commissions, principal invested, and interests of the sellers.

Regulation to the full extent of federal power, of:

(a) Holding companies which sell securities in interstate commerce;
(b) Rates of utilities companies operating across state lines;
(c) Exchanges in securities and commodities.

We advocate quicker methods of realizing on assets for the relief of depositors of suspended banks, and a more rigid supervision of national banks for the protection of depositors and the prevention of the use of their moneys in speculation to the detriment of local credits.

The severance of affiliated security companies from, and the divorce of the investment banking business from, commercial banks, and further restriction of federal reserve banks in permitting the use of federal reserve facilities for speculative purposes.

We advocate the full measure of justice and generosity for all war veterans who have suffered disability or disease caused by or resulting from actual service in time of war and for their dependents.

We advocate a firm foreign policy, including peace with all the world and the settlement of international disputes by arbitration; no interference in the internal affairs of other nations; and sanctity of treaties and the maintenance of good faith and of good will in financial obligations; adherence to the World Court with appending reservations; the Pact of Paris abolishing war as an instrument of national policy, to be made effective by provisions for consultation and conference in case of threatened violations of treaties.

International agreements for reduction of armaments and cooperation with nations of the Western Hemisphere to maintain the spirit of the Monroe Doctrine.

We oppose cancellation of the debts owing to the United States by foreign nations.

Independence for the Philippines; ultimate statehood for Puerto Rico.

The employment of American citizens in the operation of the Panama Canal.

Simplification of legal procedure and reorganization of the judicial system to make the attainment of justice speedy, certain, and at less cost.

Continuous publicity of political contributions and expenditures; strengthening of the Corrupt Practices Act and severe penalties for misappropriation of campaign funds.

We advocate the repeal of the Eighteenth Amendment. To effect such repeal we demand that the Congress immediately propose a Constitutional Amendment to truly represent the conventions in the states called to act solely on that proposal; we urge the enactment of such measures by the several states as will actually promote temperance, effectively prevent the return of the saloon, and bring the liquor traffic into the open under complete supervision and control by the states.

We demand that the Federal Government effectively exercise its power to enable the states to protect themselves against importation of intoxicating liquors in violation of their laws.

Pending repeal, we favor immediate modification of the Volstead Act; to legalize the manufacture and sale of beer and other beverages of such alcoholic content as is permissible under the Constitution and to provide therefrom a proper and needed revenue.

We condemn the improper and excessive use of money in political activities.

We condemn paid lobbies of special interests to influence members of Congress and other public servants by personal contact.

We condemn action and utterances of high public officials designed to influence stock exchange prices.

We condemn the open and covert resistance of administrative officials to every effort made by Congressional Committees to curtail the extravagant expenditures of the government and to revoke improvident subsidies granted to favorite interests.

We condemn the extravagance of the Farm Board, its disastrous action which made the government a speculator in farm products, and the unsound policy of restricting agricultural products to the demands of domestic markets.

We condemn the usurpation of power by the State Department in assuming to pass upon foreign securities offered by international bankers as a result of which billions of dollars in questionable bonds have been sold to the public upon the implied approval of the Federal Government.

And in conclusion, to accomplish these purposes and to recover economic liberty, we pledge the nominees of this convention the best efforts of a great party whose founder announced the doctrine which guides us now in the hour of our country's need: equal rights to all; special privilege to none.

— 1936 —

We hold this truth to be self-evident—that the test of a representative government is its ability to promote the safety and happiness of the people.

We hold this truth to be self-evident—that 12 years of Republican leadership left our Nation sorely stricken in body, mind, and spirit; and that three years of Democratic leadership have put it back on the road to restored health and prosperity.

We hold this truth to be self-evident—that 12 years of Republican surrender to the dictatorship of a privileged few have been supplanted by a Democratic leadership which has returned the people themselves to the places of authority, and has revived in them new faith and restored the hope which they had almost lost.

We hold this truth to be self-evident—that this three-year recovery in all the basic values of life and the reestablishment of the American way of living has been brought about by humanizing the policies of the Federal Government as they affect the personal, financial, industrial, and agricultural well-being of the American people.

We hold this truth to be self-evident—that government in a modern civilization has certain inescapable obligations to its citizens, among which are:

(1) Protection of the family and the home.
(2) Establishment of a democracy of opportunity for all the people.
(3) Aid to those overtaken by disaster.

These obligations, neglected through 12 years of the old leadership, have once more been recognized by American Government. Under the new leadership they will never be neglected.

FOR THE PROTECTION OF THE FAMILY AND THE HOME

(1) We have begun and shall continue the successful drive to rid our land of kidnappers and bandits. We shall continue to use the powers of government to end the activities of the malefactors of great wealth who defraud and exploit the people.

Savings and Investment

(2) We have safeguarded the thrift of our citizens by restraining those who would gamble with other peoples' savings, by requiring truth in the sale of securities; by putting the brakes upon the use of credit for speculation; by outlawing the manipulation of prices in stock and commodity markets; by curbing the overweening power and unholy practices of utility holding companies; by insuring fifty million bank accounts.

Old Age and Social Security

(3) We have built foundations for the security of those who are faced with the hazards of unemployment and old age; for the orphaned, the crippled, and the blind. On the foundation of the Social Security Act we are determined to erect a structure of economic security for all our people, making sure that this benefit shall keep step with the ever-increasing capacity of America to provide a high standard of living for all its citizens.

Consumer

(4) We will act to secure to the consumer fair value, honest sales and a decreased spread between the price he pays and the price the producer receives.

Rural Electrification

(5) This administration has fostered power rate yardsticks in the Tennessee Valley and in several other parts of the Nation. As a result, electricity has been made available to the people at a lower rate. We will continue to promote plans for rural electrification and for cheap power by means of the yardstick method.

Housing

(6) We maintain that our people are entitled to decent, adequate housing at a price which they can afford. In the last three years, the Federal Government, having saved more than two million homes from foreclosure, has taken the first steps in our history to provide decent housing for people of meager incomes. We believe every encouragement should be given to the building of new homes by private enterprise; and that the Government should steadily extend its housing program toward the goal of adequate housing for those forced through economic necessities to live in unhealthy and slum conditions.

Veterans

(7) We shall continue just treatment of our war veterans and their dependents.

FOR THE ESTABLISHMENT OF A DEMOCRACY OF OPPORTUNITY

Agriculture

We have taken the farmers off the road to ruin.

We have kept our pledge to agriculture to use all available means to raise farm income toward its prewar purchasing power. The farmer is no longer suffering from 15-cent corn, 3-cent hogs, $2\frac{1}{2}$-cent beef at the farm, 5-cent wool, 30-cent wheat, 5-cent cotton, and 3-cent sugar.

By Federal legislation, we have reduced the farmer's indebtedness and doubled his net income. In cooperation with the States and through the farmer's own committees, we are restoring the fertility of his land and checking the erosion of his soil. We are bringing electricity and good roads to his home.

We will continue to improve the soil conservation and domestic allotment program with payments to farmers.

We will continue a fair-minded administration of agricultural laws, quick to recognize and meet new problems and conditions. We recognize the gravity of the evils of farm tenancy, and we pledge the full cooperation of the Government in the refinancing of farm indebtedness at the lowest possible rates of interest and over a long term of years.

We favor the production of all the market will absorb, both at home and abroad, plus a reserve supply sufficient to insure fair prices to consumers; we favor judicious commodity loans on seasonal surpluses; and we favor assistance within Federal authority to enable farmers to adjust and balance production with demand, at a fair profit to the farmers.

We favor encouragement of sound, practical farm cooperatives.

By the purchase and retirement of ten million acres of sub-marginal land, and assistance to those attempting to eke out an existence upon it, we have made a good beginning toward proper land use and rural rehabilitation.

The farmer has been returned to the road to freedom and prosperity. We will keep him on that road.

Labor

We have given the army of America's industrial workers something more substantial than the Republican's dinner pail full of promises. We have increased the worker's pay and shortened his hours; we have undertaken to put an end to the sweated labor of his wife and children; we have written into the law of the land his right to collective bargaining and self-organization free from the interference of employers; we have provided Federal machinery for the peaceful settlement of labor disputes.

We will continue to protect the worker and we will guard his rights, both as wage-earner and consumer, in the production and consumption of all commodities, including coal and water power and other natural resource products.

The worker has been returned to the road to freedom and prosperity. We will keep him on that road.

Business

We have taken the American business man out of the red. We have saved his bank and given it a sounder foundation; we have extended credit; we have lowered interest rates; we have undertaken to free him from the ravages of cutthroat competition.

The American business man has been returned to the road to freedom and prosperity. We will keep him on that road.

Youth

We have aided youth to stay in school; given them constructive occupation; opened the door to opportunity which 12 years of Republican neglect had closed.

Our youth have been returned to the road to freedom and prosperity. We will keep them on that road.

MONOPOLY AND CONCENTRATION OF ECONOMIC POWER

Monopolies and the concentration of economic power, the creation of Republican rule and privilege, continue to be the master of the producer, the exploiter of the consumer, and the enemy of the independent operator. This is a problem challenging the unceasing effort of untrammeled public officials in every branch of the Government. We pledge vigorously and fearlessly to enforce the criminal and civil provisions of the existing anti-trust laws, and to the extent that their effectiveness has been weakened by new corporate devices or judicial construction, we propose by law to restore their efficacy in stamping out monopolistic practices and the concentration of economic power.

AID TO THOSE OVERTAKEN BY DISASTER

We have aided and will continue to aid those who have been visited by widespread drought and floods, and have adopted a Nation-wide flood-control policy.

Unemployment

We believe that unemployment is a national problem, and that it is an inescapable obligation of our Government to meet it in a national way. Due to our stimulation of private business, more than five million people have been reemployed; and we shall continue to maintain that the first objective of a program of economic security is maximum employment in private industry at adequate wages. Where business fails to supply such employment, we believe that work at prevailing wages should be provided in cooperation with State and local governments on useful public projects, to the end that the national wealth may be increased, the skill and energy of the worker may be utilized, his morale maintained, and the unemployed assured the opportunity to earn the necessities of life.

The Constitution

The Republican platform proposes to meet many pressing national problems solely by action of the separate States. We know that drought, dust storms, floods, minimum wages, maximum hours, child labor, working conditions in industry and monopolistic and unfair business practices cannot be adequately handled exclusively by 48 separate State legislatures, 48 separate State administrations, and 48 separate State courts. Transactions and activities which inevitably overflow State boundaries call for both State and Federal treatment.

We have sought and will continue to seek to meet these problems through legislation within the Constitution.

If these problems cannot be effectively solved by legislation within the Constitution, we shall seek such clarifying amendment as will assure to the legislatures of the several States and to the Congress of the United States, each within its proper jurisdiction, the power to enact those laws which the State and Federal legislatures, within their respective spheres, shall find necessary, in order adequately to regulate commerce, protect public health and safety and safeguard economic security. Thus we propose to maintain the letter and spirit of the Constitution.

THE MERIT SYSTEM IN GOVERNMENT

For the protection of government itself and promotion of its efficiency, we pledge the immediate extension of the merit system through the classified civil service—which was first established and fostered under Democratic auspices—to all non–policy-making positions in the Federal service.

We shall subject to the civil service law all continuing positions which, because of the emergency, have been exempt from its operation.

CIVIL LIBERTIES

We shall continue to guard the freedom of speech, press, radio, religion and assembly which our Constitution guarantees; with equal rights to all and special privileges to none.

GOVERNMENT FINANCE

The administration has stopped deflation, restored values and enabled business to go ahead with confidence.

When national income shrinks, government income is imperilled. In reviving national income, we have fortified government finance. We have raised the public credit to a position of unsurpassed security. The interest rate on Government bonds has been reduced to the lowest point in twenty-eight years. The same Government bonds which in 1932 sold under 83 are now selling over 104.

We approve the objective of a permanently sound currency so stabilized as to prevent the former wide fluctuations in value which injured in turn producers, debtors, and property owners on the one hand, and wage-earners and creditors on the other, a currency which will permit full utilization of the country's resources. We assert that today we have the soundest currency in the world.

We are determined to reduce the expenses of government. We are being aided therein by the recession in unemployment. As the requirements of relief decline and national income advances, an increasing percentage of Federal expenditures can and will be met from current revenues, secured from taxes levied in accordance with ability to pay. Our retrenchment, tax and recovery programs thus reflect our firm determination to achieve a balanced budget and the reduction of the national debt at the earliest possible moment.

FOREIGN POLICY

In our relationship with other nations, this Government will continue to extend the policy of Good Neighbor. We reaffirm our opposition to war as an instrument of national policy, and declare that disputes between nations should be settled by peaceful means. We shall continue to observe a true neutrality in the disputes of others; to be prepared resolutely to resist aggression against ourselves; to work for peace and to take the profits out of war; to guard against being drawn, by political commitments, international banking or private trading, into any war which may develop anywhere.

We shall continue to foster the increase in our foreign trade which has been achieved by this administration; to seek by mutual agreement the lowering of those tariff barriers, quotas and embargoes which have been raised against our exports of agricultural and industrial products; but continue as in the past to give adequate protection to our farmers and manufacturers against unfair competition or the dumping on our shores of commodities and goods produced abroad by cheap labor or subsidized by foreign governments.

THE ISSUE

The issue in this election is plain. The American people are called upon to choose between a Republican administration that has and would again regiment them in the service of privileged groups and a Democratic administration dedicated to the establishment of equal economic opportunity for all our people.

We have faith in the destiny of our Nation. We are sufficiently endowed with natural resources and with productive capacity to provide for all a quality of life that meets the standards of real Americanism.

Dedicated to a government of liberal American principles, we are determined to oppose equally, the despotism of Communism and the menace of concealed Fascism.

We hold this final truth to be self-evident—that the interests, the security and the happiness of the people of the United States of America can be perpetuated only under democratic government as conceived by the founders of our Nation.

— 1940 —

PREAMBLE

The world is undergoing violent change. Humanity, uneasy in this machine age, is demanding a sense of security and dignity based on human values.

No democratic government which fails to recognize this trend—and take appropriate action—can survive.

That is why the Government of this nation has moved to keep ahead of this trend; has moved with speed incomprehensible to those who do not see this trend.

Outside the Americas, established institutions are being overthrown and democratic philosophies are being repudiated by those whose creed recognizes no power higher than military force, no values other than a false efficiency.

What the founding fathers realized upon this continent was a daring dream, that men could have not only physical security, not only efficiency, but something else in addition that men had never had before—the security of the heart that comes with freedom, the peace of mind that comes from a sense of justice.

To this generation of Americans it is given to defend this democratic faith as it is challenged by social maladjustment within and totalitarian greed without. The world revolution against which we prepare our defense is so threatening that not until it has burned itself out in the last corner of the earth will our democracy be able to relax its guard.

In this world crisis, the purpose of the Democratic Party is to defend against external attack and justify by internal progress the system of government and way of life from which the Democratic Party takes its name.

FULFILLING THE AMERICAN IDEAL

Toward the modern fulfillment of the American ideal, the Democratic Party, during the last seven years, has labored successfully:

1. *To strengthen democracy by defensive preparedness against aggression, whether by open attack or secret infiltration;*
2. *To strengthen democracy by increasing our economic efficiency; and*
3. *To strengthen democracy by improving the welfare of the people.*

These three objectives are one and inseparable. No nation can be strong by armaments alone. It must possess and use all the necessary resources for producing goods plentifully and distributing them effectively. It must add to these factors of material strength the unconquerable spirit and energy of a contented people, convinced that there are no boundaries to human progress and happiness in a land of liberty.

Our faith that these objectives can be attained is made unshakable by what has already been done by the present Administration, in stopping the waste and exploitation of our human and natural resources, in restoring to the average man and woman a stake in the preservation of our democracy, in enlarging our national armaments, and in achieving national unity.

We shall hold fast to these gains. We are proud of our record. Therefore the Party in convention assembled endorses wholeheartedly the brilliant and courageous leadership of President Franklin D. Roosevelt

and his statesmanship and that of the Congress for the past seven trying years. And to our President and great leader we send our cordial greetings.

WE MUST STRENGTHEN DEMOCRACY AGAINST AGGRESSION

The American people are determined that war, raging in Europe, Asia and Africa, shall not come to America.

We will not participate in foreign wars, and we will not send our army, naval or air forces to fight in foreign lands outside of the Americas, except in case of attack. We favor and shall rigorously enforce and defend the Monroe Doctrine.

The direction and aim of our foreign policy has been, and will continue to be, the security and defense of our own land and the maintenance of its peace.

For years our President has warned the nation that organized assaults against religion, democracy and international good faith threatened our own peace and security. Men blinded by partisanship brushed aside these warnings as war-mongering and officious intermeddling. The fall of twelve nations was necessary to bring their belated approval of legislative and executive action that the President had urged and undertaken with the full support of the people. It is a tribute to the President's foresight and action that our defense forces are today at the peak of their peacetime effectiveness.

Weakness and unpreparedness invite aggression. We must be so strong that no possible combination of powers would dare to attack us. We propose to provide America with an invincible air force, a navy strong enough to protect all our seacoasts and our national interests, and a fully equipped and mechanized army. We shall continue to coordinate these implements of defense with the necessary expansion of industrial productive capacity and with the training of appropriate personnel. Outstanding leaders of industry and labor have already been enlisted by the Government to harness our mighty economic forces for national defense.

Experience of other nations gives warning that total defense is necessary to repel attack, and that partial defense is no defense.

We have seen the downfall of nations accomplished through internal dissension provoked from without. We denounce and will do all in our power to destroy the treasonable activities of disguised anti-democratic and un-American agencies which would sap our strength, paralyze our will to defend ourselves, and destroy our unity by inciting race against race, class against class, religion against religion and the people against their free institutions.

To make America strong, and to keep America free, every American must give of his talents and treasure in accordance with his ability and his country's needs. We must have democracy of sacrifice as well as democracy of opportunity.

To insure that our armaments shall be implements of peace rather than war, we shall continue our traditional policies of the good neighbor; observe and advocate international respect for the rights of others and for treaty obligations; cultivate foreign trade through desirable trade agreements; and foster economic collaboration with the Republics of the Western Hemisphere.

In self-defense and in good conscience, the world's greatest democracy cannot afford heartlessly or in a spirit of appeasement to ignore the peace-loving and liberty-loving peoples wantonly attacked by ruthless aggressors. We pledge to extend to these peoples all the material aid at our command, consistent with law and not inconsistent with the interests of our own national self-defense—all to the end that peace and international good faith may yet emerge triumphant.

We do not regard the need for preparedness as a warrant for infringement upon our civil liberties, but on the contrary we shall continue to protect them, in the keen realization that the vivid contrast between the freedom we enjoy and the dark repression which prevails in the lands where liberty is dead, affords warning and example to our people to confirm their faith in democracy.

WE MUST STRENGTHEN DEMOCRACY BY INCREASING OUR ECONOMIC EFFICIENCY

The well-being of the land and those who work upon it is basic to the real defense and security of America.

The Republican Party gives its promises to the farmer and its allegiance to those who exploit him.

Since 1932 farm income has been doubled; six million farmers, representing more than 80 per cent of all farm families, have participated in an effective soil conservation program; the farm debt and the interest rate on farm debt have been reduced, and farm foreclosures have been drastically curtailed; rural highways and farm-to-market roads have been vastly improved and extended; the surpluses on the farms have been used to feed the needy; low-cost electricity has been brought to five million farm people as a result of the rural electrification program; thousands of impoverished farm families have been rehabilitated; and steps have been taken to stop the alarming growth of farm tenancy, to increase land ownership, and to mitigate the hardships of migratory farm labor.

The Land and the Farmer

We pledge ourselves

To make parity as well as soil conservation payments until such time as the goal of parity income for agriculture is realized.

To extend and enlarge the tenant-purchase program until every deserving tenant farmer has a real opportunity to have a farm of his own.

To refinance existing farm debts at lower interest rates and on longer and more flexible terms.

To continue to provide for adjustment of production through democratic processes to the extent that excess surpluses are capable of control.

To continue the program of rehabilitation of farmers who need and merit aid.

To preserve and strengthen the ever-normal granary on behalf of the national defense, the consumer at home and abroad, and the American farmer.

To continue to make commodity loans to maintain the ever-normal granary and to prevent destructively low prices.

To expand the domestic consumption of our surpluses by the food and cotton stamp plan, the free school lunch, low-cost milk and other plans for bringing surplus farm commodities to needy consumers.

To continue our substantially increased appropriations for research and extension work through the land-grant colleges, and for research laboratories established to develop new outlets for farm products.

To conserve the soil and water resources for the benefit of farmers and the nation. In such conservation programs we shall, so far as practicable, bring about that development in forests and other permanent crops as will not unduly expand livestock and dairy production.

To safeguard the farmer's foreign markets and expand his domestic market for all domestic crops.

To enlarge the rural electrification [sic].

To encourage farmer-owned and controlled cooperatives.

To continue the broad program launched by this Administration for the coordinated development of our river basins through reclamation and irrigation, flood control, reforestation and soil conservation, stream purification, recreation, fish and game protection, low-cost power, and rural industry.

To encourage marketing agreements in aid of producers of dairy products, vegetables, fruits and specialty crops for the purpose of orderly marketing and the avoidance of unfair and wasteful practices.

To extend crop insurance from wheat to other crops as rapidly as experience justifies such extension.
To safeguard the family-sized farm in all our programs.
To finance these programs adequately in order that they may be effective.

In settling new lands reclaimed from desert by projects like Grand Coulee, we shall give priority to homeless families who have lost their farms. As these new lands are brought into use, we shall continue by Federal purchase to retire from the plow submarginal lands so that an increased percentage of our farmers may be able to live and work on good land.

These programs will continue to be in the hands of locally elected farmer committees to the largest extent possible. In this truly democratic way, we will continue to bring economic security to the farmer and his family, while recognizing the dignity and freedom of American farm life.

Industry and the Worker

Under Democratic auspices, more has been done in the last seven years to foster the essential freedom, dignity and opportunity of the American worker than in any other administration in the nation's history. In consequence, labor is today taking its rightful place as a partner of management in the common cause of higher earnings, industrial efficiency, national unity and national defense.

A far-flung system of employment exchanges has brought together millions of idle workers and available jobs. The workers' right to organize and bargain collectively through representatives of their own choosing is being enforced. We have enlarged the Federal machinery for the mediation of labor disputes. We have enacted an effective wage and hour law. Child labor in factories has been outlawed. Prevailing wages to workers employed on Government contracts have been assured.

We pledge to continue to enforce fair labor standards; to maintain the principles of the National Labor Relations Act; to expand employment training and opportunity for our youth, older workers, and workers displaced by technological changes; to strengthen the orderly processes of collective bargaining and peaceful settlement of labor disputes; and to work always for a just distribution of our national income among those who labor.

We will continue our efforts to achieve equality of opportunity for men and women without impairing the social legislation which promotes true equality by safeguarding the health, safety and economic welfare of women workers. The right to work for compensa-tion in both public and private employment is an inalienable privilege of women as well as men, without distinction as to marital status.

The production of coal is one of our most important basic industries. Stability of production, employment, distribution and price are indispensable to the public welfare. We pledge continuation of the Federal Bituminous Coal Stabilization Act, and sympathetic consideration of the application of similar legislation to the anthracite coal industry, in order to provide additional protection for the owners, miners and consumers of hard coal.

We shall continue to emphasize the human element in industry and strive toward increasingly wholehearted cooperation between labor and industrial management.

Capital and the Business Man

To make democracy strong, our system of business enterprise and individual initiative must be free to gear its tremendous productive capacity to serve the greatest good of the greatest number.

We have defended and will continue to defend all legitimate business.

We have attacked and will continue to attack unbridled concentration of economic power and the exploitation of the consumer and the investor.

We have attacked the kind of banking which treated America as a colonial empire to exploit; the kind of securities business which regarded the Stock Exchange as a private gambling club for wagering other people's money; the kind of public utility holding companies which used consumers' and investors' money to suborn a free press, bludgeon legislatures and political conventions, and control elections against the interest of their customers and their security holders.

We have attacked the kind of business which levied tribute on all the rest of American business by the extortionate methods of monopoly.

We did not stop with attack—we followed through with the remedy. The American people found in themselves, through the democratic process, ability to meet the economic problems of the average American business where concentrated power had failed.

We found a broken and prostrate banking and financial system. We restored it to health by strengthening banks, insurance companies and other financial institutions. We have insured 62 million bank accounts, and protected millions of small investors in the security and commodity markets. We have thus revived confidence, safeguarded thrift, and opened the road to all honorable business.

We have made credit at low interest rates available

to small-business men, thus unfastening the oppressive yoke of a money monopoly, and giving the ordinary citizen a chance to go into business and stay in business.

We recognize the importance of small business concerns and new enterprises in our national economy, and favor the enactment of constructive legislation to safeguard the welfare of small business. Independent small-scale enterprise, no less than big business, should be adequately represented on appropriate governmental boards and commissions, and its interests should be examined and fostered by a continuous research program.

We have provided an important outlet for private capital by stimulating home building and low-rent housing projects. More new homes were built throughout the nation last year than in any year since 1929.

We have fostered a well-balanced American merchant marine and the world's finest system of civil aeronautics, to promote our commerce and our national defense.

We have steered a steady course between a bankruptcy-producing deflation and a thrift-destroying inflation, so that today the dollar is the most stable and sought-after currency in the world—a factor of immeasurable benefit in our foreign and domestic commerce.

We shall continue to oppose barriers which impede trade among the several states. We pledge our best efforts in strengthening our home markets, and to this end we favor the adjustment of freight rates so that no section or state will have undue advantage over any other.

To encourage investment in productive enterprise, the tax-exempt privileges of future Federal, state and local bonds should be removed.

We have enforced the anti-trust laws more vigorously than at any time in our history, thus affording the maximum protection to the competitive system.

We favor strict supervision of all forms of the insurance business by the several states for the protection of policyholders and the public.

The full force of our policies, by raising the national income by thirty billion dollars from the low of 1932, by encouraging vast reemployment, and by elevating the level of consumer demand, has quickened the flow of buying and selling through every artery of industry and trade.

With mass purchasing power restored and many abuses eliminated, American business stands at the threshold of a great new era, richer in promise than any we have witnessed—an era of pioneering and progress beyond the present frontiers of economic activity—in transportation, in housing, in industrial expansion, and in the new utilization of the products of the farm and the factory.

We shall aid business in redeeming America's promise.

Electric Power

During the past seven years the Democratic Party has won the first major victories for the people of the nation in their generation-old contest with the power monopoly.

These victories have resulted in the recognition of certain self-evident principles and the realization of vast benefits by the people. These principles, long opposed by the Republican Party, are:

That the power of falling water is a gift from God, and consequently belongs not to a privileged few, but to all the people, who are entitled to enjoy its benefits;

That the people have the right through their government to develop their own power sites and bring low-cost electricity to their homes, farms and factories;

That public utility holding companies must not be permitted to serve as the means by which a few men can pyramid stocks upon stocks for the sole purpose of controlling vast power empires.

We condemn the Republican policies which permitted the victimizing of investors in the securities of private power corporations, and the exploitation of the people by unnecessarily high utility costs.

We condemn the opposition of utility power interests which delayed for years the development of national defense projects in the Tennessee Valley, and which obstructed river basin improvements and other public projects bringing low-cost electric power to the people. The successful power developments in the Tennessee and Columbia River basins show the wisdom of the Democratic Party in establishing government-owned and operated hydroelectric plants in the interests of power and light consumers.

Through these Democratic victories, whole regions have been revived and restored to prosperous habitation. Production costs have been reduced. Industries have been established which employ men and capital. Cheaper electricity has brought vast economic benefits to thousands of homes and communities.

These victories of the people must be safeguarded. They will be turned to defeat if the Republican Party should be returned to power. We pledge our Party militantly to oppose every effort to encroach upon the inherent right of our people to be provided with this primary essential of life at the lowest possible cost.

The nomination of a utility executive by the Republican Party as its presidential candidate raises squarely the issue, whether the nation's water power shall be used for all the people or for the selfish interests of a few. We accept that issue.

Development of Western Resources

We take satisfaction in pointing out the incomparable development of the public land states under the wise and constructive legislation of this Administration. Mining has been revived, agriculture fostered, reclamation extended and natural resources developed as never before in a similar period. We pledge the continuance of such policies, based primarily on the expansion of opportunity for the people, as will encourage the full development, free from financial exploitation, of the great resources—mineral, agricultural, livestock, fishing and lumber—which the West affords.

Radio

Radio has become an integral part of the democratically accepted doctrine of freedom of speech, press, assembly and religion. We urge such legislative steps as may be required to afford the same protection from censorship that is now afforded the press under the Constitution of the United States.

WE MUST STRENGTHEN DEMOCRACY BY IMPROVING THE WELFARE OF THE PEOPLE

We place human resources first among the assets of a democratic society.

Unemployment

The Democratic Party wages war on unemployment, one of the gravest problems of our times, inherited at its worst from the last Republican administration. Since we assumed office, nine million additional persons have gained regular employment in normal private enterprise. All our policies—financial, industrial and agricultural—will continue to accelerate the rate of this progress.

By public action, where necessary to supplement private reemployment, we have rescued millions from idleness that breeds weakness, and given them a real stake in their country's well being. We shall continue to recognize the obligation of Government to provide work for deserving workers who cannot be absorbed by private industry.

We are opposed to vesting in the states and local authorities the control of Federally financed work relief. We believe that this Republican proposal is a thinly disguised plan to put the unemployed back on the dole.

We will continue energetically to direct our efforts toward the employment in private industry of all those willing to work, as well as the fullest employment of money and machines. This we pledge as our primary objective. To further implement this objective, we favor calling, under the direction of the President, a national unemployment conference of leaders of government, industry, labor and farm groups.

There is work in our factories, mines, fields, forests and river basins, on our coasts, highways, railroads and inland waterways. There are houses to be built to shelter our people. Building a better America means work and a higher standard of living for every family, and a richer and more secure heritage for every American.

Social Security

The Democratic Party, which established social security for the nation, is dedicated to its extension. We pledge to make the Social Security Act increasingly effective, by covering millions of persons not now protected under its terms; by strengthening our unemployment insurance system and establishing more adequate and uniform benefits, through the Federal equalization fund principle; by progressively extending and increasing the benefits of the old-age and survivors insurance system, including protection of the permanently disabled; and by the early realization of a minimum pension for all who have reached the age of retirement and are not gainfully employed.

Health

Good health for all the people is a prime requisite of national preparedness in its broadest sense. We have advanced public health, industrial hygiene, and maternal and child care. We are coordinating the health functions of the Federal Government. We pledge to expand these efforts, and to provide more hospitals and health centers and better health protection wherever the need exists, in rural and urban areas, all through the cooperative efforts of the Federal, state and local governments, the medical, dental, nursing and other scientific professions, and the voluntary agencies.

Youth and Education

Today, when the youth of other lands is being sacrificed in war, this nation recognizes the full value of the sound youth program established by the Administration. The National Youth Administration and Civilian Conservation Corps have enabled our youth to complete their education, have maintained their health, trained them for useful citizenship, and aided them to secure employment.

Our public works have modernized and greatly expanded the nation's schools. We have increased Federal aid for vocational education and rehabilitation, and undertaken a comprehensive program of defense-industry training. We shall continue to bring to millions of children, youths and adults, the educational and economic opportunities otherwise beyond their reach.

Slum-Clearance and Low-Rent Housing

We have launched a soundly conceived plan of loans and contributions to rid America of overcrowded slum dwellings that breed disease and crime, and to replace them by low-cost housing projects within the means of low-income families. We will extend and accelerate this plan not only in the congested city districts, but also in the small towns and farm areas, and we will make it a powerful arm of national defense by supplying housing for the families of enlisted personnel and for workers in areas where industry is expanding to meet defense needs.

Consumers

We are taking effective steps to insure that, in this period of stress, the cost of living shall not be increased by speculation and unjustified price rises.

Negroes

Our Negro citizens have participated actively in the economic and social advances launched by this Administration, including fair labor standards, social security benefits, health protection, work relief projects, decent housing, aid to education, and the rehabilitation of low-income farm families. We have aided more than half a million Negro youths in vocational training, education and employment. We shall continue to strive for complete legislative safeguards against discrimination in government service and benefits, and in the national defense forces. We pledge to uphold due process and the equal protection of the laws for every citizen regardless of race, creed or color.

Veterans

We pledge to continue our policy of fair treatment of America's war veterans and their dependents, in just tribute to their sacrifices and their devotion to the cause of liberty.

Indians

We favor and pledge the enactment of legislation creating an Indian Claims Commission for the special purpose of entertaining and investigating claims presented by Indian groups, bands and tribes, in order that our Indian citizens may have their claims against the Government considered, adjusted, and finally settled at the earliest possible date.

Civil Service

We pledge the immediate extension of a genuine system of merit to all positions in the executive branch of the Federal Government except actual bona fide policy-making positions. The competitive method of selecting employees shall be improved until experience and qualification shall be the sole test in determining fitness for employment in the Federal service. Promotion and tenure in Federal service shall likewise depend upon fitness, experience and qualification. Arbitrary and unreasonable rules as to academic training shall be abolished, all to the end that a genuine system of efficiency and merit shall prevail throughout the entire Federal service.

Territories and District of Columbia

We favor a larger measure of self-government leading to statehood for Alaska, Hawaii and Puerto Rico. We favor the appointment of residents to office, and equal treatment of the citizens of each of these three territories. We favor the prompt determination and payment of any just claims by Indian and Eskimo citizens of Alaska against the United States.

We also favor the extension of the right of suffrage to the people of the District of Columbia.

TRUE FIRST LINE OF DEFENSE

We pledge to continue to stand guard on our true first line of defense—the security and welfare of the men, women and children of America.

OUR DEMOCRATIC FAITH

Democracy is more than a political system for the government of a people. It is the expression of a people's faith in themselves as human beings. If this faith is permitted to die, human progress will die with it. We believe that a mechanized existence, lacking the spiritual quality of democracy, is intolerable to the free people of this country.

We therefore pledge ourselves to fight, as our fathers fought, for the right of every American to enjoy freedom of religion, speech, press, assembly, petition, and security in his home.

It is America's destiny, in these days of rampant despotism, to be the guardian of the world heritage of liberty and to hold aloft and aflame, the torch of Western civilization.

The Democratic Party rededicates itself to this faith in democracy, to the defense of the American system of government, the only system under which men are masters of their own souls, the only system under which the American people, composed of many races and creeds, can live and work, play and worship in peace, security and freedom.

Firmly relying upon a continuation of the blessings of Divine Providence upon all our righteous endeavors to preserve forever the priceless heritage of American liberty and peace, we appeal to all the liberal-minded men and women of the nation to approve this platform and to go forward with us by wholeheartedly supporting the candidates who subscribe to the principles which it proclaims.

— 1944 —

The Democratic Party stands on its record in peace and in war.

To speed victory, establish and maintain peace, guarantee full employment and provide prosperity—this is its platform.

We do not here detail scores of planks. We cite action.

Beginning March, 1933, the Democratic Administration took a series of actions which saved our system of free enterprise.

It brought that system out of collapse and thereafter eliminated abuses which had imperiled it.

It used the powers of government to provide employment in industry and to save agriculture.

It wrote a new Magna Carta for labor.

It provided social security, including old age pensions, unemployment insurance, security for crippled and dependent children and the blind. It established employment offices. It provided federal bank deposit insurance, flood prevention, soil conservation, and prevented abuses in the security markets. It saved

farms and homes from foreclosure, and secured profitable prices for farm products.

It adopted an effective program of reclamation, hydroelectric power, and mineral development.

It found the road to prosperity through production and employment.

We pledge the continuance and improvement of these programs.

Before war came, the Democratic Administration awakened the Nation, in time, to the dangers that threatened its very existence.

It succeeded in building, in time, the best-trained and equipped army in the world, the most powerful navy in the world, the greatest air force in the world, and the largest merchant marine in the world.

It gained for our country, and it saved for our country, powerful allies.

When war came, it succeeded in working out with those allies an effective grand strategy against the enemy.

It set that strategy in motion, and the tide of battle was turned.

It held the line against wartime inflation.

It ensured a fair share-and-share-alike distribution of food and other essentials.

It is leading our country to certain victory.

The primary and imperative duty of the United States is to wage the war with every resource available to final triumph over our enemies, and we pledge that we will continue to fight side by side with the United Nations until this supreme objective shall have been attained and thereafter to secure a just and lasting peace.

That the world may not again be drenched in blood by international outlaws and criminals, we pledge:

To join with the other United Nations in the establishment of an international organization based on the principle of the sovereign equality of all peace-loving states, open to membership by all such states, large and small, for the prevention of aggression and the maintenance of international peace and security,

To make all necessary and effective agreements and arrangements through which the nations would maintain adequate forces to meet the needs of preventing war and of making impossible the preparation for war and which would have such forces available for joint action when necessary.

Such organization must be endowed with power to employ armed forces when necessary to prevent aggression and preserve peace.

We favor the maintenance of an international court of justice of which the United States shall be a member and the employment of diplomacy, conciliation, arbitration and other like methods where appropriate in the settlement of international disputes.

World peace is of transcendent importance. Our gallant sons are dying on land, on sea, and in the air. They do not die as Republicans. They do not die as Democrats. They die as Americans. We pledge that their blood shall not have been shed in vain. America has the opportunity to lead the world in this great service to mankind. The United States must meet the challenge. Under Divine Providence, she must move forward to her high destiny.

We pledge our support to the Atlantic Charter and the Four Freedoms and the application of the principles enunciated therein to the United Nations and other peace-loving nations, large and small.

We shall uphold the good-neighbor policy, and extend the trade policies initiated by the present administration.

We favor the opening of Palestine to unrestricted Jewish immigration and colonization, and such a policy as to result in the establishment there of a free and democratic Jewish commonwealth.

We favor legislation assuring equal pay for equal work, regardless of sex.

We recommend to Congress the submission of a Constitutional amendment on equal rights for women.

We favor Federal aid to education administered by the states without interference by the Federal Government.

We favor Federal legislation to assure stability of products, employment, distribution and prices in the bituminous coal industry, to create a proper balance between consumer, producer and mine worker.

We endorse the President's statement recognizing the importance of the use of water in arid land states for domestic and irrigation purposes.

We favor non-discriminatory transportation charges and declare for the early correction of inequalities in such charges.

We favor enactment of legislation granting the fullest measure of self-government for Alaska, Hawaii and Puerto Rico, and eventual statehood for Alaska and Hawaii.

We favor the extension of the right of suffrage to the people of the District of Columbia.

We offer these postwar programs:

A continuation of our policy of full benefits for ex-servicemen and women with special consideration for the disabled. We make it our first duty to assure employment and economic security to all who have served in the defense of our country.

Price guarantees and crop insurance to farmers with all practical steps:

To keep agriculture on a parity with industry and labor.

To foster the success of the small independent farmer.

To aid the home ownership of family-sized farms.

To extend rural electrification and develop broader domestic and foreign markets for agricultural products.

Adequate compensation for workers during demobilization.

The enactment of such additional humanitarian, labor, social and farm legislation as time and experience may require, including the amendment or repeal of any law enacted in recent years which has failed to accomplish its purpose.

Promotion of the success of small business.

Earliest possible release of wartime controls.

Adaptation of tax laws to an expanding peace-time economy, with simplified structure and war time taxes reduced or repealed as soon as possible.

Encouragement of risk capital, new enterprise, development of natural resources in the West and other parts of the country, and the immediate reopening of the gold and silver mines of the West as soon as manpower is available.

We reassert our faith in competitive private enterprise, free from control by monopolies, cartels, or any arbitrary private or public authority.

We assert that mankind believes in the Four Freedoms.

We believe that the country which has the greatest measure of social justice is capable of the greatest achievements.

We believe that racial and religious minorities have the right to live, develop and vote equally with all citizens and share the rights that are guaranteed by our Constitution. Congress should exert its full constitutional powers to protect those rights.

We believe that without loss of sovereignty, world development and lasting peace are within humanity's grasp. They will come with the greater enjoyment of those freedoms by the peoples of the world, and with the freer flow among them of ideas and goods.

We believe in the world right of all men to write, send and publish news at uniform communication rates and without interference by governmental or private monopoly and that right should be protected by treaty.

To these beliefs the Democratic Party subscribes.

These principles the Democratic Party pledges itself in solemn sincerity to maintain.

Finally, this Convention sends its affectionate greetings to our beloved and matchless leader and President, Franklin Delano Roosevelt.

He stands before the nation and the world, the champion of human liberty and dignity. He has rescued our people from the ravages of economic disaster. His rare foresight and magnificent courage have saved our nation from the assault of international brigands and dictators. Fulfilling the ardent hope of his life, he has already laid the foundation of enduring peace for a troubled world and the well being of our nation. All mankind is his debtor. His life and services have been a great blessing to humanity.

That God may keep him strong in body and in spirit to carry on his yet unfinished work is our hope and our prayer.

— 1948 —

The Democratic Party adopts this platform in the conviction that the destiny of the United States is to provide leadership in the world toward a realization of the Four Freedoms.

We chart our future course as we charted our course under the leadership of Franklin D. Roosevelt and Harry S. Truman in the abiding belief that democracy—when dedicated to the service of all and not to a privileged few—proves its superiority over all other forms of government.

Our party record of the past is assurance of its policies and performance in the future.

Ours is the party which was entrusted with responsibility when twelve years of Republican neglect had blighted the hopes of mankind, had squandered the fruits of prosperity and had plunged us into the depths of depression and despair.

Ours is the party which rebuilt a shattered economy, rescued our banking system, revived our agriculture, reinvigorated our industry, gave labor strength and security, and led the American people to the broadest prosperity in our history.

Ours is the party which introduced the spirit of humanity into our law, as we outlawed child labor and the sweatshop, insured bank deposits, protected millions of home-owners and farmers from foreclosure, and established national social security.

Ours is the party under which this nation before Pearl Harbor gave aid and strength to those countries which were holding back the Nazi and Fascist tide.

Ours is the party which stood at the helm and led the nation to victory in the war.

Ours is the party which, during the war, prepared for peace so well that when peace came reconversion promptly led to the greatest production and employment in this nation's life.

Ours is the party under whose leadership farm owners' income in this nation increased from less than $2.5 billions in 1933 to more than $18 billions in 1947; independent business and professional income increased from less than $3 billions in 1933 to more than $22 billions in 1947; employees' earnings increased from $29 billions in 1933 to more than 128 billions in 1947; and employment grew from 39 million jobs in 1933 to a record of 60 million jobs in 1947.

Ours is the party under which the framework of the world organization for peace and justice was formulated and created.

Ours is the party under which were conceived the instruments for resisting Communist aggression and for rebuilding the economic strength of the democratic countries of Europe and Asia, the Truman Doctrine and the Marshall Plan. They are the materials with which we must build the peace.

Ours is the party which first proclaimed that the actions and policies of this nation in the foreign field are matters of national and not just party concern. We shall go forward on the course charted by President Roosevelt and President Truman and the other leaders of Democracy.

We reject the principle—which we have always rejected, but which the Republican 80th Congress enthusiastically accepted—that government exists for the benefit of the privileged few.

To serve the interests of all and not the few; to assure a world in which peace and justice can prevail; to achieve security, full production, and full employment—this is our platform.

OUR FOREIGN POLICY

We declared in 1944 that the imperative duty of the United States was to wage the war to final triumph and to join with the other United Nations in the establishment of an international organization for the prevention of aggression and the maintenance of international peace and security.

Under Democratic leadership, those pledges were gloriously redeemed.

When the United States were treacherously and savagely attacked, our great Democratic President, Franklin D. Roosevelt, and a Democratic Congress preserved the nation's honor, and with high courage and with the invincible might of the American people, the challenge was accepted. Under his inspiring leadership, the nation created the greatest Army that ever assembled under the flag, the mightiest Air Force, the most powerful Navy on the globe, and the largest merchant marine in the world.

The nation's gallant sons on land, on sea, and in the air, ended the war in complete and overwhelming triumph. Armed aggression against peaceful peoples was resisted and crushed. Arrogant and powerful war lords were vanquished and forced to unconditional surrender.

Before the end of the war the Democratic administration turned to the task of establishing measures for peace and the prevention of aggression and the threat of another war. Under the leadership of a Democratic President and his Secretary of State, the United Nations was organized at San Francisco. The charter was ratified by an overwhelming vote of the Senate. We support the United Nations fully and we pledge our whole-hearted aid toward its growth and development. We will continue to lead the way toward curtailment of the use of the veto. We shall favor such amendments and modifications of the charter as experience may justify. We will continue our efforts toward the establishment of an international armed force to aid its authority. We advocate the grant of a loan to the United Nations recommended by the President, but denied by the Republican Congress, for the construction of the United Nations headquarters in this country.

We pledge our best endeavors to conclude treaties of peace with our former enemies. Already treaties have been made with Italy, Hungary, Bulgaria and Rumania. We shall strive to conclude treaties with the remaining enemy states, based on justice and with guarantees against the revival of aggression, and for the preservation of peace.

We advocate the maintenance of an adequate Army, Navy and Air Force to protect the nation's vital interests and to assure our security against aggression.

We advocate the effective international control of weapons of mass destruction, including the atomic bomb, and we approve continued and vigorous efforts within the United Nations to bring about the successful consummation of the proposals which our Government has advanced.

The adoption of these proposals would be a vital and most important step toward safe and effective world disarmament and world peace under a strengthened United Nations which would then truly constitute a more effective parliament of the world's peoples.

Under the leadership of a Democratic President, the United States has demonstrated its friendship for other peace-loving nations and its support of their freedom and independence. Under the Truman Doctrine vital aid has been extended to China, to Greece, and to Turkey. Under the Marshall Plan generous sums have been provided for the relief and rehabilitation of European nations striving to rebuild their economy and to secure and strengthen their safety and freedom. The Republican leadership in the House of Representatives, by its votes in the 80th Congress, has shown its reluctance to provide funds to support this program, the greatest move for peace and recovery made since the end of World War II.

We pledge a sound, humanitarian administration of the Marshall Plan.

We pledge support not only for these principles—we pledge further that we will not withhold necessary funds by which these principles can be achieved. Therefore, we pledge that we will implement with appropriations the commitments which are made in this nation's foreign program.

We pledge ourselves to restore the Reciprocal Trade Agreements program formulated in 1934 by Secretary of State Cordell Hull and operated successfully for 14 years—until crippled by the Republican 80th Congress. Further, we strongly endorse our country's adherence to the International Trade Organization.

A great Democratic President established the Good Neighbor Policy toward the nations of the Western Hemisphere. The Act of Chapultepec was negotiated at Mexico City under Democratic leadership. It was carried forward in the Western Hemisphere defense pact concluded at Rio de Janeiro, which implemented the Monroe Doctrine and united the Western Hemisphere in behalf of peace.

We pledge continued economic cooperation with the countries of the Western Hemisphere. We pledge continued support of regional arrangements within the United Nations Charter, such as the Inter-American Regional Pact and the developing Western European Union.

President Truman, by granting immediate recognition to Israel, led the world in extending friendship and welcome to a people who have long sought and justly deserve freedom and independence.

We pledge full recognition to the State of Israel. We affirm our pride that the United States under the leadership of President Truman played a leading role in the adoption of the resolution of November 29, 1947, by the United Nations General Assembly for the creation of a Jewish State.

We approve the claims of the State of Israel to the boundaries set forth in the United Nations resolution of November 29th and consider that modifications thereof should be made only if fully acceptable to the State of Israel.

We look forward to the admission of the State of Israel to the United Nations and its full participation in the international community of nations. We pledge appropriate aid to the State of Israel in developing its economy and resources.

We favor the revision of the arms embargo to accord to the State of Israel the right of self-defense. We pledge ourselves to work for the modification of any resolution of the United Nations to the extent that it may prevent any such revision.

We continue to support, within the framework of the United Nations, the internationalization of Jerusalem and the protection of the Holy Places in Palestine.

The United States has traditionally been in sympathy with the efforts of subjugated countries to attain their independence, and to establish a democratic form of government. Poland is an outstanding example. After a century and a half of subjugation, it was resurrected after the first World War by our great Democratic President, Woodrow Wilson. We look forward to development of these countries as prosperous, free, and democratic fellow members of the United Nations.

OUR DOMESTIC POLICIES

The Republican 80th Congress is directly responsible for the existing and ever increasing high cost of living. It cannot dodge that responsibility. Unless the Republican candidates are defeated in the approaching elections, their mistaken policies will impose greater hardships and suffering on large numbers of the American people. Adequate food, clothing and shelter—the bare necessities of life—are becoming too expensive for the average wage earner and the prospects are more frightening each day. The Republican 80th Congress has lacked the courage to face this vital problem.

We shall curb the Republican inflation. We shall put a halt to the disastrous price rises which have come as a result of the failure of the Republican 80th Congress to take effective action on President Truman's recommendations, setting forth a comprehensive program to control the high cost of living.

We shall enact comprehensive housing legislation, including provisions for slum clearance and low-rent housing projects initiated by local agencies. This nation is shamed by the failure of the Republican 80th Congress to pass the vitally needed general housing legislation as recommended by the President. Adequate housing will end the need for rent control. Until then, it must be continued.

We pledge the continued maintenance of those sound fiscal policies which under Democratic leadership have brought about a balanced budget and reduction of the public debt by $28 billion since the close of the war.

We favor the reduction of taxes, whenever it is possible to do so without unbalancing the nation's economy, by giving a full measure of relief to those millions of low-income families on whom the wartime burden of taxation fell most heavily. The form of tax reduction adopted by the Republican 80th Congress gave relief to those who need it least and ignored those who need it most.

We shall endeavor to remove tax inequities and to continue to reduce the public debt.

We are opposed to the imposition of a general federal sales tax.

We advocate the repeal of the Taft–Hartley Act. It was enacted by the Republican 80th Congress over the President's veto. That Act was proposed with the promise that it would secure "the legitimate rights of both employees and employers in their relations affecting commerce." It has failed. The number of labor–management disputes has increased. The number of cases before the National Labor Relations Board has more than doubled since the Act was passed, and efficient and prompt administration is becoming more and more difficult. It has encouraged litigation in labor disputes and undermined the established American policy of collective bargaining. Recent decisions by the courts prove that the Act was so poorly drawn that its application is uncertain, and that it is probably, in some provisions, unconstitutional.

We advocate such legislation as is desirable to establish a just body of rules to assure free and effective collective bargaining, to determine, in the public interest, the rights of employees and employers, to reduce to a minimum their conflicts of interests, and to enable unions to keep their membership free from communistic influences.

We urge that the Department of Labor be rebuilt and strengthened, restoring to it the units, including the Federal Mediation and Conciliation Service and the United States Employment Service, which properly belong to it, and which the Republican 80th Congress stripped from it over the veto of President Truman. We urge that the Department's facilities for collecting and disseminating economic information be expanded, and that a Labor Education Extension Service be established in the Department of Labor.

We favor the extension of the coverage of the Fair Labor Standards Act as recommended by President Truman, and the adoption of a minimum wage of at least 75 cents an hour in place of the present obsolete and inadequate minimum of 40 cents an hour.

We favor legislation assuring that the workers of our nation receive equal pay for equal work, regardless of sex.

We favor the extension of the Social Security program established under the Democratic leadership, to provide additional protection against the hazards of old age, disability, disease or death. We believe that this program should include:

Increases in old-age and survivors' insurance benefits by at least 50 percent, and reduction of the eligibility age for women from 65 to 60 years; extension of old-age and survivors' and unemployment insurance to all workers not now covered; insurance against loss of earnings on account of illness or disability; improved public assistance for the needy.

We favor the enactment of a national health program for expanded medical research, medical education, and hospitals and clinics.

We will continue our efforts to aid the blind and other handicapped persons to become self-supporting.

We will continue our efforts to expand maternal care, improve the health of the nation's children, and reduce juvenile delinquency.

We approve the purposes of the Mental Health Act and we favor such appropriations as may be necessary to make it effective.

We advocate federal aid for education administered by and under the control of the states. We vigorously support the authorization, which was so shockingly ignored by the Republican 80th Congress, for the appropriation of $300 million as a beginning of federal aid to the states to assist them in meeting the present educational needs. We insist upon the right of every American child to obtain a good education.

The nation can never discharge its debt to its millions of war veterans. We pledge ourselves to the continuance and improvement of our national program of benefits for veterans and their families.

We are proud of the sound and comprehensive program conceived, developed and administered under Democratic leadership, including the GI Bill of Rights, which has proved beneficial to many millions.

The level of veterans' benefits must be constantly re-examined in the light of the decline in the purchasing power of the dollar brought about by inflation.

Employment and economic security must be afforded all veterans. We pledge a program of housing for veterans at prices they can afford to pay.

The disabled veteran must be provided with medical care and hospitalization of the highest possible standard.

We pledge our efforts to maintain continued farm prosperity, improvement of the standard of living and the working conditions of the farmer, and to preserve the family-size farm.

Specifically, we favor a permanent system of flexible price supports for agricultural products, to maintain farm income on a parity with farm operating costs; an intensified soil conservation program; an extended crop insurance program; improvement of methods of distributing agricultural products; development and maintenance of stable export markets; adequate financing for the school lunch program; the use of agricultural surpluses to improve the diet of low-income families in case of need; continued expansion of the rural electrification program; strengthening of all agricultural credit programs; intensified research to improve agricultural practices, and to find new uses for farm products.

We strongly urge the continuance of maximum farmer participation in all these programs.

We favor the repeal of the discriminatory taxes on the manufacture and sale of oleomargarine.

We will encourage farm cooperatives and oppose any revision of federal law designed to curtail their most effective functioning as a means of achieving economy, stability and security for American agriculture.

We favor provisions under which our fishery resources and industry will be afforded the benefits that will result from more scientific research and exploration.

We recognize the importance of small business in a sound American economy. It must be protected against unfair discrimination and monopoly, and be given equal opportunities with competing enterprises to expand its capital structure.

We favor nondiscriminatory transportation charges and declare for the early correction of inequalities in such charges.

We pledge the continued full and unified regional development of the water, mineral, and other natural resources of the nation, recognizing that the progress already achieved under the initiative of the Democratic Party in the arid and semi-arid states of the West, as well as in the Tennessee Valley, is only an indication of still greater results which can be accomplished. Our natural resources are the heritage of all our people and must not be permitted to become the private preserves of monopoly.

The irrigation of arid land, the establishment of new, independent, competitive business and the stimulation of new industrial opportunities for all of our people depends upon the development and transmission of electric energy in accordance with the program and the projects so successfully launched under Democratic auspices during the past sixteen years.

We favor acceleration of the Federal Reclamation Program, the maximum beneficial use of water in the several states for irrigation and domestic supply. In this connection, we propose the establishment and maintenance of new family-size farms for veterans and others seeking settlement opportunities, the development of hydroelectric power and its widespread distribution over publicly owned transmission lines to assure benefits to the water users in financing irrigation projects, and to the power users for domestic and industrial purposes, with preference to public agencies and R.E.A. cooperatives.

These are the aims of the Democratic Party which in the future, as in the past, will place the interest of the people as individual citizens first.

We will continue to improve the navigable waterways and harbors of the nation.

We pledge to continue the policy initiated by the Democratic Party of adequate appropriations for flood control for the protection of life and property.

In addition to practicing false economy on flood control, the Republican-controlled 80th Congress was so cruel as even to deny emergency federal funds for the relief of individuals and municipalities victimized by recent great floods, tornadoes and other disasters.

We shall expand our programs for forestation, for the improvement of grazing lands, public and private, for the stockpiling of strategic minerals and the encouragement of a sound domestic mining industry. We shall carry forward experiments for the broader utilization of mineral resources in the highly beneficial manner already demonstrated in the program for the manufacture of synthetic liquid fuel from our vast deposits of coal and oil shale and from our agricultural resources.

We pledge an intensive enforcement of the antitrust laws, with adequate appropriations.

We advocate the strengthening of existing antitrust laws by closing the gaps which experience has shown have been used to promote concentration of economic power.

We pledge a positive program to promote competitive business and to foster the development of independent trade and commerce.

We support the right of free enterprise and the right of all persons to work together in cooperatives and other democratic associations for the purpose of carrying out any proper business operations free from any arbitrary and discriminatory restrictions.

The Democratic Party is responsible for the great civil rights gains made in recent years in eliminating unfair and illegal discrimination based on race, creed or color.

The Democratic Party commits itself to continuing its efforts to eradicate all racial, religious and economic discrimination.

We again state our belief that racial and religious minorities must have the right to live, the right to work, the right to vote, the full and equal protection of the laws, on a basis of equality with all citizens as guaranteed by the Constitution.

We highly commend President Harry S. Truman for his courageous stand on the issue of civil rights.

We call upon the Congress to support our President in guaranteeing these basic and fundamental American principles: (1) the right of full and equal political participation; (2) the right to equal opportunity of employment; (3) the right of security of person; (4) and the right of equal treatment in the service and defense of our nation.

We pledge ourselves to legislation to admit a minimum of 400,000 displaced persons found eligible for United States citizenship without discrimination as to race or religion. We condemn the undemocratic action of the Republican 80th Congress in passing an inadequate and bigoted bill for this purpose, which law imposes in America restrictions based on race and religion upon such admissions.

We urge immediate statehood for Hawaii and Alaska; immediate determination by the people of Puerto Rico as to their form of government and their ultimate status with respect to the United States; and the maximum degree of local self-government for the Virgin Islands, Guam and Samoa.

We recommend to Congress the submission of a constitutional amendment on equal rights for women.

We favor the extension of the right of suffrage to the people of the District of Columbia.

We pledge adherence to the principle of nonpartisan civilian administration of atomic energy, and the development of atomic energy for peaceful purposes through free scientific inquiry for the benefit of all the people.

We urge the vigorous promotion of world-wide freedom in the gathering and dissemination of news by press, radio, motion pictures, newsreels and television, with complete confidence that an informed people will determine wisely the course of domestic and foreign policy.

We believe the primary step toward the achievement of world-wide freedom is access by all peoples to the facts and the truth. To that end, we will encourage the greatest possible vigor on the part of the United Nations Commission on Human Rights and the United Nations Economic and Social Council to establish the foundations on which freedom can exist in every nation.

We deplore the repeated attempts of Republicans in the 80tth Congress to impose thought control upon the American people and to encroach on the freedom of speech and press.

We pledge the early establishment of a national science foundation under principles which will guarantee the most effective utilization of public and private research facilities.

We will continue our efforts to improve and strengthen our federal civil service, and provide adequate compensation.

We will continue to maintain an adequate American merchant marine.

We condemn Communism and other forms of totalitarianism and their destructive activity overseas and at home. We shall continue to build firm defenses against Communism by strengthening the economic and social structure of our own democracy. We reiterate our pledge to expose and prosecute treasonable activities of anti-democratic and un-American organizations which would sap our strength, paralyze our will to defend ourselves, and destroy our unity, inciting race against race, class against class, and the people against their free institutions.

We shall continue vigorously to enforce the laws against subversive activities, observing at all times the constitutional guarantees which protect free speech, the free press and honest political activity. We shall strengthen our laws against subversion to the full extent necessary, protecting at all times our traditional individual freedoms.

We recognize that the United States has become the principal protector of the free world. The free peoples of the world look to us for support in maintaining their freedoms. If we falter in our leadership, we may endanger the peace of the world—and we shall surely endanger the welfare of our own nation. For these reasons it is imperative that we maintain our military strength until world peace with justice is secure. Under the leadership of President Truman, our military departments have been united and our Government organization for the national defense greatly strengthened. We pledge to maintain adequate military strength, based on these improvements, sufficient to fulfill our responsibilities in occupation zones, defend our national interests, and to bolster those free nations resisting Communist aggression.

This is our platform. These are our principles. They form a political and economic policy which has guided our party and our nation.

The American people know these principles well. Under them, we have enjoyed greater security, greater prosperity, and more effective world leadership than ever before.

Under them and with the guidance of Divine Providence we can proceed to higher levels of prosperity and security; we can advance to a better life at home; we can continue our leadership in the world with ever-growing prospects for lasting peace.

— 1952 —

PREAMBLE

Our Nation has entered into an age in which Divine Providence has permitted the genius of man to unlock the secret of the atom.

No system of government can survive the challenge of an atomic era unless its administration is committed to the stewardship of a trustee imbued with a democratic faith, a buoyant hope for the future, the charity of brotherhood, and the vision to translate these ideals into the realities of human government. The Government of the United States, administered by the Democratic Party, is today so entrusted.

The free choice of the Democratic Party by the people of America as the instrument to achieve that purpose will mean world peace with honor, national security based on collective pacts with other free nations, and a high level of human dignity. National survival demands that these goals be attained, and the endowments of the Democratic Party alone can assure their attainment.

For twenty years, under the dedicated guidance of Franklin Delano Roosevelt and Harry S. Truman, our country has moved steadily along the road which has led the United States of America to world leadership in the cause of freedom.

We will not retreat one inch along that road. Rather, it is our prayerful hope that the people, whom we have so faithfully served, will renew the mandate to continue our service and that Almighty God may grant us the wisdom to succeed.

TWENTY YEARS OF PROGRESS

Achieving Prosperity

An objective appraisal of the past record clearly demonstrates that the Democratic Party has been the chosen American instrument to achieve prosperity, build a stronger democracy, erect the structure of world peace, and continue on the path of progress.

Democratic Party policies and programs rescued American business from total collapse from the fatal economic consequences of watered stock, unsound banks, useless and greedy holding companies, high tariff barriers, and predatory business practices, all of which prevailed under the last Republican Administrations. Democratic policies have enabled the Federal Government to help all business, small and large, to achieve the highest rate of productivity, the widest domestic and world markets, and the largest profits in the history of the Nation.

The simple fact is that today there are more than four million operating business enterprises in this country, over one million more than existed in 1932. Corporate losses in that fateful year were over three billion dollars; in 1951, corporate profits, after taxes, reached the staggering total of eighteen billion.

Democratic policies and programs rescued American agriculture from the economic consequences of blight, drought, flood and storm, from oppressive and indiscriminate foreclosures, and from the ruinous conditions brought about by the bungling incompetence and neglect of the preceding twelve years of Republican maladministration. Economic stability, soil conservation, rural electrification, farm dwelling improvement, increased production and efficiency and more than a sevenfold increase in cash income have been the return to farmers for their faith in the Democratic Party.

Democratic labor policies have rescued the wage earners in this country from mass unemployment and from sweatshop slavery at starvation wages. Under our Democratic Administrations, decent hours, decent wages, and decent working conditions have become the rule rather than the exception.

Self-organization of labor unions and collective bargaining, both of which are the keystone to labor–management peace and prosperity must be encouraged, for the good of all.

Unemployment is now less than 3 per cent of the labor force, compared with almost 25 per cent in 1932. Trade union membership has reached a total of 16 million, which is more than five times the total of 1932.

The welfare of all economic and social groups in our society has been promoted by the sound, progressive and humane policies of the Democratic Party.

Strengthening Democracy

We are convinced that lasting prosperity must be founded upon a healthy democratic society respectful of the rights of all people.

Under Democratic Party leadership more has been done in the past twenty years to enhance the sanctity of individual rights than ever before in our history. Racial and religious minorities have progressed further toward real equality than during the preceding 150 years.

Governmental services, Democratically administered, have been improved and extended. The efficiency, economy, and integration of Federal operations have been advocated and effectuated through sound programs and policies. Through cooperative programs of Federal aid,

State and local governments have been encouraged and enabled to provide many more services.

The Democratic Party has been alert to the corroding and demoralizing effects of dishonesty and disloyalty in the public service. It has exposed and punished those who would corrupt the integrity of the public service, and it has always championed honesty and morality in government. The loyalty program of President Truman has served effectively to prevent infiltration by subversive elements and to protect honest and loyal public servants against unfounded and malicious attacks.

We commend the relentless and fearless actions of Congressional Committees which, under vigorous Democratic leadership, have exposed dereliction in public service, and we pledge our support to a continuance of such actions as conditions require them.

The administration of our government by the Democratic Party has been based upon principles of justice and equity, and upon the American tradition of fair play. Men who are elected to high political office are entrusted with high responsibilities. Slander, defamation of character, deception and dishonesty are as truly transgressions of God's commandments, when resorted to by men in public life, as they are for all other men.

Building Peace with Honor

The Democratic Party has worked constantly for peace—lasting peace, peace with honor, freedom, justice and security for all nations.

The return of the Democratic Party to power in 1933 marked the end of a tragic era of isolationism fostered by Republican Administrations which had deliberately and callously rejected the golden opportunity created by Woodrow Wilson for collective action to secure the peace.

This folly contributed to the second World War. Victory in that war has presented the nations of the world a new opportunity which the Democratic Party is determined shall not be lost.

We have helped establish the instrumentalities through which the hope of mankind for universal world peace can be realized. Under Democratic leadership, our Nation has moved promptly and effectively to meet and repel the menace to world peace by Soviet imperialism.

Progress in the New Era

The Democratic Party believes that past progress is but a prelude to the human aspirations which may be realized in the future.

Under Democratic Party leadership, America has accepted each new challenge of history and has found practical solutions to meet and overcome them. This we have done without departing from the principles of our basic philosophy, that is, the destiny of man to achieve his earthly ends in the spirit of brotherhood.

A great Democrat—Franklin Delano Roosevelt—devised the programs of the New Deal to meet the pressing problems of the 1930s. Another great Democrat—Harry S. Truman—devised the programs of the Fair Deal to meet the complex problems of America in the 1940s. The Democratic Party is ready to face and solve the challenging problems of the 1950s. We dedicate ourselves to the magnificent work of these great Presidents and to mould and adapt their democratic principles to the new problems of the years ahead.

In this spirit we adopt and pledge ourselves to this, the Democratic platform for 1952:

OUR GOAL IS PEACE WITH HONOR

Peace with honor is the greatest of all our goals.

We pledge our unremitting efforts to avert another world war. We are determined that the people shall be spared that frightful agony.

We are convinced that peace and security can be safeguarded if America does not deviate from the practical and successful policies developed under Democratic leadership since the close of World War II. We will resolutely move ahead with the constructive task of promoting peace.

Supporting the United Nations

Under Democratic leadership, this country sponsored and helped create the United Nations and became a charter member and staunchly supports its aims.

We will continue our efforts to strengthen the United Nations, improve its institutions as experience requires, and foster its growth and development.

The Communist aggressor has been hurled back from South Korea. Thus, Korea has proved, once and for all, that the United Nations will resist aggression. We urge continued effort, by every honorable means, to bring about a fair and effective peace settlement in Korea in accordance with the principles of the United Nations' charter.

Strong National Defense

Our Nation has strengthened its national defenses against the menace of Soviet aggression.

The Democratic Party will continue to stand unequivocally for the strong, balanced defense forces for this country—land, sea and air. We will continue to support the expansion and maintenance of the military and civil defense forces required for our national security. We reject the defeatist view of those who say we cannot afford the expense and effort necessary to defend ourselves. We express our full confidence in the joint Chiefs of Staff. We voice complete faith in the ability and valor of our armed forces, and pride in their accomplishments.

COLLECTIVE STRENGTH FOR THE FREE WORLD

We reject the ridiculous notions of those who would have the United States face the aggressors alone. That would be the most expensive—and the most dangerous—method of seeking security. This Nation needs strong allies, around the world, making their maximum contribution to the common defense. They add their strength to ours in the defense of freedom.

The Truman Doctrine in 1947, the organization of hemisphere defense at Rio de Janeiro that same year, the Marshall Plan in 1948, the North Atlantic Treaty in 1949, the Point IV program, the resistance to Communist aggression in Korea, the Pacific Security pacts in 1951, and the Mutual Security programs now under way—all stand as landmarks of America's progress in mobilizing the strength of the free world to keep the peace.

Encouraging European Unity

We encourage the economic and political unity of free Europe and the increasing solidarity of the nations of the North Atlantic Community.

We hail the Schuman Plan to pool the basic resources of industrial Western Europe, and the European Defense Community. We are proud of America's part in carrying these great projects forward, and we pledge our continuing support until they are established.

Support for Free Germany

We welcome the German Federal Republic into the company of free nations. We are determined that Germany shall remain free and continue as a good neighbor in the European community. We sympathize with the German people's wish for unity and will continue to do everything we can by peaceful means to overcome the Kremlin's obstruction of that rightful aim.

Support for the Victims of Soviet Imperialism

We will not abandon the once-free peoples of Central and Eastern Europe who suffer now under the Kremlin's tyranny in violation of the Soviet Union's most solemn pledges at Tehran, Yalta, and Potsdam. The United States should join other nations in formally declaring genocide to be an international crime in time of peace as well as war. This crime was exposed once more by the shocking revelations of Soviet guilt as disclosed in the report filed in Congress by the special committee investigating the Katyn Forest massacre. We look forward to the day when the liberties of Poland and the other oppressed Soviet satellites, including Czechoslovakia, Hungary, Rumania, Bulgaria, Albania, Lithuania, Estonia and Latvia and other nations in Asia under Soviet domination, will be restored to them and they can again take their rightful place in the community of free nations. We will carry forward and expand the vital and effective program of the "Voice of America" for penetration of the "Iron Curtain," bringing truth and hope to all the people subjugated by the Soviet Empire.

Support for the Nations of the Middle East

We seek to enlist the people of the Middle East to work with us and with each other in the development of the region, the lifting of health and living standards, and the attainment of peace. We favor the development of integrated security arrangements for the Middle East and other assistance to help safeguard the independence of the countries in the area.

We pledge continued assistance to Israel so that she may fulfill her humanitarian mission of providing shelter and sanctuary for her homeless Jewish refugees while strengthening her economic development.

We will continue to support the tripartite declaration of May 1950, to encourage Israel and the Arab States to settle their differences by direct negotiation, to maintain and protect the sanctity of the Holy Places and to permit free access to them.

We pledge aid to the Arab States to enable them to develop their economic resources and raise the living standards of their people. We support measures for the relief and reintegration of the Palestine refugees, and we pledge continued assistance to the reintegration program voted by the General Assembly of the United Nations in January 1952.

South Asia: A Testing Ground for Democracy

In the subcontinent of South Asia, we pledge continuing support for the great new countries of India and Pakistan in their efforts to create a better life for their people and build strong democratic governments to stand as bastions of liberty in Asia, secure against the threat of Communist subversion.

Collective Security in the Pacific

We welcome free Japan as a friendly neighbor and an ally in seeking security and progress for the whole Pacific area. America's security pacts with Japan and with the Philippines, Australia, and New Zealand are indispensable steps toward comprehensive mutual security arrangements in that area. Our military and economic assistance to the Nationalist Government of China on Formosa has strengthened that vital outpost of the free world, and will be continued.

Strengthening the Americas

In the Western Hemisphere, we pledge ourselves to continue the policy of the good neighbor. We will strive constantly to strengthen the bonds of friendship and cooperation with our Latin American allies who are joined with us in the defense of the Americas.

Disarmament Remains the Goal

The free world is rearming to secure the peace. Under Democratic leadership, America always stands prepared to join in a workable system for foolproof inspection and limitation of all armaments, including atomic weapons. This Nation has taken the leadership in proposing concrete, practical plans for such a system. We are determined to carry on the effort for real, effective disarmament.

We look forward to the day when a great share of the resources now devoted to the armaments program can be diverted into the channels of peaceful production to speed the progress of America and of the underdeveloped regions of the world.

Helping Other People to Help Themselves

Even though we cannot now disarm, we will go forward as rapidly as possible in developing the imaginative and farsighted concept of President Truman embodied in the Point IV program.

We will continue to encourage use of American skills and capital in helping the people of underdeveloped lands to combat disease, raise living standards, improve land tenure and develop industry and trade. The continuance of ever stronger and more vigorous Point IV programs—sponsored both by this country and by the United Nations—is an indispensable element in creating a peaceful world.

Upholding the Principle of Self-Determination

In an era when the "satellite state" symbolizes both the tyranny of the aggressor nations and the extinction of liberty in small nations, the Democratic Party reasserts and reaffirms the Wilsonian principle of the right of national self-determination. It is part of the policy of the Democratic Party, therefore, to encourage and assist small nations and all peoples in the peaceful and orderly achievement of their legitimate aspirations toward political, geographical and ethnic integrity so that they may dwell in the family of sovereign nations with freedom and dignity.

Expanding World Trade

The Democratic Party has always stood for expanding trade among free nations. We reassert that stand today. We vigorously oppose any restrictive policies which would weaken the highly successful reciprocal trade program fathered by Cordell Hull.

Since 1934, the United States has taken the lead in fostering the expansion and liberalization of world trade.

Our own economy requires expanded export markets for our manufactured and agricultural products and a greater supply of essential imported raw materials. At the same time, our friends throughout the world will have the opportunity to earn their own way to higher living standards with lessened dependence on our aid.

Progressive Immigration Policies

Solution of the problem of refugees from communism and over-population has become a permanent part of the foreign policy program of the Democratic Party. We pledge continued cooperation with other free nations to solve it.

We pledge continued aid to refugees from communism and the enactment of President Truman's proposals for legislation in this field. In this way we can give hope and courage to the victims of Soviet brutality and can carry on the humanitarian tradition of the Displaced Persons Act.

Subversive elements must be screened out and prevented from entering our land, but the gates must be left open for practical numbers of desirable persons from abroad whose immigration to this country provides an invigorating infusion into the stream of American life, as well as a significant contribution to the solution of the world refugee and over-population problems.

We pledge continuing revision of our immigration and naturalization laws to do away with any unjust and unfair practices against national groups which have contributed some of our best citizens. We will eliminate distinctions between native-born and naturalized citizens. We want no "second-class" citizens in free America.

OUR DOMESTIC POLICY

Economic Opportunity and Growth

The United States is today a land of boundless opportunity. Never before has it offered such a large measure of prosperity, security and hope for all its people.

Horizons of even greater abundance and opportunity lie before us under a Democratic Administration responsive to the will of the people.

The Democratic Administration has had a guiding principle since taking office 20 years ago: that the prosperity and growth of this Nation are indivisible. Every step we have taken to help the farmers has also helped the workers and business. Every improvement in the status of the worker has helped both farmers and business. Every expansion of business has provided more jobs for workers and greater demand for farm products.

A STABILIZED ECONOMY

Combatting Inflation

The Democratic Administration early recognized that defense production would limit the amount of goods in civilian markets, and subject our economy to heavy inflationary pressure. To prevent this from resulting in ruinous inflation, the Administration proposed pay-as-we-go taxation to keep the national debt as low as possible and to prevent excess money pressure on scarce goods and services.

Direct controls were also proposed to channel scarce materials into highly essential defense production, and to keep prices down.

In 1951 and 1952 Republican Congressmen demonstrated their attitude toward these necessary measures when they sponsored amendments which would have destroyed all controls.

Prices

We shall strive to redress the injury done to the American people—especially to white collar workers and fixed-income families—by the weakening amendments which the Republicans in Congress have forced into our anti-inflation laws.

We pledge continuance of workable controls so long as the emergency requires them. We pledge fair and impartial enforcement of controls and their removal as quickly as economic conditions allow.

Rents

We strongly urge continued Federal rent control in critical defense areas and in the many other localities still suffering from a substantial shortage of adequate housing at reasonable prices.

Full Employment

The Democratic Administration prudently passed the Employment Act of 1946 declaring it to be national policy never again to permit large-scale unemployment to stalk the land. We will assure the transition from defense production to peace-time production without the ravages of unemployment. We pledge ourselves at all times to the maintenance of maximum employment, production, and purchasing power in the American economy.

Integrity in Government Finances

We solemnly pledge the preservation of the financial strength of the Government. We have demonstrated our ability to maintain and enhance the Nation's financial strength. In the six full fiscal years since V-J Day, our fiscal policy has produced a $4 billion budget surplus. We have reduced the public debt $17 billion from the postwar peak.

We have demonstrated our ability to make fiscal policy contribute in a positive way to economic growth and the maintenance of high-level employment. The policies which have been followed have given us the greatest prosperity in our history. Sustained economic expansion has provided the funds necessary to finance our defense and has still left our people with record high consumer incomes and business with a record volume of investment. Employment and personal incomes are at record levels. Never have Americans enjoyed a higher standard of living and saved more for contingencies and old age.

Federal Taxes

We believe in fair and equitable taxation. We oppose a Federal general sales tax. We adhere to the principle of ability to pay. We have enacted an emergency ex-

cess profits tax to prevent profiteering from the defense program and have vigorously attacked special tax privileges.

Tax Reduction

In the future, as in the past, we will hold firm to policies consistent with sound financing and continuing economic progress. As rapidly as defense requirements permit, we favor reducing taxes, especially for people with lower incomes. But we will not imperil our Nation's security by making reckless promises to reduce taxes. We deplore irresponsible assertions that national security can be achieved without paying for it.

Closing Tax Loopholes

Justice requires the elimination of tax loopholes which favor special groups. We pledge continued efforts to the elimination of remaining loopholes.

Government Expenditures

We believe in keeping Government expenditures to the lowest practicable level. The great bulk of our national budget consists of obligations incurred for defense purposes. We pledge ourselves to a vigilant review of our expenditures in order to reduce them as much as possible.

THE AMERICAN FARMER AND AGRICULTURE

We know that national prosperity depends upon a vigorous, productive and expanding agriculture.

We take great pride in our Party's record of performance and in the impressive gains made by American agriculture in the last two decades. Under programs of Democratic Administrations the net agricultural income has increased from less than two billion dollars to almost fifteen billion dollars. These programs must be continued and improved.

Resource Conservation

The soil resources of our country have been conserved and strengthened through the Soil Conservation Service, the Agricultural Conservation Program, the Forestry and the Research programs, with their incentives to increased production through sound conservation farming. These programs have revolutionized American agriculture and must be continued and expanded. We will accelerate programs of upstream flood prevention, watershed protection, and soil, forest and water conservation in all parts of the country. These conservation measures are a national necessity; they are invaluable to our farmers, and add greatly to the welfare of all Americans and of generations yet unborn.

Grass Roots Administration

We will continue the widest possible farmer participation through referenda, farmer-elected committees, local soil conservation districts, and self-governing agencies in the conduct and administration of these truly democratic programs, initiated and developed under Democratic Administrations.

Price Supports

Under the present farm program, our farmers have performed magnificently and have achieved unprecedented production. We applaud the recent Congressional action in setting aside the "sliding scale" for price support through 1954, and we will continue to protect the producers of basic agricultural commodities under the terms of a mandatory price support program at not less than ninety percent of parity. We continue to advocate practical methods for extending price supports to other storables and to the producers of perishable commodities, which account for three-fourths of all farm income.

Abundant Production

We will continue to assist farmers in providing abundant and stable supplies of agricultural commodities for the consumer at reasonable prices, and in assuring the farmer the opportunity to earn a fair return commensurate with that enjoyed by other segments of the American economy.

The agricultural adjustment programs encourage the production of abundant supplies while enabling producers to keep supply in line with consumer demand, preventing wide fluctuations and bringing stability to the agricultural income of the Nation. We pledge retention of such programs.

We pledge continued efforts to provide adequate storage facilities for grain and other farm products with sufficient capacity for needed reserves for defense, and other emergency requirements, in order to protect the integrity of the farm price support programs.

Research

We are justly proud of the outstanding achievements of our agricultural research. We favor a greatly ex-

panded research and education program for American agriculture in order that both production and distribution may more effectively serve consumers and producers alike, and thus meet the needs of the modern world. We favor especial emphasis on the development of new crops and varieties, on crop and livestock disease and pest control, and on agricultural statistics and marketing services.

Marketing

We must find profitable markets for the products of our farms, and we should produce all that these markets will absorb. To this end we will continue our efforts to reduce trade barriers, both at home and abroad, to provide better marketing and inspection facilities, and to find new uses and outlets for our foods and fibers both in domestic and foreign markets.

Farm Credit

We have provided credit facilities for all agriculture, including means by which young men, veterans of military service, and farm tenants have been encouraged to become farmers and farm homeowners, and through which low-income farmers have been assisted in establishing self-sustaining and fully productive farm units. We will not waver in our efforts to provide such incentives.

Crop Insurance

Crop insurance to protect farmers against loss from destruction of their crops by natural causes has been created and developed under Democratic Administrations into a sound business operation. This program should be expanded as rapidly as experience justifies, in order that its benefits may be made available to every farmer.

Rural Electrification

Democratic Administrations have established the great Rural Electrification Program, which has brought light and power to the rural homes of our Nation. In 1935, only 10% of the farm homes of America had the benefits of electricity. Today 85% of our rural homes enjoy the benefits of electric light and power. We will continue to fight to make electricity available to all rural homes, with adequate facilities for the generation and transmission of power. Through the Rural Telephone Program, inaugurated by the Democratic 81st Congress, we will provide the opportunity for every farm home to have this modern essential service. We pledge support of these self-liquidating farm programs.

Cooperatives

We will continue to support the sound development and growth of bonafide farm cooperatives and to protect them from punitive taxation.

Defense Needs

We will continue to recognize agriculture as an essential defense industry, and to assist in providing all the necessary tools, machinery, fertilizer, and manpower needed by farmers in meeting production goals.

Family Farming

The family farm is the keystone of American agriculture. We will strive unceasingly to make the farm homes of our country healthier and happier places in which to live. We must see that our youth continues to find attractive opportunity in the field of agriculture.

The Republican Party platform is loud in its criticism of our great farm programs. We challenge Republicans and other enemies of farm progress to justify their opposition to the program now in operation, to oppose the improvements here proposed, or to advocate repeal of a single vital part of our program.

A FAIR DEAL FOR WORKERS

Good Incomes

There can be no national prosperity unless our working men and women continue to prosper and enjoy rising living standards. The rising productivity of American workers is a key to our unparalleled industrial progress. Good incomes for our workers are the secret of our great and growing consumer markets.

Labor–Management Relations

Good labor–management relations are essential to good incomes for wage earners and rising output from our factories. We believe that to the widest possible extent consistent with the public interest, management and labor should determine wage rates and conditions of employment through free collective bargaining.

Taft–Hartley Act

We strongly advocate the repeal of the Taft–Hartley Act.

The Taft–Hartley Act has been proved to be inadequate, unworkable, and unfair. It interferes in an arbitrary manner with collective bargaining, tipping the scales in favor of management against labor.

The Taft–Hartley Act has revived the injunction as a weapon against labor in industrial relations. The Act has arbitrarily forbidden traditional hiring practices which are desired by both management and labor in many industries. The Act has forced workers to act as strikebreakers against their fellow unionists. The Act has served to interfere with one of the most fundamental rights of American workers—the right to organize in unions of their own choosing.

We deplore the fact that the Taft–Hartley Act provides an inadequate and unfair means of meeting with national emergency situations. We advocate legislation that will enable the President to deal fairly and effectively with cases where a breakdown in collective bargaining seriously threatens the national safety or welfare.

In keeping with the progress of the times, and based on past experiences, a new legislative approach toward the entire labor–management problem should be explored.

Fair Labor Standards

We pledge to continue our efforts so that Government programs designed to establish improved fair labor standards shall prove a means of assuring minimum wages, hours and protection to workers, consistent with present-day progress.

Equal Pay for Equal Work

We believe in equal pay for equal work, regardless of sex, and we urge legislation to make that principle effective.

The Physically Handicapped

We promise to further the program to afford employment opportunities both in Government and in private industry for physically handicapped persons.

Migratory Workers

We advocate prompt improvement of employment conditions of migratory workers and increased protection of their safety and health.

STRENGTHENING FREE ENTERPRISE

The free enterprise system has flourished and prospered in America during these last twenty years as never before. This has been made possible by the purchasing power of all our people and we are determined that the broad base of our prosperity shall be maintained.

Small and Independent Business

Small and independent business is the backbone of American free enterprise. Upon its health depends the growth of the economic system whose competitive spirit has built this Nation's industrial strength and provided its workers and consumers with an incomparably high standard of living.

Independent business is the best offset to monopoly practices. The Government's role is to insure that independent business receives equally fair treatment with its competitors.

Congress has established the permanent Small Business Committee of the Senate and the Special Small Business Committee of the House, which have continued to render great service to this important segment of our economy. We favor continuance of both these committees with all the powers to investigate and report conditions, correct discriminations, and propose needed legislation.

We pledge ourselves to increased efforts to assure that small business be given equal opportunity to participate in Government contracts, and that a suitable proportion of the dollar volume of defense contracts be channeled into independent small business. The Small Defense Plants Administration, which our Party caused to be established, should retain its independent status and be made a continuing agency, equipped with sufficient lending powers to assist qualified small business in securing defense contracts.

We urge the enactment of such laws as will provide favorable incentives to the establishment and survival of independent businesses, especially in the provision of tax incentives and access to equity or risk capital.

Enforcement of Anti-Trust Laws

Free competitive enterprise must remain free and competitive if the productive forces of this Nation are to remain strong. We are alarmed over the increasing concentration of economic power in the hands of a few.

We reaffirm our belief in the necessity of vigorous enforcement of the laws against trusts, combinations, and restraints of trade, which laws are vital to the safeguarding of the public interest and of small competitive business men against predatory monopolies. We will seek adequate appropriations for the Department of Justice and the Federal Trade Commission for vig-

orous investigation and for enforcement of the anti-trust laws. We support the right of all persons to work together in cooperatives and other democratic associations for the purpose of carrying out any proper business operations free from any arbitrary and discriminatory restrictions.

Protection of Investors and Consumers

We must avoid unnecessary business controls. But we cannot close our eyes to the special problems which require Government surveillance. The Government must continue its efforts to stop unfair selling practices which deceive investors, and unfair trade practices which deceive consumers.

Transportation

In the furtherance of national defense and commerce, we pledge continued Government support, on a sound financial basis, for further development of the Nation's transportation systems, land, sea and air. We endorse a policy of fostering the safest and most reliable air transportation system in the world. We favor fair, nondiscriminatory freight rates to encourage economic growth in all parts of the country.

Highways

In cooperation with State and local governmental units, we will continue to plan, coordinate, finance, and encourage the expansion of our road and highway network, including access roads, for the dual purposes of national defense and efficient motor transportation. We support expansion of farm-to-market roads.

Rivers and Harbors

We pledge continued development of our harbors and waterways.

Merchant Marine

We will continue to encourage and support an adequate Merchant Marine.

OUR NATURAL RESOURCES

The United States has been blessed with the richest natural resources of any nation on earth.

Yet, unless we redouble our conservation efforts we will become a "have-not" nation in some of the most important raw materials upon which depend our industries, agriculture, employment and high standard of living. This can be prevented by a well rounded and nation-wide conservation effort.

Land and Water Resources

We favor sound, progressive development of the Nation's land and water resources for flood control, navigation, irrigation, power, drainage, soil conservation and creation of new, small family-sized farms, with immediate action in critical areas.

We favor the acceleration of all such projects, including construction of transmission facilities to local centers for wider and more equitable distribution of electric energy at the lowest cost to the consumer with continuing preference to public agencies and REA Cooperatives.

The Democratic Party denounces all obstructionist devices designed to prevent or retard utilization of the Nation's power and water resources for the benefit of the people, their enterprises and interests.

The wise policy of the Democratic Party in encouraging multipurpose projects throughout the country is responsible for America's productive superiority over any nation in the world and is one of the greatest single factors leading toward the accomplishment of world peace. Without these projects our atomic weapons program could never have been achieved, and without additional such projects it cannot be expanded.

The Democratic Party is dedicated to a continuation of the natural resources development policy inaugurated and carried out under the Administrations of Presidents Roosevelt and Truman, and to the extension of that policy to all parts of the Nation—North, South, East, Midwest, West and the territories—to the end that the Nation and its people receive maximum benefits from these resources to which they have an inherent right.

The Democratic Party further pledges itself to protect these resources from destructive monopoly and exploitation.

River Basin Development

We pledge the continued full and unified regional development of the water, mineral and other natural resources of the Nation, recognizing that the progress already achieved under the initiative of the Democratic Party in the arid and semi-arid States of the West, as well as in the Tennessee Valley, is only an indication of still greater results which can be accomplished.

Fertilizer Development

Great farming areas, particularly of the Midwest and West, are in acute need of low-cost commercial fertilizers. To meet this demand, we favor the opening of the Nation's phosphate rock deposits in the West, through prompt provision of sufficient low-cost hydroelectric power to develop this great resource.

Forests and Public Lands

We seek to establish and demonstrate such successful policies of forest and land management on Federal property as will materially assist State and private owners in their conservation efforts. Conservation of forest and range lands is vital to the strength and welfare of the Nation. Our forest and range lands must be protected and used wisely in order to produce a continuing supply of basic raw materials for industry; to reduce damaging floods; and to preserve the sources of priceless water. With adequate appropriations to carry out feasible projects, we pledge a program of forest protection, reforestation projects and sound practices of production and harvesting which will promote sustained yields of forest crops.

We propose to increase forest access roads in order to improve cutting practices on both public and private lands.

On the public land ranges we pledge continuance of effective conservation and use programs, including the extension of water pond construction and restoration of forage cover.

Arid Areas

In many areas of the Nation assistance is needed to provide water for irrigation, domestic and industrial purposes. We pledge that in working out programs for rational distribution of water from Federal sources we will aid in delivering this essential of life cheaply and abundantly.

Minerals and Fuels

The Nation's minerals and fuels are essential to the national defense and development of our country. We pledge the adoption of policies which will further encourage the exploration and development of additional reserves of our mineral resources. We subscribe to the principles of the Stockpiling Act and will lend our efforts to strengthening and expanding its provisions and those of the Defense Production Act to meet our military and civilian needs. Additional access roads should be constructed with Government aid.

Research programs on our synthetic fuels, including monetary metals, should go forward. Laws to aid and assist these objectives will be advocated.

Domestic Fisheries

We favor increased research and exploration for conserving and better utilizing fishery resources; expanded research and education to promote new fishery products and uses and new markets; promotion of world trade in fish products; a public works and water policy providing adequate protection for domestic fishery resources; and treaties with other nations for conservation and better utilization of international fisheries.

Wildlife Recreations

In our highly complex civilization, outdoor recreation has become essential to the health and happiness of our people.

The Democratic Party has devoted its efforts to the preservation, restoration and increase of the bird, animal and fish life which abound in this Nation. State, local and private agencies have cooperated in this worthy endeavor. We have extended and vastly improved the parks, forests, beaches, streams, preserves and wilderness areas across the land.

To the 28,000,000 of our citizens who annually purchase fishing and hunting licenses, we pledge continued efforts to improve all recreational areas.

ATOMIC ENERGY

In the field of atomic energy, we pledge ourselves:

(1) to maintain vigorous and non-partisan civilian administrations, with adequate security safeguards;
(2) to promote the development of nuclear energy for peaceful purposes in the interests of America and mankind;
(3) to build all the atomic and hydrogen firepower needed to defend our country, deter aggression, and promote world peace;
(4) to exert every effort to bring about bonafide international control and inspection of all atomic weapons.

SOCIAL SECURITY

Our national system of social security, conceived and developed by the Democratic Party, needs to be extended and improved.

Old Age and Survivors Insurance

We favor further strengthening of old age and survivors insurance, through such improvements as increasing benefits, extending them to more people and lowering the retirement age for women.

We favor the complete elimination of the work clause for the reason that those contributing to the Social Security program should be permitted to draw benefits, upon reaching the age of eligibility, and still continue to work.

Unemployment Insurance

We favor a stronger system of unemployment insurance, with broader coverage and substantially increased benefits, including an allowance for dependents.

Public Assistance

We favor further improvements in public assistance programs for the blind, the disabled, the aged and children in order to help our less fortunate citizens meet the needs of daily living.

Private Plans

We favor and encourage the private endeavors of social agencies, mutual associations, insurance companies, industry–labor groups, and cooperative societies to provide against the basic hazards of life through mutually agreed upon benefit plans designed to complement our present Social Security program.

Needs of Our Aging Citizens

Our older citizens constitute an immense reservoir of skilled, mature judgment and ripened experience. We pledge ourselves to give full recognition to the right of our older citizens to lead a proud, productive and independent life throughout their years.

In addition to the fundamental improvements in Old Age and Survivors Insurance, which are outlined above, we pledge ourselves, in cooperation with the States and private industry, to encourage the employment of older workers. We commend the 82nd Congress for eliminating the age restriction on employment in the Federal Government.

Health

We will continue to work for better health for every American, especially our children. We pledge continued and wholehearted support for the campaign that modern medicine is waging against mental illness, cancer, heart disease and other diseases.

Research

We favor continued and vigorous support, from private and public sources, of research into the causes, prevention and cure of disease.

Medical Education

We advocate Federal aid for medical education to help overcome the growing shortages of doctors, nurses, and other trained health personnel.

Hospitals and Health Centers

We pledge continued support for Federal aid to hospital construction. We pledge increased Federal aid to promote public health through preventive programs and health services, especially in rural areas.

Cost of Medical Care

We also advocate a resolute attack on the heavy financial hazard of serious illness. We recognize that the costs of modern medical care have grown to be prohibitive for many millions of people. We commend President Truman for establishing the non-partisan Commission on the Health Needs of the Nation to seek an acceptable solution of this urgent problem.

Housing

We pledge ourselves to the fulfillment of the programs of private housing, public low-rent housing, slum clearance, urban redevelopment, farm housing and housing research as authorized by the Housing Act of 1949.

We deplore the efforts of special interests groups, which themselves have prospered through Government guarantees of housing mortgages, to destroy those programs adopted to assist families of low income.

Additional Legislation

We pledge ourselves to enact additional legislation to promote housing required for defense workers, middle-income families, aged persons and migratory farm laborers.

Veterans' Housing

We pledge ourselves to provide special housing aids to veterans and their families.

EDUCATION

Every American child, irrespective of color, national origin, economic status or place of residence should have every educational opportunity to develop his potentialities.

Local, State and Federal governments have shared responsibility to contribute appropriately to the pressing needs of our educational system. We urge that Federal contributions be made available to State and local units which adhere to basic minimum standards.

The Federal Government should not dictate nor control educational policy.

We pledge immediate consideration for those school systems which need further legislation to provide Federal aid for new school construction, teachers' salaries and school maintenance and repair.

We urge the adoption by appropriate legislative action of the proposals advocated by the President's Commission on Higher Education, including Federal scholarships.

We will continue to encourage the further development of vocational training which helps people acquire skills and technical knowledge so essential to production techniques.

Child Welfare

The future of America depends on adequate provision by Government for the needs of those of our children who cannot be cared for by their parents or private social agencies.

Maternity, Child Health and Welfare Services

The established national policy of aiding States and localities, through the Children's Bureau and other agencies, to insure needed maternity, child health and welfare services should be maintained and extended. Especially important are the detection and treatment of physical defects and diseases which, if untreated, are reflected in adult life in draft rejections and as handicapped workers. The Nation, as a whole, should provide maternity and health care for the wives, babies and preschool children of those who serve in our armed forces.

School Lunches

We will enlarge the school lunch program which has done so much for millions of American school children and charitable institutions while at the same time benefiting producers.

Day Care Facilities

Since several million mothers must now be away from their children during the day, because they are engaged in defense work, facilities for adequate day care of these children should be provided and adequately financed.

Children of Migratory Workers

The Nation, as a whole, has a responsibility to support health, educational, and welfare services for the children of agricultural migratory workers who are now almost entirely without such services while their parents are engaged in producing essential crops.

Veterans

The Democratic Party is determined to advance the welfare of all the men and women who have seen service in the armed forces. We pledge ourselves to continue and improve our national program of benefits for veterans and their families, to provide the best possible medical care and hospitalization for the disabled veteran, and to help provide every veteran an opportunity to be a productive and responsible citizen with an assured place in the civilian community.

STRENGTHENING DEMOCRATIC GOVERNMENT

Streamlining the Federal Government

The public welfare demands that our Government be efficiently and economically operated and that it be reorganized to meet changing needs. During the present Democratic Administration, more reorganization has been accomplished than by all its predecessors. We pledge our support to continuing reorganization wherever improvements can be made. Only constant effort by the Executive, the Congress, and the public enable our Government to render the splendid service to which our citizens are entitled.

Improving the Postal Service

We pledge a continuing increase in the services of the United States Postal Service. Through efficient handling of mail, improved working conditions for postal employees, and more frequent services, the Democratic Party promises its efforts to provide the greatest communication system in the world for the American people.

Strengthening the Civil Service

Good government requires a Civil Service high in quality and prestige. We deplore and condemn smear attacks upon the character and reputations of our Federal workers. We will continue our fight against partisan political efforts to discredit the Federal service and undermine American principles of justice and fair play.

Under President Truman's leadership, the Federal Civil Service has been extended to include a greater proportion of positions than ever before. He has promoted a record number of career appointees to top-level policy positions. We will continue to be guided by these enlightened policies, and we will continue our efforts to provide Federal service with adequate pay, sound retirement provisions, good working conditions, and an opportunity for advancement.

We will use every proper means to eliminate pressure by private interests seeking undeserved favors from the Government. We advocate the strongest penalties against those who try to exert improper influence, and against any who may yield to it.

Democracy in Federal Elections

We advocate new legislation to provide effective regulation and full disclosure of campaign expenditures in elections to Federal office, including political advertising from any source.

We recommend that Congress provide for a non-partisan study of possible improvements in the methods of nominating and electing Presidents and in the laws relating to Presidential succession. Special attention should be given to the problem of assuring the widest possible public participation in Presidential nominations.

Strengthening Basic Freedoms

We will continue to press strongly for worldwide freedom in the gathering and dissemination of news and for support to the work of the United Nations Commission on Human Rights in furthering this and other freedoms.

Equal Rights Amendment

We recommend and endorse for submission to the Congress a constitutional amendment providing equal rights for women.

Puerto Rico

Under Democratic Party leadership, a new status his been developed for Puerto Rico. This new status is based on mutual consent and common devotion to the United States, formalized in a new Puerto Rican Constitution. We welcome the dignity of the new Puerto Rican Commonwealth and pledge our support of the Commonwealth, its continued development and growth.

Alaska and Hawaii

By virtue of their strategic geographical locations, Alaska and Hawaii are vital bastions in the Pacific. These two territories have contributed greatly to the welfare and economic development of our country and have become integrated into our economic and social life. We, therefore, urge immediate statehood for these two territories.

Other Territories and Possessions

We favor increased self-government for the Virgin Islands and other outlying territories and the trust territory of the Pacific.

District of Columbia

We favor immediate home rule and ultimate national representation for the District of Columbia.

American Indians

We shall continue to use the powers of the Federal Government to advance the health, education and economic well-being of our American Indian citizens, without impairing their cultural traditions. We pledge our support to the cause of fair and equitable treatment in all matters essential to and desirable for their individual and tribal welfare.

The American Indian should be completely integrated into the social, economic and political life of the Nation. To that end we shall move to secure the prompt final settlement of Indian claims and to remove restrictions on the rights of Indians individually and through their tribal councils to handle their own fiscal affairs.

We favor the repeal of all acts or regulations that deny to Indians rights or privileges held by citizens generally.

Constitutional Government

The Democratic Party has demonstrated its belief in the Constitution as a charter of individual freedom and an effective instrument for human progress. Democratic Administrations have placed upon the statute books during the last twenty years a multitude of measures which testify to our belief in the Jeffersonian principle of local control, even in general legislation involving nation-wide programs. Selective service, Social Security, Agricultural Adjustment, Low Rent Housing, Hospital, and many other legislative programs have placed major responsibilities in States and counties and provide fine examples of how benefits can be extended through Federal–State cooperation.

In the present world crisis, with new requirements of Federal action for national security, and accompanying provision for public services and individual rights related to defense, constitutional principles must and will be closely followed. Our record and our clear commitments, in this platform, measure our strong faith in the ability of constitutional government to meet the needs of our times.

Improving Congressional Procedures

In order that the will of the American people may be expressed upon all legislative proposals, we urge that action be taken at the beginning of the 83rd Congress to improve Congressional procedures so that majority rule prevails and decisions can be made after reasonable debate without being blocked by a minority in either House.

Civil Rights

The Democratic Party is committed to support and advance the individual rights and liberties of all Americans.

Our country is founded on the proposition that all men are created equal. This means that all citizens are equal before the law and should enjoy equal political rights. They should have equal opportunities for education, for economic advancement, and for decent living conditions.

We will continue our efforts to eradicate discrimination based on race, religion or national origin.

We know this task requires action, not just in one section of the Nation, but in all sections. It requires the cooperative efforts of individual citizens and action by State and local governments. It also requires Federal action. The Federal Government must live up to the ideals of the Declaration of Independence and must exercise the powers vested in it by the Constitution.

We are proud of the progress that has been made in securing equality of treatment and opportunity in the Nation's armed forces and the civil service and all areas under Federal jurisdiction. The Department of Justice has taken an important part in successfully arguing in the courts for the elimination of many illegal discriminations, including those involving rights to own and use real property, to engage in gainful occupations and to enroll in publicly supported higher educational institutions. We are determined that the Federal Government shall continue such policies.

At the same time, we favor Federal legislation effectively to secure these rights to everyone: (1) the right to equal opportunity for employment; (2) the right to security of persons; (3) the right to full and equal participation in the Nation's political life, free from arbitrary restraints. We also favor legislation to perfect existing Federal civil rights statutes and to strengthen the administrative machinery for the protection of civil rights.

CONCLUSION

Under the guidance, protection, and help of Almighty God we shall succeed in bringing to the people of this Nation a better and more rewarding life and to the peoples of the entire world, new hope and a lasting, honorable peace.

— 1956 —

PREAMBLE

In the brief space of three and one-half years, the people of the United States have come to realize, with tragic consequences, that our National Government cannot be trusted to the hands of political amateurs, dominated by representatives of special privilege.

Four years ago they were beguiled, by empty promises and pledges, to elect as President a recent convert to Republicanism. Our people have now learned that the party of Lincoln has been made captive to big businessmen with small minds. They have found that they are now ruled by a Government which they did not elect, and to which they have not given their consent. Their awareness of this fact was demonstrated in 1954 when they returned control of the legislative machinery of the Federal Government to the 84th Democratic Congress.

From the wreckage of American world leadership under a Republican Administration, this great Democratic Congress has salvaged a portion of the world prestige our Nation enjoyed under the brilliant Administrations of Franklin Delano Roosevelt and Harry S. Truman.

Our Democratic 84th Congress made one of the greatest legislative records in the history of our country. It enacted an active program of progressive, humane legislation, which has repudiated the efforts of reactionary Republicanism to stall America's progress. When we return to the halls of Congress next January, and with a Democratic President in the White House, it will be the plan and purpose of our Party to complete restoration and rehabilitation of American leadership in world affairs. We pledge return of our National Government to its rightful owners, the people of the United States.

On the threshold of an atomic age, in the mid-Twentieth Century, our beloved Nation needs the vision, vigor and vitality which can be infused into it only by a government under the Democratic Party.

We approach the forthcoming election with a firm purpose of effecting such infusion; and with the help and assistance of Divine Providence we shall endeavor to accomplish it. To the end that the people it has served so well may know our program for the return of America to the highway of progress, the Democratic Party herewith submits its platform for 1956.

I. FOREIGN POLICY AND NATIONAL DEFENSE

The Democratic Party affirms that world peace is a primary objective of human society. Peace is more than a suspension of shooting while frenzied and fearful nations stockpile armaments of annihilation.

Achievement of world peace requires political statesmanship and economic wisdom, international understanding and dynamic leadership. True peace is the tranquillity of ordered justice on a global scale. It may be destroyed without a shot being fired. It can be fostered and preserved only by the solid unity and common brotherhood of the peoples of the world in the cause of freedom.

The hopes and aspirations of the peoples of all nations for justice and peace, depend largely upon the courageous and enlightened administration of the foreign and defense policies of the United States. We deplore the fact that the administration of both policies since 1953 has confused timidity with courage, and blindness with enlightenment.

The Republican Record of Confusion and Complacency Is the President's Responsibility

The world's hopes for lasting peace depend upon the conduct of our foreign policy, a function which the Constitution vests in the President of the United States and one which has not been effectively exercised by

President Eisenhower. Since 1953, responsibility for foreign affairs has been President Eisenhower's, his alone, and his in full.

In the past three years, his conduct of our policies has moved us into realms where we risk grave danger. He has failed to seek peace with determination, for his disarmament policy has failed to strike hard at the institution of war. His handling of the day-to-day problems of international affairs has unnecessarily and dangerously subjected the American people to the risk of atomic world war.

Our Government Lacks Leadership

We need bold leadership, yet in the three years since Stalin's death, in the full year since President Eisenhower's meeting at the "summit," the Republican Administration has not offered a single concrete new idea to meet the new-style political and economic offensive of the Soviets, which represents, potentially, an even greater challenge than Stalin's use of force: President Eisenhower and his Secretary of State talk at cross-purposes, praising neutralism one day, condemning it the next. The Republicans seem unable either to make up their minds or to give us leadership, while the unity of the free world rapidly disintegrates.

We in America need to make our peaceful purpose clear beyond dispute in every corner of the world—yet Secretary Dulles brags of "brinks of war." We need a foreign policy which rises above jockeying for partisan position or advantage—yet, not in memory has there been so little bipartisanship in the administration of our policies, so little candor in their presentation to our people, so much pretending that things are better than they are.

The Republican Bluster and Bluff

Four years ago the Republican Party boasted of being able to produce a foreign policy which was to free the Communist satellites, unleash Chang Kai-shek, repudiate the wartime agreements, and reverse the policy of containing Communist expansion.

Since 1953 they have done just the opposite, standing silent when the peoples rise in East Germany and Poland, and thereby weakening the positive Democratic policy of halting Communist expansion.

Our Friends Lose Faith in Us

Our friends abroad now doubt our sincerity. They have seen the solid assurance of collective security under a Democratic Administration give place to the un-

certainties of personal diplomacy. They have seen the ties of our international alliances and friendship weakened by inept Republican maneuvering.

They have seen traditional action and boldness in foreign affairs evaporate into Republican complacency, retrenchment and empty posturing.

The Failure Abroad

Blustering without dynamic action will not alter the fact that the unity and strength of the free world have been drastically impaired. Witness the decline of NATO, the bitter tragedy of Cyprus, the withdrawal of French forces to North Africa, the uncertainty and dangers in the Middle East, an uncertain and insecure Germany, and resentment rising against United States leadership everywhere.

In Asia—in Burma, Ceylon, Indonesia, India—anti-Americanism grows apace, aggravated by the clumsy actions of our Government, and fanned by the inept utterances of our "statesmen."

In the Middle East, the Eisenhower Administration has dawdled and drifted. The results have been disastrous, and worse threatens. Only the good offices of the United Nations in maintaining peace between Israel and her neighbors conceal the diplomatic incapacities of the Republican Administration. The current crisis over Suez is a consequence of inept and vacillating Republican policy. Our Government's mistakes have placed us in a position in the Middle East which threatens the free world with a loss of power and prestige, potentially more dangerous than any we have suffered in the past decade.

The Failure at Home

Political considerations of budget balancing and tax reduction now come before the wants of our national security and the needs of our Allies. The Republicans have slashed our own armed strength, weakened our capacity to deal with military threats, stifled our air force, starved our army and weakened our capacity to deal with aggression of any sort save by retreat or by the alternatives, "massive retaliation" and global atomic war. Yet, while our troubles mount, they tell us our prestige was never higher, they tell us we were never more secure.

The Challenge Is for Democracy to Meet

The Democratic Party believes that "waging peace" is a monumental task to be performed honestly, forthrightly, with dedication and consistent effort.

The way to lasting peace is to forego bluster and bluff, to regain steadiness of purpose, to join again in faithful concert with the community of free nations, to look realistically at the challenging circumstances which confront us, to face them candidly and imaginatively, and to return to the Democratic policy of peace through strength.

This is a task for Democrats. This facing of new problems, this rising to new challenges, has been our Party's mission and its glory for three generations past. President Truman met and mastered Stalin's challenge a decade ago, with boldness, courage and imagination, and so will we turn to the challenge before us now, pressing the search for real and lasting peace.

TO THIS WE PLEDGE:

Support for the United Nations

The United Nations is indispensable for the maintenance of world peace and for the settlement of controversies between nations small and large. We pledge our every effort to strengthen its usefulness and expand its role as guide and guardian of international security and peace. We deplore the Republicans' tendency to use the United Nations only when it suits them, ignoring or bypassing it whenever they please.

We pledge determined opposition to the admission of the Communist Chinese into the United Nations. They have proven their complete hostility to the purposes of this organization. We pledge continued support to Nationalist China.

Release of American Prisoners

We urge a continuing effort to effect the release of all Americans detained by Communist China.

Support for Effective Disarmament

In this atomic age, war threatens the very survival of civilization. To eliminate the danger of atomic war, a universal, effective and enforced disarmament system must be the goal of responsible men and women everywhere. So long as we lack enforceable international control of weapons, we must maintain armed strength to avoid war. But technological advances in the field of nuclear weapons make disarmament an ever more urgent problem. Time and distance can never again protect any nation of the world. The Eisenhower Administration, despite its highly publi-

cized proposals for aerial inspection, has made no progress toward this great objective. We pledge the Democratic Party to pursue vigorously this great goal of enforced disarmament in full awareness that irreparable injury, even total destruction, now threatens the human race.

Adequate Defense Forces

We reject the false Republican notion that this country can afford only a second-best defense. We stand for strong defense forces so clearly superior in modern weapons to those of any possible enemy that our armed strength will make an attack upon the free world unthinkable, and thus be a major force for world peace. The Republican Administration stands indicted for failing to recognize the necessity of proper living standards for the men and women of our armed forces and their families. We pledge ourselves to the betterment of the living conditions of the members of our armed services, and to a needed increase in the so-called "fringe benefits."

Training for Defense

The Democratic Party pledges itself to a bold and imaginative program devised to utilize fully the brain power of America's youth, including its talent in the scientific and technical fields.

Scholarships and loan assistance and such other steps as may be determined desirable must be employed to secure this objective. This is solely in the interest of necessary and adequate national defense.

Strengthening Civil Defense

We believe that a strong, effective civil defense is a necessary part of national defense. Advances in nuclear weapons have made existing civil defense legislation and practices obsolete.

We pledge ourselves to establish a real program for protecting the civilian population and industry of our Nation in place of the present weak and ineffective program. We believe that this is essentially a Federal responsibility.

Collective Security Arrangements

The Democratic Party inaugurated and we strongly favor collective defense arrangements, such as NATO and the Organization of American States, within the framework of the United Nations. We realize, as the Republicans have not, that mutually recognized common interests can be flexibly adapted to the varied needs and aspirations of all countries concerned.

Winning the Productivity Race

The Republican Party has not grasped one of the dominant facts of mid-century—that the growth of productive power of the Communist states presents a challenge which cannot be evaded. The Democratic Party is confident that, through the freedom we enjoy, a vast increase in the productive power of our Nation and our Allies will be achieved, and by their combined capacity they will surmount any challenge.

Economic Development Abroad

We believe that, in the cause of peace, America must support the efforts of underdeveloped countries on a cooperative basis to organize their own resources and to increase their own economic productivity, so that they may enjoy the higher living standards which science and modern industry make possible. We will give renewed strength to programs of economic and technical assistance. We support a multilateral approach to these programs, wherever possible, so that burdens are shared and resources pooled among all the economically developed countries with the capital and skills to help in this great task.

Further, while recognizing the relation of our national security to the role of the United States in international affairs, the Democratic Party believes the time has come for a realistic reappraisal of the American foreign aid program, particularly as to its extent and the conditions under which it should be continued. This reappraisal will determine the standards by which further aid shall be granted, keeping in mind America's prime objective of securing world peace.

Bringing the Truth to the World

The tools of truth and candor are even more important than economic tools. The Democratic Party believes that once our Government is purged of the confusion and complacency fostered by the Republican Administration a new image of America will emerge in the world: the image of a confident America dedicated to its traditional principles, eager to work with other peoples, honest in its pronouncements, and consistent in its policies.

Freedom for Captive Nations

We condemn the Republican Administration for its heartless record of broken promises to the unfortunate victims of Communism. Candidate Eisenhower's 1952 pledges to "liberate" the captive peoples have been disavowed and dishonored.

We declare our deepest concern for the plight of the freedom-loving peoples of Central and Eastern Europe and of Asia, now under the yoke of Soviet dictatorship. The United States, under Democratic leaders, has never recognized the forcible annexation of Lithuania, Latvia, and Estonia, or condoned the extension of the Kremlin's tyranny over Poland, Bulgaria, Rumania, Czechoslovakia, Hungary, Albania and other countries.

We look forward to the day when the liberties of all captive nations will be restored to them and they can again take their rightful place in the community of free nations.

We shall press before the United Nations the principle that Soviet Russia withdraw its troops from the captive countries, so as to permit free, fair and unfettered elections in the subjugated areas, in compliance with the Atlantic Charter and other binding commitments.

Upholding the Principle of Self-Determination

We rededicate ourselves to the high principle of national self-determination, as enunciated by Woodrow Wilson, whose leadership brought freedom and independence to uncounted millions.

It is the policy of the Democratic Party, therefore, to encourage and assist small nations and all peoples, behind the Iron Curtain and outside, in the peaceful and orderly achievement of their legitimate aspirations toward political, geographical, and ethnic integrity, so that they may dwell in the family of sovereign nations with freedom and dignity. We are opposed to colonialism and Communist imperialism.

We shall endeavor to apply this principle to the desires of all peoples for self-determination.

Reciprocal Trade Among the Nations

The Democratic Party has always worked for expanding trade among free nations. Expanding world trade is necessary not only for our friends, but for ourselves; it is the way to meet America's growing need for industrial raw materials. We shall continue to support vigorously the Hull Reciprocal Trade Program.

Under Democratic Administrations, the operation of this Act was conducted in a manner that recognized equities for agriculture, industry and labor. Under the present Republican Administration, there has been a most flagrant disregard of these important segments of our economy resulting in serious economic injury to hundreds of thousands of Americans engaged in these pursuits. We pledge correction of these conditions.

Encouraging European Unity

Through the Marshall Plan, the European Economic Organization and NATO, the Democratic Party encouraged and supported efforts to achieve greater economic and political unity among the free nations of Europe, and to increase the solidarity of the nations of the North Atlantic community. We will continue those efforts, taking into account the viewpoints and aspirations of different sectors of the European community, particularly in regard to practical proposals for the unification of Germany.

Peace and Justice in the Middle East

The Democratic Party stands for the maintenance of peace in the Middle East, which is essential to the well-being and progress of all its peoples.

We will urge Israel and the Arab States to settle their differences by peaceful means, and to maintain the sanctity of the Holy Places in the Holy Land and permit free access to them.

We will assist Israel to build a sound and viable economy for her people, so that she may fulfill her humanitarian mission of providing shelter and sanctuary for her homeless Jewish refugees while strengthening her national development.

We will assist the Arab States to develop their economic resources and raise the living standards of their people. The plight of the Arab refugees commands our continuing sympathy and concern. We will assist in carrying out large-scale projects for their resettlement in countries where there is room and opportunity for them.

We support the principle of free access to the Suez Canal under suitable international auspices. The present policies of the Eisenhower Administration in the Middle East are unnecessarily increasing the risk that war will break out in this area. To prevent war, to assure peace, we will faithfully carry out our country's pledge under the Tripartite Declaration of 1950 to oppose the use or threat of force and to take such action as may be necessary in the interest of peace, both within and outside the United Nations, to prevent any violation of the frontiers of any armistice lines.

The Democratic Party will act to redress the dangerous imbalance of arms in the area resulting from the shipment of Communist arms to Egypt, by selling or supplying defensive weapons to Israel, and will take such steps, including security guarantees, as may be required to deter aggression and war in the area.

We oppose, as contrary to American principles, the practice of any government which discriminates against American citizens on grounds of race or reli-

gion. We will not countenance any arrangement or treaty with any government which by its terms or in its practical application would sanction such practices.

Support for Free Asia

The people of Asia seek a new and freer life and they are in a commendable hurry to get it. They struggle against poverty, ill health and illiteracy. In the aftermath of war, China became a victim of Communist tyranny. But many new free nations have arisen in South and Southeast Asia. South Korea remains free, and the new Japan has abandoned her former imperial and aggressive ways. America's task and interest in Asia is to help the governments of free peoples demonstrate that they have improved living standards without yielding to Communist tyranny or domination by anyone. That task will be carried out under Democratic leadership.

Support of Our Good Neighbors to the South

In the Western Hemisphere the Democratic Party will restore the policy of the "good neighbor" which has been alternately neglected and abused by the Republican Administration. We pledge ourselves to fortify the defenses of the Americas. In this respect, we will intensify our cooperation with our neighboring republics to help them strengthen their economies, improve educational opportunities, and combat disease. We will strive to make the Western Hemisphere an inspiring example of what free peoples working together can accomplish.

Progressive Immigration Policies

America's long tradition of hospitality and asylum for those seeking freedom, opportunity, and escape from oppression, has been besmirched by the delays, failures and broken promises of the Republican Administration. The Democratic Party favors prompt revision of the immigration and nationality laws to eliminate unfair provisions under which admissions to this country depend upon quotas based upon the accident of national origin. Proper safeguards against subversive elements should be provided. Our immigration procedures must reflect the principles of our Bill of Rights.

We favor eliminating the provisions of law which charge displaced persons admitted to our shores against quotas for future years. Through such "mortgages" of future quotas, thousands of qualified persons are being forced to wait long years before they can hope for admission.

We also favor more liberal admission of relatives to eliminate the unnecessary tragedies of broken families.

We favor elimination of unnecessary distinctions between native-born and naturalized citizens. There should be no "second-class" citizenship in the United States.

The administration of the Refugee Relief Act of 1953 has been a disgrace to our country. Rescue has been denied to innocent, defenseless and suffering people, the victims of war and the aftermath of wars. The purpose of the Act has been defeated by Republican mismanagement.

Victims of Communist Oppression

We will continue to support programs providing succor for escapees from behind the Iron Curtain, and bringing help to the victims of war and Communist oppression.

The Challenge of the Next Four Years

Today new challenges call for new ideas and new methods.

In the coming years, our great necessity will be to pull together as a people, with true nonpartisanship in foreign affairs under leaders informed, courageous and responsible.

We shall need to work closely with each other as Americans. If we here indict the Republican record, we acknowledge gratefully the efforts of individual Republicans to achieve true bipartisanship. In this spirit an affirmative, cooperative policy can be developed. We shall need to work closely, also, with others all around the world. For there is much to do—to create once more the will and the power to transform the principles of the United Nations into a living reality; to awaken ourselves and others to the effort and sacrifice which alone can win justice and peace.

II. THE DOMESTIC POLICY— THE REPUBLICAN REACTION TO 20 YEARS OF PROGRESS

The Democratic Bequest

Twenty years of vivid Democratic accomplishments revived and reinforced our economic system, and wrote humanity upon the statute books. All this, the current Republican Administration inherited.

The Republican Brand of Prosperity

Substituting deceptive slogans and dismal deeds for the Democratic program, the Republicans have been telling the American people that "we are now more prosperous than ever before in peacetime." For the American farmer, the small businessman and the low-income worker, the old people living on a pittance, the young people seeking an American standard of education, and the minority groups seeking full employment opportunities at adequate wages, this tall tale of Republican prosperity has been an illusion.

The evil is slowly but surely infiltrating the entire economic system. Its fever signs are evidenced by soaring monopoly profits, while wages lag, farm income collapses, and small-business failures multiply at an alarming rate.

The first time-bomb of the Republican crusade against full prosperity for all was the hard-money policy. This has increased the debt burden on depressed farms, saddled heavier costs on small business, foisted higher interest charges on millions of homeowners (including veterans), pushed up unnecessarily the cost of consumer credit, and swelled the inordinate profits of a few lenders of money. It has wrought havoc with the bond market, with resulting financial loss to the ordinary owners of Government bonds.

The Republican tax policy has joined hands in an unholy alliance with the hard-money policy. Fantastic misrepresentation of the Government's budgetary position has been used to deny tax relief to low- and middle-income families, while tax concessions and handouts have been generously sprinkled among potential campaign contributors to Republican coffers. The disastrously reactionary farm program, the hardhearted resistance to adequate expansion of Social Security and other programs for human well-being, and favoritism in the award of Government contracts, all have watered the economic tree at the top and neglected its roots.

The Stunting of Our Economic Progress

The Republicans say that employment and production are "higher" than ever before. The fact is that our overall rate of growth has been crippled and stunted in contrast to its faster increase during the Democratic years from 1947 to 1953, after World War II.

With production lagging behind full capacity, unemployment has grown.

The Republican claim that this stunted prosperity is the price of peace is a distortion. National-security outlays have averaged a higher part of our total production (during these Republican years than during 1947–53, and yet the annual growth in total production during these Republican years has been only about 60 percent as fast as in the preceding Democratic years. The progress of low-income families toward an American standard of living, rapid during the Democratic years, has ground to a stop under the Republicans.

Federal budgetary outlays for education and health, old-age assistance and child care, slum clearance and resource development, and all the other great needs of our people have been mercilessly slashed from an annual rate of more than $57 per capita under the Democrats to $33 per capita under the Republicans, a cut of 42 percent.

The Failure of the Republican Budget-Balancers

During the Republican fiscal years 1954–1957 as a whole, the deficits have averaged larger, and the surpluses smaller, than during the Democratic fiscal years 1947–1953, financial manipulation to the contrary notwithstanding.

Democratic Principles for Full Prosperity for All

(1) We repudiate the Republican stunting of our economic growth, and we reassert the principles of the Full Employment Act of 1946;
(2) We pledge ourselves to achieve an honest and realistic balance of the Federal Budget in a just and fully prosperous American economy;
(3) We pledge ourselves to equitable tax revisions and monetary policies designed to combine economic progress with economic justice. We condemn the Republican use of our revenue and money systems to benefit the few at the expense of the vast majority of our people;
(4) We pledge ourselves to work toward the reduction and elimination of poverty in America;
(5) We pledge ourselves to full parity of income and living standards for agriculture; to strike off the shackles which the Taft–Hartley law has unjustly imposed on labor; and to foster the more rapid growth of legitimate business enterprise by founding this growth upon the expanding consuming power of the people; and
(6) We pledge ourselves to expand world trade and to enlarge international economic cooperation, all toward the end of a more prosperous and more peaceful world.

Democratic Goals to Be Achieved During Four Years of Progress

By adhering to these principles, we shall strive to attain by 1960 the following full prosperity objectives for all American families:

(1) A 500 billion dollar national economy in real terms;
(2) An increase of 20 percent or better in the average standard of living;
(3) An increase in the annual income of American families, with special emphasis on those whose incomes are below $2000;
(4) A determined drive toward parity of incomes and living standards for those engaged in the vital pursuit of agriculture;
(5) The addition of all necessary classrooms for our primary and secondary schools; the construction of needed new homes, with a proper proportion devoted to the rehousing of low- and middle-income families in urban and rural areas; the increase of benefits under the Old Age Assistance and Old Age Survivors Insurance Programs; a substantial expansion in hospital facilities and medical research; and a doubling of our programs for resource development and conservation; and
(6) National defense outlays based upon our national needs, not permitting false economy to jeopardize our very survival.

This country of ours, in the factory, in business and on the farm, is blessed with ever-increasing productive power. The Republicans have not permitted this potential abundance to be released for the mutual benefit of all. We reject this stunted Republican concept of America. We pledge ourselves to release the springs of abundance, to bring this abundance to all, and thus to fulfill the full promise of America.

These are our Democratic goals for the next four years. We set them forth in vivid contrast to Republican lip-service protestations that they, too, are for these goals. Their little deeds belie their large and hollow slogans. Our performance in the past gives validity to our goals for the future.

Our victory in 1956 will make way for the commencement of these four years of progress.

III. FREE ENTERPRISE

"Equal rights for all and special privileges for none," the tested Jeffersonian principle, remains today the only philosophy by which human rights can be preserved by government.

It is a sad fact in the history of the Republican Party that, under its control, our Government has always become an instrument of special privilege; not a government of the people, by the people, and for the people. We have had, instead, under Harding, Coolidge and Hoover, and now under Eisenhower, government of the many, by the few, and for the few.

We recognize monopolies and monopolistic practices as the real barriers between the people and their economic and political freedom. Monopolies act to stifle equality of opportunity and prevent the infusion of fresh blood into the lifestream of our economy. The Republican Administration has allowed giant corporate entities to dominate our economy. For example, forty thousand automobile dealers now know they were incapable of coping with these giants. They were, as the Democratic 84th Congress found, subjected to abuse and threatened with extinction. The result was passage of the O'Mahoney–Celler Bill giving the automobile dealers of America economic freedom. We enacted this law, and we pledge that it shall be retained upon the statute books as a monument to the Democratic Party's concern for small business.

We pledge ourselves to the restoration of truly competitive conditions in American industry. Affirmative action within the framework of American tradition will be taken to curb corporate mergers that would contribute to the growth of economic concentration.

Small and Independent Business

In contrast to the maladministration by the Republican Party of the Federal program to assist small and independent business, we pledge ourselves—

(1) To the strict and impartial enforcement of the laws originally fostered and strengthened by the Democratic Party and designed to prevent monopolies and other concentrations of economic and financial power; and to enact legislation to close loopholes in the laws prohibiting price discrimination;

(2) To tax relief for all small and independent businesses by fair and equitable adjustments in Federal taxation which will encourage business expansion, and to the realistic application of the principle of graduated taxation to such corporate income. An option should be provided to spread Federal estate taxes over a period of years when an estate consists principally of the equity capital of a closely held small business;

(3) To adoption of all practical means of making long- and short-term credit available to small and independent businessmen at reasonable rates;

(4) To the award of a substantially higher proportion of Government contracts to independent small businesses, and to the award of a far larger percentage of military procurement, by value, after competitive bids rather than by negotiation behind closed doors. We severely condemn Republican discrimination against small and independent business;

(5) To replacement of the weak and ineffective Republican conduct of the Small Business Administration, and its reconstitution as a vigorous, independent agency which will advocate the cause of small and independent businessmen, and render genuine assistance in fulfilling their needs and solving their problems. We condemn the Republican Administration for its failure to serve this important segment of our economy.

Law Enforcement

We pledge ourselves to the fair and impartial administration of justice. The Republican Administration has degraded the great powers of law enforcement. It has not used them in the service of equal justice under law, but for concealment, coercion, persecution, political advantage and special interests.

Merchant Marine

In the interest of our national security, and of the maintenance of American standards of wages and living, and in order that our waterborne overseas commerce shall not be unfairly discriminated against by low-cost foreign competition, we pledge our continued encouragement and support of a strong and adequate American Merchant Marine.

Transportation

The public and national defense interests require the development and maintenance, under the competitive free enterprise system, of a strong, efficient and financially sound system of common-carrier transportation by water, highway, rail, and air, with each mode enabled, through sound and intelligent exercise of regulatory powers, to realize its inherent economic advantages and to reflect its full competitive capabilities. Public interest also requires, under reasonable standards, the admission of new licensees, where public convenience may be served, into the transport fields. We deplore the lack of enforcement of safety regulations for protection of life and property under the present Republican Administration, and pledge strict enforcement of such regulations.

Highways

We commend the foresight of the Democratic 84th Congress for its enactment of the greatest program in history for expansion of our highway network, and we congratulate it upon its rejection of the unsound, unworkable, inadequate and unfair roads bill proposed by the present Republican Administration.

In cooperation with State and local governments, we will continue the programs developed and fostered under prior Democratic Administrations for planning, coordinating, financing and encouraging the expansion of our national road and highway network so vital to defense and transportation in the motor age. We support expansion of farm-to-market roads.

Rivers and Harbors

We pledge continued development of harbors and waterways as a vital segment of our transportation system. We denounce as capricious and arbitrary the Eisenhower pocket veto of the 1956 Rivers and Harbors Bill, which heartlessly deprived the people in many sections of our country of vitally needed public works projects.

IV. A MAGNA CHARTA FOR LABOR

Labor–Management Relations

Harmonious labor–management relations are productive of good incomes for wage earners and conducive to rising output from our factories. We believe that, to the widest possible extent consistent with the public interest, management and labor should determine wage rates and conditions of employment through free collective bargaining.

The Taft–Hartley Act passed by the Republican-dominated 80th Congress seriously impaired this relationship as established in the Wagner National Labor Relations Act, enacted under the Roosevelt Administration. The Wagner Act protected, encouraged and guaranteed the rights of workers to organize, to join unions of their own choice, and to bargain collectively through these unions without coercion.

The vicious anti-union character of the Taft–Hartley Act was expressly recognized by Candidate Eisenhower during the 1952 election campaign.

At that time, he made a solemn promise to eliminate its unjust provisions and to enact a fair law. President Eisenhower and his Administration have failed utterly, however, to display any executive initiative or forcefulness toward keeping this pledge to the workers. He was further responsible for administratively amending Taft–Hartley into a more intensely anti-labor weapon by stacking the National Labor Relations Board with biased pro-management personnel who, by administrative decision, transformed the Act into a management weapon. One such decision removed millions of workers from the jurisdiction of the NLRB, which in many cases left them without protection of either State or Federal legislation.

We unequivocally advocate repeal of the Taft–Hartley Act. The Act must be repealed because State "right-to-work" laws have their genesis in its discriminatory anti-labor provisions.

It must be repealed because its restrictive provisions deny the principle that national legislation based on the commerce clause of the Constitution normally overrides conflicting State laws.

The Taft–Hartley Act has been proven to be inadequate, unworkable and unfair. It interferes in an arbitrary manner with collective bargaining, causing imbalance in the relationship between management and labor.

Upon return of our National Government to the Democratic Party, a new legislative approach toward the entire labor–management problem will be adopted, based on past experience and the principles of the Wagner National Labor Relations Act and the Norris–La Guardia Anti-Injunction Law.

Fair Labor Standards

We commend the action of the Democratic 84th Congress which raised the minimum wage from 75 cents to $1.00 an hour despite the strenuous objection of President Eisenhower and the Republicans in Congress. However, the inadequacies of the minimum wage become apparent as the cost of living increases, and we feel it imperative to raise the minimum wage to at least $1.25 an hour, in order to approximate present-day needs more closely.

We further pledge as a matter of priority to extend full protection of the Fair Labor Standards Act to all workers in industry engaged in, or affecting, interstate commerce.

Walsh–Healey Contracts Act

We pledge revision and honest administration of the Walsh–Healey Act, to restore its effectiveness and usefulness as an instrument for maintaining fair standards of wages and hours for American workers.

Equal Pay for Equal Work

We advocate legislation to provide equal pay for equal work, regardless of sex.

The Physically Handicapped

The Democratic Party has always supported legislation to benefit the disabled worker. The physically handicapped have proved their value to Government and industry. We pledge our continued support of legislation to improve employment opportunities of physically handicapped persons.

Migratory Workers

We shall support legislation providing for the protection and improvement of the general welfare of migratory workers.

Jobs for Depressed Areas

We pledge our Party to support legislation providing for an effective program to promote industry and create jobs in depressed industrial and rural areas so that such areas may be restored to economic stability.

V. AGRICULTURE

Sustained national prosperity is dependent upon a vigorous agricultural economy.

We condemn the defeatist attitude of the Eisenhower Administration in refusing to take effective action to assure the well-being of farm families. We condemn its fear of abundance, its lack of initiative in developing domestic markets, and its dismal failure to obtain for the American farmer his traditional and deserved share of the world market. Its extravagant expenditure of money intended for agricultural benefit, without either direction or results, is a national calamity.

The Eisenhower Administration has failed utterly to develop any programs to meet the desperate needs of farmers in the face of fantastic promises, and it has sabotaged the progressive programs inherited from prior Democratic Administrations by failing to administer them properly in the interest either of farmers or of the Nation as a whole.

Specifically, we denounce President Eisenhower's veto of the constructive legislation proposed and passed by the Democratic 84th Congress to reverse the alarming fall of farm prices and restore farmers to a position of first-class economic citizenship in the sharing of benefits from American productive ability.

We also condemn the Republican Administration for its abandonment of the true principles of soil conservation and for its destruction of the Soil Conservation Service. We pledge to support continued improvements in the soil bank program passed by the Democratic 84th Congress and originally opposed by President Eisenhower and Secretary Ezra Taft Bellson. We deplore the diversion of this conservation program into a direct vote-buying scheme.

Farmers have had to struggle for three and one-half years while their net farm income has fallen more than one billion dollars a year. Their parity ratio, which under Democratic Administrations had been 100 percent or more during the eleven years prior to 1953, dropped to as low as 80 percent during the Eisenhower Administration, and the farmers' share of the consumers' food dollar shrank from 47 cents in 1952 to as low as only 38 cents. One stark fact stands out clearly for all to see—disastrously low farm prices and record high consumer prices vie with each other for the attention of responsible government. In a reduction of this incongruous spread lies the answer to some of the most vexing problems of agricultural economics.

In their courageous fight to save their homes and land, American farmers have gone deeper and deeper into debt. Last year farmers' mortgage indebtedness increased more than in any year in history with the exception of the year 1923.

The Democratic Party met similar situations forthrightly in the past with concrete remedial action. It takes legitimate pride in its consistent record of initiating and developing every constructive program designed to protect and conserve the human and natural resources so vital to our rural economy. These programs enabled consumers to obtain more abundant supplies of high-quality food and fiber at reasonable prices while maintaining adequate income for farmers and improving the level of family living in rural areas.

In order to regain the ground lost during the Eisenhower Administration, and in order better to serve both consumers and producers, the Democratic Party pledges continuous and vigorous support of the following policies:

Sponsor positive and comprehensive program to conserve our soil, water and forest resources for future generations;

Promote programs which will protect and preserve the family-type farm as a bulwark of American life, and encourage farm-home ownership, including additional assistance to family farmers and young farmers in the form of specially designed credit and price-support programs, technical aid, and enlarged soil conservation allowances.

Maintain adequate reserves of agricultural commodities strategically situated, for national security purposes. Such stockpiles should be handled as necessary strategic reserves, so that farmers will not be penalized by depressed prices for their efficiency and diligence in producing abundance;

Promote international exchange of commodities by creating an International Food Reserve, fostering commodity agreements, and vigorously administering the Foreign Agricultural Trade Development and Assistance Act;

Undertake immediately by appropriate action to endeavor to regain the full 100 percent of parity the farmers received under the Democratic Administrations. We will achieve this by means of supports on basic commodities at 90 percent of parity and by means of commodity loans, direct purchases, direct payments to producers, marketing agreements and orders, production adjustments, or a combination of these, including legislation, to bring order and stability into the relationship between the producer, the processor and the consumer;

Develop practical measures for extending price supports to feed grains and other nonbasic storables and to the producers of perishable commodities such as meat, poultry, dairy products and the like;

Inaugurate a food-stamp or other supplemental food program administered by appropriate State or local agencies to insure that no needy family shall be denied an adequate and wholesome diet because of low income;

Continue and expand school lunch and special milk programs to meet the dietary needs of all school children;

Increase the distribution of food to public institutions and organizations and qualified private charitable agencies, and increase the distribution of food and fiber to needy people in other nations through recognized charitable and religious channels;

Devise and employ effective means to reduce the spread between producers' prices and consumers' costs, and improve market facilities and marketing practices;

Expand the program of agricultural research and education for better distribution, preservation and marketing of farm products to serve both producers and consumers, and promote increased industrial use of farm surpluses;

Provide for an increased reservoir of farm credit at lower rates, designed particularly to accommodate operators of small family-type farms, and extend crop insurance to maximum coverage and protection;

Return the administration of farm programs to farmer-elected committeemen, eliminate the deplorable political abuses in Federal employment in many agricultural counties as practiced by the Eisenhower Administration, and restore leadership to the administration of soil conservation districts;

Insure reliable and low-cost rural electric and telephone service;

Exercise authority in existing law relating to imports of price-supported agricultural commodities in raw, manufactured or processed form as part of our national policy to minimize damage to our domestic economy;

Encourage bona fide farm cooperatives which help farmers reduce the cost–price squeeze, and protect such cooperatives against punitive taxation;

Expand farm forestry marketing research and price reporting on timber products, and provide adequate credit designed to meet the needs of timber farmers; and

Enact a comprehensive farm program which, under intelligent and sympathetic Democratic administration, will make the rural homes of America better and healthier places in which to live.

VI. GENERAL WELFARE

The Democratic Party believes that America can and must adopt measures to assure every citizen an opportunity for a full, healthy and happy life. To this end, we pledge ourselves to the expansion and improvement of the great social welfare programs inaugurated under Democratic Administrations.

Social Security

By lowering the retirement age for women and for disabled persons, the Democratic 84th Congress pioneered two great advances in Social Security, over the bitter opposition of the Eisenhower Administration. We shall continue our efforts to broaden and strengthen this program by increasing benefits to keep pace with improving standards of living; by raising the wage base upon which benefits depend; and by increasing benefits for each year of covered employment.

Unemployment Insurance

We shall continue to work for a stronger unemployment insurance system, with broader coverage and increased benefits consistent with rising earnings. We shall also work for the establishment of a floor to assure minimum level and duration of benefits, and fair eligibility rules.

Wage Losses Due to Illness

In 1946, a Democratic Congress enacted an insurance program to protect railroad workers against temporary wage losses due to short-term illnesses. Because this program has worked so effectively, we favor extending similar protection to other workers.

Public Assistance

We pledge improvements in the public assistance program even beyond those enacted by the Democratic 84th Congress, through increased aid for the aged, the blind, dependent children, the disabled and other needy persons who are not adequately protected by our contributory insurance programs.

Additional Needs of Our Senior Citizens

To meet the needs of the 14 million Americans aged 65 or over, we pledge ourselves to seek means of assuring these citizens greater income through expanded opportunities for employment, vocational retraining and adult education; better housing and health services for the aged; rehabilitation of the physically and mentally disabled to restore them to independent, productive lives; and intensified medical and other research aimed both at lengthening life and making the longer life more truly livable.

Health and Medical Care

The strength of our Nation depends on the health of our people. The shortage of trained medical and health personnel and facilities has impaired American health standards and has increased the cost of hospital care beyond the financial capacities of most American families.

We pledge ourselves to initiate programs of Federal financial aid, without Federal controls, for medical education.

We pledge continuing and increased support for hospital construction programs, as well as increased Federal aid to public health services, particularly in rural areas.

Medical Research

Mindful of the dramatic progress made by medical research in recent years, we shall continue to support vigorously all efforts, both public and private, to wage relentless war on diseases which afflict the bodies and minds of men. We commend the Democratic Party for its leadership in obtaining greater Congressional authorizations in this field.

Housing

We pledge our Party to immediate revival of the basic housing program enacted by the Democratic Congress in 1949, to expansion of this program as our population and resources grow, and to additional legislation to provide housing for middle-income families and aged persons. Aware of the financial burdens which press upon most American communities and prevent them from taking full advantage of Federal urban redevelopment and renewal programs, we favor increasing the Federal share of the cost of these programs.

We reaffirm the goal expressed by a Democratic Congress in 1949 that every American family is entitled to a "decent home and a suitable living environment." The Republican Administration has sabotaged that goal by reducing the public housing program to a fraction of the Nation's need.

We pledge that the housing insurance and mortgage guarantee programs will be redirected in the interest of the home owner, and that the availability of low-interest housing credit will be kept consistent with the expanding housing needs of the Nation.

We favor providing aid to urban and suburban communities in better planning for their future development and redevelopment.

Education

Every American child, irrespective of race or national origin, economic status or place of residence, has full right under the law and the Constitution, without discrimination, to every educational opportunity for developing his potentialities.

We are now faced with shortages of educational facilities that threaten national security, economic prosperity and human well-being. The resources of our States and localities are already strained to the limit. Federal aid and action should be provided, within the traditional framework of State and local control.

We pledge the Democratic Party to the following:

(1) Legislation providing Federal financing to assist States and local communities to build schools, and to provide essential health and safety services for all school children;
(2) Better educational, health and welfare opportunities for children of migratory workers;
(3) Assistance to programs for training teachers of exceptional children;
(4) Programs providing for the training of teachers to meet the critical shortage in technical and scientific fields; and
(5) Expansion of the program of student, teacher and cultural exchange with other nations.

Vocational Education

We commend the 84th Congress for voting the maximum authorized funds for vocational education under the Smith–Hughes Act for the first time in the history of the Act. We pledge continuing and increased support of vocational training for youth and adults, including aid to the States and localities for area technical–vocational schools.

Child Welfare

To keep pace with the growing need for child care and welfare, we pledge an expanded program of grants to the States. We pledge continued support of adequate day care centers to care for the children of the millions of American mothers who work to help support their families.

Aid to the Physically Handicapped

There are today several million physically handicapped citizens, many of whom could become self-supporting if given the opportunity and training for rehabilitation. We pledge support to a vastly expanded rehabilitation program for these physically handicapped, including increased aid to the States, in contrast to the grossly inadequate action of the Republican Administration.

VII. FINANCIAL POLICY

Tax Adjustment

A fully expanding economy can yield enough tax revenues to meet the inescapable obligations of government, balance the Federal Budget, and lighten the tax burden. The immediate need is to correct the inequities in the tax structure which reflect the Republican determination to favor the few at the expense of the many. We favor realistic tax adjustments, giving first consideration to small independent business and the small individual taxpayer. Lower-income families need tax relief; only a Democratic victory will assure this. We favor an increase in the present personal tax exemption of $600 to a minimum of at least $800.

Debt Management

The Republican debt management policy of higher interest rates serves only to benefit a few to the detriment of the general taxpayer, the small borrower, and the small and middle-class investor in Government bonds. We pledge ourselves to a vigilant review of our debt management policy in order to reduce interest rates in the service of our common welfare.

Protection of Investors

Effective administration of the Federal securities laws has been undermined by Republican appointees with conflicting interests. Millions of investors who have bought securities with their savings are today without adequate protection. We favor vigorous administration and revision of the laws to provide investor safeguards for securities extensively traded in the over-the-counter market, for foreign securities distributed in the United States, and against proxy contest abuses.

VIII. GOVERNMENT OPERATIONS

The Democratic Party pledges that it will return the administration of our National Government to a sound, efficient, and honest basis.

Civil Service and Federal Employee Relations

The Eisenhower Administration has failed either to understand or trust the Federal employee. Its record in personnel management constitutes a grave indictment of policies reflecting prejudices and excessive partisanship to the detriment of employee moral.

Intelligent and sympathetic programs must be immediately undertaken to insure the re-establishment of the high morale and efficiency which were characteristic of the Federal worker during 20 years of Democratic Administrations.

To accomplish these objectives, we propose:

(1) Protection and extension of the merit system through the enactment of laws to specify the rights and responsibilities of workers;
(2) A more independent Civil Service Commission in order that it may provide the intelligent leadership essential in perfecting a proper Civil Service System;
(3) Promotion within the Federal Service under laws assuring advancement on merit and proven ability;
(4) Salary increases of a nature that will insure a truly competitive scale at all levels of employment;
(5) Recognition by law of the right of employee organizations to represent their members and to participate in the formulation and improvement of personnel policies and practices; and
(6) A fair and nonpolitical loyalty program, by law, which will protect the Nation against subversion and the employee against unjust and un-American treatment.

Restoring the Efficiency of the Postal Service

The bungling policies of the Republican Administration have crippled and impaired the morale, efficiency and reputation of the U.S. Postal Service. Mail carriers and clerks and other Postal employees are compelled to work under intolerable conditions. Communication by mail and service by parcel post have been delayed and retarded with resulting hardships, business losses and inconveniences. A false concept of economy has impaired seriously the efficiency of the best communication system in the world.

We pledge ourselves to programs which will:

(1) Restore the principle that the Postal Service is a public service to be operated in the interest of improved business economy and better communication, as well as an aid to the dissemination of information and intelligence;

(2) Restore Postal employee morale through the strengthening of the merit system, with promotions by law rather than caprice or partisan politics, and payment of realistic salaries reflecting the benefits of an expanded economy;

(3) Establish a program of research and development on a scale adequate to insure the most modern and efficient handling of the mails; and

(4) Undertake modernization and construction of desperately needed Postal facilities designed to insure the finest Postal system in the world.

Conflict of Interests

Maladministration and selfish manipulation have characterized Federal administration during the Eisenhower years. Taxpayers, paying billions of dollars each year to their Government, demand and must have the highest standards of honesty, integrity and efficiency as a minimum requirement of Federal Executive conduct. We pledge a strong merit system as a substitute for cynical policies of spoils and special favor which are now the rule of the day. We seek the constant improvements of the Federal Government apparatus to accomplish these ends.

Under certain conditions, we recognize the need for the employment of personnel without compensation in the Executive Branch of the Government. But the privileges extended these dollar-a-year men have resulted in grave abuses of power. Some of these representatives of large corporations have assumed a dual loyalty to the Government and to the corporations that pay them. These abuses under the Republican Administration have been scandalous. The Democratic Party proposes that any necessary use of noncompensated employees shall be made only after the most careful scrutiny and under the most rigidly prescribed safeguards to prevent any conflict of interests.

Freedom of Information

During recent years there developed a practice on the part of Federal agencies to delay and withhold information which is needed by Congress and the general public—to make important decisions affecting their lives and destinies. We believe that this trend toward secrecy in Government should be reversed and that the Federal Government should return to its basic tradition of exchanging, and promoting the freest flow of information possible in those unclassified areas where secrets involving weapons development and bona fide national security are not involved. We condemn the Eisenhower Administration for the excesses practiced in this vital act, and pledge the Democratic Party to reverse this tendency, substituting a rule of law for that of broad claims of executive privilege.

We reaffirm our position of 1952 "to press strongly for world-wide freedom in the gathering and dissemination of news." We shall press for free access to information throughout the world for our journalists and scholars.

Clean Elections

The shocking disclosures in the last Congress of attempts by selfish interests to exert improper influence on members of Congress have resulted in a Congressional investigation now under way. The Democratic Party pledges itself to provide effective regulation and full disclosure of campaign expenditures and contributions in elections to Federal offices.

Equal Rights Amendment

We of the Democratic Party recommend and endorse for submission to the Congress a Constitutional amendment providing equal rights for women.

Veterans Administration

We are spending approximately $4\frac{3}{4}$ billion dollars per year on veterans' benefits. There are more than 22 million veterans in civil life today and approximately 4 million veterans or dependents of deceased veterans drawing direct cash benefits from the Veterans Administration. It is clear that a matter of such magnitude demands more prominence in the affairs of Government. We pledge that we will elevate the Veterans Administration to a place of dignity commensurate with its importance in national affairs.

We charge the present Administration with open hostility toward the veterans' hospital program as disclosed by its efforts to restrict severely that program in fiscal year 1954. We further charge the Administration with incompetence and gross neglect in the handling of veterans' benefits in the following particulars:

(1) The refusal to allow service connection for disabilities incurred in or aggravated by military service,

and the unwarranted reduction of disability evaluations in cases where service connection has been allowed; and

(2) The failure to give proper protection to veterans purchasing homes under the VA home loan program both by inadequate supervision of the program and in some instances, by active cooperation with unscrupulous builders, lenders and real estate brokers.

In recognition of the valiant efforts of those who served their Nation in its gravest hours, we pledge:

(1) Continuance of the Veterans Administration as an independent Federal agency handling veterans' programs;
(2) Continued recognition of war veterans, with adequate compensation for the service-connected disabled and for the survivors of those who have passed away in service or from service-incurred disabilities; and with pensions for disabled and distressed veterans, and for the dependents of those who have passed on, where they are in need or unable to provide for themselves;
(3) Maintenance of the Veterans Administration hospital system, with no impairment in the high quality of medical and hospital service;
(4) Priority of hospitalization for the service connected disabled, and the privilege of hospital care when beds are available for the non–service connected illness of veterans who are sick and without funds or unable to procure private hospitalization;
(5) Fair administration of veterans preference laws, and employment opportunities for handicapped and disabled veterans;
(6) Full hearings for war veterans filing valid applications with the review, corrective and settlement boards of the Federal Government; and
(7) Support for legislation to obtain an extension of the current law to enable veterans to obtain homes and farms through the continuance of the GT Loan Program.

Statehood for Alaska and Hawaii

We condemn the Republican Administration for its utter disregard of the rights to statehood of both Alaska and Hawaii. These territories have contributed greatly to our national economic and cultural life and are vital to our defense. They are part of America and should be recognized as such. We of the Democratic Party, therefore, pledge immediate Statehood for these two territories. We commend these territories for the action their people have taken in the adoption of constitutions which will become effective forthwith when they are admitted into the Union.

Puerto Rico

The Democratic Party views with satisfaction the progress and growth achieved by Puerto Rico since its political organization as a Commonwealth under Democratic Party leadership. We pledge, once again, our continued support of the Commonwealth and its development and growth along lines of increasing responsibility and authority, keeping as functions of the Federal Government only such as are essential to the existence of the compact of association adopted by the Congress of the United States and the people of Puerto Rico.

The progress of Puerto Rico under Commonwealth status has been notable proof of the great benefits which flow from self-government and the good neighbor policy which under Democratic leadership this country has always followed.

Virgin Islands

We favor increased self-government for the Virgin Islands to provide for an elected Governor and a Resident Commissioner in the Congress of the United States. We denounce the scandalous administration of the first Eisenhower-appointed Governor of the Virgin Islands.

Other Territories and Possessions

We favor increased self-government for Guam, other outlying territories and the Trust Territory of the Pacific.

District of Columbia

We favor immediate home rule and ultimate national representation for the District of Columbia.

American Indians

Recognizing that all American Indians are citizens of the United States and of the States in which they reside, and acknowledging that the Federal Government has a unique legal and moral responsibility for Indians which is imposed by the Constitution and spelled out in treaties, statutes and court decisions, we pledge:

Prompt adoption of a Federal program to assist Indian tribes in the full development of their human and natural resources, and to advance the health, education and economic well-being of Indian citizens, preserving their traditions without impairing their cultural heritage;

No alteration of any treaty or other Federal Indian contractual relationships without the free consent of the Indian tribes concerned; reversal of the present policies which are tending toward erosion of Indian rights, reduction of their economic base through alienation of their lands, and repudiation of Federal responsibility;

Prompt and expeditious settlement of Indian claims against the United States, with full recognition of the rights of both parties; and

Elimination of all impediments to full citizenship for American Indians.

Governmental Balance

The Democratic Party has upheld its belief in the Constitution as a charter of individual rights, an effective instrument for human progress. Democratic Administrations placed upon the statute books during their last 20 years a multitude of measures which testify to our belief in the Jeffersonian principle of local control even in general legislation involving Nation-wide programs. Selective Service, Social Security, agricultural adjustment, low-rent housing, hospital, and many other legislative programs have placed major responsibilities in States and counties, and provide fine examples of how benefits can be extended through Federal–State cooperation.

While we recognize the existence of honest differences of opinion as to the true location of the Constitutional line of demarcation between the Federal Government and the States, the Democratic Party expressly recognizes the vital importance of the respective States in our Federal Union. The Party of Jefferson and Jackson pledges itself to continued support of those sound principles of local government which will best serve the welfare of our people and the safety of our democratic rights.

Improving Congressional Procedures

In order that the will of the American people may be expressed upon all legislative proposals, we urge that action be taken at the beginning of the 85th Congress to improve Congressional procedures so that majority rule prevails and decisions can be made after reasonable debate without being blocked by a minority in either House.

IX. NATURAL RESOURCES

Our national economic strength and welfare depend primarily upon the development of our land, water, mineral and energy resources, with which this Nation has been abundantly blessed.

We pledge unstinting support to a full and integrated program of development, protection, management and conservation of all of our natural resources for all of the people.

The framework of time-tested conservation and mining policy is fixed in laws under which America has developed its natural resources for the general welfare.

The Democratic 84th Congress has remained steadfast to this traditional policy. It has built upon the tremendous conservation and development achievements of the Roosevelt and Truman Administrations by undertaking the greatest program of natural resources development ever assumed by any Congress in our Nation's history.

This constructive Democratic record, embracing all resources of land, water, energy and minerals, is in sharp contrast to the faithless performance of the Eisenhower Administration which has despoiled future generations of their heritage by utter failure to safeguard natural resources. Our people will long remember this betrayal of their heritage as symbolized by the infamous Dixon–Yates contract; the Al Sarena timber scheme; the low-level Hells Canyon Dams; and for its unreasonable resistance to authorizing the Niagara Project which would benefit so many millions in the State of New York and adjacent areas.

We condemn, and will continue to decry, this pillaging of our dwindling natural resource wealth through political manipulation and administrative subversion by the Eisenhower Administration. We pledge ourselves to halt this betrayal of the people's trust.

We shall devise for the American people a dynamic, far-reaching and progressive conservation program.

The Democratic Party proposes, and will strive to secure, this comprehensive resources program for America's future.

Land

Our land will be preserved and improved for the present and future needs of our people, and not wastefully exploited to benefit special interest groups.

Soil Conservation

In contrast to the wasteful neglect of the present Administration, soil conservation practices will be stimulated and intensified to reduce land deterioration under the vital Soil Conservation Service assistance program conceived and fostered by the Democratic Party.

National Parks, Recreation and Wildlife

We pledge adoption of an immediate and broad policy to mobilize the efforts of private and public agencies for protection of existing recreational areas, provision of new ones, and improvement of inadequate facilities. Slum conditions fostered by Republican neglect are intolerable to the tens of millions of Americans using our national parks and forests. Democratic administration will end this shocking situation.

Fish and game habitats will be guarded against encroachment for commercial purposes. All river basin development plans will take into full consideration their effect upon fish, wildlife, and national park and wilderness areas. The Fish and Wildlife Service must and will be returned to the career status from which it was removed by the political patronage policy of the present Administration.

Recreational facilities for the millions of field and stream sportsmen of America will be conserved and expanded.

Forest and Grazing Lands

Timber on Federal commercial forest lands will be harvested and managed on a sustained-yield basis.

We propose to increase forest access roads in order to improve cutting practices on both public and private lands.

Private owners of farm, forest and range lands need and must have financial and technical assistance so that all lands will be utilized to contribute more fully to the national welfare by production of food and fiber and protection of our watersheds. Any effort to transform grazing permits from a revocable license to a vested right will be rejected.

We will vigorously advocate Federally financed forestation, upstream erosion control and flood control programs on our public range, timber lands and small drainage basins to protect our watersheds and double the rate of forage and commercial timber growth. We will promote cooperative programs with Government assistance to reduce timber losses from fire, insects, and disease.

Prospecting and mining on unreserved Federal lands will be encouraged, but surface areas not needed in mining will be safeguarded by appropriate legislation.

Water

We pledge the resumption of rapid and orderly multiple-purpose river basin development throughout the country. This program will bring into reality the full potential benefits of flood control, irrigation and our domestic and municipal water supply from surface and underground waters. It will also materially aid low-cost power, navigation, recreation, fish and wildlife propagation and mineral development. We pledge our aid to the growing requirements of the semi-arid Western States for an adequate water supply to meet the vital domestic, irrigation and industrial needs of the rapidly growing urban centers. Enhanced regional economies will strengthen the economy of the Nation as a whole.

We will take appropriate and vigorous steps to prevent comprehensive drainage basin development plans from being fragmented by single purpose projects. The conservation of water is essential to the life of the Nation. The Democratic Party pledges itself to conservation of water in the public interest.

The Democratic 84th Congress has taken a long step toward reducing the pollution of our rivers and streams. We pledge continuation and expansion of this program, vital to every citizen.

The program of obtaining a large new source of fresh water supply from salt water was begun by the Democratic Party, but has been allowed to lapse by the Eisenhower Republican Administration. It will be resumed and accelerated.

Energy

We pledge ourselves to carry forward, under national policy, aggressive programs to provide abundant supplies of low-cost energy, including continued research for the development of synthetic liquid fuel from coal, shale and agricultural products. These we must have to feed our insatiable industrial economy, to enable our workers to develop their skills and increase their productivity, to provide more jobs at higher wages, to meet the ever-mounting demands for domestic and farm uses, including the production of lower-cost farm fertilizers and lower-cost power to consumers.

We will carry forward increased and full production of hydroelectric power on our rivers and of steam generation for the Tennessee Valley Authority to meet its peacetime and defense requirements. Such self-liquidating projects must go forward in a rapid and orderly manner, with appropriate financing plans. Integrated regional transmission systems will enhance exchange of power and encourage diversified industrial development.

We shall once more rigorously enforce the anti-monopoly and public body preference clauses, including the Holding Company Act, administratively circumvented by the Eisenhower Republican Administration. We shall preserve and strengthen the public power competitive yardstick in power developments under TVA, REA, Bureau of Reclamation, Bonneville, Southeast and Southwest Power Administrations and other future projects, including atomic power plants, under a policy of the widest possible use of electric energy at the lowest possible cost.

Minerals

The Republican Administration has seriously neglected and ignored one of the Nation's basic industries, metal mining. We recognize that a healthy mining industry is essential to the economy of the Nation, and therefore pledge immediate efforts toward the establishment of a realistic, long-range minerals policy. The Nation's minerals and fuels are essential to the safety, security and development of our country. We pledge the adoption of policies which will further encourage the exploration and development of additional reserves of our mineral resources.

Domestic Fisheries

We will undertake comprehensive scientific and economic research programs for the conservation and better utilization of, and new markets for, fishery products. We favor and will encourage reciprocal world trade in fish products.

We pledge ourselves to a public works and water policy providing adequate protection for domestic fishery resources.

We favor treaties with other nations for conservation and better utilization of international fisheries.

Scenic Resources

To the end that the scenic beauty of our land may be preserved and maintained for this and future generations to enjoy, we pledge accelerated support of educational programs to stimulate individual responsibility and pride in clean, attractive surroundings—from big cities to rural areas.

X. ATOMIC ENERGY

The atomic era came into being and was developed under Democratic Administrations.

The genius of American scientists, engineers and workmen, supported by the vision and courage of Franklin D. Roosevelt, made possible the splitting of the atom and the development of the first atomic bomb in time to end World War II.

With the ending of the war, the supremacy of America in atomic weapons was maintained under the leadership of President Truman, and the United States pushed ahead vigorously toward utilizing this new form of energy in peaceful pursuits, particularly in the fields of medicine, agriculture and industry. By the end of the Truman Administration, the pre-eminence of the United States in the nuclear field was clearly established, and we were on the threshold of large-scale development of industrial nuclear energy at home and as an instrument of world peace.

The Eisenhower Administration promptly reversed the field and plunged the previously independent and nonpartisan Atomic Energy Commission into partisan politics. For example, President Eisenhower ordered the Commission to sign the scandalous Dixon–Yates contract. He was later forced to repudiate the same contract, after the exposure of the illegal activities of one of his own consultants with a secret office in the Bureau of the Budget.

The Republican Administration has followed the same pattern in the field of atomic energy that it has pursued in its treatment of other natural resources— lofty words, little action, but steady service to selfish interests. While the AEC and the special private interests consult and confer, the United States is lagging instead of leading in the world race for nuclear power, international prestige and world markets.

The Democrats in Congress believed that the national interest thus became imperiled, and they moved to meet the challenge both at home and abroad. They established a nonpartisan panel of eminent Americans to study the impact of the peaceful atom.

Following the comprehensive report of this panel, the joint Congressional Committee on Atomic Energy held extensive hearings on bills to accelerate the atomic reactor demonstration program. Though the bills were reported unanimously from committee, the Republican members of Congress, under heavy pressure from the White House, insured the final defeat of this legislation in the Congress.

But the fight to bring nuclear power to the people has only begun. As the United States was first in the development of the atom as a weapon, so the United States must lead in bringing the blessings of the peaceful uses of nuclear energy to mankind.

Hence, the Democratic Party pledges itself:

(1) To restore nonpartisan administration of the vital atomic energy program and to expand and accelerate nuclear development by vigorous action:

(2) To accelerate the domestic civilian atomic power program by the construction of a variety of demonstration prototype reactors;

(3) To give reality—life and meaning—to the "Atoms for Peace" program. We will substitute deeds for words;

(4) To increase the production of fissionable material for use in a stockpile for peacetime commitments at home and abroad, and for an ever-present reserve for weapons to guarantee freedom in the world;

(5) To conduct a comprehensive survey of radiation hazards from bomb tests and reactor operations, in order to determine what additional measures are required to protect existing and future generations from these invisible dangers; and

(6) To make the maximum contribution to the defense of our Nation and the free world through the development of a balanced and flexible stockpile of nuclear weapons, containing a sufficient number and variety to support our armed services in any contingency.

XI. CIVIL RIGHTS

The Democratic Party is committed to support and advance the individual rights and liberties of all Americans. Our country is founded on the proposition that all men are created equal. This means that all citizens are equal before the law and should enjoy all political rights. They should have equal opportunities for education, for economic advancement, and for decent living conditions.

We will continue our efforts to eradicate discrimination based on race, religion or national origin. We know this task requires action, not just in one section of the Nation, but in all sections. It requires the cooperative efforts of individual citizens, and action by State and local governments. It also requires Federal action. The Federal Government must live up to the ideals of the Declaration of Independence and must exercise the powers vested in it by the Constitution.

We are proud of the record of the Democratic Party in securing equality of treatment and opportunity in the Nation's armed forces, the Civil Service, and in all areas under Federal jurisdiction. The Democratic Party pledges itself to continue its efforts to eliminate illegal discriminations of all kinds, in relation to (1) full rights to vote, (2) full rights to engage in gainful occupations, (3) full rights to enjoy security of the person, and (4) full rights to education in all publicly supported institutions.

Recent decisions of the Supreme Court of the United States relating to segregation in publicly supported schools and elsewhere have brought consequences of vast importance to our Nation as a whole and especially to communities directly affected. We reject all proposals for the use of force to interfere with the orderly determination of these matters by the courts.

The Democratic Party emphatically reaffirms its support of the historic principle that ours is a government of laws and not of men, it recognizes the Supreme Court of the United States as one of the three Constitutional and coordinate branches of the Federal Government, superior to and separate from any political party, the decisions of which are part of the law of the land. We condemn the efforts of the Republican Party to make it appear that this tribunal is a part of the Republican Party.

We condemn the Republican Administration's violation of the rights of Government employees by a heartless and unjustified confusing of "security" and "loyalty" for the sole purpose of political gain and regardless of consequences to individual victims and to the good name of the United States. We condemn the Republican Administration's misrepresentation of facts and violation of individual rights in a wicked and unprincipled attempt to degrade and destroy the Democratic Party, and to make political capital for the Republican Party.

— 1960 —

In 1796, in America's first contested national election, our Party, under the leadership of Thomas Jefferson, campaigned on the principles of "The Rights of Man."

Ever since, these four words have underscored our identity with the plain people of America and the world.

In periods of national crisis, we Democrats have returned to these words for renewed strength. We return to them today.

In 1960, "The Rights of Man" are still the issue.

It is our continuing responsibility to provide an effective instrument of political action for every American who seeks to strengthen these rights everywhere here in America, and everywhere in our 20th Century world.

The common danger of mankind is war and the threat of war. Today, three billion human beings live in fear that some rash act or blunder may plunge us all into a nuclear holocaust which will leave only ruined cities, blasted homes, and a poisoned earth and sky.

Our objective, however, is not the right to coexist in armed camps on the same planet with totalitarian ideologies; it is the creation of an enduring peace in which the universal values of human dignity, truth, and justice under law are finally secured for all men everywhere on earth.

If America is to work effectively for such a peace, we must first restore our national strength—military, political, economic, and moral.

NATIONAL DEFENSE

The new Democratic Administration will recast our military capacity in order to provide forces and weapons of a diversity, balance, and mobility sufficient in quantity and quality to deter both limited and general aggressions.

When the Democratic Administration left office in 1953, the United States was the pre-eminent power in the world. Most free nations had confidence in our will and our ability to carry out our commitments to the common defense.

Even those who wished us ill respected our power and influence.

The Republican Administration has lost that position of pre-eminence. Over the past $7\frac{1}{2}$ years, our military power has steadily declined relative to that of the Russians and the Chinese and their satellites.

This is not a partisan election-year charge. It has been persistently made by high officials of the Republican Administration itself. Before Congressional committees they have testified that the Communists will have a dangerous lead in intercontinental missiles through 1963—and that the Republican Administration has no plans to catch up.

They have admitted that the Soviet Union leads in the space race—and that they have no plans to catch up.

They have also admitted that our conventional military forces, on which we depend for defense in any non-nuclear war, have been dangerously slashed for reasons of "economy"—and that they have no plans to reverse this trend.

As a result, our military position today is measured in terms of gaps—missile gap, space gap, limited-war gap.

To recover from the errors of the past $7\frac{1}{2}$ years will not be easy.

This is the strength that must be erected:

1. Deterrent military power such that the Soviet and Chinese leaders will have no doubt that an attack on the United States would surely be followed by their own destruction.
2. Balanced conventional military forces which will permit a response graded to the intensity of any threats of aggressive force.
3. Continuous modernization of these forces through intensified research and development, including essential programs now slowed down, terminated, suspended, or neglected for lack of budgetary support.

A first order of business of a Democratic Administration will be a complete re-examination of the organization of our armed forces.

A military organization structure, conceived before the revolution in weapons technology, cannot be suitable for the strategic deterrent, continental defense, limited war, and military alliance requirements of the 1960s.

We believe that our armed forces should be organized more nearly on the basis of function, not only to produce greater military strength, but also to eliminate duplication and save substantial sums.

We pledge our will, energies, and resources to oppose Communist aggression.

Since World War II, it has been clear that our own security must be pursued in concert with that of many other nations.

The Democratic Administrations which, in World War II, led in forging a mighty and victorious alliance, took the initiative after the war in creating the North Atlantic Treaty Organization, the greatest peacetime alliance in history.

This alliance has made it possible to keep Western Europe and the Atlantic Community secure against Communist pressures.

Our present system of alliances was begun in a time of an earlier weapons technology when our ability to retaliate against Communist attack required bases all around the periphery of the Soviet Union. Today, because of our continuing weakness in mobile weapons systems and intercontinental missiles, our defenses still depend in part on bases beyond our borders for planes and shorter-range missiles.

If an alliance is to be maintained in vigor, its unity must be reflected in shared purposes. Some of our allies have contributed neither devotion to the cause of freedom nor any real military strength.

The new Democratic Administration will review our system of pacts and alliances. We shall continue to adhere to our treaty obligations, including the commitment of the UN Charter to resist aggression. But we shall also seek to shift the emphasis of our cooperation from military aid to economic development, wherever this is possible.

CIVIL DEFENSE

We commend the work of the civil defense groups throughout the nation. A strong and effective civil defense is an essential element in our nation's defense.

The new Democratic Administration will undertake a full review and analysis of the programs that should be adopted if protection is to be provided to the civilian population of our nation.

ARMS CONTROL

A fragile power balance sustained by mutual nuclear terror does not, however, constitute peace. We must regain the initiative on the entire international front with effective new policies to create the conditions for peace.

There are no simple solutions to the infinitely complex challenges which face us. Mankind's eternal dream, a world of peace, can only be built slowly and patiently.

A primary task is to develop responsible proposals that will help break the deadlock on arms control.

Such proposals should include means for ending nuclear tests under workable safeguards, cutting back nuclear weapons, reducing conventional forces, preserving outer space for peaceful purposes, preventing surprise attack, and limiting the risk of accidental war.

This requires a national peace agency for disarmament planning and research to muster the scientific ingenuity, coordination, continuity, and seriousness of purpose which are now lacking in our arms control efforts.

The national peace agency would develop the technical and scientific data necessary for serious disarmament negotiations, would conduct research in cooperation with the Defense Department and Atomic Energy Commission on methods of inspection and monitoring arms control agreements, particularly agreements to control nuclear testing, and would provide continuous technical advice to our disarmament negotiators.

As with armaments, so with disarmament, the Republican Administration has provided us with much talk but little constructive action. Representatives of the United States have gone to conferences without plans or preparation. The Administration has played opportunistic politics, both at home and abroad.

Even during the recent important negotiations at Geneva and Paris, only a handful of people were devoting full time to work on the highly complex problem of disarmament.

More than $100 billion of the world's production now goes each year into armaments. To the extent that we can secure the adoption of effective arms control agreements, vast resources will be freed for peaceful use.

The new Democratic Administration will plan for an orderly shift of our expenditures. Long-delayed reductions in excise, corporation, and individual income taxes will then be possible. We can also step up the pace in meeting our backlog of public needs and in pursuing the promise of atomic and space science in a peaceful age.

As world-wide disarmament proceeds, it will free vast resources for a new international attack on the problem of world poverty.

THE INSTRUMENTS OF FOREIGN POLICY

American foreign policy in all its aspects must be attuned to our world of change.

We will recruit officials whose experience, humanity, and dedication fit them for the task of effectively representing America abroad.

We will provide a more sensitive and creative direction to our overseas information program. And we will overhaul our administrative machinery so that America may avoid diplomatic embarrassments and at long last speak with a single confident voice in world affairs.

The "Image" of America

First, those men and women selected to represent us abroad must be chosen for their sensitive understanding of the peoples with whom they will live, We can no longer afford representatives who are ignorant of the language and culture and politics of the nations in which they represent us.

Our information programs must be more than news broadcasts and boastful recitals of our accomplishments and our material riches. We must find ways to show the people of the world that we share the same goals—dignity, health, freedom, schools for our children, a place in the sun—and that we will work together to achieve them.

Our program of visits between Americans and people of other nations will be expanded, with special emphasis upon students and younger leaders. We will encourage study of foreign languages. We favor continued support and extension of such programs as the East–West Cultural Center established at the University of Hawaii. We shall study a similar center for Latin America, with due consideration of the existing facilities now available in the Canal Zone.

National Policy Machinery

In the present Administration, the National Security Council has been used not to focus issues for decision by the responsible leaders of Government, but to paper over problems of policy with "agreed solutions" which avoid decisions.

The mishandling of the U-2 espionage flights—the sorry spectacle of official denial, retraction, and contradiction—and the admitted misjudging of Japanese public opinion are only two recent examples of the breakdown of the Administration's machinery for assembling facts, making decisions, and coordinating action.

The Democratic Party welcomes the study now being made by the Senate Subcommittee on National Policy Machinery. The new Democratic Administration will revamp and simplify this cumbersome machinery.

WORLD TRADE

World trade is more than ever essential to world peace. In the tradition of Cordell Hull, we shall expand world trade in every responsible way.

Since all Americans share the benefits of this policy, its costs should not be the burden of a few. We shall support practical measures to ease the necessary adjustments of industries and communities which may be unavoidably hurt by increases in imports.

World trade raises living standards, widens markets, reduces costs, increases profits, and builds political stability and international economic cooperation.

However, the increase in foreign imports involves costly adjustment and damage to some domestic industries and communities. The burden has been heavier recently because of the Republican failure to maintain an adequate rate of economic growth, and the refusal to use public programs to ease necessary adjustments.

The Democratic Administration will help industries affected by foreign trade with measures favorable to economic growth, orderly transition, fair competition, and the long-run economic strength of all parts of our nation.

Industries and communities affected by foreign trade need and deserve appropriate help through trade adjustment measures such as direct loans, tax incentives, defense contracts priority, and retraining assistance.

Our Government should press for reduction of foreign barriers to the sale of the products of American industry and agriculture. These are particularly severe in the case of fruit products. The present balance-of-payments situation provides a favorable opportunity for such action.

The new Democratic Administration will seek international agreements to assure fair competition and fair labor standards to protect our own workers and to improve the lot of workers elsewhere.

Our domestic economic policies and our essential foreign policies must be harmonious.

To sell, we must buy. We therefore must resist the temptation to accept remedies that deny American producers and consumers access to world markets and destroy the prosperity of our friends in the non-Communist world.

IMMIGRATION

We shall adjust our immigration, nationality and refugee policies to eliminate discrimination and to enable members of scattered families abroad to be united with relatives already in our midst.

The national-origins quota system of limiting immigration contradicts the founding principles of this nation. It is inconsistent with our belief in the rights of man. This system was instituted after World War I as a policy of deliberate discrimination by a Republican Administration and Congress.

The revision of immigration and nationality laws we seek will implement our belief that enlightened immigration, naturalization and refugee policies and humane administration of them are important aspects of our foreign policy.

These laws will bring greater skills to our land, reunite families, permit the United States to meet its fair share of world programs of rescue and rehabilitation, and take advantage of immigration as an important factor in the growth of the American economy.

In this World Refugee Year it is our hope to achieve admission of our fair share of refugees. We will institute policies to alleviate suffering among the homeless wherever we are able to extend our aid.

We must remove the distinctions between native-born and naturalized citizens to assure full protection of our laws to all. There is no place in the United States for "second-class citizenship."

The projections provided by due process, right of appeal, and statutes of limitation, can be extended to non-citizens without hampering the security of our nation.

We commend the Democratic Congress for the initial steps that have recently been taken toward liberalizing changes in immigration law. However, this should not be a piecemeal project and we are confident that a Democratic President in cooperation with Democratic Congresses will again implant a humanitarian and liberal spirit in our nation's immigration and citizenship policies.

To the peoples and governments beyond our shores we offer the following pledges:

THE UNDERDEVELOPED WORLD

To the non-Communist nations of Asia, Africa, and Latin America: We shall create with you working partnerships, based on mutual respect and understanding.

In the Jeffersonian tradition, we recognize and welcome the irresistible momentum of the world revolution of rising expectations for a better life. We shall identify American policy with the values and objectives of this revolution.

To this end the new Democratic Administration will revamp and refocus the objectives, emphasis and allocation of our foreign assistance programs.

The proper purpose of these programs is not to buy

gratitude or to recruit mercenaries, but to enable the peoples of these awakening, developing nations to make their own free choices.

As they achieve a sense of belonging, of dignity, and of justice, freedom will become meaningful for them, and therefore worth defending.

Where military assistance remains essential for the common defense, we shall see that the requirements are fully met. But as rapidly as security considerations permit, we will replace tanks with tractors, bombers with bulldozers, and tacticians with technicians.

We shall place our programs of international cooperation on a long-term basis to permit more effective planning. We shall seek to associate other capital-exporting countries with us in promoting the orderly economic growth of the underdeveloped world.

We recognize India and Pakistan as major tests of the capacity of free men in a difficult environment to master the age-old problems of illiteracy, poverty, and disease. We will support their efforts in every practical way.

We welcome the emerging new nations of Africa to the world community. Here again we shall strive to write a new chapter of fruitful cooperation.

In Latin America we shall restore the Good Neighbor Policy based on far closer economic cooperation and increased respect and understanding.

In the Middle East we will work for guarantees to insure independence for all states. We will encourage direct Arab–Israeli peace negotiations, the resettlement of Arab refugees in lands where there is room and opportunity for them, an end to boycotts and blockades, and unrestricted use of the Suez Canal by all nations.

A billion and a half people in Asia, Africa and Latin America are engaged in an unprecedented attempt to propel themselves into the 20th Century. They are striving to create or reaffirm their national identity.

But they want much more than independence. They want an end to grinding poverty. They want more food, health for themselves and their children, and other benefits that a modern industrial civilization can provide.

Communist strategy has sought to divert these aspirations into narrowly nationalistic channels, or external troublemaking, or authoritarianism. The Republican Administration has played into the hands of this strategy by concerning itself almost exclusively with the military problem of Communist invasion.

The Democratic programs of economic cooperation will be aimed at making it as easy as possible for the political leadership in these countries to turn the en-

ergy, talent and resources of their peoples to orderly economic growth.

History and current experience show that an annual per capita growth rate of at least 2% is feasible in these countries. The Democratic Administration's assistance program, in concert with the aid forthcoming from our partners in Western Europe, Japan, and the British Commonwealth, will be geared to facilitating this objective.

The Democratic Administration will recognize that assistance to these countries is not an emergency or short-term matter. Through the Development Loan Fund and otherwise, we shall seek to assure continuity in our aid programs for periods of at least five years, in order to permit more effective allocation on our part and better planning by the governments of the countries receiving aid.

More effective use of aid and a greater confidence in us and our motives will be the result.

We shall establish priorities for foreign aid which will channel it to those countries abroad which, by their own willingness to help themselves, show themselves most capable of using it effectively.

We shall use our own agricultural productivity as an effective tool of foreign aid, and also as a vital form of working capital for economic development. We shall seek new approaches which will provide assistance without disrupting normal world markets for food and fiber.

We shall give attention to the problem of stabilizing world prices of agricultural commodities and basic raw materials on which many underdeveloped countries depend for needed foreign exchange.

We shall explore the feasibility of shipping and storing a substantial part of our food abundance in a system of "food banks" located at distribution centers in the underdeveloped world.

Such a system would be an effective means of alleviating famine and suffering in times of natural disaster, and of cushioning the effect of bad harvests. It would also have a helpful anti-inflationary influence as economic development gets under way.

Although basic development requirements like transport, housing, schools, and river development may be financed by Government, these projects are usually built and sometimes managed by private enterprise. Moreover, outside this public sector a large and increasing role remains for private investment.

The Republican Administration has done little to summon American business to play its part in this, one of the most creative tasks of our generation. The Democratic Administration will take steps to recruit and organize effectively the best business talent in America for foreign economic development.

We urge continued economic assistance to Israel and the Arab peoples to help them raise their living standards. We pledge our best efforts for peace in the Middle East by seeking to prevent an arms race while guarding against the dangers of a military imbalance resulting from Soviet arms shipments.

THE ATLANTIC COMMUNITY

To our friends and associates in the Atlantic Community: We propose a broader partnership that goes beyond our common fears to recognize the depth and sweep of our common political, economic, and cultural interests.

We welcome the recent heartening advances toward European unity. In every appropriate way, we shall encourage their further growth within the broader framework of the Atlantic Community.

After World War II, Democratic statesmen saw that an orderly, peaceful world was impossible with Europe shattered and exhausted.

They fashioned the great programs which bear their names—the Truman Doctrine and the Marshall Plan—by which the economies of Europe were revived. Then in NATO they renewed for the common defense the ties of alliance forged in war.

In these endeavors, the Democratic Administrations invited leading Republicans to full participation as equal partners. But the Republican Administration has rejected this principle of bipartisanship.

We have already seen how the mutual trust and confidence created abroad under Democratic leadership have been eroded by arrogance, clumsiness, and lack of understanding in the Republican Administration.

The new Democratic Administration will restore the former high levels of cooperation within the Atlantic Community envisaged from the beginning by the NATO treaty in political and economic spheres as well as military affairs.

We welcome the progress towards European unity expressed in the Coal and Steel Community, Euratom, the European Economic Community, the European Free Trade Association, and the European Assembly.

We shall conduct our relations with the nations of the Common Market so as to encourage the opportunities for freer and more expanded trade, and to avert the possibilities of discrimination that are inherent in it.

We shall encourage adjustment with the so-called "Outer Seven" nations so as to enlarge further the area of freer trade.

THE COMMUNIST WORLD

To the rulers of the Communist World: We confidently accept your challenge to competition in every field of human effort.

We recognize this contest as one between two radically different approaches to the meaning of life—our open society which places its highest value upon individual dignity, and your closed society in which the rights of men are sacrificed to the state.

We believe your Communist ideology to be sterile, unsound, and doomed to failure. We believe that your children will reject the intellectual prison in which you seek to confine them, and that ultimately they will choose the eternal principles of freedom.

In the meantime, we are prepared to negotiate with you whenever and wherever there is a realistic possibility of progress without sacrifice of principle.

If negotiations through diplomatic channels provide opportunities, we will negotiate.

If debate before the United Nations holds promise, we will debate.

If meetings at high level offer prospects of success, we will be there.

But we will use all the power, resources, and energy at our command to resist the further encroachment of Communism on freedom—whether at Berlin, Formosa, or new points of pressure as yet undisclosed.

We will keep open the lines of communication with our opponents. Despite difficulties in the way of peaceful agreement, every useful avenue will be energetically explored and pursued.

However, we will never surrender positions which are essential to the defense of freedom, nor will we abandon peoples who are now behind the Iron Curtain through any formal approval of the status quo.

Everyone proclaims "firmness" in support of Berlin. The issue is not the desire to be firm, but the capability to be firm. This the Democratic Party will provide as it has done before.

The ultimate solution of the situation in Berlin must be approached in the broader context of settlement of the tensions and divisions of Europe.

The good faith of the United States is pledged likewise to defending Formosa. We will carry out that pledge.

The new Democratic Administration will also reaffirm our historic policy of opposition to the establishment anywhere in the Americas of governments dominated by foreign powers, a policy now being undermined by Soviet threats to the freedom and independence of Cuba. The Government of the United States under a Democratic Administration will not be deterred from fulfilling its obligations and solemn responsibilities under its treaties and agreements with the nations of the Western Hemisphere. Nor will the United States, in conformity with its treaty obligations, permit the establishment of a regime dominated by international, atheistic Communism in the Western Hemisphere.

To the people who live in the Communist World and its captive nations: We proclaim an enduring friendship which goes beyond governments and ideologies to our common human interest in a better world.

Through exchanges of persons, cultural contacts, trade in non-strategic areas, and other non-governmental activities, we will endeavor to preserve and improve opportunities for human relationships which no Iron Curtain can permanently sever.

No political platform promise in history was more cruelly cynical than the Republican effort to buy votes in 1952 with false promises of painless liberation for the captive nations.

The blood of heroic freedom fighters in Hungary tragically proved this promise a fraud. We Democrats will never be party to such cruel cultivation of false hopes.

We look forward to the day when the men and women of Albania, Bulgaria, Czechoslovakia, East Germany, Estonia, Hungary, Latvia, Lithuania, Poland, Rumania, and the other captive nations will stand again in freedom and justice. We will hasten, by every honorable and responsible means, the arrival of that day.

We shall never accept any deal or arrangement which acquiesces in the present subjugation of these peoples.

We deeply regret that the policies and actions of the Government of Communist China have interrupted the generations of friendship between the Chinese and American peoples.

We reaffirm our pledge of determined opposition to the present admission of Communist China to the United Nations.

Although normal diplomatic relations between our Governments are impossible under present conditions, we shall welcome any evidence that the Chinese Communist Government is genuinely prepared to create a new relationship based on respect for international obligations, including the release of American prisoners.

We will continue to make every effort to effect the release of American citizens and servicemen now un-

justly imprisoned in Communist China and elsewhere in the Communist empire.

THE UNITED NATIONS

To all our fellow members of the United Nations: We shall strengthen our commitments in this, our great continuing institution for conciliation and the growth of a world community.

Through the machinery of the United Nations, we shall work for disarmament, the establishment of an international police force, the strengthening of the World Court, and the establishment of world law.

We shall propose the bolder and more effective use of the specialized agencies to promote the world's economic and social development.

Great Democratic Presidents have taken the lead in the effort to unite the nations of the world in an international organization to assure world peace with justice under law.

The League of Nations, conceived by Woodrow Wilson, was doomed by Republican defeat of United States participation.

The United Nations, sponsored by Franklin Roosevelt, has become the one place where representatives of the rival systems and interests which divide the world can and do maintain continuous contact.

The United States' adherence to the World Court contains a so-called "self-judging reservation" which, in effect, permits us to prevent a Court decision in any particular case in which we are involved. The Democratic Party proposes its repeal.

To all these endeavors so essential to world peace, we, the members of the Democratic Party, will bring a new urgency, persistence, and determination, born of the conviction that in our thermonuclear century all of the other Rights of Man hinge on our ability to assure man's right to peace.

The pursuit of peace, our contribution to the stability of the new nations of the world, our hopes for progress and well-being at home, all these depend in large measure on our ability to release the full potential of our American economy for employment, production, and growth.

Our generation of Americans has achieved a historic technological breakthrough. Today we are capable of creating an abundance in goods and services beyond the dreams of our parents. Yet on the threshold of plenty the Republican Administration hesitates, confused and afraid.

As a result, massive human needs now exist side by side with idle workers, idle capital, and idle machines.

The Republican failure in the economic field has been virtually complete.

Their years of power have consisted of two recessions, in 1953–54 and 1957–60, separated by the most severe peacetime inflation in history.

They have shown themselves incapable of checking inflation. In their efforts to do so, they have brought on recessions that have thrown millions of Americans out of work. Yet even in these slumps, the cost of living has continued to climb, and it is now at an all-time high.

They have slowed down the rate of growth of the economy to about one-third the rate of the Soviet Union's.

Over the past $7\frac{1}{2}$-year period, the Republicans have failed to balance the budget or reduce the national debt. Responsible fiscal policy requires surpluses in good times to more than offset the deficits which may occur in recessions, in order to reduce the national debt over the long run. The Republican Administration has produced the deficits—in fact, the greatest deficit in any peacetime year in history, in 1958–59—but only occasional and meager surpluses. Their first seven years produced a total deficit of nearly $19 billion.

While reducing outlays for essential public services which directly benefit our people, they have raised the annual interest charge on the national debt to a level $3 billion higher than when they took office. In the eight fiscal years of the Republican Administration, these useless higher interest payments will have cost the taxpayers $9 billion.

They have mismanaged the public debt not only by increasing interest rates, but also by failing to lengthen the average maturity of Government obligations when they had a clear opportunity to do so.

ECONOMIC GROWTH

The new Democratic Administration will confidently proceed to unshackle American enterprise and to free American labor, industrial leadership, and capital, to create an abundance that will outstrip any other system.

Free competitive enterprise is the most creative and productive form of economic order that the world has seen. The recent slow pace of American growth is due not to the failure of our free economy but to the failure of our national leadership.

We Democrats believe that our economy can and must grow at an average rate of 5% annually, almost twice as fast as our average annual rate since 1953. We pledge ourselves to policies that will achieve this goal without inflation.

Economic growth is the means whereby we improve the American standard of living and produce added tax resources for national security and essential public services.

Our economy must grow more swiftly in order to absorb two groups of workers: the much larger number of young people who will be reaching working age in the 1960s, and the workers displaced by the rapid pace of technological advances, including automation. Republican policies which have stifled growth could only mean increasingly severe unemployment, particularly of youth and older workers.

AN END TO TIGHT MONEY

As the first step in speeding economic growth, a Democratic President will put an end to the present high-interest, tight-money policy.

This policy has failed in its stated purpose—to keep prices down. It has given us two recessions within five years, bankrupted many of our farmers, produced a record number of business failures, and added billions of dollars in unnecessary higher interest charges to Government budgets and the cost of living.

A new Democratic Administration will reject this philosophy of economic slowdown. We are committed to maximum employment, at decent wages and with fair profits, in a far more productive, expanding economy.

The Republican high-interest policy has extracted a costly toll from every American who has financed a home, an automobile, a refrigerator, or a television set.

It has foisted added burdens on taxpayers of state and local governments which must borrow for schools and other public services.

It has added to the cost of many goods and services, and hence has been itself a factor in inflation.

It has created windfalls for many financial institutions.

The $9 billion of added interest charges on the national debt would have been even higher but for the prudent insistence of the Democratic Congress that the ceiling on interest rates for long-term Government bonds be maintained.

CONTROL OF INFLATION

The American consumer has a right to fair prices. We are determined to secure that right.

Inflation has its roots in a variety of causes; its cure lies in a variety of remedies. Among those remedies are monetary and credit policies properly applied, budget surpluses in times of full employment, and action to restrain "administered price" increases in industries where economic power rests in the hands of a few.

A fair share of the gains from increasing productivity in many industries should be passed on to the consumer through price reductions.

The agenda which a new Democratic Administration will face next January is crowded with urgent needs on which action has been delayed, deferred, or denied by the present Administration.

A new Democratic Administration will undertake to meet those needs.

It will reaffirm the Economic Bill of Rights which Franklin Roosevelt wrote into our national conscience sixteen years ago. It will reaffirm these rights for all Americans of whatever race, place of residence, or station in life:

1. *"The right to a useful and remunerative job in the industries or shops or farms or mines of the nation."*

FULL EMPLOYMENT

The Democratic Party reaffirms its support of full employment as a paramount objective of national policy.

For nearly 30 months the rate of unemployment has been between 5 and 7.5% of the labor force. A pool of three to four million citizens, able and willing to work but unable to find jobs, has been written off by the Republican Administration as a "normal" readjustment of the economic system.

The policies of a Democratic Administration to restore economic growth will reduce current unemployment to a minimum.

Thereafter, if recessionary trends appear, we will act promptly with counter-measures, such as public works or temporary tax cuts. We will not stand idly by and permit recessions to run their course as the Republican Administration has done.

AID TO DEPRESSED AREAS

The right to a job requires action to create new industry in America's depressed areas of chronic unemployment.

General economic measures will not alone solve the problems of localities which suffer some special disadvantage. To bring prosperity to these depressed areas and to enable them to make their full contribution to the national welfare, specially directed action is needed.

Areas of heavy and persistent unemployment result from depletion of natural resources, technological change, shifting defense requirements, or trade imbalances which have caused the decline of major industries. Whole communities, urban and rural, have been left stranded in distress and despair, through no fault of their own.

These communities have undertaken valiant efforts of self-help. But mutual aid, as well as self-help, is part of the American tradition. Stricken communities deserve the help of the whole nation.

The Democratic Congress twice passed bills to provide this help. The Republican President twice vetoed them.

These bills proposed low-interest loans to private enterprise to create new industry and new jobs in depressed communities, assistance to the communities to provide public facilities necessary to encourage the new industry, and retraining of workers for the new jobs.

The Democratic Congress will again pass, and the Democratic President will sign, such a bill.

DISCRIMINATION IN EMPLOYMENT

The right to a job requires action to break down artificial and arbitrary barriers to employment based on age, race, sex, religion, or national origin.

Unemployment strikes hardest at workers over 40, minority groups, young people, and women. We will not achieve full employment until prejudice against these workers is wiped out.

COLLECTIVE BARGAINING

The right to a job requires the restoration of full support for collective bargaining and the repeal of the anti-labor excesses which have been written into our labor laws.

Under Democratic leadership a sound national policy was developed, expressed particularly by the Wagner National Labor Relations Act, which guaranteed the rights of workers to organize and to bargain collectively. But the Republican Administration has replaced this sound policy with a national anti-labor policy.

The Republican Taft–Hartley Act seriously weakened unions in their efforts to bring economic justice to the millions of American workers who remain unorganized.

By administrative action, anti-labor personnel appointed by the Republicans to the National Labor

Relations Board have made the Taft–Hartley Act even more restrictive in its application than in its language.

Thus the traditional goal of the Democratic Party—to give all workers the right to organize and bargain collectively—has still not been achieved.

We pledge the enactment of an affirmative labor policy which will encourage free collective bargaining through the growth and development of free and responsible unions.

Millions of workers just now seeking to organize are blocked by Federally authorized "right-to-work" laws, unreasonable limitations on the right to picket, and other hampering legislative and administrative provisions.

Again, in the new Labor–Management Reporting and Disclosure Act, the Republican Administration perverted the constructive effort of the Democratic Congress to deal with improper activities of a few in labor and management by turning that Act into a means of restricting the legitimate rights of the vast majority of working men and women in honest labor unions. This law likewise strikes hardest at the weak or poorly organized, and it fails to deal with abuses of management as vigorously as with those of labor.

We will repeal the authorization for "right-to-work" laws, limitations on the rights to strike, to picket peacefully and to tell the public the facts of a labor dispute, and other anti-labor features of the Taft–Hartley Act and the 1959 Act. This unequivocal pledge for the repeal of the anti-labor and restrictive provisions of those laws will encourage collective bargaining and strengthen and support the free and honest labor movement.

The Railroad Retirement Act and the Railroad Unemployment Insurance Act are in need of improvement. We strongly oppose Republican attempts to weaken the Railway Labor Act.

We shall strengthen and modernize the Walsh–Healey and Davis–Bacon Acts, which protect the wage standards of workers employed by Government contractors.

Basic to the achievement of stable labor–management relations is leadership from the White House. The Republican Administration has failed to provide such leadership.

It failed to foresee the deterioration of labor–management relations in the steel industry last year. When a national emergency was obviously developing, it failed to forestall it. When the emergency came, the Administration's only solution was government-by-injunction.

A Democratic President, through his leadership and concern, will produce a better climate for continuing constructive relationships between labor and management. He will have periodic White House conferences between labor and management to consider their mutual problems before they reach the critical stage.

A Democratic President will use the vast fact-finding facilities that are available to inform himself, and the public, in exercising his leadership in labor disputes for the benefit of the nation as a whole.

If he needs more such facilities, or authority, we will provide them.

We further pledge that in the administration of all labor legislation we will restore the level of integrity, competence and sympathetic understanding required to carry out the intent of such legislation.

PLANNING FOR AUTOMATION

The right to a job requires planning for automation, so that men and women will be trained and available to meet shifting employment needs.

We will conduct a continuing analysis of the nation's manpower resources and of measures which may be required to assure their fullest development and use.

We will provide the Government leadership necessary to insure that the blessings of automation do not become burdens of widespread unemployment. For the young and the technologically displaced workers, we will provide the opportunity for training and retraining that equips them for jobs to be filled.

MINIMUM WAGES

2. "The right to earn enough to provide adequate food and clothing and recreation."

At the bottom of the income scale are some eight million families whose earnings are too low to provide even basic necessities of food, shelter, and clothing.

We pledge to raise the minimum wage to $1.25 an hour and to extend coverage to several million workers not now protected.

We pledge further improvements in the wage, hour and coverage standards of the Fair Labor Standards Act so as to extend its benefits to all workers employed in industries engaged in or affecting interstate commerce and to raise its standards to keep up with our general economic progress and needs.

We shall seek to bring the two million men, women and children who work for wages on the farms of the United States under the protection of existing labor and social legislation; and to assure migrant labor, perhaps the most underprivileged of all, of a comprehensive program to bring them not only decent wages but also adequate standards of health, housing, Social Security protection, education and welfare services.

AGRICULTURE

3. "The right of every farmer to raise and sell his products at a return which will give him and his family a decent living."

We shall take positive action to raise farm income to full parity levels and to preserve family farming as a way of life.

We shall put behind us once and for all the timidity with which our Government has viewed our abundance of food and fiber.

We will set new high levels of food consumption both at home and abroad.

As long as many Americans and hundreds of millions of people in other countries remain underfed, we shall regard these agricultural riches, and the family farmers who produce them, not as a liability but as a national asset.

Using Our Abundance

The Democratic Administration will inaugurate a national food and fiber policy for expanded use of our agricultural abundance. We will no longer view food stockpiles with alarm but will use them as powerful instruments for peace and plenty.

We will increase consumption at home. A vigorous, expanding economy will enable many American families to eat more and better food.

We will use the food stamp programs authorized to feed needy children, the aged and the unemployed. We will expand and improve the school lunch and milk programs.

We will establish and maintain food reserves for national defense purposes near important population centers in order to preserve lives in the event of national disaster, and will operate them so as not to depress farm prices. We will expand research into new industrial uses of agricultural products.

We will increase consumption abroad. The Democratic Party believes our nation's capacity to produce food and fiber is one of the great weapons for waging war against hunger and want throughout the world. With wise management of our food abundance we will expand trade between nations, support economic and human development programs, and combat famine.

Unimaginative, outmoded Republican policies which fail to use these productive capacities of our farms have been immensely costly to our nation. They can and will be changed.

Achieving Income Parity

While farmers have raised their productive efficiency to record levels, Republican farm policies have forced their income to drop by 30%.

Tens of thousands of farm families have been bankrupted and forced off the land. This has happened despite the fact that the Secretary of Agriculture has spent more on farm programs than all previous Secretaries in history combined.

Farmers acting individually or in small groups are helpless to protect their incomes from sharp declines. Their only recourse is to produce more, throwing production still further out of balance with demand and driving prices down further.

This disastrous downward cycle can be stopped only by effective farm programs sympathetically administered with the assistance of democratically elected farmer committees.

The Democratic Administration will work to bring about full parity income for farmers in all segments of agriculture by helping them to balance farm production with the expanding needs of the nation and the world.

Measures to this end include production and marketing quotas measured in terms of barrels, bushels and bales, loans on basic commodities at not less than 90% of parity, production payments, commodity purchases, and marketing orders and agreements.

We repudiate the Republican administration of the Soil Bank Program, which has emphasized the retirement of whole farm units, and we pledge an orderly land retirement and conservation program.

We are convinced that a successful combination of these approaches will cost considerably less than present Republican programs which have failed.

We will encourage agricultural cooperatives by expanding and liberalizing existing credit facilities and developing new facilities if necessary to assist them in extending their marketing and purchasing activities, and we will protect cooperatives from punitive taxation.

The Democratic Administration will improve the marketing practices of the family-type dairy farm to reduce risk of loss.

To protect farmers' incomes in times of natural disaster, the Federal Crop Insurance Program, created and developed experimentally under Democratic

Administrations, should be invigorated and expanded nationwide.

Improving Working and Living on Farms

Farm families have been among those victimized most severely by Republican tight-money policies.

Young people have been barred from entering agriculture. Giant corporations and other non-farmers, with readier access to credit and through vertical integration methods, have supplanted hundreds of farm families and caused the bankruptcy of many others.

The Democratic Party is committed by tradition and conviction to the preservation of family agriculture.

To this end, we will expand and liberalize farm credit facilities, especially to meet the needs of family-farm agriculture and to assist beginning farmers.

Many families in America's rural counties are still living in poverty because of inadequate resources and opportunity. This blight and personal desperation should have received national priority attention long ago.

The new Democratic Administration will begin at once to eradicate neglected rural blight. We will help people help themselves with extended and supervised credit for farm improvement, local industrial development, improved vocational training and other assistance to those wishing to change to non-farm employment, and with the fullest development of commercial and recreational possibilities. This is one of the major objectives of the area redevelopment program, twice vetoed by the Republican President.

The rural electric cooperatives celebrate this year the twenty-fifth anniversary of the creation of the Rural Electrification Administration under President Franklin D. Roosevelt.

The Democratic Congress has successfully fought the efforts of the Republican Administration to cut off REA loans and force high interest rate policies on this great rural enterprise.

We will maintain interest rates for REA co-ops and public power districts at the levels provided in present law.

We deplore the Administration's failure to provide the dynamic leadership necessary for encouraging loans to rural users for generation of power where necessary.

We promise the co-ops active support in meeting the ever-growing demand for electric power and telephone service, to be filled on a complete area-coverage basis without requiring benefits for special-interest power groups.

In every way we will seek to help the men, women, and children whose livelihood comes from the soil to achieve better housing, education, health, and decent earnings and working conditions.

All these goals demand the leadership of a Secretary of Agriculture who is conversant with the technological and economic aspects of farm problems, and who is sympathetic with the objectives of effective farm legislation not only for farmers but for the best interest of the nation as a whole.

SMALL BUSINESS

4. *"The right of every businessman, large and small, to trade in an atmosphere of freedom from unfair competition and domination by monopolies at home and abroad."*

The new Democratic Administration will act to make our free economy really free—free from the oppression of monopolistic power, and free from the suffocating impact of high interest rates. We will help create an economy in which small businesses can take root, grow, and flourish.

We Democrats pledge:

1. Action to aid small business in obtaining credit and equity capital at reasonable rates. Small business which must borrow to stay alive has been a particular victim of the high-interest policies of the Republican Administration.

The loan program of the Small Business Administration should be accelerated, and the independence of that agency preserved. The Small Business Investment Act of 1958 must be administered with a greater sense of its importance and possibilities.

2. Protection of the public against the growth of monopoly.

The last $7\frac{1}{2}$ years of Republican government has been the greatest period of merger and amalgamation in industry and banking in American history. Democratic Congresses have enacted numerous important measures to strengthen our anti-trust laws. Since 1950 the four Democratic Congresses have enacted laws like the Celler–Kefauver Anti-Merger Act, and improved the laws against price discriminations and tie-in sales.

When the Republicans were in control of the 80th and 83rd Congresses they failed to enact a single measure to strengthen or improve the antitrust laws.

The Democratic Party opposes this trend to monopoly.

We pledge vigorous enforcement of the antitrust laws.

We favor requiring corporations to file advance notice of mergers with the antitrust enforcement agencies.

We favor permitting all firms to have access at reasonable rates to patented inventions resulting from

Government-financed research and development contracts.

We favor strengthening the Robinson–Patman Act to protect small business against price discrimination.

We favor authorizing the Federal Trade Commission to obtain temporary injunctions during the pendency of administrative proceedings.

3. A more equitable share of Government contracts to small and independent business.

We will move from almost complete reliance on negotiation in the award of Government contracts toward open, competitive bidding.

HOUSING

5. *"The right of every family to a decent home."*

Today our rate of home building is less than that of ten years ago. A healthy, expanding economy will enable us to build two million homes a year, in wholesome neighborhoods, for people of all incomes.

At this rate, within a single decade we can clear away our slums and assure every American family a decent place to live.

Republican policies have led to a decline of the home building industry and the production of fewer homes. Republican high-interest policies have forced the cost of decent housing beyond the range of many families. Republican indifference has perpetuated slums.

We record the unpleasant fact that in 1960 at least 40 million Americans live in substandard housing.

One million new families are formed each year and need housing, and 300,000 existing homes are lost through demolition or other causes and need to be replaced. At present, construction does not even meet these requirements, much less permit reduction of the backlog of slum units.

We support a housing construction goal of more than two million homes a year. Most of the increased construction will be priced to meet the housing needs of middle- and low-income families who now live in substandard housing and are priced out of the market for decent homes.

Our housing programs will provide for rental as well as sales housing. They will permit expanded cooperative housing programs and sharply stepped up rehabilitation of existing homes.

To make possible the building of two million homes a year in wholesome neighborhoods, the home building industry should be aided by special mortgage assistance, with low interest rates, long-term mortgage periods and reduced down payments.

Where necessary, direct Government loans should be provided.

Even with this new and flexible approach, there will still be need for a substantial low-rent public housing program authorizing as many units as local communities require and are prepared to build.

HEALTH

6. *"The right to adequate medical care and the opportunity to achieve and enjoy good health."*

Illness is expensive. Many Americans have neither incomes nor insurance protection to enable them to pay for modern health care. The problem is particularly acute with our older citizens, among whom serious illness strikes most often.

We shall provide medical care benefits for the aged as part of the time-tested Social Security insurance system. We reject any proposal which would require such citizens to submit to the indignity of a means test—a "pauper's oath."

For young and old alike, we need more medical schools, more hospitals, more research laboratories to speed the final conquest of major killers.

Medical Care for Older Persons

Fifty million Americans—more than a fourth of our people—have no insurance protection against the high cost of illness. For the rest, private health insurance pays, on the average, only about one-third of the cost of medical care.

The problem is particularly acute among the 16 million Americans over 65 years old, and among disabled workers, widows and orphans.

Most of these have low incomes and the elderly among them suffer two to three times as much illness as the rest of the population.

The Republican Administration refused to acknowledge any national responsibility for health care for elder citizens until forced to do so by an increasingly outraged demand. Then, its belated proposal was a cynical sham built around a degrading test based on means or income—a "pauper's oath."

The most practicable way to provide health protection for older people is to use the contributory machinery of the Social Security system for insurance covering hospital bills and other high-cost medical services. For those relatively few of our older people who have never been eligible for Social Security coverage, we shall provide corresponding benefits by appropriations from the general revenue.

Research

We will step up medical research on the major killers and crippling diseases—cancer, heart disease, arthritis, mental illness. Expenditures for these purposes should be limited only by the availability of personnel and promising lines of research. Today such illness costs us $35 billion annually, much of which could be avoided. Federal appropriations for medical research are barely 1% of this amount.

Heart disease and cancer together account for two out of every three deaths in this country. The Democratic President will summon to a White House conference the nation's most distinguished scientists in these fields to map a coordinated long-run program for the prevention and control of these diseases.

We will also support a cooperative program with other nations on international health research.

Hospitals

We will expand and improve the Hill–Burton hospital construction program.

Health Manpower

To ease the growing shortage of doctors and other medical personnel we propose Federal aid for constructing, expanding and modernizing schools of medicine, dentistry, nursing and public health.

We are deeply concerned that the high cost of medical education is putting this profession beyond the means of most American families. We will provide scholarships and other assistance to break through the financial barriers to medical education.

Mental Health

Mental patients fill more than half the hospital beds in the country today. We will provide greatly increased Federal support for psychiatric research and training, and community mental health programs, to help bring back thousands of our hospitalized mentally ill to full and useful lives in the community.

7. "The right to adequate protection from the economic fears of old age, sickness, accidents, and unemployment."

A PROGRAM FOR THE AGING

The Democratic Administration will end the neglect of our older citizens. They deserve lives of usefulness, dignity, independence, and participation. We shall assure them not only health care but employment for those who want work, decent housing, and recreation.

Already 16 million Americans—about one in ten—are over 65, with the prospect of 26 million by 1980.

Health

As stated, we will provide an effective system for paid-up medical insurance upon retirement, financed during working years through the Social Security mechanism and available to all retired persons without a means test. This has first priority.

Income

Half of the people over 65 have incomes inadequate for basic nutrition, decent housing, minimum recreation and medical care. Older people who do not want to retire need employment opportunity and those of retirement age who no longer wish to or cannot work need better retirement benefits.

We pledge a campaign to eliminate discrimination in employment due to age. As a first step we will prohibit such discrimination by Government contractors and subcontractors.

We will amend the Social Security Act to increase the retirement benefit for each additional year of work after 65, thus encouraging workers to continue on the job full time.

To encourage part-time work by others, we favor raising the $1200-a-year ceiling on what a worker may earn while still drawing Social Security benefits.

Retirement benefits must be increased generally, and minimum benefits raised from $33 a month to $50.

Housing

We shall provide decent and suitable housing which older persons can afford. Specifically we shall move ahead with the program of direct Government loans for housing for older people initiated in the Housing Act of 1959, a program which the Republican Administration has sought to kill.

Special Services

We shall take Federal action in support of state efforts to bring standards of care in nursing homes and other institutions for the aged up to desirable minimums.

We shall support demonstration and training programs to translate proven research into action in such fields as health, nutritional guidance, home care, counseling, and recreational activity.

Taken together, these measures will affirm a new charter of rights for the older citizens among us—the right to a life of usefulness, health, dignity, independence and participation.

WELFARE

Disability Insurance

We shall permit workers who are totally and permanently disabled to retire at any age, removing the arbitrary requirement that the worker be 50 years of age.

We shall also amend the law so that after six months of total disability, a worker will be eligible for disability benefits, with restorative services to enable him to return to work.

Physically Handicapped

We pledge continued support of legislation for the rehabilitation of physically handicapped persons and improvement of employment opportunities for them.

Public Assistance

Persons in need who are inadequately protected by social insurance are cared for by the states and local communities under public assistance programs.

The Federal Government, which now shares the cost of aid to some of these, should share in all, and benefits should be made available without regard to residence.

Unemployment Benefits

We will establish uniform minimum standards throughout the nation for coverage, duration, and amount of unemployment insurance benefits.

Equality for Women

We support legislation which will guarantee to women equality of rights under the law, including equal pay for equal work.

Child Welfare

The Child Welfare Program and other services already established under the Social Security Act should be expanded. Federal leadership is required in the nationwide campaign to prevent and control juvenile delinquency.

Intergroup Relations

We propose a Federal bureau of intergroup relations to help solve problems of discrimination in housing, education, employment, and community opportunities in general. The bureau would assist in the solution of problems arising from the resettlement of immigrants and migrants within our own country, and in resolving religious, social and other tensions where they arise.

EDUCATION

8. *"The right to a good education."*
America's young people are our greatest resource for the future. Each of them deserves the education which will best develop his potentialities.

We shall act at once to help in building the classrooms and employing the teachers that are essential if the right to a good education is to have genuine meaning for all the youth of America in the decade ahead.

As a national investment in our future we propose a program of loans and scholarship grants to assure that qualified young Americans will have full opportunity for higher education, at the institutions of their choice, regardless of the income of their parents.

The new Democratic Administration will end eight years of official neglect of our educational system.

America's education faces a financial crisis. The tremendous increase in the number of children of school and college age has far outrun the available supply of educational facilities and qualified teachers. The classroom shortage alone is interfering with the education of 10 million students.

America's teachers, parents and school administrators have striven courageously to keep up with the increased challenge of education.

So have states and local communities. Education absorbs two-fifths of all their revenue. With limited resources, private educational institutions have shouldered their share of the burden.

Only the Federal Government is not doing its part. For eight years, measures for the relief of the educational crisis have been held up by the cynical maneuvers of the Republican Party in Congress and the White House.

We believe that America can meet its educational obligations only with generous Federal financial support, within the traditional framework of local control. The assistance will take the form of Federal grants to states for educational purposes they deem most pressing, including classroom construction and teachers' salaries. It will include aid for the construction of academic facilities as well as dormitories at colleges and universities.

We pledge further Federal support for all phases of vocational education for youth and adults; for libraries and adult education; for realizing the potential of educational television; and for exchange of students and teachers with other nations.

As part of a broader concern for young people we recommend establishment of a Youth Conservation Corps, to give underprivileged young people a rewarding experience in a healthful environment.

The pledges contained in this Economic Bill of Rights point the way to a better life for every family in America.

They are the means to a goal that is now within our reach—the final eradication in America of the age-old evil of poverty.

Yet there are other pressing needs on our national agenda.

NATURAL RESOURCES

A thin layer of earth, a few inches of rain, and a blanket of air make human life possible on our planet.

Sound public policy must assure that these essential resources will be available to provide the good life for our children and future generations.

Water, timber and grazing lands, recreational areas in our parks, shores, forests and wildernesses, energy, minerals, even pure air—all are feeling the press of the enormously increased demands of a rapidly growing population.

Natural resources are the birthright of all the people.

The new Democratic Administration, with the vision that built a TVA and a Grand Coulee, will develop and conserve that heritage for the use of this and future generations. We will reverse Republican policies under which America's resources have been wasted, depleted, underdeveloped, and recklessly given away.

We favor the best use of our natural resources, which generally means adoption of the multiple-purpose principle to achieve full development for all the many functions they can serve.

Water and Soil

An abundant supply of pure water is essential to our economy. This is a national problem.

Water must serve domestic, industrial and irrigation needs and inland navigation. It must provide habitat for fish and wildlife, supply the base for much outdoor recreation, and generate electricity. Water must also be controlled to prevent floods, pollution, salinity and silt.

The new Democratic Administration will develop a comprehensive national water resource policy. In cooperation with state and local governments, and interested private groups, the Democratic Administration will develop a balanced, multiple-purpose plan for each major river basin, to be revised periodically to meet changing needs. We will erase the Republican slogan of "no new starts" and will begin again to build multiple-purpose dams, hydroelectric facilities, flood-control works, navigation facilities, and reclamation projects to meet mounting and urgent needs.

We will renew the drive to protect every acre of farm land under a soil and water conservation plan, and we will speed up the small-watershed program.

We will support and intensify the research effort to find an economical way to convert salt and brackish water. The Republicans discouraged this research, which holds untold possibilities for the whole world.

Water and Air Pollution

America can no longer take pure water and air for granted. Polluted rivers carry their dangers to everyone living along their courses; impure air does not respect boundaries.

Federal action is needed in planning, coordinating and helping to finance pollution control. The states and local communities cannot go it alone. Yet President Eisenhower vetoed a Democratic bill to give them more financial help in building sewage treatment plants.

A Democratic President will sign such a bill.

Democrats will step up research on pollution control, giving special attention to:

1. the rapidly growing problem of air pollution from industrial plants, automobile exhausts, and other sources, and
2. disposal of chemical and radioactive wastes, some of which are now being dumped off our coasts without adequate knowledge of the potential consequences.

Outdoor Recreation

As population grows and the work week shortens and transportation becomes easier and speedier, the need for outdoor recreation facilities mounts.

We must act quickly to retain public access to the oceans, gulfs, rivers, streams, lakes and reservoirs, and their shorelines, and to reserve adequate camping and recreational areas while there is yet time. Areas near major population centers are particularly needed.

The new Democratic Administration will work to improve and extend recreation opportunities in national parks and monuments, forests, and river development projects, and near metropolitan areas. Emphasis will be on attractive, low-cost facilities for all the people and on preventing undue commercialization.

The National Park System is still incomplete; in particular, the few remaining suitable shorelines must be included in it. A national wilderness system should be created for areas already set aside as wildernesses. The system should be extended but only after careful consideration by the Congress of the value of areas for competing uses.

Recreational needs of the surrounding area should be given important consideration in disposing of Federally owned lands.

We will protect fish and game habitats from commercial exploitation and require military installations to conform to sound conservation practices.

Energy

The Republican Administration would turn the clock back to the days before the New Deal, in an effort to divert the benefits of the great natural energy resources from all the people to a favored few. It has followed for many years a "no new starts" policy.

It has stalled atomic energy development; it has sought to cripple rural electrification.

It has closed the pilot plant on getting oil from shale.

It has harassed and hampered the TVA.

We reject this philosophy and these policies. The people are entitled to use profitably what they already own.

The Democratic Administration instead will foster the development of efficient regional giant power systems from all sources, including water, tidal, and nuclear power, to supply low-cost electricity to all retail electric systems, public, private, and cooperative.

The Democratic Administration will continue to develop "yardsticks" for measuring the rates of private utility systems. This means meeting the needs of rural electric cooperatives for low-interest loans for distribution, transmission and generation facilities; Federal transmission facilities, where appropriate, to provide efficient low-cost power supply; and strict enforcement of the public preference clause in power marketing.

The Democratic Administration will support contin-

ued study and research on energy fuel resources, including new sources in wind and sun. It will push forward with the Passamaquoddy tidal power project with its great promise of cheaper power and expanded prosperity for the people of New England.

We support the establishment of a national fuels policy.

The $15 billion national investment in atomic energy should be protected as a part of the public domain.

Federal Lands and Forests

The record of the Republican Administration in handling the public domain is one of complete lethargy. It has failed to secure existing assets. In some cases, it has given away priceless resources for plunder by private corporations, as in the Al Sarena mining incident and the secret leasing of game refuges to favored oil interests.

The new Democratic Administration will develop balanced land and forest policies suited to the needs of a growing America.

This means intensive forest management on a multiple-use and sustained-yield basis, reforestation of burnt-over lands, building public access roads, range reseeding and improvement, intensive work in watershed management, concern for small business operations, and insuring free public access to public lands for recreational uses.

Minerals

America uses half the minerals produced in the entire Free World. Yet our mining industry is in what may be the initial phase of a serious long-term depression. Sound policy requires that we strengthen the domestic mining industry without interfering with adequate supplies of needed materials at reasonable costs.

We pledge immediate efforts toward the establishment of a realistic long-range minerals policy.

The new Democratic Administration will begin intensive research on scientific prospecting for mineral deposits.

We will speed up the geologic mapping of the country, with emphasis on Alaska.

We will resume research and development work on use of low-grade mineral reserves, especially oil shale, lignites, iron ore taconite, and radioactive minerals. These efforts have been halted or cut back by the Republican Administration.

The Democratic Party favors a study of the problem of non-uniform seaward boundaries of the coastal states.

Government Machinery for Managing Resources

Long-range programming of the nation's resource development is essential. We favor creation of a council of advisers on resources and conservation, which will evaluate and report annually upon our resource needs and progress.

We shall put budgeting for resources on a businesslike basis, distinguishing between operating expense and capital investment, so that the country can have an accurate picture of the costs and returns. We propose the incremental method in determining the economic justification of our river basin programs. Charges for commercial use of public lands will be brought into line with benefits received.

CITIES AND THEIR SUBURBS

A new Democratic Administration will expand Federal programs to help urban communities clear their slums, dispose of their sewage, educate their children, transport suburban commuters to and from their jobs, and combat juvenile delinquency.

We will give the city dweller a voice at the Cabinet table by bringing together within a single department programs concerned with urban and metropolitan problems.

The United States is now predominantly an urban nation.

The efficiency, comfort, and beauty of our cities and suburbs influence the lives of all Americans.

Local governments have found increasing difficulty in coping with such fundamental public problems as urban renewal, slum clearance, water supply, mass transportation, recreation, health, welfare, education and metropolitan planning. These problems are, in many cases, interstate and regional in scope.

Yet the Republican Administration has turned its back on urban and suburban America. The list of Republican vetoes includes housing, urban renewal and slum clearance, area redevelopment, public works, airports and stream pollution control. It has proposed severe cutbacks in aid for hospital construction, public assistance, vocational education, community facilities and sewage disposal.

The result has been to force communities to thrust an ever-greater tax load upon the already overburdened property taxpayer and to forgo needed public services.

The Democratic Party believes that state and local governments are strengthened—not weakened—by financial assistance from the Federal Government. We will extend such aid without impairing local administration through unnecessary Federal interference or red tape.

We propose a ten-year action program to restore our cities and provide for balanced suburban development, including the following:

1. The elimination of slums and blight and the restoration of cities and depressed areas within the next ten years.
2. Federal aid for metropolitan area planning and community facility programs.
3. Federal aid for comprehensive metropolitan transportation programs, including bus and rail mass transit, commuter railroads as well as highway programs, and construction of civil airports.
4. Federal aid in combating air and water pollution.
5. Expansion of park systems to meet the recreation needs of our growing population.

The Federal Government must recognize the financial burdens placed on local governments, urban and rural alike, by Federal installations and land holdings.

TRANSPORTATION

Over the past seven years, we have watched the steady weakening of the nation's transportation system. Railroads are in distress. Highways are congested. Airports and airways lag far behind the needs of the jet age.

To meet this challenge we will establish a national transportation policy, designed to coordinate and modernize our facilities for transportation by road, rail, water, and air.

Air

The jet age has made rapid improvement in air safety imperative. Rather than "an orderly withdrawal" from the airport grant programs as proposed by the Republican Administration, we pledge to expand the program to accommodate growing air traffic.

Water

Development of our inland waterways, our harbors, and Great Lakes commerce has been held back by the Republican President.

We pledge the improvement of our rivers and harbors by new starts and adequate maintenance.

A strong and efficient American-flag merchant marine is essential to peacetime commerce and defense emergencies. Continued aid for ship construction and operation to offset cost differentials favoring foreign shipping is essential to these goals.

Roads

The Republican Administration has slowed down, stretched out and greatly increased the costs of the interstate highway program.

The Democratic Party supports the highway program embodied in the Acts of 1956 and 1958 and the principle of Federal–state partnership in highway construction.

We commend the Democratic Congress for establishing a special committee which has launched an extensive investigation of this highway program. Continued scrutiny of this multi-billion-dollar highway program can prevent waste, inefficiency and graft and maintain the public's confidence.

Rail

The nation's railroads are in particular need of freedom from burdensome regulation to enable them to compete effectively with other forms of transportation. We also support Federal assistance in meeting certain capital needs, particularly for urban mass transportation.

SCIENCE

We will recognize the special role of our Federal Government in support of basic and applied research.

Space

The Republican Administration has remained incredibly blind to the prospects of space exploration. It has failed to pursue space programs with a sense of urgency at all close to their importance to the future of the world.

It has allowed the Communists to hit the moon first, and to launch substantially greater payloads. The Republican program is a catchall of assorted projects with no clearly defined, long-range plan of research.

The new Democratic Administration will press forward with our national space program in full realization of the importance of space accomplishments to our national security and our international prestige. We shall reorganize the program to achieve both efficiency and speedy execution. We shall bring top scientists into positions of responsibility. We shall undertake long-term basic research in space science and propulsion.

We shall initiate negotiations leading toward the international regulation of space.

Atomic Energy

The United States became pre-eminent in the development of atomic energy under Democratic Administrations.

The Republican Administration, despite its glowing promises of "Atoms for Peace," has permitted the gradual deterioration of United States leadership in atomic development both at home and abroad.

In order to restore United States leadership in atomic development, the new Democratic Administration will:

1. Restore truly nonpartisan and vigorous administration of the vital atomic energy program.
2. Continue the development of the various promising experimental and prototype atomic power plants which show promise, and provide increasing support for longer-range projects at the frontiers of atomic energy application.
3. Continue to preserve and support national laboratories and other Federal atomic installations as the foundation of technical progress and a bulwark of national defense.
4. Accelerate the Rover nuclear rocket project and auxiliary power facilities so as to achieve world leadership in peaceful outer space exploration.
5. Give reality to the United States international atoms-for-peace programs, and continue and expand technological assistance to underdeveloped countries.
6. Consider measures for improved organization and procedure for radiation protection and reactor safety, including a strengthening of the role of the Federal Radiation Council, and the separation of quasi-judicial functions in reactor safety regulations.
7. Provide a balanced and flexible nuclear defense capability, including the augmentation of the nuclear submarine fleet.

Oceanography

Oceanographic research is needed to advance such important programs as food and minerals from our Great Lakes and the sea. The present Administration has neglected this new scientific frontier.

GOVERNMENT OPERATIONS

We shall reform the processes of Government in all branches—Executive, Legislative, and Judicial. We will clean out corruption and conflicts of interest, and improve Government services.

The Federal Service

Two weeks before this Platform was adopted, the difference between the Democratic and Republican attitudes toward Government employees was dramatically illustrated. The Democratic Congress passed a fully justified pay increase to bring Government pay scales more nearly into line with those of private industry.

The Republican President vetoed the pay raise.

The Democratic Congress decisively overrode the veto.

The heavy responsibilities of modern government require a Federal service characterized by devotion to duty, honesty of purpose and highest competence. We pledge the modernization and strengthening of our Civil Service system.

We shall extend and improve the employees' appeals system and improve programs for recognizing the outstanding merits of individual employees.

Ethics in Government

We reject totally the concept of dual or triple loyalty on the part of Federal officials in high places.

The conflict-of-interest statutes should be revised and strengthened to assure the Federal service of maximum security against unethical practices on the part of public officials.

The Democratic Administration will establish and enforce a Code of Ethics to maintain the full dignity and integrity of the Federal service and to make it more attractive to the ablest men and women.

Regulatory Agencies

The Democratic Party promises to clean up the Federal regulatory agencies. The acceptance by Republican appointees to these agencies of gifts, hospitality, and bribes from interests under their jurisdiction has been a particularly flagrant abuse of public trust.

We shall bring all contacts with commissioners into the open, and will protect them from any form of improper pressure.

We shall appoint to these agencies men of ability and independent judgment who understand that their function is to regulate these industries in the public interest.

We promise a thorough review of existing agency practices, with an eye toward speedier decisions, and a clearer definition of what constitutes the public interest.

The Democratic Party condemns the usurpation by the Executive of the powers and functions of any of the independent agencies and pledges the restoration of the independence of such agencies and the protection of their integrity of action.

The Postal Service

The Republican policy has been to treat the United States postal service as a liability instead of a great investment in national enlightenment, social efficiency and economic betterment.

Constant curtailment of service has inconvenienced every citizen.

A program must be undertaken to establish the Post Office Department as a model of efficiency and service. We pledge ourselves to:

1. Restore the principle that the postal service is a public service.
2. Separate the public service costs from those to be borne by the users of the mails.
3. Continue steady improvement in working conditions and wage scales, reflecting increasing productivity.
4. Establish a long-range program for research and capital improvements compatible with the highest standards of business efficiency.

Law Enforcement

In recent years, we have been faced with a shocking increase in crimes of all kinds. Organized criminals have even infiltrated into legitimate business enterprises and labor unions.

The Republican Administration, particularly the Attorney General's office, has failed lamentably to deal with this problem despite the growing power of the underworld. The new Democratic Administration will take vigorous corrective action.

Freedom of Information

We reject the Republican contention that the workings of Government are the special private preserve of the Executive.

The massive wall of secrecy erected between the Executive branch and the Congress as well as the citizen must be torn down. Information must flow freely, save in those areas in which the national security is involved.

Clean Elections

The Democratic Party favors realistic and effective limitations on contributions and expenditures, and full disclosure of campaign financing in Federal elections.

We further propose a tax credit to encourage small contributions to political parties. The Democratic Party affirms that every candidate for public office has a moral obligation to observe and uphold traditional American principles of decency, honesty and fair play in his campaign for election.

We deplore efforts to divide the United States into regional, religious and ethnic groups.

We denounce and repudiate campaign tactics that substitute smear and slander, bigotry and false accusations of bigotry, for truth and reasoned argument.

District of Columbia

The capital city of our nation should be a symbol of democracy to people throughout the world. The Democratic Party reaffirms its long-standing support of home rule for the District of Columbia, and pledges to enact legislation permitting voters of the District to elect their own local government.

We urge the legislatures of the 50 states to ratify the 23rd Amendment, passed by the Democratic Congress, to give District citizens the right to participate in Presidential elections.

We also support a Constitutional amendment giving the District voting representation in Congress.

Virgin Islands

We believe that the voters of the Virgin Islands should have the right to elect their own Governor, to have a delegate in the Congress of the United States and to have the right to vote in national elections for a President and Vice President of the United States.

Puerto Rico

The social, economic, and political progress of the Commonwealth of Puerto Rico is a testimonial to the sound enabling legislation, and to the sincerity and understanding with which the people of the 50 states and Puerto Rico are meeting their joint problems.

The Democratic Party, under whose administration the Commonwealth status was established, is entitled to great credit for providing the opportunity which the people of Puerto Rico have used so successfully.

Puerto Rico has become a show place of world-wide interest, a tribute to the benefits of the principles of self-determination. Further benefits for Puerto Rico under these principles are certain to follow.

CONGRESSIONAL PROCEDURES

In order that the will of the American people may be expressed upon all legislative proposals, we urge that action be taken at the beginning of the 87th Congress to improve Congressional procedures so that majority rule prevails and decisions can be made after reason-able debate without being blocked by a minority in either House.

The rules of the House of Representatives should be so amended as to make sure that bills reported by legislative committees reach the floor for consideration without undue delay.

CONSUMERS

In an age of mass production, distribution, and advertising, consumers require effective Government representation and protection.

The Republican Administration has allowed the Food and Drug Administration to be weakened. Recent Senate hearings on the drug industry have revealed how flagrant profiteering can be when essential facts on costs, prices, and profits are hidden from scrutiny. The new Democratic Administration will provide the money and the authority to strengthen this agency for its task.

We propose a consumer counsel, backed by a suitable staff, to speak for consumers in the formulation of Government policies and represent consumers in administrative proceedings.

The consumer also has a right to know the cost of credit when he borrows money. We shall enact Federal legislation requiring the vendors of credit to provide a statement of specific credit charges and what these charges cost in terms of true annual interest.

VETERANS AFFAIRS

We adhere to the American tradition dating from the Plymouth Colony in New England in 1636:

"... any soldier injured in defense of the colony shall be maintained competently by the colony for the remainder of his life."

We pledge adequate compensation for those with service-connected disabilities and for the survivors of those who died in service or from service-connected disabilities. We pledge pensions adequate for a full and dignified life for disabled and distressed veterans and for needy survivors of deceased veterans.

Veterans of World War I, whose Federal benefits have not matched those of veterans of subsequent service, will receive the special attention of the Democratic Party looking toward equitable adjustments.

We endorse expanded programs of vocational rehabilitation for disabled veterans, and education for orphans of servicemen.

The quality of medical care furnished to the disabled

veterans has deteriorated under the Republican Administration. We shall work for an increased availability of facilities for all veterans in need and we shall move with particular urgency to fulfill the need for expanded domiciliary and nursing-home facilities.

We shall continue the veterans home loan guarantee and direct loan programs and educational benefits patterned after the G.I. Bill of Rights.

AMERICAN INDIANS

We recognize the unique legal and moral responsibility of the Federal Government for Indians in restitution for the injustice that has sometimes been done them. We therefore pledge prompt adoption of a program to assist Indian tribes in the full development of their human and natural resources and to advance the health, education, and economic well-being of Indian citizens while preserving their cultural heritage.

Free consent of the Indian tribes concerned shall be required before the Federal Government makes any change in any Federal–Indian treaty or other contractual relationship.

The new Democratic Administration will bring competent, sympathetic, and dedicated leadership to the administration of Indian affairs which will end practices that have eroded Indian rights and resources, reduced the Indians' land base and repudiated Federal responsibility. Indian claims against the United States can and will be settled promptly, whether by negotiation or other means, in the best interests of both parties.

THE ARTS

The arts flourish where there is freedom and where individual initiative and imagination are encouraged. We enjoy the blessings of such an atmosphere.

The nation should begin to evaluate the possibilities for encouraging and expanding participation in and appreciation of our cultural life.

We propose a Federal advisory agency to assist in the evaluation, development, and expansion of cultural resources of the United States. We shall support legislation needed to provide incentives for those endowed with extraordinary talent, as a worthy supplement to existing scholarship programs.

CIVIL LIBERTIES

With democratic values threatened today by Communist tyranny, we reaffirm our dedication to the Bill of Rights. Freedom and civil liberties, far from being incompatible with security, are vital to our national strength. Unfortunately, those high in the Republican Administration have all too often sullied the name and honor of loyal and faithful American citizens in and out of Government.

The Democratic Party will strive to improve Congressional investigating and hearing procedures. We shall abolish useless disclaimer affidavits such as those for student educational loans. We shall provide a full and fair hearing, including confrontation of the accuser, to any person whose public or private employment or reputation is jeopardized by a loyalty or security proceeding.

Protection of rights of American citizens to travel, to pursue lawful trade and to engage in other lawful activities abroad without distinction as to race or religion is a cardinal function of the national sovereignty.

We will oppose any international agreement or treaty which by its terms or practices differentiates among American citizens on grounds of race or religion.

The list of unfinished business for America is long. The accumulated neglect of nearly a decade cannot be wiped out overnight. Many of the objectives which we seek will require our best efforts over a period of years.

Although the task is far-reaching, we will tackle it with vigor and confidence. We will substitute planning for confusion, purpose for indifference, direction for drift and apathy.

We will organize the policymaking machinery of the Executive branch to provide vigor and leadership in establishing our national goals and achieving them.

The new Democratic President will sign, not veto, the efforts of a Democratic Congress to create more jobs, to build more homes, to save family farms, to clean up polluted streams and rivers, to help depressed areas, and to provide full employment for our people.

FISCAL RESPONSIBILITY

We vigorously reject the notion that America, with a half-trillion-dollar gross national product, and nearly half of the world's industrial resources, cannot afford to meet our needs at home and in our world relationships.

We believe, moreover, that except in periods of recession or national emergency, these needs can be met with a balanced budget, with no increase in present tax rates, and with some surplus for the gradual reduction of our national debt.

To assure such a balance we shall pursue a four-point program of fiscal responsibility.

First, we shall end the gross waste in Federal expenditures which needlessly raises the budgets of many Government agencies.

The most conspicuous unnecessary item is, of course, the excessive cost of interest on the national debt. Courageous action to end duplication and competition among the armed services will achieve large savings. The cost of the agricultural program can be reduced while at the same time prosperity is being restored to the nation's farmers.

Second, we shall collect the billions in taxes which are owed to the Federal Government but not now collected.

The Internal Revenue Service is still suffering from the cuts inflicted upon its enforcement staff by the Republican Administration and the Republican Congress in 1953.

The Administration's own Commissioner of Internal Revenue has testified that billions of dollars in revenue are lost each year because the Service does not have sufficient agents to follow up on tax evasion.

We will add enforcement personnel, and develop new techniques of enforcement, to collect tax revenue which is now being lost through evasion.

Third, we shall close the loopholes in the tax laws by which certain privileged groups legally escape their fair share of taxation.

Among the more conspicuous loopholes are depletion allowances which are inequitable, special consideration for recipients of dividend income, and deductions for extravagant "business expenses" which have reached scandalous proportions.

Tax reform can raise additional revenue and at the same time increase legitimate incentives for growth, and make it possible to ease the burden on the general taxpayer who now pays an unfair share of taxes because of special favors to the few.

Fourth, we shall bring in added Federal tax revenues by expanding the economy itself. Each dollar of additional production puts an additional 18 cents in tax revenue in the national treasury. A 5% growth rate, therefore, will mean that at the end of four years the Federal Government will have had a total of nearly $50 billion in additional tax revenues above those presently received.

By these four methods we can sharply increase the Government funds available for needed services, for correction of tax inequities, and for debt or tax reduction.

Much of the challenge of the 1960s, however, remains unforeseen and unforeseeable.

If, therefore, the unfolding demands of the new decade at home or abroad should impose clear national responsibilities that cannot be fulfilled without higher taxes, we will not allow political disadvantage to deter us from doing what is required.

As we proceed with the urgent task of restoring America's productivity, confidence, and power, we will never forget that our national interest is more than the sum total of all the group interests in America.

When group interests conflict with the national interest, it will be the national interest which we serve.

On its values and goals the quality of American life depends. Here above all our national interest and our devotion to the Rights of Man coincide.

Democratic Administrations under Wilson, Roosevelt, and Truman led the way in pressing for economic justice for all Americans.

But man does not live by bread alone. A new Democratic Administration, like its predecessors, will once again look beyond material goals to the spiritual meaning of American society.

We have drifted into a national mood that accepts payola and scandals, tax evasion and false expense accounts, soaring crime rates, influence peddling in high Government circles, and the exploitation of sadistic violence as popular entertainment.

For eight long critical years our present national leadership has made no effective effort to reverse this mood.

The new Democratic Administration will help create a sense of national purpose and higher standards of public behavior.

CIVIL RIGHTS

We shall also seek to create an affirmative new atmosphere in which to deal with racial divisions and inequalities which threaten both the integrity of our democratic faith and the proposition on which our nation was founded—that all men are created equal. It is our faith in human dignity that distinguishes our open free society from the closed totalitarian society of the Communists.

The Constitution of the United States rejects the notion that the Rights of Man means the rights of some men only. We reject it too.

The right to vote is the first principle of self-government. The Constitution also guarantees to all Americans the equal protection of the laws.

It is the duty of the Congress to enact the laws necessary and proper to protect and promote these constitutional rights. The Supreme Court has the power to interpret these rights and the laws thus enacted.

It is the duty of the President to see that these rights are respected and that the Constitution and laws as interpreted by the Supreme Court are faithfully executed.

What is now required is effective moral and political leadership by the whole Executive branch of our

Government to make equal opportunity a living reality for all Americans.

As the party of Jefferson, we shall provide that leadership.

In every city and state in greater or lesser degree there is discrimination based on color, race, religion, or national origin.

If discrimination in voting, education, the administration of justice or segregated lunch counters are the issues in one area, discrimination in housing and employment may be pressing questions elsewhere.

The peaceful demonstrations for first-class citizenship which have recently taken place in many parts of this country are a signal to all of us to make good at long last the guarantees of our Constitution.

The time has come to assure equal access for all Americans to all areas of community life, including voting booths, schoolrooms, jobs, housing, and public facilities.

The Democratic Administration which takes office next January will therefore use the full powers provided in the Civil Rights Acts of 1957 and 1960 to secure for all Americans the right to vote.

If these powers, vigorously invoked by a new Attorney General and backed by a strong and imaginative Democratic President, prove inadequate, further powers will be sought.

We will support whatever action is necessary to eliminate literacy tests and the payment of poll taxes as requirements for voting.

A new Democratic Administration will also use its full powers—legal and moral—to ensure the beginning of good-faith compliance with the Constitutional requirement that racial discrimination be ended in public education.

We believe that every school district affected by the Supreme Court's school desegregation decision should submit a plan providing for at least first-step compliance by 1963, the 100th anniversary of the Emancipation Proclamation.

To facilitate compliance, technical and financial assistance should be given to school districts facing special problems of transition.

For this and for the protection of all other Constitutional rights of Americans, the Attorney General should be empowered and directed to file civil injunction suits in Federal courts to prevent the denial of any civil right on grounds of race, creed, or color.

The new Democratic Administration will support Federal legislation establishing a Fair Employment Practices Commission to secure effectively for everyone the right to equal opportunity for employment.

In 1949 the President's Committee on Civil Rights recommended a permanent Commission on Civil Rights. The new Democratic Administration will broaden the scope and strengthen the powers of the present commission and make it permanent.

Its functions will be to provide assistance to communities, industries, or individuals in the implementation of Constitutional rights in education, housing, employment, transportation, and the administration of justice.

In addition, the Democratic Administration will use its full executive powers to assure equal employment opportunities and to terminate racial segregation throughout Federal services and institutions, and on all Government contracts. The successful desegregation of the armed services took place through such decisive executive action under President Truman.

Similarly, the new Democratic Administration will take action to end discrimination in Federal housing programs, including Federally assisted housing.

To accomplish these goals will require executive orders, legal actions brought by the Attorney General, legislation, and improved Congressional procedures to safeguard majority rule.

Above all, it will require the strong, active, persuasive, and inventive leadership of the President of the United States.

The Democratic President who takes office next January will face unprecedented challenges. His Administration will present a new face to the world.

It will be a bold, confident, affirmative face. We will draw new strength from the universal truths which the founder of our Party asserted in the Declaration of Independence to be "self-evident."

Emerson once spoke of an unending contest in human affairs, a contest between the Party of Hope and the Party of Memory.

For $7\frac{1}{2}$ years America, governed by the Party of Memory, has taken a holiday from history.

As the Party of Hope it is our responsibility and opportunity to call forth the greatness of the American people.

In this spirit, we hereby rededicate ourselves to the continuing service of the Rights of Man—everywhere in America and everywhere else on God's earth.

— 1964 —

ONE NATION, ONE PEOPLE

America is One Nation, One People. The welfare, progress, security and survival of each of us reside in the common good—the sharing of responsibilities as well as benefits by all our people.

Democracy in America rests on the confidence that people can be trusted with freedom. It comes from the conviction that we will find in freedom a unity of purpose stronger than all our differences.

We have drawn upon that unity when the forces of ignorance, hate, and fear fired an assassin's bullet at the nation's heart, incited violence in our land, and attacked the outposts of freedom around the world.

Because of this unity, those who traffic in fear, hate, falsehood, and violence have failed to undermine our people's deep love of truth and quiet faith in freedom.

Our program for the future is to make the national purpose—the human purpose of us all—fulfill our individual needs.

Accordingly, we offer this platform as a covenant of unity.

We invite all to join us who believe that narrow partisanship takes too small account of the size of our task, the penalties for failure and the boundless rewards to all our people for success.

We offer as the goal of this covenant peace for all nations and freedom for all peoples.

PEACE

Peace should be the first concern of all governments as it is the prayer of all men.

At the start of the third decade of the nuclear age, the preservation of peace requires the strength to wage war and the wisdom to avoid it. The search for peace requires the utmost intelligence, the clearest vision, and a strong sense of reality.

Because for four years our nation has patiently demonstrated these qualities and persistently used them, the world is closer to peace today than it was in 1960.

In 1960, freedom was on the defensive. The Communists—doubting both our strength and our will to use it—pressed forward in Southeast Asia, Latin America, Central Africa and Berlin.

President Kennedy and Vice President Johnson set out to remove any question of our power or our will. In the Cuban crisis of 1962 the Communist offensive shattered on the rock of President Kennedy's determination—and our ability—to defend the peace.

Two years later, President Johnson responded to another Communist challenge, this time in the Gulf of Tonkin. Once again power exercised with restraint repulsed Communist aggression and strengthened the cause of freedom.

Responsible leadership, unafraid but refusing to take needless risk, has turned the tide in freedom's favor. No nation, old or new, has joined the Communist bloc since Cuba during the preceding Republican Administration. Battered by economic failures, challenged by recent American achievements in space, torn by the Chinese–Russian rift, and faced with American strength and courage international Communism has lost its unity and momentum.

NATIONAL DEFENSE

By the end of 1960, military strategy was being shaped by the dictates of arbitrary budget ceilings instead of the real needs of national security. There were, for example, too few ground and air forces to fight limited war, although such wars were a means to continued Communist expansion.

Since then, and at the lowest possible cost, we have created a balanced, versatile, powerful defense establishment, capable of countering aggression across the entire spectrum of conflict, from nuclear confrontation to guerrilla subversion.

We have increased our intercontinental ballistic missiles and Polaris missiles from fewer than 100 to more than 1,000, more than four times the force of the Soviet Union. We have increased the number of combat ready divisions from 11 to 16.

Until such time as there can be an enforceable treaty providing for inspected and verified disarmament, we must, and we will, maintain our military strength, as the sword and shield of freedom and the guarantor of peace.

Specifically, we must and we will:

Continue the overwhelming supremacy of our Strategic Nuclear Forces.

Strengthen further our forces for discouraging limited wars and fighting subversion.

Maintain the world's largest research and development effort, which has initiated more than 200 new programs since 1961, to ensure continued American leadership in weapons systems and equipment.

Continue the nationwide Civil Defense program as an important part of our national security.

Pursue our examination of the Selective Service program to make certain that it is continued only as long as it is necessary and that we meet our military manpower needs without social or economic injustice.

Attract to the military services the highest caliber of career men and women and make certain they are adequately paid and adequately housed.

Maintain our Cost Reduction Program, to ensure a dollar's worth of defense for every dollar spent, and minimize the disruptive effects of changes in defense spending.

BUILDING THE PEACE

As citizens of the United States, we are determined that it be the most powerful nation on earth.

As citizens of the world, we insist that this power be exercised with the utmost responsibility.

Control of the use of nuclear weapons must remain solely with the highest elected official in the country—the President of the United States.

Through our policy of never negotiating from fear but never fearing to negotiate, we are slowly but surely approaching the point where effective international agreements providing for inspection and control can begin to lift the crushing burden of armaments off the backs of the people of the world.

In the Nuclear Test Ban Treaty, signed now by over 100 nations, we have written our commitment to limitations on the arms race, consistent with our security. Reduced production of nuclear materials for weapons purposes has been announced and nuclear weapons have been barred from outer space.

Already the air we and our children breathe is freer of nuclear contamination.

We are determined to continue all-out efforts through fully enforceable measures to halt and reverse the arms race and bring to an end the era of nuclear terror.

We will maintain our solemn commitment to the United Nations, with its constituent agencies, working to strengthen it as a more effective instrument for peace, for preventing or resolving international disputes, and for building free nations through economic, technical, and cultural development. We continue to oppose the admission of Red China to the United Nations.

We believe in increased partnership with our friends and associates in the community which spans the North Atlantic. In every possible way we will work to strengthen our ties and increase our cooperation, building always more firmly on the sure foundation of the NATO treaty.

We pledge unflagging devotion to our commitments to freedom from Berlin to South Vietnam. We will:

Help the people of developing nations in Asia, Africa and Latin America raise their standards of living and create conditions in which freedom and independence can flourish.

Place increased priority on private enterprise and development loans as we continue to improve our mutual assistance programs.

Work for the attainment of peace in the Near East as an urgent goal, using our best efforts to prevent a military unbalance, to encourage arms reductions and the use of national resources for internal development and to encourage the resettlement of Arab refugees in lands where there is room and opportunity. The problems of political adjustment between Israel and the Arab countries can and must be peacefully resolved and the territorial integrity of every nation respected.

Support the partnership of free American Republics in the Alliance for Progress.

Move actively to carry out the Resolution of the Organization of American States to further isolate Castroism and speed the restoration of freedom and responsibility in Cuba.

Support our friends in and around the rim of the Pacific, and encourage a growing understanding among peoples, expansion of cultural exchanges, and strengthening of ties.

Oppose aggression and the use of force or the threat of force against any nation.

Encourage by all peaceful means the growing independence of the captive peoples living under Communism and hasten the day that Albania, Bulgaria, Czechoslovakia, East Germany, Estonia, Hungary, Latvia, Lithuania, Poland, Rumania and the other captive nations will achieve full freedom and self-determination. We deplore Communist oppression of Jews and other minorities.

Encourage expansion of our economic ties with other nations of the world and eliminate unjustifiable tariff and non-tariff barriers, under authority of the Trade Expansion Act of 1962.

Expand the Peace Corps.

Use even more of our Food for Peace.

THE CONQUEST OF SPACE

In four vigorous years we have moved to the forefront of space exploration. The United States must never again settle for second place in the race for tomorrow's frontiers.

We will continue the rapid development of space technology for peaceful uses.

We will encourage private industry to increase its efforts in space research.

We will continue to ensure that any race in space is won for freedom and for peace.

THE LEADERSHIP WE OFFER

The complications and dangers in our restless, constantly changing world require of us consummate understanding and experience. One rash act, one thoughtless decision, one unchecked reaction—and cities could become smoldering ruins and farms parched wasteland.

The leadership we offer has already been tested in the crucible of crisis and challenge. To this nation and to all the world we reaffirm President Johnson's resolve to ". . . use every resource at the command of the Government . . . and the people . . . to find the road to peace."

We offer this platform as a guide for that journey.

FREEDOM AND WELL BEING

There can be full freedom only when all of our people have the opportunity for education to the full extent of their ability to learn, followed by the opportunity to employ their learning in the creation of something of value to themselves and to the nation.

The Individual

Our task is to make the national purpose serve the human purpose: that every person shall have the opportunity to become all that he or she is capable of becoming.

We believe that knowledge is essential to individual freedom and to the conduct of a free society. We believe that education is the surest and most profitable investment a nation can make.

Regardless of family financial status, therefore, education should be open to every boy and girl in America up to the highest level which he or she is able to master.

In an economy which will offer fewer and fewer places for the unskilled, there must be a wide variety of educational opportunities so that every young American, on leaving school, will have acquired the training to take a useful and rewarding place in our society.

It is increasingly clear that more of our educational resources must be directed to pre-school training as well as to junior college, college and post-graduate study.

The demands on the already inadequate sources of state and local revenues place a serious limitation on education. New methods of financial aid must be explored, including the channeling of Federally collected revenues to all levels of education, and, to the extent permitted by the Constitution, to all schools. Only in

this way can our educational programs achieve excellence throughout the nation, a goal that must be achieved without interfering with local control and direction of education.

In order to insure that all students who can meet the requirements for college entrance can continue their education, we propose an expanded program of public scholarships, guaranteed loans, and work–study grants.

We shall develop the potential of the Armed Forces for training young men who might otherwise be rejected for military service because their work skills are underdeveloped.

The health of the people is important to the strength and purpose of our country and is a proper part of our common concern.

In a nation that lacks neither compassion nor resources, the needless suffering of people who cannot afford adequate medical care is intolerable:

We will continue to fight until we have succeeded in including hospital care for older Americans in the Social Security program, and have insured adequate assistance to those elderly people suffering from mental illness and mental retardation.

We will go forward with research into the causes and cures of disease, accidents, mental illness and mental retardation.

We will further expand our health facilities, especially medical schools, hospitals, and research laboratories.

America's veterans who served their Nation so well must, in turn, be served fairly by a grateful Nation. First-rate hospitals and medical care must be provided veterans with service-connected injuries and disabilities, and their compensation rates must insure an adequate standard of living. The National Service Life Insurance program should be reopened for those who have lost their insurance coverage, and an equitable and just pension system must help meet the need of those disabled veterans and their survivors who require financial assistance.

Democracy of Opportunity

The variety of our people is the source of our strength and ought not to be a cause of disunity or discord. The rights of all our citizens must be protected and all the laws of our land obeyed if America is to be safe for democracy.

The Civil Rights Act of 1964 deserves and requires full observance by every American and fair, effective enforcement if there is any default.

Resting upon a national consensus expressed by the overwhelming support of both parties, this new law impairs the rights of no American; it affirms the rights of all Americans. Its purpose is not to divide, but to end division; not to curtail the opportunities of any, but to increase opportunities for all; not to punish, but to promote further our commitment to freedom, the pursuit of justice, and a deeper respect for human dignity.

We reaffirm our belief that lawless disregard for the rights of others is wrong—whether used to deny equal rights or to obtain equal rights.

We cannot and will not tolerate lawlessness. We can and will seek to eliminate its economic and social causes.

True democracy of opportunity will not be served by establishing quotas based on the same false distinctions we seek to erase, nor can the effects of prejudice be neutralized by the expedient of preferential practices.

The immigration laws must be revised to permit families to be reunited, to welcome the persecuted and oppressed, and to eliminate the discriminatory provisions which base admission upon national origins.

We will support legislation to carry forward the progress already made toward full equality of opportunity for women as well as men.

We will strive to eliminate discrimination against older Americans, especially in their employment.

Ending discrimination based on race, age, sex, or national origin demands not only equal opportunity but the opportunity to be equal. We are concerned not only with people's right to be free, but also with their ability to use their freedom.

We will:

Carry the War on Poverty forward as a total war against the causes of human want.

Move forward with programs to restore those areas, such as Appalachia, which the Nation's progress has by-passed.

Help the physically handicapped and mentally disadvantaged develop to the full limit of their capabilities.

Enhance the security of older Americans by encouraging private retirement and welfare programs, offering opportunities like those provided for the young under the Economic Opportunities Act of 1964, and expanding decent housing which older citizens can afford.

Assist our Indian people to improve their standard of living and attain self-sufficiency, the privileges of equal citizenship, and full participation in American life.

The Social Security program, initiated and developed under the National leadership of the Democratic Party and in the face of ceaseless partisan opposition, contributes greatly to the strength of the Nation. We must insure that those who have contributed to the system shall share in the steady increase in our standard of living by adjusting benefit levels.

We hold firmly to the conviction, long embraced by Democratic Administrations, that the advancing years of life should bring not fear and loneliness, but security, meaning, and satisfaction.

We will encourage further support for the arts, giving people a better chance to use increased leisure and recognizing that the achievements of art are an index of the greatness of a civilization.

We will encourage the advance of science and technology—for its material rewards, and for its contribution to an understanding of the universe and ourselves.

The Economy

The American free enterprise system is one of the great achievements of the human mind and spirit. It has developed by a combination of the energetic efforts of working men and women, bold private initiative, the profit motive and wise public policy, until it is now the productive marvel of mankind.

In spite of this, at the outset of 1961, America was in the depths of the fourth postwar recession.

Since then, in 42 months of uninterrupted expansion under Presidents Kennedy and Johnson, we have achieved the longest and strongest peacetime prosperity in modern history:

Almost four million jobs have been added to the economy—almost $1\frac{1}{2}$ million since last December.

Workers' earnings and corporate profits are at the highest level in history.

Prices have been more stable than in any other industrial nation in the free world.

This did not just happen. It has come about because we have wisely and prudently used our increasing understanding of how the economy works.

It is the national purpose, and our commitment, to continue this expansion of the American economy toward its potential, without a recession, with continued stability, and with an extension of the benefits of this growth and prosperity to those who have not fully shared in them.

This will require continuation of flexible and innovative fiscal, monetary, and debt management policies, recognizing the importance of low interest rates.

We will seek further tax reduction—and in the process we need to remove inequities in our present tax laws. In particular we should carefully review all our excise taxes and eliminate those that are obsolete. Consideration should be given to the development of fiscal policies which would provide revenue sources to hard-pressed state and local governments to assist them with their responsibilities.

Every penny of Federal spending must be accounted for in terms of the strictest economy, efficiency and integrity. We pledge to continue a frugal government, getting a dollar's value for a dollar spent, and a government worthy of the citizen's confidence.

Our goal is a balanced budget in a balanced economy.

Our enviable record of price stability must be maintained—through sound fiscal and monetary policies and the encouragement of responsible private wage and price policies. Stability is essential to protect our citizens—particularly the retired and handicapped—from the ravages of inflation. It is also essential to maintain confidence in the American dollar; this confidence has been restored in the past four years through sound policies.

Radical changes in technology and automation contribute to increased productivity and a higher standard of living. They must not penalize the few while benefiting the many. We maintain that any man or woman displaced by a machine or by technological change should have the opportunity, without penalty, to another job. Our common responsibility is to see that this right is fulfilled.

Full employment is an end in itself and must be insisted upon as a priority objective.

It is the national purpose, and our commitment, that every man or woman who is willing and able to work is entitled to a job and to a fair wage for doing it.

The coverage of the Fair Labor Standards Act must be extended to all workers employed in industries affecting interstate commerce, and the minimum wage level and coverage increased to assure those at the bottom of the economic scale a fairer share in the benefits of an ever-rising standard of American living.

Overtime payment requirements must be increased to assure maximum employment consistent with business efficiency. The matter of the length of work periods should be given continuing consideration.

The unemployment insurance program must be basically revised to meet the needs of the unemployed and of the economy, and to assure that this program meets the standards the nation's experience dictates.

Agricultural and migratory workers must be given legal protection and economic encouragement.

We must develop fully our most precious resource—our manpower. Training and retraining programs must be expanded. A broad-gauge manpower program must be developed which will not only satisfy the needs of the economy but will also give work its maximum meaning in the pattern of human life.

We will stimulate as well as protect small business, the seedbed of free enterprise and a major source of employment in our economy.

The antitrust laws must be vigorously enforced.

Our population, which is growing rapidly and becoming increasingly mobile, and our expanding economy are placing greater demands upon our transportation system than ever before. We must have fast, safe, and economic modes of transportation. Each mode should be encouraged to develop in accordance with its maximum utility, available at the lowest cost under the principles of fair competition. A strong and efficient American Flag merchant marine is essential to peacetime commerce and defense emergencies.

The industrial democracy of free, private collective bargaining and the security of American trade unions must be strengthened by repealing Section 14(b) of the Taft–Hartley Act. The present inequitable restrictions on the right to organize and to strike and picket peaceably must also be eliminated.

In order to protect the hard-earned American consumers, as well as promote their basic consumer rights, we will make full use of existing authority, and continue to promote efforts on behalf of consumers by industry, voluntary organizations, and state and local governments. Where protection is essential, we will enact legislation to protect the safety of consumers and to provide them with essential information. We will continue to insist that our drugs and medicines are safe and effective, that our food and cosmetics are free from harm, that merchandise is labeled and packaged honestly and that the true cost of credit is disclosed.

It is the national purpose, and our commitment to increase the freedom and effectiveness of the essential private forces and processes in the economy.

RURAL AMERICA

The roots of our economy and our life as a people lie deep in the soil of America's farm land. Our policies and programs must continue to recognize the significant role of agricultural and rural life.

To achieve the goals of higher incomes to the farm and ranch, particularly the family-sized farm, lower prices for the consumer, and lower costs to the government, we will continue to carry forward this three-dimensional program:

1. Commodity Programs to strengthen the farm income structure and reach the goal of parity of income in every aspect of American agriculture. We will continue to explore and develop new domestic

and foreign markets for the products of our farms and ranches.

2. Consumer Programs including expansion of the Food Stamp Program and the school lunch and other surplus food programs, and acceleration of research into new industrial uses of farm products, in order to assure maximum use of and abundance of wholesome foods at fair prices here and abroad. We will also study new low-cost methods and techniques of food distribution for the benefit of our housewives to better feed their families.

3. Community Programs and agricultural cooperatives to assure rural America decent housing, economic security and full partnership in the building of the great society. We pledge our continued support of the rural telephone program and the Rural Electrification Administration, which are among the great contributions of the Democratic Party to the well-being and comfort of rural America.

THE NATION'S NATURAL RESOURCES

America's bountiful supply of natural resources has been one of the major factors in achieving our position of world leadership, in developing the greatest industrial machine in the world's history, and in providing a richer and more complete life for every American. But these resources are not inexhaustible. With our vastly expanding population—an estimated 325 million people by the end of the century—there is an ever-increasing responsibility to use and conserve our resources wisely and prudently if we are to fulfill our obligation to the trust we hold for future generations. Building on the unsurpassed conservation record of the past four years, we shall:

Continue the quickened pace of comprehensive development of river basins in every section of the country, employing multi-purpose projects such as flood control, irrigation and reclamation, power generation, navigation, municipal water supply, fish and wildlife enhancement and recreation where appropriate to realize the fullest possible benefits.

Provide the people of this nation a balanced outdoor recreation program to add to their health and well-being, including the addition or improved management of national parks, forests, lake shores, seashores and recreation areas.

Preserve for us and our posterity through the means provided by the Wilderness Act of 1964 millions of acres of primitive and wilderness areas, including countless beautiful lakes and streams.

Increase our stock of wildlife and fish.

Continue and strengthen the dynamic program inaugurated to assure fair treatment for American fishermen and the preservation of fishing rights.

Continue to support balanced land and forest development through intensive forest management on a multiple-use and sustained yield basis, reforestation of burned land, providing public access roads, range improvement, watershed management, concern for small-business operations and recreational uses.

Unlock the resources of the sea through a strong oceanography program.

Continue the attack we have launched on the polluted air that envelops our cities and on eliminating the pollution of our rivers and streams.

Intensify our efforts to solve the critical water problems of many sections of this country by desalinization.

Sustain and promote strong, vigorous domestic minerals, metals, petroleum and fuels industries.

Increase the efficient use of electrical power through regional inter-ties and more extensive use of high-voltage transmission.

Continue to promote the development of new and improved methods of generating electric power, such as the recent important gains in the field of atomic energy and the Passamaquoddy tidal power project.

Preserve the T.V.A., which has played such an instrumental role in the revitalization of the area it serves and which has been the inspiration for regional development programs throughout the world.

THE CITY

The vitality of our cities is essential to the healthy growth of American civilization. In the next 40 years urban populations will double, the area of city land will double and we will have to construct houses, highways and facilities equal to all those built since this country was first settled.

Now is the time to redouble our efforts, with full cooperation among local, State and Federal governments, for these objectives:

The goal of our housing program must be a decent home for every American family.

Special effort must be made in our cities to provide wholesome living for our young people. We must press the fight against narcotics and, through the war against poverty, increase educational and employment opportunities, turning juvenile delinquents into good citizens and tax-users into tax payers.

We will continue to assist broad community and regional development, urban renewal, mass transit, open-space and other programs for our metropolitan areas.

We will offer such aid without impairing local administration through unnecessary Federal interference.

Because our cities and suburbs are so important to the welfare of all our people, we believe a department devoted to urban affairs should be added to the President's cabinet.

THE GOVERNMENT

We, the people, are the government.

The Democratic Party believes, as Thomas Jefferson first stated that "the care of human life and happiness is the first and only legitimate object of good government:"

The government's business is the people's business. Information about public affairs must continue to be freely available to the Congress and to the public.

Every person who participates in the government must be held to a standard of ethics which permits no compromise with the principles of absolute honesty and the maintenance of undivided loyalty to the public interest.

The Congress of the United States should revise its rules and procedures to assure majority rule after reasonable debate and to guarantee that major legislative proposals of the President can be brought to a vote after reasonable consideration in committee.

We support home rule for the District of Columbia. The seat of our government shall be a workshop for democracy, a pilot-plant for freedom, and a place of incomparable beauty.

We also support a constitutional amendment giving the District voting representation in Congress and, pending such action, the enactment of legislation providing for a non-voting delegate from the District of Columbia to the House of Representatives.

We support the right of the people of the Virgin Islands to the fullest measure of self-government, including the right to elect their Governor.

The people of Puerto Rico and the people of the United States enjoy a unique relationship that has contributed greatly to the remarkable economic and political development of Puerto Rico. We look forward to the report on that relationship by a commission composed of members from Puerto Rico and the United States, and we are confident that it will contribute to the further enhancement of Puerto Rico and the benefit that flows from the principles of self-determination.

The Democratic Party holds to the belief that government in the United States—local, state and Federal—was created in order to serve the people. Each level of government has appropriate powers and each has specific responsibilities. The first responsibility of government at every level is to protect the basic freedoms of the people. No government at any level can properly complain of violation of its power, if it fails to meet its responsibilities.

The Federal government exists not to grow larger, but to enlarge the individual potential and achievement of the people.

The Federal government exists not to subordinate the states, but to support them.

All of us are Americans. All of us are free men. Ultimately there can be no effective restraint on the powers of government at any level save as Americans exercising their duties as citizens insist upon and maintain free, democratic processes of our constitutional system.

ONE NATION, ONE PEOPLE

On November 22, 1963, John Fitzgerald Kennedy was shot down in our land.

We honor his memory best—and as he would wish—by devoting ourselves anew to the larger purposes for which he lived.

Of first priority is our renewed commitments to the values and ideals of democracy.

We are firmly pledged to continue the Nation's march towards the goals of equal opportunity an equal treatment for all Americans regardless of race, creed, color or national origin.

We cannot tolerate violence anywhere in our land—north, south, east or west. Resort to lawlessness is anarchy and must be opposed by the government and all thoughtful citizens.

We must expose, wherever it exists, the advocacy of hatred which creates the clear and present danger of violence.

We condemn extremism, whether from the Right or Left, including the extreme tactics of such organizations as the Communist Party, the Ku Klux Klan and the John Birch Society.

We know what violence and hate can do. We have seen the tragic consequences of misguided zeal and twisted logic.

The time has come now for all of us to understand and respect one another, and to seek the unity of spirit and purpose from which our future greatness will grow—for only as we work together with the object of liberty and justice for all will the peace and freedom of each of us be secured.

These are the principles which command our cause and strengthen our effort as we cross the new frontier and enter upon the great society.

AN ACCOUNTING OF STEWARDSHIP, 1961–1964

One hundred and twenty-four years ago, in 1840, the Democratic National Convention meeting in Baltimore adopted the first platform in the history of a national political party. The principles stated in that platform are as valid as ever:

"Resolved, That the liberal principles embodied by Jefferson in the Declaration of Independence, and sanctioned in the Constitution, which makes ours the land of liberty, and the asylum of the oppressed of every nation, have ever been cardinal principles in the democratic faith."

One hundred and twenty years later, in 1960, our nation had grown from 26 to 50 states, our people from 17 million to 179 million.

That year, in Los Angeles, the Democratic National Convention adopted a platform which reflected, in its attention to 38 specific subjects, the volume of unfinished business of the American people which had piled up to the point of national crisis.

The platform declared that as a Party we would put the people's business first, and stated in plain terms how we proposed to get on with it.

Four year have passed, and the time has come for the people to measure our performance against our pledges.

We welcome the comparison; we seek it.

For the record is one of four years of unrelenting effort, and unprecedented achievement—not by a political party, but by a people.

THE RECORD

National Defense

In 1960, we proposed to—

"Recast our military capacity in order to provide forces and weapons of a diversity, balance, and mobility sufficient in quantity and quality to deter both limited and general aggression."

Since January 1961, we have achieved:

A 150% increase in the number of nuclear warheads and a 200% increase in total megatonnage available in the Strategic Alert Forces.

A 60% increase in the tactical nuclear strength in Western Europe.

A 45% increase in the number of combat-ready Army divisions.

A 15,000-man increase in the strength of the Marine Corps.

A 75% increase in airlift capability.

A 100% increase in ship construction to modernize our fleet.

A 44% increase in the number of tactical fighter squadrons.

An 800% increase in the special forces trained to deal with counter-insurgency threats.

In 1960, we proposed to create—

"Deterrent military power such that the Soviet and Chinese leaders will have no doubt that an attack on the United States would surely be followed by their own destruction."

Since 1961, we have increased the intercontinental ballistic missiles and Polaris missiles in our arsenal from fewer than 100 to more than 1,000.

Our Strategic Alert Forces now have about 1,100 bombers, including 550 on 15-minute alert, many of which are equipped with decoy missiles and other penetration aids to assure that they will reach their targets.

In 1960, we proposed—

"Continuous modernization of our forces through intensified research and development, including essential programs slowed down, terminated, suspended, or neglected for lack of budgetary support."

Since 1961, we have—

Increased funds for research and development by 50% over the 1957–60 level.

Added 208 major new research and development projects, including 77 weapons programs with costs exceeding $10 million each, among which are the SR-71 long-range, manned, supersonic strategic military reconnaissance aircraft, the NIKE-X anti-ballistic missile system, the A7A navy attack aircraft, and the F-111 fighter-bomber and a new main battle tank.

Increased, by more than 1,000%, the funds for the development of counter-insurgency weapons and equipment, from less than $10 million to over $103 million per year.

In 1960, we proposed—

"Balanced conventional military forces which will permit a response graded to the intensity of any threats of aggressive force."

Since 1961, we have—

Increased the regular strength of the Army by 100,000 men, and the numbers of combat-ready Army divisions from 11 to 16.

Increased the number of tactical fighter squadrons from 55 to 79 and have substantially increased the procurement of tactical fighters.

Trained over 100,000 officers in counter-insurgency

skills necessary to fight guerilla and antiguerilla warfare, and increased our special forces trained to deal with counter-insurgency by 800%.

Acquired balanced stocks of combat consumables for all our forces so that they can engage in combat for sustained periods of time.

In reconstructing the nation's defense establishment, the Administration has insisted that the services be guided by these three precepts:

Buy only what we need.

Buy only at the lowest sound price.

Reduce operating costs through standardization, consolidation, and termination of unnecessary operations.

As a result, our expanded and reconstituted defense force has cost billions of dollars less than it would have cost under previous inefficient and unbusinesslike methods of procurement and operation. These savings amounted to more than $1 billion in the fiscal year 1963, and to $2.5 billion in the fiscal year just completed. Furthermore, under the cost reduction program we have established, we will be saving $4.6 billion each year, every year, by Fiscal Year 1968.

We have successfully met the challenges of Berlin and Cuba, and attacks upon our naval forces on the high seas, thus decreasing the prospect of further such challenges and brightening the outlook for peace.

Arms Control

In 1960, we proposed—

"A national peace agency for disarmament planning and research to muster the scientific ingenuity, coordination, continuity, and seriousness of purpose which are now lacking in our arms control efforts."

In 1961, the United States became the first nation in the world to establish an "agency for peace"—the Arms Control and Disarmament Agency.

This agency is charged by law with the development of a realistic arms control and disarmament policy to promote national security and provide an impetus towards a world free from the threat of war. Working closely with the senior military leaders of the Department of Defense, the Arms Control and Disarmament Agency has enabled the United States to lead the world in a new, continuous, hard-headed and purposeful discussion, negotiation and planning of disarmament.

In 1960, we proposed—

"To develop responsible proposals that will help break the deadlock on arms control."

In the aftermath of the Cuban crisis the United States pressed its advantage to seek a new breakthrough for peace. On June 10, 1963, at American University, President Kennedy called on the Soviet leadership to join in concrete steps to abate the nuclear arms race. After careful negotiations experienced American negotiators reached agreement with the Russians on a Nuclear Test Ban Treaty—an event that will be marked forever in the history of mankind as a first step on the difficult road of arms control.

One hundred and six nations signed or acceded to the treaty.

In the United States it was supported by the joint Chiefs of Staff, and ratified in the Senate by an 80–20 vote.

To insure the effectiveness of our nuclear development program in accord with the momentous Test Ban Treaty, the joint Chiefs of Staff recommended, and the Administration has undertaken:

A comprehensive program of underground testing of nuclear explosives.

Maintenance of modern nuclear laboratory facilities.

Preparations to test in the atmosphere if essential to national security, or if the treaty is violated by the Soviet Union.

Continuous improvement of our means for detecting violations and other nuclear activities elsewhere in the world.

In 1960, we proposed—

"To the extent we can secure the adoption of effective arms control agreements, vast resources will be freed for peaceful use."

In January and April 1964, President Johnson announced cutbacks in the production of nuclear materials: twenty percent in plutonium production and forty percent in enriched uranium. When the USSR followed this United States initiative with a similar announcement, the President welcomed the response as giving hope "that the world may yet, one day, live without the fear of war."

Instruments of Foreign Policy

In 1960, we proposed that—

"American foreign policy in all its aspects must be attuned to our world of change.

"We will recruit officials whose experience, humanity and dedication fit them for the task of effectively representing America abroad.

"We will provide a more sensitive and creative direction to our overseas information program."

Since 1961, the Department of State has had its self-respect restored, and has been vitalized by more vigorous recruitment and more intensive training of foreign service officers representing all elements of the American people.

Forty days after taking office President Kennedy established the Peace Corps. The world did not change overnight. Neither will it ever be quite the same again. The foreign minister of one large Asian nation has called the Peace Corps "the most powerful idea in recent times."

One hundred thousand Americans have volunteered for the Peace Corps. Nine thousand have served in a total of 45 countries.

Nearly every country to which volunteers have been sent has asked for more. Two dozen new countries are on the waiting list.

Volunteer organizations on the Peace Corps model are already operating in 12 countries and there has been a great expansion of volunteer service in many others.

An International Secretariat for Volunteer Service is working in 32 economically advanced and developing nations.

The United States Information Agency has been transformed into a powerful, effective and respected weapon of the free world. The new nations of the world have come to know an America that is not afraid to tell the truth about itself and so can be believed when it tells the truth about Communist imperialism.

World Trade

In 1960, we said—

". . . We shall expand world trade in every responsible way.

"Since all Americans share the benefits of this policy, its costs should not be the burden of a few. We shall support practical measures to ease the necessary adjustments of industries and communities which may be unavoidably hurt by increases in imports.

"Our government should press for reduction of foreign barriers on the sale of the products of American industry and agriculture."

This pledge was fulfilled in the Trade Expansion Act of 1962.

The Trade Expansion Act of 1962, gives the President power to negotiate a 50 percent across-the-board cut in tariff barriers to take place over a five-year period.

Exports have expanded over 10 percent—by over $2 billion—since 1961.

Foreign trade now provides jobs for more than 4 million workers.

Negotiations now under way will permit American businessmen and farmers to take advantage of the greatest trading opportunity in history—the rapidly expanding European market.

The Trade Expansion Act provides for worker training and moving allowances, and for loans, tax rebates and technical assistance for businesses if increased imports resulting from concessions granted in trade agreements result in unemployment or loss of business.

Where American agriculture or industrial products have been unfairly treated in order to favor domestic products, prompt and forceful action has been taken to break down such barriers. These efforts have opened new United States export opportunities for fruits and vegetables, and numerous other agricultural and manufactured products to Europe and Japan.

The Long Term Cotton Textile Agreement of 1962 protects the textile and garment industry against disruptive competition from imports of cotton textiles. The Cotton Act of 1964 enables American manufacturers to buy cotton at the world market price, so they can compete in selling their products at home and abroad.

Immigration

In 1960, we proposed to—

"Adjust our immigration, nationality and refugee policies to eliminate discrimination and to enable members of scattered families abroad to be United with relatives already in our midst.

"The national-origins quota system of limiting immigration contradicts the founding principles of this nation. It is inconsistent with our belief in the rights of men."

The immigration law amendments proposed by the Administration, and now before Congress, by abolishing the national-origin quota system, will eliminate discrimination based upon race and place of birth and will facilitate the reunion of families.

The Cuban Refugee Program begun in 1961 has resettled over 81,000 refugees, who are now self-supporting members of 1,800 American communities. The Chinese Refugee Program, begun in 1962, provides for the admission to the United States of 12,000 Hong Kong refugees from Red China.

The Underdeveloped World

In 1960, we pledged—

"To the non-Communist nations of Asia, Africa, and Latin America: We shall create with you working partnerships based on mutual respect and understanding" and "will revamp and refocus the objectives, emphasis and allocation of our foreign assistance programs."

In 1961, the Administration created the Agency for International Development, combining the three separate agencies that had handled foreign assistance activities into an orderly and efficient instrument of national policy.

Since 1961, foreign aid has been conducted on a spartan, cost-conscious basis, with emphasis on self-help, reform and performance as conditions of American help.

These new policies are showing significant returns.

Since the beginning of the Marshall Plan in 1948, U.S. economic assistance has been begun and ended in 17 countries. In 14 other countries in Asia, Africa and Latin America, the transition to economic self-support is well under way, and U.S. assistance is now phasing out. In the 1965 AID program, 90 percent of economic assistance will go to just 25 countries.

In 1960, only 41 percent of aid-financed commodities were purchased in America. In 1964, under AID, 85 percent of all aid-financed commodities were U.S. supplied.

The foreign aid appropriation of $3.5 billion for fiscal year 1965 represents the smallest burden on U.S. resources that has been proposed since foreign aid began after World War II.

Since 1961, the United States has insisted that our allies in Europe and Japan must share responsibility in the field of foreign assistance, particularly to their former colonies. They have responded with major programs. Several nations now contribute a larger share of their gross national production to foreign assistance than does the United States.

The Alliance for Progress, launched at the Conference of Punta del Este in Uruguay in 1961, has emerged as the greatest undertaking of social reform and international cooperation in the history of the Western Hemisphere.

The American republics agreed to work together "To make the benefits of economic progress available to all citizens of all economic and social groups through a more equitable distribution of national income, raising more rapidly the income and standard of living of the needier sectors of the population, at the same time that a higher proportion of the national product is devoted to investment."

The results so far:

Major tax reform legislation has been adopted in eight countries.

Agrarian reform legislation has been introduced in twelve countries, and agricultural credit, technical assistance and resettlement projects are going forward in sixteen countries.

Fifteen countries have self-help housing programs,

and savings and loan legislation has been adopted by nine countries.

Private or public development banks have been established or are being established in eight countries, providing new sources of capital for the small businessman.

Education budgets have risen by almost 13 percent a year, and five million more children are going to school. U.S. aid has helped build 23,000 schoolrooms.

A Latin American school lunch program is feeding 10 million children at least one good meal every day, and the program will reach 12 million by the end of the year.

The Alliance for Progress has immeasurably strengthened the collective will of the nations of the Western Hemisphere to resist the massive efforts of Communist subversion that conquered Cuba in 1959 and then headed for the mainland.

In 1960, we urged—

". . . Continued economic assistance to Israel and the Arab peoples to help them raise their living standards.

"We pledge our best efforts for peace in the Middle East by seeking to prevent an arms race while guarding against the dangers of a military imbalance resulting from Soviet arms shipments."

In the period since that pledge was made the Middle East has come closer to peace and stability than at any time since World War II.

Economic and technical assistance to Israel and Arab nations continues at a high level, although with more and more emphasis on loans as against grants. The United States is determined to help bring the revolution in the technology of desalinization to the aid of the desert regions of this area.

The Atlantic Community

In 1960, we said—

"To our friends and associates in the Atlantic Community: We propose a broader partnership that goes beyond our common fears to recognize the depth and sweep of our common political, economic, and cultural interests."

In 1961, the United States ratified the conventions creating the Organization for Economic Cooperation and Development, a body made up of ourselves, Canada and 18 European states which carries forward on a permanent basis the detailed cooperation and mutual assistance that began with the Marshall Plan.

Since 1961, we have progressed in the building of mutual confidence, unity, and strength. NATO has frequently been used for consultation on foreign policy issues. Strong Atlantic unity emerged in response to

Soviet threats in Berlin and in Cuba. Current trade negotiations reflect the value of the Trade Expansion Act and the utility of arrangements for economic cooperation. NATO military forces are stronger in both nuclear and conventional weapons.

The United States has actively supported the proposal to create a multilateral, mix-manned, seaborne nuclear missile force which could give all NATO countries a direct share in NATO's nuclear deterrent without proliferating the number of independent, national nuclear forces.

The Communist World

In 1960, we said—

"To the rulers of the Communist World: We confidently accept your challenge to competition in every field of human effort.

"We believe your Communist ideology to be sterile, unsound, and doomed to failure. . . .

". . . We are prepared to negotiate with you whenever and wherever there is a realistic possibility of progress without sacrifice of principle.

"But we will use all the will, power, resources, and energy at our command to resist the further encroachment of Communism on freedom whether at Berlin, Formosa or new points of pressure as yet undisclosed."

Following the launching of Sputnik in 1957, the Soviet Union began a world-wide offensive. Russian achievements in space were hailed as the forerunners of triumph on Earth.

Now, seven years later, the Communist influence has failed in its efforts to win Africa. Of the 31 African nations formed since World War II, not one has chosen Communism.

Khrushchev had to back down on his threat to sign a peace treaty with East Germany. Access to West Berlin remains free.

In Latin America, the Alliance for Progress has begun to reduce the poverty and distress on which Communism breeds.

In Japan, where anti-American riots in 1960 prevented a visit from the President, relations with the United States have been markedly improved.

In the United Nations the integrity of the office of Secretary General was preserved despite the Soviet attack on it through the Troika proposal.

When Red China attacked India, the U.S. promptly came to India's aid with modern infantry supplies and equipment.

On the battlefield of the Cold War one engagement after another has been fought and won.

Frustrated in its plans to nibble away at country after country, the Soviet Union conceived a bold stroke designed to reverse the trend against it. With extreme stealth Soviet intermediate range and medium range offensive missiles were brought into Cuba in 1962.

Shortly after the missiles arrived in Cuba, and before any of them became operational, they were discovered and photographed by U.S. reconnaissance flights.

The U.S. response was carefully planned and prepared, and calmly, deliberately, but effectively executed. On October 22, President Kennedy called on the Soviet Union to dismantle and remove the weapons from Cuba. He ordered a strict quarantine on Cuba enforced by the U.S. Navy.

The Organization of American States acted swiftly and decisively by a unanimous vote of 20 to 0 to authorize strong measures, including the use of force, to ensure that the missiles were withdrawn from Cuba and not reintroduced.

At the end of a tense week Khrushchev caved in before this demonstration of Western power and determination. Soviet ships, closely observed by U.S. pilots, loaded all the missiles and headed back to Russia. U.S. firmness also compelled withdrawal of the IL-28 bombers.

A turning point of the Cold War had been reached.

The record of world events in the past year reflects the vigor and successes of U.S. policy:

Berlin, October–November 1963

Communist efforts to interfere with free Western access to Berlin were successfully rebuffed.

Venezuela, March 1964

Despite the threats and terror tactics of Castro-inspired agitators, over 90 percent of the people voted in the election that chose President Leoni to succeed Romulo Betancourt—the first democratic succession in that office in Venezuela's history.

Panama, 1964

Patient negotiation achieved a resumption of diplomatic relations, which had been severed after the riots in January; President Johnson achieved a dignified and an honorable solution of the crisis.

Vietnam, August 1964

Faced with sudden unprovoked attacks by Communist PT boats on American destroyers on the high sea, President Johnson ordered a sharp immediate retaliation on the hostile vessels and their supporting facilities.

Speaking on that occasion, the President said:

"Aggression—deliberate, willful and systematic aggression has unmasked its face to the world. The world remembers—the world must never forget—that aggression unchallenged is aggression unleashed.

"We of the United States have not forgotten.

"That is why we have answered this aggression with action."

Cuba, 1961–1964

Cuba and Castro have been virtually isolated in the Hemisphere.

Only 2 out of 20 OAS countries maintain diplomatic relations with Cuba.

Cuban trade with the Free World has dropped sharply from the 1958 level.

Free world shipping to Cuba has fallen sharply.

Isolation of Cuba by air has tightened greatly.

Hundreds of thousands of Cubans have left the island or have indicated their desire to come to the United States.

The Castro regime has been suspended from participation in the OAS.

The Cuban economy is deteriorating: the standard of living is 20 percent below pre-Castro levels, with many items rationed; industrial output is stagnant; sugar production is at the lowest level since the 1940's.

The United Nations

In 1960, we pledged—

"To our fellow members of the United Nations: we shall strengthen our commitments in this, our great continuing institution for conciliation and the growth of a world community."

Over the past four years the Administration has fulfilled this pledge as one of the central purposes of foreign policy.

During that time the United States has supported—and frequently led—efforts within the United Nations:

- to strengthen its capacity as peacekeeper and peacemaker—with the result that the UN remained on guard on armistice lines in Korea, Kashmir and the Middle East; preserved peace in the Congo, West New Guinea and Cyprus; provided a forum for the U.S. during crises in the Caribbean and the Gulf of Tonkin; began to develop a flexible call-up system for emergency peacekeeping forces; and moved toward a revival of the Security Council as the primary organ for peace and security without loss of the residual powers of the General Assembly.
- to discover and exploit areas of common interest for the reduction of world dangers and world tensions—with the result that the orbiting of weapons

of mass destruction has been banned and legal principles adopted for the use of outer space; projects of scientific cooperation in meteorology, oceanography, Antarctic exploration and peaceful uses of atomic energy have been promoted; and the search for further moves toward arms control has been pursued to supplement the limited test ban treaty.

- to further the work of the United Nations in improving the lot of mankind—with the result that the Decade of Development has been launched; the World Food Program undertaken; aid to children extended; projects to promote economic and social progress in the developing world have been expanded; and the impact of technology and world trade upon development has been explored.
- to maintain the integrity of the organization—its Charter and its Secretariat—with the result that the Troika proposal was defeated; the functions of the Secretary-General have been kept intact; the authority of the General Assembly to levy assessments for peacekeeping has been sustained despite attempted financial vetoes by Communist and other members.

In fulfilling its pledge to the United Nations, the Administration has helped to strengthen peace, to promote progress, and to find areas of international agreement and cooperation.

Economic Growth

In 1960, we said—

"The new Democratic Administration will confidently proceed to unshackle American enterprise and to free American labor, industrial leadership, and capital, to create an abundance that will outstrip any other system.

"We Democrats believe that our economy can and must grow at an average rate of 5 percent annually, almost twice as fast as our average annual rate since 1953. We pledge ourselves to policies that will achieve this goal without inflation."

In January 1961, the nation was at the bottom of the fourth recession of the postwar period—the third in the eight-year period, 1953–60. More men and women were out of work than at any time since the Great Depression of the 1930's. In February 1961, the unemployment rate was 6.8 percent, with a total of 5,705,000 unemployed.

Today we are in the midst of the longest peacetime expansion in our history. During the past 42 months of unbroken economic expansion:

Our economic growth rate has risen now to over 5 percent—twice the average rate for the 1953–60 period.

3,900,000 jobs have been added to the economy, and the unemployment rate was down in July 1964 to 4.9 percent.

The Gross National Product has risen by $120 billion in less than four years! No nation in peacetime history has ever added so much to its wealth in so short a time.

The average manufacturing worker's weekly earnings rose from $89 in January 1961, to $103 in July 1964—an increase of over 15 percent.

Industrial production has increased 28 percent; average operating rates in manufacturing have risen from 78 percent of capacity to 87 percent.

Profits after taxes have increased 62 percent—from an annual rate of $19.2 billion in early 1961 to an estimated $31.2 billion in early 1964.

Total private investment has increased by 43 percent—from an annual rate of $61 billion in early 1961 to $87 billion in the spring of 1964.

There are a million and a half more Americans at work today than there were a year ago.

Our present prosperity was brought about by the enterprise of American business, the skills of the American work force, and by wise public policies.

The provision in the Revenue Act of 1962 for a credit for new investment in machinery and equipment, and the liberalization of the depreciation allowance by administrative ruling, resulted in a reduction of $2.5 billion in business taxes.

The Revenue Act of 1964 cut individual income taxes by more than $9 billion, increasing consumer purchasing power by that amount; and corporate taxes were cut another $2.5 billion, with the effect of increasing investment incentives. Overall individual Federal income taxes were cut an average of 19 percent; taxpayers earning $3,000 or less received an average 40 percent cut.

The Temporary Extended Unemployment Compensation Act of 1961 provided $800 million to 2.8 million jobless workers who had exhausted their benefits.

The Area Redevelopment Act of 1961 has meant a $227 million Federal investment in economically hard-hit areas, creating 110,000 new jobs in private enterprise.

The Accelerated Public Works Act of 1962 added $900 million for urgently needed State and local government construction projects.

An End to Tight Money

In 1960, we proposed—

"As the first step in speeding economic growth, a Democratic President will put an end to the present high-interest, tight money policy.

"This policy has failed in its stated purpose to keep prices down. It has given us two recessions within five years, bankrupted many of our farmers, produced a record number of business failures, and added billions of dollars in unnecessary higher interest charges to government budgets and the cost of living."

Since 1961, we have maintained the free flow of credit so vital to industry, home buyers, and State and local governments.

Immediately, in February 1961, the Federal Housing Agency interest rate was cut from $5\frac{3}{4}$ percent to $5\frac{1}{2}$ percent. It is now down to $5\frac{1}{4}$ percent.

Today's home buyer will pay about $1,700 less for FHA-insured financing of a 30-year $15,000 home mortgage than he would have had he taken the mortgage in 1960.

Today after 42 months of expansion, conventional home mortgage rates are lower than they were in January 1961, in the midst of a recession. So are borrowing costs for our States and municipalities, and for long-term corporate issues.

Short-term interest rates have been brought into reasonable balance with interest rates abroad, reducing or eliminating incentives to place short-term funds abroad and thus reducing gold outflow.

We have prudently lengthened the average maturity of the Federal debt, in contrast to the steady shortening that characterized the 1950's.

Control of Inflation

In 1960, we asserted—

"The American consumer has a right to fair prices. We are determined to secure that right.

"A fair share of the gains from increasing productivity in many industries should be passed on to the consumer through price reductions."

Today, after 42 months of economic expansion, wholesale prices are lower than they were in January 1961, in the midst of a recession! The Wholesale Price Index was 101.0 in January 1961; in July 1964, it is 100.4.

The Consumer Price Index, which measures the price of goods and services families purchase, has been brought back to stability, averaging now less than a 1.3% increase per year—as compared, for example, with an increase rate about three times this large in the European common market countries.

Since January 1961, the increase in average after-tax family income has been twice the increase in price.

The Administration has established guideposts for price and wage movements alike, based primarily on productivity developments, and designed to protect the economy against inflation.

In the single year 1960, the overall balance of payments deficit reached $3.9 billion, and we lost $1.7 billion in gold. Now for 1964, the prospective balance of payments deficit has been cut to $2 billion, and the gold outflow has ceased.

Full Employment

In 1960, we reaffirmed our—

"support of full employment as a paramount objective of national policy."

In July 1964, total employment in the United States rose to the historic peak of 72,400,000 jobs. This represents an increase of 3,900,000 jobs in 42 months.

In the past twelve months, total civilian employment has increased by 1,600,000 jobs, and non-farm employment by 1,700,000. Most of this job expansion has occurred in the past eight months.

In July 1964, the jobless total was one-half million below a year ago, and was at its lowest July level since 1959.

In July, 1964, the overall unemployment rate was 4.9%—compared with 6.5% in January 1961; and the jobless rate for men who are heads of families was down to 2.7%.

There have been more than a million full-time jobs added to the private profit sector of the economy in the past 12 months. This is the largest increase in any one-year period in the past decade.

We have brought ourselves now within reach of the full employment objective.

Aid to Depressed Areas

In 1960, we recognized that—

"General economic measures will not alone solve the problems of localities which suffer some special disadvantage. To bring prosperity to these depressed areas and to enable them to make their full contribution to the national welfare, specially directed action is needed."

The Area Redevelopment Administration was created in 1961 to help depressed areas organize their human and material resources for economic growth. Since its establishment, the ARA has:

Approved 512 financial assistance projects involving a Federal investment of $243.5 million.

Created, in partnership with local government, private workers and other investors, 118,000 new jobs in private enterprise.

Provided retraining programs, with tuition and subsistence, for 37,327 jobless workers, equipping them with new skills to fill available jobs in their areas.

In 1961, Congress authorized $900 million for the Accelerated Public Works Program to speed construction of urgently needed public facilities and increase employment in areas which had failed to recover from previous recessions.

Between October 1962, when the first appropriations were made available, and April 1, 1964, 7,762 projects, involving an estimated 2,500,000 man-months of employment, were approved.

In early 1961, there were 101 major areas in the United States in which unemployment was 6 percent or more, discounting seasonal or temporary factors. By July 1964, this number had been cut two-thirds, to a total of 35.

The concept of "depressed areas" has been broadened in these $3\frac{1}{2}$ years to include clear recognition of the inequity and waste of poverty wherever it exists, and in the Economic Opportunity Act of 1964 the nation has declared, in historic terms, a War on Poverty.

Title I of the Economic Opportunity Act creates the Job Corps, Work–Training programs, and Work–Study programs to provide useful work for about 400,000 young men and women. Job Corps volunteers will receive work and vocational training, part of which will involve conservation work in rural areas. The Work–Training, or Neighborhood Youth Corps program, is open to young persons living at home, including those who need jobs in order to remain in school. The Work–Study programs will enable youth from poor families to earn enough income to enable them to attend college.

Title II of the Act authorized $340 million for the Community Action programs to stimulate urban and rural communities to mobilize their resources to combat poverty through programs designed especially to meet local needs.

Title III provides for special programs to combat poverty in rural areas, including loans up to $1,500 for low-income farmers, and loans up to $2,500 for families, to finance non-agricultural enterprises—which will enable such families to supplement their incomes. This section of the law provides funds for housing, sanitation, education, and day care of children of migrant farm workers.

Title IV of the Act provides for loans up to $25,000 for small businesses to create jobs for the long-term unemployed.

Title V of the Act provides constructive work experience and other needed training to persons who are unable to support or care for themselves or their families.

The Report of the President's Appalachian Regional Commission, submitted to President Johnson in April 1964, proposed a wide-ranging development program.

The Appalachian Redevelopment Act, now before Congress, provides for a more than $1.1 billion investment in needed basic facilities in the area, together with a regional organization to help generate the full development potential of the human and material resources of this mountain area.

Registration and regulation of migrant labor crew chiefs has been provided to require that crew chiefs or labor brokers, who act on behalf of domestic migrant labor and operate across state lines, shall be registered, show financial responsibility, and meet certain requirements as to moral character and honest dealing with their clients.

Discrimination in Employment

In 1960, we insisted that—

"The right to a job requires action to break down artificial and arbitrary barriers to employment based on age, race, sex, religion, or national origin."

The great Civil Rights Act of 1964 is the strongest and most important law against discrimination in employment in the history of the United States.

It states unequivocally that "It shall be an unlawful employment practice for an employer . . . an employment agency . . . or a labor organization" to discriminate against any person because of his or her "race, color, religion, sex, or national origin."

On March 6, 1961, President Kennedy issued an Executive Order establishing the President's Committee on Equal Employment Opportunity to combat racial discrimination in the employment policies of Government agencies and private firms holding Government contracts. Then–Vice President Johnson, in his capacity as Chairman of the new Committee, assumed personal direction of this program.

As a consequence of the enforcement of the Executive Order, not only has discrimination been eliminated in the Federal Government, but strong affirmative measures have been taken to extend meaningful equality of opportunity to compete for Federal employment to all citizens.

The private employers of 8,076,422 men and women, and trade unions with 12,500,000 members, have signed public agreements establishing non-discriminatory practices.

The Equal Pay Act of 1963 guarantees equal pay to women doing the same work as men, by requiring employers who are covered by the Fair Labor Standards Act to pay equal wages for equal work, regardless of the sex of their workers.

Executive Order 11141, issued by President Johnson on February 12, 1964, establishes for the first time in history a public policy that "contractors and subcontractors engaged in the performance of Federal contracts shall not, in connection with the employment, advancement, or discharge of their employees, or in connection with the terms, conditions, or privileges of their employment, discriminate against persons because of their age."

Collective Bargaining

In 1960, we pledged—

"an affirmative labor policy which will encourage free collective bargaining through the growth and development of free and responsible unions."

These have been good years for labor–management relations. Time lost from strikes is at the lowest point in history.

The President's Advisory Committee on Labor Management Policy, made up of distinguished leaders of business and trade unions, has spoken out consistently in favor of creative and constructive solutions to common problems.

Executive Order 10988, issued by President Kennedy on January 17, 1962, extended the rights of union recognition to Federal employees—a goal which some employee organizations had been trying to reach for three quarters of a century.

In the spring of 1964, under President Johnson's personal leadership, the five-year-old railroad dispute that would have resulted in a critical nationwide strike, was at last ended—by free collective bargaining. A cause many thought lost was won; industrial self-government was saved from a disastrous setback.

Planning for Automation

In 1960, we proposed to: "provide the government leadership necessary to insure that the blessings of automation do not become burdens of widespread unemployment. For the young and the technologically displaced workers, we will provide the opportunity for training and retraining that equips them for jobs to be filled."

The Manpower Development and Training Act of 1962 provides for the training or retraining of unemployed or underemployed people, particularly those threatened or displaced by technological advances. The 1963 amendments to the Act emphasize the problem of youth employment.

In the two years of the administration of this program, training projects for 240,471 persons have been approved, and more than 54,000 persons have completed their training.

Under the Manpower Development and Training Act an active manpower policy is being developed to keep the nation ahead of the problems of automation.

Congress has now enacted, in August 1964, legislation creating a National Commission on Technology, Automation and Economic Progress to undertake a searching inquiry into the problems created by automation, and means by which they can be prevented or solved.

In its own activities, the Federal Government has taken full account of human considerations in instituting technological developments.

Minimum Wages

In 1960, we pledged—

"To raise the minimum wage to $1.25 an hour and to extend coverage to several million workers not now covered."

The Fair Labor Standards Act Amendments of 1961 raised the minimum wage to $1.25 over a three-year period, and extended the coverage of the Act to 3.6 million additional workers.

The Administration has proposed further amendments to the Fair Labor Standards Act, which are now before the Congress, and which would extend minimum wage coverage to nearly three quarters of a million workers in laundry and dry cleaning establishments. Overtime coverage would be extended to an additional 2.6 million workers.

It has proposed a Fringe Benefit amendment to the Bacon–Davis law to provide that the cost of fringe benefits should be included in the definition of "prevailing wage" under the Bacon–Davis law, so that wage rates required in government construction contracts will be in accord with prevailing practice.

Agriculture

In 1960, we said—

"In every way we will seek to help the men, women, and children whose livelihood comes from the soil to achieve better housing, education, and decent earnings and working conditions."

This is the record:

Total net farm income in 1961–63 averaged nearly a billion dollars a year higher than in 1960.

Total net income per farm was 18 percent higher in 1963 than in 1960.

Farm purchasing power, or gross farm income, rose from $37.9 billion in 1960 to nearly $42 billion in 1963.

Percent of family income spent for food today has declined. In 1960, 20 percent of disposable family income was spent for food. This has now been reduced to less than 19 percent.

Grain surpluses have been brought down to manageable levels; wheat surpluses this year will be the lowest since 1958, and feed grains have been reduced from 80 to 70 million tons.

Reduction of wheat and feed grain surpluses from their 1960 levels to present levels has resulted in an accumulated savings of about a quarter of a billion dollars in storage, transportation, interest and other costs.

Total farm exports have increased 35 percent in 4 years, and have reached a record high in fiscal 1964 of $6.1 billion.

Credit resources administered by the Farmers Home Administration are up 141 percent over 1960, and are averaging now $687 million a year.

Commodity programs to strengthen the farm income structure and reach the goal of parity of income in every aspect of American agriculture. We also cite the parity program providing American cotton to American factories and processes at the same price at which they are exported.

The Rural Areas Development program has helped create an estimated 125,000 new jobs, and more than 12,000 projects in the process of approval will provide new employment for as many as 200,000 persons.

Participation in the Agricultural Conservation Program has increased 20 percent since 1960.

More than 20,000 farmers have received technical help to develop recreation as an income-making "crop" on land which had been producing surpluses.

Over 600 rural communities have been aided in providing modern water services.

During the winter of 1964, a special lunch program was instituted for 315 schools and 12,000 children in rural areas where families have extremely low incomes.

Since January 1, 1961, $1.1 billion in electric loans has been made by the Rural Electrification Administration, to rural electric cooperatives, or some $350 million more than in the previous $3\frac{1}{2}$ years. Improved service, as a result, has meant customer savings of $7.5 million a year.

American farmers, in 1964, have protected crop investments totaling $500.5 million with Federal All-Risk Crop Insurance—more than double the amount of insurance in force three years ago, and an all-time record.

Soil and water conservation activities in the past $3\frac{1}{2}$ years have shown a constant upward trend in their contributions to the physical, social and economic welfare of rural areas.

289 new small upstream watershed projects were authorized.

3,000 local soil and water conservation districts have updated their long-range programs to reflect the broadened concepts of economic development.

The Great Plains Conservation Program has been extended for 10 years and 36 counties have been added to the program.

In June 1964, Congress authorized the creation of a National Commission on Food Marketing to investigate the operation of the food industry from producer to consumer.

On January 24, 1961, President Kennedy established by executive order, the Food for Peace program to utilize America's agricultural abundance "to promote the interests of peace . . . and to play an important role in helping to provide a more adequate diet for peoples all around the world."

In the last $3\frac{1}{2}$ years, over $5 billion worth of surplus farm commodities went overseas under Public Law 480 programs. This is one and one-half billion dollars more than during the previous $3\frac{1}{2}$ years.

Small Business

In 1960, we pledged—

"Action to aid small business in obtaining credit and equity capital at reasonable rates.

"Protection of the public against the growth of monopoly.

"A more equitable share of government contracts to small and independent business."

Through liberalizing amendments to the Small Business Investment Act in 1961 and 1964, and special tax considerations, the investment of equity capital and long-term loan funds in small businesses has been greatly accelerated by privately owned and operated small business investment companies licensed under that Act. Moreover, since January 1961, over 21,000 small businesses have obtained SBA business loans, totalling over $1.14 billion, as a result of liberalized and simplified procedures.

The Federal Trade Commission has stepped up its activities to promote free and fair competition in business, and to safeguard the consuming public against both monopolistic and deceptive practices.

The reorganized Antitrust Division of the Department of Justice has directed special emphasis to price fixing, particularly on consumer products, by large companies who distribute through small companies. These include eyeglasses, salad oil, flour, cosmetics, swimsuits, bread, milk, and even sneakers.

Since January 1961, some 166,000 government contracts worth $6.2 billion have been set aside for small

business. In the preceding $3\frac{1}{2}$ years there were 77,838 contracts set aside, with a worth of $2.9 billion.

Housing

In 1960 we proposed—

"To make possible the building of 2,000,000 homes a year in wholesome neighborhoods, the home building industry should be aided by special mortgage assistance, with low interest rates, long-term mortgage periods and reduced down payments.

"There will still be need for a substantial low-rent public housing program authorizing as many units as local communities require and are prepared to build."

The Housing Act of 1961 provides many of the necessary new and improved tools for providing housing for low- and moderate-income families, and for housing for the elderly.

For the $3\frac{1}{2}$-year period ending June 30, 1964, some 5.3 million new units of public and private housing have been built at a cost of approximately $65 billion. The construction rate has risen above 1.5 million units a year, with an annual output of over $20 billion, and we are moving close now to the goal of 2 million a year.

Since January 1961, nearly 400 local housing authorities have been formed to provide housing for low-income families. More than 100,000 new units have been approved for construction, at an annual rate about three times that of 1960.

The annual rate of grant assistance for Urban Renewal has risen from $262 million per year (1956 through 1961) to a rate of better than $630 million during the past 12 months.

In the past $3\frac{1}{2}$ years, more than 750 new urban renewal transactions have been approved, equal to nearly 90 percent of the number approved for the entire period from 1949 to 1960.

Cities with community Urban Renewal programs jumped from a cumulative total of seven in December 1960 to 118 by mid-1964.

To house families whose income is not quite low enough to qualify for public housing, a new rental housing program providing a "below market" interest rate (currently $3\frac{7}{8}$%) insured by FHA, has been made available. Mortgage purchase funds have been allocated for about 78,000 such rental units.

Reflecting the fuller recognition of the special equities and needs of older people:

FHA mortgage insurance written on housing projects for the elderly since 1961 has provided more than 3 times as many units as were being provided prior to that time.

Low-rent public housing under Federal assistance is being provided senior citizens at an annual rate more than twice that for 1960.

Direct loan authorizations for housing for the elderly increased from $50 million in 1961 to $275 million in 1963.

Maximum loan amounts have been increased to 100% of development cost.

The Housing Act of 1961 expanded and strengthened the Federal program in this area.

The Senior Citizens Housing Act of 1962 moved us another long step forward.

Applications for the provision of nursing homes increased from 30 in January 1961 to more than 580 by the middle of 1964, involving more than 50,000 beds for community nursing homes.

Assistance has been given for more than 1,000 college housing projects including housing for more than 290,000 students and faculty, plus dining halls and other school facilities.

The 1963 Executive Order on Equal Opportunity in Housing assures that the benefits of Federal housing programs and assistance are available without discrimination as to race, color, creed or national origin.

Health

In 1960, we proposed to—

"Provide medical care benefits for the aged as part of the time-tested Social Security system.

"Step up medical research on the major killers and crippling diseases.

"Expand and improve the Hill–Burton hospital construction program.

"Federal aid for construction, expanding and modernizing schools of medicine, dentistry, nursing and public health.

"Greatly increased Federal support for psychiatric research and training and community mental health programs."

More health legislation has been enacted during the past $3\frac{1}{2}$ years than during any other period in American history.

The Community Health Services and Facilities Act of 1961 has made possible 149 projects for testing and demonstrating new or improved services in nursing homes, home care services, central information and referral centers; and providing additional personnel to serve the chronically ill and aged. It has also provided additional Federal funds for the construction of nursing homes.

The Hill–Burton Amendments of 1964, extend the program of Federal grants for construction of hospitals, public health centers, long-term facilities, rehabilitation facilities and diagnostic or treatment centers for five additional years. For the first time provision is made for the modernization and renovation of hospitals and health facilities. Funds for the construction of nursing homes and other long-term care facilities are substantially increased.

The Mental Retardation Facilities and Community Mental Health Construction Act of 1963, authorized grants of $150,000,000 to States for constructing community Mental Health Centers, which emphasize the new approach to the care of the mentally ill, centered on care and treatment in the patients' home communities. Thirty-six States have already budgeted more than 75% of their share of Federal funds for planning these new systems.

The Maternal and Child Health and Mental Retardation Planning Amendments of 1963, along with the Mental Retardation Facilities and Community Mental Health Construction Act of 1963, authorized a broad program to prevent, treat, and ameliorate mental retardation. The program provides States and communities needed research, manpower developments, and facilities for health, education rehabilitation, and vocational services to the retarded.

As part of the Federal Government's program to employ the mentally retarded in suitable Federal jobs, the State rehabilitation agencies are certifying persons as qualified for specific suitable Federal jobs. A rising number of placements already made in Federal installations all over the country constitutes an encouraging start.

The current need for another 200,000 qualified teachers for the estimated 6 million handicapped children of school age, has been recognized in legislation authorizing grants-in-aid for the training of professional personnel.

Other legislation provides funds for training teachers of the deaf.

A 1962 amendment to the Public Health Act authorizes a new program of project grants to help meet critical health needs of domestic migratory workers and their families through establishment of family health service clinics.

Forty-nine projects in 24 States have received grants to assist an estimated 300,000 migrant workers.

One out of every ten migrant laborers is estimated to have received some health services through these projects.

The National Institute of Child Health and Human Development, authorized in 1962, is now supporting research and training in eight major areas.

The National Institute of General Medical Sciences,

also authorized in 1962, gives recognition to the significance of research training in the sciences basic to medicine. Two thousand research projects are currently being supported.

A $2 million Radiological Health Grant Program was established in 1962 to provide matching grants to assist States in assuming responsibility for adequate radiation control and protection. During Fiscal Year 1964, forty-nine States and Puerto Rico and the Virgin Islands participated.

After two years of scientific evaluation of research and findings, the Report of the Surgeon General's Advisory Committee on Smoking and Health was released in January 1964, calling attention to the health hazards of smoking. An information clearinghouse and a public education program directed toward preventing young people from acquiring the smoking habit are being developed.

A Program for the Aging

In 1960, we proposed to—

"End the neglect of our older citizens. They deserve lives of usefulness, dignity, independence, and participation. We shall assure them not only health care, but employment for those who want to work, decent housing, and recreation."

The Social Security Act Amendments of 1961 broadened benefits to 5.3 million persons, increased minimum benefits for retired workers from $33 to $40 per month, permitted men as well as women to begin collecting reduced benefits at age 62.

The Social Security program now provides $1.3 billion in benefits each month to 19.5 million persons. One out of every ten Americans receives a Social Security check every month.

The Welfare and Pension Plans Disclosure Act Amendments of 1962 put "enforcement teeth" into this measure, protecting workers' assets in pension programs.

The Housing Act of 1961 increased the scope of Federal housing aids for the elderly by raising from $50 million to $125 million the authorization for low-interest-rate direct loans. In 1962, this was raised further to $225 million and in 1963 to $275 million.

Insurance written by the Federal Housing Administration for mortgage insurance for the elderly since 1961 provides three times as many units as during the preceding Administration.

Low-rent public housing under Federal assistance has been provided senior citizens at an annual rate more than twice that for 1960.

The Community Health Services and Facilities Act of 1961 raised the ceiling on appropriations for the construction of nursing homes under the Hill–Burton legislation from $10 million to $20 million; and authorized $10 million per year for a 5-year program of special project grants for the development of new or improved methods of providing health services outside the hospital for the chronically ill or aged.

Executive Order 11114, issued by President Johnson on February 12, 1964, establishes for the first time the policy of non-discrimination in employment based on age by Federal contractors.

Welfare

In 1960, we proposed to—

"Permit workers who are totally and permanently disabled to retire at any age, removing the arbitrary requirement that the worker be 50 years of age.

"Amend the law so that after six months of total disability, a worker will be eligible for disability benefits, with restorative services to enable the worker to return to work.

"Continued support of legislation for the rehabilitation of physically handicapped persons and improvement of employment opportunities for them.

"Persons in need who are inadequately protected by social insurance are cared for by the States and local communities under public assistance programs. The Federal Government, which now shares the cost of aid to some of these, should share in all, and benefits should be made available without regard to residence.

"Uniform minimum standards throughout the nation for coverage, duration, and amount of unemployment insurance benefits.

"Legislation which will guarantee to women equality of rights under the law, including equal pay for equal work.

"The Child Welfare Program and other services already established under the Social Security Act should be expanded. Federal leadership is required in the nationwide campaign to prevent and control juvenile delinquency.

"A Federal bureau of inter-group relations to help solve problems of discrimination in housing, education, employment and community opportunities in general. The bureau would assist in the solution of problems arising from the resettlement of immigrants and migrants within our own country, and in resolving religious, social and other tensions where they arise."

The 1961 Public Assistance Amendments extended aid for the first time to families with dependent children in which the parent is unemployed. Currently, 18 States have adopted this program. Aid is being provided to about 75,000 families with nearly 280,000 children.

The food stamp program is providing improved purchasing powers and a better diet for families and persons receiving general assistance.

The 1962 Public Welfare amendments provide the authority and financial resources for a new approach to the problems of prolonged dependency and some of the special needs of children.

Under these enactments and related provisions: 49 States have now qualified for increased Federal financial aid to provide help to families with economic and social problems, and to assist families dependent on public assistance back to economic independence.

9 pilot projects have been initiated to help children stay in school.

41 demonstration projects have been designed to improve public assistance operations and to find ways of helping low-income families and individuals to become independent.

18,000 unemployed fathers in needy families are currently on community work and training projects.

Three million children are now covered by the program of aid to families with dependent children; and under the 1962 amendments these children receive, in addition to financial assistance, other needed help toward normal growth and development.

46 States now have approved plans for day care services.

Grants for research and demonstrations in child welfare were first awarded in 1962, and 62 projects have since been approved.

Starting for the first time in 1963, grants for training child welfare workers have been made to 58 institutions of higher learning.

Approximately 453,000 older persons received medical assistance under the Kerr–Mills program in Fiscal Year 1964.

The Temporary Extended Unemployment Compensation Act of 1961 provided 13 additional weeks of benefits to the long-term unemployed. 2.8 million jobless workers received $800 million in assistance.

The Juvenile Delinquency and Youth Offenses Control Act of 1961 made possible the establishment of training centers at 12 universities. By the end of Fiscal Year 1964, the program will have reached 12,500 trainees for work in delinquency prevention and control.

The Equal Pay Act of 1963 and the work of the President's Commission on the Status of Women, which reported to the President that same year, were events of historic importance in the struggle for equal opportunity and full partnership for women. The inclusion of women in the employment provisions of the Civil Rights Act of 1964 makes equality in employment at long last the law of the land.

Title X of the Civil Rights Act of 1964 establishes a Community Relations Service "to provide assistance to communities and persons therein in resolving disputes, disagreements, or difficulties relating to discriminatory practices based on race, color, or national origin.

Education

In 1960, we pledged—

"We believe that America can meet its educational obligations only with generous Federal financial support, within the traditional framework of local control. The assistance will take the form of Federal grants to States for educational purposes they deem most pressing, including classroom construction and teachers' salaries. It will include aid for the construction of academic facilities as well as dormitories at colleges and universities.

"We pledge further Federal support for all phases of vocational education for youth and adults; for libraries and adult education; for realizing the potential of educational television; and for exchange of students and teachers with other nations.

"As part of a broader concern for young people we recommend establishment of a Youth Conservation Corps, to give underprivileged young people a rewarding experience in a healthful environment."

The Higher Education Facilities Act of 1963 provides $1.2 billion for college construction over a three-year period. Over 2,000 institutions are eligible to benefit from its provisions in helping them meet current enrollment increases of 350,000 students each year.

The Health Professions Educational Assistance Act of 1963 will increase the number of professional health personnel through construction grants for health teaching facilities, and through low-interest student loans to assist up to 10,000 students of medicine, dentistry, or osteopathy to pay for their high-cost education.

The Vocational Education Act of 1963 authorizes a $956 million increase in Federal support for vocational education over the next five fiscal years—1964 through 1968. It is estimated that 7,000,000 students will be enrolled in vocational education in 1968, an increase of about 3,000,000 over present annual enrollment.

Legislation approved in 1963, which increased authorization for loans to needy students for college education, will mean that in the coming school year approximately 280,000 students will be borrowing about $142 million from the loan funds to help pay for their higher education, as compared with 115,450 students borrowing $50,152,000 in 1960.

In the last three fiscal years, there have been grants of $153.1 million in Federal funds to the States for purchases of equipment and materials, and remodeling classrooms to strengthen instruction in science, mathematics, and modern foreign languages.

A $32 million program of grants to help establish non-commercial educational television stations was approved in 1962. Thirty-seven grants have been approved, totaling $6.1 million—18 for new stations and 19 for expansion.

The Library Services and Construction Act of 1964 broadened Federal aid to cover urban as well as rural areas, and to provide construction grants in addition to other library services. The new legislation increased the authorization for Federal aid to develop libraries from $7.5 million to the present level of $25 million and included a new program of assistance for public library construction, with an appropriation for Fiscal Year 1965 of $30 million.

The Youth Conservation Corps envisioned by the 1960 proposal is provided for under Title I of the Economic Opportunity Act of 1964.

Natural Resources

In 1960, we said—

"A thin layer of earth, a few inches of rain, and a blanket of air makes human life possible on our planet.

"Sound public policy must assure that these essential resources will be available to provide the good life for our children and future generations."

After the 1960 election President Kennedy and President Johnson implemented this platform by a whole series of new conservation policies and programs, some of which emanated from the first White House Conference on Conservation called by any President since the 1908 conference called by President Theodore Roosevelt.

During this Administration two historic conservation measures were enacted. These were:

The Wilderness Bill and the Land and Water Conservation Fund Bill which will together do more to help conserve outdoor America than any legislation passed in a generation.

In addition to this landmark legislation new emphasis has been placed on science as the modern midwife of conservation, and new impetus has been given across the board in the conservation of natural resources.

In the Field of Water Conservation

Twenty-one new major water resources projects have been authorized or started in the West;

A highwater mark has been achieved in the annual level of national investment in water resource projects;

The saline water conversion effort has been, quadru-

pled, and should achieve a dramatic cost-break-through during the next Administration.

In Electric Power

Ending 16 years of argument, a bold plan was developed under President Johnson's personal leadership to interconnect the electric power systems of the Pacific Northwest and the Southwest, thus providing benefits for power users in 11 Western States; under this plan, construction will soon begin on the first direct current long-distance lines in the United States, stretching all the way from the Columbia River to Los Angeles—and a new era of public and private power cooperation will commence.

Federal hydroelectric generating capacity has been increased by 2,600,000 kilowatts, and 5,150,000 kilowatts of non-Federal capacity has been licensed by the Federal Power Commission.

3,350 miles of vital transmission lines have been added to Federal systems and about 25,000 miles of new transmission lines have also been built by non-Federal power systems.

The FCC has conducted a National Power Survey to encourage both public and private power companies to join in power pools which are bringing lower-cost electricity to consumers throughout the nation.

The world's largest atomic electric power plant (at Hanford, Washington) was funded and will soon be generating as much power as two Bonneville dams.

Federal REA loans have made it possible to open up the lignite coal fields of the Dakotas, and to exploit the coal fields of Western Colorado.

In addition, the Congress authorized the Delaware Basin Compact to permit the multi-purpose development of that river, and the Senate ratified the Columbia River Treaty which enables the joint U.S.–Canadian development of the full potential of that great river to begin later this year.

In Outdoor Recreation

The Congress created three superb new national seashores at Cape Cod (Massachusetts), Padre Island (Texas) and Point Reyes (California).

Pioneering a new park concept, Ozark Rivers National Riverway (Missouri) was established as the first river preservation national park in the nation, and 12 other major new additions to the Park System were recommended for action by future Congresses,

A Bureau of Outdoor Recreation was created. As a vital part of the war on poverty, during the next year, 20 thousand young Americans will set to work in conservation camps across the land tackling the big backlog of work in the land and water areas owned by all of the people.

In the Conservation and Development of Mineral Resources

Research helped coal production surge upward, and there were initiated a series of action steps (including activation of the huge Rifle, Colorado, research center) which will lead to the orderly development of the vast oil shale resources of the Colorado plateau.

For Wildlife

Enactment of the Wetlands Bill of 1961 made it possible to create more new Waterfowl Refuges (27) than during any previous four-year period in our history.

The Clean Air Act of 1963 is already providing the first full-scale attack on the air pollution problems that blight living conditions in so many of our cities.

Enactment of the Federal Water Pollution Control Act of 1961 launched the first massive attack on this conservation problem which has already resulted in 1,300 municipal waste treatment plants and the approval of projects that have improved the water quality in 18,000 miles of streams that provide water for 22 million people.

Cities and Their Suburbs

In 1960, we declared—

"A new Democratic administration will expand Federal programs to aid urban communities to clear their slums, dispose of their sewage, educate their children, transport suburban commuters to and from their jobs, and combat juvenile delinquency."

The Housing Act of 1961 marked the beginning of a new era of Federal commitment to the problems of a nation in which three-fourths of the population has come to live in urban areas.

Under that Act, funds available for urban planning grants were increased by $55 million and a new $50 million Federal grant program to assist localities in the acquisition of permanent open-space land to be used as parks and playgrounds was established.

The Housing Act of 1961 and the Area Redevelopment Act of 1961 authorized public facilities loans of $600 million.

The Juvenile Delinquency and Youth Offenses Control Act of 1961 launched a broad attack on youth problems by financing demonstration projects, training personnel in delinquency work, and providing technical assistance for community youth programs.

In 1960, we pledged "Federal aid for comprehensive metropolitan transportation programs, including bus and rail mass transit, commuter railroads as well as highway programs and construction of civil airports."

The Housing Act of 1961 launched the first efforts to help metropolitan and other urban areas solve their mass transportation problems; $75 million in loans and demonstration grants were provided to States and localities to construct and improve mass transportation systems.

The Urban Mass Transportation Act of 1964 establishes a new long-range program for this purpose and authorizes $375 million in Federal grants, over 3 years, for capital construction and improvement which local transit systems cannot otherwise finance.

Transportation

In 1960, we observed—

"Over the past seven years we have watched the steady weakening of the Nation's transportation system, and we noted the need for 'a national transportation policy.'"

The National Transportation policy was enunciated in the first Presidential message ever to be sent to the Congress dealing solely with transportation.

The Highway Act of 1961 resolved the nagging problem of financing the 41,000-mile interstate highway program, and the finished construction rate has almost doubled.

The Federal Maritime Commission has been established as an independent agency to guard against prejudice or discrimination harmful to the growth of U.S. World Trade.

The Maritime Administration, U.S. Department of Commerce, was set up to give its full attention to promoting a vigorous policy of strengthening and modernizing our merchant fleet. Seventy big modern cargo and cargo–passenger ships have been added to the U.S. merchant fleet. The *Savannah*, the world's first nuclear-powered merchant ship, is now on her first foreign voyage.

The far-reaching decision has been made that the United States will design and build a supersonic air transport plane—and thereby maintain our leadership position in international aviation. Congress has provided $60 million for the development of detailed designs. Twenty airlines already have placed orders.

On August 13, President Johnson signed a new highway bill to provide better primary and secondary highways on a 50–50 basis with the states. In addition, it will support needed efforts to improve forest highways, public land roads and national park roads.

Science

In 1960, we declared—

"We will recognize the special role of our Federal

Government in support of basic and applied research," mentioning in particular Space, Atomic Energy, and Oceanography.

Space

Since 1961, the United States has pressed vigorously forward with a 10-year, $35-billion national space program for clear leadership in space exploration, space use, and all important aspects of space science and technology.

Already this program has enabled the United States to challenge the early Soviet challenge in space booster power and to effectively counter the Soviet bid for recognition as the world's leading nation in science and technology.

In the years 1961–1964, the United States has

Successfully flown the Saturn I rocket, putting into orbit the heaviest payloads of the space age to date.

Moved rapidly forward with much more powerful launch vehicles, the Saturn IB and the Saturn V. The Saturn IB, scheduled to fly in 1966, will be able to orbit a payload of 16 tons; and Saturn V, scheduled to fly in 1967 or 1968, will be able to orbit 120 tons or send 45 tons to the moon or 35 tons to Mars or Venus.

Mastered the difficult technology of using liquid hydrogen as a space rocket fuel in the Centaur upper-stage rocket and the Saturn I second-stage—assuring American leadership in space science and manned space flight in this decade.

Successfully completed six manned space flights in Project Mercury, acquiring 54 hours of space flight experience.

Successfully flight-tested the two-man Gemini spacecraft and Titan II space rocket so that manned Gemini flights can begin late in 1964 or early in 1965.

Developed the three-man Apollo spacecraft which will be able to spend up to two months in Earth orbit, operate out to a quarter of a million miles from Earth, and land our first astronaut explorers on the moon.

Taken all actions to conduct a series of manned space flights in the Gemini and Apollo programs which will give the United States some 5,000 man-hours of flight experience in Earth orbit, develop U.S. capabilities for rendezvous and joining of spacecraft in orbit, and prove out man's ability to perform valuable missions during long stays in space.

Made man's first close-up observations of another planet during the highly successful Mariner II fly-by of Venus.

Obtained the first close-up pictures of the moon, taken and relayed to earth by Ranger VII.

Initiated an ambitious long-range program for scientific investigations in space utilizing large, versatile spacecraft called Orbiting Observatories for geophysical, solar and stellar studies.

Operated the world's first weather satellites (Tiros).

Set up, under the Communications Satellite Act of 1962, the Communications Satellite Corporation, which is well on the way to establishing a global satellite communications system to provide reliable, low-cost telephone, telegraph, and television services to all parts of the world.

In short, the United States has matched rapid progress in manned space flight with a balanced program for scientific investigations in space, practical uses of space, and advanced research and technological pioneering to assure that the new challenges of space in the next decade can also be met, and U.S. leadership maintained.

Atomic Energy

The number of civilian nuclear power plants has increased from 3 to 14 since January 1961; and now the advent of economic nuclear power provides utilities a wider choice of competitive power sources in many sections of the country.

The world's largest nuclear power reactor, the Atomic Energy Commission's Production Reactor near Richland, Washington, achieved a controlled, self-sustained nuclear reaction on December 31, 1963.

The first deep-sea anchored, automatic weather station powered by nuclear energy has gone into unattended operation in the Gulf of Mexico, and the first lighthouse powered by nuclear energy flashes now in Chesapeake Bay.

Nuclear energy was extended to space for the first time in 1961. Compact nuclear generators supplied part of the power for instruments in two satellites, and in 1963 provided all of the power needs of two other satellites.

Vigorous support has been given to basic research in atomic energy. The world's highest energy accelerator, the AGS, has come into productive operation.

Oceanography

For the first time in history the United States is building a fleet expressly designed for oceanographic research. Since 1961, 29 ships have been completed or are currently under construction. Shoreside facilities and training programs have been established as part of a major government-wide effort, begun in 1961, to capture the enormous potential rewards of research in this area which until now have been almost as remote and inaccessible as space itself.

Government Operations

"We shall reform the processes of government in all branches—executive, legislative, and judicial. We will clean out corruption and conflicts of interest, and improve government services."

This Administration has brought the personnel, morale, ethics, and performance of the Federal service to a point of high excellence. To accomplish this transformation it made improvements in a broad range of activities affecting the operation of the government.

The conflict of interest laws were strengthened by the first major revision in a century. The comprehensive new law eliminates ambiguities and inconsistencies in existing laws, and increases the range of government matters in which conflict of interest is prohibited. In addition, President Kennedy issued an Executive Order which established more rigid standards of conduct for Federal officials and employees.

The regulatory agencies were made more effective by reorganization programs and by the appointment of highly qualified officials dedicated to protecting the public interest.

The Department of Justice has cracked down effectively on organized crime under new anti-racketeering statutes, has uncovered and prosecuted important foreign spies, and has made progress toward more effective procedures for protecting the rights of poor defendants to bail and counsel.

Federal Employee Organizations, many of which have existed for over half a century, were at last extended formal recognition under Executive Order 10988, issued by President Kennedy.

The Federal Pay Raise Act of 1964 updated the pay structure for Federal employees on a basis of equal salary rates for comparable levels of work in private industry. Completing the reforms initiated in the Act of 1962, it provided for long-needed increases in salary for top-level Government administrators upon whom major responsibility for program results must rest. In President Johnson's words, this law established a basis for a standard of "brilliance" and "excellence" in the Federal Government.

Congressional Procedures

In 1960, we urged action—

"To improve Congressional procedures so that majority rule prevails."

In 1961, the House Rules Committee was enlarged from 12 to 15 members, making it more representative of the views of the majority, and thereby enabling much important legislation to be reported to the floor for a vote by the entire House membership.

In 1964, for the first time in history, the Senate voted to limit debate on a civil rights measure, thus permitting the Civil Rights Act to come to a vote, and thereby to be enacted.

Consumers

In 1960, we proposed—

"Effective Government representation and protection" for consumers.

In 1962, President Kennedy became the first Chief Executive to send a message to Congress on consumer matters.

This executive action was closely followed by the creation of a Consumer Advisory Council.

In 1964, President Johnson appointed the first Special Assistant to the President for Consumer Affairs, and created a new President's Committee on Consumer Interests.

The Kefauver–Harris Drug Amendments of 1962 were the most far-reaching improvements in the Food, Drug and Cosmetics Act since 1938. Under these amendments:

Effective legal tools were provided to insure greater safety in connection with the manufacture, distribution and use of drugs.

Vital safeguards were added for drug research and manufacture.

Interstate distribution of new drugs for testing was barred until an adequate plan of investigation was made available to the Food and Drug Administration.

Domestic drug manufacturing establishments will now be required to register annually and be inspected by the FDA at least once a year.

The Administration has vigorously supported Truth-in-Lending, Truth-in-Packaging, and Truth-in-Securities bills.

The titles of these bills explain their objectives. Together, they form a triple armor of protection: for buyers of packaged goods, from prevailing deceptive practices; for borrowers of money, from hidden and unscrupulous interest and carrying charges; and for investors in securities from unfair practices threatening to vital savings. The first two bills are still awaiting Congressional action; the third is now a law.

The upward spiral in the price of natural gas which took place in the decade of the 1950's has been halted by vigorous regulatory action of the Federal Power

Commission and the nation's 36 million consumers of natural gas have benefited from rate reductions and refunds in excess of $600 million. Natural gas moving largely in interstate pipelines now supplies almost a third of the nation's energy requirements. Regulation to insure its availability in ample supply and at reasonable prices is an important consumer protection function which is now being effectively discharged.

Veterans Affairs

In 1960, we proposed—

"Adequate compensation for those with service-connected disabilities," and "pensions adequate for a full and dignified life for disabled and distressed veterans and for needy survivors of deceased veterans."

Since 1961, we have achieved:

Increased disability payments for veterans with service-connected disabilities. In the first year alone, this increase provided veterans with additional payments of about $98 million.

An increase of about 10 percent a month in the compensation for widows, children, and parents of veterans who died of service-connected disabilities.

An increase from $112 to $150 a month in the dependency and indemnity compensation payable to widows of veterans who died of service-connected disabilities.

Increased compensation benefits to veterans disabled by blindness, deafness, and kidney disorders, and increased benefits to widows and orphans of veterans whose deaths were service-connected.

In 1960, we endorsed—

"Expanded programs of vocational rehabilitation for disabled veterans, and education for orphans of servicemen."

Since 1961, vocational rehabilitation and training has enabled thousands of GIs to choose occupations and acquire valuable training. For the first time, veterans with peacetime service-connected disabilities have been afforded vocational rehabilitation training. In addition, vocational rehabilitation was extended to blinded World War II and Korean conflict veterans, and war orphans' educational assistance was extended in behalf of certain reservists called to active duty.

In 1960, we stated—

"The quality of medical care furnished to the disabled veterans has deteriorated. . . . We shall work for an increased availability of facilities for all veterans in need and we shall move with particular urgency to fulfill the need for expanded domiciliary and nursing-home facilities."

Since 1961, we have—

Approved the construction of new, modern hospitals, a number of which are being built near medical schools to improve veterans' care and research.

Added more full-time doctors to the VA staff, bringing it to an all-time high of nearly 5,000.

Provided hospital and medical care, including outpatient treatment, to peacetime ex-servicemen for service-connected disabilities on the same basis furnished war veterans.

Stepped up medical research programs, which have made outstanding contributions to American medicine.

In 1960, we pledged—

"We shall continue the veterans home loan guarantee and direct loan programs and education benefits patterned after the GI Bill of Rights."

Since 1961, legislation has extended veterans home loans for both World War II and Korean conflict veterans. The GI Bill of Rights for Korean veterans was also extended for the benefit of certain reservists called to active duty.

Despite this considerably increased activity, the Veterans Administration has reduced its operating costs.

American Indians

In 1960, we pledged—

"Prompt adoption of a program to assist Indian tribes in the full development of their human and natural resources and to advance the health, education and economic well-being of Indian citizens while preserving their cultural heritage."

In these $3\frac{1}{2}$ years:

New classrooms have been provided for more than 7,000 Indian children; summer educational programs have been expanded tenfold so they now serve more than 20,000 students; and a special institute to train artistically gifted Indian youth has been established.

Indian enrollment in vocational training programs has been doubled.

For the first time in history, Federal low-rent housing programs have been launched on Indian reservations, and more than 3,100 new housing units have now been authorized.

Industrial plants offering employment opportunities for thousands of Indians are being opened on Indian reservations.

Accelerated Public Works projects on 89 reservations in 21 States have provided nearly 30,000 man-months of employment.

The Vocational Education Act and the Adult Indian Vocational Training Act have been amended to provide improved training for Indians.

The Arts

In 1960, we observed—

"The arts flourish where there is freedom and where individual initiative and imagination are encouraged."

No single quality of the new Administration was more immediately evident to the Nation and the world than the recognition it gave to American artists.

President Kennedy early created an advisory commission to assist in the growth and development of the arts, and the Administration secured amendments to the Educational and Cultural Exchange Act to improve the quality and effectiveness of the international educational and cultural exchange programs. This past year, the John F. Kennedy Center for the Performing Arts was established to stimulate widespread interest in the arts.

On Washington's Birthday 1963, President Kennedy, by Executive Order, created a new Presidential Medal of Freedom as the highest civil honor conferred by the President in peacetime upon persons who have made distinctive contributions to the security and national interest of the United States, to world peace, or to cultural activities. Henceforth, those men and women selected by the President for the Medal will be announced annually on the Fourth of July and will be presented with medals at an appropriate White House ceremony.

In his address to the University of Michigan in May 1964, President Johnson proposed that we begin to build the Great Society first of all in the cities of America, restoring the beauty and dignity which urban centers have lost.

That same month the President's Council on Pennsylvania Avenue presented to him a sweeping proposal for the reconstruction of the center of the City of Washington. The proposal has been hailed as "a blueprint for glory . . . a realistic and far-seeing redevelopment scheme that may be Washington's last chance to save its 'Avenue of Presidents.' "

Civil Liberties

In 1960, we reaffirmed—

"Our dedication to the Bill of Rights. Freedom and civil liberties, far from being incompatible with security, are vital to our national strength."

The era of fear and suspicion brought on by accusa-tions, true and false, of subversive activities and security risks has passed. The good sense of the American people and the overwhelming loyalty of our citizenry have combined to restore balance and calm to security activities, without in any way diminishing the scope or effectiveness of those activities.

The Administration has jealously guarded the right of each American to protect his good name. Except in those instances where the national security is overriding, confrontation of the accuser is now required in all loyalty hearings. Individuals whose loyalty is being questioned must also be notified of the charges in sufficient time for them to prepare their defense.

The Criminal Justice Act of 1964, now before the President for signature, will for the first time in history ensure that poor defendants in criminal cases will have competent legal counsel in defending themselves in Federal courts.

Fiscal Responsibility

In 1960, we promised—

"We shall end the gross waste in Federal expenditures which needlessly raises the budgets of many Government agencies."

Since 1961, we have moved boldly and directly to eliminate waste and duplication wherever it occurs.

For example, the Department of Defense has embarked on a far-reaching program to realize savings through improvements in its efficiency and management. This program has already produced savings of more than $1 billion in Fiscal Year 1963 and $2.5 billion in the Fiscal Year just completed. By 1964, it is expected that the program will produce yearly savings of over $4 billion.

At the close of the past Fiscal Year Federal employment had been reduced by 22,000 over the total one year earlier. The 1965 budget calls for lower expenditures than in the preceding year—only the second time such a feat has been accomplished in the past 10 years.

In 1960, we pledged—

"We shall collect the billions in taxes which are owed to the Federal Government but are not now collected."

To handle additional work in income tax collection, 3,971 new employees were added to the Internal Revenue Service by the Congress in fiscal 1961; 2,817 new positions were added in fiscal 1963; and about 1,000 more in fiscal 1964. The additional revenue which these employees will produce will far exceed the cost of their employment.

In 1960, we pledged—

"We shall close the loopholes in the tax laws by which certain privileged groups legally escape their fair share of taxation."

The Revenue Acts of 1962 and 1964 eliminated more loopholes than all the revenue legislation from 1941 to 1962 combined. They raised $1.7 billion annually in new revenue, nine times the sum raised in this manner during the 1953–60 period. These bills sharply limited expense account abuses, special preferences to U.S. firms and individuals operating abroad, escapes from taxation through personal holding companies and many other unjustified advantages.

Civil Rights

In 1960, we pledged—

"We shall . . . seek to create an affirmative new atmosphere in which to deal with racial divisions and inequalities which threaten both the integrity of our democratic faith and the proposition on which our Nation was founded—that all men are created equal."

That pledge was made from the deepest moral conviction.

It was carried out on the same basis.

From the establishment of the President's Committee on Equal Employment Opportunity, under the chairmanship of the then Vice President Lyndon B. Johnson, on March 6, 1961, to this moment, the efforts of the Administration to provide full and equal civil rights for all Americans have never relaxed.

The high point of achievement in this effort was reached with the passage of the Civil Rights Act of 1964, the greatest civil rights measure in the history of the American people.

This landmark of our Democracy bars discrimination in the use of public accommodations, in employment, and in the administering of Federally assisted programs. It makes available effective procedures for assuring the right to vote in Federal elections, directs Federal technical and financial assistance to local public school systems in desegregation, and strengthens the Civil Rights Commission. This comprehensive legislation resolves many of the festering conflicts which had been a source of irritating uncertainty, and smooths the way for favorable resolution of these problems.

We have also insisted upon non-discrimination in apprenticeship, and have made free, unsegregated access a condition for Federal financial assistance to public libraries, programs for training of teachers of the handicapped, counseling, guidance and foreign language institutes, adult civil defense classes, and manpower development and training programs.

In supporting construction of Hill–Burton hospitals, mental retardation and community health facilities, we have required nondiscrimination in admission and provision of services and granting of staff privileges.

We have been equally firm in opposing any policy of quotas or "discrimination in reverse," and all other arbitrary or irrelevant distinctions in American life.

This, then, is the accounting of our stewardship:

The 1960 platform was not directed to any one sector or group of Americans with particular interests.

It proclaimed, rather, the Rights of Man.

The platform asserted the essential fact of that moment in our history—that the next Administration to take office would face as never before the "responsibility and opportunity to call forth the greatness of the American people."

That responsibility was met; that opportunity was seized. The years since have been times of towering achievement.

We are proud to have been a part of this history. The task of leadership is to lead, and that has been our purpose. But the achievements of the nation over this period outreach the contribution of any party: they are the work of the American people.

In the 1,000 days of John F. Kennedy, in the eventful and culminating months of Lyndon B. Johnson, there has been born new American greatness.

Let us continue.

— 1968 —

THE TERMS OF OUR DUTY

America belongs to the people who inhabit it. The source of the nation's strength is the people's freedom to be the source of the laws governing them. To uphold this truth, when Thomas Jefferson and James Madison brought the Democratic Party to birth 175 years ago, they bound it to serve the people and their government as a united whole.

Today, in our 175th anniversary year, the Democratic Party in national convention assembled, again renews the covenant of our birth. We affirm the binding force of our inherited duty to serve the people and their government. We here, therefore, account for what we have done in the Democratic years since 1961. We here state what we will do when our party is again called to lead the nation.

In America and in the world over, strong forces for change are on the move. Systems of thought have been jarred, ways of life have been uprooted, institutions are under siege. The governed challenge those who govern.

We are summoned, therefore, to a fateful task—to ensure that the turmoil of change will prove to be the turmoil of birth instead of decay. We cannot stand still until we are overtaken by events. We dare not entrust our lives to the blind play of accident and force. By reflection and choice, we must make the impulse for change the agent of orderly progress.

There is no alternative.

In the world around us, people have patiently lived with hopes long deferred, with grievances long endured. They are now impatient with patience. Their demands for change must not only be heard, they must be answered.

This is the reality the world as a whole faces.

In America itself, now, and not later, is the right time to strengthen the fabric of our society by making justice and equity the cornerstones of order. Now, and not later, is the right time to uphold the rule of law by securing to all the people the natural rights that belong to them by virtue of their being human. Now, and not later, is the right time to unfurl again the flag of human patriotism and rededicate ourselves under it, to the cause of peace among nations. Now, and not later, is the right time to reclaim the strength spent in quarrels over the past and to apply that strength to America's future. Now is the right time to proceed with the work of orderly progress that will make the future become what we want it to be.

It has always been the object of the Democratic Party to march at the head of events instead of waiting for them to happen. It is our resolve to do that in the years ahead—just as we did in the Democratic years since 1961 when the nation was led by two Democratic Presidents and four Democratic Congresses.

THIS WE HAVE DONE

Our pride in the achievements of these Democratic years in no way blinds us to the large and unfinished tasks which still lie ahead. Just as we know where we have succeeded, we know where our efforts still fall short of our own and the nation's hopes. And we candidly recognize that the cost of trying the untried, of ploughing new ground, is bound to be occasional error. In the future, as in the past, we will confront and correct such errors as we carry our program forward.

In this, we are persuaded that the Almighty judges in a different scale those who err in warmly striving to promote the common good, and those who are free from error because they risked nothing at all and were icily indifferent to good and evil alike. We are also persuaded of something else. What we have achieved with the means at hand—the social inventions we have made since 1961 in all areas of our internal life, and the

initiatives we have pressed along a broad front in the world arena—gives us a clear title of right to claim that we know how to move the nation forward toward the attainment of its highest goal in a world of change.

The Economy

In presenting first the record of what we have achieved in the economic life of the American people, we do not view the economy as being just dollar signs divorced from the flesh-and-blood concerns of the people. Economics, like politics, involves people and it means people. It means for them the difference between what they don't want and what they do want. It means the difference between justice or injustice, health or sickness, better education or ignorance, a good place to live or a rat-infested hovel, a good job or corrosive worry.

In the Democratic years since 1961, under the leadership of Presidents Kennedy and Johnson, we managed the national economy in ways that kept the best aspirations of people in clear view, and brought them closer to fulfillment.

The case was different in the 1950's, when the Republicans held the trust of national leadership. In those years, the American economy creaked and groaned from recurrent recessions. One wasteful recession came in 1954, another in 1958, and a third in 1960. The loss in national production from all three recessions and from a sluggish rate of growth—a loss that can fairly be called the GOP-gap—was a staggering $175 billion, computed in today's prices.

The Democratic Party, seeing the Republican inertia and the dangers it led to, promised to get America moving again. President Kennedy first made that promise for us, and we kept it. We brought an end to recurring recessions, each one of which had followed closer on the heels of the last. Full cooperation between our government officials and all sectors of American life led to new public policies which unlocked the creative power of America's free enterprise system. The magnificent response of all the people comprising that system made the world stand in awe of the results.

Since 1961, we have seen:

A 90-month period of recession-free prosperity, the longest and strongest period of sustained economic growth in American history;

A slash in the unemployment rate from 7 to under 4 percent;

An increase of nearly 40 percent in real wages and salaries and nearly one-third in the average person's real income;

And, on the eight-year average, a reduction in the rate levels of the individual income tax.

America's private enterprise system flourished as never before in these years of Democratic leadership. Compared with the preceding eight Republican years, private enterprise in the Democratic 1960's grew twice as fast, profits increased twice as rapidly, four times as many jobs were created, and thirteen million Americans—or one-third of those in poverty in 1960—have today escaped its bondage.

Democrats, however, were not satisfied. We saw—and were the first to see—that even sustained prosperity does not eliminate hardcore unemployment. We were the first to see that millions of Americans would never share in America's abundance unless the people as a whole, through their government, acted to supplement what free enterprise could do.

So, under the leadership of President Johnson, this nation declared war on poverty—a war in which the government is again working in close cooperation with leaders of the free enterprise system.

It would compromise the integrity of our words to claim that the war on poverty and for equal opportunity has been won. Democrats are the first to insist that it has only begun—while 82 percent of the House Republicans and 69 percent of the Senate Republicans voted against even beginning it at all. Democrats know that much more remains to be done. What we have done thus far is to test a series of pilot projects before making them bigger, and we have found that they DO work.

Thus:

The new preschool program known as Head Start has proven its effectiveness in widening the horizons of over two million poor children and their parents.

The new programs known as the Job Corps and the Neighborhood Youth Corps, entailing close cooperation between the government and private enterprise, have helped nearly two million unskilled boys and girls—most of them drop-outs from school—get work in the community and in industry.

The new program known as Upward Bound has helped thousands of poor but talented young men and women prepare themselves for college.

The new structure of neighborhood centers brings modern community services directly to the people who need them most.

The People

We emphasize that the coldly stated statistics of gains made in the war on poverty must be translated to mean people, in all their yearnings for personal fulfill-ment. That is true as well of all other things in the great outpouring of constructive legislation that surpassed even the landmark years of the early New Deal.

Education is one example. From the beginning of our Party history, Democrats argued that liberty and learning must find in each other the surest ground for mutual support. The inherited conviction provided the motive force behind the educational legislation of the 1960's that we enacted:

Because of the Elementary and Secondary Education Act of 1965, local education has been enriched to the benefit of over 13 million young Americans;

Because of the Higher Education Act of 1965, new college classrooms, laboratories and libraries have been built to assure that higher education will not be the monopoly of the few but the right of the many;

Because of federal assistance to students, the doors to college have been opened for over a million young men and women coming from families with modest means—so that about one out of every five college students is now pursuing his higher education with some kind of federal help;

Because Democrats are convinced that the best of all investments is in the human resources represented by the youth of America, we brought about a fourfold increase in the federal investment in education since 1960. The level now approaches $12 billion annually.

As it promoted better education, so did Democratic leadership promote better health for all.

The program of mercy and justice known as health care for the aged, which President Truman originally proposed and Presidents Kennedy and Johnson fought for, finally became law in the summer of 1965. Because of it, more than seven million older citizens each year are now receiving modern medical care in dignity—no longer forced to depend on charity, no longer a burden on relatives, no longer in physical pain because they cannot afford to pay for the healing power of modern medicine. Virtually all older Americans, the well and the sick alike, are now protected, their lives more secure, their afflictions eased.

To deal with other aspects of the nation's health needs, measures were enacted in the Democratic years representing an almost fourfold increase in the government's investment in health. Programs were enacted to cope with the killing diseases of heart, cancer and stroke; to combat mental retardation and mental illness; to increase the manpower supply of trained medical technicians; to speed the construction of new hospitals.

Democrats in the Presidency and in the Congress have led the fight to erase the stain of racial discrimination that tarnished America's proudly announced proposition that all men are created equal.

We knew that racial discrimination was present in every section of the country. We knew that the enforcement of civil rights and general laws is indivisible. In this conviction, Democrats took the initiative to guarantee the right to safety and security of the person, the right to all the privileges of citizenship, the right to equality of opportunity in employment, and the right to public services and accommodations and housing. For example:

Because of the Civil Rights Act of 1964, all men born equal in the eyes of their Creator are by law declared to be equal when they apply for a job, or seek a night's lodging or a good meal;

Because of the Voting Rights Act of 1965, the right to the ballot box—the right on which all other rights depend—has been reinforced by law;

Because of the Civil Rights Act of 1968, all families will have an equal right to live where they wish.

The Nation

The frontier on which most Americans live is the vertical frontier of the city. It is a frontier whose urgent needs hold a place of very high priority on the national agenda—and on the agenda of the Democratic Party.

Democrats recognize that the race to save our cities is a race against the absolute of time itself. The blight that threatens their future takes many forms. It is the physical decay of homes and neighborhoods. It is poverty and unemployment. It is broken homes and social disintegration. It is crime. It is congestion and pollution. The Democratic program attacked all of these forms of blight—and all at once.

Since we know that the cities can be saved only by the people who live there, Democrats have invigorated local effort through federal leadership and assistance. In almost every city, a community action agency has mounted a many-sided assault on poverty. Through varied neighborhood organizations, the poor themselves are tackling their own problems and devising their own programs of self-help. Under Model Cities legislation, enacted in 1966, seventy-five cities are now launching the most comprehensive programs of economic, physical, and social development ever undertaken—and the number of participating cities will be doubled soon. In this effort, the residents of the areas selected to become the model neighborhoods are participating fully in planning their future and deciding what it will be.

In a series of housing acts beginning in 1961, Democrats have found ways to encourage private enterprise to provide modern, decent housing for low-income and moderate-income families. The Housing and Urban Development Act of 1968 is the most far-reaching housing legislation in America's history. Under its terms, the genius of American business will combine with the productivity of American labor to meet a 10-year goal of 26 million new housing units—6 million of them for the poor. The objective is to enable the poor to own their own homes, to rebuild entire neighborhoods, to spur the pace of urban renewal, and to deal more humanely with the problems of displaced people.

To give our cities a spokesman of Cabinet rank, Democrats in 1965 took the lead in creating a Department of Housing and Urban Development.

Democratic Presidents and Congresses have moved with equal vigor to help the people of America's vast hinterland outside the metropolitan centers to join the march of economic progress. Of the 101 major areas classified as "depressed areas" when the Democrats assumed office in 1961, 90 have now solved their problems of excessive unemployment and the others are on their way. The Area Redevelopment Act, the expansion of resource development programs, and the massive effort to restore Appalachia and other lagging regions to economic health assisted the people of these areas in their remarkable progress.

In these legislative undertakings of primary concern to people—American people—it is to the credit of some Republicans that they joined the Democratic majority in a common effort. Unfortunately, however, most Republicans sat passively by while Democrats wrote the legislation the nation's needs demanded. Worse, and more often, Republicans did what they could to obstruct and defeat the measures that were approved by Democrats in defiance of hostile Republican votes. Thus:

In the case of the Elementary and Secondary Education Act, 73 percent of the Republicans in the House voted to kill it.

In the case of medical care for the aged, 93 percent of the Republicans in the House and 64 percent in the Senate voted to kill it.

In the case of the Model Cities program, 88 percent of the Republicans in the House voted to kill it.

In the case of the program to help Appalachia, 81 percent of House Republicans and 58 percent of Senate Republicans voted to kill it, and 75 percent of House Republicans voted to kill corresponding programs of aid for other depressed regions of the country.

The same negative attitude was present among Republicans in the 1950's, and one of the results was a crisis in the farm sector of the economy—which the Democrats inherited in the 1960's. In the late Republican 1950's, the glut of farm surpluses amounted to over $8 billion, and the taxpayers were forced to pay $1 billion every year in interest and storage charges alone. Democrats, however, set out resolutely to reverse the picture. Democratic farm programs supported farm income, expanded farm exports and domestic consumption, helped farmers adjust their production to the size of the expanded markets, and reduced farm surpluses and storage costs to the lowest level since 1952.

Democrats have also acted vigorously to assure that American science and technology shall continue to lead the world.

In atomic energy, in space exploration, in communications, in medicine, in oceanology, in fundamental and applied research in many fields, we have provided leadership and financial aid to the nation's scientists and engineers. Their genius has, in turn, powered our national economic growth.

Other measures affected all Americans everywhere.

Under our Constitutional system of federalism, the primary responsibility for law enforcement rests with selected local officials and with governors, but the federal government can and should play a constructive role in support of state and local authorities.

In this conviction, Democratic leadership secured the enactment of a law which extended financial assistance to modernize local police departments, to train law enforcement personnel, and to develop modern police technology. The effect of these provisions is already visible in an improved quality of law enforcement throughout the land.

Under Democratic leadership, furthermore, the juvenile delinquency Prevention and Control Act was passed to aid states and communities to plan and carry out comprehensive programs to prevent and combat youth crime. We have added more personnel to strengthen the Federal Bureau of Investigation and the enforcement of narcotics laws, and have intensified the campaign against organized crime. The federal government has come swiftly to the aid of cities needing help to bring major disturbances under control, and Democratic leadership secured the enactment of a new gun control law as a step toward putting the weapons of wanton violence beyond the reach of criminal and irresponsible hands.

To purify the air we breathe and the water we drink, Democrats led the way to the enactment of landmark anti-pollution legislation.

To bring order into the administration of transportation programs and to coordinate transportation policy, Democrats in 1966 established a new Cabinet-level Department of Transportation.

For the consumer, new standards of protection were enacted—truth-in-lending and truth-in-packaging, the Child Safety Act, the Pipeline Safety Act, the Wholesome Meat and Wholesome Poultry Acts.

For America's 100 million automobile drivers, auto and highway safety legislation provided protection not previously known.

For every American family, unparalleled achievements in conservation meant the development of balanced outdoor recreation programs involving magnificent new national parks, seashores, and lakeshores—all within an afternoon's drive of 110 million Americans. For the first time, we are beating the bulldozer to the nation's remaining open spaces.

For the sake of all living Americans and for their posterity, the Wilderness Preservation Act of 1964 placed in perpetual trust millions of acres of primitive and wilderness areas.

For America's sons who manned the nation's defenses, a new GI bill with greatly enlarged equitable benefits was enacted gratefully and proudly.

America's senior citizens enjoyed the largest increase in Social Security since the system was inaugurated during the Democratic Presidency of Franklin D. Roosevelt.

For the hungry, our food distribution programs were expanded to provide more than $1 billion worth of food a year for domestic use, giving millions of children, for the first time, enough to eat.

A new minimum wage law raised paychecks and standards of living for millions, while a new network of training programs enabled more than a million Americans to learn new skills and become productive workers in the labor force.

A new Immigration Act removed the harsh injustice of the national-origins quota system and opened our shores without discrimination to those who can contribute to the growth and strength of America.

Many more measures enacted under Democratic leadership could be added to this recital of achievements in our internal life since 1961. But what we could list shares the character of what we have listed. All the measures alike are a witness to our desire to serve the people as a united whole, to chart the way for their orderly progress, to possess their confidence—by striving through our conduct to deserve to possess it.

The World

The conscience of the entire world has been shocked by the brutal and unprovoked Soviet aggression against Czechoslovakia. By this act, Moscow has confessed that it is still the prisoner of its fear of freedom. And the Czechoslovakian people have shown that the love of freedom, in their land and throughout Eastern Europe, can never be crushed.

This severe blow to freedom and self-determination reinforces our commitment to the unending quest for peace and security in the world. These dark days should not obscure the solid achievements of the past eight years. Nuclear war has been avoided. West Berlin and Western Europe are still free.

The blend of American power and restraint, so dramatically demonstrated in the Cuban missile crisis, earned the respect of the world and prepared the way for a series of arms control agreements with the Soviet Union. Long and patient negotiation by Presidents Kennedy and Johnson resulted in the Nuclear Test Ban, Nuclear Non-Proliferation, and Space treaties and the "hot line." These hard-won agreements provide the base for pursuing other measures to reduce the risk of nuclear war.

The unprecedented expansion of the American economy has invigorated the whole free world. Many once skeptical nations, including some communist states, now regard American economic techniques and institutions as a model.

In Asia the tragic Vietnam war has often blinded us to the quiet and constructive developments which affect directly the lives of over a billion people and the prospects for peace everywhere.

An economically strong and democratic Japan has assumed a more active role in the development of the region. Indonesia has a nationalist, non-communist government seeking to live at peace with its neighbors. Thailand, Taiwan, Singapore, Malaysia, and the Republic of Korea have more stable governments and steadily growing economies. They have been aided by American economic assistance and by the American military presence in the Pacific. They have also been encouraged by a confidence reflecting successive Presidential decisions to assist nations to live in peace and freedom.

Elsewhere in the developing world, there has been hopeful political and economic progress. Though Castro's Cuba is still a source of subversion, the other Latin American states are moving ahead under the Alliance for Progress. In Africa, many of the new states have chosen moderate leaders committed to peaceful nation-building. They are beginning to cooperate with their neighbors in regional agencies of their own design. And like developing countries on other continents, they are for the first time giving serious attention to agricultural development. This new emphasis on food will buy time to launch effective programs of population control.

In all these constructive changes America, under Democratic leadership, has played a significant role. But we Democrats do not believe in resting on past achievements. We view any success as a down payment on the hard tasks that lie ahead. There is still much to be done at home and abroad and we accept with confidence the challenge of the future.

THIS WE WILL DO

Toward a Peaceful World

In the pursuit of our national objectives and in the exercise of American power in the world, we assert that the United States should:

Continue to accept its world responsibilities, not turn inward and isolate ourselves from the cares and aspirations of mankind;

Seek a world of diversity and peaceful change, where men can choose their own governments and where each nation can determine its own destiny without external interference;

Resist the temptation to try to mold the world, or any part of it, in our own image, or to become the self-appointed policeman of the world;

Call on other nations, great and small, to contribute a fair share of effort and resources to world peace and development;

Honor our treaty obligations to our allies;

Seek always to strengthen and improve the United Nations and other international peacekeeping arrangements and meet breaches or threatened breaches of the peace according to our carefully assessed interests and resources;

In pursuing these objectives, we will insure that our policies will be subject to constant review so they reflect our true national interests in a changing world.

National Defense

The tragic events in Czechoslovakia are a shocking reminder that we live in a dangerous and unpredictable world. The Soviet attack on and invasion of a small country that only yesterday was Moscow's peaceful ally, is an ominous reversal of the slow trend toward greater freedom and independence in Eastern Europe. The reimposition of Soviet tyranny raises the spectre of the darkest days of the Stalin era and increases the risk of war in Central Europe, a war that could become a nuclear holocaust.

Against this somber backdrop, whose full portent cannot now be seen, other recent Soviet military moves take on even greater significance. Though we have a significant lead in military strength and in all vital areas of military technology, Moscow has steadily increased its strategic nuclear arsenal, its missile-firing nuclear submarine fleet, and its anti-missile defenses. Communist China is providing political and military support for so-called wars of national liberation. A growing nuclear power, Peking has disdained all arms control efforts.

We must and will maintain a strong and balanced defense establishment adequate to the task of security and peace. There must be no doubt about our strategic nuclear capability, our capacity to meet limited challenges, and our willingness to act when our vital interests are threatened.

To this end, we pledge a vigorous research and development effort. We will also continue to pursue the highly successful efforts initiated by Democratic administrations to save tax dollars by eliminating waste and duplication.

We face difficult and trying times in Asia and in Europe. We have responsibilities and commitments we cannot escape with honor. But we are not alone. We have friends and allies around the world. We will consult with them and ask them, to accept a fair share of the burdens of peace and security.

North Atlantic Community

The North Atlantic Community is strong and free. We must further strengthen our ties and be constantly alert to new challenges and opportunities. We support a substantially larger European contribution to NATO.

Soviet troops have never stepped across the border of a NATO country. By harassment and threat the Kremlin has repeatedly attempted to push the West out of Berlin. But West Berlin is still free. Western Europe is still free. This is a living tribute to the strength and validity of the NATO alliance.

The political differences we have had with some of our allies from time to time should not divert us from our common task of building a secure and prosperous Atlantic community based on the principles of mutual respect and mutual dependence. The NATO alliance has demonstrated that free nations can build a common shield without sacrificing their identity and independence.

Arms Control

We must recognize that vigilance calls for the twin disciplines of defense and arms control. Defense measures and arms control measures must go hand in hand, each serving national security and the larger interests of peace.

We must also recognize that the Soviet Union and the United States still have a common interest in avoiding nuclear war and preventing the spread of nu-

clear weapons. We also share a common interest in reducing the cost of national defense. We must continue to work together. We will press for further arms control agreements, insisting on effective safeguards against violations.

For almost a quarter of a century America's pre-eminent military strength, combined with our political restraint, has deterred nuclear war. This great accomplishment has confounded the prophets of doom.

Eight years ago the Democratic Party pledged new efforts to control nuclear weapons. We have fulfilled that pledge. The new Arms Control and Disarmament Agency has undertaken and coordinated important research. The sustained initiatives of President Kennedy and President Johnson have resulted in the "hot line" between the White House and the Kremlin, the limited Nuclear Test Ban Treaty, the Non-Proliferation Treaty, and the treaty barring the orbiting of weapons of mass destruction.

Even in the present tense atmosphere, we strongly support President Johnson's effort to secure an agreement with the Soviet Union under which both states would refrain from deploying anti-missile systems. Such a treaty would result in the saving of billions of dollars and would create a climate for further arms control measures. We support concurrent efforts to freeze the present level of strategic weapons and delivery systems, and to achieve a balanced and verified reduction of all nuclear and conventional arms.

The Middle East

The Middle East remains a powder keg. We must do all in our power to prevent a recurrence of war in this area. A large Soviet fleet has been deployed to the Mediterranean. Preferring short-term political advantage to long-range stability and peace, the Soviet Union has rushed arms to certain Arab states to replace those lost in the Arab–Israeli War of 1967. As long as Israel is threatened by hostile and well-armed neighbors, we will assist her with essential military equipment needed for her defense, including the most advanced types of combat aircraft.

Lasting peace in the Middle East depends upon agreed and secured frontiers, respect for the territorial integrity of all states, the guaranteed right of innocent passage through all international waterways, a humane resettlement of the Arab refugees, and the establishment of a non-provocative military balance. To achieve these objectives, we support negotiations among the concerned parties. We strongly support efforts to achieve an agreement among states in the area and those states supplying arms to limit the flow of military equipment to the Middle East.

We support efforts to raise the living standards throughout the area, including desalinization and regional irrigation projects which cut across state frontiers.

Vietnam and Asia

Our most urgent task in Southeast Asia is to end the war in Vietnam by an honorable and lasting settlement which respects the rights of all the people of Vietnam. In our pursuit of peace and stability in the vital area of Southeast Asia we have borne a heavy burden in helping South Vietnam to counter aggression and subversion from the North.

We reject as unacceptable a unilateral withdrawal of our forces which would allow that aggression and subversion to succeed. We have never demanded, and do not now demand, unconditional surrender by the communists.

We strongly support the Paris talks and applaud the initiative of President Johnson which brought North Vietnam to the peace table. We hope that Hanoi will respond positively to this act of statesmanship.

In the quest for peace no solutions are free of risk. But calculated risks are consistent with the responsibility of a great nation to seek a peace of reconciliation.

Recognizing that events in Vietnam and the negotiations in Paris may affect the timing and the actions we recommend, we would support our government in the following steps:

Bombing.   Stop all bombing of North Vietnam when the action would not endanger the lives of our troops in the field; this action should take into account the response from Hanoi.

Troop Withdrawal.   Negotiate with Hanoi an immediate end or limitation of hostilities and the withdrawal from South Vietnam of all foreign forces—both United States and allied forces, and forces infiltrated from North Vietnam.

Election of Postwar Government.   Encourage all parties and interests to agree that the choice of the postwar government of South Vietnam should be determined by fair and safeguarded elections, open to all major political factions and parties prepared to accept peaceful political processes. We would favor an effective international presence to facilitate the transition from war to peace and to assure the protection of minorities against reprisal.

Interim Defense and Development Measures.   Until the fighting stops, accelerate our efforts to train and equip the South Vietnamese army so that it can defend its own country and carry out cutbacks of U.S. military involvement as the South Vietnamese forces are able to take over their larger responsibilities. We should si-

multaneously do all in our power to support and encourage further economic, political and social development and reform in South Vietnam, including an extensive land reform program. We support President Johnson's repeated offer to provide a substantial U.S. contribution to the postwar reconstruction of South Vietnam as well as to the economic development of the entire region, including North Vietnam. Japan and the European industrial states should be urged to join in this postwar effort.

For the future, we will make it clear that U.S. military and economic assistance in Asia will be selective. In addition to considerations of our vital interests and our resources, we will take into account the determination of the nations that request our help to help themselves and their willingness to help each other through regional and multilateral cooperation.

We want no bases in South Vietnam; no continued military presence and no political role in Vietnamese affairs. If and when the communists understand our basic commitment and limited goals and are willing to take their chances, as we are, on letting the choice of the postwar government of South Vietnam be determined freely and peacefully by all of the South Vietnamese people, then the bloodshed and the tragedy can stop.

Japan, India, Indonesia, and most of the smaller Asian nations are understandably apprehensive about Red China because of its nuclear weapons, its support of subversive efforts abroad, and its militant rhetoric. They have been appalled by the barbaric behavior of the Red Guards toward the Chinese people, their callous disregard for human life and their mistreatment of foreign diplomats.

The immediate prospect that China will emerge from its self-imposed isolation is dim. But both Asians and Americans will have to coexist with the 750 million Chinese on the mainland. We shall continue to make it clear that we are prepared to cooperate with China whenever it is ready to become a responsible member of the international community. We would actively encourage economic, social and cultural exchange with mainland China as a means of freeing that nation and her people from their narrow isolation.

We support continued assistance to help maintain the independence and peaceful development of India and Pakistan.

Recognizing the growing importance of Asia and the Pacific, we will encourage increased cultural and educational efforts, such as those undertaken in multiracial Hawaii, to facilitate a better understanding of the problems and opportunities of this vast area.

The Developing World

The American people share the aspirations for a better life in the developing world. But we are committed to peaceful change. We believe basic political rights in most states can be more effectively achieved and maintained by peaceful action than by violence.

In their struggle for political and economic development, most Asian, African, and Latin American states are confronted by grinding poverty, illiteracy and a stubborn resistance to constructive change. The aspirations and frustrations of the people are frequently exploited by self-serving revolutionaries who employ illegal and violent means.

Since World War II, America's unprecedented program of foreign economic assistance for reconstruction and development has made a profound contribution to peace, security, and a better life for millions of people everywhere. Many nations formerly dependent upon American aid are now viable and stable as a result of this aid.

We support strengthened U.S. and U.N. development aid programs that are responsive to changing circumstances and based on the recognition, as President Johnson put it, that "self-help is the lifeblood of economic development." Grant aid and government loans for long-term projects are part of a larger transfer of resources between the developed and underdeveloped states, which includes international trade and private capital investment as important components.

Like the burden of keeping the peace, the responsibility for assisting the developing world must be shared by Japan and the Western European states, once recipients of U.S. aid and now donor states.

Development aid should be coordinated among both donors and recipients. The World Bank and other international and regional agencies for investment and development should be fully utilized. We should encourage regional cooperation by the recipients for the most efficient use of resources and markets.

We should press for additional international agreements that will stimulate mutually beneficial trade and encourage a growing volume of private investment in the developing states. World-wide commodity agreements that stabilize prices for particular products and other devices to stabilize export earnings will also spur development.

We believe priority attention should be given to agricultural production and population control. Technical assistance which emphasizes manpower training is also of paramount importance. We support the Peace Corps which has sent thousands of ambassadors of good will to three continents.

Cultural and historic ties and a common quest for peace with freedom and justice have made Latin America an area of special concern and interest to the United States. We support a vigorous Alliance for Progress program based upon the Charter of Punta del Este which affirms that "free men working through the institutions for representative democracy can best satisfy man's aspirations."

We support the objective of Latin American economic integration endorsed by the presidents of the American Republics in April 1967 and urge further efforts in the areas of tax reform, land reform, educational reform, and economic development to fulfill the promise of Punta del Este.

United Nations

Since the birth of the United Nations, the United States has pursued the quest for peace, security and human dignity through United Nations channels more vigorously than any other member state. Our dedication to its purpose and its work remains undiminished.

The United Nations contributed to dampening the fires of conflict in Kashmir, the Middle East, Cyprus and the Congo. The agencies of the United Nations have made a significant contribution to health, education and economic well-being in Asia, Africa and Latin America. These efforts deserve continued and expanded support. We pledge that support.

Since we recognize that the United Nations can be only as effective as the support of its members, we call upon other states to join with us in a renewed commitment to use its facilities in the great tasks of economic development, the non-military use of atomic energy, arms control and peacekeeping. It is only with member nations working together that the organization can make its full contribution to the growth of a world community of peace under law, rather than by threat or use of military force.

We are profoundly concerned about the continued repression of Jews and other minorities in the Soviet Union and elsewhere, and look forward to the day when the full light of liberty and freedom shall be extended to all countries and all peoples.

Foreign Trade and Financial Policy

World trade is essential to economic stability. The growing interdependence of nations, particularly in economic affairs, is an established fact of contemporary life. It also spells an opportunity for constructive international cooperation that will bring greater well-being for all and improve the prospects for international peace and security.

We shall build upon the Trade Expansion Act of 1962 and the Kennedy round of trade negotiations, in order to achieve greater trade cooperation and progress toward freer international trade. In future negotiations, which will require careful preparation, we shall: 1) seek continued reciprocal reduction and elimination of tariff barriers, based on the most favored nation principle; 2) negotiate the reciprocal removal of non-tariff barriers to international trade on all products, including agriculture; 3) give special attention to the needs of the developing countries for increased export earnings; and 4) develop and improve the rules governing fair international competition affecting both foreign commerce and investment.

To lessen the hardships suffered by industries and workers as the result of trade liberalization, we support improvements in the adjustment assistance provisions of present law. Provision of law to remedy unfair and destructive import competition should be reviewed and strengthened, and negotiated international agreements to achieve this purpose should be employed where appropriate.

The United States has experienced balance-of-payments deficits for over a decade, mainly because of our security obligations in the free world. Faced with these deficits, we have behaved responsibly by avoiding both economic deflation at home and severe unilateral restrictive measures on international transactions, which would have weakened the international economy and international cooperation.

We shall continue to take the path of constructive measures by relying on steps to increase our exports and by the development of further cooperative arrangements with the other countries. We intend, as soon as possible, to dismantle the restrictions placed on foreign investment and finance, so that American free enterprise can play its full part as the agent of economic development. We will continue to encourage persons from other lands to visit America.

Steps of historical importance have already been taken to improve the functioning of the international monetary system, most notably the new special drawing rights under the International Monetary Fund. We shall continue to work for the further improvement of the international monetary system so as to reduce its vulnerability to monetary crises.

Economic Growth and Stability

The Democratic policies that more than doubled the nation's rate of economic expansion in the past eight years can double and redouble our national income by the end of this century. Such a rate of economic growth will enable us to win total victory in our wars on ignorance, poverty, and the misery of the ghettos.

But victory will not come automatically. To realize our full economic potential will require effective, businesslike planning and cooperation between government and all elements of private economy. The Democratic Party pledges itself to achieve that purpose in many ways.

Fiscal and Monetary Policy

Taxes were lowered in 1962, 1964, and 1965 to encourage more private spending and reach full employment; they were raised in 1966 and 1968 to help prevent inflation, but with a net reduction in the eight Democratic years. We will continue to use tax policy to maintain steady economic growth by helping through tax reduction to stimulate the economy when it is sluggish and through temporary tax increases to restrain inflation. To promote this objective, methods must be devised to permit prompt, temporary changes in tax rates within prescribed limits with full participation of the Congress in the decisions.

The goals of our national tax policy must be to distribute the burden of government equitably among our citizens and to promote economic efficiency and stability. We have placed major reliance on progressive taxes, which are based on the democratic principle of ability to pay. We pledge ourselves to continue to rely on such taxes, and to continue to improve the way they are levied and collected so that every American contributes to government in proportion to his ability to pay.

A thorough revamping of our federal taxes has been long overdue to make them more equitable as between rich and poor and as among people with the same income and family responsibilities. All corporation and individual preferences that do not serve the national interest should be removed. Tax preferences, like expenditures, must be rigorously evaluated to assure that the benefit to the nation is worth the cost.

We support a proposal for a minimum income tax for persons of high income based on an individual's total income regardless of source in order that wealthy persons will be required to make some kind of income tax contribution, no matter how many tax shelters they use to protect their incomes. We also support a reduction of the tax burden on the poor by lowering the income tax rates at the bottom of the tax scale and increasing the minimum standard deduction. No person or family below the poverty level should be required to pay federal income taxes.

Our goal is a balanced budget in a balanced economy. We favor distinguishing current operating expenditures from long-term capital outlays and repayable loans, which should be amortized consistent with sound accounting principles. All government expenditures should be subject to firm tests of efficiency and essentiality.

An effective policy for growth and stability requires careful coordination of fiscal and monetary policies. Changes in taxes, budgets, interest rates, and money supply must be carefully blended and flexibly adjusted to assure:

Adaptation to changing economic conditions;

Adequate supplies of money and credit for the expansion of industry, commerce, and housing;

Maintenance of the lowest possible interest rates;

Avoidance of needless hardships on groups that depend heavily on credit.

Cooperation between fiscal and monetary authorities was greatly strengthened in the past eight years, and we pledge ourselves to continue to perfect this cooperation.

Price Stability with Growth

Price stability continues to be an essential goal of expansive economic policy. Price inflation hurts most of the weak among us and could interfere with the continued social gains we are determined to achieve in the immediate years ahead.

The answer to rising prices will never be sought, under Democratic administrations, in unemployment and idle plant facilities. We are firmly committed to the twin objectives of full employment and price stability.

To promote price stability in a dynamic and growing economy, we will:

Pursue flexible fiscal and monetary policies designed to keep total private and public demand in line with the economy's rising productive capacity.

Work effectively with business, labor, and the public in formulating principles for price and wage policies that are equitable and sound for consumers as well as for workers and investors.

Strictly enforce antitrust and trade practice laws to combat administered pricing, supply limitations and other restrictive practices.

Strengthen competition by keeping the doors of world trade open and resisting the protectionism of captive markets.

Stimulate plant modernization, upgrade labor skills, and speed technological advance to step up productivity.

Agriculture

Twice in this century the Republican Party has brought disaster to the American farmer—in the thirties and in the fifties. Each time, the American farmer was rescued by the Democratic Party, but his prosperity has not yet been fully restored.

Farmers must continue to be heard in the councils of government where decisions affecting agriculture are taken. The productivity of our farmers—already the world's most productive—must continue to rise, making American agriculture more competitive abroad and more prosperous at home.

A strong agriculture requires fair income to farmers for an expanding output. Family farmers must be protected from the squeeze between rising production costs and low prices for their products. Farm income should grow with productivity just as industrial wages rise with productivity. At the same time, market prices should continue to reflect supply and demand conditions and American farm products must continue to compete effectively in world markets. In this way, markets at home and abroad will continue to expand beyond the record high levels of recent years.

To these ends, we shall:

Take positive action to raise farm income to full parity level in order to preserve the efficient, full-time family farm. This can be done through present farm programs when these programs are properly funded, but these programs will be constantly scrutinized with a view to improvement.

Actively seek out and develop foreign commercial markets, since international trade in agricultural products is a major favorable factor in the nation's balance of payments. In expanding our trade, we shall strive to ensure that farmers get adequate compensation for their production going into export.

Expand our food assistance programs to America's poor and our Food for Peace program to help feed the world's hungry.

Establish a Strategic Food and Feed Reserve Plan whereby essential commodities such as wheat, corn and other feed grains, soybeans, storable meat and other products will be stockpiled as a safeguard against crop failures, to assist our nation and other nations in time of famine or disaster, and to ensure adequate supplies for export markets, as well as to protect our own farm industry. This reserve should be insulated from the market.

Support the right of farmers to bargain collectively in the market place on a commodity-by-commodity basis. Labor and industry have long enjoyed this right to bargain collectively under existing legislation. Protective legislation for bargaining should be extended to agriculture.

Continue to support and encourage agricultural co-operatives by expanded and liberal credit and to protect them from punitive taxation.

Support private or public credit on reasonable terms to young farmers to enable them to purchase farms on long-term, low-interest loans.

Support the federal crop insurance program.

Reaffirm our support of the rural electrification program, recognizing that rural America cannot be revitalized without adequate low-cost electric power. We pledge continued support of programs to assure supplemental financing to meet the growing generating and distributing power needs of rural areas. We support the rural telephone program.

Support a thorough study of the effect of unlimited payments to farmers. If necessary, we suggest graduated open-end limitations of payments to extremely large corporate farms that participate in government programs.

Take a positive approach to the public interest in the issue of health and tobacco at all levels of the tobacco economy. We recommend a cooperative effort in health and tobacco research by government, industry and qualified scientific bodies, to ascertain relationships between human health and tobacco growth, curing, storage and manufacturing techniques, as well as specific medical aspects of tobacco smoke constituents.

Small Business

Small business plays a vital role in a dynamic, competitive economy; it helps maintain a strong social fabric in communities across the land; it builds concerned community leadership deriving from ownership of small enterprises; and it maintains the challenge and competition essential to a free enterprise system.

To assure a continuing healthy environment for small business, the Democratic Party pledges to:

Assure adequate credit at reasonable costs;

Assure small business a fair share of government contracts and procurement;

Encourage investment in research and development of special benefit to small enterprise;

Assist small business in taking advantage of technological innovations;

Provide centers of information on government procurement needs and foreign sales opportunities.

The Democratic Party is pledged to develop programs that will enable members of minority groups to obtain the financing and technical management assistance needed to succeed in launching and operating new enterprises.

Labor–Management Relations

Private collective bargaining and a strong and independent labor movement are essential to our system of free enterprise and economic democracy. Their development has been fostered under each Democratic administration in this century.

We will thoroughly review and update the National Labor Relations Act to assure an effective opportunity to all workers to exercise the right to organize and to bargain collectively, including such amendments as:

Repeal of the provision permitting states to enact compulsory open-shop laws;

Extension of the Act's protection to farm workers, employees of private non-profit organizations, and other employees not now covered;

Removal of unreasonable restrictions upon the right of peaceful picketing, including situs picketing;

Speedier decisions in unfair labor practice cases and representation proceedings;

Greater equality between the remedies available under the Act to labor and those available to management;

Effective opportunities for unions as well as employers to communicate with employees, without coercion by either side or by anyone acting in their behalf.

The federal government will continue to set an example as an employer to private business and to state and local governments. The government will not do business with firms that repeatedly violate federal statutes prohibiting discrimination against employees who are union members or refuse to bargain with duly authorized union representatives.

By all these means, we will sustain the right of workers to organize in unions of their own choosing and will foster truly effective collective bargaining to provide the maximum opportunity for just and fair agreements between management and labor.

Consumer Protection

Rising incomes have brought new vigor to the market place. But the march of technology which has brought unparalleled abundance and opportunity to the consumer has also exposed him to new hazards and new complexities. In providing economic justice for consumers, we shall strengthen business and industry and improve the quality of life for all 200 million Americans.

We commend the Democratic Congress for passing

the landmark legislation of the past several years which has ushered in a new era of consumer protection—truth-in-lending, truth-in-packaging, wholesome meat and poultry, auto and highway safety, child safety, and protection against interstate land swindles.

We shall take steps, including necessary legislation, to minimize the likelihood of massive electric power failures, to improve the safety of medical devices and drugs, to penalize deceptive sales practices, and to provide consumer access to product information now being compiled in the federal government.

We will help the states to establish consumer fraud and information bureaus, and to update consumer credit laws.

A major objective of all consumer programs, at all levels, must be the education of the buying public, particularly the poor, who are the special targets of unscrupulous and high-pressure salesmanship.

We will make the consumer's voice increasingly heard in the councils of government. We will strengthen consumer education and enforcement programs by consolidation of functions now dispersed among various agencies, through the establishment of an Office of Consumer Affairs to represent consumer interests within the government and before courts and regulatory agencies.

Housing

For the first time in history, a nation is able to rebuild or replace all of its substandard housing, even while providing housing for millions of new families.

This means rebuilding or replacing 4.5 million dwelling units in our urban areas and 3.9 million in rural areas, most in conditions of such dilapidation that they are too often dens of despair for millions of Americans.

Yet this performance is possible in the next decade because of goals and programs fashioned by Democratic Presidents and Democratic Congresses in close partnership with private business.

The goal is clear and pressing—"a decent home and a suitable living environment for every American family," as set forth in the 1949 Housing Act by a Democratic Congress and administration.

To achieve this goal in the next ten years:

We will assist private enterprise to double its volume of homebuilding, to an annual rate of 2.6 million units a year—a ten-year total of 26 million units. This is the specific target of the history-making Housing and Urban Development Act of 1968.

We will give the highest priority to federally-assisted home-building for low-income families, with special attention given to ghetto dwellers, the elderly, the physically handicapped, and families in neglected areas of rural America, Indian reservations, territories of the United States, and migratory worker camps. All federal subsidy programs—whether in the form of public housing, interest rates at 1%, rent supplements, or direct loans—will be administered to favor these disadvantaged families, with full participation by the neighborhood residents themselves.

We will cooperate with private home builders to experiment boldly with new production technology, with financial institutions to marshal capital for housing where it is most needed, and with unions to expand the labor force needed for a doubling of production.

Above all, we will work toward the greatest possible freedom of choice—the opportunity for every family, regardless of race, color, religion, or income, to choose home ownership or rental, high-rise or low-rise, cooperatives or condominiums, detached or town house, and city, suburban or country living.

We urge local governments to shape their own zoning laws and building codes to favor consumers and hold down costs.

Rigid enforcement of state and local health and building codes is imperative to alleviate conditions of squalor and despair in deteriorating neighborhoods.

Democrats are proud of their housing record. But we are also painfully aware of how much more needs to be done to reach the final goal of decent shelter for all Americans and we pledge a steadfast pursuit of that goal.

Transportation

America is a nation on the move. To meet the challenge of transportation, we propose a dynamic partnership between industry and government at all levels.

Of utmost urgency is the need to solve congestion in air traffic, especially in airports and between major metropolitan centers. We pledge intensified efforts to devise equitable methods of financing new and improved airport and airway facilities.

Urban and inter-urban transportation facilities are heavily overburdened. We support expanded programs of assistance to mass transit in order to avoid unnecessary congestion in air traffic, especially at airlink residential and work areas.

Despite the tremendous progress of our interstate highway program, still more super-highways are needed for safe and rapid motor transport. We need to establish local road networks to meet regional requirements.

The efficiency of our railroads has improved greatly but there is need for further strengthening of the nation's railroads so that they can contribute more fully to the nation's transport requirements. In particular, we will press forward with the effort to develop high-speed passenger trains to serve major urban areas.

To assume our proper place as a leading maritime nation, we must launch an aggressive and balanced program to replace and augment our obsolete merchant ships with modern vessels built in American shipyards. We will assist U.S. flag operators to overcome the competitive disparity between American and foreign costs.

We will continue to foster development of harbors, ports, and inland waterways, particularly regional waterways systems, and the St. Lawrence Seaway, to accommodate our expanded water-borne commerce. We support modernization of the Panama Canal.

We pledge a greater investment in transportation research and development to enhance safety and increase speed and economy; to implement the acts that have been passed to control noxious vehicle exhausts; and to reduce aircraft noise.

The expansion of our transportation must not be carried out at the expense of the environment through which it moves. We applaud the leadership provided by the First Lady to enhance the highway environment and initiate a national beautification program.

Communications

America has the most efficient and comprehensive communications system in the world. But a healthy society depends more on the quality of what is communicated than on either the volume or form of communication.

Public broadcasting has already proven that it can be a valuable supplement to formal education and a direct medium for non-formal education. We pledge our continuing support for the prompt enactment of a long-range financing plan that will help ensure the vigor and independence of this potentially vital but still underdeveloped new force in American life.

We deplore the all too frequent exploitation of violence as entertainment in all media.

In 1962 the Democratic Party sensed the great potential of space communication and quickly translated this awareness into the Communications Satellite Act. In a creative partnership between government and business, this revolutionary idea soon became a reality. Six years later we helped establish a consortium of 61 nations devoted to the development of a global satellite network.

We will continue to develop new technology and utilize communications to promote world-wide understanding as an essential pre-condition of world peace. But, in view of rapidly changing technology, the entire federal regulatory system dealing with telecommunication should be thoroughly reappraised.

Science and Technology

We lead the world in science and technology. This has produced a dramatic effect on the daily lives of all of us. To maintain our undisputed national leadership in science and further its manifold applications for the betterment of mankind, the federal government has a clear obligation to foster and support creative men and women in the research community, both public and private.

Our pioneering space program has helped mankind on Earth in countless ways. The benefits from improved weather forecasting which can soon be available to satellite observations and communications will by themselves make the space efforts worthwhile.

Observation by satellite of crops and other major Earth resources will for the first time enable man to see all that is available to him on Earth, and therefore to take maximum advantage of it. High endurance metals developed for spacecraft help make commercial planes safer; similarly, micro-electronics are now found in consumer appliances. Novel space food-preservation techniques are employed in the tropical climates of underdeveloped countries. We will move ahead in aerospace research and development for their unimagined promise for man on Earth as well as their vital importance to national defense.

We shall continue to work for our goal of leadership in space. To this end we will maximize the effectiveness and efficiency of our space programs through utilization of the best program, planning and budgeting systems.

To maintain our leadership in the application of energy, we will push forward with research and development to assure a balanced program for the supply of energy for electric power, both public and private. This effort should go hand in hand with development of "breeder" reactors and large-scale nuclear desalting plants that can provide pure water economically from the sea for domestic use and agricultural and industrial development in arid regions, and with broadened medical and biological applications of atomic energy.

In addition to the physical sciences, the social sciences will be encouraged and assisted to identify and deal with the problem areas of society.

Opportunity for All

We of the Democratic Party believe that a nation wealthy beyond the dreams of most of mankind—a nation with a twentieth of the world's population, possessing half the world's manufactured goods—has the capacity and the duty to assure to all its citizens the opportunity to enjoy the full measure of the blessings of American life.

For the first time in the history of the world, it is within the power of a nation to eradicate from within its borders the age-old curse of poverty.

Our generation of Americans has now made those commitments. It remains to implement and adequately fund the host of practical measures that demonstrate their effectiveness and to continue to devise new approaches.

We are guided by the recommendations of the National Advisory Commission on Civil Disorders concerning jobs, housing, urban renewal, and education on a scale commensurate with the needs of the urban ghettos. We are guided by the report of the Commission on Rural Poverty in tackling the equally compelling problems of the rural slums.

Economic growth is our first antipoverty program. The best avenue to an independent, confident citizenry is a dynamic, full-employment economy. Beyond that lie the measures necessary to assure that every American, of every race, in every region, truly shares in the benefits of economic progress.

Those measures include rehabilitation of the victims of poverty, elimination of the urban and rural slums where poverty is bred, and changes throughout the system of institutions that affect the lives of the poor.

In this endeavor, the resources of private enterprise—not only its economic power but its leadership and ingenuity—must be mobilized. We must marshal the power that comes from people working together in communities—the neighborhood communities of the poor and the larger communities of the city, the town, the village, the region.

We support community action agencies and their programs, such as Head Start, that will prevent the children of the poor from becoming the poor of the next generation. We support the extension of neighborhood centers. We are committed to the principle of meaningful participation of the poor in policy-making and administration of community action and related programs.

Since organizations of many kinds are joined in the war on poverty, problems of coordination inevitably arise. We pledge ourselves to review current antipoverty efforts to assess how responsibility should be distributed among levels of government, among private and public agencies, and between the permanent agencies of the federal government and an independent antipoverty agency.

Toward a Single Society

We acknowledge with concern the findings of the report of the bi-partisan National Advisory Commission on Civil Disorders and we commit ourselves to implement its recommendations and to wipe out, once and for all, the stain of racial and other discrimination from our national life. "The major goal," the Commission wrote, "is the creation of a true union—a single society and a single American identify." A single society, however, does not mean social or cultural uniformity. We are a nation of many social, ethnic and national groups. Each has brought richness and strength to America.

The Civil Rights Act of 1964 and 1968 and the Voting Rights Act of 1965, all adopted under the vigorous leadership of President Johnson, are basic to America's long march toward full equality under the law.

We will not permit these great gains to be chipped away by opponents or eroded by administrative neglect. We pledge effective and impartial enforcement of these laws. If they prove inadequate, or if their compliance provisions fail to serve their purposes, we will propose new laws. In particular, the enforcement provisions of the legislation prohibiting discrimination in employment should be strengthened. This will be done as a matter of first priority.

We have also come to recognize that freedom and equality require more than the ending of repression and prejudice. The victims of past discrimination must be encouraged and assisted to take full advantage of opportunities that are now opening to them.

We must recognize that for too long we have neglected the abilities and aspirations of Spanish-speaking Americans to participate fully in American life. We promise to fund and implement the Bilingual Education Act and expand recruitment and training of bilingual federal and state employees.

The American Indian has the oldest claim on our national conscience. We must continue and increase federal help in the Indian's battle against poverty, unemployment, illiteracy, ill health and poor housing. To this end, we pledge a new and equal federal–Indian partnership that will enable Indian communities to provide for themselves many services now furnished by the federal government and federal sponsorship of industrial development programs owned, managed, and run by Indians. We support a quick and fair settlement of land claims of Indian, Eskimo and Aleut citizens of Alaska.

The Inner City

In the decaying slums of our larger cities, where so many of our poor are concentrated, the attack on poverty must embrace many inter-related aspects of development—economic development, the rehabilitation or replacement of dilapidated and unsafe housing, job training and placement, and the improvement of education, health, recreation, crime control, welfare, and other public services.

As the framework of such an effort, we will continue to support the Model Cities program under which communities themselves are planning and carrying out the most comprehensive plans ever put together for converting their worst slum areas into model neighborhoods—with full participation and leadership by the neighborhood residents themselves. The Model Cities program will be steadily extended to more cities and more neighborhoods and adequately financed.

The resources and leadership of private enterprise must be marshaled in the attack on slums and poverty, and such incentives as may be essential for that purpose we will develop and enact.

Some of the most urgent jobs in the revival of the inner city remain undone because the hazards are too great and the rewards too limited to attract sufficient private capital. To meet this problem, we will charter a new federal banking structure to provide capital and investment guarantees for urban projects planned and implemented through local initiative—neighborhood development corporations, minority programs for self-employment, housing development corporations, and other urban construction and planning operations. We will also enact legislation providing tax incentives for new business and industrial enterprises in the inner city. Our experience with aid to small business demonstrates the importance of increased local ownership of business enterprises in the inner city.

We shall aid the universities to concentrate their resources more fully upon the problems of the cities and facilitate their cooperation with municipal agencies and local organizations in finding solutions to urban problems.

Rural Development

Balanced growth is essential for America. To achieve that balanced growth, we must greatly increase the growth of the rural non-farm economy. One-third of our people live in rural areas, but only one rural family in ten derives its principal income from farming. Almost thirty percent of the nation's poor are non-farm people in rural areas.

The problem of rural poverty and the problem of migration of poor people from rural areas to urban ghettos are mainly non-farm problems. The creation of productive jobs in small cities and towns can be the best and least costly solution of these problems.

To revitalize rural and small-town America and assure equal opportunity for all Americans wherever they live, we pledge to:

Create jobs by offering inducements to new enterprises—using tax and other incentives—located in small towns and rural areas;

Administer existing federal programs and design new programs where necessary to overcome the disparity between rural and urban areas in opportunities for education, for health services, for low-income housing, for employment and job training, and for public services of all kinds;

Encourage the development of new towns and new growth centers;

Encourage the creation of comprehensive planning and development agencies to provide additional leadership in non-metropolitan areas, and assist them financially.

The experience of the Appalachian and other regional commissions indicates that municipalities, counties, and state and federal agencies can work together in a common development effort.

Jobs and Training

Every American in need of work should have opportunity not only for meaningful employment, but also for the education, training, counselling, and other services that enable him to take advantage of available jobs.

To the maximum possible extent, our national goal of full employment should be realized through creation of jobs in the private economy, where six of every seven Americans now work. We will continue the Job Opportunities in the Business Sector (JOBS) program, which for the first time has mobilized the energies of business and industry on a nationwide scale to provide training and employment to the hardcore unemployed. We will develop whatever additional incentives may be necessary to maximize the opportunities in the private sector for hardcore unemployed.

We will continue also to finance the operation by local communities of a wide range of training programs for youth and retraining for older workers whose skills have become obsolete, coupled with related services necessary to enable people to undertake training and accept jobs—including improved recruitment and placement services, day-care centers, and transportation between work and home.

For those who can work but cannot find jobs, we pledge to expand public job and job-training programs, including the Neighborhood Youth Corps, to provide meaningful employment by state and local government and non-profit institutions.

For those who cannot obtain other employment, the federal government will be the employer of last resort, either through federal assistance to state and local projects or through federally sponsored projects.

Employment Standards

American workers are entitled to more than the right to a job. They have the right to fair and safe working conditions and to adequate protection in periods of unemployment or disability.

In the last thirty years Democratic administrations and Congress have enacted, extended and improved a series of measures to provide safeguards against exploitation and distress. We pledge to continue these efforts.

The minimum standards covering terms and conditions of employment must be improved:

By increasing the minimum wage guarantee to assure those at the bottom of the economic scale a fairer share in rising living standards;

By extending the minimum wage and overtime provision of the Fair Labor Standards Act to all workers;

By enacting occupational health and safety legislation to assure the material reduction of the present occupational death rate of 14,500 men and women each year, and the disabling accident rate of over 2 million per year;

By assuring that the "green card" worker does not depress wages and conditions of employment for American workers;

By updating of the benefit provisions of the Longshoremen and Harbor Workers Act.

The unemployment compensation program should be modernized by national minimum standards for level and duration of benefits, eligibility, and universal coverage.

Older Citizens

A lifetime of work and effort deserves a secure and satisfying retirement.

Benefits, especially minimum benefits, under Old Age, Survivors, and Disability Insurance should be raised to overcome present inadequacies and thereafter should be adjusted automatically to reflect increases in living costs.

Medical care for the aged should be expanded to include the costs of prescription drugs.

The minimum age for public assistance should be lowered to correspond to the requirements for Social Security.

America's self-employed citizens should be encouraged by tax incentive legislation to supplement Social Security benefits for themselves and their employees to the same extent that employees of corporations are encouraged.

In addition to improving Social Security, we must develop in each community a wide variety of activities to enrich the lives of our older citizens, to enable them to continue to contribute to our society, and to permit them to live in dignity. The aged must have access to better housing, opportunities for regular or part-time employment and community volunteer services, and cultural and recreational activities.

People in Need

Every American family whose income is not sufficient to enable its members to live in decency should receive assistance free of the indignities and uncertainties that still too often mar our present programs. To support family incomes of the working poor a number of new program proposals have recently been developed. A thorough evaluation of the relative advantages of such proposals deserves the highest priority attention by the next administration. This we pledge to do.

Income payments and eligibility standards for the aged, the blind, the disabled and dependent children should be determined and financed on a federal basis—in place of the present inequitable, under-financed hodgepodge of state plans. This would, among other things, assure the eligibility in all states of needy children of unemployed parents who are now denied assistance in more than half the states as long as the father remains in the home.

Assistance payments should not only be brought to adequate levels but they should be kept adequate by providing for automatic adjustment to reflect increases in living costs.

Congress has temporarily suspended the restrictive amendment of 1967 that placed an arbitrary limit on the number of dependent children who can be aided in each state. We favor permanent repeal of that restriction and of the provision requiring mothers of young children to work.

The new federal–state program we propose should provide for financial incentives and needed services to enable and encourage adults on welfare to seek employment to the extent they are able to do so.

The time has come when we should make a national commitment that no American should have to go hungry or undernourished. The Democratic Party here and now does make that commitment. We will move rapidly to implement it through continued improvement and expansion of our food programs.

The Democratic Congress this year has already enacted legislation to expand and improve the school lunch and commodity distribution programs, and shortly will complete action on legislation now pending to expand the food stamp program. We will enact further legislation and appropriations to assure on a permanent basis that the school lunch program provides free and reduced-price meals to all needy school children.

Health

The best of modern medical care should be made available to every American. We support efforts to overcome the remaining barriers of distance, poverty, ignorance, and discrimination that separate persons from adequate medical services.

During the last eight years of Democratic administrations, this nation has taken giant steps forward in assuring life and health for its citizens. In the years ahead, we Democrats are determined to take those final steps that are necessary to make certain that every American, regardless of economic status, shall live out his years without fear of the high costs of sickness.

Through a partnership of government and private enterprise we must develop new coordinated approaches to stem the rise in medical and drug costs without lowering the quality or availability of medical care. Out-of-hospital care, comprehensive group practice arrangements, increased availability of neighborhood health centers, and the greater rise of sub-professional aides can all contribute to the lowering of medical costs.

We will raise the level of research in all fields of health, with special programs for development of the artificial heart and the heart transplant technique, development of drugs to treat and prevent the recurrence of heart diseases, expansion of current task forces in cancer research and the creation of new ones including cancer of the lung, determination of the factors in mental retardation and reduction of infant mortality, development of drugs to reduce the incidence of suicide, and construction of health research facilities and hospitals.

We must build new medical, dental and medical service schools, and increase the capacity of existing ones, to train more doctors, dentists, nurses, and medical technicians.

Medical care should be extended to disabled beneficiaries under the Old Age, Survivors and Disability Insurance Act to the same extent and under the same system that such care is available to the aged.

Thousands of children die, or are handicapped for life, because their mothers did not receive proper prenatal medical attention or because the infants were unattended in the critical first days of life. Maternal and child health centers, located and designed to serve the needs of the poor, and voluntary family planning information centers should be established throughout the country. Medicaid programs administered by the states should have uniform standards so that no mother or child is denied necessary health services. Finally, we urge consideration of a program comparable to Medicare to finance prenatal care for mothers and postnatal care for children during the first year of life.

Veterans

American veterans deserve our enduring gratitude for their distinguished service to the nation.

In 1968 some 750,000 returning servicemen will continue their education with increased benefits under the new GI Bill passed by an education-minded Democratic Congress. Two million disabled veterans and survivors of those killed in action are receiving larger pensions and higher disability payments.

Guided by the report of the Veterans Advisory Commission, established by the Democratic administration, we will:

Continue a strong one-stop agency vested with sole responsibility for all veterans programs;

Sustain and upgrade veteran medical services and expand medical training in VA hospitals;

Maintain compensation for disabled veterans and for widows and dependents of veterans who die of service-connected causes, in line with the rise in earnings and living standards;

Assure every veteran the right of burial in a national cemetery;

Provide incentives for veterans to aid their communities by serving in police, fire departments, educational systems and other public endeavors;

Make veterans and their widows eligible for pension benefits at the same age at which Social Security beneficiaries may receive old-age benefits.

We recommend the establishment of a standing Committee on Veteran Affairs in the Senate.

Education

Education is the chief instrument for making good the American promise. It is indispensable to every man's chance to achieve his full potential. We will seek to open education to all Americans.

We will assure equal opportunity to education and equal access to high-quality education. Our aim is to maintain state–local control over the nation's educational system with federal financial assistance and help in stimulating changes through demonstration and technical assistance. New concepts of education and training employing new communications technology must be developed to educate children and adults.

Every citizen has a basic right to as much education and training as he desires and can master—from preschool through graduate studies—even if his family cannot pay for his education.

We will marshal our national resources to help develop and finance new and effective methods of dealing with the educationally disadvantaged—including expanded preschool programs to prepare all young children for full participation in formal education, improved teacher recruitment and training programs for inner city and rural schools, the Teacher Corps, assistance to community controlled schools to encourage pursuit of innovative practices, university participation in research and operation of school programs, a vocational education system that will provide imaginative new ties between school and the world of work, and improved and more wide-spread adult education programs.

We will fully fund Title I of the Elementary and Secondary Education Act of 1965, which provides federal funds for improving education in schools serving large numbers of students from low-income families.

The financial burden of education continues to grow as enrollments spiral and costs increase. The home owner's property tax burden must be eased by increased levels of financial aid by both the states and the federal government.

Our rapidly expanding educational frontiers require a redoubling of efforts to insure the vitality of a diverse higher education system—public and private, large and small, community and junior colleges, vocational and technical schools, and great universities. We also pledge support for high-quality graduate and medical education.

We will enlarge the federal scholarship program to remove the remaining financial barriers to post-secondary education for low-income youths, and increase assistance to students in the form of repayable loans out of future income.

We will encourage support for the arts and the humanities, through the national foundations established by a Democratic Congress, to provide incentives for those endowed with extraordinary talent, enhance the quality of our life, and make productive leisure available to all our people.

We recommend greater stress on the arts and humanities in elementary and secondary curricula to ensure a proper educational balance.

Youth

For generations, the Democratic Party has renewed its vitality with young people and new ideas. Today, young people are bringing a new vigor and a deep concern for social justice into the political process, yet many feel excluded from full participation.

We of the Democratic Party welcome the bold thinking and exciting ideas of youth. We recognize, with deep satisfaction, that their healthy desire for participation in the democratic system must lead to a series of reforms in the direction of a greater democracy and a more open America.

The Democratic Party takes pride in the fact that so many of today's youth have channeled their interests and energies into our Party. To them, and to all young Americans we pledge the fullest opportunity to participate in the affairs of our Party at the local, state, and national levels. We call for special efforts to recruit young people as candidates for public office.

We will support a Constitutional amendment lowering the voting age to 18.

We will favor an increase in youth representation on state delegations in future Democratic conventions.

Steps should be taken to include youth advisers on all government studies, commissions, and hearings which are relevant to their lives.

Every young person should have an opportunity to contribute to the social health of his community or to humanitarian service abroad. The extraordinary experience of the Teacher Corps, VISTA, and the Peace Corps points the way for broadening the opportunities for such voluntary service. Hundreds of thousands of America's youth have sought to enlist in these programs, but only tens of thousands have been able to serve. We will expand these opportunities.

The lives of millions of young men are deeply affected by the requirement for military service. The present system leaves them in uncertainty through much of their early manhood. Until our manpower needs can be fully met by voluntary enlistment, the Democratic Party will insist upon the most equitable and just selection system that can be devised. We support a random system of selection which will reduce the period of eligibility to one year, guarantee fair selection, and remove uncertainty.

We urge review of draft board memberships to make them more representative of the communities they serve.

Environment, Conservation and Natural Resources

These United States have undergone 200 years of continuous change and dramatic development resulting in the most technologically advanced nation in the world. But with rapid industrialization, the nation's air and water resources have been degraded, the public health and welfare endangered, the landscape scarred and littered, and the very quality of our national life jeopardized.

We must assure the availability of a decent environment for living, working and relaxation.

To this end, we pledge our efforts:

To accelerate programs for the enhancement of the quality of the nation's waters for the protection of all legitimate water uses, with special emphasis on public water supplies, recreation, fish and wildlife;

To extend the national emission control program to all moving sources of air pollution;

To work for programs for the effective disposal of wastes of our modern industrial society;

To support the efforts on national, state, and local levels to preserve the historic monuments and sites of our heritage;

To assist in planning energy production and transportation to fit into the landscape, to assure safety, and to avoid interference with more desirable uses of land for recreation and other public purposes;

To continue to work toward abating the visual pollution that plagues our land;

To focus on the outdoor recreation needs of those who live in congested metropolitan areas;

To continue to work toward strong measures for the reclamation of mined and depleted lands and the conservation of soil.

Public Domain

We pledge continued support of the Public Land Law Review Commission, which is reviewing public land laws and policies to assure maximum opportunity for all beneficial uses of the public lands, including lands under the sea, and to develop a comprehensive land use policy.

We support sustained yield management of our forests, and expanded research for control of forest insects, disease, and fires.

We plan to examine the productivity of the public lands in goods, services, and local community prosperity; with a view to increasing such productivity.

We shall enforce existing federal statutes governing federal timber.

We support the orderly use and development of mineral resources on federal lands.

Recreation

We will continue the vigorous expansion of the public recreational domain to meet tomorrow's increasing needs. We will add national parks, recreation areas and seashores, and create national systems of scenic and wild rivers and of trails and scenic roads. We will support a growing wilderness preservation system, preservation of our redwood forests, and conservation of marshlands and estuarine areas.

Recognizing that the bulk of the task of acquisition and development must be accomplished at the state and local levels we shall foster federal assistance to encourage such action, as well as recreational expansion by the private sector. To this end, we shall build upon the landmark Land and Water Conservation Fund Act, which has assured a foundation of a recreational heritage for future generations. We will assist communities to rehabilitate and expand inadequate and deteriorating urban park systems, and develop open space, waterways, and waterfront renovation facilities.

Resources of the Oceans

In and beneath the seas are resources of untold dimension for the benefit of mankind. Recognizing and protecting the paramount public interest in the seas, Congress under Democratic leadership enacted the Sea Grant College Act of 1965 and the Marine Resources and Engineering Development Act of 1966, which established for the first time a comprehensive long-range policy and program for the marine sciences. We pledge to pursue vigorously the goals of that Act. Specifically, we will:

Foster marine application of new technology—spacecraft, buoys, data networks, and advanced navigation systems—and develop an engineering capability to work on and under the sea at any depth;

Encourage development of underseas resources by intensified research and better weather forecasting, with recognition to the coastal, insular and other littoral states of their unique interest and responsibility;

Foster an extensive program of oceanologic research and development, financed by a portion of the mineral-royalty receipts from the outer continental shelf;

Accelerate public and private programs for the development of food and other marine resources to meet world-wide malnutrition, to create new industries, and to utilize underemployed manpower living near the waterfront;

Promote our fisheries by providing incentives for private investment, enforcing our 12-mile fishing zone, and discouraging other nations from excessive territorial and fishery claims;

Conclude an appropriate Ocean Space treaty to secure rules and agreements that will facilitate public and private investment, guarantee security of investment and encourage efficient and orderly development of the sea's resources.

The Government

In the coming four years, the Democratic President and Democratic Congress will give priority to simplifying and streamlining the processes of government, particularly in the management of the great innovative programs enacted in the 1960's.

The Executive branch of the federal government is the largest and most complicated enterprise in the world, with programs distributed among 150 separate departments, agencies, bureaus, and boards. This massive operation contributes to and often results in duplication, administrative confusion, and delay.

We will seek to streamline this machinery by improving coordination and management of federal programs.

We realize that government must develop the capacity to anticipate problems. We support a thorough study of agency operations to determine priorities for governmental action and spending, for examination of the structure of these agencies, and for establishing more systematic means of attacking our nation's problems.

We recognize that citizen participation in government is most meaningful at the levels of government closest to the people. For that reason, we recognize the necessity of developing a true partnership between state, local, and federal governments, with each carrying its share of the financial and administrative load. We acknowledge the tremendous strides made by President Johnson in strengthening federal–state relations through open communication with the governors and local officials, and we pledge to continue and expand on this significant effort.

The complexities of federal–state–local relationships must be simplified, so that states and local communities receiving federal aid will have maximum freedom to initiate and carry out programs suited to their own particular needs. To give states and communities greater flexibility in their programs, we will combine individual grant programs into broader categories.

As the economy grows, it is the federal revenue system that responds most quickly, yet it may be the states and local governments whose responsibilities mount most rapidly. To help states and cities meet their fiscal challenges, we must seek new methods for states and local governments to share in federal revenues while retaining responsibility for establishing their own priorities and for operating their own programs. To this end, we will seek out new and innovative approaches to government to assure that our federal system does, in fact, deliver to the people the services for which they are paying.

Public Employees

The Democratic administration has moved vigorously in the past eight years—particularly with regard to pay scales—to improve the conditions of public service.

We support:

A federal service that rewards new ideas and leadership;

Continued emphasis on education and training programs for public employees, before and during their service;

Parity of government salaries with private industry;

A proper respect for the privacy and independence of federal employees;

Equal opportunities for career advancement.

Continued application of the principles of collective bargaining to federal employment;

Encouragement to state and local governments to continue to upgrade their personnel systems in terms of pay scales and training;

Interchange of employees between federal and state government.

Elections

We are alarmed at the growing costs of political participation in our country and the consequent reliance of political parties and candidates on large contributors, and we want to assure full public information on campaign expenditures. To encourage citizen participation we urge that limited campaign contributions be made deductible as a credit from the federal income tax.

We fully recognize the principle of one man, one vote in all elections. We urge that due consideration be given to the question of presidential primaries throughout the nation. We urge reform of the electoral college and election procedures to assure that the votes of the people are fully reflected.

We urge all levels of our Party to assume leadership in removing all remaining barriers to voter registration.

We will also seek to eliminate disenfranchisement of voters who change residence during an election year.

The District of Columbia

With the reorganization of the government of the District of Columbia, the nation's capitil has for the first time in nearly a century the strong leadership provided by a mayor–council form of government. This, however, is no substitute for an independent and fiscally autonomous District government. We support a federally funded charter commission—controlled by District residents—to determine the most appropriate form of government for the District, and the prompt implementation of the Commission's recommendations.

The Democratic Party supports full citizenship for residents of the District of Columbia and a Constitutional amendment to grant such citizenship through voting representation in Congress. Until this can be done, we propose nonvoting representation.

Puerto Rico

In accordance with the democratic principle of self-determination the people of Puerto Rico have expressed their will to continue in permanent union with the United States through commonwealth status. We pledge our continued support to the growth of the commonwealth status which the people of Puerto Rico overwhelmingly approved last year.

Virgin Islands and Guam

We favor an elected governor and a nonvoting delegate in the House of Representatives for the Virgin Islands and Guam, and will consider methods by which American citizens residing in American territories can participate in presidential elections.

Justice and Law

We are firm in our commitment that equal justice under law shall be denied to no one. The duty of government at every level is the safety and security of its people. Yet the fact and fear of crime are uppermost in the minds of Americans today. The entire nation is united in its concern over crime , in all forms and wherever it occurs. America must move aggressively to reduce crime and its causes.

Democratic Presidents, governors and local officials are dedicated to the principle that equal justice under law shall remain the American creed. Those who take the law into their own hands undermine that creed. Anyone who breaks the law must be held accountable. Organized crime cannot be accepted as a way of life, nor can individual crime or acts of violence be permitted.

As stated in the report of the National Advisory Commission on Civil Disorders, the two fundamental questions confronting the American people are:

"How can we as a people end the resort to violence while we build a better society?

"How can the nation realize the promise of a single society—one nation indivisible—which yet remains unfulfilled?"

This platform commits the Democratic Party to seek resolution of these questions.

We pledge a vigorous and sustained campaign against lawlessness in all its forms—organized crime, white collar crime, rioting, and other violations of the rights and liberties of others. We will further this campaign by attack on the root causes of crime and disorder.

Under the recent enactments of a Democratic Congress we will continue and increase federal financial support and technical assistance to the states and their local governments to:

Increase the numbers, raise the pay, and improve the training of local police officers;

Reduce delays and congestion in our criminal courts;

Rehabilitate and supervise convicted offenders, to return offenders to useful, decent lives, and to protect the public against habitual criminals;

Develop and deploy the most advanced, effective techniques and equipment for the public safety;

Assure the availability in every metropolitan area of quick, balanced, coordinated control forces, with ample manpower, thoroughly trained and properly equipped, to suppress rioting;

Encourage responsible and competent civic associations and business and labor groups to cooperate with the law enforcement agencies in new efforts to combat organized crime, build community support for police work, and assist in rehabilitating convicted offenders—and for the attainment of these ends, encourage our police to cooperate with any such groups and to establish links of communication with every element of the public they serve, building confidence and respect;

Establish and maintain open and responsive channels of communication between the public and the police through creative police–community relations programs;

Develop innovative programs to reduce the incidence of juvenile delinquency;

Promote the passage and enforcement of effective federal, state and local gun control legislation.

In all these efforts, our aim is to strengthen state and local law enforcement agencies so that they can do their jobs. In addition, the federal government has a clear responsibility for national action. We have accepted that responsibility and will continue to accept it with these specific objectives:

Prompt and effective federal support, upon request of appropriate authorities, to suppress rioting: improvement of the capabilities of all agencies of law enforcement and justice—the police, the military, the courts—to handle more effectively problems attending riots;

A concentrated campaign by the federal government to wipe out organized crime: by employment of additional federal investigators and prosecutors; by computerizing the present system of collecting information; by enlarging the program of technical assistance teams to work with the states and local governments that request assistance in this fight; by launching a nationwide program for the country's business and labor leaders to alert them to the problems of organized crime;

Intensified enforcement, research, and education to protect the public from narcotics and other damaging drugs: by review of federal narcotics laws for loopholes and difficulties of enforcement; by increased surveillance of the entire drug traffic; through negotiations with those foreign nations which grow and manufacture the bulk of drug derivatives;

Vigorous federal leadership to assist and coordinate state and local enforcement efforts, and to ensure that all communities benefit from the resources and knowledge essential to the fight on crime;

Further implementation of the recommendations of the President's crime commission;

Creation in the District of Columbia of a model system of criminal justice;

Federal research and development to bring to the problems of law enforcement and the administration of justice the full potential of the scientific revolution.

In fighting crime we must not foster injustice. Lawlessness cannot be ended by curtailing the hard-won liberties of all Americans. The right of privacy must be safeguarded. Court procedures must be expedited. Justice delayed is justice denied.

A respect for civil peace requires also a proper respect for the legitimate means of expressing dissent. A democratic society welcomes criticism within the limits of the law. Freedom of speech, press, assembly and association, together with free exercise of the franchise, are among the legitimate means to achieve change in democratic society. But when the dissenter resorts to violence he erodes the institutions and values which are the underpinnings of our democratic society. We must not and will not tolerate violence.

As President Johnson has stated, "Our test is to rise above the debate between the rights of the individual and the rights of society by securing the rights of both."

We freely admit that the years we live in are years of turbulence. But the wisdom of history has something hopeful to say about times like these. It tells us that the giant American nation, on the move with giant strides, has never moved—and can never move—in silence.

We are an acting, doing, feeling people. We are a people whose deepest emotions are the source of the creative noise we make—precisely because of our ardent desire for unity, our wish for peace, our longing for concord, our demand for justice, our hope for material well-being, our impulse to move always toward a more perfect union.

In that never-ending quest, we are all partners together—the industrialist and the banker, the workman and the storekeeper, the farmer and the scientist, the clerk and the engineer, the teacher and the student, the clergyman and the writer, the men of all colors and of all the different generations.

The American dream is not the exclusive property of any political party. But we submit that the Democratic Party has been the chief instrument of orderly progress in our time. As heirs to the longest tradition of any political party on earth, we Democrats have been trained over the generations to be a party of builders. And that experience has taught us that America builds best when it is called upon to build greatly.

We sound that call anew. With the active consent of the American people, we will prove anew that freedom is best secured by a government that is responsive and compassionate and committed to justice and the rule of law.

— 1972 —

I. NEW DIRECTIONS: 1972–76

Skepticism and cynicism are widespread in America. The people are *skeptical* of platforms filled with political platitudes—of promises made by opportunistic politicians.

The people are *cynical* about the idea that a rosy future is just around the corner.

And is it any wonder that the people are skeptical and cynical of the whole political process?

Our traditions, our history, our Constitution, our laws, all say that America belongs to its people.

But the people no longer believe it.

They feel that the government is run for the privileged few rather than for the many—and they are right.

No political party, no President, no government can by itself restore a lost sense of faith. No Administration can provide solutions to all our problems. What we can do is to recognize the doubts of Americans, to speak to those doubts, and to act to begin turning those doubts into hopes.

As Democrats, we know that we share responsibility for that loss of confidence. But we also know, as Democrats, that at decisive moments of choice in our past, our Party has offered leadership that his tapped the best within our country.

Our party—standing by its ideals of domestic progress and enlightened internationalism—has served America well. We have nominated or elected men of the high calibre of Woodrow Wilson, Franklin Delano Roosevelt, Harry S. Truman, Adlai E. Stevenson, John Fitzgerald Kennedy, Lyndon Baines Johnson—and in the last election Hubert Humphrey and Edmund S. Muskie. In that proud tradition we are now prepared to move forward.

We know that our nation cannot tolerate any longer a government that shows no regard for the people's basic needs and no respect for our right to the truth from those who lead us.

What do the people want?

They want three things:

They want a personal life that makes us all feel that life is worth living;

They want a social environment whose institutions promote the good of all; and

They want a physical environment whose resources are used for the good of all.

They want an opportunity to achieve their aspirations and their dreams for themselves and their children.

We believe in the rights of citizens to achieve to the limit of their talents and energies. We are determined to remove barriers that limit citizens because they are black, brown, young or women; because they never had the chance to gain an education; because there was no possibility of being anything but what they were.

We believe in hard work as a fair measure of our own willingness to achieve. We are determined that millions should not stand idle while work demands to be done. We are determined that the dole should not become a permanent way of life for any. And we are determined that government no longer tax the product of hard work more rigorously than it taxes inherited wealth, or money that is gained simply by having money in the first place.

We believe that the law must apply equally to all, and that it must be an instrument of justice.

We are determined that the citizen must be protected in his home and on his streets. We are determined also that the ordinary citizen should not be imprisoned for a crime before we know whether he is guilty or not while those with the right friends and the

right connections can break the law without ever facing the consequences of their actions.

We believe that war is a waste of human life. We are determined to end forthwith a war which has cost 50,000 American lives, $150 billion of our resources, that has divided us from each other, drained our national will and inflicted incalculable damage to countless people. We will end that war by a simple plan that need not be kept secret: The immediate total withdrawal of all Americans from Southeast Asia.

We believe in the right of an individual to speak, think, read, write, worship, and live free of official intrusion. We are determined that our government must no longer tap the phones of law-abiding citizens nor spy on those who have broken no law. We are determined that never again shall government seek to censor the newspapers and television. We are determined that the government shall no longer mock the supreme law of the land, while it stands helpless in the face of crime which makes our neighborhoods and communities less and less safe.

Perhaps most fundamentally, we believe that government is the servant, not the master, of the people. We are determined that government should not mean a force so huge, so impersonal, that the complaint of an ordinary citizen goes unheard.

That is not the kind of government America was created to build. Our ancestors did not fight a revolution and sacrifice their lives against tyrants from abroad to leave us a government that does not know how to listen to its own people.

The Democratic Party is proud of its past; but we are honest enough to admit that we are part of the past and share in its mistakes. We want in 1972 to begin the long and difficult task of reviewing existing programs, revising them to make them work and finding new techniques to serve the public need. We want to speak for, and with, the citizens of our country. Our pledge is to be truthful to the people and to ourselves, to tell you when we succeed, but also when we fail or when we are not sure. In 1976, when this nation celebrates its 200th anniversary, we want to tell you simply that we have done our best to give the government to those who formed it—the people of America.

Every election is a choice: In 1972, Americans must decide whether they want their country back again.

II. JOBS, PRICES AND TAXES

"I went to school here and I had some training for truck driver school and I go to different places and put in applications for truck driving but they say, 'We can't hire you without the experience.' Now, I don't have the experience. I don't get the experience without the job first. I have four kids, you know, and I'm on unemployment. And when my unemployment runs out, I'll probably be on relief, like a lot of other people. But, being that I have so many kids, relief is just not going to be enough money. I'm looking for maybe the next year or two, but if I don't get a job, they'll probably find me down at the county jail, because I have to do something."—Robert Coleman, Pittsburgh Hearing, June 2, 1972.

The Nixon Administration has deliberately driven people out of work in a heartless and ineffective effort to deal with inflation. Ending the Nixon policy of creating unemployment is the first task of the Democratic Party.

The Nixon "game plan" called for more unemployment. Tens of millions of families have suffered joblessness or work cutbacks in the last four years in the name of fighting inflation . . . and for nothing.

Prices rose faster in early 1972 than at any time from 1960 to 1968.

Today there are 5.5 million unemployed. The nation will have suffered $175 billion in lost production during the Nixon Administration by election day. Twenty per cent of our people have suffered a period without a job each year in the last three.

Business has lost more in profits than it has gained from this Administration's business-oriented tax cuts.

In pockets of cities, up to 40 per cent of our young people are jobless.

Farmers have seen the lowest parity ratios since the Great Depression.

For the first time in 30 years, there is substantial unemployment among aerospace technicians, teachers and other white-collar workers.

The economic projections have been manipulated for public relations purposes.

The current Nixon game plan includes a control structure which keeps workers' wages down while executive salaries soar, discourages productivity and distributes income away from those who need it and has produced no significant dent in inflation, as prices for food, clothes, rent and basic necessities soar.

These losses were unnecessary. They are the price of a Republican Administration which has no consistent economic philosophy, no adequate regard for the human costs of its economic decisions and no vision of what a full employment economy could mean for all Americans.

Jobs, Income and Dignity

Full employment—guaranteed jobs for all—is the primary economic objective of the Democratic Party. The Democratic Party is committed to a job for every American who seeks work. Only through full employment can we reduce the burden on working people. We are determined to make economic security a matter of right. This means a job with decent pay and good working conditions for everyone willing and able to work and an adequate income for those unable to work. It means abolition of the present welfare system.

To assure jobs and economic security for all, the next Democratic Administration should support:

A full employment economy, making full use of fiscal and monetary policy to stimulate employment;

Tax reform directed toward equitable distribution of income and wealth and fair sharing of the cost of government;

Full enforcement of all equal employment opportunity laws, including federal contract compliance and federally regulated industries and giving the Equal Employment Opportunity Commission adequate staff and resources and power to issue cease-and-desist orders promptly;

Vastly increased efforts to open education at all levels and in all fields to minorities, women and other under-represented groups;

An effective nation-wide job placement system to enhance worker mobility;

Opposition to arbitrarily high standards for entry to jobs;

Overhaul of current manpower programs to assure training—without sex, race or language discrimination—for jobs that really exist with continuous skill improvement and the chance for advancement;

Economic development programs to ensure the growth of communities and industry in lagging parts of the nation and the economy;

Use of federal depository funds to reward banks and other financial institutions which invest in socially productive endeavors;

Improved adjustment assistance and job creation for workers and employers hurt by foreign competition, reconversion of defense-oriented companies, rapid technological change and environmental protection activities;

Closing tax loopholes that encourage the export of American jobs by American-controlled multinational corporations;

Assurance that the needs of society are considered when a decision to close or move an industrial plant is to be made and that income loss to workers and revenue loss to communities does not occur when plants are closed;

Assurance that, whatever else is done in the income security area, the Social Security system provides a decent income for the elderly, the blind and the disabled and their dependents, with escalators so that benefits keep pace with rising prices and living standards;

Reform of Social Security and government employment security programs to remove all forms of discrimination by sex; and

Adequate federal income assistance for those who do not benefit sufficiently from the above measures.

The last is not least, but it is last for good reason. The present welfare system has failed because it has been required to make up for too many other failures. Millions of Americans are forced onto public assistance because public policy too often creates no other choice.

The heart of a program of economic security based on earned income must be creating jobs and training people to fill them. Millions of jobs—real jobs, not make-work—need to be provided. Public service employment must be greatly expanded in order to make the government the employer of last resort and guarantee a job for all. Large sections of our cities resemble bombed-out Europe after World War II. Children in Appalachia cannot go to school when the dirt road is a sea of mud. Homes, schools and clinics, roads and mass transit systems need to be built.

Cleaning up our air and water will take skills and people in large numbers. In the school, the police department, the welfare agency or the recreation program, there are new careers to be developed to help ensure that social services reach the people for whom they are intended.

It may cost more, at least initially, to create decent jobs than to perpetuate the hand-out system of present welfare. But the return—in new public facilities and services, in the dignity of bringing a paycheck home and in the taxes that will come back in—far outweigh the cost of the investment.

The next Democratic Administration must end the present welfare system and replace it with an income security program which places cash assistance in an appropriate context with all of the measures outlined above, adding up to an earned income approach to ensure each family an income substantially more than the poverty level and ensuring standards of decency and health, as officially defined in the area. Federal income assistance will supplement the income of working poor people and assure an adequate income for those unable to work. With full employment and simpler, fair administration, total costs will go down, and with federal financing the burden on local and state budgets will be eased. The program will protect current benefit goals during the transitional period.

The system of income protection which replaces welfare must be a part of the full employment policy which assures every American a job at a fair wage under conditions which make use of his ability and provide an opportunity for advancement.

H.R. 1, and its various amendments, is not humane and does not meet the social and economic objectives that we believe in, and it should be defeated. It perpetuates the coercion of forced work requirements.

Economic Management

Every American family knows how its grocery bill has gone up under Nixon. Every American family has felt the bite of higher and higher prices for food and housing and clothing. The Administration's attempts to stop price rises have been dismal failures—for which the working people have paid in lost jobs, missed raises and higher prices.

This nation achieved its economic greatness under a system of free enterprise, coupled with human effort and ingenuity, and thus it must remain. This will be the attitude and objective of the Democratic Party.

There must be an end to inflation and the ever increasing cost of living. This is of vital concern to the laborer, the housewife, the farmer and the small businessman, as well as the millions of Americans dependent upon their weekly or monthly income for sustenance. It wrecks the retirement plans and lives of our elderly who must survive on pensions or savings gauged by the standards of another day.

Through greater efficiency in the operation of the machinery of government, so badly plagued with duplication, overlapping and excesses in programs, we will ensure that bureaucracy will cease to exist solely for bureaucracy's own sake. The institutions and functions of government will be judged by their efficiency of operation and their contribution to the lives and welfare of our citizens.

A first priority of a Democratic Administration must be eliminating the unfair, bureaucratic Nixon wage and price controls.

When price rises threaten to or do get out of control—as they are now—strong, fair action must be taken to protect family income and savings. The theme of that action should be swift, tough measures to break the wage–price spiral and restore the economy. In that kind of economic emergency, America's working people will support a truly fair stabilization program which affects profits, investment earnings, executive salaries and prices, as well as wages. The Nixon controls do not meet that standard. They have forced the American worker, who suffers most from inflation, to pay the price of trying to end it.

In addition to stabilizing the economy, we propose;

To develop automatic instruments protecting the livelihood of Americans who depend on fixed incomes, such as savings bonds with purchasing power guarantees and cost-of-living escalators in government Social Security and income support payments;

To create a system of "recession insurance" for states and localities to replace lost local revenues with federal funds in economic downturns, thereby avoiding reduction in public employment or public services;

To establish longer-term budget and fiscal planning; and

To create new mechanisms to stop unwarranted price increases in concentrated industries.

Toward Economic Justice

The Democratic Party deplores the increasing concentration of economic power in fewer and fewer hands. Five per cent of the American people control 90 per cent of our productive national wealth. Less than one per cent of all manufacturers have 88 per cent of the profits. Less than two per cent of the population now owns approximately 80 per cent of the nation's personally held corporate stock, 90 per cent of the personally held corporate bonds and nearly 100 per cent of the personally held municipal bonds. The rest of the population—including all working men and women—pay too much for essential products and services because of national policy and market distortions.

The Democratic Administration should pledge itself to combat factors which tend to concentrate wealth and stimulate higher prices.

To this end, the federal government should:

Develop programs to spread economic growth among the workers, farmers and businessmen;

Help make parts of the economy more efficient—such as medical care—where wasteful and inefficient practices now increase prices;

Step up anti-trust action to help competition, with particular regard to laws and enforcement curbing conglomerate mergers which swallow up efficient small business and feed the power of corporate giants;

Strengthen the anti-trust laws so that the divestiture remedy will be used vigorously to break up large conglomerates found to violate the anti-trust laws;

Abolish the oil import quota that raises prices for consumers;

Deconcentrate shared monopolies such as auto, steel and tire industries which administer prices, create unemployment through restricted output and stifle technological innovation;

Assure the right of the citizen to recover costs and attorneys fees in all successful suits including class actions involving Constitutionally-guaranteed rights, or rights secured by federal statutes;

Adjust rate-making and regulatory activities, with particular attention to regulations which increase prices for food, transportation and other necessities;

Remove artificial constraints in the job market by better job manpower training and strictly enforcing equal employment opportunity;

Stiffen the civil and criminal statutes to make corporate officers responsible for their actions; and

Establish a temporary national economic commission to study federal chartering of large multinational and international corporations, concentrated ownership and control in the nation's economy.

Tax Reform

The last ten years have seen a massive shift in the tax burden from the rich to the working people of America. This is due to cuts in federal income taxes simultaneous with big increases in taxes which bear heavily on lower incomes—state and local sales and property taxes and the payroll tax. The federal tax system is still grossly unfair and over-complicated. The wealthy and corporations get special tax favors; major reform of the nation's tax structure is required to achieve a more equitable distribution of income and to raise the funds needed by government. The American people neither should nor will accept anything less from the next Administration.

The Nixon Administration, which fought serious reform in 1969, has no program, only promises, for tax reform. Its clumsy administrative favoring of the well-off has meant quick action on corporate tax giveaways like accelerated depreciation, while over-withholding from workers' paychecks goes on and on while the Administration tries to decide what to do.

In recent years, the federal tax system has moved precipitously in the wrong direction. Corporate taxes have dropped from 30 per cent of federal revenues in 1954 to 16 per cent in 1973, but payroll taxes for Social Security—regressive because the burden falls more heavily on the worker than on the wealthy—have gone from ten per cent to 29 per cent over the same period. If legislation now pending in Congress passes, payroll taxes will have increased over 500 per cent between 1960 and 1970—from $144 to $755—for the average wage earner. Most people earning under $10,000 now pay more in regressive payroll tax than in income tax.

Now the Nixon Administrion—which gave corporations the largest tax cut in American history—is considering a hidden national sales tax (Value Added Tax) which would further shift the burden to the average wage earner and raise prices of virtually everything ordinary people buy. It is cruel and unnecessary to pretend to relieve one bad tax, the property tax, by a new tax which is just as bad. We oppose this price-raising, unfair tax in any form.

Federal Income Tax

The Democratic Party believes that all unfair corporate and individual tax preferences should be removed. The tax law is clogged with complicated provisions and special interests, such as percentage oil depletion and other favors for the oil industry, special rates and rules for capital gains, fast depreciation unrelated to useful life, easy-to-abuse "expense-account" deductions and the ineffective minimum tax. These hidden expenditures in the federal budget are nothing more than billions of "tax welfare" aid for the wealthy, the privileged and the corporations.

We, therefore, endorse as a minimum step the Mills–Mansfield Tax Policy Review Act of 1972, which would repeal virtually all tax preferences in the existing law over the period 1974–1976, as a means of compelling a systematic review of their value to the nation. We acknowledge that the original reasons for some of these tax preferences may remain valid, but believe that none should escape close scrutiny and full public exposure. The most unjustified of the tax loopholes should, however, be closed immediately, without waiting for a review of the whole system.

After the implementation of the minimum provisions of the Mills–Mansfield Act, the Democratic Party, to combat the economically depressing effect of a regressive income tax scheme, proposes further revision of the tax law to ensure economic equality of opportunity to ordinary Americans.

We hold that the federal tax structure should reflect the following principles:

The cost of government must be distributed more fairly among income classes. We reaffirm the long-established principle of progressive taxation—allocating the burden according to ability to pay—which is all but a dead letter in the present tax code.

The cost of government must be distributed fairly among citizens in similar economic circumstances.

Direct expenditures by the federal government which can be budgeted are better than tax preferences as the means for achieving public objectives. The lost income of those tax preferences which are deemed desirable should be stated in the annual budget.

When relief for hardship is provided through federal tax policy, as for blindness, old age or poverty, benefits should be provided equally by credit rather than deductions which favor recipients with more income, with special provisions for those whose credits would exceed the tax they owe.

Provisions which discriminate against working women and single people should be corrected. In addition to greater fairness and efficiency, these principles would mean a major redistribution of personal tax burdens and permit considerable simplification of the tax code and tax forms.

Social Security Tax

The Democratic Party commits itself to make the Social Security tax progressive by raising substantially the ceiling on earned income. To permit needed increases in Social Security benefits, we will use general revenues as necessary to supplement payroll tax receipts. In this way, we will support continued movement toward general revenue financing for Social Security.

Property Tax

Greater fairness in taxation at the federal level will have little meaning for the vast majority of American households if the burden of inequitable local taxation is not reduced. To reduce the local property tax for all American families, we support equalization of school spending and substantial increases in the federal share of education costs and general revenue sharing.

New forms of federal financial assistance to states and localities should be made contingent upon property tax reforms, including equal treatment and full publication of assessment ratios.

Tax policy should not provide incentives that encourage overinvestment in developed countries by American business, and mechanisms should be instituted to limit undesirable capital exports that exploit labor abroad and damage the American worker at home.

Labor–Management Relations

Free private collective bargaining between management and independent labor unions has been, and must remain, the cornerstone of our free enterprise system. America achieved its greatness through the combined energy and efforts of the working men and women of this country. Retention of its greatness rests in their hands. Through their great trade union organizations, these men and women have exerted tremendous influence on the economic and social life of the nation and have attained a standard of living known to no other nation. The concern of the Party is that the gains which labor struggled so long to obtain not be lost to them, whether through inaction or subservience to illogical Republican domestic policies.

We pledge continued support for our system of free collective bargaining and denounce any attempt to substitute compulsory arbitration for it. We, therefore, oppose the Nixon Administration's effort to impose arbitration in transportation disputes through its last-offer-selection bill.

The National Labor Relations Act should be updated to ensure:

Extension of protection to employees of non-profit institutions;
Remedies which adequately reflect the losses caused by violations of the Act;
Repeal of section 14(b), which allows states to legislate the open shop and remove the ban on common-situ picketing; and
Effective opportunities for unions, as well as employers, to communicate with employees, without coercion by either side or by anyone acting on their behalf.

The Railway Labor Act should be updated to ensure:

That strikes on a single carrier or group of carriers cannot be transformed into nation-wide strikes or lockouts; incentives for bargaining which would enable both management and labor to resolve their differences without referring to government intervention; and
Partial operation of struck railroads to ensure continued movement of essential commodities.

New legislation is needed to ensure:

Collective bargaining rights for government employees;
Universal coverage and longer duration of the Unemployment Insurance and Workmen's Compensation programs and to establish minimum federal standards, including the establishment of equitable wage-loss ratios in those programs, including a built-in escalator clause that fairly reflects increases in average wage rates; and
That workers covered under private pension plans actually receive the personal and other fringe benefits to which their services for their employer entitle them. This requires that the fixed right to benefits starts early in employment, that reserves move with the worker from job to job and that re-insurance protection be given pension plans.

Labor Standards

American workers are entitled to job safety at a living wage. Most of the basic projections needed have been recognized in legislation already enacted by Congress.

The Fair Labor Standards Act should be updated, however, to:

Move to a minimum wage of $2.50 per hour, which allows a wage earner to earn more than a poverty level income for 40 hours a week, with no sub-minimums for special groups or age differentials;
Expand coverage to include the 16 million workers not presently covered, including domestic workers, service workers, agricultural employees and employees of governmental and non-profit agencies; and
Set overtime premiums which give an incentive to hire new employees rather than to use regular employees for extended periods of overtime.

The Longshoremen and Harbor Workers' Compensation Act should be updated to provide adequate protection for injured workers and federal standards for workmen's compensation should be set by Congress.

The Equal Pay Act of 1963 should be extended to be fully effective, and to cover professional, executive and administrative workers.

Maternity benefits should be made available to all working women. Temporary disability benefits should cover pregnancy, childbirth, miscarriage and recovery.

Occupational Health and Safety

Each year over 14,000 American workers are killed on their jobs, and nine million injured. Unknown millions more are exposed to long-term danger and disease from exposure to dangerous substances. Federal and state laws are supposed to protect workers; but these laws are not being enforced. This Administration has hired only a handful of inspectors and proposes to turn enforcement over to the same state bureaucracies that have proven inadequate in the past. Where violations are detected, only token penalties have been assessed.

We pledge to fully and rigorously enforce the laws which protect the safety and health of workers on their jobs and to extend those laws to all jobs, regardless of number of employees. This must include standards that truly protect against all health hazards, adequate federal enforcement machinery backed up by rigorous penalties and an opportunity for workers themselves to participate in the laws' enforcement by sharing responsibility for plant inspection.

We endorse federal research and development of effective approaches to combat the dehumanizing debilitating effects of monotonous work.

Farm Labor

The Sixties and Seventies have seen the struggle for unionization by the poorest of the poor in our country—America's migrant farm workers.

Under the leadership of Cesar Chavez, the United Farm Workers have accomplished in the non-violent tradition what was thought impossible only a short time ago. Through hard work and much sacrifice, they are the one group that is successfully organizing farm workers.

Their movement has caught the imagination of millions of Americans who have not eaten grapes so that agribusiness employers will recognize their workers as equals and sit down with them in meaningful collective bargaining.

We now call upon all friends and supporters of this movement to refrain from buying or eating non-union lettuce.

Furthermore, we support the farm workers' movement and the use of boycotts as a non-violent and potent weapon for gaining collective bargaining recognition and contracts for agricultural workers. We oppose the Nixon Administration's effort to enjoin the use of the boycott.

We also affirm the right of farm workers to organize free of repressive anti-labor legislation, both state and federal.

III. RIGHTS, POWER AND SOCIAL JUSTICE

"We're just asking, and we don't ask for much. Just to give us the opportunity to live as human beings as other people have lived."—Dorothy Bolden, Atlanta Hearing, June 9, 1972.

"All your platform has to say is that the rights, opportunities and political power of citizenship will be extended to the lowest level, to neighborhoods and individuals. If your party can live up to that simple pledge, my faith will be restored."—Bobby Westbrooks, St. Louis Hearing, June 17, 1972.

"We therefore urge the Democratic Party to adopt

the principle that America has a responsibility to offer every American family the best in health care, whenever they need it, regardless of income or any other factor. We must devise a system which will assure that . . . every American receives comprehensive health services from the day he is born to the day he dies, with an emphasis on preventive care to keep him healthy." Joint Statement of Senator Edward M. Kennedy and Representative Wilbur Mills, St. Louis Hearing, June 17, 1972.

The Democratic Party commits itself to be responsive to the millions of hard working, lower- and middle-income Americans who are traditionally courted by politicians at election time, get bilked at tax-paying time, and are too often forgotten the balance of the time.

This is an era of great change. The world is fast moving into a future for which the past has not prepared us well; a future where to survive, to find answers to the problems which threaten us as a people, we must create qualitatively new solutions. We can no longer rely on old systems of thought, the results of which were partially successful programs that were heralded as important social reforms in the past. It is time now to rethink and reorder the institutions of this country so that everyone—women, blacks, Spanish-speaking, Puerto Ricans, Indians, the young and the old—can participate in the decision-making process inherent in the democratic heritage to which we aspire. We must restructure the social, political and economic relationships throughout the entire society in order to ensure the equitable distribution of wealth and power.

The Democratic Party in 1972 is committed to resuming the march toward equality; to enforcing the laws supporting court decisions and enacting new legal rights as necessary, to assuring every American true opportunity, to bringing about a more equal distribution of power, income and wealth and equal and uniform enforcement in all states and territories of civil rights statutes and acts.

In the 1970's, this commitment requires the fulfillment—through laws and policies, through appropriations and directives; through leadership and exhortation—of a wide variety of rights:

The right to full participation in government and the political process;

The rights of free speech and free political expression, of freedom from official intimidation, harassment and invasion of privacy, as guaranteed by the letter and the spirit of the Constitution;

The right to a decent job and an adequate income, with dignity;

The right to quality, accessibility and sufficient quantity in tax-supported services and amenities—including educational opportunity, health care, housing and transportation;

The right to quality, safety and the lowest possible cost on goods and services purchased in the market place;

The right to be different, to maintain a cultural or ethnic heritage or lifestyle, without being forced into a compelled homogeneity;

The rights of people who lack rights: Children, the mentally retarded, mentally ill and prisoners, to name some; and

The right to legal services, both civil and criminal, necessary to enforce secured rights.

Free Expression and Privacy

The new Democratic Administration should bring an end to the pattern of political persecution and investigation, the use of high office as a pulpit for unfair attack and intimidation and the blatant efforts to control the poor and to keep them from acquiring additional economic security or political power.

The epidemic of wiretapping and electronic surveillance engaged in by the Nixon Administration and the use of grand juries for purposes of political intimidation must be ended. The rule of law and the supremacy of the Constitution, as these concepts have traditionally been understood, must be restored.

We strongly object to secret computer data banks on individuals. Citizens should have access to their own files that are maintained by private commercial firms and the right to insert corrective material. Except in limited cases, the same should apply to government files. Collection and maintenance by federal agencies of dossiers on law-abiding citizens, because of their political views and statements, must be stopped, and files which never should have been opened should be destroyed. We firmly reject the idea of a National Computer Data Bank.

The Nixon policy of intimidation of the media and Administration efforts to use government power to block access to media by dissenters must end, if free speech is to be preserved. A Democratic Administration must be an open one, with the fullest possible disclosure of information, with an end to abuses of security classifications and executive privilege, and with regular top-level press conferences.

The Right to Be Different

The new Democratic Administration can help lead America to celebrate the magnificence of the diversity within its population, the racial, national, linguistic and religious groups which have contributed so much to the vitality and richness of our national life. As things are, official policy too often forces people into a mold of artificial homogeneity.

Recognition and support of the cultural identity and pride of black people are generations overdue. The American Indians, the Spanish-speaking, the Asian Americans—the cultural and linguistic heritage of these groups is too often ignored in schools and communities. So, too, are the backgrounds, traditions and contributions of white national, ethnic, religious and regional communities ignored. All official discrimination on the basis of sex, age, race, language, political belief, religion, region or national origin must end. No American should be subject to discrimination in employment or restriction in business because of ethnic background or religious practice. Americans should be free to make their own choice of lifestyles and private habits without being subject to discrimination or prosecution. We believe official policy can encourage diversity while continuing to place full emphasis on equal opportunity and integration.

We urge full funding of the Ethnic Studies bill to provide funds for development of curriculum to preserve America's ethnic mosaic.

Rights of Children

One measure of a nation's greatness is the care it manifests for all of its children. The Nixon Administration has demonstrated a callous attitude toward children repeatedly through veto and administrative decisions. We, therefore, call for a reordering of priorities at all levels of American society so that children, our most precious resource, and families come first.

To that end, we call for:

The federal government to fund comprehensive development child care programs that will be family centered, locally controlled and universally available. These programs should provide for active participation of all family members in the development and implementation of the program. Health, social service and early childhood education should be part of these programs, as well as a variety of options most appropriate to their needs. Child care is a supplement, not a substitute, for the family;

The establishment of a strong child advocacy program, financed by the federal government and other sources, with full ethnic, cultural, racial and sexual representation;

First priority for the needs of children, as we move toward a National Health Insurance Program;

The first step should be immediate implementation of the federal law passed in the 1967 Social Security Amendments providing for "early and periodic screening, diagnosis and treatment" of children's health problems;

Legislation and administrative decisions to drastically reduce childhood injuries—prenatal, traffic, poisoning, burns, malnutrition, rat bites—and to provide health and safety education;

Full funding of legislation designed to meet the needs of children with special needs: The retarded, the physically and mentally handicapped, and those whose environment produces abuse and neglect and directs the child to anti-social conduct;

Reaffirmation of the rights of bilingual, handicapped or slow-learning children to education in the public schools, instead of being wrongly classified as retarded or uneducable and dismissed;

Revision of the juvenile court system; dependency and neglect cases must be removed from the corrections system, and clear distinctions must be drawn between petty childhood offenses and the more serious crimes;

Allocation of funds to the states to provide counsel to children in juvenile proceedings, legal or administrative; and

Creation by Congress of permanent standing committees on Children and Youth.

Rights of Women

Women historically have been denied a full voice in the evolution of the political and social institutions of this country and are therefore allied with all underrepresented groups in a common desire to form a more humane and compassionate society. The Democratic Party pledges the following:

A priority effort to ratify the Equal Rights Amendment;

Elimination of discrimination against women in public accommodations and public facilities, public education and in all federally assisted programs and federally contracted employment:

Extension of the jurisdiction of the Civil Rights Commission to include denial of civil rights on the basis of sex;

Full enforcement of all federal statutes and executive laws barring job discrimination on the basis of sex, giving the Equal Employment Opportunities Commission adequate staff and resources and power to issue cease-and-desist orders promptly;

Elimination of discriminatory features of criminal laws and administration;

Increased efforts to open educational opportunities at all levels, eliminating discrimination against women in access to education, tenure, promotion and salary;

Guarantee that all training programs are made more equitable, both in terms of the numbers of women involved and the job opportunities provided; jobs must be available on the basis of skill, not sex;

Availability of maternity benefits to all working women; temporary disability benefits should cover pregnancy, childbirth, miscarriage and recovery;

Elimination of all tax inequities that affect women and children, such as higher taxes for single women;

Amendment of the Social Security Act to provide equitable retirement benefits for families with working wives, widows, and women heads of households and their children;

Amendment of the Internal Revenue Code to permit working families to deduct from gross income as a business expense, housekeeping and child care costs;

Equality for women in credit, mortgage, insurance, property, rental and financial contracts;

Extension of the Equal Pay Act to all workers, with amendment to read "equal pay for comparable work";

Appointment of women to positions of top responsibility in all branches of the federal government to achieve an equitable ratio of women and men. Such positions include Cabinet members, agency and division heads and Supreme Court justices; inclusion of women advisors in equitable ratios on all government studies, commissions and hearings; and

Laws authorizing federal grants on a matching basis for financing State Commissions on the Status of Women.

Rights of Youth

In order to ensure, maintain and secure the proper role and functions of youth in American government, politics and society, the Democratic Party will endeavor to:

Lower the age of legal majority and consent to 18;

Actively encourage and assist in the election of youth to federal, state and local offices;

Develop special programs for employment of youth, utilizing governments' resources to guarantee development, training and job placement and secure the electoral reforms called for under "People and the Government."

Rights of Poor People

Poor people, like all Americans, should be represented at all levels of the Democratic Party in reasonable proportion of their numbers in the general population. Affirmative action must be taken to ensure their representation at every level. The Democratic Party guidelines guaranteeing proportional representation to "previously discriminated against groups" (enumerated as "women, young people and minorities") must be extended to specifically include poor people.

Political parties, candidates and government institutions at all levels must be committed to working with, and supporting poor people's organizations and ending the tokenism and co-optation that has characterized past dealings.

Welfare rights organizations must be recognized as representative of welfare recipients and be given access to regulations, policies and decision-making processes, as well as being allowed to represent clients at all governmental levels.

The federal government must protect the right of tenants to organize tenant organizations and negotiate collective bargaining agreements with private landlords and encourage the participation of the tenants in the management and control of all subsidized housing.

Rights of American Indians

We support rights of American Indians to full rights of citizenship. The federal government should commit all necessary funds to improve the lives of Indians, with no division between reservation and non-reservation Indians. We strongly oppose the policy of termination, and we urge the government to provide unequivocal advocacy for the protection of the remaining Indian land and water resources. All land rights due American Indians, and Americans of Spanish and Mexican descent, on the basis of treaties with the federal government will be protected by the federal government. In addition we support allocation of federal surplus lands to American Indians on a first priority basis.

American Indians should be given the right to receive bilingual medical services from hospitals and physicians of their choice.

Rights of the Physically Disabled

The physically disabled have the right to pursue meaningful employment and education, outside a hospital environment, free from unnecessary discrimination, living in adequate housing, with access to public mass transportation and regular medical care. Equal opportunity employment practices should be used by the government in considering their application for federal jobs and equal access to education from preschool to the college level guaranteed. The physically disabled, like all disadvantaged peoples, should be represented in any group making decisions affecting their lives.

Rights of the Mentally Retarded

The mentally retarded must be given employment and educational opportunities that promote their dignity as individuals and ensure their civil rights. Educational treatment facilities must guarantee that these rights always will be recognized and protected. In addition, to assure these citizens a more meaningful life, emphasis must be placed on programs of treatment that respect their right to life in a non-institutional environment.

Rights of the Elderly

Growing old in America for too many means neglect, sickness, despair and, all too often, poverty. We have failed to discharge the basic obligation of a civilized people—to respect and assure the security of our senior citizens. The Democratic Party pledges, as a final step to economic security for all, to end poverty—as measured by official standards—among the retired, the blind and the disabled. Our general program of economic and social justice will benefit the elderly directly. In addition, a Democratic Administration should:

Increase Social Security to bring benefits in line with changes in the national standard of living;

Provide automatic adjustments to assure that benefits keep pace with inflation;

Support legislation which allows beneficiaries to earn more income, without reduction of Social Security payments;

Protect individual's pension rights by pension reinsurance and early vesting;

Lower retirement eligibility age to 60 in all government pension programs;

Expand housing assistance for the elderly;

Encourage development of local programs by which senior citizens can serve their community in providing education, recreation, counseling and other services to the rest of the population;

Establish federal standards and inspection of nursing homes and full federal support for qualified nursing homes;

Take the needs of the elderly and the handicapped into account in all federal programs, including construction of federal buildings, housing and transportation planning;

Pending a full national health security system, expand Medicare by supplementing trust funds with general revenues in order to provide a complete range of care and services; eliminate the Nixon Administration cutbacks in Medicare and Medicaid; eliminate the Part B premium under Medicare and include under Medicare and Medicaid the costs of eyeglasses, dentures, hearing cards, and all prescription drugs and establish uniform national standards for Medicaid to bring to an end the present situation which makes it worse to be poor in one state than in another.

The Democratic Party pledges itself to adopt rules to give those over 60 years old representation on all Party committees and agencies as nearly as possible in proportion to their percentage in the total population.

Rights of Veterans

It is time that the nation did far more to recognize the service of our 28 million living veterans and to serve them in return. The veterans of Vietnam must get special attention, for no end of the war is truly honorable which does not provide these men the opportunities to meet their needs.

The Democratic Party is committed to extending and improving the benefits available to American veterans and society, to ending the neglect shown by the Nixon Administration to these problems and to the human needs of our ex-servicemen.

Medical Care

The federal government must guarantee quality medical care to ex-servicemen, and to all disabled veterans, expanding and improving Veterans Administration facilities and manpower and preserving the independence and integrity of the VA hospital program. Staff–patient ratios in these hospitals should be made comparable to ratios in community hospitals. Meanwhile, there should be an increase in the VA's ability to deliver out-patient care and home health services, wherever possible treating veterans as part of a family unit.

We support future coordination of health care for veterans with the national health care insurance program, with no reduction in scale or quality of existing veterans care and with recognition of the special health needs of veterans.

The VA separate personnel system should be ex-panded to take in all types of health personnel, and especially physician's assistants; and VA hospitals should be used to develop medical schools and area health education centers.

The VA should also assume responsibility for the care of wives and children of veterans who are either permanently disabled or who have died from service-connected causes. Distinction should no longer be made between veterans who have seen "wartime," as opposed to "peacetime," service.

Education

Educational benefits should be provided for Vietnam-era veterans under the GI Bill at levels comparable to those of the original Bill after World War II, supplemented by special veteran's education loans. The VA should greatly expand and improve programs for poor or educationally disadvantaged veterans. In addition, there should be a program under which servicemen and women can receive high school, college or job training while on active duty. GI Bill trainees should be used more extensively to reach out to other veterans who would otherwise miss these educational opportunities.

Drug Addiction

The Veterans Administration should provide either directly or through community facilities, a comprehensive, individually tailored treatment and rehabilitation program for all drug- and alcohol-addicted veterans, on a voluntary and confidential basis, and regardless of the nature of their discharge or the way in which they acquired their condition.

Unemployment

There should be an increase in unemployment compensation provided to veterans, and much greater emphasis on the Veterans Employment Service of the Department of Labor, expanding its activities in every state. There should be a greatly enlarged effort by the federal government to employ Vietnam-era veterans and other veterans with service-connected disabilities. In addition, veterans' preferences in hiring should be written into every federal contract or subcontract and for public service employment.

Rights of Servicemen and Servicewomen

Military discipline must be maintained, but unjustifiable restriction on the Constitutional rights of members of the armed services must cease.

We support means to ensure the protection of GI rights to express political opinion and engage in off-base political activity.

We should explore new procedures for providing review of discharges other than honorable, in cases involving political activity.

We oppose deferential advancement, punishment assignment or any other treatment on the basis of race, and support affirmative action to end discrimination.

We support rights of women in the armed forces to be free from unfair discrimination.

We support an amendment of the Uniform Code of Military justice to provide for fair and uniform sentencing procedures.

Rights of Consumers

Consumers need to be assured of a renewed commitment to basic rights and freedoms. They must have the mechanisms available to allow self-protection against the abuses that the Kennedy and Johnson programs were designed to eliminate. We propose a new consumer program:

In the Executive Branch

The Executive Branch must use its power to expand consumer information and protection:

Ensure that every policy-making level of government concerned with economic or procurement decisions should have consumer input either through a consumer advisory committee or through consumer members on policy advisory committees;

Support the development of an independent consumer agency providing a focal point on consumer matters with the right to intervene on behalf of the consumer before all agencies and regulatory bodies; and

Expand all economic policy-making mechanisms to include an assessment of social as well as economic indicators of human well-being.

In the Legislative Branch

We support legislation which will expand the ability of consumers to defend themselves:

Ensure an extensive campaign to get food, drugs and all other consumer products to carry complete informative labeling about safety, quality and cost. Such labeling is the first step in ensuring the economic and physical health of the consumer. In the food area, it should include nutritional unit pricing, full ingredients by percentage, grade, quality and drained weight information. For drugs, it should include safety, quality, price and operation data, either on the label or in an enclosed manual;

Support a national program to encourage the development of consumer cooperatives, patterned after the rural electric cooperatives in areas where they might help eliminate inflation and restore consumer rights; and

Support federal initiatives and federal standards to reform automobile insurance and assure coverage on a first-party, no-fault basis.

In the Judicial Branch

The courts should become an effective forum to hear well-founded consumer grievances.

Consumer Class Action. Consumers should be given access to the federal courts in a way that allows them to initiate group action against fraudulent, deceitful, or misleading or dangerous business practices.

Small Claims Court. A national program should be undertaken to improve the workings of small claims courts and spread their use so that consumers injured in economically small, though individually significant amounts (e.g. $500), can bring their complaints to the attention of a court and collect their damages without self-defeating legal fees.

The Quality and Quantity of Social Service

The new Democratic Administration can begin a fundamental reexamination of all federal domestic social programs and the patterns of service delivery they support. Simply advocating the expenditure of more funds is not enough, although funds are needed, for billions already have been poured into federal government programs—programs like urban renewal, current welfare and aid to education, with meager results. The control, structure, and effectiveness of every institution and government grant system must be fully examined and these institutions must be made accountable to those they are supposed to serve.

We will, therefore, pursue the development of new rights of two kinds: Rights to the service itself and rights to participate in the delivery process.

Health Care

Good health is the least this society should promise its citizens. The state of health services in this country indicates the failure of government to respond to this fundamental need. Costs skyrocket while the availability of services for all but the rich steadily declines.

We endorse the principle that good health is a right of all Americans.

America has a responsibility to offer to every American family the best in health care whenever they need it, regardless of income or where they live or any other factor.

To achieve this goal the next Democratic Administration should:

Establish a system of universal National Health Insurance which covers all Americans with a comprehensive set of benefits including preventive medicine, mental and emotional disorders, and complete protection against catastrophic costs, and in which the rule of free choice for both provider and consumer is protected. The program should be federally financed and federally administered. Every American must know he can afford the cost of health care whether given in a hospital or doctor's office;

Incorporate in the National Health Insurance System incentives and controls to curb inflation in health care costs and to assure efficient delivery of all services;

Continue and evaluate Health Maintenance Organizations;

Set up incentives to bring health service personnel back to inner-cities and rural areas;

Continue to expand community health centers and availability of early screening diagnosis and treatment;

Provide federal funds to train added health manpower including doctors, nurses, technicians and paramedical workers;

Secure greater consumer participation and control over health care institutions;

Expand federal support for medical research including research in heart disease, hypertension, stroke, cancer, sickle cell anemia, occupational and childhood diseases which threaten millions and in preventive health care;

Eventual replacement of all federal programs of health care by a comprehensive National Health Insurance System;

Take legal and other action to curb soaring prices for vital drugs using anti-trust laws as applicable and amending patent laws to end price-raising abuses, and require generic-name labeling of equally effective drugs; and

Expand federal research and support for drug abuse treatment and education, especially development of non-addictive treatment methods.

Family Planning

Family planning services, including the education, and comprehensive medical and social services necessary to permit individuals freely to determine and achieve the number and spacing of their children, should be available to all, regardless of sex, age, marital status, economic group or ethnic origin, and should be administered in a non-coercive and nondiscriminatory manner.

Puerto Rico

The Democratic Party respects and supports the frequently expressed desire of the people of Puerto Rico to freely associate in permanent union with the United States, as an autonomous commonwealth. We are committed to Puerto Rico's right to enjoy full self-determination and a relationship that can evolve in ways that will most benefit both parties.

To this end, we support equal treatment for Puerto Rico in the distribution of all federal grants-in-aid, amendment of federal laws that restrict aid to Puerto Rico; and we pledge no further restrictions in future laws. Only in this way can the people of Puerto Rico come to participate more fully in the many areas of social progress made possible by Democratic efforts, on behalf of all the people.

Finally, the Democratic Party pledges to end all naval shelling and bombardment of the tiny, inhabited island of Culebra and its neighboring keys, not later than June 1, 1975. With this action, and others, we will demonstrate the concern of the Democratic Party to develop and maintain a productive relationship between the Commonwealth and the United States.

Virgin Islands, Guam, American Samoa and the Trust Territories of the Pacific

We pledge to include all of these areas in federal grant-in-aid programs on a full and equitable basis.

We praise the Democratic Congress for providing a non-voting delegate to the House of Representatives from Guam and the Virgin Islands and urge that these elected delegates be accorded the full vote in the committees to which they are assigned.

We support the right of American Samoans to elect their Governor, and will consider methods by which American citizens residing in American territories can participate in Presidential elections.

IV. CITIES, COMMUNITIES, COUNTIES AND THE ENVIRONMENT

"When the Democratic Platform is written and acted on in Miami, let it be a blueprint for the life and survival of our cities and our people."—Mayor Kenneth

A. Gibson, U.S. Conference of Mayors, New Orleans, June 19, 1972.

Introduction

Always the vital center of our civilization, the American city since World War II has been suffering growing pains, partly by the change of the core city into a metropolitan city and partly by the movement of people from towns and rural areas into the cities.

The burgeoning of the suburbs—thrust outward with too little concern for social, economic and environmental consequences—has both broadened the city's limits and deepened human and neighborhood needs.

The Nixon Administration has failed to meet most of these needs. It has met the problem of urban decay with tired, decaying "solutions" that are unworthy of the name. It could act to revitalize our urban areas; instead, we see only rising crime, fear and flight, racial and economic polarization, loss of confidence and depletion of community resources.

This Administration has ignored the cities and permitted taxes to rise and services to decline; housing to deteriorate faster than it can be replaced, and morale to suffer. It actually has impounded funds appropriated by a Democratic Congress to help cities in crisis.

The Administration has ignored the needs of city and suburban residents for public services, for property tax relief and for the planning and coordination that alone can assure that housing, jobs, schools and transportation are built and maintained in suitable locations and in needed numbers and quality.

Meanwhile, the Nixon Administration has forgotten small-town America, too, refusing to provide facilities that would make it an attractive alternative to city living.

This has become the American crisis of the 1970's. Today, our highest national priority is clear and precise: To deal effectively and now with the massive, complex and urgent needs of our cities, suburbs and towns.

The federal government cannot solve all the problems of these communities. Too often, federal bureaucracy has failed to deliver the services and keep the promises that are made. But only the federal government can be the catalyst to focus attention and resources on the needs of every neighborhood in America.

Under the Nixon Administration, piecemeal measures, poorly funded and haphazardly applied, have proved almost totally inadequate. Words have not halted the decline of neighborhoods. Words have not relieved the plight of tenants in poorly managed, shoddy housing. Our scarce urban dollars have been wasted, and even the Republican Secretary of Housing and Urban Development has admitted it.

The Democratic Party pledges to stop the rot in our cities, suburbs and towns, and stop it now. We pledge commitment, coordination, planning and funds:

Commitment to make our communities places where we are proud to raise our children;

Coordination and planning to help all levels of government achieve the same goals, to ensure that physical facilities meet human needs and to ensure that land—a scarce resource—is used in ways that meet the needs of the entire nation; and funds to reduce the burden of the inequitable property tax and to help local government meet legitimate and growing demands for public facilities and services.

The nation's urban areas must and can be habitable. They are not only centers of commerce and trade, but also repositories of history and culture, expressing the richness and variety of their region and of the larger society. They are worthy of the best America can offer. They are America.

Partnership Among Governments

The federal government must assist local communities to plan for their orderly growth and development, to improve conditions and opportunities for all their citizens and to build the public facilities they need.

Effective planning must be done on a regional basis. New means of planning are needed that are practical and realistic, but that go beyond the limits of jurisdictional lines. If local government is to be responsive to citizen needs, public services and programs must efficiently be coordinated and evolved through comprehensive regional planning and decision-making. Government activities should take account of the future as well as the present.

In aiding the reform of state and local government, federal authority must insist that local decisions take into account the views and needs of all citizens, white and black, haves and have-nots, young and old, Spanish and other non-English-speaking, urban, suburban and rural.

Americans ask more and more of their local government, but the regressive property tax structure makes it impossible for cities and counties to deliver. The Democratic Party is committed to ensure that state and local governments have the funds and the capacity to achieve community service and development goals—goals that are nationally recognized. To this end:

> We fully support general revenue sharing and the principle that the federal income tax should be used to raise more revenues for local use;

We pledge adequate federal funds to halt property tax increases and to begin to roll them back. Turning over federal funds to local governments will permit salaries of underpaid state and local government employees to climb to acceptable levels; and it will reduce tax pressures on the aged, the poor, Spanish- and other non-English-speaking Americans and young couples starting out in life;

We further commit ourselves to reorganize categorical grant programs. They should be consolidated, expanded and simplified. Funding should be adequate, dependable, sustained, long-term and related to state and local fiscal timetables and priorities. There should be full funding of all programs, without the impounding of funds by the Executive Branch to thwart the will of Congress. And there should be performance standards governing the distribution of all federal funds to state and local governments; and

We support efforts to eliminate gaps and costly overlaps in services delivered by different levels of government.

Urban Growth Policy

The Nixon Administration has neither developed an effective urban growth policy designed to meet critical problems, nor concerned itself with the needed re-creation of the quality of life in our cities, large and small. Instead, it has severely over-administered and under-funded existing federal aid programs. Through word and deed, the Administration has widened the gulf between city and suburb, between core and fringe, between haves and have-nots.

The nation's urban growth policies are seen most clearly in the legitimate complaints of suburban householders over rising taxes and center-city families over houses that are falling apart and services that are often non-existent. And it is here, in the center city, that the failure of Nixon Administration policies is most clear to all who live there.

The Democratic Party pledges:

• A national urban growth policy to promote a balance of population among cities, suburbs, small towns and rural areas, while providing social and economic opportunities for everyone. America needs a logical urban growth policy, instead of today's inadvertent, chaotic and haphazard one that doesn't work. An urban growth policy that truly deals with our tax and mortgage insurance and highway policies will require the use of federal policies as leverage on private investment;

• A policy on housing—including low- and middle-income housing—that will concentrate effort in areas where there are jobs, transportation, schools, health care and commercial facilities. Problems of over-growth are not caused so much by land scarcity, as by the wrong distribution of people and the inadequate servicing of their needs; and

• a policy to experiment with alternative strategies to reserve land for future development—land banks— and a policy to recoup publicly created land values for public benefit.

The Cities

Many of the worst problems in America are centered in our cities. Countless problems contribute to their plight: decay in housing, the drain of welfare, crime and violence, racism, failing schools, joblessness and poor mass transit, lack of planning for land use and services.

The Democratic Party pledges itself to change the disastrous policies of the Nixon Administration toward the cities and to reverse the steady process of decay and dissolution. We will renew the battle begun under the Kennedy and Johnson Administrations to improve the quality of life in our cities. In addition to pledging the resources critically needed, we commit ourselves to these actions:

Help localities to develop their own solutions to their most pressing problems— federal government should not stifle or usurp local initiative;

Carry out programs developed elsewhere in this Platform to assure every American decent shelter, freedom from hunger, good health care, the opportunity to work, adequate income and a decent education;

Provide sufficient management and planning funds for cities, to let them increase staff capacity and improve means of allocating resources;

Distribute funds according to standards that will provide center cities with enough resources to revitalize old neighborhoods and build new ones, to expand and improve community services and to help local governments better to plan and deliver these services; and

Create and fund a housing strategy that will recognize that housing is neighborhood and community as well as a shelters strategy that will serve all the nation's areas and all the American people.

Housing and Community Development

The 1949 Housing Act pledged "a decent home and suitable living environment for every American family." Twenty-three years later, this goal is still far away.

Under this Administration, there simply has been no progress in meeting our housing needs, despite the Democratic Housing Act of 1968. We must build 2.6 million homes a year, including two-thirds of a million units of federally subsidized low- and middle-income housing. These targets are not being met. And the lack of housing is particularly critical for people with low and middle incomes.

In the cities, widespread deterioration and abandonment are destroying once sound homes and apartments, and often entire neighborhoods, faster than new homes are built.

Federal housing policy creates walled compounds of poor, elderly and ethnic minorities, isolating them in the center city.

These harmful policies include the Administration's approach to urban renewal, discrimination against the center city by the Federal Housing Administration, highway policies that destroy neighborhoods and create ghettoes and other practices that work against housing for low- and middle-income families.

Millions of lower- and middle-class Americans—each year the income level is higher—are priced out of housing because of sharply rising costs.

Under Republican leadership, the Federal Housing Administration (FHA) has become the biggest slumlord in the country. Some unsophisticated home buyers have purchased homes with FHA mortgage insurance or subsidies. These consumers, relying on FHA appraisals to protect them, often have been exploited by dishonest real estate speculators. Unable to repair or maintain these houses, the buyers often have no choice but to abandon them. As a result, the FHA will acquire a quarter million of these abandoned houses at a cost to the taxpayers of billions of dollars.

Under the Republican Administration, the emphasis has been on housing subsidies for the people who build and sell houses rather than for those people who need and live in them. In many cases, the only decent shelter provided is a tax shelter.

To correct this inequity the Democratic Party pledges:

> To overhaul completely the FHA to make it a consumer-oriented agency;
> To use the full faith and credit of the Treasury to provide direct, low-interest loans to finance the construction and purchase of decent housing for the American people; and
> To insist on building practices, inspection standards and management that will assure quality housing.

The next Administration must build and conserve housing that not only meets the basic need for shelter, but also provides a wider choice of quality housing and living environments. To meet this challenge, the Democratic Party commits itself to a housing approach that:

> Prevents the decay and abandonment of homes and neighborhoods. Major rehabilitation programs to conserve and rehabilitate housing are needed. Consumers should be aided in purchasing homes, and low-income housing foreclosed by the FHA should be provided to poor families at minimal cost as an urban land grant. These houses should be rehabilitated and lived in, not left to rot;
> Provides federal funds for preservation of existing neighborhoods. Local communities should decide whether they want renewal or preservation. Choosing preservation should not mean steady deterioration and inadequate facilities;
> Provides for improved housing quality for all families through strict enforcement of housing quality standards and full compliance with state and local health and safety laws;
> Provides effective incentives to reduce housing costs—to the benefit of poor and middle-income families alike—through effective use of unused, undeveloped land, reform of building practices and the use of new building techniques, including factory-made and modular construction;
> Assures that residents have a strong voice in determining the destiny of their own neighborhoods;
> Promotes free choice housing—the right of all families, regardless of race, color, religion or income, to choose among a wide range of homes and neighborhoods in urban, suburban and rural areas—through the greater use of grants to individuals for housing, the development of new communities offering diversified housing and neighborhood options and the enforcement of fair housing laws; and
> Assures fair and equitable relationships between landlords and tenants.

New Towns

New towns meet the direct housing and community needs of only a small part of our populations. To do more, new towns must be developed in concert with massive efforts to revitalize central cities and enhance the quality of life in still growing suburban areas.

The Democratic Party pledges:

> To strengthen the administration of the New Towns program; to reduce onerous review requirements that delay the start of New Towns and thus

thwart Congressional mandates; to release already appropriated monies and provide new planning and development funds needed to assure the quality of life in New Towns; and

To assure coordination between development of New Towns and renewed efforts to improve the quality of life in established urban and suburban areas. We also promise to use effectively the development of New Towns to increase housing choices for people now living in central and suburban areas.

Transportation

Urban problems cannot be separated from transportation problems. Whether tying communities together, connecting one community to another or linking our cities and towns to rural areas, food transportation is essential to the social and economic life of any community. It joins workers to jobs; makes commercial activity both possible and profitable and provides the means for expanding personal horizons and promoting community cultural life.

Today, however, the automobile is the principal form of transportation in urban areas. The private automobile has made a major contribution to economic growth and prosperity in this century. But now we must have better-balanced transportation—more of it public. Today, 15 times as much federal aid goes to highways as to mass transit; tomorrow this must change. At the same time, it is important to preserve and improve transportation in America's rural areas, to end the crisis in rural mobility.

The Democratic Party pledges:

To create a single Transportation Trust Fund, to replace the Highway Trust Fund, with such additional funds as necessary to meet our transportation crisis substantially from federal resources. This fund will allocate monies for capital projects on a regional basis, permitting each region to determine its own needs under guidelines that will ensure a balanced transportation system and adequate funding of mass transit facilities.

Moreover, we will:

Assist local transit systems to meet their capital operating needs;

End the deterioration of rail and rural transportation and promote a flexible rural transportation system based on local, state and regional needs;

Take steps to meet the particular transportation problems of the elderly, the handicapped and others with special needs; and

Assist development of airport terminals, facilities

and access to them, with due regard to impact on environment and community.

Environment, Technology and Resources

Every American has the right to live, work and play in a clean, safe and healthy environment. We have the obligation to ourselves and to our children. It is not enough simply to prevent further environmental deterioration and the despoliation of our natural endowment. Rather, we must improve the quality of the world in which we and they will live.

The Nixon Administration's record on the environment is one of big promises and small actions.

Inadequate enforcement, uncertain requirements, reduced funding and a lack of manpower have undercut the effort commenced by a Democratic Administration to clean up the environment.

We must recognize the costs all Americans pay for the environmental destruction with which we all live: Poorer health, lessened recreational opportunities, higher maintenance costs, lower land productivity and diminished beauty in our surroundings. Only then can we proceed wisely, yet vigorously, with a program of environmental protection which recognizes that, although environmental protection will not be cheap, it is worth a far greater price, in effort and money, than we have spent thus far.

Such a program must include adequate federal funding for waste management, recycling and disposal and for purification and conservation of air and water resources.

The next Administration must reconcile any conflicts among the goals of cleaner air and water, inexpensive power and industrial development and jobs in specific places. These difficulties do exist—to deny them would be deceptive and irresponsible. At the same time, we know they can be resolved by an Administration with energy, intelligence and commitment—qualities notably absent from the current Administration's handling of the problem.

We urge additional financial support to the United States Forest Service for planning and management consistent with the environmental ideal stated in this Platform.

Choosing the Right Methods of Environmental Protection

The problem we face is to choose the most efficient, effective and equitable techniques for solving each new environmental problem. We cannot afford to waste resources while doing the job, any more than we can afford to leave the job undone.

We must enforce the strict emission requirements on all pollution sources set under the 1970 Clean Air Act.

We must support the establishment of a policy of no harmful discharge into our waters by 1985.

We must have adequate staffing and funding of all regulatory and enforcement agencies and departments to implement laws, programs and regulations protecting the environment, vigorous prosecution of violators and a Justice Department committed to enforcement of environmental law.

We must fully support laws to assure citizens' standing in federal environmental court suits.

Strict interstate environmental standards must be formulated and enforced to prevent pollution from high-density population areas being dumped into low-density population areas for the purpose of evasion of strict pollution enforcement.

The National Environmental Policy Act should be broadened to include major private as well as public projects, and a genuine commitment must be made to making the Act work.

Our environment is most threatened when the natural balance of an area's ecology is drastically altered for the sole purpose of profits. Such practices as "clear cut" logging, strip mining, the indiscriminate destruction of whole species, creation of select ocean crops at the expense of other species and the unregulated use of persistent pesticides cannot be justified when they threaten our ability to maintain a stable environment.

Where appropriate, taxes need to be levied on pollution, to provide industry with an incentive to clean up.

We also need to develop new public agencies that can act to abate pollution—act on a scale commensurate with the size of the problem and the technology of pollution control.

Expanded federal funding is required to assist local governments with both the capital and operating expenses of water pollution control and solid waste management.

Jobs and the Environment

The United States should not be condemned to the choice between the development of resources and economic security or preservation of those resources.

A decent job for every American is a goal that need not, and must not, be sacrificed to our commitment to a clean environment. Far from slowing economic growth, spending for environmental protection can create new job opportunities for Americans. Nevertheless, some older and less efficient plants might find themselves in a worse competitive position due to environmental protection requirements. Closely monitored adjustment as-

sistance should be made available to those plants willing to modernize and institute environmental protection measures.

Science and Technology

For years, the United States was the world's undisputed leader in science and technology. Now that leadership is being challenged, in part because of the success of efforts in other countries, and in part because of the Nixon Administration's neglect of our basic human and material resources in this field.

As Democrats, we understand the enormous investment made by the nation in educating and training hundreds of thousands of highly skilled Americans in science and technology. Many of these people are now unemployed, as aerospace and defense programs are slowly cut back and as the Administration's economic policies deprive these Americans, as well as others, of their livelihood.

So far, however, the Nixon Administration has paid scant attention to these problems. By contrast, the Democratic Party seeks both to increase efforts by the federal government and to stimulate research in private industry.

In addition, the Democratic Party is committed to increasing the overall level of scientific research in the United States, which has been allowed to fall under the Nixon Administration. And we are eager to take management methods and technicalities devised for the space and defense programs, as well as our technical resources, and apply them to the city, the environment, education, energy, transportation, health care and other urgent domestic needs. We propose also to work out a more effective relationship between government and industry in this area, to stimulate the latter to a greater research and development effort, thus helping buoy up the economy and create more jobs.

Finally, we will promote the search for new approaches in science and technology, so that the benefits of progress may be had without further endangering the environment—indeed, so that the environment may be better preserved. We must create a systematic way to decide which new technologies will contribute to the nation's development, and which will cause more problems than they solve. We are committed to a role for government in helping to bring the growth of technology into a harmonious relationship with our lives.

Energy Resources

The earth's natural resources, once in abundant and seemingly unlimited supply, can no longer be taken for granted. In particular, the United States is facing major changes in the pattern of energy supply that will force us to reassess traditional policies. By 1980, we may well have to depend on imports from the Eastern Hemisphere for as much as 30 to 50 per cent of our oil supplies. At the same time, new forms of energy supply—such as nuclear, solar or geothermal power—lag far behind in research and development.

In view of these concerns, it is shocking that the Nixon Administration still steadfastly refuses to develop a national energy policy.

The Democratic Party would remedy that glaring oversight. To begin with, we should:

Promote greater research and development, both by government and by private industry, of unconventional energy sources, such as solar power, geothermal power, energy from water and a variety of nuclear power possibilities to design clean breeder fission and fusion techniques. Public funding in this area needs to be expanded, while retaining the principle of public administration of public funds;

Re-examine our traditional view of national security requirements in energy to reconcile them with our need for long-term abundant supplies of energy at reasonable cost;

Expand research on coal technology to minimize pollution, while making it possible to expand the efficiency of coal in meeting our energy needs;

Establish a national power plant siting prodecure to examine and protect environmental values;

Reconcile the demand for energy with the demand to protect the environment;

Redistribute the cost of power among consumers, so that all, especially the poor, may be guaranteed adequate power at reasonable costs;

Develop a national power grid to improve the reliability and efficiency of our electricity system;

End the practice of allowing promotional utility advertising as an expense when rates are set; and

Find new techniques to encourage the conservation of energy. We must also require full disclosure of the energy needs of consumer products and home heating to enable consumers to make informed decisions on their use of energy.

The Oceans

As with the supply of energy, no longer can we take for granted the precious resources we derive from the oceans. Here, too, we need comprehensive national and international policies to use and protect the vast potential contained in the sea. In particular we must:

Agree with other nations on stopping pollution of the seas, if they are not one day to become one large sewer, or be filled with dangerous poisons that will deprive us of vital food resources;

Agree with other nations on the conservation of food resources in the seas and promote the use of management techniques that will end the decline of the world's fish catch on the continental shelf through international cooperation for fishing gear regulations and species quota and preserve endangered species;

Agree on an international accord for the seas, so resources can be shared equitably among the world's nations. We must be prepared to act constructively at next year's Conference on the Law of the Seas;

Begin to reconcile competing interests in the future of the seas, including our national security objectives, to protect ocean resources in cooperation with other nations; and

Support strongly the protection of ocean mammals (seal, whale, walrus) from indiscriminate destruction by both foreign and tuna fishing industries, but specifically exempting those native Americans whose subsistence depends completely on their total use of the ocean's resources.

Ninety per cent of all salt water fish species live on our continental shelves, where plant life is plentiful. For this reason, we support monitoring and strict enforcement of all safety regulations on all offshore drilling equipment and on environmentally safe construction of all tankers transporting oil.

Public Lands

For generations, Americans have been concerned with preserving the natural treasures of our country: Our lakes and rivers, our forests and mountains. Enlightened Americans of the past decided that the federal government should take a major role in protecting these treasures, on behalf of everyone. Today, however, neglect on the part of the Nixon Administration is threatening this most valued heritage—and that of our children. Never before in modern history have our public lands been so neglected and the responsible agencies so starved of funds.

The Democratic Party is concerned about preserving our public lands, and promoting policies of land management in keeping with the broad public interest. In particular, it is imperative to restore lost funds for land, park and forest management. It is imperative that decisions about the future use of our public lands be opened up to all the people for widespread public debate and discussion. Only through such an open process can we set ground rules that appropriately limit the influence of special interests and allow for cohesive guidelines for national land-use planning.

We are particularly aware of the potential conflicts among the use of land, rivers, lakes and the seashore for economic development, large-scale recreation and for preservation as unspoiled wilderness. We recognize that there are competing goals, and shall develop means for resolving these conflicts in a way that reflects the federal government's particular responsibilities as custodian for the public. We need more National Seashores and expansion of the National Park system. Major steps must be taken to follow up on Congressional commitment to scenic riverways. Recreation areas must be made available to people where they live. This includes the extension of our national wilderness preserves to include de facto wilderness areas and their preservation free of commercialization. In this way, we will help to preserve and improve the quality of life for millions of our people.

With regard to the development of the vast natural resources on our public lands, we pledge a renewed commitment to proceed in the interests of all our citizens.

V. EDUCATION

"The American people want overwhelmingly to give to our children and adults equitable educational opportunities of the highest possible quality, not predicated on race, not predicated on past social accomplishment or wealth, except in a compensatory way to those who have been deprived in the past."— Governor Jimmy Carter, Atlanta Hearing, June 9, 1972.

Our schools are failing our children. Never, more than now, have we needed the schools to play their traditional role—to create a sense of national unity and to reconcile ethnic, religious and racial conflicts. Yet the Nixon Administration—ignoring the plight of the nation's schools, by twice vetoing funds for education— has contributed to this failure.

America in the 1970's requires something the world has never seen: Masses of educated people—educated to feel and to act, as well as to think. The children who enter school next fall still will be in the labor force in the year 2030; we cannot even imagine what American society will be like then, let alone what specific jobs they may hold. For them, education must be done by teaching them how to learn, how to apply man's wisdom to new problems as they arise and how to recognize new problems as they arise. Education must prepare students not just to earn a living but to live a life—a creative, humane and sensitive life.

School Finance

Achieving educational excellence requires adequate financial support. But today local property taxes— which do not keep pace with inflation—can no longer support educational needs. Continued reliance on this revenue source imposes needless hardship on the American family without supplying the means for good schools. At the same time, the Nixon recession has sapped the resources of state government, and the Administration's insensitivity to school children has meant inadequate federal expenditures in education.

The next Democratic Administration should:

Support equalization in spending among school districts. We support court decisions holding unconstitutional the disparities in school expenditures produced by dependence on local property taxes. We pledge equality of spending as a way to improve schools and to assure equality of access to good education for all children;

Increase federal financial aid for elementary and secondary education to enhance achievement of quality education everywhere, and by fully funding the programs passed by the Congress and by fully funding ESEA Title I;

Step up efforts to meet the special needs and costs of educationally disadvantaged children handicapped by poverty, disability or non-English-speaking family background;

Channel financial aid by a Constitutional formula to children in nonpublic schools;

Support suburban–urban cooperation in education to share resources and expenses;

Develop and implement the retraining of displaced black and other minority teachers affected by desegregation; and

Continue with full federal funding the breakfast and lunch programs for all children and the development of other programs to combat hunger.

Early Childhood Education

Our youngest children are most ignored by national policy and most harshly treated by the Nixon Administration. President Nixon's cruel, irresponsible veto of the Comprehensive Child Development Act of 1971 indicates dramatically the real values of the present Administration.

That legislation struck down by President Nixon remains the best program to bring support to family units threatened by economic and social pressures; to eliminate educational handicaps which leave disadvantaged children unable to compete in school; to prevent early childhood disease before it results in adult disability; to interrupt the painful, destructive cycle of welfare dependence, and, most important, to allow all children happy lives as children and the opportunity to develop their full potential.

We support legislation for positive and preventive approaches to early childhood education.

These approaches should be designed to help eliminate educational handicaps before they require remedial treatment. A Democratic President will support and sign a program for universal comprehensive child development.

We should give reality to the right of mentally retarded children to adequate health care and educational opportunities through such measures as including necessary care under national health insurance and federal aid to assure an opportunity for education for all retarded persons.

Equal Access to Quality Education

The Supreme Court of the United States in Brown v. Board of Education established the Constitutional principle that states may not discriminate between school children on the basis of their race and that separate but equal has no place in our public education system. Eighteen years later the provision of integration is not a reality.

We support the goal of desegregation as a means to achieve equal access to quality education for all our children. There are many ways to desegregate schools: School attendance lines may be redrawn; schools may be paired; larger physical facilities may be built to serve larger, more diverse enrollments; magnet schools or educational parks may be used. Transportation of students is another tool to accomplish desegregation. It must continue to be available according to Supreme Court decisions to eliminate legally imposed segregation and improve the quality of education for all children.

Bilingual Education

Ten per cent of school children in the United States speak a language other than English in their homes and communities. The largest of the linguistic and cultural groups—Spanish-speaking and American Indians—are also among the poorest people in the United States. Increasing evidence indicates an almost total failure of public education to educate these children.

The drop-out rates of Spanish-speaking and Indian

children are the worst of any children in the country. The injury is compounded when such children are placed in special "compensatory" programs or programs for the "dumb" or the "retarded" on the basis of tests and evaluations conducted in English.

The passage of the Bilingual Education Act of 1967 began a commitment by the nation to do something about the injustices committed against the bilingual child. But for 1972–73, Congress appropriated $35 million—enough to serve only two per cent of the children who need help.

The next Democratic Administration should:

Increase federal support for bilingual, bicultural educational programs, pre-school through secondary school, including funding of bilingual Adult Basic Education;

Ensure sufficient teacher training and curriculum development for such schools;

Implement an affirmative action program to train and to hire bilingual–bicultural Spanish-speaking persons at all levels in the educational system;

Provide inventories for state and local districts to initiate bilingual–bicultural education programs;

Require testing of bilingual–bicultural children in their own languages; and

Prohibit discrimination against bilingual–bicultural children in school.

Career Education

Academic accomplishment is not the only way to financial success, job satisfaction or rewarding life in America. Many young Americans think that college is the only viable route when for some a vocational–technical career offers as much promise of a full life. Moreover, the country desperately needs skilled workers and technicians, men and women who understand and can handle the tools and equipment that mean growth and jobs. By 1975 the need for skilled craftsmen will increase 18 per cent while the need for college-trained persons will remain stable.

Young people should be permitted to make a career choice consistent with their interests, aptitudes and aspirations. We must create an atmosphere where the dignity of work is respected, where diversity of talent and taste is encouraged and where continuing opportunity exists to keep pace with change and gives a saleable skill.

To aid this, the next Democratic Administration can:

Give vocational–technical education the same priority in funds and emphasis previously given academic education;

Support full appropriations for the recently passed Occupational Education Act;

Strengthen the career counseling programs in elementary, secondary and postsecondary education so that young people are made aware of all of the opportunities open to them and provide special kinds of vocational–technical education and experience to meet specific area needs;

Develop and promote a climate conducive to free, rational choice by young people, dispelling the current prejudices that influence career decisions for most young people almost from birth;

Establish a lifetime system of continuing education to enhance career mobility, both vertically and laterally, so that the career choice made at 18 or 20 years of age does not have to be the only or the final choice; and

Grant equal representation to minorities and women in vocational–technical education.

Higher Education

We support universal access to opportunities to post-secondary education. The American education system has always been an important path toward social and economic advance. Federal education policy should ensure that our colleges and universities continue as an open system. It must also stimulate the creative development and expansion of higher education to meet the new social, economic and environmental problems confronting society. To achieve the goals of equal opportunity in education, to meet the growing financial crisis in higher education and to stimulate reform of educational techniques, the next Democratic Administration should:

- Support guaranteed access for all students to loan funds with long-term repayment based on future earnings. Not only the poor, but families with moderate incomes must be provided relief from the cost of a college and professional education;

- Grant supplements and contingent loans to institutions, based on enrollment of federally aided students;

- Provide research funds to stimulate a partnership between postsecondary, secondary and primary education, in an effort to find new patterns for learning and to provide training and retraining of teachers, especially in urban areas;

- Develop broad opportunities for lifelong learning including encouragement for postsecondary education throughout adult years and permit "stopping-off " during higher education;

- Develop affirmative programs in universities and colleges for recruitment of minorities and women for administrative and teaching positions and as students; and

- Create incentives for nontraditional education which recognize the contribution of experience to an individual's educational status.

Arts and Humanities

Support for the arts and humanities is one of the benchmarks of a civilized society. Yet, the continued existence of many of America's great symphonies, theatres and museums, our film institutes, dance companies and other art forms, is now threatened by rising costs, and the public contribution, far less than in most advanced industrial societies, is a fraction of the need.

We should expand support of the arts and humanities by direct grants through the National Foundation for the Arts and Humanities, whose policy should be to stimulate the widest variety of artistic and scholarly expression.

We should support long-range financing for public broadcasting, insulated from political pressures. We deplore the Nixon Administration's crude efforts to starve and muzzle public broadcasting, which has become a vital supplement to commercial television.

VI. CRIME, LAW AND JUSTICE

"I think we can reduce crime. Society has no more important challenge because crime is human conduct and more than any other activity of people it reflects the moral character of a nation."—Ramsey Clark, Washington Hearing, June 23, 1972.

We advocate and seek a society and a government in which there is an attitude of respect for the law and for those who seek its enforcement and an insistence on the part of our citizens that the judiciary be ever mindful of their primary duty and function of punishing the guilty and protecting the innocent. We will insist on prompt, fair and equal treatment for all persons before the bar of justice.

The problem of crime in America is real, immediate and fundamental; its costs to the nation are staggering; nearly three-quarters of a million victims of violent crime in one year alone; more than 15,000 murders, billions of dollars of property loss.

The indirect, intangible costs are even more ominous. A frightened nation is not a free nation. Its citizens are prisoners, suspicious of the people they meet, restricted in when they go out and when they return, threatened even in their own homes. Unless government at all levels can restore a sense of confidence and security to its people, there is the ever-present danger that alarm will turn to panic, triggering short-cut remedies that jeopardize hard-won liberties.

When law emforcement breaks down, not only the victims of street violence suffer; the worker's health and safety is imperiled by unsafe, illegal conditions on the job; the society is defenseless against fraud and pollution; most tragically of all, parents and communities are ravaged by traffic in dangerous drugs.

The Nixon Administration campaigned on a pledge to reduce crime—to strengthen the "peace forces" against the "criminal forces." Despite claims to the contrary, that pledge has been broken:

Violent crime has increased by one-third, to the highest levels in our history;

Fueled by immense profits of narcotics traffic, organized crime has thrust its corruption farther and farther, into law enforcement agencies and the halls of justice;

The Department of Justice has become the handmaiden of the White House political apparatus, offering favors to those special interests which buy their "law" in Washington;

The Justice Department has failed to enforce laws protecting key legal rights, such as the Voting Rights Act of 1965;

Nixon and Mitchell use federal crime control funds for political purposes, squandering $1.5 billion.

To reverse this course, through equal enforcement of the law, and to rebuild justice the Democratic Party believes:

The impact of crime in America cuts across racial, geographic and economic lines;

Hard-line rhetoric, pandering to emotion, is both futile and destructive;

We can protect all people without undermining fundamental liberties by ceasing to use "law and order" as justification for repression and political persecution, and by ceasing to use stop-gap measures as preventive detention, "no-knock" entry, surveillance, promiscuous and unauthorized use of wire taps, harassment, and secret dossiers; and

The problems of crime and drug abuse cannot be isolated from the social and economic conditions that give rise to them.

Preventing Crime

Effective law enforcement requires tough planning and action. This Administration has given us nothing

but tough words. Together with unequal law enforcement by police, prosecutors and judges, the result is a "turnstile" system of justice, where most of those who commit crime are not arrested, most of those arrested are not prosecuted, and many of those prosecuted are not convicted. Under this Administration, the conviction rate for federal prosecutions has decline to one-half its former level. Tens of thousands of offenders simply never appear in court and are heard from again only when they commit another crime. This system does not deter crime. It invites it. It will be changed only when all levels of government act to return firmness and fairness to every part of the criminal justice system.

Fear of crime, and firm action against it, is not racism. Indeed the greatest victims of crime today—whether of business fraud or of the narcotics plague—are the people of the ghetto, black and brown. Fear now stalks their streets far more than it does the suburbs.

So that Americans can again live without fear of each other the Democratic Party believes:

There must be equally stringent law enforcement for rich and poor, corporate and individual offenders;

Citizens must be actively involved with the police in a joint effort;

Police forces must be upgraded, and recruiting of highly qualified and motivated policemen must be made easier through federally assisted pay commensurate with the difficulty and importance of their job, and improved training with comprehensive scholarship and financial support for anyone who is serving or will contract to serve for an appropriate period of police service;

The complex job of policing requires a sensitivity to the changing social demands of the communities in which police operate;

We must provide the police with increased technological facilities and support of efficient use of police resources, both human and material;

When a person is arrested, both justice and effective deterrence of crime require that he be speedily tried and convicted and promptly sentenced. To this end we support financial assistance to local courts, prosecutors, and independent defense counsel for expansion, streamlining, and upgrading, with trial in 60 days as the goal;

To train local and state police officers, a Police Academy on a par with the other service academies should be established as well as an Academy of Judicial Administration;

We will provide every assistance to our law enforcement agencies at federal and local levels in the training of personnel and the improvement of techniques and will encourage mutual cooperation between each in its own sphere of responsibility;

We will support needed legislation and action to seek out and bring to justice the criminal organization of national scope operating in our country;

We will provide leadership and action in a national effort against the usage of drugs and drug addiction, attacking this problem at every level and every source in a full-scale campaign to drive this evil from our society. We recognize drug addiction as a health problem and pledge that emphasis will be put on rehabilitation of addicts;

We will provide increased emphasis in the area of juvenile delinquency and juvenile offenses in order to deter and rehabilitate young offenders;

There must be laws to control the improper use of hand guns. Four years ago a candidate for the presidency was slain by a hand gun. Two months ago, another candidate for that office was gravely wounded. Three out of four police officers killed in the line of duty are slain with hand guns. Effective legislation must include a ban on the sale of hand guns known as Saturday night specials which are unsuitable for sporting purposes;

A comprehensive fully funded program is needed to improve juvenile justice, to ensure mininimum standards, to expand research into rehabilition techniques, including alternatives to reform schools, and coordinate existing programs for treating juvenile delinquency; and

The block-grant system of the Law Enforcement Assistance Administration which has produced ineffectiveness, waste and corruption should be eliminated. Funds should go directly to operating agencies that are committed to change and improvement in local law enforcement, including agencies concerned with research, rehabilitation, training and treatment.

Narcotic Drugs

Drug addiction and alcoholism are health problems. Drugs prey on children, destroy lives and communities, force crimes to satisfy addicts, corrupt police and government and finance the expansion of organized crime. A massive national effort, equal to the scale and complexity of the problem, is essential.

The next Democratic Administration should support:

A massive law enforcement effort, supported by increased funds and personnel, against the suppliers and distributors of heroin and other dangerous drugs, with increased penalties for major narcotics traffickers;

Full use of all existing resources to halt the illegal entry of narcotics into the United States, including suspension of economic and military assistance to any country that fails to take appropriate steps to prevent narcotic drugs produced or processed in that country from entering the United States illegally, and increases in customs personnel fighting smuggling of hard drugs;

An all-out investigative and prosecutory effort against corruption in government and law enforcement. Where corruption exists it is a major factor in permitting criminal activity, especially large-scale narcotics distribution, to flourish. It also destroys respect for the law in all who are conscious of its operation. We are determined that our children—whether in the ghetto or in a suburban high school—shall no longer be able to see a pusher protected from prosecution, openly plying his trade;

Strict regulation and vigorous enforcement of existing quotas regulating production and distrubiton of dangerous drugs, including amphetamines and barbiturates, to prevent diversion into illegal markets, with legislation for strong criminal penalties against drug manufacturers engaging in illegal overproduction, distribution and importation;

Expanded research into dangerous drugs and their abuse, focusing especially on heroin addiction among the young and development of effective, non-addictive heroin treatment methods;

Concentration of law enforcement efforts on major suppliers and distributors, with most individual users diverted into treatment before prosecution;

Immediate placement in medical or psychiatric treatment, available to any individual drug abuser without fear of disclosure or harassment. Work opportunities should be provided for addicts in treatment by supported work and other programs; and

Drug education in schools based on fact, not scare tactics to teach young people the dangers of different drugs, and full treatment opportunities for youthful drug abusers. Hard drug trafficking in schools must be met with the strongest possible law enforcement.

Organized and Professional Crime

We are determined to exert the maximum power and authority of the federal government to protect the many victims who cannot help themselves against great criminal combinations.

Against the organized criminal syndicates, we pledge an expanded federal enforcement effort; one not restricted to criminals of any particular ethnic group, but which recognizes that organized crime in the United States cuts across all boundaries of race, national origin and class.

Against white-collar crime, we pledge to enforce the maximum penalties provided by law. Justice cannot survive when, as too often is the case, a boy who steals a television set is sentenced to a long jail term, while a stock manipulator who steals millions is only commanded to sin no more.

At least where life or personal injury are at stake, we pledge to seek expanded criminal penalties for the violation of federal laws. Employers who violate the worker safety and health laws, or manufacturers who knowingly sell unsafe products or drugs profit from death and injury as knowingly as the common mugger. They deserve equally severe punishment.

Rehabilitation of Offenders

Few institutions in America are as uniformly condemned and as consistently ignored as our existing prison system. Many prisons that are supposed to rehabilitate and separate, in fact train their inmates for nothing but brutality and a life of further crime. Only when public understanding recognizes that our existing "corrections" system *contributes* to escalating crime, will we get the massive effort necessary for fundamental restructuring.

Therefore, the Democratic Party commits itself to:

Restoration, after release, of rights to obtain driver's licenses and to public and private employment, and, after completion of sentence and conditions of parole, restoration of civil rights to vote and hold public office;

Revision of sentencing procedures and greater use of community-based rehabilitation facilities, especially for juveniles;

Recognition of the constitutional and human rights of prisoners; realistic therapeutic, vocational, wage-earning, education, alcoholism and drug treatment programs;

Making correctional personnel an integral part of the rehabilitative process; and

Emergency, educational and work-release furlough programs as an available technique, support for "self-help" programs.

The Quality of Justice

Justice is not merely effective law enforcement—though that is an essential part of it. Justice, rather, ex-presses the moral character of a nation and its commitment to the rule of law, to equality of all people before the law.

The Democratic Party believes that nothing must abridge the faith of the American citizens in their system of law and justice.

We believe that the quality of justice will be enhanced by:

Equal treatment for all citizens in the court without fear or favor—corporations as well as individual offenders;

Swift trials for accused persons;

Equitable pre-trial release systems and the elimination of plea bargaining abuses;

Ending subversion of the legal system for political gain in court appointments, in anti-trust cases and in administration of law enforcement programs;

Administering the laws and funding enacted by the Congress;

Respecting and abiding by Constitutional protections of due process; and

Abolishing capital punishment, recognized as an ineffective deterrent to crime, unequally applied and cruel and excessive punishment.

VII. FARMING AND RURAL LIFE

"A blight hangs over the land caused by misguided farm policies."—Tony Dechant, Sioux City Hearing, June 16, 1972.

For many decades, American agriculture has been the envy of the world; and American farmers and American ranchers have made possible a level of nutrition and abundance for our people that is unrivaled in history, while feeding millions of people abroad.

The basis for this success—and its promise for the future—lies with the family-type farm. It can and must be preserved, in the best interests of all Americans and the nation's welfare.

Today, as dwindling income forces thousands of family farmers into bankruptcy each year, the family-type farm is threatened with extinction. American farming is passing to corporate control.

These trends will benefit few of our people, while hurting many. The dominance of American food production by the large corporation would destroy individual enterprise and links that millions of our people have with the land; and it would lead to higher prices and higher food costs for everyone.

Major efforts must be made to prevent this disaster for the fabric of rural life, for the American farmer, rancher, farm worker and for the consumer and other rural people throughout our nation;

Farm income must be improved to enable farmers, ranchers and farm workers to produce a steady and dependable supply of food and fiber products in return for full parity; and

We must recognize and fulfill the social contract that exists between the family-farm producers of food and the non-farm consumer.

The Democratic Party understands these urgent needs; the Nixon Administration does not and has failed the American farmer. Its record today is consistent with the Republican record of the past: Low prices, farm surpluses that depress the market and callous disregard for the people in rural America.

This Administration has sold out agriculture to interests bent on eliminating family-type farmers and bent on delivering agriculture to conglomerates, agribusiness giants and rich investors seeking to avoid taxes.

Its policies have driven farm income as low as 67 per cent of parity, unequalled since the Depression. Between 50,000 and 75,000 farm families are driven off the land each year. Hundreds of thousands of demoralized people are being forced into overcrowded cities, emptying the countryside and bankrupting small business in rural towns and cities.

The Nixon Administration tries to hide its failures by misleading the people, juggling the parity formula to make prices look higher, distorting reports to make corporate farming look insignificant and trying to break up the U.S. Department of Agriculture and still the farmer's voice.

The Democratic Party will reverse these disastrous policies, and begin to re-create a rural society of widespread family farming, individual opportunity and private and cooperative enterprises, where honest work will bring a decent income.

We repudiate the Administration's set-aside program, which pushes up the cost of farm programs while building huge surpluses that depress prices.

We repudiate the Report of the USDA Young Executives Committee which would eliminate the family-type farm by ending price support, loan and purchasing programs on all farm commodities and which would put farm people on the welfare rolls.

We repudiate a Presidential commission report recommending that future federal investment in many small towns and cities should make their decline merely more bearable rather than reverse it.

In place of these negative and harmful policies, the Democratic Party pledges itself to take positive and decisive action:

We will replace the 1970 Farm Act, when it expires next year, with a permanent law to provide fair prices to family-type farm and ranch operators. This law will include loans and payments to farmers and effective supply management to raise family farm income to 100 per cent of parity, based on the 1910–14 ratios;

We will resist a price ceiling on agricultural products until farm prices reach 110 per cent of parity, based on the 1910–14 ratios, and we will conduct a consumer education program to inform all Americans of the relationship between the prices of raw commodities and retail prices;

We will end farm program benefits to farm units larger than family-size; and

We will work for production adjustment that will assure adequate food and fiber for all our people, including low-income families and individuals whose purchasing power is supplemented with food stamps and that can provide enough commodities for export and for the Food for Peace Program.

Exporting Our Abundance

For many years, farm exports have made a major contribution to our balances of trade and payments. But this benefit for the entire nation must not be purchased with depressed prices for the producer.

The Democratic Party will ensure that:

Prices for commodities sent abroad as exports or aid return the cost of production plus a profit for the American farmer;

We will negotiate international commodity agreements to include prices that guarantee prices to producers based on cost of production plus a reasonable profit;

We will require U.S. corporations producing commodities outside the country for consumption here to pay duties high enough to prevent unfair competition for domestic producers;

We will assure that the same rigid standards for inspection of domestic dairy products and meat will be applied to imports; and

We will create a strategic reserve of storable commodities, insulated from the market, rotated regularly to maintain quality and stored to the extent possible on farms.

Strengthening the Family Farm

These policies and actions will not be enough on their own to strengthen the family farm. The Democratic Party also recognizes that farmers and ranchers must be able to gain economic strength in the marketplace by organizing and bargaining collectively for the sale of their products. And they need to be free of unfair competition from monopoly and other restrictive corporate practices. We therefore pledge:

To remove all obstacles to farm bargaining for the sale of products;

To extend authority for marketing orders to all farm commodities including those used for processing;

To prohibit farming, or the gaining of monopolistic control of production, on the part of corporations whose resources and income derive primarily from non-farm sources;

To investigate violations and enforce anti-trust laws in corporation–agriculture–agribusiness interlocks;

To prohibit corporations and individuals from setting up tax shelters or otherwise engaging in agriculture primarily for the purpose of tax avoidance or tax loss;

To encourage and support the use of cooperatives and membership associations in all areas of the country, which we pledge to protect from interference, punitive taxation or other hindrances; and

To assist small rural cooperatives to promote projects in housing, health, social services, marketing, farming, employment and transportation for rural areas with such things as technical assistance and credit.

Guaranteeing Farm People a Voice

None of these policies can begin to work unless farmers, ranchers, farm workers and other rural people have full rights of participation in our democratic institutions of government. The Democratic Party is committed to seeing that family-type farmers and ranchers will be heard and that they will have ample opportunity to help shape policies affecting agriculture and rural America. To this end:

We support the appointment of a farmer or rancher as Secretary of Agriculture;

We oppose all efforts to abolish or dismantle the U.S. Department of Agriculture;

We will require that decisions relating to dams and other public land-use projects in rural areas involving federal funds be considered at well-publicized public hearings. Government is not now giving adequate protection to individual rights in condemnation procedures. It must set new and better procedures and requirements to assure individual rights;

We support the United Farm Workers in their nonviolent efforts to gain collective bargaining recognition and contracts. We also support unemployment insurance compensation benefits, workman's compensation benefits and delivery of health services for farm workers; and

We support the removal of sugar workers from the custody of the U.S. Department of Agriculture.

Revitalizing Rural America

Sound rural development must start with improved farm income, which also promotes the prosperity of the small businesses that serve all rural people. But there must be other efforts, as well, to ensure equity for farm and rural people in the American economy. The Democratic Party Pledges:

To support the rural cooperative electrification and telephone programs and to implement rural transportation programs as explained in the section Cities, Communities, Counties and the Environment of this Platform. We will extend the agricultural exemption in the Motor Carriers Act to products and supplies and ensure rural areas an equitable share of Highway Trust Funds;

To apply general revenue sharing in ways that will permit state and local taxation of family farm lands on the basis of value for farm use rather than value for land speculation;

To guarantee equal treatment of rural and urban areas in the provision of federal funds for schools, poverty programs, health facilities, housing, highways, air services, pollution control, senior citizen programs and employment opportunities and manpower and training programs;

To provide loans to aid young farm families and small businesses to get established in rural areas; and

To ensure agricultural research toward an examination of the social and economic consciences of technology.

The prime goal of land grant colleges and research should be to help family farms and rural people.

VIII. FOREIGN POLICY

"The Administration is continuing a war—continuing the killing of Americans and Vietnamese—when our national security is not at stake.

"It is our duty as the opposition party to point out the Administration's errors and to offer a responsible alternative."—W. Averell Harriman, New York Hearing, June 22, 1972.

Strength in defense and wisdom in foreign affairs are essential to prosperity and tranquility. In the modern world, there can be no isolationism in reality or policy. But the measure of our nation's rank in the world must be our success in achieving a just and peaceful society at home.

For the Nixon Administration, foreign policy results have fallen short of the attention and the slogans:

After four years of "Vietnamization," the war in Southeast Asia continues and Nixon's plan is still a secret;

Vital foreign policy decisions are made without consultation with Congress or our allies; and

Executive secrecy runs wild with unparalleled efforts to intimidate the media and suppress those who seek to put a different view before the American people.

The next Democratic Administration should:

End American participation in the war in Southeast Asia;

Re-establish control over military activities and reduce military spending, where consistent with national security;

Defend America's real interests and maintain our alliances, neither playing world policeman nor abandoning old and good friends;

Not neglect America's relations with small third-world nations in placing reliance in great power relationships;

Return to Congress, and to the people, a meaningful role in decisions on peace and war; and

Make information public, except where real national defense interests are involved.

Vietnam

Nothing better describes the need for a new American foreign policy than the fact that now, as for the past seven years, it begins with the war in Vietnam.

The task now is still to end the war, not to decide who is to blame for it. The Democratic Party must share the responsibility for this tragic war. But, elected with a secret plan to end this war, Nixon's plan is still secret, and we—and the Vietnamese—have had four more years of fighting and death.

It is true that our involvement on the ground has been reduced. Troops are coming home. But the war has been extended in Laos and Cambodia; the bombing of North Vietnam has been expanded to levels of destruction undreamed of four years ago; North Vietnam has been blockaded; the number of refugees increases each day, and the Secretary of Defense warns us of still further escalation.

All this has accomplished nothing except to prolong the war.

The hollowness of "Vietnamization"—a delusive slogan seeming to offer cheap victory—has been exposed by the recent offensive. The Saigon Government, despite massive U.S. support, is still not viable. It is militarily ineffective, politically corrupt and economically near collapse. Yet it is for this regime that Americans still die, and American prisoners still rot in Indo-China camps.

The plight of these American prisoners justly arouses the concern of all Americans. We must insist that any resolution of the war include the return of all prisoners held by North Vietnam and other adversary forces and the fullest possible accounting for the missing. With increasing lack of credibility, the Nixon Administration has sought to use the prisoners of war as an excuse for its policies. It has refused to make the simple offer of a definite and final end to U.S. participation in the war, in conjunction with return of all U.S. prisoners.

The majority of the Democratic Senators have called for full U.S. withdrawal by October 1, 1972. We support that position. If the war is not ended before the next Democratic Administration takes office, we pledge, as the first order of business, an immediate and complete withdrawal of all U.S. forces in Indo-China. All U.S. military action in Southeast Asia will cease. After the end of U.S. direct combat participation, military aid to the Saigon Government, and elsewhere in Indo-China, will be terminated.

The U.S. will no longer seek to determine the political future of the nations of Indo-China. The issue is not whether we will depose the present South Vietnamese Government, rather when we will cease insisting that it must be the core of any political settlement. We will do what we can to foster an agreement on an acceptable political solution—but we recognize that there are sharp limits to our ability to influence this process, and to the importance of the outcome to our interest.

Disengagement from this terrible war will not be a "defeat" for America. It will not imply any weakness in America's will or ability to protect its vital interests from attack. On the contrary, disengagement will enable us to heal domestic divisions and to end the distortion of our international priorities which the war has caused.

A Democratic Administration will act to ease the hard transitions which will come with the end of this war. We pledge to offer to the people of Vietnam humanitarian assistance to help them repair the ravages of 30 years of war to the economy and to the people of that devastated land.

To our own people, we pledge a true effort to extend the hand of reconciliation and assistance to those most affected by the war.

To those who have served in this war, we pledge a full GI Bill of Rights, with benefits sufficient to pay for an education of the veteran's choice, job training programs and the guarantee of employment and the best medical care this country can provide, including a full program of rehabilitation for those who have returned addicted to dangerous drugs. To those who for reasons of conscience refused to serve in this war and were prosecuted or sought refuge abroad, we state our firm intention to declare an amnesty, on an appropriate basis, when the fighting has ceased and our troops and prisoners of war have returned.

Military Policy

We propose a program of national defense which is both prudent and responsible, which will be a deterrent to potential aggressors.

Military strength remains an essential element of a responsible international policy. America must have the strength required for effective deterrence.

But military defense cannot be treated in isolation from other vital national concerns. Spending for military purposes is greater by far than federal spending for education, housing, environmental protection, unemployment insurance or welfare. Unneeded dollars for the military at once add to the tax burden and preempt funds from programs of direct and immediate benefit to our people. Moreover, too much that is now spent on defense not only adds nothing to our strength but makes us less secure by stimulating other countries to respond.

Under the Nixon stewardship of our defense policy, lack of sound management controls over defense projects threatens to price us out of an adequate defense. The reaction of the Defense Department to exposure of cost overruns has been to strike back at the critics instead of acting to stop the waste.

Needless projects continue and grow, despite evidence of waste, military ineffectiveness and even affirmative danger to real security. The "development" budget starts pressures for larger procurement budgets in a few years. Moral and military effectiveness deteriorate as drugs, desertion and racial hatred plagues the armed forces, especially in Vietnam.

The Democratic Party pledges itself to maintain adequate military forces for deterrence and effective support of our international position. But we will also insist on the firm control of specific costs and projects that are essential to ensure that each defense dollar makes a real contribution to national security. Specifically, a Democratic Administration should:

Plan military budgets on the basis of our present needs and commitments, not past practices or force levels;

Stress simplicity and effectiveness in new weapons and stop goldplating and duplication which threatens to spawn a new succession of costly military white elephants; avoid commitment to new weapons unless and until it becomes clear that they are needed;

Reject calls to use the SALT agreement as an excuse for wasteful and dangerous acceleration of our military spending;

Reduce overseas bases and forces; and

Rebuild the morale and military tradition of our armed forces through creative programs to combat drug abuse, racial tensions and eroded pride in service. We will support reforms of the conditions of military life to restore military service as an attractive career for men and women from all segments of our society.

By these reforms and this new approach to budgeting, coupled with a prompt end to U.S. involvement in the war in Indo-China, the military budget can be reduced substantially with no weakening of our national security. Indeed a leaner, better-run system will mean added strength, efficiency and morale for our military forces.

Workers and industries now dependent on defense spending should not be made to pay the price of altering our priorities. Therefore, we pledge reconversion policies and government resources to assure jobs and new industrial opportunities for all those adversely affected by curtailed defense spending.

Draft

We urge abolition of the draft.

Disarmament and Arms Control

The Democratic Party stands for keeping America strong; we reject the concept of unilateral reductions below levels needed for adequate military defense. But effective international arms control and disarmament do not threaten American security; they enhance it.

The last Democratic Administration took the lead in pressing for U.S.–Soviet agreement on strategic arms limitation. The recent SALT agreement is an important and useful first step.

The SALT agreement should be quickly ratified and taken as a starting point for new agreements. It must not be used as an excuse for new "bargaining chip" military programs or the new round of the arms race.

The next Democratic Administration should:

Carry on negotiations to expand the initial SALT agreement to other areas, especially to seek limits to the qualitative arms race and to begin reducing force levels on each side;

Seek a comprehensive ban on all nuclear testing, verified, as SALT will be, by national means;

Press for wide adherence to the Non-Proliferation Treaty, signed in 1968, and for extension of the concept of nuclear-free regions;

Seek ratification of the Protocol on Chemical Warfare without reservations;

In concert with our allies, pursue with the U.S.S.R. mutual force reductions in Europe; and widen the range of arms control discussions to include new subjects, such as mutual budget cuts, control of arms transfer to developing countries, restrictions on naval force deployments and other measures to limit conventional forces.

U.S. and the World Community

A new foreign policy must be adequate for a rapidly changing world. We welcome the opportunity this brings for improved relations with the U.S.S.R. and China. But we value even more America's relations with our friends and allies in the Western Hemisphere, in Western Europe, Japan and other industrialized countries, Israel and the Middle East, and in the developing nations of Asia and Africa. With them, our relations must be conducted on a basis of mutual trust and consultation, seeking to strengthen our ties and to resolve differences on a basis of mutual advantage. Throughout the world, the focus of our policy should be a commitment to peace, self-determination, development, liberty and international cooperation, without distortion in favor of military points of view.

Europe

Europe's increasing economic and political strength and the growing cooperation and self-confidence of its people have made the Atlantic alliance a partnership of equals. If we face the challenge of this new relationship, our historic partnership can endure.

The next Democratic Administration should:

Reduce U.S. troop levels in Europe in close consultation with our allies, as part of a program to adjust NATO to changed conditions. What is essential in our relations with the other NATO nations is not a particular troop level, but our continued commitment to collective defense;

Pledge to work in greater cooperation with the European economic communities to ensure that integration in Europe does not serve as a formula for discrimination against American goods and enterprises;

Cease American support for the repressive Greek military government; and

Make the voice of the United States heard in Northern Ireland against violence and terror and against the discrimination, repression and deprivation which brought about that awful civil strife.

We welcome every improvement in relations between the United States and the Soviet Union and every step taken toward reaching vital agreements on trade and other subjects. However, in our pursuit of improved relations, America cannot afford to be blind to the continued existence of serious differences between us. In particular, the United States should, by diplomatic contacts, seek to mobilize world opinion to express concern at the denial to the oppressed peoples of Eastern Europe and the minorities of the Soviet Union, including the Soviet Jews, of the right to practice their religion and culture and to leave their respective countries.

Middle East

The United States must be unequivocally committed to support of Israel's right to exist within secure and defensible boundaries. Progress toward a negotiated political settlement in the Middle East will permit Israel and her Arab neighbors to live at peace with each other, and to turn their energies to internal development. It will also free the world from the threat of the explosion of Mid-East tensions into world war. In working toward a settlement, our continuing pledge to the security and freedom of Israel must be both clear and consistent.

The next Democratic Administration should:

Make and carry out a firm, long-term public commitment to provide Israel with aircraft and other military equipment in the quantity and sophistication she needs to preserve her deterrent strength in the face of Soviet arsenaling of Arab threats of renewed war;

Seek to bring the parties into direct negotiations toward a permanent political solution based on the necessity of agreement on secure and defensible national boundaries;

Maintain a political commitment and a military

force in Europe and at sea in the Mediterranean ample to deter the Soviet Union from putting unbearable pressure on Israel;

Recognize and support the established status of Jerusalem as the capital of Israel, with free access to all its holy places provided to all faiths. As a symbol of this stand, the U.S. Embassy should be moved from Tel Aviv to Jerusalem; and

Recognize the responsibility of the world community for a just solution to the problems of the Arab and Jewish refugees.

Africa

The central feature of African politics today is the struggle against racism and colonialism in Southern Africa. There should be no mistake about which side we are on. We stand for full political, civil and economic rights for black and other nonwhite peoples in Southern Africa. We are against white-minority rule. We should not underwrite a return to the interventionism of the past. But we can end United States complicity with such governments.

The focus of America's concern with Africa must be on economic and social development. Economic aid to Africa, without political conditions, should be expanded, and African states assured an adequate share of the aid dollar. Military aid and aid given for military purposes should be sharply reduced.

All military aid to Portugal should be stopped and the Nixon $435-million deal for unneeded Azores bases should be canceled.

U.N. sanctions against the illegal racist regime in Southern Rhodesia should be supported vigorously, especially as they apply to chrome imports.

The U.S. should give full support to U.N. assertion of its control over Namibia (South West Africa), in accordance with the World Court's ruling.

The U.S. should make clear its opposition to the radical totalitarianism of South Africa. The U.S. government should act firmly to press U.S. businesses in South Africa to take measures for the fullest possible justice for their black employees. Blacks should be assigned at all levels to U.S. offices in South Africa, and throughout Africa. The South African sugar quota should be withdrawn.

No U.S. company or its subsidiary should be given U.S. tax credit for taxes paid to white-minority–ruled countries of Africa.

Japan

Our relations with Japan have been severely strained by a series of "Nixon shocks." We must restore our friendship with Japan, the leading industrial nation of Asia and a growing world power. There are genuine issues between us and Japan in the economic area, but accommodation of trade problems will be greatly eased by an end to the Nixon Administration's calculated insensitivity to Japan and her interests, marked by repeated failures to afford advance warnings, much consultation over sudden shifts in U.S. diplomatic and economic policy that affect Japan.

India, Pakistan and Bangla Desh

A Democratic Administration should work to restore the damage done to America's friendship with India as a result of the Administration's folly in "tilting" in favor of Pakistan and against Bangla Desh. The alienation by the Nixon Administration of India, the world's largest democracy, and the continued suspension of economic aid to India have seriously damaged the status of the United States in Asia. We pledge generous support for the essential work of reconstruction and reconciliation in Bangla Desh. At the same time, we will maintain friendship and developmental assistance to the "new" Pakistan which has emerged from these sad events.

China

The beginnings of a new U.S.–China relationship are welcome and important. However, so far, little of substance has changed, and the exaggerated secrecy and rhetoric of the Nixon Administration have produced unnecessary complications in our relationship with our allies and friends in Asia and with the U.S.S.R.

What is needed now is serious negotiation on trade, travel exchanges and progress on more basic issues. The U.S. should take the steps necessary to establish regular diplomatic relations with China.

Other Asian Countries

The future of Asia will be determined by its people, not by the United States. We should support accommodation and cooperation among all Asian countries and continue to assist in economic development.

Canada

A Democratic Administration should restore close U.S.–Canadian cooperation and communication, respecting Canada's nationhood and pride. In settling economic issues, we should not compromise our interests; but seek mutually advantageous and equitable solutions. In areas such as environmental protection and social policies, the Americans and Canadians share common problems and we must act together.

Latin America

The Good Neighbor policy of Franklin Roosevelt and the Alliance for Progress of John Kennedy set still-living goals—insulation from external political conflicts, mutual non-interference in internal affairs, and support for political liberty, social justice and economic progress. The Nixon Administration has lost sight of these goals, and the result is hostility and suspicion of the U.S. unmatched in generations.

The next Democratic Administration should:

Re-establish an inter-American alliance of equal sovereign nations working cooperatively for development;

Sharply reduce military assistance throughout the area;

Strive to deepen the exchange of people and ideas within the Hemisphere;

Take account of the special claims of democratically elected governments on our resources and sympathy;

Pursue a policy of non-intervention by military means in domestic affairs of Latin American nations;

Recognize that, while Cuba must not be permitted to become a foreign military base, after 13 years of boycott, crisis and hostility, the time has come to re-examine our relations with Cuba and to seek a way to resolve this cold war confrontation on mutually acceptable terms; and

Re-establish a U.S.–Mexico border commission, with representatives, to develop a comprehensive program to desalinate and eradicate pollution of the Colorado River and other waterways flowing into Mexico, and conduct substantial programs to raise the economic level on both sides of the border. This should remove the economic reasons which contribute to illegal immigration and discourage run-away industries. In addition, language requirements for citizenship should be removed.

The United Nations

The U.N. cannot solve all the great political problems of our time, but in an increasingly interdependent world, a world body is essential and its potential must be increasingly relied upon.

The next Democratic Administration should:

Re-establish the U.N. as a key forum for international activity, and assign representatives with the highest qualifications for diplomacy;

Give strong Executive Branch leadership for U.S. acceptance of its obligations for U.N. financing, while renegotiating arrangement for sharing U.N. costs;

Abide by the binding U.N. Security Council decision on Rhodesia sanctions, and support U.N. peace-keeping efforts;

Work for development of enforceable world law as a basis for peace, and endorse repeal of the Connally Reservation on U.S. acceptance of World Court jurisdiction; and

Work to involve the U.N. increasingly on the complex technical and social problems such as pollution policy, which are worldwide in scope and demand a worldwide approach, and help provide the means for these U.N. efforts and for U.N. economic development functions.

International Economic Policy

In a prosperous economy, foreign trade has benefits for virtually everyone. For the consumer, it means lower prices and a wider choice of goods. For the worker and the businessman, it means new jobs and new markets. For nations, it means greater efficiency and growth.

But in a weak economy—with over five million men and women out of work—foreign imports bring hardships to many Americans. The automobile or electrical worker, the electronics technician, the small businessman—for them, and millions of others, foreign competition coinciding with a slack economy has spelled financial distress. Our national commitment to liberal trade policies takes its toll when times are bad, but yields its benefits when the economy is fully employed.

The Democratic Party proposes no retreat from this commitment. Our international economic policy should have these goals: To expand jobs and business opportunities in this country and to establish two-way trade relations with other nations. To do this, we support the following policies.

End the high-unemployment policy of the Nixon Administration. When a job is available for everyone who wants to work, imports will no longer be a threat. Full employment is a realistic goal, it is a goal which has been attained under Democratic Administrations, and it is a goal we intend to achieve again;

Adopt broad programs to ease dislocations and relieve the hardship of workers injured by foreign competition;

Seek higher labor standards in the advanced nations where productivity far outstrips wage rates, thus providing unfair competition to American workers and seek to limit harmful flows of American capital, which exploit both foreign and American workers;

Adhere to liberal trade policies, but we should oppose actions and policies which harm American workers through unfair exploitation of labor abroad and the encouragement of American capital to run after very low-wage opportunities for quick profits that will damage the economy of the United States and further weaken the dollar;

Negotiate orderly and reciprocal reductions of trade barriers to American products. Foreign nations with access to our markets should no longer be permitted to fence us out of theirs;

Support reform of the international monetary system. Increased international reserves, provision for large margins in foreign exchange fluctuations and strengthened institutions for the coordination of national economic policies can free our government and others to achieve full employment;

Support efforts to promote exports of American farm products; and

Develop ground rules for pollution controls with our industrialized trading partners so that no country gains competitive advantage at the expense of the environment.

Developing Nations

Poverty at home or abroad is part of a common problem. Great and growing income gaps among nations are no more tenable than such gaps among groups in our own country. We should remain committed to U.S. support for economic and social development of countries in need. Old ways of providing aid must be revised—to reduce U.S. involvement in administration, to encourage other nations to contribute jointly with its. But funding must be adequate to help poor countries achieve accelerated rates of growth.

Specifically, the next Democratic Administation should support:

Provision of more assistance through international organizations, along with measures to strengthen the development agencies of the U.N.;

A curtailment of military aid;

Improved access to the markets of industrial nations for the products of the developing countries;

A greater role in international monetary affairs for poor countries; in particular distributing the new Special Drawing Rights in support of the poor countries; and

A fair share for poor countries in the resources of the seabeds.

The Methods and Structures of U.S. Foreign and Military Policy

The needed fundamental reordering of U.S. foreign and military policy calls for changes in the structure of decision-making as well as in particular policies. This means:

Greater sharing with Congress of real decisions on issues of war and peace, and providing Congress with the information and resources needed for a more responsible role;

More honest information policies, beginning with a fundamental reform of the document classification system and including regular press conferences by the President, his Cabinet and senior advisors;

Ending the present drastic overbalance in favor of military opinion by redefining the range of agencies and points of view with a proper claim to be heard on foreign and military policies;

Subjecting the military budget to effective civilian control and supervision;

Establishing effective executive control and legislative oversight of the intelligence agencies;

Ending political domination of USIA's reporting and Peace Corps dedication and, in general, making it clear that the White House understands the crucial distinction between dissent and disloyalty; and

Urging the appointment of minority Americans to top positions of ambassadors and diplomats, to let the world know that America is a multi-racial nation and proud of it.

IX. THE PEOPLE AND THE GOVERNMENT

"Our people are dispirited because there seems to be no way by which they can call to office a government which will cut the ties to the past, meeting the challenge of leadership and begin a new era of bold action.

"Bold action by innovative government—responsive to the people's needs and desires—is essential to the achievement of our national hopes."—Leonard Woodcock, President, United Auto Workers, New York Hearing, June 22, 1972.

Representative democracy fails when citizens cannot know:

When public officials ignore or work against the principles of due process;

How their public officials conduct the public's business;

Whether public officials have personal financial stakes in the very matters they are legislating, administering or enforcing; and

What special interest pressures are being exerted on public officials by lobbyists.

Today, it is imperative that the Democratic Party again take the lead in reforming those practices that limit the responsiveness of government and remove it from the control of the people.

Seniority

The seniority system is one of the principal reasons that party platforms—and parties themselves—have lost meaning and importance in our political life. Seniority has weakened Congress as an effective and responsive institution in a changing society. It has crippled effective Congressional leadership and made it impossible to present and enact a coherent legislative program. It has permitted the power of the Democratic majority to be misused and abused. It has stifled initiative and wasted the talents of many members by making length of service the only criterion for selection to the vital positions of Congressional power and leadership.

We, therefore, call on the Democratic Members of the Congress to use the powers inherent in their House and Senate caucuses to implement the policies and programs of the National Democratic Party. It is specifically not intended that Democratic members be directed how to vote on issues on the floor. But, in order that they be responsive to broad party policies and programs, we nonetheless call upon Members of Congress to:

Choose committee chairpeople as provided in existing caucus rules and procedures, but by separate open ballot; chairpeople should be chosen who will carry out party policies and programs which come within the jurisdiction of their committees;

Assure that Democratic programs and policies receive full and fair consideration and are brought to a vote in each house;

Discipline committee members, including chairpeople, who refuse to comply with caucus instructions regarding the reporting of legislation from their committees; and

Withhold any seniority benefits from a Member of Congress who fails to overtly identify with the Democratic organization in his state which is recognized by the National Democratic Party.

Secrecy

Public business should be transacted publicly, except when national security might be jeopardized.

To combat secrecy in government, we call on the Democratic Members of Congress and state legislatures to:

Enact "open meetings" legislation, barring the practice of conducting the public business behind closed doors. This should include so-called mark-up sessions by legislative committees, but should allow for exceptions involving national security and invasions of privacy. To the extent possible, the same principle should apply to the Executive Branch;

Assure that all committee and floor votes are taken in open session, recorded individually for each legislator; record caucus votes, and make all of these available to the public;

Urge reservation of executive privilege for the President alone;

Urge that the judgment in the U.S. Senate in a contested election case be rendered in open Senate session;

Immediately strengthen the Federal Freedom of Information Act. Congress should improve its oversight of executive secrecy by requiring federal agencies to report annually on every refusal to grant information requested under the Act. Citizens should have full recourse to the courts to deal with violation or circumvention of the Act. It should be amended to allow courts to review the reasonableness of a claim of executive privilege; and

Administer the security system so as to limit the number of officials who can make a document secret, and provide for frequent declassification of documents. Congress should be given the means to obtain documents necessary to fulfill its responsibilities.

We also call on the Democratic Members of the House of Representatives to take action through their caucus to end the "closed rule," which is used to prevent amendments and votes on vital tax matters and other important issues, and we call on the Democratic Members of the Senate to liberalize the cloture rule, which is used to prevent votes in that body, so that after full and extensive debate majority rule can prevail.

Administrative Agencies

There is, among more and more citizens, a growing revolt against large, remote and impersonal government agencies that are not responsive to human needs. We pledge to build a representative process into the Executive Branch, so that individuals affected by agency programs can be involved in formulating, implementing and revising them. This requires a basic restructuring of procedures—public hearings before guidelines and regulations are handed down, the processing of citizen complaints, the granting of citizen standing and the recovery of litigation fees for those who win suits against the government.

We recommend these specific changes in the rule making and adjudication process of the federal government:

There should be no non-written communication between an agency and outside parties about pending decisions. All written communications should promptly be made a part of the public record;

All communications between government employees and outside parties about possible future action should be made a part of the public record;

All government employees involved in rule making and adjudication should be subject to conflict of interest laws;

The Justice Department should make available to the public any consent decree 90 days prior to its submission to court, to allow any interested party to comment on it to the court; and

The Justice Department should report to Congress each year, to explain its action on major suits.

In addition, we must more effectively protect consumer rights before the government. The consumer must be made an integral part of any relationship between government and institutions (public or private) at every level of proceedings whether formal or informal.

A Democratic Administration would instruct all federal agencies to identify American Indians, Asian Americans and Spanish-speaking Americans in separate categories in all statistical data that note racial or ethnic heritage. Only in this way can these Americans be assured their rights under federal programs.

Finally, in appropriate geographical areas, agencies of the federal government should be equipped to conduct business in such a fashion that Spanish-speaking citizens should not be hampered by language difficulties.

Conflict of Interest

The public interest must not be sacrificed to personal gain. Therefore, we call for legislation requiring full disclosure of the financial interests of Members of Congress and their staffs and high officials of the Executive Branch and independent agencies. Disclosure should include business directorships held

and associations with individuals or firms lobbying or doing business with the government.

Further, Congress should forbid its members to engage in the practice of law or to retain association with a law firm while in office. Legislators serving on a committee whose jurisdiction includes matters in which they have a financial interest should divest themselves of the interest or resign from the committee.

Campaign Finance

A total overhaul of the present system of financing elections is a national necessity. Candidates should not be dependent on large contributors who seek preferential treatment. We call for Congressional action to provide for public financing of more election costs by 1974. We recommend a statutory ceiling on political gifts at a reasonable limit. Publicly owned communications facilities such as television, radio and the postal service should be made available, but on a limited basis, to candidates for federal office.

Regulation of Lobbyists

We also call upon Congress to enact rigorous lobbying disclosure legislation, to replace the present shockingly ineffective law. There should be full disclosure of all organized lobbying—including names of lobbyists, identity of the source of funds, total receipts and expenditures, the nature of the lobbying operation and specific target issues or bills. Reports should be filed at least quarterly, with criminal penalties for late filing.

Lobbying regulations should cover attempts to influence both Legislative and Executive Branch decisions. The legislation should specifically cover lobbying appeals in subscription publications.

As a safeguard, we urge the availability of subpoena and cease-and-desist powers to enforce these conflict of interest, campaign financing and lobby disclosure laws. We also affirm the citizens' right to seek enforcement through the courts, should public officials fail in enforcement.

Taking Part in the Political Process

The Presidential primary system today is an unacceptable patchwork. The Democratic Party supports federal laws that will embody the following principles:

Protect the opportunity for less-known candidates to build support;

Establish uniform ground rules;

Reduce the cost of primary campaigns;

Promote maximum voter turnout;

Ensure that issues are clarified;

Foster the selection of nominees with broad popular support to assure the continued viability of the two-party system;

Ensure every citizen the ability to take part in the Presidential nomination process; and

Equalize the ability of people from all income levels to participate in the political decision-making processes of the Democratic Party, by providing financial assistance through party funds for delegates, alternates and standing committee members to state and national conventions.

We also call for full and uniform enforcement of the Voting Rights Act of 1965. But further steps are needed to end *all* barriers to participation in the political process:

Universal voter registration by post card;

Bilingual means of registration and voting;

Bilingual voter education programs;

Liberalized absentee voting;

Lower minimum age requirements for service in the Senate and House of Representatives;

Minimum residency requirements of 30 days for all elections, including primaries;

Student voting where they attend schools;

Study and review of the Hatch Act, to see what can be done to encourage good citizenship and reasonable participation by government employees;

Full home rule for the District of Columbia, including an elected mayor–city council government, broad legislative power, control over appointments, automatic federal payment and voting representation in both Houses of Congress;

No discriminatory districting;

We favor a Constitutional change to abolish the Electoral College and to give every voter a direct and equal voice in Presidential elections. The amendment should provide for a run-off election, if no candidate received more than 40 percent of the popular vote;

Early ratification of the Equal Rights Amendment to the Constitution;

Appointment of women to positions of top responsibilities in all branches of the federal government, to achieve an equitable ratio of women and men;

Inclusion of women advisors in equitable ratios in all government studies, commissions and hearings; and

Laws authorizing federal grants on a matching basis for financing state commissions on the status of women.

These changes in themselves will not solve the problems of government for all time. As our society changes, so must the ways we use to make government more responsive to the people. Our challenge, today, as always, is to ensure that politics and institutions belong in spirit and in practice to all the people of our nation. In 1972, Americans are deciding that they want their country back again.

— 1976 —

PREAMBLE

We meet to adopt a Democratic platform, and to nominate Democratic candidates for President and Vice President of the United States, almost 200 years from the day that our revolutionary founders declared this country's independence from the British crown.

The founder of the Democratic Party—Thomas Jefferson of Virginia—set forth the reasons for this separation and expressed the basic tenets of democratic government: That all persons are created equal, that they are endowed by their creator with unalienable rights, that among these are Life, Liberty, and the Pursuit of Happiness—That to secure these rights, Governments are instituted among People, deriving their just powers from the consent of the governed.

These truths may still be self-evident, but they have been tragically abused by our national government during the past eight years.

Two Republican administrations have both misused and mismanaged the powers of national government, obstructing the pursuit of economic and social opportunity, causing needless hardship and despair among millions of our fellow citizens.

Two Republican administrations have betrayed the people's trust and have created suspicion and distrust of government through illegal and unconstitutional actions.

We acknowledge that no political party, nor any President or Vice President, possesses answers to all of the problems that face us as a nation, but neither do we concede that every human problem is beyond our control. We recognize further that the present distrust of government cannot be transformed easily into confidence.

It is within our power to recapture, in the governing of this nation, the basic tenets of fairness, equality, opportunity and rule of law that motivated our revolutionary founders.

We do pledge a government that has as its guiding concern, the needs and aspirations of all the people, rather than the perquisites and special privilege of the few.

We do pledge a government that listens, that is truthful, and that is not afraid to admit its mistakes.

We do pledge a government that will be committed to a fairer distribution of wealth, income and power.

We do pledge a government in which the new Democratic President will work closely with the leaders of the Congress on a regular, systematic basis so that the people can see the results of unity.

We do pledge a government in which the Democratic members in both houses of Congress will seek a unity of purpose on the principles of the Party.

Now, as we enter our 200th year as a nation, we as a party, with a sense of our obligations, pledge a reaffirmation of this nation's founding principles.

In this platform of the Democratic Party, we present a clear alternative to the failures of preceding administrations and a projection of the common future to which we aspire: a world at peace; a just society of equals; a society without violence; a society in consonance with its natural environment, affording freedom to the individual and the opportunity to develop to the fullest human potential.

I. FULL EMPLOYMENT, PRICE STABILITY AND BALANCED GROWTH

The Democratic Party's concern for human dignity and freedom has been directed at increasing the economic opportunities for all our citizens and reducing the economic deprivation and inequities that have stained the record of American democracy.

Today, millions of people are unemployed. Unemployment represents mental anxiety, fear of harassment over unpaid bills, idle hours, loss of self-esteem, strained family relationships, deprivation of children and youth, alcoholism, drug abuse and crime. A job is a key measure of a person's place in society—whether as a full-fledged participant or on the outside. jobs are the solution to poverty, hunger and other basic needs of workers and their families. Jobs enable a person to translate legal rights of equality into reality.

Our industrial capacity is also wastefully underutilized. There are houses to build, urban centers to rebuild, roads and railroads to construct and repair, rivers to clean, and new sources of energy to develop. Something is wrong when there is work to be done, and the people who are willing to do it are without jobs. What we have lacked is leadership.

Republican Mismanagement

During the past 25 years, the American economy has suffered five major recessions, all under Republican administrations. During the past eight years, we have had two costly recessions with continuing unprecedented peacetime inflation. "Stagflation" has become a new word in our language just as it has become a product of Republican economic policy. Never before have we had soaring inflation in the midst of a major recession.

Stagnation, waste and human suffering are the legacy left to the American people by Republican economic policies. During the past five years, U.S. economic growth has averaged only $1\frac{1}{2}$ per cent per year compared with an historical average of about 4 per cent. Because of this shortfall, the nation has lost some $500 billion in the production of goods and services, and, if Republican rule continues, we can expect to lose another $600–$800 billion by 1980.

Ten million people are unemployed right now, and twenty to thirty million were jobless at some time in each of the last two years. For major groups in the labor force—minorities, women, youth, older workers, farm, factory and construction workers—unemployment has been, and remains, at depression levels.

The rising cost of food, clothing, housing, energy and health care has eroded the income of the average American family, and has pushed persons on fixed incomes to the brink of economic disaster. Since 1970, the annual rate of inflation has averaged more than 6 per cent and is projected by the Ford administration to continue at an unprecedented peacetime rate of 6 to 7 per cent until 1978.

The depressed production and high unemployment rates of the Nixon–Ford administrations have produced federal deficits totaling $242 billion. Those who should be working and paying taxes are collecting unemployment compensation or other welfare payments in order to survive. For every one per cent increase in the unemployment rate—for every one million Americans out of work—we all pay $3 billion more in unemployment compensation and $2 billion in welfare and related costs, and lose $14 billion in taxes. In fiscal 1976, $76 billion was lost to the federal government through increased recession-related expenditures and lost revenues. In addition, state and local governments lost $27 billion in revenues. A return to full employment will eliminate such deficits. With prudent management of existing programs, full employment revenues will permit the financing of national Democratic initiatives.

For millions of Americans, the Republican Party has substituted welfare for work. Huge sums will be spent on food stamps and medical care for families of the unemployed. Social insurance costs are greatly increased. This year alone the federal government will spend nearly $20 billion on unemployment compensation. In contrast, spending on job development is 2\frac{1}{2}$ billion. The goal of the new Democratic administration will be to turn unemployment checks into pay checks.

What Democrats Can Achieve

In contrast to the record of Republican mismanagement, the most recent eight years of Democratic leadership, under John F. Kennedy and Lyndon B. Johnson, produced economic growth that was virtually uninterrupted. The unemployment rate dropped from 6.7 per cent in 1961 to 3.6 per cent in 1968, and most segments of the population benefited. Inflation increased at an average annual rate of only 2 per cent, and the purchasing power of the average family steadily increased. In 1960, about 40 million people were living in poverty. Over the next eight years, 14 $\frac{1}{2}$ million people moved out of poverty because of training opportunities, increased jobs and higher incomes. Since 1968, the number of persons living in poverty has remained virtually unchanged.

We have met the goals of full employment with stable prices in the past and can do it again. The Democratic Party is committed to the right of all adult Americans willing, able and seeking work to have opportunities for useful jobs at living wages. To make that commitment meaningful, we pledge ourselves to the support of legislation that will make every responsible effort to reduce adult unemployment to 3 per cent within 4 years.

Modernizing Economic Policy

To meet our goals we must set annual targets for employment, production and price stability; the Federal Reserve must be made a full partner in national economic decisions and become responsive to the economic goals of Congress and the President; credit must be generally available at reasonable interest rates; tax, spending and credit policies must be carefully coordinated with our economic goals, and coordinated within the framework of national economic planning.

Of special importance is the need for national economic planning capability. This planning capability should provide roles for Congress and the Chief Executive as equal partners in the process and provide for full participation by the private sector, and state and local government. Government must plan ahead just like any business, and this type of planning can be implemented without the creation of a new bureaucracy but rather through the well-defined use of existing bodies and techniques. If we do not plan, but continue to react to crisis after crisis, our economic performance will be further eroded.

Full Employment Policies

Institutional reforms and the use of conventional tax, spending and credit policies must be accompanied by a broad range of carefully targeted employment programs that will reduce unemployment in the private sector, and in regions, states and groups that have special employment problems.

The lack of formal coordination among federal, state and local governments is a major obstacle to full employment. The absence of economic policy coordination is particularly visible during times of high unemployment. Recessions reduce tax revenues, and increase unemployment-related expenditures for state and local governments. To maintain balanced budgets or reduce budget deficits these governments are forced to increase taxes and cut services—actions that directly undermine federal efforts to stimulate the economy.

Consistent and coherent economic policy requires federal anti-recession grant programs to state and local government, accompanied by public employment, public works projects and direct stimulus to the private sector. In each case, the programs should be phased in automatically when unemployment rises and phased out as it declines.

Even during periods of normal economic growth there are communities and regions of the country—particularly central cities and rural areas—that do not fully participate in national economic prosperity. The Democratic Party has supported national economic policies which have consciously sought to aid regions in the nation which have been afflicted with poverty, or newer regions which have needed resources for development. These policies were soundly conceived and have been successful. Today, we have different areas and regions in economic decline and once again face a problem of balanced economic growth. To restore balance, national economic policy should be designed to target federal resources in areas of greatest need. To make low-interest loans to businesses and state and local governments for the purpose of encouraging private sector investment in chronically depressed areas, we endorse consideration of programs such as a domestic development bank or federally insured taxable state and local bonds with adequate funding, proper management and public disclosure.

Special problems faced by young people, especially minorities, entering the labor force persist regardless of the state of the economy. To meet the needs of youth, we should consolidate existing youth employment programs; improve training, apprenticeship, internship and job-counseling programs at the high school and college levels; and permit youth participation in public employment projects.

There are people who will be especially difficult to employ. Special means for training and locating jobs for these people in the private sector, and, to the extent required, in public employment, should be established. Every effort should be made to create jobs in the private sector. Clearly, useful public jobs are far superior to welfare and unemployment payments. The federal government has the responsibility to ensure that all Americans able, willing and seeking work are provided opportunities for useful jobs.

Equal Employment Opportunity

We must be absolutely certain that no person is excluded from the fullest opportunity for economic and social participation in our society on the basis of sex, age, color, religion or national origin. Minority unemployment has historically been at least double the aggregate unemployment rate, with incomes at two-thirds the national average. Special emphasis must be placed on closing this gap.

Accordingly, we reaffirm this Party's commitment to full and vigorous enforcement of all equal opportunities laws and affirmative action. The principal agencies charged with anti-discrimination enforcement in jobs—the Equal Employment Opportunity Commission, the Department of Labor, and the Justice Department—are locked into such overlapping and uncoordinated strategies that a greatly improved government-wide system for the delivery of equal job and promotion opportunities must be developed and adequate funding committed to that end. New remedies to provide equal opportunities need exploration.

Anti-Inflation Policies

The economic and social costs of inflation have been enormous. Inflation is a tax that erodes the income of our workers, distorts business investment decisions, and redistributes income in favor of the rich. Americans on fixed incomes, such as the elderly, are often pushed into poverty by this cruel tax.

The Ford administration and its economic advisors have been consistently wrong about the sources and cures of the inflation that has plagued our nation and our people. Fighting inflation by curtailing production and increasing unemployment has done nothing to restrain it. With the current high level of unemployment and low level of capacity utilization, we can increase production and employment without rekindling inflation.

A comprehensive anti-inflation policy must be established to assure relative price stability. Such a program should emphasize increased production and productivity and should take other measures to enhance the stability and flexibility of our economy.

The see-saw progress of our economy over the past eight years has disrupted economic growth. Much of the instability has been created by stop-and-go monetary policies. High interest rates and the recurring underutilization of our manufacturing plants and equipment have retarded new investment. The high cost of credit has stifled small business and virtually halted the housing industry. Unemployment in the construction industry has been raised to depression levels and home ownership has been priced beyond the reach of the majority of our people.

Stable economic growth with moderate interest rates will not only place downward pressure on prices through greater efficiency and productivity, but will reduce the prospects for future shortages of supply by increasing the production of essential goods and services and by providing a more predictable environment for business investment.

The government must also work to improve the ability of our economy to respond to change. Competition in the private sector, a re-examination, reform and consolidation of the existing regulatory structure, and promotion of a freer but fair system of international trade will aid in achieving that goal.

At times, direct government involvement in wage and price decisions may be required to ensure price stability. But we do not believe that such involvement requires a comprehensive system of mandatory controls at this time. It will require that business and labor must meet fair standards of wage and price change. A strong domestic council on price and wage stability should be established with particular attention to restraining price increases in those sectors of our economy where prices are "administered" and where price competition does not exist.

The federal government should hold public hearings, investigate and publish facts on price, profit, wage and interest rate increases that seriously threaten national price stability. Such investigations and proper planning can focus public opinion and awareness on the direction of price, profit, wage and interest rate decisions.

Finally, tax policy should be used if necessary to maintain the real income of workers as was done with the 1975 tax cut.

Economic Justice

The Democratic Party has a long history of opposition to the undue concentration of wealth and economic power. It is estimated that about three-quarters of the country's total wealth is owned by one-fifth of the people. The rest of our population struggles to make ends meet in the face of rising prices and taxes.

Anti-trust Enforcement

The next Democratic administration will commit itself to move vigorously against anti-competitive concentration of power within the business sector. This can be accomplished in part by strengthening the anti-trust laws and insuring adequate commitment and resources for the enforcement of these laws. But we must go beyond this negative remedy to a positive policy for encouraging the development of small business, including the family farm.

Small Businesses

A healthy and growing small business community is a prerequisite for increasing competition and a thriving national economy. While most people would accept this view, the federal government has in the past impeded the growth of small business.

To alleviate the unfavorable conditions for small business, we must make every effort to assure the availability of loans to small business, including direct government loans at reasonable interest rates particularly to those in greatest need, such as minority-owned businesses. For example, efforts should be made to strengthen minority business programs, and increase minority opportunities for business ownership. We support similar programs and opportunities for women. Federal contract and procurement opportunities in such areas as housing, transportation and energy should support efforts to increase the volume of minority and small business involvement. Regulatory agencies and the regulated small business must work together to see that federal regulations are met, without applying a strangle-hold on the small firm or farm and with less paperwork and red tape.

Tax Reform

Economic justice will also require a firm commitment to tax reform at all levels. In recent years there has been a shift in the tax burden from the rich to the working people of this country. The Internal Revenue Code offers massive tax welfare to the wealthiest income groups in the population and only higher taxes for the average citizen. In 1973, there were 622 people with adjusted income of $100,000 or more who still managed to pay no tax. Most families pay between 20 and 25 per cent of their income in taxes.

We have had endless talk about the need for tax reform and fairness in our federal tax system. It is now time for action.

We pledge the Democratic Party to a complete overhaul of the present tax system, which will review all special tax provisions to ensure that they are justified and distributed equitably among our citizens. A responsible Democratic tax reform program could save over $5 billion in the first year with larger savings in the future.

We will strengthen the internal revenue tax code so that high-income citizens pay a reasonable tax on all economic income.

We will reduce the use of unjustified tax shelters in such areas as oil and gas, tax-loss farming, real estate, and movies.

We will eliminate unnecessary and ineffective tax provisions to business and substitute effective incentives to encourage small business and capital formation in all businesses. Our commitment to full employment and sustained purchasing power will also provide a strong incentive for capital formation.

We will end abuses in the tax treatment of income from foreign sources; such as special tax treatment and incentives for multinational corporations that drain jobs and capital from the American economy.

We will overhaul federal estate and gift taxes to provide an effective and equitable structure to promote tax justice and alleviate some of the legitimate problems faced by farmers, small business men and women and others who would otherwise be forced to liquidate assets in order to pay the tax.

We will seek and eliminate provisions that encourage uneconomic corporate mergers and acquisitions.

We will eliminate tax inequities that adversely affect individuals on the basis of sex or marital status.

We will curb expense account deductions.

And we will protect the rights of all taxpayers against oppressive procedures, harassment and invasions of privacy by the Internal Revenue Service.

At present, many federal government tax and expenditure programs have a profound but unintended and undesirable impact on jobs and on where people and business locate. Tax policies and other indirect subsidies have promoted deterioration of cities and regions. These policies should be reversed.

There are other areas of taxation where change is also needed. The Ford administration's unwise and unfair proposal to raise the regressive Social Security tax gives new urgency to the Democratic Party's goal of redistributing the burden of the Social Security tax by raising the wage base for earnings subject to the tax with effective exemptions and deductions to ease the impact on low-income workers and two-earner families. Further revision in the Social Security program will be required so that women are treated as individuals.

The Democratic Party should make a reappraisal of the appropriate sources of federal revenues. The historical distribution of the tax burden between corporations and individuals, and among the various types of federal taxes, has changed dramatically in recent years. For example, the corporate tax share of federal revenue has declined from 30 per cent in 1954 to 14 per cent in 1975.

Labor Standards and Rights

The purpose of fair labor standards legislation has been the maintenance of the minimum standards necessary for the health, efficiency and general well-being of workers. Recent inflation has eroded the real value of the current minimum wage. This rapid devaluation of basic income for working people makes a periodic review of the level of the minimum wage essential. Such a review should insure that the minimum wage rate at least keep pace with the increase in the cost of living.

Raising the pay standard for overtime work, additional hiring of part-time persons and flexible work schedules will increase the independence of workers and create additional job opportunities, especially for women. We also support the principle of equal pay for comparable work.

We are committed to full implementation and enforcement of the Equal Credit Opportunity Act.

Over a generation ago this nation established a labor policy whose purpose is to encourage the practice and procedure of collective bargaining and the right of workers to organize to obtain this goal. The Democratic Party is committed to extending the benefit of the policy to all workers and to removing the barriers to its administration. We support the right of public employees and agricultural workers to organize and bargain collectively. We urge the adoption of appropriate federal legislation to ensure this goal.

We will seek to amend the Fair Labor Standards Act to speed up redress of grievances of workers asserting their legal rights.

We will seek to enforce and, where necessary, to amend the National Labor Relations Act to eliminate delays and inequities and to provide for more effective remedies and administration.

We will support the full right of construction workers to picket a job site peacefully.

We will seek repeal of Section 14(b) of the Taft–Hartley Act which allows states to legislate the anti-union open shop.

We will maintain strong support for the process of voluntary arbitration, and we will enact minimum federal standards for workers compensation laws and for eligibility, benefit amounts, benefit duration and other essential features of the unemployment insurance program. Unemployment insurance should cover all wage and salary workers.

The Occupational Safety and Health Act of 1970 should cover all employees and be enforced as intended when the law was enacted. Early and periodic review of its provisions should be made to insure that they are reasonable and workable.

The Democratic Party will also seek to enact a comprehensive mine safety law, utilizing the most effective and independent enforcement by the federal government and support special legislation providing adequate compensation to coal miners and their dependents who have suffered disablement or death as a result of the black lung disease.

We believe these policies will put America back to work, bring balanced growth to our economy and give all Americans an opportunity to share in the expanding prosperity that will come from a new Democratic administration.

II. GOVERNMENT REFORM AND BUSINESS ACCOUNTABILITY

The current Republican administration did not invent inept government, but it has saddled the country with ineffective government; captive government, subservient to the special pleading of private economic interests; insensitive government, trampling over the rights of average citizens; and remote government, secretive and unresponsive.

Democrats believe that the cure for these ills is not the abandonment of governmental responsibility for addressing national problems, but the restoration of legitimate popular control over the organs and activities of government.

There must be an ever-increasing accountability of government to the people. The Democratic Party is pledged to the fulfillment of four fundamental citizen rights of governance: the right to competent government; the right to responsive government; the right to integrity in government; the right to fair dealing by government.

The Right to Competent Government

The Democratic Party is committed to the adoption of reforms such as zero-based budgeting, mandatory reorganization timetables, and sunset laws which do not jeopardize the implementation of basic human and political rights. These reforms are designed to terminate or merge existing agencies and programs, or to renew them, only after assuring elimination of duplication, overlap, and conflicting programs and authorities, and the matching of funding levels to public needs. In addition, we seek flexibility to reflect changing public needs, the use of alternatives to regulation and the elimination of special interest favoritism and bias.

To assure that government remains responsive to the people's elected representatives, the Democratic Party supports stepped-up congressional agency oversight and program evaluation, including full implementation of the congressional budget process; an expanded, more forceful role for the General Accounting Office in performing legislative audits for Congress; and restraint by the President in exercising executive privilege designed to withhold necessary information from Congress.

The Right to Responsive Government

To begin to restore the shaken faith of Americans that the government in Washington is *their* government—responsive to their needs and desires, not the special interests of wealth, entrenched political influence, or bureaucratic self-interest—government decision-making must be opened up to citizen advocacy and participation.

Governmental decision-making behind closed doors is the natural enemy of the people. The Democratic Party is committed to openness throughout government: at regulatory commissions, advisory committee meetings and at hearings. Public calendars of scheduled meetings between regulators and the regulated, and freedom of information policies, should be designed to facilitate rather than frustrate citizen access to documents and information.

All persons and citizen groups must be given standing to challenge illegal or unconstitutional government action in court and to compel appropriate action. Where a court or an agency finds evidence of government malfeasance or neglect those who brought forward such evidence should be compensated for their reasonable expenses in doing so.

Democrats have long sought—against fierce Republican and big business opposition—the creation and maintenance of an independent consumer agency with the staff and power to intervene in regulatory matters on behalf of the consuming and using public. Many states have already demonstrated that such independent public or consumer advocates can win important victories for the public interest in proceedings before state regulatory agencies and courts.

This nation's Civil Service numbers countless strong and effective public servants. It was the resistance of earnest and steadfast federal workers that stemmed the Nixon–Ford efforts to undermine the integrity of the Civil Service. The reorganization of government which we envision will protect the job rights of civil servants and permit them to more effectively serve the public.

The Democratic Party is committed to the review and overhaul of Civil Service laws to assure: insulation from political cronyism, accountability for nonfeasance as well as malfeasance, protection for the public servant who speaks out to identify corruption or failure, performance standards and incentives to reward efficiency and innovation and to assure nondiscrimination and affirmative action in the recruitment, hiring and promotion of civil service employees.

We support the revision of the Hatch Act so as to extend to federal workers the same political rights enjoyed by other Americans as a birthright, while still protecting the Civil Service from political abuse.

The Right to Integrity in Government

The Democratic Party is pledged to the concept of full public disclosure by major public officials and urges appropriate legislation to effectuate this policy.

We support divestiture of all financial holdings which directly conflict with official responsibilities and the development of uniform standards, review procedures and sanctions to identify and eliminate potential conflicts of interest.

Tough, competent regulatory commissioners with proven commitment to the public interest are urgently needed.

We will seek restrictions on "revolving door" careerism—the shuttling back and forth of officials between jobs in regulatory or procurement agencies and in regulated industries and government contractors.

All diplomats, federal judges and other major officials should be selected on a basis of qualifications. At all levels of government services, we will recruit, appoint and promote women and minorities.

We support legislation to ensure that the activities of lobbyists be more thoroughly revealed both within the Congress and the executive agencies.

The Democratic Party has led the fight to take the

presidency off the auction block by championing the public financing of presidential elections. The public has responded with enthusiastic use of the $1 income tax check-off. Similar steps must now be taken for congressional candidates. We call for legislative action to provide for partial public financing on a matching basis of the congressional elections, and the exploration of further reforms to insure the integrity of the electoral process.

The Right to Fair Dealing by Government

A citizen has the right to expect fair treatment from government. Democrats are determined to find a means to make that right a reality.

An Office of Citizen Advocacy should be established as part of the executive branch, independent of any agency, with full access to agency records and with both the power and the responsibility to investigate complaints.

Freedom of information requirements must be interpreted in keeping with the right of the individual to be free from anonymous accusation or slander. Each citizen has the right to know and to review any information directly concerning him or her held by the government for any purpose whatsoever under the Freedom of Information Act and the Privacy Act of 1974, other than those exceptions set out in the Freedom of Information Act. Such information should be forthcoming promptly, without harassment and at a minimal cost to the citizen.

Appropriate remedies must be found for citizens who suffer hardship as the result of abuse of investigative or prosecutorial powers.

Business Accountability

The Democratic Party believes that competition is preferable to regulation and that government has a responsibility to seek the removal of unreasonable restraints and barriers to competition, to restore and, where necessary, to stimulate the operation of market forces. Unnecessary regulation should be eliminated or revised, and the burden of excessive paperwork and red tape imposed on citizens and businesses should be removed.

The Democratic Party encourages innovation and efficiency in the private sector.

The Democratic Party also believes that strengthening consumer sovereignty—the ability of consumers to exercise free choice, to demand satisfaction, and to obtain direct redress of grievances—is similarly prefer-

able to the present indirect government protection of consumers. However, government must not shirk its responsibility to impose and rigorously enforce regulations where necessary to ensure health, safety and fairness. We reiterate our support for unflinching antitrust enforcement, and for the selection of an Attorney General free of political obligation and committed to rigorous antitrust prosecution.

We shall encourage consumer groups to establish and operate consumer cooperatives that will enable consumers to provide themselves marketplace alternatives and to provide a competitive spur to profit-oriented enterprises.

We support responsible cost savings in the delivery of professional services including the use of low-cost paraprofessionals, efficient group practice and federal standards for state no-fault insurance programs.

We reiterate our support for full funding of neighborhood legal services for the poor.

The Democratic Party is also committed to strengthening the knowledge and bargaining power of consumers through government-supported systems for developing objective product performance standards; advertising and labeling requirements for the disclosure of essential consumer information; and efficient and low-cost redress of consumer complaints including strengthened small claims courts, informal dispute settlement mechanisms, and consumer class actions.

The Democratic Party is committed to making the U.S. Postal Service function properly as an essential public service.

We reaffirm the historic Democratic commitment to assure the wholesomeness of consumer products such as food, chemicals, drugs and cosmetics, and the safety of automobiles, toys and appliances. Regulations demanding safe performance can be developed in a way that minimizes their own costs and actually stimulates product innovation beneficial to consumers.

III. GOVERNMENT AND HUMAN NEEDS

The American people are demanding that their national government act more efficiently and effectively in those areas of urgent human needs such as welfare reform, health care and education.

However, beyond these strong national initiatives, state and local governments must be given an increased, permanent role in administering social programs. The federal government's role should be the constructive one of establishing standards and goals with increased state and local participation. There is a need for a new blueprint for the public sector, one which identifies and responds to national problems, and recognizes the proper point of administration for both new and existing programs. In shifting administrative responsibility, such programs must meet minimum federal standards.

Government must concentrate, not scatter, its resources. It should not divide our people by inadequate and demanding programs. The initiatives we propose do not require larger bureaucracy. They do require committed government.

The Democratic Party realizes that accomplishing our goals in the areas of human needs will require time and resources. Additional resources will become available as we implement our full-employment policies. Federal revenues also grow over time. After full employment has been achieved, $20 billion of increased revenue will be generated by a fully operating economy each year. The program, detailed in the areas of human needs, cannot be accomplished immediately, but an orderly beginning can be made and the effort expanded as additional resources become available.

Health Care

In 1975, national health expenditures averaged $547 per person—an almost 40 per cent increase in four years. Inflation and recession have combined to erode the effectiveness of the Medicare and Medicaid programs.

An increasingly high proportion of health costs have been shifted back to the elderly. An increasing Republican emphasis on restricting eligibility and services is emasculating basic medical care for older citizens who cannot meet the rising costs of good health.

We need a comprehensive national health insurance system with universal and mandatory coverage. Such a national health insurance system should be financed by a combination of employer–employee shared payroll taxes and general tax revenues. Consideration should be given to developing a means of support for national health insurance that taxes all forms of economic income. We must achieve all that is practical while we strive for what is ideal, taking intelligent steps to make adequate health services a right for all our people. As resources permit, this system should not discriminate against the mentally ill.

Maximum personal interrelationships between patients and their physicians should be preserved. We should experiment with new forms of medical care delivery to mold a national health policy that will meet our needs in a fiscally responsible manner.

We must shift our emphasis in both private and public health care away from hospitalization and acute-care services to preventive medicine and the early detection of the major cripplers and killers of the American people. We further support increased federal aid to the government laboratories as well as private institutions to seek the cure to heart disease, cancer, sickle cell anemia, paralysis from spinal cord injury, drug addiction and other such afflictions.

National health insurance must also bring about a more responsive consumer-oriented system of health care delivery. Incentives must be used to increase the number of primary health care providers, and shift emphasis away from limited application, technology-intensive programs. By reducing the barriers to primary preventive care, we can lower the need for costly hospitalization. Communities must be encouraged to avoid duplication of expensive technologies and meet the genuine needs of their populations. The development of community health centers must be resumed. We must develop new health careers, and promote a better distribution of health care professionals, including the more efficient use of paramedics. All levels of government should concern themselves with increasing the number of doctors and paramedical personnel in the field of primary health care.

A further need is the comprehensive treatment of mental illness, including the development of Community Mental Health Centers that provide comprehensive social services not only to alleviate, but to prevent mental stresses resulting from social isolation and economic dislocation. Of particular importance is improved access to the health care system by underserved population groups.

We must have national health insurance with strong built-in cost and quality controls. Rates for institutional care and physicians' services should be set in advance, prospectively. Alternative approaches to health care delivery, based on prepayment financing, should be encouraged and developed.

Americans are currently spending $133 billion for health care—8.3% of our Gross National Product. A return to full employment and the maintenance thereafter of stable economic growth will permit the orderly and progressive development of a comprehensive national health insurance program which is federally financed. Savings will result from the removal of inefficiency and waste in the current multiple public and private insurance programs and the structural integration of the delivery system to eliminate duplication and waste. The cost of such a program need not exceed the share of the GNP this nation currently expends on health care; but the resulting improvement of health service would represent a major improvement in the quality of life enjoyed by Americans at all economic levels.

Welfare Reform

Fundamental welfare reform is necessary. The problems with our current chaotic and inequitable system of public assistance are notorious. Existing welfare programs encourage family instability. They have few meaningful work incentives. They do little or nothing for the working poor on substandard incomes. The patchwork of federal, state and local programs encourages unfair variations in benefit levels among the states, and benefits in many states are well below the standards for even lowest-income budgets.

Of the current programs, only Food Stamps give universal coverage to all Americans in financial need. Cash assistance, housing aid and health care subsidies divide recipients into arbitrary categories. People with real needs who do not fit existing categories are ignored altogether.

The current complexity of the welfare structure requires armies of bureaucrats at all levels of government. Food Stamps, Aid to Families with Dependent Children, and Medicaid are burdened by unbelievably complex regulations, statutes and court orders. Both the recipients of these benefits, and the citizen who pays for them, suffer as a result. The fact that our current system is administered and funded at different levels of government makes it difficult to take initiatives to improve the status of the poor.

We should move toward replacement of our existing inadequate and wasteful system with a simplified system of income maintenance, substantially financed by the federal government, which includes a requirement that those able to work be provided with appropriate available jobs or job training opportunities. Those persons who are physically able to work (other than mothers with dependent children) should be required to accept appropriate available jobs or job training. This maintenance system should embody certain basic principles. First and most important, it should provide an income floor both for the working poor and the poor not in the labor market. It must treat stable and broken families equally. It must incorporate a simple schedule of work incentives that guarantees equitable levels of assistance to the working poor. This reform may require an initial additional investment, but it offers the prospect of stabilization of welfare costs over the long run, and the assurance that the objectives of this expenditure will be accomplished.

As an interim step, and as a means of providing immediate federal fiscal relief to state and local governments, local governments should no longer be required to bear the burden of welfare costs. Further, there should be a phased reduction in the states' share of welfare costs.

Civil and Political Rights

To achieve a just and healthy society and enhance respect and trust in our institutions, we must insure that all citizens are treated equally before the law and given the opportunity, regardless of race, color, sex, religion, age, language or national origin, to participate fully in the economic, social and political processes and to vindicate their legal and constitutional rights.

In reaffirmation of this principle, an historic commitment of the Democratic Party, we pledge vigorous federal programs and policies of compensatory opportunity to remedy for many Americans the generations of injustice and deprivation; and full funding of programs to secure the implementation and enforcement of civil rights.

We seek ratification of the Equal Rights Amendment, to insure that sex discrimination in all its forms will be ended, implementation of Title IX, and elimination of discrimination against women in all federal programs.

We support the right of all Americans to vote for President no matter where they live; vigorous enforcement of voting rights legislation to assure the constitutional rights of minority and language-minority citizens; the passage of legislation providing for registration by mail in federal elections to erase existing barriers to voter participation; and full home rule for the District of Columbia, including authority over its budget and local revenues, elimination of federal restrictions in matters which are purely local and voting representation in the Congress, and the declaration of the birthday of the great civil rights leader, Martin Luther King, Jr., as a national holiday.

We pledge effective and vigorous action to protect citizens' privacy from bureaucratic technological intrusions, such as wiretapping and bugging without judicial scrutiny and supervision; and a full and complete pardon for those who are in legal or financial jeopardy because of their peaceful opposition to the Vietnam War, with deserters to be considered on a case-by-case basis.

We fully recognize the religious and ethical nature of the concerns which many Americans have on the subject of abortion. We feel, however, that it is undesirable to attempt to amend the U.S. Constitution to overturn the Supreme Court decision in this area.

The Democratic Party reaffirms and strengthens its legal and moral trust responsibilities to the American Indian. We believe it is honorable to obey and implement our treaty obligations to the first Americans. In discharging our duty, we shall exert all and necessary assistance to afford the American Indians the protection of their land, their water and their civil rights.

Federal laws relating to American Indians and the functions and purposes of the Bureau of Indian Affairs should be reexamined.

We support a provision in the immigration laws to facilitate acquisition of citizenship by Resident Aliens.

We are committed to Puerto Rico's right to enjoy full self-determination and a relationship that can evolve in ways that will most benefit U.S. citizens in Puerto Rico. The Democratic Party respects and supports the present desire of the people of Puerto Rico to freely associate in permanent union with the United States, as an autonomous commonwealth or as a State.

Education

The goal of our educational policy is to provide our citizens with the knowledge and skills they need to live successfully. In pursuing this goal, we will seek adequate funding, implementation and enforcement of requirements in the education programs already approved by Congress.

We should strengthen federal support of existing programs that stress improvement of reading and math skills. Title I of the Elementary and Secondary Education Act must reach those it is intended to benefit to effectively increase these primary skills. "Breakthroughs" in compensatory education require a concentration of resources on each individual child and a mix of home and school activities that is not possible with the underfunded Republican programs. Compensatory education is realistic only when there is a stable sequence of funding that allows proper planning and continuity of programs, an impossibility under Republican veto and impoundment politics.

We should also work to expand federal support in areas of educational need that have not yet been addressed sufficiently by the public schools—education of the handicapped, bilingual education and vocational education, and early childhood education. We propose federally financed, family-centered developmental and educational child care programs—operated by the public schools or other local organizations, including both private and community—and that they be available to all who need and desire them. We support efforts to provide for the basic nutritional needs of students.

We recognize the right of all citizens to education, pursuant to Title VI of the Civil Rights Act of 1968, and the need in affected communities for bilingual and bicultural educational programs. We call for compliance with civil rights requirements in hiring and promotion in school systems.

For the disadvantaged child, equal opportunity requires concentrated spending. And for all children, we must guarantee that jurisdictions of differing financial capacity can spend equal amounts on education. These goals do not conflict but complement each other.

The principle that a child's education should depend on the property wealth of his or her school jurisdiction has been discredited in the last few years. With increased federal funds, it is possible to enhance educational opportunity by eliminating spending disparities within state borders. State-based equalizations, even state takeover of education costs, to relieve the overburdened property taxpayer and to avoid the inequities in the existing finance system, should be encouraged.

The essential purpose of school desegregation is to give all children the same educational opportunities. We will continue to support that goal. The Supreme Court decision of 1954 and the aftermath were based on the recognition that separate educational facilities are inherently unequal. It is clearly our responsibility as a party and as citizens to support the principles of our Constitution.

The Democratic Party pledges its concerted help through special consultation, matching funds, incentive grants and other mechanisms to communities which seek education, integrated both in terms of race and economic class, through equitable, reasonable and constitutional arrangements. Mandatory transportation of students beyond their neighborhoods for the purpose of desegregation remains a judicial tool of the last resort for the purpose of achieving school desegregation. The Democratic Party will be an active ally of those communities which seek to enhance the quality as well as the integration of educational opportunities. We encourage a variety of other measures, including the redrawing of attendance lines, pairing of schools, use of the "magnet school" concept, strong fair housing enforcement, and other techniques for the achievement of racial and economic integration.

The Party reaffirms its support of public school education. The Party also renews its commitment to the support of a constitutionally acceptable method of providing tax aid for the education of all pupils in nonsegregated schools in order to insure parental freedom in choosing the best education for their children. Specifically, the Party will continue to advocate constitutionally permissible federal education legislation which provides for the equitable participation in federal programs of all low- and moderate-income pupils attending all the nation's schools.

The Party commits itself to support of adult education and training which will provide skills upgrading.

In higher education, our Party is strongly committed to extending postsecondary opportunities for students from low- and middle-income families, including older students and students who can attend only part-time. The Basic Educational Opportunity Grants should be funded at the full payment schedule, and campus-based programs of aid must be supported to provide a reasonable choice of institutions as well as access. With a coordinated and reliable system of grants, loans and work study, we can relieve the crisis in costs that could shut all but the affluent out of our colleges and universities.

The federal government and the states must develop strategies to support institutions of higher education from both public and private sources. The federal government should directly provide the cost of education payments to all higher education institutions, including predominantly black colleges, to help cover per-student costs, which far exceed those covered by tuition and fees.

Finally, government must systematically support basic and applied research in the liberal arts, the sciences, education and the professions—without political interference or bureaucratic restraint. The federal investment in graduate education should be sustained and selectively increased to meet the need for highly trained individuals. Trainee-ships and fellowships should be provided to attract the most talented students, especially among minority groups and women.

Libraries should receive continuous guaranteed support and the presently impounded funds for nationwide library planning and development should be released immediately.

Social Services

The Nixon–Ford administration would limit eligibility for federally subsidized social services to the very poor. Social services can make significant changes in the lives of the non-poor, as well. The problems of alcoholism, drug abuse, mental retardation, child abuse or neglect, and mental illness arise at every income level, and quality daycare has become increasingly urgent for low- and middle-income families. Federal grants to the states should support a broad community-based program of social services to low- and middle-income families, to assure that these programs reach their intended populations.

The states are now being required to take over an increasing share of existing social service programs. In 1972, the ceiling for federal social service grants was frozen at $2.5 billion, and subsequent inflation of 28 per cent has reduced the effective federal aid to existing programs. While there must certainly be a ceiling on such grants, it should be raised to compensate for inflation and to encourage states and localities to expand social services to low- and moderate-income families.

Disabled Citizens

We support greater recognition of the problems of the disabled and legislation assuring that all people with disabilities have reasonable access to all public accommodations and facilities. The Democratic Party supports affirmative action goals for employment of the disabled.

Older Citizens

The Democratic Party has always emphasized that adequate income and health care for senior citizens are basic federal government responsibilities. The recent failure of government to reduce unemployment and alleviate the impact of the rising costs of food, housing and energy have placed a heavy burden on those who live on fixed and limited incomes, especially the elderly. Our other platform proposals in these areas are designed to help achieve an adequate income level for the elderly.

We will not permit an erosion of Social Security benefits, and while our ultimate goal is a health security system ensuring comprehensive and quality care for all Americans, health costs paid by senior citizens under the present system must be reduced.

We believe that Medicare should be made available to Americans abroad who are eligible for Social Security.

Democrats strongly support employment programs and the liberalization of the allowable earnings limitation under Social Security for older Americans who wish to continue working and living as productive citizens. We will put an end to delay in implementation of nutrition programs for the elderly and give high priority to a transportation policy for senior citizens under the Older Americans Act. We pledge to enforce vigorously health and safety standards for nursing homes, and seek alternatives which allow senior citizens where possible to remain in their own homes.

Veterans

America's veterans have been rhetorically praised by the Nixon–Ford administration at the same time that they have been denied adequate medical, educational, pension and employment benefits.

Vietnam veterans have borne the brunt of unemployment and economic mismanagement at home. As late as December 1975, the unemployment rate for Vietnam veterans was over 10 per cent. Younger Vietnam veterans (ages 20–24) have had unemployment rates almost twice the rate of similarly aged nonveterans. Job training, placement, and information and counseling programs for veterans are inadequate.

The Veterans Administration health care program requires adequate funding and improved management and health care delivery in order to provide high-quality service and effectively meet the changing needs of the patient population.

The next Democratic administration must act to rescue pensioner veterans below the poverty line. Thirty per cent of the veterans and 50 per cent of the widows receiving pensions have total incomes below the poverty line. Cost of living increases should be automatic in the veterans' pension and disability system.

Educational assistance should be expanded two years for those veterans already enrolled and drawing benefits in VA-approved educational and training programs.

The Arts and Humanities

We recognize the essential role played by the arts and humanities in the development of America. Our nation cannot afford to be materially rich and spiritually poor. We endorse a strong role for the federal government in reinforcing the vitality and improving the economic strength of the nation's artists and arts institutions, while recognizing that artists must be absolutely free of any government control. We would support the growth and development of the National Endowments for the Arts and Humanities through adequate funding, the development of special anti-recession employment programs for artists, copyright reforms to protect the rights of authors, artists and performers, and revision of the tax laws that unfairly penalize artists. We further pledge our support for the concept and adequate financing of public broadcasting.

IV. STATES, COUNTIES AND CITIES

More than eight years ago, the Kerner Commission on Civil Disorders concluded that the disorders of the 1960s were caused by the deteriorating conditions of life in our urban centers—abject poverty, widespread unemployment, uninhabitable housing, declining services, rampant crime and disintegrating families. Many of these same problems plagued rural America as well. Little has been done by the Republican administrations to deal with the fundamental challenges to our society. This policy of neglect gives the lie to the current administration's rhetorical commitment to state and local governments.

By tolerating intolerable unemployment, by vetoing programs for the poor, the old, and the ill, by abandoning the veterans and the young, and by withholding necessary funds for the decaying cities, the Nixon–Ford years have been years of retrogression in the nation's efforts to meet the needs of our cities. By abdicating responsibility for meeting these needs at the national level, the current administration has placed impossible burdens on fiscally hard-pressed state and local governments. In turn, local governments have been forced to rely excessively on the steadily diminishing and regressive property tax—which was originally designed to cover property related services and was never intended to support the services now required in many of our cities and towns.

Federal policies and programs have inadvertently exacerbated the urban crisis. Within the framework of a new partnership of federal, state and local governments, and the private sector, the Democratic Party is pledged to the development of America's first national urban policy. Central to the success of that policy are the Democratic Party's commitments to full employment, incentives for urban and rural economic development, welfare reform, adequate health care, equalization of education expenditures, energy conservation and environmental quality. If progress were made in these areas, much of the inappropriately placed fiscal burden would be removed, and local governments could better fulfill their appropriate responsibilities.

To assist further in relieving both the fiscal and service delivery problems of states and local governments, the Democratic Party reaffirms its support for general revenue sharing as a base for the fiscal health of all levels of government, acknowledging that the civil rights and citizens' participation provisions must be strengthened. We further believe that there must be an increase in the annual funding to compensate for the erosion of inflation. We believe the distribution formula should be adjusted to reflect better community and state needs, poverty levels, and tax effort.

Finally, to alleviate the financial burden placed on our cities by the combination of inflation and recession, the Democratic Party restates its support for emergency anti-recession aid to states and cities particularly hard-hit by recession.

Housing and Community Development

In the past eight Republican years, housing has become a necessity priced as a luxury. Housing prices have nearly doubled in the past six years and housing starts have dropped by almost one-quarter. The effect is that over three-fourths of American families cannot afford to buy an average-priced home. The basic national goal of providing decent housing and available shelter has been sacrificed to misguided tax, spending and credit policies which were supposed to achieve price stability but have failed to meet that goal. As a result, we do not have decent housing or price stability. The vision of the Housing Act of 1968, the result of three decades of enlightened Democratic housing policy, has been lost. The Democratic Party reasserts these goals, and pledges to achieve them.

The Democratic Party believes it is time for a housing and urban development policy which recognizes the needs and difficulties of both the buying and renting public and the housing industry. We support a revitalized housing program which will be able to meet the public's need for housing at reasonable cost and the industry's need for relief from years of stagnation and now-chronic unemployment.

We support direct federal subsidies and low-interest loans to encourage the construction of low- and moderate-income housing. Such subsidies shall not result in unreasonable profit for builders, developers or credit institutions.

We support the expansion of the highly successful programs of direct federal subsidies to provide housing for the elderly.

We call for greatly increased emphasis on the rehabilitation of existing housing to rebuild our neighborhoods—a priority which is undercut by the current pattern of federal housing money which includes actual prohibitions on the use of funds for rehabilitation.

We encourage public and private commitments to the preservation and renovation of our country's historic landmarks so that they can continue as a vital part of our commercial and residential architectural heritage.

We will work to assure that credit institutions make greater effort to direct mortgage money into the financing of private housing.

We will take all necessary steps to prohibit the practice of red-lining by private financial institutions, the FHA, and the secondary mortgage market which have had the effect of depriving certain areas of the necessary mortgage funds which they need to upgrade themselves. We will further encourage an increase in loans and subsidies for housing and rehabilitation, especially in poverty stricken areas.

We support greater flexibility in the use of community development block grants at the local level.

The current Housing and Community Development Act should be reformed and restructured so that its allocation, monitoring, and citizen participation features better address the needs of local communities, major cities and underdeveloped rural areas.

The revitalization of our cities must proceed with an understanding that housing, jobs and related community facilities are all critical to a successful program. The Democratic Party will create the necessary incentives to insure that private and public jobs are available to meet the employment needs of these communities and pledges a more careful planning process for the location of the federal government's own employment-creating facilities.

The Democratic Party proposes a revitalization of the Federal Housing Administration as a potent institution to stabilize new construction and existing housing markets. To this end, the Agency's policies must be simplified, its operating practices and insurance rate structures modernized and the sense of public service which was the hallmark of the FHA for so many years must be restored. In addition, we propose automatic triggering of direct production subsidies and a steady flow of mortgage funds during periods when housing starts fall below acceptable levels.

Women, the elderly, single persons and minorities are still excluded from exercising their right to select shelter in the areas of their choice, and many "high-risk" communities are systematically denied access to the capital they require. The Democratic Party pledges itself to the aggressive enforcement of the Fair Housing Act; to the promotion and enforcement of equal opportunity in housing; and to the pursuit of new regulatory and incentive policies aimed at providing minority groups and women with equal access to mortgage credit.

In addition to direct attacks upon such known violations of the law, a comprehensive approach to these problems must include policies aimed at the underlying causes of unequal credit allocations. The Democratic Party pledges itself to aggressive policies designed to assure lenders that their commitments will be backed by government resources, so that investment risks will be shared by the public and private sectors.

The Special Needs of Older Cities

The Democratic Party recognizes that a number of major, older cities—including the nation's largest city—have been forced to undertake even greater social responsibilities, which have resulted in unprecedented fiscal crises. There is a national interest in helping such cities in their present travail, and a new Democratic

President and the Congress shall undertake a massive effort to do so.

Law Enforcement and Law Observance

The total crime bill in the United States has been estimated at $90 billion a year, almost as much as the cost of our national defense. But over and above the economic impact, the raging and unchecked growth of crime seriously impairs the confidence of many of our citizens in their ability to walk on safe streets, to live securely in peaceful and happy homes, and to work safely in their places of business. Fear mounts along with the crime rate. Homes are made into fortresses. In large sections of every major city, people are afraid to go out at night. Outside big cities, the crime rate is growing even faster, so that suburbs, small towns and rural areas are no longer secure havens.

Defaulting on their "law and order" promises, the Republicans in the last eight years have let the rising tide of crime soil the highest levels of government, allowed the crime rate to skyrocket and failed to reform the criminal justice system. Recognizing that law enforcement is essentially a local responsibility, we declare that control of crime is an urgent national priority and pledge the efforts of the Democratic Party to insure that the federal government act effectively to reverse these trends and to be an effective partner to the cities and states in a well-coordinated war on crime.

We must restore confidence in the criminal justice system by insuring that detection, conviction and punishment of lawbreakers is swift and sure; that the criminal justice system is just and efficient; that jobs, decent housing and educational opportunities provide a real alternative to crime to those who suffer enforced poverty and injustice.

We pledge equally vigorous prosecution and punishment for corporate crime, consumer fraud and deception; programs to combat child abuse and crimes against the elderly; criminal laws that reflect national needs; application of the law with a balanced and fair hand; a judiciary that renders equal justice for all; criminal sentences that provide punishment that actually punishes and rehabilitation that actually rehabilitates; and a correctional system emphasizing effective job training, educational and post-release programs. Only such measures will restore the faith of the citizens in our criminal justice system.

Toward these ends, we support a major reform of the criminal justice system, but we oppose any legislative effort to introduce repressive and anti–civil libertarian measures in the guise of reform of the criminal code.

The Law Enforcement Assistance Administration has not done its job adequately. Federal funding for crime-fighting must be wholly revamped to more efficiently assist local and state governments in strengthening their law enforcement and criminal justice systems, rather than spend money on the purchase of expensive equipment, much of it useless.

Citizen confidence in law enforcement can be enhanced through increased citizen participation, by informing citizens of police and prosecutor policies, assuring that police departments reflect a cross-section of the communities they serve, establishing neighborhood forums to settle simple disputes, restoring the grand jury to fair and vigorous independence, establishing adequate victim compensation programs, and reaffirming our respect for the individual's right to privacy.

Coordinated action is necessary to end the vicious cycle of drug addiction and crime. We must break up organized crime syndicates dealing in drugs, take necessary action to get drug pushers off the streets, provide drug users with effective rehabilitation programs, including medical assistance, ensure that all young people are aware of the costs of a life of drug dependency, and use worldwide efforts to stop international production and trafficking in illicit drugs.

A Democratic Congress in 1974 passed the Juvenile Justice and Delinquency Prevention Act to come to grips with the fact that juveniles account for almost half of the serious crimes in the United States, and to remedy the fact that federal programs thus far have not met the crisis of juvenile delinquency. We pledge funding and implementation of this Act, which has been ignored by the Republican administration.

Handguns simplify and intensify violent crime. Ways must be found to curtail the availability of these weapons. The Democratic Party must provide the leadership for a coordinated federal and state effort to strengthen the presently inadequate controls over the manufacture, assembly, distribution and possession of handguns and to ban Saturday night specials.

Furthermore, since people and not guns commit crimes, we support mandatory sentencing for individuals convicted of committing a felony with a gun.

The Democratic Party, however, affirms the right of sportsmen to possess guns for purely hunting and target-shooting purposes.

The full implementation of these policies will not in themselves stop lawlessness. To insure professionally trained and equitably rewarded police forces, law enforcement officers must be properly recruited and trained, and provided with decent wages, working conditions, support staff, and federal death benefits for those killed in the line of duty. Effective police forces cannot operate without just and speedy court systems. We must reform bail and pre-trial detention procedures. We must assure speedy trials and ease court congestion by increasing the number of judges, prosecutors and public defenders. We must improve and streamline courthouse management procedures, require criminal justice records to be accurate and responsible, and establish fair and more uniform sentencing for crimes.

Courts should give priority to crimes which are serious enough to deserve imprisonment. Law enforcement should emphasize the prosecution of crimes against persons and property as a higher priority than victimless crimes. Current rape laws need to be amended to abolish archaic evidence rules that discriminate against rape victims.

We pledge that the Democratic Party will not tolerate abuses of governmental processes and unconstitutional action by the government itself. Recognizing the value of legitimate intelligence efforts to combat espionage and major crime, we call for new legislation to ensure that these efforts will no longer be used as an excuse for abuses such as bugging, wiretaps, mail opening and disruption aimed at lawful political and private activities.

The Attorney General in the next Democratic administration will be an independent, non-political official of the highest integrity. If lawlessness is found at any level, in any branch, immediate and decisive action will be taken to root it out. To that end, we will establish the machinery for appointing an independent Special Prosecutor whenever needed.

As a party, as a nation, we must commit ourselves to the elimination of injustice wherever it plagues our government, our people and our future.

Transportation

An effective national transportation policy must be grounded in an understanding of all transportation systems and their consequences for costs, reliability, safety, environmental quality and energy savings. Without public transportation, the rights of all citizens to jobs and social services cannot be met.

To that end, we will work to expand substantially the discretion available to states and cities in the use of federal transportation money, for either operating expenses or capital programs on the modes of transportation which they choose. A greater share of Highway Trust Fund money should also be available on a flexible basis.

We will change further the current restrictive limits on the use of mass transit funds by urban and rural localities so that greater amounts can be used as operating subsidies; we emphatically oppose the Republican administration's efforts to reduce federal operating subsidies.

We are committed to dealing with the transportation needs of rural America by upgrading secondary roads and bridges and by completion of the original plan of 1956 for the interstate highway system where it benefits rural Americans. Among other benefits, these measures would help overcome the problems of getting products to market, and services to isolated persons in need.

We will take whatever action is necessary to reorganize and revitalize our nation's railroads.

We are also committed to the support of healthy trucking and bus, inland waterway and air transport systems.

A program of national rail and road rehabilitation and improved mass transit would not only mean better transportation for our people, but it would also put thousands of unemployed construction workers back to work and make them productive tax-paying citizens once again.

Further, it would move toward the Democratic Party's goal of assuring balanced transportation services for all areas of the nation—urban and rural. Such a policy is intended to reorganize both pressing urban needs and the sorry state of rural public transportation.

Rural Development

The problems of rural America are closely linked to those of our cities. Rural poor and the rural elderly suffer under the same economic pressures and have at least as many social needs as their counterparts in the cities. The absence of rural jobs and rural vitality and the continuing demise of the family farm have promoted a migration to our cities which is beyond the capacity of the cities to absorb. Over 20 million Americans moved to urban areas between 1940 and 1960 alone. We pledge to develop programs to make the family farm economically healthy again so as to be attractive to young people.

To that end, the Democratic Party pledges to strengthen the economy and thereby create jobs in our great agricultural and rural areas by the full implementation and funding of the Rural Development Act of 1972 and by the adoption of an agricultural policy which recognizes that our capacity to produce food and fiber is one of our greatest assets.

While it is bad enough to be poor, or old, or alone in the city, it is worse in the country. We are therefore committed to overcome the problems of rural as well as urban isolation and poverty by insuring the existence of adequate health facilities, critically needed community facilities such as water supply and sewage disposal systems, decent housing, adequate educational opportunity and needed transportation throughout rural America.

As discussed in the transportation section, we believe that transportation dollars should be available in a manner to permit their flexible use. In rural areas this means they could be used for such needs as secondary road improvement, taxi systems, buses, or other systems to overcome the problems of widely dispersed populations, to facilitate provisions of social services and to assure access of citizens to meet human needs.

Two thousand family farms are lost per week. To help assure that family farms stay in the family where they belong, we will push increases in relevant estate tax exemptions. This increased exemption, when coupled with programs to increase generally the vitality of rural America, should mean that the demise of the family farm can be reversed.

We will seek adequate levels of insured and guaranteed loans for electrification and telephone facilities.

Only such a coordinated program can make rural America again attractive and vigorous, as it needs to be if we are to deal with the challenges facing the nation as a whole.

Administration of Federal Aid

Federal aid programs impose jurisdictional and administrative complications which substantially diminish the good accomplished by the federal expenditure of about $50 billion annually on state and local governments. An uncoordinated policy regarding eligibility requirements, audit guidelines, accounting procedures and the like comprise the over 800 categorical aid programs and threaten to bog down the more broadly conceived flexible block grant programs. The Democratic Party is committed to cutting through this chaos and simplifying the grant process for both recipient governments and program administrators.

The Democratic Party also reaffirms the role of state and general purpose local governments as the principal governments in the orderly administration of federal aid and revenue sharing programs.

V. NATURAL RESOURCES AND ENVIRONMENTAL QUALITY

Energy

Almost three years have passed since the oil embargo. Yet, by any measure, the nation's energy lifeline is in far greater peril today. America is running out of energy—natural gas, gasoline and oil.

The economy is already being stifled. The resulting threat of unemployment and diminished production is already present.

If America, as we know it, is to survive, we must move quickly to develop renewable sources of energy.

The Democratic Party will strive to replace the rapidly diminishing supply of petroleum and natural gas with solar, geothermal, wind, tide and other forms of energy, and we recommend that the federal government promptly expand whatever funds are required to develop new systems of energy.

We have grown increasingly dependent on imported oil. Domestic production, despite massive price increases, continues to decline. Energy stockpiles, while authorized, are yet to be created. We have no agreements with any producing nations for security of supply. Efforts to develop alternative energy sources have moved forward slowly. Production of our most available and plentiful alternative—coal—is not increasing. Energy conservation is still a slogan, instead of a program.

Republican energy policy has failed because it is based on illusions; the illusion of a free market in energy that does not exist, the illusion that ever-increasing energy prices will not harm the economy, and the illusion of an energy program based on unobtainable independence.

The time has come to deal with the realities of the energy crisis, not its illusions. The realities are that rising energy prices, falling domestic supply, increasing demand, and the threat to national security of growing imports, have not been contained by the private sector.

The Democratic energy platform begins with a recognition that the federal government has an important role to play in insuring the nation's energy future, and that it must be given the tools it needs to protect the economy and the nation's consumers from arbitrary and excessive energy price increases and help the nation embark on a massive domestic energy program focusing on conservation, coal conversion, exploration and development of new technologies to insure an adequate short-term and long-term supply of energy for the nation's needs. A nation advanced enough and wealthy enough to send a man to the moon must develop alternate sources of energy.

Energy Pricing

Enactment of the Energy Policy and Conservation Act of 1975 established oil ceiling prices at levels sufficient to maximize domestic production but still below OPEC equivalents. The act was a direct result of the

Democratic Congress' commitment to the principle that beyond certain levels, increasing energy prices simply produce high-cost energy—without producing any additional energy supplies.

This oil-pricing lesson should also be applied to natural gas. Those now pressing to turn natural gas price regulation over to OPEC, while arguing the rhetoric of so-called deregulation, must not prevail. The pricing of new natural gas is in need of reform. We should narrow the gap between oil and natural gas prices with new natural gas ceiling prices that maximize production and investment while protecting the economy and the consumer. Any reforms in the pricing of new natural gas should not be at the cost of severe economic dislocations that would accelerate inflation and increase unemployment.

An examination must be made of advertising cost policies of utilities and the imposition of these costs on the consumer. Advertising costs used to influence public policy ought to be borne by stockholders of utility companies and not by the consumers.

Domestic Supply and Demand

The most promising neglected domestic option for helping balance our energy budget is energy conservation. But major investments in conservation are still not being made.

The Democratic Party will support legislation to establish national building performance standards on a regional basis designed to improve energy efficiency. We will provide new incentives for aiding individual homeowners, particularly average-income families and the poor in undertaking conservation investments. We will support the reform of utility rate structures and regulatory rules to encourage conservation and ease the utility rate burden on residential users, farmers and other consumers who can least afford it; make more efficient use of electrical generating capacity; and we will aggressively pursue implementation of automobile efficiency standards and appliance labeling programs already established by Democratic initiative in the Energy Policy and Conservation Act.

Coal currently comprises 80 per cent of the nation's energy resources, but produces only 16 per cent of the nation's energy. The Democratic Party believes that the United States' coal production can and must be increased without endangering the health and safety of miners, diminishing the land and water resources necessary for increased food production, and sacrificing the personal and property rights of farmers, ranchers and Indian tribes.

We must encourage the production of the highest-quality coal, closest to consumer markets, in order to insure that investments in energy production reinforce the economics of energy producing and consuming regions. Improved rail transportation systems will make coal available where it is actually needed, and will insure a rail transport network required for a healthy industrial and agricultural economy.

We support an active federal role in the research and development of clean burning and commercially competitive coal burning systems and technologies, and we encourage the conversion to coal of industrial users of natural gas and imported oil. Air quality standards that make possible the burning of coal without danger to the public health or degradation of the nation's clean air must be developed and implemented.

The Democratic Party wants to put an end to the economic depression, loss of life and environmental destruction that has long accompanied irresponsible coal development in Appalachia. Strip mining legislation designed to protect and restore the environment, while ending the uncertainty over the rules governing future coal mining, must be enacted.

The huge reserves of oil, gas and coal on federal territory, including the outer continental shelf, belong to all the people. The Republicans have pursued leasing policies which give the public treasury the least benefit and the energy industry the most benefit from these public resources. Consistent with environmentally sound practices, new leasing procedures must be adopted to correct these policies, as well as insure the timely development of existing leases.

Major federal initiatives, including major governmental participation in early high-risk development projects, are required if we are to harness renewable resources like solar, wind, geothermal, the oceans, and other new technologies such as fusion, fuel cells and the conversion of solid waste and starches into energy. The Ford administration has failed to provide those initiatives, and, in the process, has denied American workers important new opportunities for employment in the building and servicing of emerging new energy industries.

U.S. dependence on nuclear power should be kept to the minimum necessary to meet our needs. We should apply stronger safety standards as we regulate its use. And we must be honest with our people concerning its problems and dangers as well as its benefits.

An increasing share of the nuclear research dollar must be invested in finding better solutions to the problems of nuclear waste disposal, reactor safety and nuclear safeguards—both domestically and internationally.

Competition in the Domestic Petroleum Industry

Legislation must be enacted to insure energy administrators and legislators access to information they need for making the kind of informed decisions that future energy policy will require. We believe full disclosure of data on reserves, supplies and costs of production should be mandated by law.

It is increasingly clear that there is no free, competitive market for crude oil in the United States. Instead, through their control of the nation's oil pipelines, refineries and marketing, the major oil producers have the capability of controlling the field and often the downstream price of almost all oil.

When competition inadequate to insure free markets and maximum benefit to American consumers exists, we support effective restrictions on the right of major companies to own all phases of the oil industry.

We also support the legal prohibition against corporate ownership of competing types of energy, such as oil and coal. We believe such "horizontal" concentration of economic power to be dangerous both to the national interest and to the functioning of the competitive system.

Improved Energy Planning

Establishment of a more orderly system for setting energy goals and developing programs for reaching those goals should be undertaken. The current proliferation of energy jurisdictions among many executive agencies underscores the need for a more coordinated system. Such a system should be undertaken, and provide for centralization of overall energy planning in a specific executive agency and an assessment of the capital needs for all priority programs to increase production and conservation of energy.

Mineral Resources

As with energy resources, many essential mineral resources may soon be inadequate to meet our growing needs unless we plan more wisely than we have with respect to energy. The Democratic Party pledges to undertake a long-range assessment of the supply of our mineral reserves as well as the demand for them.

Agriculture

As a nation, we are blessed with rich resources of land, water and climate. When the supporting technology has been used to preserve and promote the family ownership and operation of farms and ranches, the people have been well served.

America's farm families have demonstrated their ability and eagerness to produce food in sufficient quantity to feed their fellow citizens and share with hungry people around the world as well. Yet this national asset has been neither prudently developed nor intelligently used.

The eight-year record of the Nixon–Ford adminis-

tration is a record of lost opportunities, failure to meet the challenges of agricultural statesmanship, and favoritism to the special pleading of giant corporate agricultural interests.

Republican misrule in agriculture has caused wide fluctuations in prices to producers, inflated food prices to consumers, unconscionable profiteering on food by business, unscrupulous shipping practices by grain traders, and the mishandling of our abundance in export markets. Republican agricultural policy has spelled high food prices, unstable farm income, windfalls for commodity speculators and multinational corporations, and confrontations between farmer and consumer.

Foremost attention must be directed to the establishment of a national food and fiber policy which will be fair to both producer and consumer, and be based on the family farm agricultural system which has served the nation and the world so well for so long.

Maximum agricultural production will be the most effective means of achieving an adequate food and fiber supply and reasonable price stability to American consumers. Without parity income assurance to farmers, full production cannot be achieved in an uncertain economy. We must assure parity return to farmers based on costs of production plus a reasonable profit.

We must continue and intensify efforts to expand agriculture's long-term markets abroad, and at the same time we must prevent irresponsible and inflationary sales from the American granary to foreign purchasers. Aggressive but stable and consistent export policy must be our goal. The production of food and fiber in America must be used as part of a constructive foreign policy based on long-term benefits at home and abroad, but not at the expense of the farmers.

Producers shall be encouraged to produce at full capacity within the limits of good conservation practices, including the use of recycled materials, if possible and desirable, to restore natural soil fertility. Any surplus production needed to protect the people of the world from famine shall be stored on the farm in such a manner as to isolate it from the marketplace.

Excess production beyond the needs of the people for food shall be converted to industrial purposes.

Farmers as individual producers must deal constantly with organized suppliers and marketers, and compete with non-farm conglomerates. To assist them in bargaining for the tools of production, and to strengthen the institution of the family farm, the Democratic Party will: support the Capper–Volstead Act in its present form; curb the influence of non-farm conglomerates which, through the elimination of competition in the marketplace, pose a threat to farmers; support the farmer cooperatives and bargaining associations; scrutinize and remedy any illegal concentrations and price manipulations of farm equipment and supply industries; revitalize basic credit programs for farmers; provide adequate credit tailored to the needs of young farmers; assure access for farmers and rural residents to energy, transportation, electricity and telephone services; reinstate sound, locally administered soil conservation programs; eliminate tax shelter farming; and overhaul federal estate and gift taxes to alleviate some of the legal problems faced by farm families who would otherwise be forced to liquidate their assets to pay the tax.

Long overdue are programs of assistance to farm workers in housing, employment, health, social services and education.

To protect the health of our citizens the government shall insure that all agricultural imports must meet the same quality standards as those imposed on agricultural products produced in the United States and that only quality American agricultural products be exported.

Fisheries

America's fisheries must be protected and enhanced as a renewable resource through ecologically sound conservation practices and meaningful international agreements and compacts between individual states.

Environmental Quality

The Democratic Party's strong commitment to environmental quality is based on its conviction that environmental protection is not simply an aesthetic goal, but is necessary to achieve a more just society. Cleaning up air and water supplies and controlling the proliferation of dangerous chemicals is a necessary part of a successful national health program. Protecting the worker from workplace hazards is a key element of our full employment program. Occupational disease and death must not be the price of a weekly wage.

The Democratic Party, through the Congress, has recognized the need for basic environmental scrutiny, and has authored a comprehensive program to achieve this objective. In eight years, the efforts to implement that program have been thwarted by an administration committed only to unfounded allegations that economic growth and environmental protection are incompatible.

Quite to the contrary, the Democratic Party believes that a concern for the environment need not and must not stand in the way of a much needed policy of high economic growth.

Moreover, environmental protection creates jobs.

Environmental legislation enacted since 1970 already has produced more than one million jobs, and we pledge to continue to work for additional laws to protect, restore and preserve the environment while providing still more jobs.

Today, permanently harmful chemicals are dispersed, and irrecoverable land is rendered worthless. If we are to avoid repeated environmental crises, we must now renew our efforts to restore both environmental quality and economic growth.

Those who would use the environment must assume the burden of demonstrating that it will not be abused. For too long this burden has been on government agencies, representing the public, to assess and hopefully correct the damage that has already been done.

Our irreplaceable natural and aesthetic resources must be managed to ensure abundance for future generations. Strong land and ocean use planning is an essential element of such management. The artifacts of the desert, the national forests, the wilderness areas, the endangered species, the coastal beaches and barrier dunes and other precious resources are in danger. They cannot be restored. They must be protected.

Economic inequities created by subsidies for virgin materials to the disadvantage of recycled materials must be eliminated. Depletion allowances and unequal freight rates serve to discourage the growing numbers of businesses engaged in recycling efforts.

Environmental research and development within the public sector should be increased substantially. For the immediate future, we must learn how to correct the damage we have already done, but more importantly, we need research on how to build a society in which renewable and nonrenewable resources are used wisely and efficiently.

Federal environmental anti-pollution requirement programs should be as uniform as possible to eliminate economic discrimination. A vigorous program with national minimum environmental standards fully implemented, recognizing basic regional differences, will ensure that states and workers are not penalized by pursuing environmental programs.

The technological community should be encouraged to produce better pollution-control equipment, and more importantly, to produce technology which produces less pollution.

VI. INTERNATIONAL RELATIONS

The next Democratic administration must and will initiate a new American foreign policy.

Eight years of Nixon–Ford diplomacy have left our nation isolated abroad and divided at home. Policies have been developed and applied secretly and arbitrarily by the executive department from the time of secret bombing in Cambodia to recent covert assistance in Angola. They have been policies that relied on ad hoc, unilateral maneuvering, and a balance-of-power diplomacy suited better to the last century than to this one. They have disdained traditional American principles which once earned the respect of other peoples while inspiring our own. Instead of efforts to foster freedom and justice in the world, the Republican administration has built a sorry record of disregard for human rights, manipulative interference in the internal affairs of other nations, and, frequently, a greater concern for our relations with totalitarian adversaries than with our democratic allies. And its efforts to preserve, rather than reform, the international status quo betray a self-fulfilling pessimism that contradicts a traditional American belief in the possibility of human progress.

Defense policy and spending for military forces must be consistent with meeting the real security needs of the American people. We recognize that the security of our nation depends first and foremost on the internal strength of American society—economic, social and political. We also recognize that serious international threats to our security, such as shortages of food and raw materials, are not solely military in nature and cannot be met by military force or the threat of force. The Republican administration has, through mismanagement and misguided policies, undermined the security of our nation by neglecting human needs at home while, for the first time in our nation's history, increasing military spending after a war. Billions of dollars have been diverted into wasteful, extravagant and, in some instances, destabilizing military programs. Our country can—and under a Democratic administration it will—work vigorously for the adoption of policies of full employment and economic growth which will enable us to meet both the justified domestic needs of our citizens and our needs for an adequate national defense.

A Democratic administration will work to create a foreign policy that does justice to the strength and decency of the American people through adherence to these fundamental principles and priorities:

We will act on the premise that candor in policy-making, with all its liabilities, is preferable to deceit. The Congress will be involved in the major international decisions of our government, and our foreign policies will be openly and consistently presented to the American people. For even if diplomatic tactics

and national security information must sometimes remain secret, there can be no excuse for formulating and executing basic policy without public understanding and support.

Our policy must be based on our nation's commitment to the ideal of individual freedom and justice. Experience has taught us not to rely solely on military strength or economic power, as necessary as they are, in pursuit of our international objectives. We must rely too on the moral strength of our democratic values—the greatest inspiration to our friends and the attribute most feared by our enemies. We will ensure that human needs are not sacrificed to military spending, while maintaining the military forces we require for our security.

We will strengthen our ties to the other great democracies, working together to resolve common economic and social problems as well as to keep our defenses strong.

We will restore the Democratic tradition of friendship and support to Third World nations.

We must also seek areas of cooperation with our traditional adversaries. There is no other option, for human survival itself is at stake. But pursuit of detente will require maintenance of a strong American military deterrent, hard bargaining for our own interest, recognition of continuing competition, and a refusal to oversell the immediate benefits of such a policy to the American public.

We will reaffirm the fundamental American commitment to human rights across the globe. America must work for a release of all political prisoners—men and women who are in jail simply because they have opposed peacefully the policies of their governments or have aided others who have in all countries. America must take a firm stand to support and implement existing U.S. law to bring about liberalization of emigration policy in countries which limit or prohibit free emigration. America must be resolute in its support of the right of workers to organize and of trade unions to act freely and independently, and in its support of freedom of the press. America must continue to stand as a bulwark in support of human liberty in all countries. A return to the politics of principle requires a reaffirmation of human freedom throughout the world.

The Challenge of Interdependence

The International Economy

Eight years of mismanagement of the American economy have contributed to global recession and inflation. The most important contribution a Democratic administration will make to the returning health of the world economy will be to restore the health of our own economy, with all that means to international economic stability and progress.

We are committed to trade policies that can benefit a full employment economy—through creation of new jobs for American workers, new markets for American farmers and businesses, and lower prices and a wider choice of goods for American consumers. Orderly reductions in trade barriers should be negotiated on a reciprocal basis that does not allow other nations to deny us access to their markets while enjoying access to ours. These measures must be accompanied by improved programs to ease dislocations and to relieve the hardship of American workers affected by foreign competition.

The Democratic Party will also seek to promote higher labor standards in those nations where productivity far outstrips wage rates, harming American workers through unfair exploitation of foreign labor, and encouraging American capital to pursue low-wage opportunities that damage our own economy and weaken the dollar.

We will exert leadership in international efforts to strengthen the world economic system. The Ford administration philosophy of reliance on the international "market economy" is insufficient in a world where some governments and multinational corporations are active in managing and influencing market forces.

We pledge constant efforts to keep world monetary systems functioning properly in order to provide a reasonably stable economic environment for business and to prevent the importation of inflation. We will support reform of the international monetary system to strengthen institutional means of coordinating national economic policies, especially with our European and Japanese allies, thus facilitating efforts by our government and others to achieve full employment.

The Democratic Party is committed to a strong and competitive merchant fleet, built in the United States and manned by American seamen, as an instrument of international relations and national security. In order to revitalize our merchant fleet, the party pledges itself to a higher level of coordination of maritime policy, reaffirmation of the objectives of the Merchant Marine Acts of 1936 and 1970, and the development of a national cargo policy which assures the U.S. fleet a fair participation in all U.S. trade.

A Democratic administration will vigorously pursue international negotiations to ensure that the multinational activities of corporations, whether American or foreign, be made more responsible to the international community. We will give priority attention to the establishment of an international code of conduct for multinational corporations and host countries.

We will encourage multinational corporations before they relocate production across international boundaries to make ancient advance arrangements for the workers whose jobs will be affected.

We will eliminate bribery and other corrupt practices.

We will prevent these corporations from interfering in the political systems of the countries in which they operate.

If such a code cannot be negotiated or proves to be unenforceable, our country should reserve the right to take unilateral action directed toward each of these problems, specifically including the outlawing of bribes and other improper payments to government officials of other nations.

In pursuit of open and fair international economic relationships, we will seek mechanisms, including legislation, to ensure that foreign governments cannot introduce third party boycotts or racial and religious discrimination into the conduct of American foreign commerce.

Energy

The United States must be a leader in promoting cooperation among the industrialized countries in developing alternative energy sources and reducing energy consumption, thus reducing our dependence on imports from the Middle East and restraining high energy prices. Under a Democratic administration, the United States also will support international efforts to develop the vast energy potential of the developing countries.

We will also actively seek to limit the dangers inherent in the international development of atomic energy and in the proliferation of nuclear weapons. Steps to be given high priority will include: revitalization of the Nonproliferation Treaty, expansion of the International Atomic Energy Agency and other international safeguards and monitoring of national facilities, cooperation against potential terrorism involving nuclear weapons, agreement by suppliers not to transfer enrichment or reprocessing facilities, international assurance of supply of nuclear fuel only to countries cooperating with strict non-proliferation measures, subsidization of multinational nuclear facilities, and gradual conversion to international control of non-weapon fissionable material.

The Developing World

We have a historic opportunity in the next decade to improve the extent and quality of cooperation between the rich and poor countries. The potential benefits to our nation of a policy of constructive cooperation with the developing world would be considerable: uninterrupted access at reasonable cost to raw materials and to basic commodities; lower rates of global inflation; improved world markets for our goods; and a more benign atmosphere for international negotiation in general. Above all, the prospects for the maintenance of peace will be vastly higher in a world in which fewer and fewer people suffer the pangs of hunger and the yoke of economic oppression.

We support efforts to stabilize and increase export earnings of developing countries through our participation in reasonable commodity arrangements. We support strengthening of global financing mechanisms and trade liberalization efforts. We will assist in promoting greater developing country capital markets.

Because our country provides food and fiber to all the world, the American farmer is heavily dependent on world markets. These markets must be developed in a way that prevents the wild gyrations of food prices and the periodic shortages that have been common under recent Republican administrations. We pledge significant financial support to the International Fund for Agricultural Development; more effective food aid through further revision of the U.S. Food for Peace program; significant contributions to a multinational world food reserve system, with appropriate safeguards for American farmers; and continuing efforts to promote American food exports.

The proliferation in arms, both conventional and nuclear, is a principal potential source of conflict in the developing as well as the industrialized world. The United States should limit significantly conventional arms sales and reduce military aid to developing countries, should include conventional arms transfers on the arms control agenda, and should regulate country-by-country justification for U.S. arms transfers, whether by sales or aid. Such sales or aid must be justified in terms of foreign policy benefits to the United States and not simply because of their economic value to American weapons producers.

A primary object of American aid, both military and economic, is first of all to enhance the condition of freedom in the world. The United States should not provide aid to any government—anywhere in the world—which uses secret police, detention without charges, and torture to enforce its powers. Exceptions to this policy should be rare, and the aid provided should be limited to that which is absolutely necessary. The United States should be open and unashamed in its exercise of diplomatic efforts to encourage the observance of human rights in countries which receive American aid.

Current world population growth is a threat to the long-range well-being of mankind. We pledge to support effective voluntary family planning around the world, as well as at home, and to recognize officially the link between social and economic development and the willingness of the individual to limit family size.

To be true to the traditional concern of Americans for the disadvantaged and the oppressed, our aid programs should focus on alleviating poverty and on support of the quest for human liberty and dignity. We will work to see that the United States does its fair share in international development assistance efforts, including participation in the fifth replenishment of the World Bank's International Development Association. We will implement a foreign assistance policy which emphasizes utilization of multilateral and regional development institutions, and one that includes a review of aid programs, country by country, to reinforce those projects whose financial benefits go to the people most in need and which are consistent with overall United States foreign policy goals.

The World Environment

Decay of the environment knows no national boundary. A government committed to protect our environment at home must also seek international cooperation in defending the global environment.

Working through and supporting such organizations as the United Nations Environmental Program, we will join other governments in more effective efforts to preserve the quality and resources of the oceans; to preserve endangered species of fish and wildlife; to reverse the encroachment of the deserts, the erosion of the world's agricultural lands, and the accelerating destruction of its forests; to limit pollution of the atmosphere; and to control alterations of the global climate.

Criminal Justice Rights of Americans Abroad

We will protect the rights and interests of Americans charged with crimes or jailed in foreign countries by vigorously exerting all appropriate efforts to guarantee humane treatment and due process and to secure extradition to the United States where appropriate.

International Drug Traffic

We call for the use of diplomatic efforts to stop international production and trafficking in illicit drugs including the possible cut-off of foreign aid to noncooperating countries.

Defense Policy

The size and structure of our military forces must be carefully related to the demands of our foreign policies in this new era. These should be based on a careful assessment of what will be needed in the long run to deter our potential adversaries; to fight successfully, if necessary, conventional wars in areas in which our national security is threatened; and to reassure our allies and friends—notably in Western Europe, Japan and the Near East. To this end, our strategic nuclear forces must provide a strong and credible deterrent to nuclear attack and nuclear blackmail. Our conventional forces must be strong enough to deter aggression in areas whose security is vital to our own. In a manner consistent with these objectives, we should seek those disarmament and arms control agreements which will contribute to mutual reductions in both nuclear and conventional arms.

The hallmarks of the Nixon–Ford administration's defense policy, however, have been stagnation and vulnerability.

By its reluctance to make changes in those features of our armed forces which were designed to deal with the problems of the past, the administration has not only squandered defense dollars, but also neglected making improvements which are needed to increase our forces' fighting effectiveness and their capability to deter future aggression.

By its undue emphasis on the overall size of the defense budget as the primary measure of both our national resolve and the proficiency of our armed forces, the administration has forgotten that we are seeking not to outspend, but to be able to deter and, if necessary, outfight our potential adversaries. While we must spend whatever is legitimately needed for defense, cutbacks on duplication and waste are both feasible and essential. Barring any major change in the international situation, with the proper management, with the proper kind of investment of defense dollars, and with the proper choice of military programs, we believe we can reduce present defense spending by about $5 billion to $7 billion. We must be tough-minded about the development of new weapons systems which add only marginal military value. The size of our defense budget should not be dictated by bureaucratic imperatives or the needs of defense contractors but by our assessment of international realities. In order to provide for a comprehensive review of the B-1 test and evaluation program, no decision regarding B-1 production should be made prior to February 1977.

The Pentagon has one of the federal government's most overgrown bureaucracies. The Department of Defense can be operated more effectively and efficiently and its budget reduced, without in any way compromising our defense posture. Our armed forces have many more admirals and generals today than during World War II, when our fighting force was much larger than now. We can reduce the ratio of officers to men and of support forces to combat troops.

Misdirected efforts such as the construction of pork-barrel projects under the jurisdiction of the Defense Department can be terminated. Exotic arms systems which serve no defense or foreign policy purpose should not be initiated.

By ignoring opportunities to use our advanced technology innovatively to obtain maximum effectiveness in weapons and minimize complexity and cost, the Republican administration has failed to reverse the trend toward increasingly intricate and expensive weapons systems. Thus, it has helped to put our forces—particularly the Navy—on the dangerous path of becoming both smaller in numbers and more vulnerable.

A new approach is needed. Our strategic nuclear forces should be structured to ensure their ability to survive nuclear attack, thereby assuring deterrence of nuclear war. Successful nuclear deterrence is the single most important task of our armed forces. We should, however, avoid becoming diverted into making expenditures which have only symbolic or prestige value or which themselves contribute to nuclear instability.

The United States Navy must remain the foremost fleet in the world. Our naval forces should be improved to stress survivability and our modern technology should be used in new ways to keep the essential sea lanes open. Concretely, we should put more stress on new sensors and armaments, and give priority to a navy consisting of a greater number of smaller and less vulnerable vessels.

Our land forces should be structured to fight effectively in support of our political and military commitments. To this end, modern, well-equipped and highly mobile land forces are more important than large numbers of sparsely equipped infantry divisions.

Our tactical air forces should be designed to establish air superiority quickly in the event of hostilities, and to support our land and naval forces.

We can and will make significant economies in the overhead and support structure of our military forces.

The defense procurement system should be reformed to require, wherever possible and consistent with efforts to encourage full participation by small and minority businesses, advertised competitive bids and other improvements in procurement procedure so as to encourage full and fair competition among potential contractors and to cut the current waste in defense procurement. A more equitable formula should be considered for distribution of defense contracts and other federal procurement on a state or regional basis.

The United States and other nations share a common interest in reducing military expenditures and transferring the savings into activities which raise living standards. In order to smooth the path for such changes, the Executive Branch and the Congress should encourage long-range planning by defense-dependent communities and managements of defense firms and unions. This process should take place within the context of the Democratic Party's commitment to planned full employment.

Our civilian and military intelligence agencies should be structured to provide timely and accurate information and analysis of foreign affairs and military matters. Covert action must be used only in the most compelling cases where the national security of the U.S. is vitally involved; assassination must be prohibited. There should be full and thorough congressional oversight of our intelligence agencies. The constitutional rights of American citizens can and must be fully protected, and intelligence abuses corrected, without endangering the confidentiality of properly classified intelligence or compromising the fundamental intelligence mission.

U.S.–U.S.S.R. Relations

The United States and the Soviet Union are the only powers who, by rivalry or miscalculation, could bring general nuclear war upon our civilization. A principal goal must be the continued reduction of tension with the U.S.S.R. This can, however, only be accomplished by fidelity to our principles and interests and through business-like negotiations about specific issues, not by the bad bargains, dramatic posturing, and the stress on general declarations that have characterized the Nixon–Ford administration's detente policy.

Soviet actions continue to pose severe threats to peace and stability in many parts of the world and to undermine support in the West for fruitful negotiations toward mutually beneficial agreements. The U.S.S.R. has undertaken a major military buildup over the last several years in its navy, in its strategic forces, and in its land forces stationed in Eastern Europe and Asia. It has sought one-sided advantages in negotiations, and has exerted political and military pressure in such areas as the Near East and Africa, not hesitating to dispatch to Angola its own advisors as well as the expeditionary forces of its clients.

The continued U.S.S.R. military dominance of many Eastern European countries remains a source of oppression for the peoples of those nations, an oppression we do not accept and to which we are morally opposed. Any attempt by the Soviet Union similarly to

dominate other parts of Europe—such as Yugoslavia—would be an action posing a grave threat to peace. Eastern Europe will not truly be an area of stability until these countries regain their independence and become part of a large European framework.

Our task is to establish U.S.–U.S.S.R. relations on a stable basis, avoiding excesses of both hope and fear. Patience, a clear sense of our own priorities, and a willingness to negotiate specific firm agreements in areas of mutual interest can return balance to relations between the United States and the Soviet Union.

In the field of nuclear disarmament and arms control we should work toward: limitations on the international spread of fissionable materials and nuclear weapons; specific strategic arms limitation agreements which will increase the stability of the strategic balance and reduce the risk of nuclear war, emphasizing mutual reductions and limitations on future weapons deployment which most threaten the strategic balance because their characteristics indicate a potential first-strike use; a comprehensive ban on nuclear tests; mutual reduction with the Soviet Union and others, under assured safeguards, of our nuclear arsenals, leading ultimately to the elimination of such arsenals; mutual restrictions with the Soviet Union and others on sales or other transfers of arms to developing countries; and conventional arms agreements and mutual and balanced force reductions in Europe.

However, in the area of strategic arms limitation, the U.S. should accept only such agreements that would not overall limit the U.S. to levels of intercontinental strategic forces inferior to the limits provided for the Soviet Union.

In the long run, further development of more extensive economic relations between the United States and the Soviet Union may bring significant benefit to both societies. The U.S.S.R. has sought, however, through unfair trade practices to dominate such strategic fields as merchant shipping. Rather than effectively resisting such efforts, the Nixon–Ford administration has looked favorably on such steps as subsidizing U.S.–U.S.S.R. trade by giving the Soviet Union concessionary credits, promoting trade increases because of a short-run hope of using trade to modify political behavior, and even placing major United States energy investment in pawn to Soviet Union policy. Where bilateral trade agreements with the U.S.S.R. are to our economic advantage, we should pursue them, but our watch-words should be tough bargaining and concrete economic, political or other benefits for the United States. We should also press the Soviet Union to take a greater share of responsibility in multilateral solutions to such problems as creating adequate world grain reserves.

Our stance on the issue of human rights and political liberties in the Soviet Union is important to American self-respect and our moral standing in the world. We should continually remind the Soviet Union, by word and conduct, of its commitments in Helsinki to the free flow of people and ideas and of how offensive we and other free people find its violations of the Universal Declaration of Human Rights. As part of our programs of official, technical, trade, cultural and other exchanges with the U.S.S.R., we should press its leaders to open their society to a genuine interchange of people and ideas.

We must avoid assuming that the whole of American–Soviet relations is greater than the sum of its parts, that any agreement is superior to none, or that we can negotiate effectively as supplicants. We must realize that our firmness can help build respect for us and improve the long-run opportunities for mutually beneficial concrete agreements. We must beware of the notion that Soviet–American relations are a seamless web in which concessions in one area will bring us benefits in others. By the same token, we must husband our resources to concentrate on what is most important to us. Detente must be military as well as political.

More fundamentally, we must recognize that the general character of our foreign policies will not be set by our direct relationship with the Soviet Union. Our allies and friends must come first. Nor can the pursuit of our interests elsewhere in the world be dominated by concern for Soviet views. For example, American policy toward China should continue to be based on a desire for a steady improvement and broadening of relations, whatever the tenor and direction of Chinese–Soviet relations.

Above all, we must be open, honest, mature and patient with ourselves and with our allies. We must recognize that, in the long run, an effective policy toward the Soviet Union can only be grounded on honest discussion, and on a national and, to some extent, an international consensus. Our own institutions, especially the Congress, must be consulted and must help formulate our policy. The governments of our allies and friends must be made partners in our undertakings. Haste and secret bilateral executive arrangements in our dealings with the U.S.S.R. can only promote a mood of uncertainty and suspicion which undermines the public support essential to effective and stable international relations.

America in the World Community

Many of the critical foreign policy issues we face require global approaches, but an effective international role for the United States also demands effective working with the special interests of specific foreign nations and regions. The touchstone of our policy must be our own interests, which in turn means that we should not seek or expect to control events everywhere. Indeed, intelligent pursuit of our objectives demands a realization that even where our interests are great and our involvement essential, we do not act alone, but in a world setting where others have interests and objectives as well.

We cannot give expression to our national values without continuing to play a strong role in the affairs of the United Nations and its agencies. Firm and positive advocacy of our positions is essential.

We should make a major effort at reforming and restructuring the U.N. systems. The intensity of interrelated problems is rapidly increasing, and it is likely that in the future, the issues of war and peace will be more a function of economic and social problems than of the military security problems that have dominated international relations since 1945.

The heat of debate at the General Assembly should not obscure the value of our supporting United Nations involvement in keeping the peace and in the increasingly complex technical and social problems—such as pollution, health, economic development and population growth—that challenge the world community. But we must let the world know that anti-American polemics are no substitute for sound policy and that the United Nations is weakened by harsh rhetoric from other countries or by blasphemous resolutions such as the one equating Zionism and racism.

A Democratic administration should seek a fair and comprehensive Law-of-the-Sea Treaty that will balance the interests of the developed and less developed countries.

Europe

The nations of Western Europe, together with Japan, are among our closest allies. Except for our closest neighbors in this hemisphere, it is in these regions where our interests are most strongly linked with those of other nations. At the same time, the growing economic and political strength of Europe and Japan creates areas of conflict and tension in a relationship both sides must keep close and healthy.

On the great economic issues—trade, energy, employment, international finance, resources—we must work with the Europeans, the Japanese and other nations to serve our long-run mutual interests in stability and growth, and in the development of poorer nations.

The military security of Europe is fundamental to our own. To that end, NATO remains a vital commitment. We should retain in Europe a U.S. contribution to NATO forces so that they are sufficient to deter or defeat attack without premature resort to nuclear weapons. This does not exclude moderate reductions in manpower levels made possible by more efficiency, and it affirmatively requires a thorough reform and overhaul of NATO forces, plans and deployments. We encourage our European allies to increase their share of the contributions to NATO defense, both in terms of troops and hardware. By mutual agreement or through modernization, the thousands of tactical nuclear weapons in Europe should be reduced, saving money and manpower and increasing our own and international security.

Europe, like the rest of the world, faces substantial political change. We cannot control that process. However, we can publicly make known our preference for developments consistent with our interests and principles. In particular, we should encourage the most rapid possible growth of stable democratic institutions in Spain, and a continuation on the path of democracy of Portugal and Greece, opposing authoritarian takeover from either left or right. We can make clear our sense of the risks and dangers of Communist participation in Western European governments, while being equally clear that we will work on a broad range of nonmilitary matters with any legally constituted government that is prepared to do the same with us. We similarly must reaffirm our support for the continued growth and cohesion of the institutions of the European community.

The voice of the United States should be heard in Northern Ireland against violence and terror, against the discrimination, repression and deprivation which brought about that civil strife, and for the efforts of the parties toward a peaceful resolution of the future of Northern Ireland. Pertinent alliances such as NATO and international organizations such as the United Nations should be fully apprised of the interests of the United States with respect to the status of Ireland in the international community of nations.

We must do all that is possible, consistent with our interest in a strong NATO in Southern Europe and stability in the Eastern Mediterranean, to encourage a fair settlement of the Cyprus issue, which continues to extract human costs.

Middle East

We shall continue to seek a just and lasting peace in the Middle East. The cornerstone of our policy is a firm commitment to the independence and security of the State of Israel. This special relationship does not prejudice improved relations with other nations in the region. Real peace in the Middle East will permit Israel and her Arab neighbors to turn their energies to internal development, and will eliminate the threat of world conflict spreading from tensions there.

The Middle East conflict is complex, and a realistic, pragmatic approach is essential. Our policy must be based on firm adherence to these fundamental principles of Middle East policy:

We will continue our consistent support of Israel, including sufficient military and economic assistance to maintain Israel's deterrent strength in the region, and the maintenance of U.S. military forces in the Mediterranean adequate to deter military intervention by the Soviet Union.

We steadfastly oppose any move to isolate Israel in the international arena or suspend it from the United Nations or its constituent organizations.

We will avoid efforts to impose on the region an externally devised formula for settlement, and will provide support for initiatives toward settlement, based on direct face-to-face negotiation between the parties and normalization of relations and a full peace within secure and defensible boundaries.

We vigorously support the free passage of shipping in the Middle East—especially in the Suez Canal.

We recognize that the solution to the problems of Arab and Jewish refugees must be among the factors taken into account in the course of continued progress toward peace. Such problems cannot be solved, however, by recognition of terrorist groups which refuse to acknowledge their adversary's right to exist, or groups which have no legitimate claim to represent the people for whom they purport to be speaking.

We support initiation of government enforcement action to insure that stated U.S. policy in opposition to boycotts against friendly countries is fully and vigorously implemented.

We recognize and support the established status of Jerusalem as the capital of Israel, with free access to all its holy places provided to all faiths. As a symbol of this stand, the U.S. Embassy should be moved from Tel Aviv to Jerusalem.

Asia

We remain a Pacific power with important stakes and objectives in the region, but the Vietnam War has taught us the folly of becoming militarily involved where our vital interests were not at stake.

Friendship and cooperation with Japan are the cornerstone of our Asian interests and policy. Our commitment to the security of Japan is central to our own, and it is an essential condition to a constructive, peaceful role for that nation in the future of Asia. In our economic dealings with Japan, we must make clear our insistence on mutuality of benefits and opportunities, while focusing on ways to expand our trade, avoiding economic shocks and resultant retaliation on either side. We must avoid the "shocks" to Japan which have resulted from Republican foreign policy.

We reaffirm our commitment to the security of the Republic of Korea, both in itself and as a key to the security of Japan. However, on a prudent and carefully planned basis, we can redeploy, and gradually phase out, the U.S. ground forces, and can withdraw the nuclear weapons now stationed in Korea without endangering that support, as long as our tactical air and naval forces in the region remain strong. Our continued resolve in the area should not be misunderstood. However, we deplore the denial of human rights in the Republic of Korea, just as we deplore the brutal and aggressive acts of the regime in North Korea.

We have learned, at a tragically high price, certain lessons regarding Southeast Asia. We should not seek to control the political future of that region. Rather, we should encourage and welcome peaceful relations with the nations of that area. In conjunction with the fullest possible accounting of our citizens still listed as missing in action, we should move toward normalized relations with Vietnam.

No foreign policy that reflects traditional American humanitarian concerns can be indifferent to the plight of the peoples of the Asian subcontinent.

The recent improvement in relations with China, which has received bipartisan support, is a welcome recognition that there are few areas in which our vital interests clash with those of China. Our relations with China should continue to develop on peaceful lines, including early movement toward normalizing diplomatic relations in the context of a peaceful resolution of the future of Taiwan.

The Americas

We recognize the fundamental importance of close relations and the easing of economic tension with our Canadian and Mexican neighbors.

In the last eight years, our relations with Latin America have deteriorated amid high-level indifference, increased military domination of Latin American governments, and revelations of extensive American interference in the internal politics of Chile and other nations. The principles of the Good Neighbor Policy and the Alliance for Progress, under which we are committed to working with the nations of the Americas as equals, remain valid today

but seem to have been forgotten by the present administration.

The U.S. should adopt policies on trade, aid and investment that include commodity agreements and an appropriate system of trade preferences.

We must make clear our revulsion at the systematic violations of basic human rights that have occurred under some Latin American military regimes.

We pledge support for a new Panama Canal treaty, which insures the interests of the United States in that waterway, recognizes the principles already agreed upon, takes into account the interests of the Canal work force, and which will have wide hemispheric support.

Relations with Cuba can only be normalized if Cuba refrains from interference in the internal affairs of the United States, and releases all U.S. citizens currently detained in Cuban prisons and labor camps for political reasons. We can move towards such relations if Cuba abandons its provocative international actions and policies.

Africa

Eight years of indifference, accompanied by increasing cooperation with racist regimes, have left our influence and prestige in Africa at an historical low. We must adopt policies that recognize the intrinsic importance of Africa and its development to the United States, and the inevitability of majority rule on that continent.

The first task is to formulate a rational African policy in terms of enlightened U.S.–African priorities, not as a corollary of U.S.–Soviet policy. Angola demonstrated that we must have sound relations with Black Africa and disassociate our policies from those of South Africa to achieve the desired African response to Soviet expansionism in Africa. Our policy must foster high-level U.S.–Africa communications and establish a sound basis for dealing when crises arise.

The next Democratic administration will work aggressively to involve black Americans in foreign policy positions, at home and abroad, and in decisions affecting African interests.

To promote African economic development, the U.S. should undertake increased bilateral and multilateral assistance, continue congressional initiatives in food assistance and food production, with special aid to the Sahel and implementation of the Sahel Development Plan; and carry forward our commitment to negotiate with developing countries on key trade and economic issues such as commodity arrangements and trade preferences.

Our policy must be reformulated towards unequivocal and concrete support of majority rule in Southern Africa, recognizing that our true interests lie in peaceful progress toward a free South Africa for all South Africans, black and white. As part of our commitment to the development of a free and democratic South Africa, we should support the position of African nations in denying recognition to "homelands" given pseudo independence by the South African government under its current policy of "separate development. "

The Republican administration's relaxation of the arms embargo against South Africa must be ended, and the embargo tightened to prevent transfers of military significance, particularly of nuclear material. The U.S. government should not engage in any activity regarding Namibia that would recognize or support the illegal South African administration, including granting tax credits to U.S. companies doing business in Namibia and paying taxes to South Africa. Moreover, the U.S. government should deny tax advantages to all corporations doing business in South Africa and Rhodesia who support or participate in apartheid practices and policies.

The U.S. government should fully enforce the U.N.-ordered Rhodesia sanctions, seek universal compliance with such measures, and repeal the Byrd Amendment.

Efforts should be made to normalize relations with Angola.

— 1980 —

PREAMBLE

In its third century, America faces great challenges and an uncertain future. The decade that America now enters presents us with decisions as monumental and fundamental as those we faced during the Civil War, during two World Wars, and during the Great Depression. Our current task is different from each of these historic challenges. But in many ways the challenge is the same: to marshall the talents and spirit of the American people, to harness our enormous resources, and to face the future with confidence and hope.

The task now before us is as global as the worldwide energy shortage, and as local as the plight of children in Appalachia. It reaches from the condition of older Eastern cities and the industries of the snowbelt, to the complex new demands of our sunbelt region and the special needs of our Western states. It is as basic as the entitlement of minorities and women to real equality in every aspect of the nation's life. It is as immediate as the refugee crisis in Miami and the natural disaster at Mount St. Helens. It is as futuristic as the exploration of space and the oceans. It is as idealistic as the spirit of liberty which imbues our Constitution. It requires nothing less than a continued dedication to Democratic principles by each element in our society—government, business, labor, and every citizen—to the promise and potential of our nation.

We live in a time when effective policy requires an understanding of the web of competing values and interests which exist in our country. We must combine compassion with self-discipline. We must forego simplistic answers for long-term solutions to our problems.

With the Republican leadership closing its eyes to the realities of our time and running for the Presidency on a program of the easy answer, of the pleasant sounding political promise, it is time to take a page from Adlai Stevenson's 1952 presidential campaign—it is time "to talk sense to the American people." It is time to talk bluntly and candidly about our problems and our proposed solutions; to face up to our problems and respond to them.

If we fail in this important task, if we fail to lay the issues squarely before the American people, we could well allow the federal government to revert to four years of Republicanism—neglect of the poor and disadvantaged, disdain for working men and women, compassion only for the rich and the privileged, failure to meet the challenges of energy, inflation and unemployment, and a breakdown of the partnership among local, state and federal governments. We as Democrats must not let this happen.

After nearly four years in office, we Democrats have not solved all of America's problems.

Most of these problems we inherited. Eight years of Republican politics left this nation weak, rudderless, unrespected and deeply divided.

As a result of this legacy, despite our progress, inflation still erodes the standard of living of every American.

As a result of this legacy, despite our progress, too many Americans are out of work.

As a result of this legacy, despite our progress, complete equality for all citizens has yet to be achieved.

As a result of this legacy, despite our progress, we still live in a very dangerous world, where competing ideologies and age-old animosities daily threaten the peace.

As a result of this legacy, our nation is still subject to the oil pricing and production decisions of foreign countries.

We will not run from these problems, nor will we fail. The record of the past four years is a testament to what the Democrats can do working together.

Time and time again in these past four years, a Democratic Congress and a Democratic President proved that they were willing to make the tough decisions.

Today, because of that Democratic partnership, we are a stronger nation.

Today, because of that Democratic partnership, we are at peace.

Today, because of that Democratic partnership, we are a more just nation.

Today, because of that Democratic partnership, honor and truth and integrity have been restored to our government and to our political process.

And so this Party looks to the future with determination and confidence.

We have been and we shall remain the Party of all Americans. We seek solutions that not only meet the needs of the many, but reaffirm our commitment to improve the conditions of the least fortunate in our society.

In this platform we offer programs and solutions that represent our dedication to Democratic principles. They define a spirit as well as a program . . . a set of beliefs as well as a set of ideas. Time and events may alter their priority or prospects. But nothing will alter the defining spirit and values of the Democratic Party.

The platform of the Democratic Party is a contract with the people. We believe that accountability for Democratic principles goes hand in hand with dedication to those principles. The Democratic Party is proud of its historic heritage of commitment to the people of America. Fulfilling this platform will permit us to keep faith with that tradition.

CHAPTER I: THE ECONOMY

A Commitment to Economic Fairness

The Democratic Party will take no action whose effect will be a significant increase in unemployment—no fiscal action, no monetary action, no budgetary action—if it is the assessment of either the Council of Economic Advisers or the Congressional Budget Office that such action will cause significantly greater unemployment.

In all of our economic programs, the one overriding principle must be fairness. All Americans must bear a fair share of our economic burdens and reap a fair share of our economic benefits. High interest rates impose an unfair burden on farmers, small businesses, and younger families buying homes. Recession im-

poses an unfair burden on those least able to bear it. Democratic economic policy must assure fairness for workers, the elderly, women, the poor, minorities and the majority who are middle-income Americans. In 1980, we pledge a truly Democratic economic policy to secure a prosperous economic future.

ECONOMIC STRENGTH

While the past three and a half years of Democratic leadership have been years of growth for our economy, we now find ourselves in a recession.

The Democratic Party is committed to taking the necessary steps to combat the current recession. However, we cannot abandon our fight against inflation. We must fight both of these problems at the same time; we are committed to do so. We will continue to pursue the fight against inflation in ways not designed or intended to increase unemployment.

Our current economic situation is unique. In 1977, we inherited a severe recession from the Republicans. The Democratic Administration and the Democratic Congress acted quickly to reduce the unacceptably high levels of unemployment and to stimulate the economy. And we succeeded. We recovered from that deep recession and our economy was strengthened and revitalized. As that fight was won, the enormous increases in foreign oil prices—120 percent last year—and declining productivity fueled an inflationary spiral that also had to be fought. The Democrats did that, and inflation has begun to recede. In working to combat these dual problems, significant economic actions have been taken.

Two tax cuts have been enacted, in 1977 and 1978, reducing taxes on individuals and businesses by an amount equal, this year, to about $40 billion.

While meeting our national security and pressing domestic needs, the Democratic Partnership has restrained the increase in government spending in ways which have steadily reduced the deficit we inherited.

Airline and banking regulatory reforms have been enacted; further regulatory reforms are now under consideration.

In the effort to restrain inflation, a voluntary pay advisory committee has been established with labor, business, and public representatives pursuant to a National Accord.

The first national export policy was developed; export and trade responsibilities were reorganized and strengthened; the Multilateral Trade Negotiations were completed; and the MTN Agreement was approved by the Congress.

To ensure a greater impact for scarce federal dollars, grant and loan programs have been redirected to the areas of greatest need, and the formula programs have been redesigned to target the areas with the most serious problems.

As a result of these economic actions:

- *Employment*—More than 8.5 million new jobs have been added to the workforce; about 1 million of those jobs are held by Blacks, and nearly an additional 1 million are held by Hispanics. Gains have been made by all groups—more men, more women, more minorities, and more young people are working than ever before in our history. Despite these gains, current unemployment is too high and must be lowered.
- *Inflation*—A strong anti-inflation program has been initiated and pursued aggressively, to deal both with the short-term inflation problem and with the long-term causes of inflation. The effects of the short-term effort are now evident: inflation is beginning to come down. Although some interest rates remain high, they are falling at record rates. This progress will continue as short-term actions continue to work and long-term initiatives begin to take hold.
- *Economic Growth*—Despite the economic declines of the past few months, for the first three years of the Carter Administration our economy was strong. For the 1977–1979 period:
- Gross National Product increased by 11.8 percent in real terms.
- Real after-tax income per person increased by 10.3 percent.
- Industrial production increased by 14.8 percent.
- Dividends increased by 36 percent.
- Real business fixed investment increased by 22.9 percent.
- *Energy*—Our dependence on foreign oil has decreased—in 1977 we imported 8.8 million barrels of oil per day, and our nation is now importing approximately 6.5 million per day, a decline of 26 percent.

Solving Economic Problems

The Democratic Party commits itself to a strong economic program—one that builds on the progress we have made to date, one that corrects the very real problems we face now, one that is responsible, one that offers realistic hope, and one that can unify our Party. Such a Democratic program would contrast dramatically with the simplistic rhetoric and the traditional economic policies of the Republican Party.

Full Employment

We specifically reaffirm our commitment to achieve all the goals of the Humphrey–Hawkins Full Employment Act within the currently prescribed dates in the Act, especially those relating to a joint reduction in unemployment and inflation. Full employment is important to the achievement of a rising standard of living, to the pursuit of sound justice, and to the strength and vitality of America.

Anti-Recession Assistance

Immediately, we must undertake a short-term anti-recession program to reverse the tide of deepening recession and rising unemployment. Each percentage point increase in the unemployment rate adds $25 billion to the federal deficit.

A Democratic anti-recession program must recognize that Blacks, Hispanics, other minorities, women and older workers bear the brunt of recession. We pledge a $12 billion anti-recession jobs program, providing at least 800,000 additional jobs, including full funding of the counter-cyclical assistance program for the cities, a major expansion of the youth employment and training program to give young people in our inner cities new hope, expanded training programs for women and displaced homemakers to give these workers a fair chance in the workplace, and new opportunities for the elderly to contribute their talents and skills.

Coupling our need to rehabilitate our railroads with the need to create new job opportunities, we must commit ourselves to a $1 billion railroad renewal program which can employ 20,000 workers.

We must take steps to restore the housing industry, including effective implementation of the Brooke–Cranston program, and the addition of 200,000 new units a year for low- and moderate-income families.

National Accord

The National Accord with labor must be strengthened and continued. This enhances the unique opportunity afforded by a Democratic Administration for government, labor and business to work together to solve our inflationary and other economic problems.

Tax Reductions

We commit ourselves to targeted tax reductions designed to stimulate production and combat recession as soon as it appears so that tax reductions will not have a disproportionately inflationary effect. We must avoid untargeted tax cuts which would increase inflation. Any tax reduction must, if it is to help solve pressing economic problems, follow certain guiding principles:

- The inflationary impact must be minimized;
- Reductions provided to individuals must be weighted to help low- and middle-income individuals and families, to improve consumer purchasing power, and to enhance a growing economy while maintaining and strengthening the overall progressive nature of the tax code;
- Productivity, investment, capital formation, as well as incentives, must be encouraged, particularly in distressed areas and industries;
- The effect on our economy must be one which encourages job formation and business growth.

Federal Spending

Spending restraint must be sensitive to those who look to the federal government for aid and assistance, especially to our nation's workers in times of high unemployment. At the same time, as long as inflationary pressures remain strong, fiscal prudence is essential to avoid destroying the progress made to date in reducing the inflation rate.

Fiscal policy must remain a flexible economic tool. We oppose a constitutional amendment requiring a balanced budget.

Interest Rates

The Democratic Party has historically been committed to policies that result in low interest rates in order to help our nation's workers, small businesses, farmers and homeowners. Therefore, we must continue to pursue a tough anti-inflationary policy which will lead to an across-the-board reduction in interest rates on loans.

In using monetary policy to fight inflation, the government should be sensitive to the special needs of areas of our economy most affected by high interest rates. The Federal Reserve shall use the tool of reserve requirements creatively in its effort to fight inflation. The Federal Reserve should also take particular care to make certain that it is aware of the concerns of labor, agriculture, housing, consumers and small business in its decision-making process. Finally, its Open Market Committee should continue to provide regular information to the public about its activities.

Regulatory Reform

Consistent with our basic health, safety, and environmental goals, we must continue to deregulate overregulated industries and to remove other unnecessary regulatory burdens on state and local governments and on the private sector, particularly those which inhibit competition.

Targeting and Regional Balance

From the time of Franklin Roosevelt, the Democratic Party has dedicated itself to the principle that the federal government has a duty to ensure that all regions, states and localities share in the benefits of national economic prosperity and that none bears more than its share of economic adversity.

Our 1976 platform stated: *Even during periods of normal economic growth there are communities and regions of the country—particularly central cities and urban areas—that do not fully participate in national economic prosperity. The Democratic Party has supported national economic policies which have conscientiously sought to aid regions in the nation which have been afflicted with poverty, or newer regions which have needed resources for development. These policies were soundly conceived and have been successful. Today, we have different areas and regions in economic decline and once again face a problem of balanced economic growth. To restore balance, national economic policy should be designed to target federal resources in areas of greatest need.*

A Democratic Administration has welcomed and encouraged the sustained growth of the West and Southwest in recent years. Policies now in place ensure that this growth will continue and bring the greatest benefits to the nation as a whole.

At the same time, a Democratic Administration will be committed to the economic growth and prosperity of the other regions of the nation. The era of federal policies directed exclusively to the development of one region or another should be succeeded by government-wide policies designed to bring about balanced and shared growth in all regions.

To restore balance, we must continue to improve the targeting of federal programs in order to maximize their benefit to those most in need. To involve the private sector in solving our economic problems, and to reduce the burden on government, we must leverage federal dollars with funds from the private sector.

Rebuilding American Industry by Increasing Economic Productivity and Competitiveness

The Democratic Party has a long tradition of innovation, foresight, and flexibility in creating policies to solve the nation's most urgent economic needs. We now stand at another watershed in our economic history which demands our Party's full attention, creative powers, resources, and skills. To revive productivity and revitalize our economy, we need a national effort to strengthen the American economy. It must include new tax depreciation rules to stimulate selective capital investment; a simplified tax code to assist business planning; removal of governmental regulations which are unnecessary and stifle business initiative; effective incentives for saving that do not discriminate against low- and middle-income taxpayers; reform in patent rules and new incentives for research and development, especially by small business; cooperative efforts with labor and management to retool the steel, auto and shipbuilding industries; and strengthened worker training programs to improve job opportunities and working skills.

Encouraging investment, innovation, efficiency and downward pressure on prices also requires new measures to increase competition in our economy. In regulated sectors of our economy, government serves too often to entrench high price levels and stifle competition. Regulations must balance protective benefits against potentially adverse effects on competitiveness. Necessary regulations should be achieved at minimum cost and at reduced burden to industry. In unregulated sectors of the economy, we must increase antitrust enforcement; greatly improve the speed and efficiency of antitrust litigation; and renew efforts to prevent the concentration of economic power—both in specific industries and across the economy as a whole—which operate to stifle growth and to fuel inflation.

United States non-farm exports have risen 50 percent in real terms in the last three years. A Democratic President and a Democratic Congress have recognized and strengthened the export trade functions of the federal government. To create new markets for American products and strengthen the dollar, we must seek out new opportunities for American exports; help establish stable, long-term commercial relationships between nations; offer technical assistance to firms competing in world markets; promote reciprocal trading terms for nations doing business here; and help ensure that America's domestic retooling is consistent with new opportunities in foreign trade.

One of our main goals in this effort will be to enable American industry to compete more effectively with foreign products. We must intensify our efforts to promote American exports and to ensure that our domestic industries and workers are not affected adversely by unfair trade practices, such as dumping. We must make international trade a major focus of our domestic and international policy. We will continue to support the development of trading companies which will compete more effectively in world markets. We must ensure that our efforts to lower tariff barriers are reciprocated by our trading partners. We recognize the superior productivity of American agriculture and the importance of agricultural exports to the balance of trade. We support continuing efforts to promote agricultural exports.

ENSURING ECONOMIC EQUITY

Budget

The budget policy that has been put forth by the Democratic Party traditionally has been based on providing adequate federal resources to meet our nation's urgent needs. The current Democratic Partnership has continued that tradition while restraining the growth of the federal budget.

We have increased support for vital domestic programs. We have increased funding for education by 75 percent over the Ford budget. We have increased Head Start by 73 percent, basic skills programs by 233 percent, bilingual education by 113 percent, Native American education by 124 percent, summer jobs by 66 percent, Job Corps by 157 percent, employment and training programs by 115 percent, Medicare by 54 percent, National Health Service Corps by 179 percent, Child Nutrition by 43 percent, and Women, Infants and Children (WIC) Program by 300 percent.

We have been able to do this, while restraining the growth in federal spending, because the country has had a growing economy; tax cuts have been moderate; waste and fraud have been reduced; and aid has been targeted to those most in need.

International events have required increased defense spending. The Soviet challenge cannot be ignored. We have had to reverse the steady decline in defense spending that occurred under the Republican Administration. A Democratic Administration and a Democratic Congress have done this; real defense spending has increased, in part through the elimination of waste and the emphasis on increased efficiency.

In the eight years preceding the first Carter budget, real federal spending had been growing at an average rate of 3 percent each year. By contrast, between FY 1978 and 1981, real federal spending will have declined at an average annual rate of 0.6 percent.

The federal budget has not been and must not be permitted to be an inflationary nor a recessionary force in our economy, but it also must not be permitted to ignore pressing human needs.

We support the discipline of attempting to live within the limits of our anticipated revenues. Government must set the example of fiscal responsibility for all our citizens who are helping in the fight against inflation. Spending discipline allows us to concentrate our resources to meet our most pressing human needs.

We as Democrats will continue our policy of opposing drastic cuts in social programs which impose un-fair burdens on the poor and the aged, on women, on children and on minorities. We have always opposed and will continue to oppose imposition of ever greater burdens on the poor, who can least afford them.

We also recommit ourselves to operating our gov-ernment more efficiently, and concentrating our efforts on eliminating waste, fraud, and abuse in government programs to make our tax dollars go further.

Worker Protection

The Democratic Administration has worked with Congress to take actions which protect our nation's workers from declining incomes, unsafe working con-ditions, and threats to their basic rights. The Democratic Party will not pursue a policy of high interest rates and unemployment as the means to fight inflation. We will take no action whose effect will be a significant increase in unemployment—no fiscal action, no monetary ac-tion, no budgetary action. The Democratic Party re-mains committed to policies that will not produce high interest rates or high unemployment.

But much more needs to be done to protect our na-tion's workers. The Democratic Party has a long and proud tradition in this area and we must pledge to continue our efforts over the next four years.

Over a generation ago this nation established a labor policy whose purpose is to encourage the practice and procedure of collective bargaining and the right of workers to organize to obtain this goal. The Demo-cratic Party is committed to extending the benefit of this policy to all workers and to removing the barriers to its administration.

In the future the Democratic Party will concentrate on the following areas.

Our labor laws should be reformed to permit better administration and enforcement, and particularly to prevent the inordinate delays and outright defiance by some employers of our labor laws. We can no longer tolerate the fact that certain employers are will-ing to bear the cost of sanctions which are in our cur-rent laws in order to violate the rights of those at-tempting to organize.

OSHA projections should be properly administered, with the concern of the worker being the highest pri-ority; legislative or administrative efforts to weaken OSHA's basic worker protection responsibilities are unacceptable. OSHA has significantly reduced work-place accidents and fatalities. We will not limit its scope for any reason, including the size of business, since all workers face significant workplace dangers. The Democratic Party strongly opposes and urges all

actions to defeat legislation which weakens OSHA's critical projections.

Hatch Act reforms should be enacted to give federal workers their basic First Amendment rights. We must protect federal workers from interruptions in their pay due to delays in the federal appropriations process and must seek ways to assure the comparability to pay scales between the federal and private sectors.

We support the right of public employees and a agri-cultural workers to organize and bargain collectively.

We urge the adoption of appropriate federal legisla-tion to ensure this goal.

Legislation must be enacted to allow building trades workers the same peaceful picketing rights currently afforded industrial workers.

All fair labor standards acts, such as the minimum wage and Davis–Bacon projections, must continue to be effectively enforced against employers seeking to circumvent their worker projections.

Section 14-b of the Taft–Hartley Act should be repealed.

Special assistance should be made available for un-employed workers in a distressed industry, such as the automobile, steel, and shipbuilding industries.

We must improve and strengthen our trade adjust-ment assistance programs.

We support federal legislation designed to give pro-tection and human rights to those workers affected by plant closings.

Just as we must protect workers in their workplace, so must we protect them when they are disabled by ac-cidents or sicknesses resulting from their work. The Democratic Party supports federal legislation to assure adequate minimum benefit levels to those who are un-employed, including expansion of coverage to all wage and salary workers and extended benefits for the long-term unemployed. It must not artificially disre-gard those who have already been unemployed for a long time.

We will continue to oppose a sub-minimum wage for youth and other workers and to support increases in the minimum wage so as to ensure an adequate in-come for all workers.

Small Business

The prosperity of small business is an important na-tional priority. Over half of the major innovations in the past twenty years have come from firms with less than 1,000 employees, and technological innovation has accounted for nearly half of America's economic growth. Small firms have a cost-per-scientist or engi-neer half that of larger firms. Ninety-six percent of the six million jobs created in the private sector between

1968 and 1976 came from small businesses—primarily firms in business less than four years, employing less than 20 workers. In contrast, the biggest 500 manufacturing companies—accounting for 80 percent of national output—employed precisely the same number of workers in 1968 as they did in 1976.

Of course, larger firms may offer other economic benefits to society, but the contribution of small business is vital and unique, and no overall program for economic recovery will succeed unless it relies heavily on small businesses. For this reason, the Democratic Party commits itself to the first comprehensive program for small business in American history. That program will include the following measures:

A prompt review and response for the recommendations of the White House Conference on Small Business.

Legislation to transfer from the SBA to the Farmers Home Administration responsibility for providing loans to farmers in financial need.

Allocation of a fair percentage of federal research funds to small business.

Protection of small and independent businesses against takeover by giant conglomerates.

Continued efforts to end federal regulations which reinforce barriers to entry by new and small firms, and which thereby entrench the dominance of market leaders.

A review of regulations and requirements which impose unnecessary burdens upon smaller firms.

Results should provide relief for smaller firms which now pay $12.7 billion a year to fill 850 million pages of government paperwork. We will adopt regulatory requirements to meet the needs of smaller firms, where such action will not interfere with the objectives of the regulation.

Minority Business

A Democratic Congress and a Democratic Administration have worked together to increase opportunities for minority businesses, which have suffered from inadequate capitalization. Enormous progress has been made in the last four years.

Federal procurement from minority-owned firms has increased by nearly two and a half times.

Federal deposits in minority-owned banks have already doubled.

Minority ownership of radio and television stations has increased by 65 percent.

Almost 15 percent of the funds spent under the Local Public Works Act went to minority-owned firms.

The Section 8(a) program operated by the Small Business Administration has been reformed and strengthened.

The Democratic Party pledges itself to advance minority businesses, including Black, Hispanic, Asian/Pacific Americans, Native Americans and other minorities to:

- Increase the overall level of support and the overall level of federal procurement so that minority groups will receive additional benefits and opportunities.
- Triple the 1980 level of federal procurement from minority-owned firms as we have tripled the 1977 levels in the past three years.
- Increase substantially the targeting of Small Business Administration loans to minority-owned businesses.
- Increase ownership of small businesses by minorities, especially in those areas which have traditionally been closed to minorities, such as communications and newspapers.
- Expand management, technical, and training assistance for minority firms, and strengthen minority capital development under the SBA's Minority Enterprise Small Business Investment Company (MESBIC) program.
- Establish a Minority Business Development Agency in the Department of Commerce under statutory mandate.
- Implement vigorously all set-aside provisions for minority businesses.

Women in Business

The Democrats have exercised effective leadership in the field of support to women-owned businesses. A national policy was developed to support women's business enterprises, and SBA created the first program to help women entrepreneurs. President Carter has issued an Executive Order creating a national women's business enterprise policy and prescribing arrangements for developing, coordinating, and implementing a national program for women's business enterprise.

Support of this program must be expanded through effective implementation of the Executive Order to ensure an equitable distribution of government prime and subcontracts to women business owners. Cabinet Secretaries and agency heads, working with the Office of Federal Procurement Policy, must monitor realistic goals established for the award of government business and financial support to women-owned businesses.

As the key office within the federal government for these programs, the Office of Women's Business

Enterprise in the SBA must be strengthened through adequate staffing and funding, and should receive continued emphasis by key White House and Office of Management and Budget personnel.

Women and the Economy

We pledge to secure the rights of working women, homemakers, minority women and elderly women to a fair share of our economy. A sound economy in the next four years is of vital importance to women, who are often at the bottom of the economic ladder. But if our economy is to be truly fair, additional steps are required to address the inequities that women now face.

Special attention must be paid to the employment needs of women. Today, women who can find work earn, on average, only fifty-nine cents for every dollar earned by men.

The Democratic Party, therefore, commits itself to strong steps to close the wage gap between men and women, to expand child care opportunities for families with working parents, to end the tax discrimination that penalizes married working couples, and to ensure that women can retire in dignity.

We will strictly enforce existing anti-discrimination laws with respect to hiring, pay and promotions. We will adopt a full employment policy, with increased possibilities for part-time work. Vocational programs for young women in our high schools and colleges will be equalized and expanded. Fields traditionally reserved for men—from construction to engineering—must be opened to women, a goal which must be promoted through government incentives and federally sponsored training programs.

Perhaps most important, the Democratic Party is committed to the principle of equal pay for work of comparable value. Through new job classification studies by the Department of Labor, job reclassification by the Office of Personnel Management and new legislation from Congress if necessary, we will ensure that women in both the public and private sectors are not only paid equally for work which is identical to that performed by men, but are also paid equally for work which is of comparable value to that performed by men.

The Democratic Party must lead the way in ensuring that women and minorities are afforded real equality in the work force, neither displacing the other. As the nation's single largest employer, the hiring and promotion practices of the federal government must set an example. Every branch of government will be mandated not only to hire qualified women and minorities, but also affirmatively to seek out able minorities and women within the government for training and promotion. Opportunities for part-time work will be expanded and pay equalized to reflect the value of the work which is done.

Economic Inequities Facing Minorities

We must expand jobs and job training including apprenticeship training programs for those who have special problems—groups such as the young, veterans, older workers, minorities, those with limited fluency in English, and the handicapped. The Democratic Party pledges that anyone who wants to learn the skills necessary to secure a job will be able to do so.

We also must improve the quality of the programs designed to help the structurally unemployed. We must give trainees a better sense of what work will be like, assure a higher level of training, and undertake greater efforts to place people in jobs and help them adjust to the world of work. We should explore several methods for making such improvements, including performance funding. More money should go to those training programs which prove most successful. Particular emphasis should be given to training programs run by community-based organizations which have a superior record of success.

Where public agencies have trouble reaching those who seem unemployable, and where the training they provide is not effective, we should assist business to provide that training. We should ensure that business is not paid merely for hiring those that would be hired anyway, and that federal subsidies are truly training subsidies and not disguised wage subsidies.

A major effort must be undertaken to address youth employment. Half the unemployed are under twenty-five. Teenage inner city unemployment is at disastrous levels of 50 percent or higher. The problem is one of both employment and employability—a lack of jobs and a lack of skills.

We need new combinations of work experience and training for young people, new links between schools and the workplace, new ways to reach out to those who are out of school and out of work, but who have special need for skill development and job experience.

Consumer Protection

Since the first Administration of Franklin Roosevelt, the Democratic Party has stood as the Party which championed consumer rights. It is our tradition to support and enact policies which guarantee that the consumer is sovereign in the market place. It is our history to institute necessary government programs to protect the health, safety and economic well-being of the American consumer. And it is our way of governing to ensure that consumers have full opportunity to participate in the decision-making processes of government.

Working together, the Democratic Administration and Congress have maintained that tradition. Prominent consumer advocates have been appointed to key government positions. A new National Consumer Cooperative Bank has been created, and a Fair Debt Collection Practices Act has been enacted. Each federal agency has been directed to establish procedures so that consumer needs and interests are adequately considered and addressed on a continual basis. The basic consumer protection authorities of the Federal Trade Commission have been preserved.

Over the next four years, we must continue to guarantee and enhance the basic consumer rights to safety, to information, to choice and to a fair hearing.

Government must continue its efforts to create a strong independent voice to ensure that the consumer's interest is considered in government proceedings. We pledge continued support for an independent consumer protection agency to protect the rights and interests of consumers. Until one is created, we must ensure that each department and agency of the government has established and adequately funded a consumer program which complies with the requirements of Executive Order 12160. Each agency must provide ample opportunity for public involvement in its proceedings and should strive to adopt a program to provide funds for consumers and small businesses to participate in those proceedings.

We must continue our support of basic health, safety, environmental and consumer protection regulatory programs and must undertake the following new initiatives to provide additional basic projections to consumers:

- Comprehensive review of food safety and drug statutes, with particular emphasis on food labeling which discloses product ingredients.
- Requirements for full warranties for new automobiles.
- Class action reform to remove unnecessarily burdensome and expensive procedures.
- Reform of requirements for legal standing to seek judicial redress.
- Protection for consumers against dangerous products, including standards for automobile safety, clothing flammability, new drugs and chemicals, and food and children's products.
- Vigorous enforcement of truth-in-lending, anti-redlining, and fair credit reporting laws.
- Curtailment of abuses in sale of credit life insurance.

While consumer regulatory programs are necessary to achieve social goals, we recognize that an effective competition policy frees the market place from regulation. Therefore, we support vigorous enforcement and strengthening of the antitrust laws. Legislation should be enacted to overturn the Illinois Brick case and allow consumers who are injured as a result of a violation of the antitrust laws to seek redress, whether or not they have dealt directly with the violator.

We are committed to ensuring that America's poor do not suffer from lack of food. To this end, we support continued funding of the Food Stamp Program and expansion of the Women, Infant and Children (WIC) program.

We support the efforts of the National Consumer Cooperative Bank to assist grassroots consumer organizations to undertake self-help programs.

We support a nationwide program of consumer education to enable citizens to fully understand their rights in the market place, to be informed of the opportunities for participation in government decision-making, and to be equipped to make intelligent, rational consumer decisions.

Antitrust Enforcement

America must commit itself to a free, open and competitive economy. We pledge vigorous antitrust enforcement in those areas of the economy which are not regulated by government and in those which are, we pledge an agency-by-agency review to prevent regulation from frustrating competition.

To accomplish these goals, we must:

- Enact the Illinois Brick legislation.
- Permit consumers and other interested parties to seek enforcement of consent decrees issued in antitrust cases brought by government.
- Prevent anti-competitive pricing by firms in concentrated industries, and combat price signalling and other forms of anti-competitive conduct which do not fall into the current legal categories of either monopoly or collusion.
- Control conglomerate mergers, when such mergers undermine important economic, social and political values without offsetting economic benefits.
- Reform antitrust procedures to speed up cases and deter dilatory conduct by any party.
- Provide strong support for antitrust enforcement by the federal enforcement agencies.
- Provide technical and financial support for the antitrust enforcement efforts of the state attorneys-general and other state antitrust agencies.
- Develop a "single stop" clearance procedure to allow exporters to determine whether specific export agreements are permissible under the antitrust law.

CHAPTER II: GOVERNMENT AND HUMAN NEEDS

The Democratic Party has properly been known as the Party of the people. We Democrats believe in making government responsive to the needs of the people— making it *work* for the people. We do not claim that government has all the answers to our problems, but we do believe that government has a legitimate role to play in searching for those answers and in applying those answers.

The Democratic Party has a proud record of responding to the human needs of our citizens. After eight years of Republican government and systematic Republican efforts to dismantle all of the hard-won New Frontier and Great Society social programs, the Carter Administration and the Democratic Congress have resurrected, preserved and strengthened those programs which have proven effective.

In the areas of health care, housing, education, welfare and social services, civil rights, and care for the disabled, elderly and veterans, a Democratic President and a Democratic Congress have put the federal government back in the business of serving our people.

Our progress has been significant, and in many areas unprecedented. In 1980, the people must decide whether our country will continue that progress, or whether we will allow the federal government to revert to four years of Republicanism—which means neglect of the poor and disadvantaged, disdain for working men and women, and compassion only for the rich and the privileged.

We will not allow this to happen. We pledge to build on the Democratic record of the past four years—to continue the process we have begun.

While we recognize the need for fiscal restraint and have proposed specific steps toward that goal, we pledge as Democrats that for the sole and primary purpose of fiscal restraint alone, we will not support reductions in the funding of any program whose purpose is to serve the basic human needs of the most needy in our society—programs such as unemployment, income maintenance, food stamps, and efforts to enhance the educational, nutritional or health needs of children.

Health

The Carter Administration and the Congress have worked closely together to improve the health care provided to all Americans. In many vital areas, there has been clear progress.

The United States spent over $200 billion for health care in 1979. Despite these high expenditures and although we possess some of the finest hospitals and health professionals in the world, millions of Americans have little or no access to health care services. Incredibly, costs are predicted to soar to $400 billion by 1984, without improvement in either access to care or coverage of costs. Health care costs already consume ten cents of every dollar spent for goods and services.

The answer to runaway medical costs is not, as Republicans propose, to pour money into a wasteful and inefficient system. The answer is not to cut back on benefits for the elderly and eligibility for the poor. The answer is to enact a comprehensive, universal national health insurance plan.

To meet the goals of a program that will control costs and provide health coverage to every American, the Democratic Party pledges to seek a national health insurance program with the following features:

- Universal coverage, without regard to place of employment, sex, age, marital status, or any other factor;
- Comprehensive medical benefits, including preventive, diagnostic, therapeutic, health maintenance and rehabilitation services, and complete coverage of the costs of catastrophic illness or injury;
- Aggressive cost containment provisions along with provisions to strengthen competitive forces in the marketplace;
- Enhancement of the quality of care;
- An end to the widespread use of exclusions that disadvantage women and that charge proportionately higher premiums to women;
- Reform of the health care system, including encouragement of health maintenance organizations and other alternative delivery systems;
- Building on the private health care delivery sector and preservation of the physician–patient relationship;
- Provision for maximum individual choice of physician, other provider, and insurer;
- Maintenance of the private insurance industry with appropriate public regulation;
- Significant administrative and organizational roles for state and local government in setting policy and in resource planning;
- Redistribution of services to ensure access to health care in underserved areas;
- Improvement of non-institutional health services so that elderly, disabled, and other patients may remain in their homes and out of institutions; and

Child Health Assurance Program

We must continue to emphasize preventive health care for all citizens. As part of this commitment, we call for the enactment of legislation during the 96th Congress to expand the current Medicaid program and make an additional 5 million low-income children eligible for Medicaid benefits and an additional 200,000 low-income pregnant women eligible for prenatal and postnatal care.

Mental Health Systems Act

We must enact legislation to help the mentally ill, based on the recommendations of the President's Commission on Mental Health. The legislation should focus on de-institutionalization of the chronically mentally ill, increased program flexibility at the local level, prevention, and the development of community-based mental health services. It is imperative that there be ongoing federal funding for the community-based mental health centers established under the 1963 Mental Health Act and that sufficient federal funding be provided for adequate staffing. We also endorse increased federal funding for ongoing training of mental health personnel in public facilities.

In the 1980s we must move beyond these existing health care initiatives and tackle other problems as well.

Long-Term Care

We must develop a new policy on long-term care for our elderly and disabled populations that controls the cost explosion and at the same time provides more humane care. We must establish alternatives to the present provisions for long-term care, including adequate support systems and physical and occupational therapy in the home and the community, to make it unnecessary to institutionalize people who could lead productive lives at home.

We must support legislation to expand home health care services under Medicare and other health programs. Visits from doctors, nurses and other health personnel are a cost-effective and necessary program for the elderly who often cannot travel to medical facilities. Without home health services, many elderly citizens would be forced to give up their homes and shift their lives to institutions.

Multilingual Needs

We must support the utilization of bilingual interpreters in English–Spanish and other appropriate languages at federal- and state-supported health care facilities. In addition, we support broader, more comprehensive health care for migrants.

Health Care Personnel

This nation must maintain an adequate supply of health professionals and personnel. Particular empha-

sis should be given to programs which educate nurses and other health professionals and related personnel, especially for the traditionally underserved rural and inner city areas.

The rising cost of education in health fields bars many who wish to enter these fields from doing so. In order to expand representation in the health professions of traditionally underrepresented groups, we support programs of financial assistance such as capitation grants. These programs must increase the presence of men and minorities in nursing, and must be targeted toward women and minorities in other health professions.

Minority and Women Health Care Professionals

We recognize the need for a significant increase in the number of minority and women health care professionals. We are committed to placing greater emphasis on enrollment and retention of minorities and women in medical schools and related health education professional programs.

We are also committed to placing a greater emphasis on medical research and services to meet the needs of minorities, women and children.

Reproductive Rights

We fully recognize the religious and ethical concerns which many Americans have about abortion. We also recognize the belief of many Americans that a woman has a right to choose whether and when to have a child.

The Democratic Party supports the 1973 Supreme Court decision on abortion rights as the law of the land and opposes any constitutional amendment to restrict or overturn that decision.

Furthermore, we pledge to support the right to be free of environmental and worksite hazards to the reproductive health of women and men.

We further pledge to work for programs to improve the health and safety of pregnancy and childbirth, including adequate prenatal care, family planning, counseling, and services with special care to the needs of the poor, the isolated, the rural, and the young.

Financially Distressed Public Hospitals

Frequently, the only source of medical care for much of the inner city population is the public general hospital. The ever-increasing costs of providing high-quality hospital services and the lack of insurance coverage for many of the patients served have jeopardized the financial stability of these institutions. Immediate support is required for financially distressed public hospitals that provide a major community service in urban and rural areas.

In underserved areas where public hospitals have already been closed because of financial difficulty, we must explore methods for returning the needed hospitals to active service.

We must develop financial stability for these hospitals. Our approach should stress system reforms to assure that more primary medical care is provided in free-standing community centers, while the hospital is used for referral services and hospitalization.

Medicaid Reimbursement

The Democratic Party supports programs to make the Medicaid reimbursement formulae more equitable.

Unnecessary Prescriptions

We must reduce unnecessary prescribing of drugs and guarantee the quality and safety of products that reach the market through improved approval procedures.

Substance Abuse

Alcoholism and drug abuse are unique illnesses which not only impair the health of those who abuse those products, but impose costs on society as a whole—in production losses, in crimes to supply habits, and in fatalities on the highway.

The Democratic Partnership has worked to reduce the serious national problem of substance abuse, and progress has been made.

As a result, in part, of a major adolescent drug abuse prevention campaign, levels of drug abuse among adolescents have begun to decline. However, as long as abuse still exists, we consider it a major problem requiring our attention.

Because of a coordinated, concerted attack on drug trafficking, heroin availability in the U.S. over the past four years has decreased by 44 percent; heroin-related injuries have declined by 50 percent.

Progress made since 1977 must be continued.

We must continue to focus on preventing substance abuse in the early years of adolescence by working with grassroots organizations and parent groups throughout the country.

Special efforts must be made to strengthen prevention and rehabilitation resources in the major urban areas that are so acutely affected by drug and alcohol abuse problems because of the cumulative effect of joblessness, poor housing conditions and other factors.

We must provide adequate funding for alcohol and drug abuse research and treatment centers designed to meet the special needs of women, and end the currently widespread discrimination, based on sex, age, race, and ethnicity, in alcohol and drug abuse programs.

We must treat addiction as a health problem and seek flexibility in administering Medicare and Medicaid for substance abuse treatment, especially alcohol and drug services.

We must reduce the availability of heroin and other illicit narcotics in this country and in the source countries.

We must conduct investigations leading to the prosecution and conviction of drug traffickers and to the forfeiture of financial and other assets acquired by their organizations.

Older Americans

In other sections of this platform (for example, Health and the extensive section on Social Security), we have listed programs and commitments for improving the status of older Americans. As a Party, we are aware of the demographic and biomedical developments that call for a high-priority approach to the issues of retirement, work, and income maintenance for the growing number of older citizens.

The Democratic Party stands for the achievement and maintenance of the quality of life for Americans in their later years. We speak for our future selves, as well as for the elderly of today.

There has been substantial progress, but much remains to be done. Too many senior citizens (especially among minority groups) live close to or below the poverty line, in isolated conditions, and without access to needed services.

The Democratic Party pledges to continue to improve the policies and programs which ensure a high quality of life for older Americans. This includes the following measures.

All Americans, regardless of age, must be afforded an opportunity to participate in the mainstream of society, and in activities at local and national levels, as useful citizens. The 1967 Age Discrimination in Employment Act, and the milestone amendments to that Act in 1978, are concrete examples of this principle. So are programs such as senior centers, nutrition services, and home attendants, as well as those programs under ACTION, the Administration on Aging, and the Community Services Administration.

Such programs have helped to diminish the conditions of dependency, isolation, and unnecessary institutionalization. We propose to continue and expand these programs to reach underserved areas and all segments of the elderly.

The Democratic Party is proud of the passage of legislation to protect and improve private pensions through the Employees Retirement Income Security Act (ERISA), as well as current proposals to extend such protection to larger numbers of workers. No worker, after long years of employment, should lose his or her pension rights because of mobility, poor management, or economic reasons.

Other priorities include working with the private sector to assure maintenance and expansion of employer–employee pension systems and continuing support of the federal–state partnership in SSI (Supplemental Security Income) for the least fortunate.

A comprehensive program of long-term care services is a goal of the Democratic Party. The fastest growing segment of our population is the "very old" and the "frail elderly." The Democratic Party will continue to be concerned with the provision of services for these groups, increasingly composed of women without access to family care. This will include home attendant care, day centers, and quality institutional care for those elderly with functional disabilities who cannot rely on non-institutional alternatives.

For many older citizens, continuing participation in the mainstream means continuing employment, or a return to the labor force as a result of widowhood or the "empty nest." In addition to increasing employment opportunities by raising the allowable mandatory retirement age, we must continue existing, and create new, programs for the retention and re-entry of adult and older Americans in our labor force, including the private and community service sectors.

The Democratic Party will encourage the development of services by the public and private sectors to provide meals-on-wheels for those who need them; senior day centers; friendly visiting services; and similar supportive, educational–recreational, and outreach services.

We pledge to make the elderly secure in the necessities of life. The Democratic Party pledges that it will seek to increase the number of meals served under Title III of the Older Americans Act until it covers at least a quarter of all older people at or near the poverty level while at least maintaining current services for those who are not in poverty. The Democratic Party will seek expanded funding provided for the Section 202 housing program for the elderly.

Social Security

No group in our society deserves the commitment and respect of the Democratic Party more than the elderly. They have built the factories and mills of the nation. They have fought to defend our country. They have paid taxes to finance the growth of our cities and towns. They have worked and sacrificed for a lifetime to give their children a better chance to achieve their dreams. They have a continuing reservoir of talent, skill and experience to contribute to our future.

The basic program and guarantee for older citizens is Social Security. It is the single most successful social program ever undertaken by the federal government. Ninety-five percent of those reaching 65 are eligible for this program; without it, 60 percent of the elderly would have incomes below the poverty level,

The Democratic Party will oppose any effort to tamper with the Social Security system by cutting or taxing benefits as a violation of the contract the American government has made with its people. We hereby make a covenant with the elderly of America that as we have kept the Social Security trust fund sound and solvent in the past, we shall keep it sound and solvent in the years ahead.

In 1977, the Social Security system faced bankruptcy. The Carter Administration and the Congress enacted legislation ensuring the Social Security system's financial stability and making certain that each of the 35 million recipients received his or her monthly check without interruption. They also worked together to strengthen the benefits provided to Social Security recipients. As a result of our actions:

- Workers have been protected against inflation;
- Minimum benefit payments have been reformed to protect low-paid, long-time participants;
- A 3 percent increase in primary benefit amounts has been added;
- The retirement test has been liberalized.

Despite our efforts, much remains to be done if the elderly are to receive the respect and dignity they have earned. Elderly households have only half the income of younger households. For women, the annual median income of those over 65 is only $2,800. One out of seven persons over 65 lives in poverty. Three-quarters of all elderly unmarried, widowed, or divorced women live in poverty. Millions of elderly persons live in special fear of crime. Health care costs for the elderly are now three and a half times the level for younger people. Actual out-of-pocket health expenditures for the elderly today are greater in real dollars than when Medicare was enacted.

In the 1980s we must continue to work for a financially strong Social Security system. The levels and types of benefits, as well as rates and systems of financing, must be continually reviewed in light of current circumstances. Decisions affecting Social Security benefits should be measured by the standards of Social Security's goals, not by the program's impact on the federal budget.

The Democratic Party is responsible for the adjustments of Social Security benefits to keep pace with increases in the cost of living. We remain committed to ensuring that these adjustments continue. We oppose any caps on Social Security benefits. No change in the index which determines cost-of-living adjustments should be made for the purpose of achieving smaller adjustments than those granted under the current index.

We oppose efforts to raise the age at which Social Security benefits will be provided. Our Party seeks to protect and assist those most in need. We continue to be sensitive to the economic and physical plight of the older worker and the elderly. We therefore stand unalterably opposed to the taxation of any portion of Social Security benefits. Taxing Social Security benefits would mean real hardship for millions of retired Americans. If government needs to expand the tax base, additional taxation should be borne by those most able to pay.

While these steps are critically important, they will not, standing alone, secure adequate income for the elderly women of this nation. To reach this goal, we must also move immediately to eliminate all the gender-based classifications in the Social Security system. We must consider the special needs of elderly women in future benefit increases. We must end the unfairness in the current system that penalizes two-worker families. We must devise a practical way for the Social Security system to recognize the contributions of homemakers, and thus ensure the resources they need to live in dignity in old age.

Finally, the Democratic Party vehemently opposes all forms of age discrimination and commits itself to eliminating mandatory retirement. With the surety of a guillotine, mandatory retirement severs productive persons from their livelihood, shears their sense of self-worth, and squanders their talents.

Pensions

Our nation's complex and uneven pension system is a continuing source of concern. To help address this important problem, President Carter created a Presidential Commission on Pension Policy, charged with developing recommendations to improve public and private, federal, state and local pension systems. We applaud this initiative. We must achieve an equitable pension system with improved benefit safeguards and adequate benefit levels.

We urge the Commission to give special attention to recommendations which address the discrimination and hardships imposed on women in pension plans. Problem areas include pension rights in divorce pro-

ceedings, lack of pension benefits for survivors when a worker dies before retirement age, the rules for establishing Individual Retirement Accounts, the vesting rules and participation in pension plans.

We support strong programs of portability in teacher and other public employee retirement programs and private pension plans in order to offer employees involved in geographic employment moves the opportunity to continue retirement security.

Welfare Reform

The nation's welfare system continues to be inequitable and archaic. The existing organization of our delivery system is chaotic. The roles of the federal, state, and local governments, and of the courts, are scrambled, with each vying for power and control over delivery. This confusion lends credence to public outrage.

States and cities which make an honest effort to meet the welfare crisis find themselves in deepening fiscal difficulty. In the past few years, the federal share of welfare costs in many of these states has actually declined.

The fiscal crisis of welfare recipients has also deepened, since states and localities are unable or unwilling to adjust benefits to prevent inflation from robbing them of their worth.

The fiscal crisis for taxpayers continues, as states have little ability or incentive to reduce welfare error rates.

Incentives continue that cause families to break apart and fathers to leave home so that children may survive. Disincentives continue for welfare families to seek work on their own; no regular method links welfare recipients to the work force.

We are at a crossroads in the delivery of welfare. Serious reform is necessary if the inequities are to be remedied and administration improved.

The various components must be reorganized and simplified, with each level of government performing those services most suited to its organizational structure, taking advantage of economies allowed by large-scale delivery where appropriate, and of customized services where they are required, always treating each person with fairness and equity.

The components of an effective human service delivery system are these.

Employment

We must require work or necessary training leading to work of every capable person, except for the elderly and those responsible for the care of small children. However, we cannot make this requirement effective unless we can assure employment first through the private sector and, if that is insufficient, through public employment. We must provide an income floor both for the working poor and the poor not in the labor market. We must adopt a simple schedule of work incentives that guarantees equitable levels of assistance to the working poor.

The training and job program must emphasize supported work programs, in which welfare recipients receive intensive training, personnel counseling and help in the job search. Such services can lead to large increases in job placement, lower government expenditures and more productive workers.

Income Transfer

For those persons who cannot work and who have no independent means of support, we must provide assistance in an integrated, humane, dignified, and simple manner. These problems are national in scope and require a unified, national response.

Social Services

As society becomes more complex and faster-paced, people such as senior citizens, handicapped, children, families, and those who need protection are under greater pressure and find it more difficult to find the help they need. As these issues vary among communities, communities should take the lead in design and provision of these services.

Social services must continue to be developed and operated at the local level, close to the users, with knowledge of and sensitivity to both the particular problems of each case and the community's unique infrastructure, resources, and support networks.

We must develop a community-level system for coordinating existing public and voluntary programs that support the family and individual initiative, and develop programs to fill existing gaps in order to provide the variety and extent of social services appropriate for each locality.

Food Stamps

Hunger is one of the most debilitating and urgently felt human needs. A government pledged to a fairer distribution of wealth, income, and power, and to holding as a guiding concern the needs and aspirations of all, must also be a government which seeks to alleviate the hunger that results from economic conditions or personal circumstances. Over the years, the Food Stamp Program, expanded and made more responsive by a Democratic Congress and Administration, has become the bulwark of this nation's efforts to relieve hunger among its citizens.

The only form of assistance which is available to all those in financial need—food stamps—provides an important cushion for poor people, including those whose incomes are temporarily disrupted by layoffs or regional unemployment, or whose age or physical handicap leaves them unable to work.

As state and local governments modify other benefit programs on which low-income people depend, the Food Stamp Program becomes increasingly important. We will continue to work toward full employment in recognition of the importance of self-support. Until that goal can be attained, and for those who cannot be self-supporting, we remain committed to our current policy of full funding for the Food Stamp Program.

Medical Care

Provision of medical care for the poor remains essential. This is a critical part of the national health debate, and should be handled as such.

These reforms may require an additional investment, but they offer the prospect of stabilization of welfare costs over the long run, and the assurance that the objective of this expenditure will be accomplished.

Toward these goals, President Carter proposed welfare reform to the Congress in the form of the Work and Training Opportunities Act and the Social Welfare Reform Amendments Act. These two Acts would lift over two million people out of poverty by providing assistance to individuals and families to enable them to meet minimum income standards and by providing employment to those able to work. We must continue to work to ensure the passage of these two very important acts.

As a means of providing immediate federal fiscal relief to state and local governments, the federal government will assume the local government's burden of welfare costs. Further, there should be a phased reduction in the states' share of welfare costs in the immediate future.

The Democratic Party pledges in the immediate future to introduce legislation to accomplish these purposes in the next year.

Welfare policies significantly affect families. Most persons receiving Aid to Families with Dependent Children, for example, are children or the mothers of young children. Many of these young mothers want to work. So, too, many others receiving welfare are well-suited to work and want to work. A companion to any effective welfare reform must be provision for adequate and available child care, so that parents can participate in training programs and in the work force.

Government should not encourage the break-up of intact families. On the contrary, we must provide the help a family needs to survive a crisis together. In 1962, America took an action which has been one of the greatest contributors to family stability in the history of federal policy. For the first time, states were permitted to provide assistance to families with both parents, and still be eligible for federal reimbursement. We reaffirm our support for the 1962 action and urge that states not providing assistance to unified families begin to do so. We must treat stable and broken families equally.

The thirty-day waiting period for placement on the welfare rolls poses serious problems for individuals and families in dire need of assistance. We support efforts to streamline processing of new welfare recipients which also attempt to address the problem of administrative errors. Simplified rules and better administrative machinery would significantly improve the operation of the welfare system.

We strongly reject the Republican Platform proposal to transfer the responsibility for funding welfare costs entirely to the states. Such a proposal would not only worsen the fiscal situation of state and local governments, but would also lead to reduced benefits and services to those dependent on welfare programs. The Democratic policy is exactly the opposite—to provide greater assistance to state and local governments for their welfare costs and to improve benefits and services for those dependent on welfare.

Low-Income Energy Assistance

Our citizens see their family budgets stretched to the breaking point by an explosion of energy costs, while the profits of oil companies multiply to record levels. Last year's 120 percent increase in energy prices by OPEC led to a drastic decrease in the ability of needy families to pay for other necessities of life. The recently enacted low-income energy assistance legislation is helping, but it is providing only $1 of help for every $4 in increased costs that have been imposed upon the poor. Significant expansion of this program is urgently needed, and we support such action as a major priority of our Party.

Veterans

This Administration has worked to strengthen the federal government's commitment to our nation's veterans. The Veterans Administration has been given Cabinet-level participation. There have been three consecutive annual increases in VA compensation. The Veterans' and Survivors' Pension Improvement Act has assured veterans of an adequate minimum income. A treatment and rehabilitation program has been established for veterans with alcohol and drug-

dependency disabilities. G.I. educational benefits have been considerably expanded. Unemployment among Vietnam veterans has been reduced. Veterans' health care has been improved. A process has been initiated for veterans to upgrade less than honorable discharges from the Vietnam War era.

During the 1980s, we must commit ourselves to:

- Equal opportunity and full voluntary participation in the military regardless of sex. We oppose quotas and/or percentages, rules, policies and practices which restrict or bar women from equal access to educational training and employment benefits which accrue during and after military service.
- Continue improving education and training benefits and opportunities for veterans, especially those who are economically or educationally disadvantaged and those who are disabled.
- Initiate and complete comprehensive epidemiological studies on veterans exposed to certain defoliants used during the Vietnam War as well as on veterans or civilians exposed to above-ground nuclear explosion. We then must establish appropriate and sensitive VA health care programs for those determined to have suffered from such exposure or service.
- Complete promptly the current Cabinet-level study on Agent Orange.
- Strive to maintain and improve quality health care in an independent VA health care system.
- Continue priority care to veterans with service-connected disabilities and seek ways of improving and developing special treatment for the ever-increasing aging veterans population, including burial benefit programs sensitive to the needs of veterans and their families in rural areas.
- Provide authority for the construction of a memorial in the nation's capital to those who died in service to their country in Southeast Asia.

Education

Perhaps the single most important factor in spurring productivity in our society is a skilled work force. We must begin to think of federal expenditures as capital investments, favoring those which are productive and which reduce future costs. In this context, education must be one of our highest priorities. Education is also the indispensable prerequisite for effective democracy. As Daniel Webster said, "On the diffusion of education among people rests the preservation and perpetuation of free institutions."

The Democratic Party is strongly committed to education as the best hope for America's future. We applaud the leadership taken by a Democratic President and a Democratic Congress in strengthening federal programs for education.

In the past four years:

- Federal aid to education has increased by 73 percent—the greatest income increase in such a short period in our history.
- Strong financial and administrative support has been provided for programs that enhance educational opportunities for women, minorities, American Indians and other native Americans, the handicapped, and students with limited English-speaking ability and other special needs;
- The Middle Income Student Assistance Act was adopted, expanding eligibility for need-based student financial aid to approximately one-third of the students enrolled in post-secondary education;
- A number of legislative, regulatory, and other administrative actions were taken to enhance benefits received by private school children from federal education programs; and
- A new Department of Education was created to give education a stronger, more direct voice at the federal level, while at the same time reserving control over educational policy-making and operations to states, localities, and public and private institutions.

Over the next four years, we pledge to continue our strong commitment to education. We will continue to support the Department of Education and assist in its all-important educational enterprise that involves three out of ten Americans.

In this regard, we endorse the language of the legislation which emphasized the intent of Congress "to protect the rights of state and local governments and public and private institutions in the areas of educational policies and administration of programs. . . ."

It is now a decade and a half since the passage—by a Democratic Congress at the behest of a Democratic Administration—of the landmark Elementary and Secondary Education Act of 1965. At the time, there were sound and compelling reasons to undergird all federal aid to education with specific purposes. The specific purposes remain compelling and the specific programs addressed to them must be maintained.

Federal aid to education plays a significant role in guaranteeing that jurisdictions of differing financial capacity can spend equal amounts on schooling. We favor a steady increase in federal support with an emphasis on reducing inter- and intrastate disparities in ability to support quality education. The federal government and the states should be encouraged to equal-

ize or take over educational expenses, relieving the overburdened property taxpayer.

The Democratic Party renews its commitment to eliminating discrimination in education because of sex and demands full and expeditious enforcement of Title IX of the 1972 education amendments.

The Democratic Party strongly urges that the federal government be sensitive to mandating state and local programs without adequate provision for funding. Such mandates force the state and/or local governments to increase taxes to fund such required programs.

Equal educational opportunity is at the heart of the Democratic program for education. Equality of opportunity must sometimes translate to compensatory efforts. For the disadvantaged, the handicapped, those with limited English-language skills, American Indians/Alaska Natives, Native Hawaiians, and other minorities, compensatory programs require concentrated federal spending.

The Democratic Administration and Congress have supported a comprehensive program of compensatory education and have expanded it to include secondary education. We will continue to target categorical assistance to low-income and low-achieving students.

We reaffirm our strong support for Title I concentration grants for remedial instruction for low income students. The Democratic Party pledges to achieve full funding of concentration grants under Title I and to expand the Head Start and Follow-through programs.

The Democratic Party will continue to advocate quality education in the Bureau of Indian Affairs and in tribally contracted schools to meet American Indian educational needs. The Democratic Party opposes the closing of schools serving American Indians and Alaska Natives without consultation with the tribes involved.

The Democratic Party recognizes the need to maintain quality education for children in school districts affected by federal activities and installations. We therefore will continue to be sensitive to the financial problems of these school districts.

School desegregation is an important tool in the effort to give all children equal educational opportunity. The Democratic Party continues to support programs aimed at achieving communities integrated both in terms of race and economic class through constitutional means. We encourage redrawing of attendance lines, pairing of schools, utilizing the "magnet school concept" as much as possible, and enforcing fair housing standards. Mandatory transportation of students beyond their neighborhoods for the purpose of desegregation remains a judicial tool of last resort.

We call for strict compliance with civil rights requirements in hiring and promotion in school systems.

We support an effective bilingual program to reach all limited-English-proficiency people who need such assistance.

The Democratic Party supports efforts to broaden students' knowledge and appreciation of other cultures, languages and countries.

We also support vocational and technical education through increased support for teacher training, personnel development, and upgrading and modernizing equipment and facilities to provide the skill and technical training to meet the work force needs for business, industry, and government services. Increased emphasis on basic skills is essential to the success of vocational and technical training. Vocational and technical education is a viable tool for establishing people in their own business through entrepreneurship programs. Vocational and technical education contributes to the economic development and productivity of our nation by offering every person an opportunity to develop a marketable skill.

The Party reaffirms its support of public school education and would not support any program or legislation that would create or promote economic, sociological or racial segregation. Our primary purpose in assisting elementary and secondary education must be to assure a quality public school system for all students.

Private schools, particularly parochial schools, are also an important part of our diverse educational system. The Party accepts its commitment to the support of a constitutionally acceptable method of providing tax aid for the education of all pupils in schools which do not racially discriminate, and excluding so-called segregation academies. Specifically, the Party will continue to advocate constitutionally permissible federal education legislation which provides for the equitable participation in federal programs of all low- and moderate-income pupils.

The Democratic Party reaffirms its commitment to the concept and promise that every handicapped child should have a full and appropriate public education in the least restrictive environment. To assure the best placement and program for handicapped students, we support maximum involvement of the regular classroom teacher in placement planning for handicapped students with assurance of barrier-free access. We further support increasing the federal share of the costs of education for the handicapped.

We applaud the actions taken by the government in strengthening federal programs for higher education. The nation must continue to ensure that our colleges and universities can provide quality higher education in the coming period of declining enrollment and rising operating costs.

We are especially interested in extending post-secondary opportunities to students from low- and middle-income families, older students, and minorities. We believe that no able student should be denied a college education for reasons of cost.

The Democratic Party is committed to a federal scholarship program adequate to meet the needs of all the underprivileged who could benefit from a college education. When those who are qualified for post-secondary education cannot afford to enter college, the nation ignores talent we cannot afford to lose. Basic Education Opportunity Grants, which offer both access to a college education and the choice of a college, must continue to be strengthened and should be funded at full payment schedule.

Likewise, campus-based programs of aid must be supported. With a coordinated and reliable system of grants, loans and work study, we can relieve the crisis in costs that could close all but the affluent colleges and universities.

Since entry to institutions of higher learning is dependent upon a student's score on a standardized test, we support testing legislation which will assure that students will receive sufficient information relative to their performance on the test to determine their strengths and weaknesses on the tests.

Our institutions of higher education deserve both public and private backing. The Party supports the continuation of tax deductions for charitable gifts, recognizing that such gifts represent the margin of excellence in higher education and foster scholarly independence within our institutions of higher learning.

The Democratic Party commits itself to the strengthening of graduate education and the support of basic and applied research. Graduate education, scholarship and research are of immense importance to the nation's economic and cultural development. Universities conduct most of the nation's basic research. Their graduate and research programs are the training grounds for the research personnel and professionals who discover knowledge and translate that knowledge into action.

The federal role is critical to the quality of these endeavors. We reaffirm the federal responsibility for stable support of knowledge production and development of highly trained personnel in all areas of fundamental scientific and intellectual knowledge to meet social needs.

High priority should be assigned to strengthening the national structure for graduate education, scholarship and research and ensuring that the most talented students, especially women and minorities, can gain access to these programs.

Historically Black colleges and universities have

played a pivotal role in educating minority students. The Democratic Party affirms its commitment to ensuring the financial viability and independence of these worthy institutions and supports expanded funding for Black institutions. The Democratic Party pledges to work vigorously for significant increases in programs which have traditionally provided funding for historically Black colleges and universities. Particular attention should be given to substantially increasing the share of funding Black colleges receive. We will substantially increase the level of participation of Black colleges in all federal programs for which they are eligible. In addition, we urge the establishment of an office within the Office of the Secretary of Education to ensure full executive implementation of the President's Black College Directive. Similarly, colleges serving Hispanic, American Indian/Alaska Native, and Asian/Pacific Islander students should receive equal consideration in federal policies affecting their survival.

Finally, educational quality should be strengthened through adequate support for libraries, federal leadership in educational research and development, and improved teacher training.

The Democratic Party further urges the federal government to take into account the geographical barriers to access to educational and library materials which particularly affect the non-contiguous territories of the United States. A study should be conducted to review the possibility of sending airmail, at surface mail rates, to and from the mainland U.S. and the non-contiguous territories of the U.S.

The Party believes that improved teacher in-service training, building upon the successful "Teacher Center Model" implemented under this Administration, could contribute substantially to educational quality. We support the establishment of federally funded teacher centers in every state and will work toward a steady increase in the number of teachers served. Teacher centers should address such issues as bilingual, multicultural, non-racist, and non-sexist curricula.

The Party continues to support adult education and training to upgrade basic skills.

We propose federally financed family-centered developmental and educational child care programs available to all who need and desire them.

We support efforts to provide for the basic nutritional needs of students. We support the availability of nutritious school breakfast, milk and lunch programs. Students who are hungry or malnourished can experience serious learning difficulties. The Democratic Party affirms its commitment to restore fair eligibility requirements for this program and to set fees at a level which does not unfairly deny students the ability to participate.

The Democratic Party recognizes the importance of family and community involvement in public schools, and the impact their involvement can have on the quality of a child's educational environment. We support initiatives that will encourage parents and all members of the community to take an active interest in the educational future of our children.

Child Care

While the American family structure has changed radically in recent years, the family remains the key unit of our society. When the needs of families and children are ignored, the nation as a whole ultimately suffers. It is not only morally right, but also far less expensive, for government to assist children in growing up whole, strong and able, than to pay the bill later for children and adults with health, social and educational problems. Government cannot and should not attempt to displace the responsibilities of the family; to the contrary, the challenge is to formulate policies which will strengthen the family.

The Democratic Party shall seek vigorously to enact an adequately funded, comprehensive quality child-care program based upon a national commitment to meet the health, safety, and educational needs of *all* children. Such a program shall provide for alternative low-cost child care arrangements so that parents may decide what is in the best interests of their children. To ensure the availability of choices, the Child Care Tax Credit shall be revised to benefit low- and moderate-income families. National policies shall ensure the availability of child care services for all parents. Our programs shall also address themselves vigorously to the issues of flex-time work programs, job sharing, and incentives for child care in private industry, in recognition of the social responsibilities of all citizens to children and their parents as the guardians of our future.

Juvenile Justice

Juvenile delinquency and other problems of young people, like truancy and running away, are often manifestations of serious problems in other areas—family, school, employment, or emotional disturbance. We are committed to maintaining and strengthening the juvenile justice and Delinquency Prevention Act of 1974 and the Runaway Youth Act to help deal with these problems. In particular, we reaffirm our commitment to ending unnecessary institutionalization of young people who have not committed serious crimes and strengthening preventive efforts and other services at the community level to help young people and their families in the sometimes difficult transition to adulthood. Equally important, we are committed to continuing reform in the juvenile courts to assure right of due process and adequate counsel to young people who become enmeshed in the juvenile justice system.

We must continue and strengthen efforts at prison reform to upgrade the safety of our penal institutions. Our penal institutions enhance rehabilitation to offenders, and lower the recidivism level.

Families

The Democratic Party supports efforts to make federal programs more sensitive to the needs of the family, in all its diverse forms.

Housing

Since 1976, the Administration's efforts in the area of housing have concentrated on achieving an adequate housing supply. From 1977–1979, housing starts increased substantially over the level of the prior Republican Administration. Additionally, increased emphasis has been placed on saving our existing housing stock through rehabilitation.

But the momentum to increase the housing supply for the 1980s has been threatened by the high rate of inflation. The downturn in economic activity during the first half of 1980 has created a period of severe difficulty for the housing industry and for those Americans in need of housing. These circumstances make it imperative that the Democratic Party redouble its efforts to meet the goal of a decent home in a suitable environment for every citizen. It is essential that we expand the construction and availability of affordable housing in order to match the growing needs of Americans during the 1980s and to help stabilize housing costs.

Housing shortages and deterioration, and the need for economic development, are among the most critical problems facing local government today.

Through a patchwork of programs and tax incentives developed over the past fifty years, this nation is now spending between $25 and $30 billion each year on housing and economic development. These funds must be redirected in a cogent manner, to provide a comprehensive response to the housing problem. This effort should be pressed forward with the same national will that put a man on the moon, and will be a major step toward the revitalization of our local economies.

During the 1980s, we must work to meet the nation's need for available, affordable housing by:

- Achieving steady, high levels of production;
- Continuing progress toward a non-inflationary environment with lower interest rates;
- Pursuing monetary and credit policies which are especially sensitive to the needs of the housing and construction industries in order to help provide jobs;
- Continuing progress toward eliminating substandard housing and meeting the housing needs of this nation's low- and moderate-income families, the elderly, and the handicapped, including a substantial increase in the authorization for public housing and Section 8 rental housing assistance;
- Expanding the coverage of the Fair Housing laws to prohibit discrimination against single parents or single persons;
- Ensuring that federal housing projects meet the needs of single-parent families;
- Strengthening our efforts to provide higher levels of multi-family housing production to meet the rental housing needs of the postwar generation in the 1980s;
- Continuing the development and expansion of new financial instruments designed to attract increased capital to the housing sector throughout the interest rate cycle;
- Continuing to improve the efficiency and management of our housing programs;
- Continuing support for efforts to improve our housing codes;
- Expanding urban homestead and rehabilitation programs which will preserve neighborhoods in our cities for the people who live there;
- Financing moderate-income housing at below-market interest rates;
- Adopting condominium conversion policies which protect tenants, particularly the elderly, against unfair and unreasonable conversion practices; and
- Assisting cities, counties, and states which have effective programs to combat the growing and dangerous problem of housing abandonment.

Transportation

Since 1977, the Carter Administration has worked closely with the Congress to improve all the transportation modes so essential to our nation. These efforts have resulted in the elimination of unnecessary regulations, the expansion of the federal commitment to mass transit, and the savings of billions of dollars for consumers. In the 1980s we must continue our efforts in the same direction.

The Democratic Party commits itself to a balanced, competitive transportation system for the efficient movement of people and goods.

The trucking industry must be deregulated, and legislation to do that is now in place. This legislation would open entry to new truckers, lift restrictions on the goods truckers may haul and the routes they may use, promote vigorous price competition, reduce regulatory delays and improve road safety.

To improve their long-term viability, we must give railroads more flexibility in setting rates, without burdening excessively shippers dependent on rail service. Congress is now progressing on comprehensive legislation in this area. We expect regulatory reform of the railroad industry to speed the elimination of wasteful regulations and improve the facilities and equipment of railroads.

Coal is a centerpiece of our nation's energy policy. We are concerned about the cost of transporting coal to its markets, particularly the cost of rail transportation. Within the context of regulatory reform, we must therefore be especially sensitive to the effects of railroad rates on coal. A healthy rail industry is of critical importance to our economy and our society.

We must ensure, through such efforts as completion of high-speed rail passenger service in the Northeast Corridor, that railroads are an efficient means for personal travel. The decline in the nation's railroad system must be reversed. Tracks must be rehabilitated, equipment modernized and maintenance improved if the nation is to have a rail system that adequately meets the needs of passengers and shippers. We must ensure that flexibility in setting rates does not become a license either for anti-competitive pricing at the expense of consumers, or for anti-competitive mergers that create or maintain inordinate market power at the expense of consumers.

The vital artery of urban America is mass transit. It saves energy by providing fuel-efficient alternatives to the automobile. For the poor, the elderly, the disabled, and many other city dwellers, there is no other transportation. If they are to travel at all, to go to work or to shop, they must rely on mass transit. Mass transit serves them, as well as the employers for whom they work and the businesses where they shop. It aids all of us, by unclogging our cities, cleansing our air, and increasing the economic health of our urban areas.

The Democratic Party pledges to strengthen the nation's mass transit systems. Federal funds must be provided for maintenance and repair of deteriorating systems, and for new equipment purchases for growing systems, Federal aid formulae should be amended to give greater weight to ridership in the allocation of dollars. Reasonable operating subsidies must be provided to help subsidize rider fares.

Mass transit is a high priority in our national transportation policy. We pledge support for significant increases in capital and operating subsidies for mass transit, to enhance the reliability, safety, and affordability of existing and expanding systems.

The auto industry and its workers must be assisted during this difficult time. We are committed to an intensive review of the automobile industry's fundamental problems, and to prompt, effective action to help ameliorate those problems. We are also committed to a strong trade adjustment program to help currently unemployed auto workers.

To meet the needs of international commerce and national security, this nation must have a strong, competitive and efficient American-flag ocean transportation system. In recent years, there has been a significant reduction in the ability of our merchant marine to compete for the carriage of world commerce because of economic policies pursued by other nations. Action must be taken to revitalize our merchant marine.

To achieve this objective, we must develop a coherent, consistent, and responsive maritime policy which will encourage the development and maintenance of an American-flag ocean transportation system, staffed with trained and efficient American personnel, and capable of carrying a substantial portion of our international trade in a competitive and efficient manner. Our maritime policy must also lead to the development and maintenance of a domestic shipbuilding and ship repair mobilization base adequate to satisfy the commercial and national security requirements of the United States. Furthermore, we pledge continued commitment to the Merchant Marine Act of 1970 and greater utilization of the private merchant marine by the Navy for its support functions.

Urban Policy

During the campaign of 1975–1976, our nation's great cities and urban counties were mired in a depression. Unemployment was well above 10 percent in many cities and counties; private sector investment and jobs were leaving the great urban centers; poverty and other serious social problems were left unattended; a severe budget squeeze was causing layoffs and cutbacks in essential city services; and the public works of our cities had been allowed to decay. The nation's mayors spent a portion of the year urging Congress to override the Republican Administration's veto of vitally important anti-recession programs. Most seriously, the leadership and citizens of our great urban centers had lost the hope that the future would be better.

Upon taking office, the Democratic Administration responded to these conditions immediately with an $11 billion anti-recession package and, one year later, with the nation's first comprehensive urban policy. The urban policy was the product of a unique effort which actively involved the elected officials of state and local government, representatives of labor, neighborhood organizations, civil rights groups and the members of Congress.

These deliberations produced a blueprint to guide federal action toward cities. The Democratic Administration, in partnership with the Democratic Congress, has moved aggressively to implement parts of the urban policy. Some of these programs have already begun to contribute to the revitalization of the nation's older cities and to assure the continued health of the nation's growing cities. For example, the urban policy has:

- Created the Urban Development Action Grant (UDAG) Program to encourage private investment and jobs to locate or remain in our nation's major cities. UDAG, which is funded at $675 million annually, has already leveraged more than $7 billion of private investment and created more than 200,000 permanent jobs;
- Targeted federal government procurement, facilities and jobs to the high-unemployment central cities;
- Increased funding for the Community Development Block Grant program by more than 30 percent and proposed a formula change that provides substantial new aid to the older, more distressed cities and urban counties; and
- Proposed a massive increase in the urban development programs of the Economic Development Administration.

Although many gains have been made, we recognize that a great deal more remains to be done. This is especially true in those cities which have borne the brunt of the current recession. We recognize that no urban policy can completely succeed in a period of high inflation and deepening recession.

In this platform, the Democratic Party dedicates itself to the strength and survival of urban America. We are committed to developing imaginative, compassionate steps to deal with the causes and effects of rising unemployment, to make our cities fiscally strong, to provide jobs and economic growth, to preserve neighborhoods and communities and to meet the basic human needs of urban residents.

Our policies must include the following features:

- A strong jobs policy which supports productive employment of people in the public sector and encourages employment in the private sector by attracting and strengthening business in the cities. This jobs policy—and the need to guarantee a job for every American who is able to work—is our single highest domestic priority, and will take precedence over all other domestic priorities.
- Public works programs which help rebuild our cities' infrastructure and which provide the unemployed with the opportunity to rebuild their own neighborhoods;
- Incentives for energy conservation by residents, business and industry in urban areas including incentives to convert oil facilities to coal and the construction of new coal-fired replacement plants;
- Increased education and training programs with special attention to employment of youth, women, and minorities and to training people for private sector jobs;
- National economic policies intended to maintain growth in our economy and reduce the inflation rate, thereby easing the fiscal burden on cities and their residents;
- Prompt enactment of the Carter Administration's proposal to expand the economic development initiative programs of the Department of Commerce. When fully implemented, this initiative will provide more than $1 billion in new loan guarantees to our urban centers and will double the amount of economic development grants available;
- Prompt enactment of the Administration's five-year extension of the local government revenue sharing program, including a $500 million transitional aid program for the areas most in need;
- A serious examination of the urban impact of the federal tax code, to ensure that businesses have substantial incentives to invest in our nation's neediest locales; and
- Renewed efforts to consolidate existing grants-in-aid programs in order to provide state and local governments with the flexibility to use these programs efficiently.

In the last analysis, we must recognize that America's cities are centers of people with needs—needs for jobs, decent housing and health care, affordable mass transit, quality education and streets where they can walk in safety. Each is a crucial part of any effective urban program. The Democratic Party is committed to placing the highest priority in our budgets and our programs on meeting these needs of city-dwellers.

Neighborhoods

From the beginning of the Carter Administration, the government has worked to revitalize neighborhoods and to make them a central component of urban life. As a result of these efforts, the federal government now has a strong neighborhoods policy.

During the 1980s we must continue to strengthen neighborhoods by:

- Making neighborhood organizations partners with government and private sectors in neighborhood revitalization projects;
- Continuing to make neighborhood concerns a major element of our urban policy;
- Developing urban revitalization programs that can be achieved without displacing neighborhood residents; and
- Continuing to reduce discriminatory redlining practices in the mortgage and insurance industries.

Small Community and Rural Development

This Democratic Administration instituted the nation's first comprehensive small community and rural development policy. This policy establishes specific goals, directs numerous organizational and management changes, and initiates an extensive program of action to improve the quality of life for all rural Americans including American Indians/Alaska Natives, rural Hispanics, rural Blacks, and other minorities. Its principles emphasize the need for a strong partnership between the public and private sectors and among all levels of government. Recognizing rural America's great diversity and the limits of the federal role, the Administration's policy invites the nation's governors to establish rural affairs councils to define state rural development strategies and to advance federal–state coordination in addressing priority needs.

Since assuming office in 1977, the Democratic Administration has acted to increase rural access to credit and capital, expand job opportunities, alleviate persistent rural poverty, rehabilitate substandard housing, address the shortage of health professionals in rural areas, improve the mobility of the rural transportation disadvantaged, and enhance educational and training opportunities for disadvantaged rural youth. For example, we have:

- Addressed the problem of substandard housing through substantial increases in rural housing and community development assistance, and through revisions in minimum property standards to permit housing construction which is less expensive and better suited to rural conditions.

- Improved rural access to credit and capital by tripling the economic development resources of the Farmers Home Administration.
- Alleviated rural unemployment by doubling Department of Labor employment and training assistance to rural areas.
- Addressed the shortage of doctors and other health professionals in rural areas through the Rural Health Clinic Services Act and a special initiative to construct 300 rural primary care health clinics by the end of 1981 in medically underserved areas.

For the future, we must move aggressively to address longstanding rural problems and to implement fully the Administration's small-community and rural development policy, with emphasis on:

- Synthesizing efforts to improve the quality of life for American Indians/Alaska Natives. We must provide incentives for the development of an economic base that will improve the quality of life on reservations;
- Ensuring that federal programs are administered in ways which encourage local solutions to local problems; target assistance to communities and individuals most in need; make federal investments in ways that leverage private sector investments and complement local and tribal investments; and make federal programs more accessible to rural jurisdictions, better adapted to rural circumstances and needs, and better coordinated in their administration and delivery;
- Promoting rural energy self-sufficiency through improved rural transit and the application of alternative energy technologies on farms and in our rural homes and communities;
- Passing satisfactory welfare reform legislation, with special attention to the needs of the rural disadvantaged;
- Protecting prime agricultural land as rural populations and the rural economy continue to grow;
- Continuing to upgrade substandard rural housing to make it safe, decent, and sanitary;
- Giving full attention to the health, education, and other basic needs of rural citizens, especially the young, the old, and the poor; and
- Providing low-cost electric and telephone services to rural areas through the Rural Electrification Administration and the hundreds of rural cooperatives that provide these services.

Science and Technology

The Nixon–Ford Administration permitted serious decline in the state of science and technology in our country.

There had been a decade of erosion of federal support of research and development. The funding of basic research in particular was far below its peak level of the mid-1960s.

Science and technology advice had been seriously downgraded and removed from the White House, until pressures from the science and engineering community had it restored through an act of Congress.

The previous decline in support had affected opportunities in science and engineering. It had resulted in the inadequate replacement of facilities and instrumentation and their growing obsolescence in the face of new scientific advances and needs.

Not only the work of our academic research centers, but also our technological innovation and economic competitiveness were impaired by this erosion of federal support.

To counter these conditions and help revitalize the country's science and technology, the Carter Administration, working with Congress, has taken a number of steps. The Office of Science and Technology Policy has been strengthened and upgraded. Growth has been restored in the budgets for federal research and development activities. Basic biomedical research has been strengthened to increase our fundamental knowledge of health and disease.

These are just a few of the innovations that have been made. Our scientific and technological agenda remains unfinished. The 1980s offer great promise. During the next four years, we will work to:

- Continue to strengthen our science and technology and provide for continuity and stability of support to research and development;
- Continue to monitor the flow of talent into science and engineering and provide the appropriate training and opportunities to ensure an adequate number of well-trained scientists and engineers in the coming years, with particular emphasis on women and minorities;
- Pay continued attention to the support of research facilities to make certain they remain among the best in the world;
- Successfully launch the Space Shuttle, take advantage of the many opportunities it offers to make space activities more economic and productive, and release new resources for the future scientific exploration of space; and
- Expand our programs of cooperation in science and technology with all nations who seek development and a stable, peaceful world.

In sum, we must continue to expand our scientific and technological capabilities and apply them to the needs of people everywhere.

Arts and the Humanities

The arts and humanities are a precious national resource.

Federal commitment to the arts and humanities has been strengthened since 1977 by expanding government funding and services to arts institutions, individual artists, scholars, and teachers. The budgets for the National Endowment for the Arts and the National Endowment for the Humanities have increased substantially. The Federal Council on the Arts and Humanities has been reactivated. Policies of the Carter Administration have fostered high standards of creativity across our nation. The Administration has encouraged the arts and humanities through appropriate federal programs for the citizens of our smallest communities, as well as those of our largest cities. During the 1980s, the Party is committed to:

- Continuing federal encouragement and support for institutions relating to the arts and to learning in the humanities;
- Encouraging business participation in a comprehensive effort to achieve a truly mixed economy of support for the arts and humanities by individuals, foundations, corporations and governments at every level;
- Exploring a variety of mechanisms to nurture the creative talent of our citizens and build audiences for their work;
- Supporting strong, active National Endowments both for the Arts and the Humanities, and strengthening the Public Broadcasting System; and
- Seeking greater recognition for the rich cultural tradition of the nation's minorities. We will work to meet the cultural needs of minorities, encourage their greater participation in the performing arts on a national level, and provide grants for the arts in low-income neighborhoods.

ENSURING BASIC RIGHTS AND LIBERTIES

Equal Rights Amendment

The Democratic Party recognizes that every issue of importance to this nation and its future concerns women as well as men. As workers and consumers, as parents and heads of households, women are vitally concerned with the economy, energy, foreign policy, and every other issue addressed in this platform. The concerns of women cannot be limited to a portion to the platform; they must be reflected in every section of our Party's policy.

There is, however, a particular concern of women which deserves special emphasis—their entitlement to full equality in our society.

Women are a majority of the population. Yet their equality is not recognized in the Constitution or enforced as the law of the land. The choices faced by women—such as whether to seek employment or work at home, what career or profession to enter, and how to combine employment and family responsibilities continue to be circumscribed by stereotypes and prejudices. Minority women face the dual discrimination of racism and sexism.

In the 1980s, the Democratic Party commits itself to a Constitution, economy, and society open to women on an equal basis with men.

The primary route to that new horizon is ratification of the Equal Rights Amendment. A Democratic Congress, working with women's leaders, labor, civil and religious organizations, first enacted ERA in Congress and later extended the deadline for ratification. Now, the Democratic Party must ensure that ERA at last becomes the 27th Amendment to the Constitution. We oppose efforts to rescind ERA in states which have already ratified the amendment, and we shall insist that past rescisions are invalid.

In view of the high priority which the Democratic Party places on ratification of the ERA, the Democratic National Committee renews its commitment not to hold national or multi-state meetings, conferences, or conventions in states which have not yet ratified the ERA. The Democratic Party shall withhold financial support and technical campaign assistance from candidates who do not support the ERA. The Democratic Party further urges all national organizations to support the boycott of the unratified states by not holding national meetings, conferences, or conventions in those states.

Furthermore, the Democratic Party shall seek to eliminate sex-based discrimination and inequities from all aspects of our society.

Civil Rights

The Democratic Party firmly commits itself to protect the civil rights of every citizen and to pursue justice and equal treatment under the law for all citizens.

In the 1960s, enormous progress was made in authorizing civil rights for all our citizens. In many areas, the promises of the civil rights efforts of the 1960s have been met, but much more remains to be done.

An effective affirmative action program is an essential component of our commitment to expanding civil rights projections. The federal government must be a model for private employers, making special efforts in recruitment, training, and promotion to aid minority Americans in overcoming both the historic patterns and the historic burdens of discrimination.

We call on the public and private sectors to live up to and enforce all civil rights laws and regulations, i.e., Equal Employment Opportunity Programs, Title VI and Title VII of the Civil Rights Act, the Fair Housing Laws, and affirmative action requirements.

We advocate strengthening the Office of Civil Rights in the Department of Education and in the Department of Health and Human Resources.

We oppose efforts to undermine the Supreme Court's historic mandate of school desegregation, and we support affirmative action goals to overturn patterns of discrimination in education and employment.

Ethnic, racial and other minorities continue to be victims of police abuse, persistent harassment and excessive use of force. In 1979, the Community Relations Service of the Department of Justice noted that "alleged use of deadly force by police and the reaction of minorities was a major cause of racial unrest in the nation in 1978." In response to this finding:

- We call for the Department of Justice's Civil Rights Division to develop uniform federal guidelines and penalties for the use of undue force by local law enforcement agencies;
- We call for the Department of Justice's Civil Rights Division to establish civil rights units at appropriate U.S. Attorneys' offices; and
- We call on the Department of Justice to move concurrently with federal prosecutors so that if a failure to obtain conviction takes place at the state or local level, federal prosecution can occur swiftly.

The Democratic Party strongly condemns the Ku Klux Klan and the American Nazi Party. We pledge vigorous federal prosecution of actions by the Klan and American Nazi Party that violate federal law, including the creation of such laws in jurisdictions where they do not exist. We further condemn those acts, symbols, and rituals, including cross-burnings, associated with anti–civil rights activities. We urge every state and local government to pursue vigorous prosecution of actions by the Klan and Nazi Party that violate state or local law.

The Democratic Party asserts that the Immigration and Naturalization Service, in enforcing the immigration laws, must recognize its obligation to respect fully the human and constitutional rights of all within our borders. Such respect must include an end to practices affecting Hispanic, Caribbean, and Asian/Pacific American communities such as "neighborhood sweeps" and stop-and-search procedures which are discriminatory or without probable cause.

Our commitment to civil rights embraces not only a commitment to legal equality, but a commitment to economic justice as well. It embraces a recognition of the right of every citizen—Black and Hispanic, American Indian and Alaska Native, Asian/Pacific Americans, and the majority who are women—to a fair share in our economy. When that opportunity is denied, and the promise of social justice is unfulfilled, the risks of tension and disorder in our cities are increased. The Democratic Party condemns violence and civil disorder wherever they occur. But we also pledge to attack the underlying injustices that contribute to such violence so that no person need feel condemned to a life of poverty and despair.

The Democratic record provides a solid basis for future progress. There should be little doubt that virtually no progress would occur under a Republican Administration. Over the next four years, our Party must strengthen and improve what has already been accomplished.

Both the ERA and District of Columbia Voting Rights Amendments to the Constitution must be ratified and our full commitment must be given to those efforts.

The Fair Housing Act must be amended to give the Department of Housing and Urban Development greater enforcement ability, including cease-and-desist authority.

The Equal Pay and the Age Discrimination Acts must be strongly and effectively enforced by the Equal Employment Opportunity Commission.

To end discrimination against language minorities, we must enforce vigorously the amendments to the Voting Rights Act of 1975 to assist Hispanic citizens. We must recognize the value of cultural diversity in education, expand bilingual facilities, and guarantee full protection of the civil and human rights of all workers.

We must affirm the dignity of all people and the right of each individual to have equal access to and participation in the institutions and services of our society. All groups must be protected from discrimination based on race, color, religion, national origin, language, age, sex or sexual orientation. This includes specifically the right of foreign citizens to enter this country. Appropriate legislative and administrative actions to achieve these goals should be undertaken.

We are concerned about the opportunity for minorities to be adequately represented on trial juries if the trend toward smaller juries continues. Efforts must be initiated to correct this possible underrepresentation.

Civil Liberties

The Democratic Party has been actively committed to protecting fundamental civil liberties. Toward that end,

over the past four years, the Carter Administration and the Democratic Congress have enacted legislation to control the use of wiretaps by the government in the pursuit of foreign intelligence; developed the government's first comprehensive program to protect privacy; and worked to enact a criminal code which scrupulously protects civil liberties.

As we enter the 1980s, we must enact grand jury reform; revise the Uniform Code of Military justice; enact charters for the FBI and the intelligence agencies which recognize vital civil liberty concerns while enabling those agencies to perform their important national security tasks; shape legislation to overturn the Supreme Court *Stanford Daily* decision; and enact a criminal code which meets the very real concerns about protecting civil liberties, and which does not interfere with existing workers' rights.

We call for passage of legislation to charter the purposes, prerogatives, and restraints on the Federal Bureau of Investigation, the Central Intelligence Agency, and other intelligence agencies of government with full protection for the civil rights and liberties of American citizens living at home or abroad. Under no circumstances should American citizens be investigated because of their beliefs.

We support the concept that no employee should be discharged without just cause.

Privacy

Social and technological changes are threatening our citizens' privacy. To meet this challenge, the Carter Administration has developed the first comprehensive privacy policy. Under this policy, administrative action has been taken to cut the number of federal files on individuals and legislation has been passed to protect the privacy of telephone conversations and bank accounts.

In the 1980s we must complete this privacy agenda. Broad legislation must be enacted to protect financial, insurance, medical, and research records. We must have these safeguards to preserve a healthy balance between efficiency and privacy.

The Democratic Party recognizes reproductive freedom as a fundamental human right. We therefore oppose government interference in the reproductive decisions of Americans, especially those government programs or legislative restrictions that deny poor Americans their right to privacy by funding or advocating one or a limited number of reproductive choices only.

Specifically, the Democratic Party opposes involuntary or uninformed sterilization for women and men, and opposes restrictions on funding for health services for the poor that deny poor women especially the right to exercise a constitutionally-guaranteed right to privacy.

Federal legislation is also necessary to protect workers from the abuse of their rights and invasion to their privacy resulting from increased employer use of polygraphs and other so-called "truth test" devices. Workers should have the right to review all records retained by their employers relating to medical and employment information.

Appointments

One of President Carter's highest priorities has been to increase significantly the number of women, Blacks, Hispanics and other minorities in the federal government. That has been done.

More women, Blacks and Hispanics have been appointed to senior government positions than during any other Administration in history.

Of the six women who have served in Cabinet positions, three have been Carter appointees.

More women, Blacks and Hispanics have been appointed to federal judgeships during the Carter Administration than during all previous Administrations in history.

Of the 39 women federal judges, 35 have been Carter appointees; of the 38 Black federal judges, 19 have been Carter appointees; of the 14 Hispanic judges, 5 have been Carter appointees.

This record must be continued. The Democratic Party is committed to continue and strengthen the policy of appointing more women and minorities to federal positions at all levels including the Supreme Court.

Handicapped

Great strides have been made toward ending discrimination against the handicapped, through increased employment and education opportunities and greater access to public facilities and services.

In the 1980s, we must continue to work towards the goals of eliminating discrimination and opening opportunities.

All federal agencies must complete their Section 504 regulations and implement them effectively.

We must continue to expand opportunities for independent living.

The Fair Housing Act and Title VI of the Civil Rights Act must be amended to include the handicapped.

We must face the task of making federal facilities and modes of transportation fully accessible.

Job opportunities and job training for the handicapped, including apprenticeship training programs, must be expanded.

We must make the most basic American civil right—the right to vote—fully available to the handicapped.

Dr. Martin Luther King Jr.

Dr. Martin Luther King Jr. led this nation's effort to provide all of its citizens with civil rights and equal opportunities. His commitment to human rights, peace and non-violence stands as a monument to humanity and courage. To honor this outstanding national leader, we must enact legislation that will commemorate his birthday as a national holiday.

Domestic Violence

Each year, 3 to 6 million Americans are injured in acts of domestic violence. To combat this violence the Carter Administration has initiated a government-wide effort to assist and educate victims and rehabilitate victimizers, including:

- The formation of a new Office of Domestic Violence in the Department of Health and Human Services, and
- Amendments to the Child Abuse Prevention and Treatment Act which provides funds to state and community groups.

The President has signed the Protection of Children Against Sexual Exploitation Act; HUD has developed demonstration projects for shelters for battered women; the Community Services Administration has established a pilot Family Crisis Center Program to assist low-income battered women and children; and the U.S. Commission on Civil Rights held a Consultation on Battered Women in 1978.

Existing federal programs have been coordinated through the Interdepartmental Committee on Domestic Violence, chaired by the Secretary of Health and Human Services. The Democratic Administration must continue to support the passage of the legislation before the Congress, HR 2977, which would provide direct, immediate assistance to victims effectively and sensitively.

Insular Areas

We must be firmly committed to self-determination for the Virgin Islands, Guam, American Samoa and the Northern Mariana Islands, and vigorously support the realization of whatever political status aspirations are democratically chosen by their peoples. The unique cultures, fragile economies, and locations of our Caribbean and Pacific Islands are distinct assets to the United States which require the sensitive application of policy. We are committed to pursuing initiatives we have begun to stimulate insular economic development, enhance treatment under federal programs, provide vitally needed special assistance and coordinate and rationalize policies. These measures will result in greater self-sufficiency and balanced growth.

Puerto Rico

We are committed to Puerto Rico's right to enjoy full self-determination and a relationship that can evolve in ways that will most benefit U.S. citizens in Puerto Rico. The Democratic Party respects and supports the desire of the people of Puerto Rico to associate, by their own will freely expressed in a peaceful and democratic process, in permanent union with the United States either as a commonwealth or as a state, or to become an independent nation. We are also committed to respect the cultural heritage of the people of Puerto Rico and to the elimination of discriminatory or unfair treatment of Puerto Ricans, as American citizens under federal programs.

American Indians

The Carter Administration has upheld and defended the historic special relationship between the federal government and Indian tribes. In addition, it has strongly supported the policy of self-determination and the right to practice the ancestral religions that are important to many tribal members. More than $24 million over the next ten years has been committed to assist Indian tribes with energy resources and in making decisions about the development and protection of these resources. The Administration has firmly reiterated its fundamental opposition to the policy of termination which was so detrimental to Indians and their relationship with the federal government.

These policies must continue as the federal government finds better means of dealing effectively and compassionately with Indian tribes and individuals. The federal government must honor its treaty commitments. The federal government must redouble its efforts to improve the housing, health care, education and general welfare of Indians. Finally, the federal government must work as an equal partner with tribes as they decide for themselves the best means of managing their substantial energy resources.

Ethnic America

President Carter has stated that the composition of American society is analogous to a beautiful mosaic. Each separate part retains its own integrity and identity while adding to and being part of the whole.

America is a pluralistic society. Each of us must learn to live, communicate, and cooperate with persons of other cultures. Our public policies and programs must reflect this pluralism. Immigrants from every nation and their descendants have made numerous contributions to this country, economically, politically and socially. They have traditionally been the backbone of the labor movement and an integral part of the Democratic Party.

Ethnic Americans share the concerns of all Americans. They too are concerned about decent housing, health care, equal employment opportunities, care of the elderly, and education. In addition, ethnic Americans have some concerns of their own. They want to preserve the culture and language of their former homeland. They want to be integrated into the political, social and economic mainstream of American society, but at the same time they are concerned about the foreign policy issues that affect their native countries. We as a nation must be sensitive to their concerns.

President Carter established the Office of Ethnic Affairs and charged it with a broad and diverse mission. The predominant functions of the office are to link the Administration and its ethnic constituents, to foster the concept of pluralism, and to enable all Americans to partake equally in the American way of life.

Americans Living Abroad

Almost 3 million American citizens live overseas, both as government employees and private citizens. We know only too well the dangers and sacrifices some of these government officials face in serving their country. With the threat of terrorism and political unrest always present, we are committed to improving the security of our embassies and missions abroad. Our government must work with other governments to ensure that Americans are protected while performing their vital duties in the interest of the United States.

We also recognize the contributions of private citizens living overseas in bringing American ideals and culture to other lands and in helping the U.S. economy by promoting exports and increased trade with other countries.

The President's Export Council has recommended that in order to encourage American exports and redress trade imbalances, the United States should conform with the practices of other major trading nations. Existing disincentives should be removed, so that Americans working abroad can compete more equitably and effectively with citizens from other nations.

The Administration must continue to support changes in the law which make it simpler for American parents to ensure that their children born overseas are not denied U.S. citizenship.

We also believe that Medicare should be made available to Americans abroad who are eligible for Social Security.

CHAPTER III: GOVERNMENT OPERATION AND REFORM

Making Government Effective and Efficient

The Democratic Party has long stood for an active, responsive, vigorous government. Democrats of our generation have a special obligation to ensure that government is also efficient and well managed.

We understand full well the importance of this obligation. We realize that even the most brilliantly conceived federal programs are doomed to failure if they are not intelligently and efficiently managed.

The kind of government we Democrats stand for is a government that cares and knows how to translate that caring into effective action; a government whose heart and head are working in concert.

Over the last four years the Democratic Administration and the Democratic Congress have built a dramatic government reform record. In the years ahead we must carefully implement the changes we have made, and we must pursue additional measures to provide the efficient government the people have a right to expect.

Regulatory Reform

Federal regulations are needed to protect consumers and providers in the areas of health, safety, and the environment. Four years ago, however, the overall regulatory machine desperately needed an overhaul. Some rules served only to protect favored industries against competition, at the public's expense. Others imposed conflicting or needlessly costly requirements.

For decades, the economy has been hamstrung by anticompetitive regulations. A Democratic Administration and a Democratic Congress are completing the most sweeping deregulation in history. Actions already taken and bills currently pending are revamping the rules governing airlines, banking, trucking, railroads, and telecommunications. Airline deregulation in its first year of operation alone has saved passengers over 2.5 billion dollars.

For the regulatory programs our country does need, the Administration has established a new management system. Under Executive Order 12044, agencies are reviewing and eliminating outdated rules and analyzing the full impact of new rules before they are issued. They are developing alternative regulatory approaches which can reduce compliance costs without sacrificing goals. They are increasing public participation in the regulatory process. The Regulatory Council is publishing the first government-wide list of upcoming rules, the Regulatory Calendar, and is using it to eliminate conflict and duplication.

The challenges of the eighties will place great demands on our regulatory system. The reforms we have put in place are building machinery that can meet those challenges. However, much work lies ahead to implement the steps we have taken and go further.

We must continue to conduct an agency-by-agency review to make regulation less intrusive and more effective.

We must find and remove barriers that prevent steady progress toward competition in each industry.

On the management side, we must increase the use of cost-effective regulatory techniques, without adversely affecting worker health or safety.

We must strengthen our research programs to ensure that we set sensible priorities for regulatory action.

We must eliminate those delays, layers of review, and litigation that unduly tie up the process.

We must make the regulatory process accessible to all members of the public who are affected.

We must oppose special interest efforts to undermine the ability of federal agencies to protect consumers, the environment, or public health and safety; and efforts to enable federal agencies to override or exempt state or federal protections of the environment or public health and safety.

Tax Reform

In 1976, this Party pledged to seek fundamental tax reform, for we believed that our tax system had lost much of its needed fairness and equity. President Carter honored that pledge by proposing to Congress the most comprehensive and far-reaching set of tax reform proposals ever made by any Administration. That proposal would have closed over $9 billion worth of tax loopholes, simplified our tax laws, and provided funds for substantial tax reduction for low- and middle-income taxpayers.

Once again, we call on Congress to legislate meaningful tax reform. We cannot any longer allow the special interests to preserve their particular benefits and loopholes at the expense of the average taxpayers. The fight for tax reform must go forward, and the Party pledges to be a part of that important effort. Therefore, we pledge to seek tax reforms which:

- Encourage savings by low- and middle-income taxpayers;
- Close tax loopholes which benefit only special interests at the expense of the average taxpayer and use the proceeds to bring relief to low- and middle-income Americans;
- Simplify the tax code and ease the burden on taxpayers in the preparation of their tax returns;
- Encourage capital formation, innovation and new production in the United States;
- Curb tax deductions, like those for three-martini lunches, conventions, first class travel, and other expense account deductions, which encourage consumption, discourage saving, and thus impede productivity;
- End tax discrimination that penalizes married working couples; and
- End abuses in the tax treatment of foreign sources, such as special tax treatment and incentives for multi-national corporations that drain jobs and capital from the American economy.

Capital formation is essential both to control inflation and to encourage growth. New tax reform efforts are needed to increase savings and investment, promote the principle of progressive taxation, close loopholes, and maintain adequate levels of federal revenue.

Management

The need to restrain federal spending means that every dollar of the budget must be spent in the most efficient way possible. To achieve this, the Democratic Partnership has been working to streamline the management of the federal government and eliminate waste and fraud from federal programs. Real progress has been made in these important areas.

While these reforms have produced substantial savings for the taxpayers, they must be sustained in the coming years to realize their full potential.

The Civil Service Reform Act can be used to encourage improved productivity of the federal government.

More business-like control of our assets, placing the government's operations on a sound financial basis, must be used to produce real savings.

Special investigations and improved accounting systems must be used to attack fraud, abuse and wasteful practices.

Efforts must be continued to improve the delivery of services to citizens through greater accountability, consolidation and coordination in program administration, and elimination of unnecessary red tape and duplication.

Government Openness and Integrity

Under the Nixon–Ford Administration the federal government was closed to all but a privileged few and the public had lost faith in the integrity of its public servants.

The Democratic Party takes pride in its long and outstanding record of leadership in opening up the processes of government to genuine participation by the people, and in making government truly responsive to the basic needs of all the American people.

For the last four years, the Carter Administration and the Democratic Congress have devoted a great deal of time and resources to opening government processes and ensuring the integrity of government officials.

The Ethics in Government Act now requires all senior government officials to make a full financial disclosure and severely limits the "revolving door" practice that has developed among former federal employees of representing private parties before the federal agencies in which they recently held significant positions.

A statutory provision has now been made for the appointment of a special prosecutor in cases of alleged wrong-doing by senior government officials.

"Whistle-blowers" in the federal government (those who report waste and illegalities) have now been given special statutory protection to prevent possible retribution.

An Executive Order has been issued significantly reducing the amount of classified information, and increasing the amount of classified material to be released over the next decade by about 250 million pages.

As a result of actions such as these, trust and confidence in government officials have been restored. In the coming years, we must ensure full implementation of these initiatives. We must also work toward lobby law reform which is needed to ensure full disclosure of Congressional and executive lobbying activities.

Law Enforcement

Numerous changes were necessary when the Democrats took office in 1976. The essential trust between police officers and the public they protect had deteriorated. Funds committed by Congress had been terribly misspent during the eight Republican years.

The Carter Administration has taken solid steps toward correcting this serious problem. It has formalized the relationship between federal and state law enforcement officials to ensure maximum cooperation between federal and state agencies. It has taken long strides toward creating and implementing uniform national guidelines for federal prisons and encouraging state penal institutions to use the same guidelines.

The Democratic Party supports the enactment of a revised federal criminal code which simplifies the currently complex federal criminal law in order to make our federal criminal justice efforts more effective, and repeals antiquated laws while fully protecting all civil liberties. As that effort proceeds, we must ensure that the rights of workers to engage in peaceful picketing during labor disputes are fully protected.

The Democratic Party affirms the right of sportsmen to possess guns for purely hunting and targetshooting purposes. However, handguns simplify and intensify violent crime. Ways must be found to curtail the availability of these weapons. The Democratic Party supports enactment of federal legislation to strengthen the presently inadequate regulations over the manufacture, assembly, distribution, and possession of handguns and to ban "Saturday night specials."

Most important, the government has used its own resources to resolve satisfactorily concerns over the use of deadly force. The Administration has made progress toward the preparation of uniform guidelines for all police departments. They have also utilized the conciliation services available through the Community Relations Service to establish closer working ties among the police and community organizations.

The Democratic Party is pledged to continuing its strong record of providing needed assistance to local law enforcement. The new Law Enforcement Assistance Act, enacted by a Democratic Administration and a Democratic Congress, provides an important framework for this purpose. We are committed to using this framework effectively, in close cooperation with state and local law enforcement authorities.

We reaffirm our support for the Juvenile Justice and Delinquency Act and the Runaway Youth Act as responses to the serious challenge of youth crime.

We must continue and strengthen efforts at prison reform, to upgrade the safety of our penal institutions, to enhance rehabilitation of offenders, and to lower the recidivism level.

We support federal assistance to the victims of crime, including special programs to assist the elderly and to aid the victims of rape and domestic violence. Further efforts should be made to demonstrate the feasibility of restitution by the perpetrators of crime.

As we work toward improved law enforcement, we must not permit or sanction excessive or illegal police force.

Minorities in some areas have been discriminated against by such police actions, and we must take every action at the federal, state, and local level to prevent that from happening in the future, including a renewed commitment to affirmative action in the hiring of law enforcement personnel, establishment of civil rights units at appropriate U.S. Attorneys' offices, and swift investigation and prosecution of suspected civil rights violations.

Paperwork Reduction

Over the years the federal government has imposed more and more paperwork on the private sector. The Carter Administration has stopped that trend and worked to cut the paperwork burden. We have eliminated unnecessary forms, simplified and consolidated needed forms, and discouraged creation of new paperwork requirements. As a result, the federal paperwork burden has been cut 15 percent, or 127 million manhours.

The Administration is currently putting into place the tools we will need to continue and expand this program. In November 1979, President Carter signed an Executive Order that created the first "paperwork budget." This program will limit the reporting time each agency can impose on the public. In addition, the President has ordered agencies to tailor their forms to reduce the burden on individuals and small business.

We need further legislation. We urge a continuation of the effort to reduce government documents to simple English, easily understandable by all. The Administration is working with Congress to pass a Paperwork Reduction Act, which will close wide loopholes in the current oversight process.

Election Reform

Recent reforms in the election process have aided immeasurably in opening the process to more people and have begun to reduce the influence of special interests. The limitations on campaign contributions and the public financing of Presidential elections are two reforms which have worked very well. Business political action committees continue to spend excessively, however. Further reform in this area is essential. In the 1980s we need to enact reforms which will:

- Provide for public financing of Congressional campaigns;
- Lower contribution limits for political action committees;
- Close the loophole that allows private spending in Presidential elections contrary to the intent of the election law reforms;
- Encourage voter participation in elections through use of simplified procedures for registration in

states that lack mail or election day registration procedures, and by resisting efforts to reduce access to bilingual ballots; and

- Increase opportunities for full participation in all areas of party and government affairs by the low- and moderate-income majority of Americans.

Postal Service

The private expression statutes guarantee the protection and security of the mail for all Americans. They are essential to the maintenance of a national postal system, which will require an adequate public service subsidy to assure the delivery of mail to all Americans.

CHAPTER IV: ENERGY, NATURAL RESOURCES, ENVIRONMENT AND AGRICULTURE

Energy

For the past four years, the Democratic Party's highest legislative priority has been the development of our nation's first comprehensive energy policy. Our actions were necessitated by the Republican Administration's policy that fostered dependence on foreign oil. This Republican legacy led to America's petroleum paralysis, which weakened our security, undermined our strength abroad, threatened our environment and endangered our economic health.

In perhaps no other domestic area did we inherit such a dangerous situation:

- Domestic production of oil and natural gas was steadily declining, with price controls discouraging exploration and production;
- Natural gas shortages were regularly plaguing parts of our country;
- Our dependence on foreign oil was increasing every year;
- Wasteful energy practices existed in our industries, homes and transportation;
- Solar and other renewable energy resources were being almost completely ignored;
- Synthetic fuel production had been stalled;
- The federal government was not promoting energy conservation;
- Our allies were unwilling to make adequate efforts to reduce their energy consumption; and
- Our energy policy was being made by nearly a dozen different agencies and bureaus throughout the federal government.

The struggle to develop an energy policy was difficult and time-consuming. Tough decisions, especially in the area of oil price decontrol, were necessary to reduce our dependence on foreign oil.

Not all of our energy problems have been solved. Yet the achievements of the past four years leave little doubt that we are finally serious about the problems caused by our excessive reliance on foreign oil. As a result of our national energy policy, oil imports will be cut in half by the end of this decade, saving our nation hundreds of billions of dollars. A framework is now in place that will permit further progress in the 1980s. Our economic security demands that we drastically reduce the massive flow of dollars into the OPEC treasuries and oil company bank accounts at the expense of American consumers and business.

Our progress on energy has been realized because we have achieved four principal goals:

- Incentives have been provided for the production of new energy sources;
- Incentives for new oil production have been added, together with a windfall profits tax, which will fund low-income energy assistance and energy research and development;
- Incentives have been provided to encourage conservation of our existing energy resources; and
- Improved international energy cooperation has reduced our dependence on OPEC.

These actions have produced enormous energy benefits to our nation:

- We are importing one million barrels of oil a day less than last year;
- Domestic natural gas exploration and production are at record-high levels;
- Domestic oil exploration is at a 20-year high, and the decline in domestic production has been averted;
- Per capita energy consumption is decreasing;
- Use of solar energy has increased considerably, and gasohol production has increased by 600 percent;
- Coal production has increased, and foreign markets for our coal have been developed;
- Gasoline consumption is 8 percent less than last year.

In the 1980s, this program can be improved, as the framework laid in the last four years is used to ensure our energy security for all time.

America's energy future requires a continued strong national policy based on two fundamental principles: efficient use of energy that will conserve our resources, preserve our economy and create jobs for Americans; and development of secure, environmentally safe and reasonably priced energy sources.

It is—and must be—the goal of the Democratic

Party to mobilize this nation to use energy efficiently without asking Americans to suffer the loss of our strong economy and hard-earned standard of living. Energy efficiency, especially in buildings, transportation, and industrial production, must be made this nation's top priority.

The following specific actions must be taken.

We must make energy conservation our highest priority, not only to reduce our dependence on foreign oil, but also to guarantee that our children and grandchildren have an adequate supply of energy. If we can convince one of every four drivers exceeding the 55-mile-per-hour speed limit to reduce their speed, we can save 100,000 barrels a day. Conservation is the cheapest form of energy production.

We must establish a massive residential energy conservation grant program. We must provide subsidized loans, direct financial assistance, and other substantial incentives to make all residences in the United States energy efficient, through upgraded insulation, heating, cooling and waterheating. Special incentives should be afforded for the use of renewable energy resources such as passive and active solar energy systems. Our goal should be to ensure that all economically justified energy efficiency investments are made by 1990.

We should use our energy programs to aid in rebuilding the industrial heartland. Industry must be given financial incentives to improve the energy efficiency of industrial processes and to build substantial amounts of generating capacity through co-generation.

We must implement mandatory Building Energy Performance Standards (BEPS) to encourage the design and construction of energy efficient buildings. Energy efficiency standards should apply to all new construction. Implementation of energy efficiency standards should begin with federal government buildings. In addition, the federal government should lead the way in implementing solar and energy efficiency improvement programs through its loan and insurance agencies by requiring energy conservation standards for federally assisted properties.

In recognition of the potential for substantial energy savings if our most efficient methods of transportation are utilized, we must provide direct economic assistance where private capital is unavailable to improve those means of transport.

Major new efforts must be launched to develop synthetic and alternative renewable energy sources. In pursuing a strong program of synthetic fuel plants we must also be sensitive to environmental and water concerns. The federal government must help eliminate red tape involved in the construction of vital energy facilities. The Energy Mobilization Board, an essential mechanism to speed the construction of vital energy facilities, should be able to override state and local substantive law only with the consent of Congress and the President.

The Democratic Party regards coal as our nation's greatest energy resource. It must play a decisive role in America's energy future. We must increase our use of coal. To accomplish this, we must see that shippers are not overburdened with excessive rates for transportation. Severance taxes levied for depletion of natural resources should be equitable. We must make clean coal conversion a reality. To this end, we will assist utilities that are large enough to permit coal conversion while maintaining or improving air quality. We must also provide incentives for industrial boiler coal conversion. Coal conversion can and must be accomplished in a manner that protects public health, nationally, regionally and locally. It can and must increase the use of coal, reduce the demand for oil, and provide employment where jobs are needed the most.

The federal government should accept its responsibility as trustee for the American Indian and Alaska Native tribes to ensure that tribal resources develop at a pace that preserves the existing life-style and that the tribes participate in the contracting process for resource development with full knowledge of the environmental tradeoffs. The federal government must continue to cooperate with tribal governments in such matters as changes in the use of sacred and religious areas. The Democratic Party believes that American Indian and Alaska Native reservations should remain the permanent homeland for these peoples.

We recognize that Hawaii, U.S. territories and Trust territories in the Pacific Basin are particularly vulnerable because of their total dependence on imported oil for meeting their energy needs. These insular areas do not have access to the alternative sources of energy that are available elsewhere. Consequently, the Democratic Party recommends that these areas, where feasible, be chosen as sites for demonstration and/or pilot alternative energy projects, especially ocean thermal energy conversion, solar and wind.

We must lead the Western World in developing a program for increased use of coal in Europe, Japan, and the developing nations.

Oil exploration on federal lands must be accelerated, consistent with environmental projections.

Offshore energy leasing and development should be conditioned on full protection of the environment and marine resources. Lease sales should proceed only after appropriate safeguards necessary to preserve and protect vital natural resources are put in place. The determination of what safeguards are needed must be based on a complete assessment of the effects of offshore activity on the marine and coastal environment, and must be made in conjunction with the Environmental Protection Agency and the National Oceanic and Atmospheric Agency, the federal agencies charged with protecting our nation's fisheries and other environmental resources.

Solar energy use must be increased, and strong efforts, including continued financial support, must be undertaken to make certain that we achieve the goal of having solar energy account for 20 percent of our total energy by the year 2000.

To ensure that we reach the 20 percent goal, the Democratic Party commits itself to a federal program for solar or other renewable resources that exceeds the federal commitment to synthetic fuels. A greater share of federal funds should be committed to basic research and must be devoted to the development of renewable energy resources and fusion research and development. Moreover, we support the commercialization of solar, wind, low-head hydro, biomass and other renewable resources as quickly as possible through direct assistance, investment and loan guarantees in addition to monies available from the solar bank. The Democratic Party vigorously supports substantial funding for the construction of an engineering test facility for fusion technology. Fusion energy is a safe, clean alternative source of energy which can be used to generate electricity efficiently.

We must encourage research and development of hydrogen- or electric-powered vehicles. We must fully commit ourselves to an alcohol fuel program. The federal government should expand its use of alcohol fuels in government and military vehicles. This will help reduce surplus feed grain and help to stabilize prices. The Democratic Party pledges that production of fuel grade alcohol will be increased until at least a target of 500 million barrels of ethanol by 1981 is achieved.

A stand-by gasoline rationing plan must be adopted for use in the event of a serious energy supply interruption. In times of supply interruption, rationing is essential for equitable and prompt distribution of gas to the public. The Strategic Petroleum Reserve should be filled as market conditions permit, consistent with the requirements of existing law.

We must impose a moratorium on the acquisition of competing coal companies and solar energy companies by major oil companies.

Legislation must be enacted to prohibit purchases by oil companies of energy or non-energy companies unless the purchase would enhance competition.

The major oil companies must be responsible and accountable in their production, importation and distribution of fossil fuels. Oil is as basic to our economy, defense, and general welfare as electric power and money. Consequently, the oil companies must be in-

vested with public purpose. To accomplish this objective, we support strengthened leasing regulations, reporting requirements and monitoring by the Departments of Energy and Justice.

Thorough investigations of the compliance of the oil companies with energy price laws and regulations must be continued, and tough penalties imposed in the event of non-compliance. The Department of Energy, consistent with the law, should share its energy data with the Department of Justice and the Federal Trade Commission.

We must make conservation and renewable energy our nation's energy priorities for the future. Through the federal government's commitment to renewable energy sources and energy efficiency, and as alternative fuels become available in the future, we will retire nuclear power plants in an orderly manner.

We must give the highest priority to dealing with the nuclear waste disposal problem. Current efforts to develop a safe, environmentally sound nuclear waste disposal plan must be continued and intensified.

The NRC shall issue no licenses or permits for new nuclear plants until the Kemeny Commission recommendations are fully implemented.

Existing plants must be required to meet the safety recommendations of the Kemeny Commission. The Democratic Party supports prompt implementation of their recommendations. No plant unable to meet these standards can be allowed to operate.

Safe permanent disposal of all high-level radioactive waste and transuranic waste should be the primary responsibility of the federal government, in consultation and concurrence with state, local, tribal, and territorial governments throughout the entire decision-making process, including the actual siting and operation of repositories. Neither the federal government nor the state or tribal or territorial governments should be permitted to act in a manner that forces an unsafe resolution of this problem or prevents a safe resolution from being accomplished. It is, therefore, essential that state and tribal governments, acting according to their constitutional processes, have the power to reject unsafe sites within their borders. Clear standards should be developed so that the courts may determine whether the federal government or a state or tribe is acting in an arbitrary manner. Every state should be responsible for the management and disposal of all low-level waste generated by non-defense sources within its boundaries. Where appropriate, this responsibility should be exercised through state regional compacts. There should be more federal funding for research and development of safer, more efficient methods of radioactive waste disposal.

Funds generated by the Windfall Profits Tax must be used to expand mass transit. Federal assistance should be provided for construction and operation costs.

Environment

We are charged with the stewardship of an irreplaceable environment. The Democratic Party must continue to be as environmentally progressive in the future as it has been in the past. Progress in environmental quality—a major achievement of the 1970s—must continue in the 1980s. The environmental problems we face today are, if anything, more challenging and urgent than those of ten years ago.

The great strides we have taken during the past few years are the best evidence of our commitment to resource conservation and environmental restoration. We have compiled a proud record.

During the next four years, we must carry forward vigorously with these important policies, and move to address a series of new challenges.

We must move decisively to protect our countryside and our coastline from overdevelopment and mismanagement. Major efforts are now under way to solve such problems as disappearing farmland and development on our barrier islands. These efforts should help forge a strong national consensus behind the realization that protection must be balanced with the need to properly manage and utilize our land resources during the 1980s.

We must develop new and improved working relationships among federal, state, local, tribal, and territorial governments and private interests, to manage effectively our programs for increased domestic energy production and their impact on people, water, air, and the environment in general. All of our energy development efforts should be carried out without sacrificing environmental quality.

We must continue on the path to a sustainable energy future—a future based increasingly on renewable resources and energy conservation. Our national goal of having 20 percent of our energy from renewable resources in the year 2000 must become a working target, not a forgotten slogan. Conservation must remain the cornerstone of our national energy supply.

New efforts at home and abroad will be required in the early 1980s to face squarely such global problems as the destruction of forests, the loss of countless irreplaceable species, growing world population, acid rain, and carbon dioxide buildup.

Passage by Congress of the hazardous waste cleanup proposal will provide the basis for a major effort beginning in 1981 to clean up the thousands of hazardous waste dump sites across the country. Toxic chemicals are a serious threat to the health of our people. We must continue our programs to improve agency performance in many areas, such as protection of groundwaters, in order to better protect the public.

We must strive to ensure that environmental regulations cost no more than necessary and are streamlined to eliminate waste, duplication and delay. We must not lose sight of the fact that the benefits of these regulations far outweigh their costs. We must work to reform legislation without deforming it.

We support the allocation of resources to the Environmental Protection Agency and other environmental agencies sufficient to carry out their mandates.

We support strict adherence to automobile pollution standards.

We will support policies to eliminate acid rain pollution from power plant emissions.

We will commit ourselves to efficient transportation alternatives, including mass transit, car pooling, van pooling, employer based commuter plans, and hydrogen and electric commuter vehicles.

We will continue to fight noise pollution in our urban centers and job sites.

We will encourage the recycling of municipal solid waste.

We will seek a strong "super-fund" law financed by government and industry.

We must continue to pursue offshore energy leasing to stimulate our domestic oil and gas production and reduce our dependence on foreign oil consistent with environmental and marine concerns.

We will fund adequately the Land and Water Conservation Fund to protect our national park system.

We will implement vigorously the Toxic Substances Control Act.

Often, actions by one nation affect the economic growth and the quality of life in other nations. Such actions can be influenced by international agreement and incentives.

To defend against environmental risks that cross national frontiers, international cooperation must be extended to new areas, such as acid rain, deforestation and decertification, buildup of carbon dioxide in the atmosphere, thinning of the ozone shield, air and water pollution, oil spills, chemicals in the environment, and disposal of radioactive waste.

Water

Water is a necessity to all, and represents life itself to much of the American Union. We recognize especially the singular dependence of the Western states on scarce water supplies. The development of navigation, irrigation, flood control, and hydroelectric projects is vital to the economic health of the West, and correspondingly to the entire nation.

Working with Congress, the Democratic Administration will implement a national water policy which recognizes the special needs of the West. Toward this end, we support the modern standards and valid cost–benefit analysis suggested by the Federal Water Resources Council. We support a federal study, in partnership with the affected states, to explore possibilities and recommend alternatives relative to importation of water into arid and semi-arid states. We also support state, local, and tribal participation in all phases of water programs within their respective jurisdictions.

Recently, water programs across the nation have become enmeshed in controversy and conflicting values. It is not unusual for a federal water project to take a generation from the time it is authorized to the time construction actually begins.

Yet the national need for expanded and accelerated investment in water development grows ever more pressing, and is increasingly acknowledged. If, as but one example, we are to develop our unequaled coal resources as a substitute for imported oil, we will require expansion of water transportation and improvement of seaports beyond the imagination of even those early Americans who sensed the path to empire in our inland waterways. The development of synthetic fuels, which must of necessity be concentrated in states with sparse water supplies, is an enormous challenge to engineering and science.

Similarly, the task of reindustrialization requires that we recognize the water development needs of all sections of the nation.

Water to supply steel mills and automobile factories, to provide for the needs of commercial cities and associated suburbs, makes a legitimate and pressing claim on national priorities.

We recognize the need to develop a truly national water program which responds to the needs of each region of our country in an active and effective manner and which recognizes the social effects of water projects.

The Democratic Party strongly supports the desalinization of sea water and the development of water resources in those areas of the country where water is scarce.

Agriculture

America's farmers are among the most vital economic forces of the nation. Because of their extraordinary productivity, America's farm workers provide more food and fiber per person at a lower cost than their counterparts in any other country. American con-

sumers have a more certain food supply than consumers in any other nation, even though a third of our farm production is sold abroad each year.

In 1977, the Democratic Administration inherited a farm economy marked by serious over-production and badly outdated price support programs. Farm prices and incomes were plummeting, partly in response to misguided attempts at price controls. The livestock sector was in its third straight year of loss, and a herd liquidation of unprecedented scale was under way.

Because of actions taken by the Democratic Administration and Democratic Congress, this situation was turned around in 1978 and 1979. U.S. agriculture was put back on a track of steady, sustained growth and improvement. The sharp decline of farm prices and farm incomes was reversed. An aggressive program of export promotion resulted in record high agricultural exports in each of the past three years.

Recently, however, the nation's farm economy has been hurt by reduced prices; high costs of production, including energy, inflation, equipment, and high interest rates. As a result, our nation's farmers are facing a time of hardship.

Agricultural policy in the 1980s must strengthen the forces which made American farmers the most productive in the world and American agriculture the hope of hungry people everywhere. In this way, we can ensure a decade of prosperity for farmers and of agricultural abundance for America's consumers.

The Democratic Party pledges itself to the following goals.

Continued Attention to Expanding Farm Exports. American agriculture's long-run interests remain firmly tied to the sale of U.S. farm products abroad. Despite the significant progress made to date, it is important that we continue to work at breaking down barriers to trade and capitalizing on our nation's enormous advantage in the production of food and fiber.

If food is to be used as an instrument of foreign policy, it is imperative that farm income be protected. Farmers must have access to free markets.

Recognizing the patriotic sacrifices made by the American farmer during the agricultural embargo protesting the invasion of Afghanistan, we commend the agricultural community's contribution in the field of foreign affairs. Except in time of war or grave threats to national security, the federal government should impose no future embargoes on agricultural products.

Protecting Farm Prices and Farm Income. Rapidly rising costs of production, especially energy costs, make it imperative that we increase the level of support for farm prices and income by increasing target prices to cover the cost of production. For those farm products not covered by target prices, such as soybeans, cattle, hogs, poultry, sugar cane, and sugar beets, we pledge support programs that will maintain viable domestic production. Low-cost farm credit should be extended with the least possible delay in times of stress from decreased farm income or disasters.

It is in the nation's long-run interest that returns to farmers keep pace with rising costs to ensure a fair return on investment.

Measures to Protect and Further Enhance Agricultural Productivity. Although agricultural productivity remains high in comparison with productivity in the non-farm sector, its rate of increase has slowed over the past two or three decades. This trend must be reversed through greater attention to the effects of regulatory actions, increased support for agricultural research, and intensified efforts to conserve our vital land and water resources.

Rebuilding Our Agricultural Transportation System. The transportation system which moves our agricultural products to their final markets, including ports for export shipment, has been strained to the limit. While needed improvements have begun, through such measures as trucking and rail deregulation and the expansion of Lock and Dam 26 on the Mississippi River at Alton, Illinois, more intensive efforts will be required in the future. In the case of railroads, a rebuilding effort will be required.

Protecting Our Soil Resource. American agriculture is critically dependent on the productivity of its soil. Without careful and consistent stewardship of this important resource, it can become depleted. An assessment of our nation's conservation needs is now under way. We must be prepared to act on the findings of this assessment. Emergency procedures should be enacted to increase soil conservation incentives for construction of watersheds, tile intake terraces, and other soil saving practices.

Protecting Family Farms. The real genius of American agriculture is the role and prominence of the farm family. It is this form of organization that provides agriculture with its vitality, independent spirit, and progressiveness. We must protect farmers from land speculators, giant farm combinations, and foreign buyers. We support laws requiring disclosure of all foreign ownership of farmland and we will continue to monitor such ownership to determine its impact on our farms.

While we recognize the need to modernize the 1902 Reclamation Act, we reaffirm our support for its intent—to assure that the federal subsidy program assists only family farmers.

We support reforms in the estate tax to strengthen the stability of family farms.

Farmer Involvement. There is a continuing need to devise better ways of involving people in the decisions of their government, particularly in those decisions that have direct and important effects on their lives. We realize the need for a strong cattle industry and for ranchers' involvement in the development of farm programs. Considerable progress has been made in this regard, but more is required.

Capper–Volstead Act. We reaffirm our strong support for agricultural cooperatives and bargaining associations to engage in vigorous programs to pack, process and market their members' crops as provided for in the Capper–Volstead Act.

Farm Labor. We must vigorously enforce existing laws relating to farm labor organization and recognize the right of farm workers to bargain collectively, while ensuring the legal rights of farmers.

Farm Mechanization. We support retraining programs for farm workers displaced by mechanized farming.

Forestry

America's national forests contain a national treasure that provides recreation, wilderness, fish and wildlife, and timber products.

We reaffirm the Democratic Party's traditional support for multiple-use management to ensure the survival of these precious resources for this generation and generations to come.

We call for the speedy resolution by Congress of the Roadless Area Review and Evaluation, stimulated by this Administration, to determine which areas are best suited for wilderness and which should be released for timber harvest and multiple-use management.

We support continued assistance to private, non-industrial forest owners to increase their management potential.

On federal lands identified as part of our timber resource, we support:

- Management policies which, consistent with sound, complete land management plans, will result in the highest timber yields, when trees are mature, and which can be sustained over the long term;
- Concentration of timber sales on areas of greatest potential;
- Management of these irreplaceable and environmentally unique areas to maintain perpetually their value; and

- Provision of adequate access facilities for all of these uses.

We shall insist that administration of public lands by the Department of Interior be fair and equitable. The interest of the state within which such public lands lie must be of paramount importance in the decision-making process. We encourage all federal agencies to consult with the states on such matters.

Fisheries

Under the Democratic Administration the U.S. fishing industry has made substantial progress, as evidenced by the following:

- Commercial landings of fish in 1979 were up 45 percent in value and 21 percent in quantity compared with 1977;
- The U.S. share of the catch in our 200-mile fisheries conservation zone increased from 27 percent in 1978 to 33 percent in 1979;
- Over the same period, the foreign catch of fish in the U.S. 200-mile zone dropped 6 percent, and 29 percent from the average for the five preceding years;
- The U.S. has moved from fifth in the world in 1977 to fourth in 1978 in total commercial fish landings; and
- Exports of U.S. edible fishery products in 1979 were up 116 percent in value and 67 percent in quantity compared with 1977.

While such trends are encouraging, there remains a tremendous potential for growth. By volume, 67 percent, and by value, 34 percent of the harvest in the fishery conservation zone is still taken by foreign vessels. The value of the catch to foreign fishermen was $470 million in 1979.

The need for more rapid growth of the U.S. fishing industry is illustrated by the fact that imports of fisheries' products outweighed exports by $1.7 billion last year. With full development of our industry, this deficit could be erased. Moreover, 43,000 new jobs could be created.

One-fifth of the world's fish are found in waters off the United States. We pledge to continue the development of our fishing industry so that the U.S. achieves self-sufficiency in this sector and fully utilizes the valuable and abundant fisheries resources off our shores. To this end, continuing effort in the following areas is needed:

- Develop a balanced U.S. harvesting, processing and marketing capability on a geographical and fishery-by-fishery basis;
- Continue to phase out foreign fishing within our 200-mile zone;

- Target efforts to stimulate and expand those fisheries that are presently unutilized and underutilized;
- Increase research and development through cooperative federal-private efforts with emphasis on industry initiatives;
- Encourage the availability of capital in sectors where it is particularly needed;
- Promote market development, and to that end, continue to allocate surplus fishery resources of the U.S. 200-mile zone to foreign nations in order to stimulate improved access to their markets for our fish products;
- Enhance conservation and management of U.S. fishery resources and in that effort, increase observer coverage of foreign fishing operations in the 200-mile zone;
- Work toward ensuring that a fair share of the costs of conservation, management, research and enforcement in the 200-mile zone is borne by foreign fishermen who enjoy access to our surplus fishery resources;
- Assist the U.S. distant-water fleets through international agreements;
- Support an international ocean regime for fisheries management through successful completion of Law-of-the-Sea negotiations;
- Encourage development of a diversified U.S. aquaculture industry;
- Protect, restore and enhance fish habitats;
- Continue support for research, propagation and management of our anadromous fish resource; and
- In recognition of its economic and recreational importance, accord a high priority to maintaining and improving marine sports fishing.

CHAPTER V: FOREIGN POLICY

Introduction

When the Democratic Party came into office almost four years ago, the most dangerous threat to America's position in the world was the profound disillusionment and mistrust which the American people felt for their own government. This had reached the point where the very term "national security" had become synonymous with the abuse of power, deceit and violation of public trust. It undermined our capacity to defend our interests and to play our proper role in the world at a time when Soviet power was continuing to grow.

The hallmark of the previous eight years of Republican Administration had been to emphasize the primacy of power politics irrespective of compatibility with American values and with the increasing power of the Soviet Union. The result was disrespect abroad and discontent at home.

The Democratic Party was determined to make our values a central factor in shaping American foreign policy. The one-sided emphasis of the previous Republican Administration had led many Americans to a suspicion of power, and in some respects, even to rejection of military strength. The American people longed to see their country once again identified with widespread human aspirations. The Democratic Party understood, if the Republicans did not, that this is essential to preserve our long-term interest in the world.

The Democratic Administration sought to reconcile these two requirements of American foreign policy—principle and strength. Both are required to maintain a constructive and secure relationship between America and the rest of the world. We have tried to make clear the continuing importance of American strength in a world of change. Without such strength, there is a genuine risk that global change will deteriorate into anarchy to be exploited by our adversaries' military power. Thus, the revival of American strength has been a central preoccupation of the Democratic Administration.

The use of American power is necessary as a means of shaping not only a more secure, but also a more decent world. To shape a decent world, we must pursue objectives that are moral, that make clear our support for the aspirations of mankind and that are rooted in the ideals of the American people.

That is why the Democrats have stressed human rights. That is why America once again has supported the aspirations of the vast majority of the world's population for greater human justice and freedom. As we continue to strive to solve our own internal problems, we are proud of the values for which the United States has always stood. We should continue to be a beacon of liberty around the world and to effectively and positively state America's case for freedom to the world through various governmental and non-governmental channels.

A foreign policy which seeks to blend our ideals and our strength does not easily reduce itself to simple statements.

First, we must consistently strengthen our relations with like-minded industrial democracies. In meeting the dangers of the coming decade the United States will consult closely with our allies to advance common security and political goals. As a result of annual summit meetings, coordinated economic policies and effective programs of international energy conservation have been fashioned. With the cooperation of rich and poor nations alike, a new international trade agreement has been reached which safeguards our free enterprise system from protectionism and gives us greater economic opportunity in the world, while it gives the developing world a stake in the stability of the world's economy.

Second, we must continue to improve our relations with the Third World by being sensitive to their legitimate aspirations. The United States should be a positive force for peaceful change in responding to ferment in the Third World. Today, thanks to a number of steps that have been taken—strengthening the international aid institutions, the Panama Canal treaties, the Zimbabwe settlement, the normalization of relations with China—the United States has a healthier and more productive relationship with these countries.

Our third objective must be peace in the Middle East. The Carter Administration has pursued this objective with determination and together with the leaders of Israel and Egypt, has overcome great obstacles in the last three years. America made this commitment for two fundamental reasons—morality and national security.

Our nation feels a profound moral obligation to stustain and assure the security of Israel. That is why our relationship with Israel is, in most respects, a unique one. Israel is the single democracy, the most stable government, the most strategic asset and our closest ally in the region.

To fulfill this imperative, we must move towards peace in the Middle East. Without peace, there is a growing prospect, indeed inevitability, that this region will become radicalized, susceptible to foreign intrusion, and possibly involved in another war. Thus, peace in the Middle East also is vital for our national security interests.

The strength of these two impulses—our moral commitment and national security—has sustained the Democratic Administration in many difficult trials. The result has been the first peace ever between Israel and an Arab country, as well as the eventual prospect of a wider comprehensive agreement which will assure peace and security to all parties concerned. Our goal is to make the Middle East an area of stability and progress in which the United States can play a full and constructive role.

Our fourth major objective is to strengthen the military security of the United States and our allies at a time when trends in the military balance have become increasingly adverse. America is now, and will continue to be, the strongest power on earth. It was the Democratic Party's greatest hope that we could, in fact, reduce our military effort. But realities of the world situation, including the unremitting buildup of Soviet military forces, required that we begin early to reverse the decade-long decline in American defense efforts.

In 1977, the United States joined with NATO to develop, for the first time in the history of the Alliance, a long-term defense program calling for 3 percent annual real growth in our collective defense efforts. This is being fulfilled. In the first year, the Democratic Administration decided that the U.S. needed an enhanced strategic posture and policy to deal with the increased first-strike capability of the Soviet Union. To this end basic commitments were made regarding U.S. strategic capabilities for the late 1980s, in particular, the MX land-based mobile ICBM deterrent. Finally, development is now under way of a rapid deployment force capable of defending our interests and protecting our friends in those parts of the world where American military forces are not regularly present.

At the same time, the Democratic Administration has determined to cut waste in defense spending. The B-1 bomber was cancelled because it was technologically obsolete. A defense bill containing unnecessary expenditures for a new nuclear carrier, while neglecting the readiness of our day-to-day forces, was vetoed and the veto was sustained. These decisions involved difficult choices, but the result is a leaner, stronger American military posture.

As a fifth objective the Democrats have been and remain committed to arms control, especially to strategic arms limitations, and to maintain a firm and balanced relationship with the Soviet Union. Our resolve to pursue this goal remains as strong as ever.

To avoid the danger to all mankind from an intensification of the strategic arms competition, and to curb a possible acceleration of the nuclear arms race while awaiting the ratification of the SALT II Treaty, we endorse the policy of continuing to take no action which would be inconsistent with its object and purpose, so long as the Soviet Union does likewise.

Arms control and strategic arms limitation are of crucial importance to us and to all other people. The Salt II Agreement is a major accomplishment of the Democratic Administration. It contributes directly to our national security, and we will seek its ratification at the earliest feasible time.

Defense

America's military strength is and must be unsurpassed. The Democratic Administration has moved to reverse the threatened decline in America's world position. While claiming concern for our nation's defense preparedness, the Nixon–Ford Administration presided over a steady decline of 33 percent in real U.S. military spending between 1968 and 1976.

As a result of the joint efforts of the Democratic Administration and Congress, there has been a real increase in our defense spending every year since 1976. This increase is necessary in order to compensate for the decline in U.S. military strength over the previous eight years and to assure a high quality of military personnel, an effective nuclear deterrent capability, a capable conventional fighting force and an improved intelligence capability. We will act to further improve intelligence gathering and analysis.

We must be careful that our defense dollars are spent wisely. We must make sure that we develop and deploy practical weapons and that we have the resources to ensure that the men and women who must operate these weapons have the skill to do so.

The serious question of manpower shortages must be addressed promptly. In order to prevent the necessity of a peacetime draft, the all-volunteer force must have wage standards which will retain experienced personnel or recruit new personnel upon whom an increasingly sophisticated military heavily depends.

We will upgrade the combat readiness of our armed forces. We will give the highest priority to combat training, to an effective Reserve and Guard force, and to sufficient supplies, spare parts, fuel and ammunition. Registration of 18-year-olds is intended to enable the United States to mobilize more rapidly in the event of an emergency, which is the only time it should be used. We do not favor a peacetime draft or the exclusion of women from registration. We will seek ways to expand voluntary service in both the armed forces and non-military programs such as VISTA, the Young Adult Conservation Corps, and the Peace Corps.

We need to go forward to protect our retaliatory capabilities in the face of continuing Soviet advances in their strategic forces.

The nation has moved to modernize its strategic deterrent through the MX, Trident, and cruise missile systems. The MX missile deployment will enhance the survivability of our land-based intercontinental ballistic missile force. Cruise missiles will modernize our strategic air deterrent, and the new Trident submarine, with a missile range of over 4,000 miles, will both improve and help guarantee the invulnerability of our nuclear deterrent.

The United States has acted to correct the dangerous military imbalance which had developed in Europe, by initiating and obtaining Allied support for a long overdue NATO long-term defense program and proceeding toward the deployment in Europe of long-range theater nuclear deterrents to counter the Soviet buildup of such weaponry in Europe. Our commitment to increase defense spending by at least 3 percent per year is crucial to the maintenance of allied consensus and confidence in this regard. We need to modernize our conventional military capabilities so that we can better protect American lives and American interests abroad.

The Democratic Administration has acted to improve our ability to make rapid responses to contingencies by organizing and supporting rapid deployment forces capable of responding to military problems in any part of the world where our vital interests are threatened. To that end, we favor the development and production of a new fleet of cargo aircraft with intercontinental range, the design and procurement of a force of Maritime Prepositioning ships that will carry heavy equipment and supplies for three Marine Corps brigades, and an increase in regional military exercises, in cooperation with friendly states. We have given particular attention to developing the facilities and capabilities to further support the policy of the United States with regard to the Persian Gulf enunciated by President Carter in the State of the Union address on January 23, 1980: "Let our position be absolutely clear: an attempt by any outside force to gain control of the Persian Gulf region will be regarded as an assault on the vital interests of the United States of America and such an assault will be repelled by any means necessary, including military force."

We are confident that the negotiation of American overseas military facilities in support of this effort as well as in other areas of the world will be conducted with respect for the independence, integrity and cultural values of the host countries.

The Democratic Party recognizes the strategic value of Israel and that peace in the Middle East requires a militarily secure Israel. Because Middle East nations that have not joined the peace process have been able to purchase the latest sophisticated Soviet and other weaponry, the technological advantage which Israel holds over its adversaries has been jeopardized. The progress of the peace talks means that Israel has gained considerable security advantages from peace with Egypt. At the same time, Israel will lose some of the tactical advantages previously provided by territory occupied in 1967. Any further war Israel fights could take place close to its population centers. Therefore, we pledge a continued high level of U.S. military support for Israel.

U.S.–Soviet Relations

A strong, consistent, and principled policy toward the Soviet Union is a vital element of our foreign policy everywhere. The Democratic Administration will use all its resources—including both firm diplomacy and military power—to deter adventurism and to make restraint the only acceptable course available to our adversaries.

We stand ready to pursue good faith negotiations with the Soviet Union at every opportunity on a wide range of issues including strategic arms, forces in the European theater, and other matters which would contribute to peace and a more genuine and reciprocal detente.

At the heart of our policy toward the Soviet Union must be a clear recognition of the reality of Soviet power. We must reject the easy mythology that the Soviets see the world as we do. A long-term strategy for the late 80s requires a clear view of the Soviet Union, a view without illusion that our adversary is either benign or omnipotent.

The Soviet attack on Afghanistan, the murder of its leaders, and the ruthless effort to exterminate those resisting the Soviet invasion have violated all norms of international law and practice and have been thoroughly condemned by the international community.

This attempt to subjugate an independent, non-aligned Islamic people is a callous violation of international law, the United Nations Charter, and the principle of restraint which underlies detente.

This invasion places the Soviet armed forces within fighter aircraft range of the Straits of Hormuz, the lifeline of the bulk of the world's exportable oil.

It creates fear and instability among our friends in the region who are already buffeted by the disintegration of Iran as a stabilizing force.

More broadly, the success or failure of Soviet military aggression will affect present and future Soviet leaders' readiness to use force to gain their ends.

Hence, it is a threat not only to our strategic interests in the region but to world peace.

A strong American response to the illegal and brutal invasion of Afghanistan serves our nation's security interests. It must and will be sustained, as long as Soviet troops remain there.

In response to the Soviet invasion, the United States has cut grain exports, curbed high-technology trade and interrupted scientific and cultural relations.

The United States has also committed itself to a boycott of Moscow as the site of the Olympic Games. To attend while the Soviet armed might brutally seeks to crush the national liberation movement in Afghanistan would be a travesty of the Olympic spirit.

We must continue to support U.S. actions such as the Olympic boycott and trade restrictions in order to show determined opposition to Soviet aggression. We insist on immediate Soviet withdrawal from Afghanistan and the reestablishment of a non-aligned, independent government which is supported by the people of Afghanistan. The Soviet invasion of Afghanistan makes it extremely important that the United States be ready to aid those in the Third World resisting Soviet, Cuban, and East German domination.

While the invasion of Afghanistan has sidetracked our pursuit of a productive relationship with the Soviet Union, the Democratic Party supports efforts to strengthen ties to the nations of Eastern Europe. Treating each of those nations with sensitivity to its individual situation, the U.S. has steadily improved relations with the people of Hungary, Poland, and Romania. While Soviet conduct has profoundly damaged East–West relations, the U.S. should continue to draw distinctions, to the extent possible, between the sanctions it imposes on economic dealings with Moscow and similar relations with some other members of the Warsaw Pact, as long as they are not diverting that trade, in grain or items under export control, to the use of the Soviet Union and as long as they are willing to maintain a constructive dialogue on issues of concern and significance to the United States.

Through the measures now being taken, including both denial of economic benefits and the Olympic boycott, as well as our efforts to enhance the security of the region more directly affected, the objective should be to make the Soviets pay a price for their act of international aggression. We should continue to do so along with efforts to strengthen our national defense. We cannot permit this attack across an international border, with the threat it poses to the region and thus to the strategic balance, to go unanswered. Only firmness now can prevent new adventures later.

The Democratic Administration will also seek to reverse the recent sharp downturn in Soviet Jewish emigration and to obtain the release of dissidents now detained in the Soviet Union, including 41 members of the Helsinki Watch Group who are in Soviet prisons, labor camps and banishment for their human rights activity. We will pursue our human rights concerns as a necessary part of overall progress on the range of political, military and economic issues between the United States and the Soviet Union—including the possibility of improved, mutually beneficial economic relations between our two countries.

Consideration of human rights should be a permanent feature of U.S.–Soviet relations. We salute those Soviet citizens active in the Moscow, Ukrainian, Lithuanian, Armenian, and Georgian Helsinki Monitoring Groups, assert our support of the courageous human rights advocate, Nobel Peace Prize winner, Dr. Andrei Sakharov, and call for Dr. Sakharov's release from forced exile as well as the release of all political prisoners in the U.S.S.R.

We pledge that a Democratic Administration will raise the question of the Soviet violation of human rights at all appropriate international forums.

Arms Control

The SALT II Treaty also serves our security interests. It is a vital step in an arms control process that can begin to lift from humanity the shadow of nuclear war. That process, also, must be sustained.

Soviet aggression against Afghanistan has delayed the course of ratification of the SALT II Treaty, but we must continue to pursue both security priorities: deterrence of Soviet aggression and balanced arms control agreements. Both the response to Afghanistan and the SALT II Treaty serve this purpose.

The SALT Treaty is in the U.S. interest because it is an important way of restraining Soviet behavior.

Without SALT II, the Soviets could have hundreds more missiles and thousands more nuclear warheads than the Treaty permits. Under the Treaty, they would have to eliminate many nuclear weapons they already have.

The Treaty helps sustain a strong American position in the world. Our allies and other nations around the world know the SALT II Treaty serves their security interests as well as ours. American support for arms control is important to our standing in the international community, the same community that has rebuked the Soviets for their attempted suppression of Afghanistan. It is also important to our efforts to organize an enduring response to the growing threat to Europe of the Soviet SS-20 nuclear missiles and to Soviet aggression in Afghanistan.

Along with support for SALT, we seek to maintain a stable conventional and theater nuclear balance in Europe. We will support modernization programs in which European countries bear their fair share of the cost and other burdens. At the same time, we will ensure that no possibility for effective limits on theater nuclear weapons is left unexplored. The Democratic Administration will join with our NATO allies in making far-reaching, equitable, and verifiable proposals for nuclear and conventional arms control in Europe.

The Democratic Party wants an arms control process to continue, just as it wants to sustain strong policies against Soviet aggression in Afghanistan. We understand that both build peace and make our nation more secure. Accordingly, we must persist in a strong policy regarding the Soviet aggression, and we must seek ratification of SALT as soon as it is feasible.

A Democratic Administration will not accept an indefinite deferral of strategic arms control. On the basis of review and planning of U.S. security requirements in the coming decade, we are determined to pursue negotiations with the Soviet Union, aimed at the achievement of strategic stability and, for the first time, of major reductions and qualitative limits on strategic systems. The American SALT proposals in March 1977 were the first effort to seek such reductions, which remain the goal and justification of arms control. A Democratic Administration will treat the Soviet government's readiness to negotiate verifiable, substantial and significant reductions and qualitative limits as a test of its seriousness about arms control and the compatibility of its approach to arms control with that of the United States.

We will pursue other arms control opportunities that can enhance both our national security and the prospects of peace. In particular, the Democratic Administration will pursue a Comprehensive Nuclear Test Ban Treaty. Such a treaty is vital to our hopes to control the proliferation of nuclear weapons. Following the 1980 Review Conference on the Nuclear Non-Proliferation Treaty, we will step up our efforts to expand adherence to the treaty, to strengthen international safeguards and controls over nuclear materials, equipment and technology, and to forestall the spread of nuclear explosive capabilities. In any peaceful nuclear supply, we will continue to seek the full application of international safeguards and undertakings not to explode nuclear devices.

We have placed significant limits on our conventional arms transfers and will vigorously press other arms suppliers and recipients to accept mutual restraints.

The Democratic Administration has increased our capacity to counter national terrorism, both on a national basis and in coordination with other governments, and to deal with acts of terrorism including hostage-taking committed either by individuals or by governments. We will strengthen multilateral arrangements for contingency planning, information sharing, military coordination, and the isolation of countries that harbor terrorists.

Human Rights

In the area of international affairs, the Democratic Administration has placed America's power in the service of a more decent world by once again living up to our own values and working in a formal, deliberate way to foster the principles set out in the Universal Declaration of Human Rights.

This has been accomplished through a strong commitment to human rights, which must be seen not only as a moral imperative but as the only secure and enduring basis upon which a truly stable world order can be fashioned. There have been successes in Asia, Latin America, and elsewhere in the world. We must be undaunted by the increasing repression in the Soviet Union. We support measures designed to restrict trade with the Soviet Union until such time as Soviet emigration policy is made fair and non-restrictive.

We must be vigilant about human rights violations in any country in which they occur including South Africa. We note in particular that many of the Communist-dominated countries are persistent violators of the most basic human freedoms—the right to free speech, the right to religious freedom, the right to travel and emigrate, and the right to be free from arbitrary harassment.

We support Senate ratification of the Genocide Convention and the International Covenant on Human Rights as soon as possible.

We support continuation of the leadership role taken by the United States in the area of human rights and urge that the Democratic Administration continue to speak out openly and forcefully on human rights violations whenever and wherever they occur.

We will fulfill the letter and the spirit of current law by denying assistance to governments that violate fundamental human rights, except for that aid which is clearly humanitarian. We also recognize the exception for assistance that is required for overriding security purposes, but that exception should not be used as an excuse for ignoring abuses of human rights.

We will provide additional assistance and support, as needed, to governments that strive successfully for greater political liberty and protection of human rights.

Refugees and Migration

America's roots are found in the immigrants and refugees who have come to our shores to build new lives in a new world. The Democratic Party pledges to honor our historic commitment to this heritage.

The first comprehensive reform of this nation's refugee policies in over 25 years was completed with the signing in March 1980 of the Refugee Act of 1980, based on legislation submitted to Congress by the Carter Administration in March 1979.

This Act offers a comprehensive alternative to the chaotic movement and the inefficient and inequitable administration of past refugee programs in the United States. We favor the full use of refugee legislation now to cope with the flow of Cuban and Haitian refugees, and to help the states, local communities and voluntary agencies resettle them across our land. We urge that monies be distributed to voluntary agencies fairly so that aid is distributed to all refugees without discrimination.

The Administration also established the first refugee coordination office in the Department of State under the leadership of a special ambassador and coordinator for refugee affairs and programs.

The new legislation and the coordinator's office will bring common sense and consolidation to our nation's previously fragmented, inconsistent, and, in many ways, outdated refugee and immigration policies.

A Select Commission on Immigration and Refugee Policy is now at work to further reform the system. We pledge our support to the goals and purposes of the Commission, and we urge the Administration to move aggressively in this area once the Commission submits its report.

Once that report has been completed, we must work to resolve the issue of undocumented residents in a fair and humane way. We will oppose any legislation designed to allow workers into the country to undercut U.S. wages and working conditions, and which would reestablish the bracero program of the past.

World population projections, as well as international economic indicators—especially in the Third World—forewarn us that migration pressures will mount rapidly in many areas of the world in the decade ahead. Our own situation of undocumented workers underscores how difficult it is to deal with economic and employment forces that are beyond any nation's immediate control. Most of Europe, and many parts of Latin America and Asia, face similar dilemmas. For example, Mexico faces the pressure of migration from Central America.

We will work with other nations to develop international policies to regularize population movement and to protect the human rights of migrants even as we protect the jobs of American workers and the economic interest of the United States. In this hemisphere, such a policy will require close cooperation with our neighbors, especially Mexico and Canada.

We must also work to resolve the difficult problems presented by the immigration from Haiti and from the more recent immigration from Cuba. In doing so, we must ensure that there is no discrimination in the treatment afforded to the Cubans or Haitians. We must also work to ensure that future Cuban immigration is handled in an orderly way, consistent with our laws. To ameliorate the impact on state and local communities and school districts of the influx of new immigrants from Cuba and Haiti, we must provide the affected areas with special fiscal assistance.

We support continued financial backing of international relief programs such as those financed by the United States, the International Red Cross, UNICEF and the private, non-profit organizations to aid the starving people of Kampuchea. We also endorse such support for the Cambodian refugees and encourage participation in the campaign of the National Cambodian Crisis Committee.

We support, through U.S. contributions to the UN High Commissioner for Refugees and other means, aid for the mounting Afghan refugee population in Pakistan and other desperate refugee situations.

The Middle East

When the Democratic Administration began in 1977, the prospects for peace in the Middle East were bleak. Despite efforts over thirty years, Israel still faced an Arab world that was totally hostile to it; it was still denied any movement towards its dream of living at peace with its neighbors, behind secure and recognized frontiers.

Almost immediately after his inauguration, President Carter undertook to move the peace process forward. Following the historic visit of President Sadat to Jerusalem, the Administration's efforts led to Camp David, where the two presidents and Prime Minister Begin in thirteen days created the Camp David Accords—the most promising effort in three decades for creating a genuine and lasting peace in the Middle East.

Following President Carter's trip to the Middle East in March 1979, Prime Minister Begin and President Sadat signed the Israel–Egypt peace treaty at the White House. A year later, that treaty has led to the transfer of two-thirds of the Sinai to Egypt—along with the Sinai oil fields; ambassadors have been exchanged; borders have been opened; and normalization of relations is well under way. Israel has finally gained peace with its largest Arab neighbor. In sum, this Democratic Administration has done more to achieve Israel's dream of peace than any other Administration in thirty years.

Negotiations are continuing under the Camp David framework on full autonomy for the inhabitants of the West Bank and Gaza, in order to preserve fully Israel's security while permitting the Palestinians living in the territories to participate in determining their own future. The United States is a full partner in negotiations between Israel and Egypt to provide for a five-year transitional regime in the West Bank and Gaza.

It is recognized that the Democratic Administration has to proceed with special care and sensitivity resulting from its deep engagement in the delicate process of promoting a wider peace for Israel.

At the same time, the United States' commitment to the independence, security, and future of Israel has been strengthened. Nearly half of all U.S. aid to Israel since its creation as a sovereign state—more than $10 billion—has been requested during the last three and a half years. We provide Israel with modern military equipment and we fully support Israel's efforts to create a just and lasting peace with all of its Arab neighbors.

U.S. policy is—and should continue to be—guided also by the following principles:

UN Security Council Resolution 242, unchanged, and the Camp David Accords are the basis for peace in the Middle East.

We support Israel's security, and will continue to provide generous military and economic aid to that end.

We pledge not to provide Israel's potential enemies with sophisticated offensive equipment that could endanger the security of Israel.

Jerusalem should remain forever undivided, with free access to the holy places for people of all faiths.

We oppose creation of an independent Palestinian state.

We will not negotiate with or recognize the Palestinian Liberation Organization, unless and until it accepts Israel's right to exist and UN Security Council Resolutions 242 and 338. It is also long past time for an end to all terrorism and other acts of violence against Israel.

We have not and will not use our aid to Israel as a bargaining tool; and we will never permit oil policies to influence our policy toward peace or our support for Israel.

As stated in the 1976 platform, the Democratic Party recognizes and supports "the established status of Jerusalem as the capital of Israel, with free access to all its holy places provided to all faiths. As a symbol of this stand, the U.S. Embassy should be moved from Tel Aviv to Jerusalem."

Elsewhere in the Middle East, we support the improvement of relations with moderate Arab states. We support the independence, sovereignty, and integrity of Lebanon. We call upon all states in the region to support the historic efforts of Israel and Egypt to build a comprehensive peace.

We believe a cooperative effort among the nations of the Middle East and the United States can help provide needed assistance to Israel and her Middle East neighbors engaging in the peace process with Israel in the vital areas of refugee resettlement, agricultural development, water development, health and medical facilities, and productivity and trade. A planning group should be created to pursue an effort to provide this type of assistance.

The Democratic Administration will also take needed measures to protect American interests in the Persian Gulf, including energy security, regional stability, and national independence. This will require sophisticated diplomacy as well as military capability. We will seek both to counter external threats and to encourage necessary political and economic development. In the end, our allies have an equal or greater interest than we in the security of oil supply and regional stability, and the Democratic Administration will continue to cooperate with them in a common strategy and to share common burdens.

We condemn the government of Iran for its outrageous conduct in the taking of our diplomatic personnel as hostages. We insist upon respect for the principle—as repeatedly enunciated by the UN Security Council and the International Court of Justice—of the inviolability for diplomatic personnel. We call upon all governments to abide by and uphold this basic tenet of civilized international conduct.

In the region as a whole, we must end our dangerous dependence on foreign oil. Only in this way can our foreign policy counter effectively the pressures of OPEC and of Soviet power poised above the Persian Gulf in Afghanistan. The Democratic Administration will fulfill its commitments to the Strategic Petroleum Reserve to protect America against an oil embargo. As we reduce oil consumption and dependence on OPEC, we will be able to bargain on equal terms with the OPEC states for an assurance of more certain supplies of oil at more stable prices.

Europe and Japan

America and her allies must continue the mutual confidence and commitment, the sense of common purpose, that marked our relations for decades. The problems we face are global in scope. We cannot begin to solve them if each of us goes a separate way. We must learn to work in partnership, on an increasing range of problems, in areas such as Africa and the Persian Gulf, and on worldwide economic and security issues.

The Democratic Administration will be committed to a strong NATO and a stable military balance in Europe. We will pursue both modernization of NATO conventional and nuclear forces and equitable limitations between NATO and the Warsaw Pact.

The Democratic Administration will seek collective solutions to the common economic problems of inflation, unemployment, energy, trade and monetary relations which confront us and our allies. This will require increased cooperation and coordination among all OECD countries.

The Democratic Administration will continue to support the growth and cohesion of the European community, and will increase our support for Greece, Spain and Portugal, which have rejoined the ranks of democracy.

We have been particularly concerned about the need to maintain strategic stability in the eastern Mediterranean. To this end, we have worked with Congress toward the resolution of differences between Greece and Turkey over Cyprus and other divisive issues. We have worked toward a balanced treatment of both countries in our assistance programs.

We will give priority to the reintegration of Greece into NATO's military structure and to the strengthening of NATO's southern flank, including the economic progress of each of our allies in southern Europe.

We have worked towards a fair settlement of the Cyprus issue by giving our support to the United Nations efforts to encourage intercommunal talks. We agree with Secretary General Waldheim's opinion that such talks, if properly used, represent the best possible solution to a just and lasting political settlement of the Cyprus problem based on the legitimate rights of the two communities.

We must do all that is possible, consistent with our interest in a strong NATO in southern Europe and stability in the eastern Mediterranean, to encourage a fair settlement of the Cyprus issue, which has caused so much suffering in that area.

We will press strongly for the full implementation of UN Resolution 3212 in order to bring about an agreed resolution to the tragic conflict in Cyprus; including the withdrawal of all Turkish military forces from Cyprus, the safe return of all refugees to their homes, full cooperation of all parties with a negotiated solution and a full peace and respect for human rights in Cyprus.

Consistent with our traditional concern for peace and human rights, the next Democratic Administration will play a positive role in seeking peace in Northern Ireland. We condemn the violence on all sides. We will encourage progress toward a long-term solution based upon consent of all parties to the conflict, based on the principle of Irish unity. We take note of the Saint Patrick's Day statement ". . . that the solution offering the greatest promise of permanent peace is to end the division of the Irish people" and its urging of ". . . the British Government to express its interest in the unity of Ireland and to join with the government of Ireland in working to achieve peace and reconciliation." New political structures which are created should protect human rights, and should be acceptable to both Great Britain and Ireland and to both parts of the community of Northern Ireland.

Our relations with Japan have moved to a new level of maturity and cooperation. The United States is able to deal with patience and understanding on a wide range of difficult and contentious economic issues. In the foreign policy and security area, Japan's record in support of U.S. foreign policy objectives is second to none. We will continue to nurture this relationship.

The International Economy

A vigorous American foreign policy and a sustained defense effort depend on the strength of the U.S. economy and its ability to compete in the international market place.

Through annual economic summits in London, Bonn, Tokyo, and Venice, we have established a sound basis for economic progress in the 1980s by improving the coordination of our economic policies. We have sought to strengthen international institutions to deal with our common problems; to reduce worldwide inflation, which undermines Western security and prosperity; to encourage investment and innovation to increase productivity; and simultaneously to find ways to reduce unemployment, especially among our youth. We have made substantial progress, but the battle continues.

The Democratic Administration, which has wrestled with these issues over the past three and a half years, pledges a renewed effort to revitalize the world economy and to maintain our position as the leader of the free world's economic forces.

Trade

In 1976, we called for trade policies that would benefit economic growth. Trade promotes new jobs for American workers, new markets for farmers and businessmen, and lower prices for consumers. But trade can also cause dislocations within the economy, and we have sought—and will continue to seek—ways to ease the burden of adjustment to foreign competition without impeding the process of structural change so vital to our economic health. We favor a free international trading system, but that system must also be fair. We will not allow our workers and industries to be displaced by unfair import competition. We have entered orderly marketing agreements and other arrangements in areas such as color television, footwear and textiles, to help promote the competitive position of American industry. Others may be necessary.

Last year, we successfully concluded the Multilateral Trade Negotiations, an ambitious set of negotiations designed to reduce barriers to international trade. Before the Democratic Administration took office, these negotiations had proceeded at a snail's pace, and there had been a growing risk of failure which could have sparked a trade war damaging to our interests. It was the imaginative leadership of this Administration which breathed new life into an otherwise somnolent negotiation.

To strengthen the U.S. economy and improve our competitive position in the world economy, U.S. export–import policy must be based on the principle of fair trade that will enhance our exports while safeguarding domestic industry from unfair trade practices. In assuring orderly foreign trade, the U.S. must require observance of our trade laws, as well as cooperation with our trade policies if economic disruption is to be avoided. This will require:

- Encouragement of export expansion through vigorous negotiations to open foreign markets and enforce U.S. rights;
- The government to take swift, effective anti-dumping actions and enforce all U.S. trade laws to assure an end to unfair trade practices that lead to the export of American jobs;
- Regulations of imports of textiles and apparel in accordance with current laws and agreements;
- Enforcement of customs laws through the assessment of appropriate penalties. Imports, exports, technology transfers, money flows and investments must be reported in accordance with current laws, monitored and regulated to protect U.S. interests; and
- Implementation of the government procurement code only as negotiated and on a truly reciprocal basis.

We bargained long and hard to obtain concessions which would benefit Americans and open new markets to U.S. producers of both agricultural and industrial goods. The agreements, which won the overwhelming support of the U.S. Congress, achieved that objective. They represent a sensible balance of benefits. At the same time, they will ensure a liberal, but fair, international trading environment for the 1980s.

Monetary Affairs

We will continue to take whatever actions are necessary to maintain a sound and stable dollar. We will cooperate with other nations to minimize exchange rate disturbances. We fully support efforts under way to strengthen the ability of international financial institutions to adapt to changing needs and to facilitate the recycling of funds from the surplus oil–producing nations to those countries facing large, oil-induced deficits. We will urge OPEC countries to participate constructively in this process.

International Energy Cooperation

We have cooperated with other industrial countries, at summit meetings and in the International Energy Agency, in developing joint programs to conserve oil and increase production of alternative energy sources. Only through a truly global effort can the present imbalance between energy supply and demand be redressed. We will continue to support such efforts, showing our leadership by continuing the actions that have reduced oil consumption and imports by a greater proportion in the U.S. than in any other industrial country in the last year. We will work with our partners abroad to elicit increased effort by them, even as we seek increased U.S. effort at home, to the same ends.

The Developing World

Under the previous Republican Administration, the nations of the Third World viewed the United States as uninterested in or hostile to the need to treat the North–South economic issues which are of greatest importance to developing countries. Since then, the United States has adopted a range of economic policies on trade (MTN, Generalized System of Preferences expansion), commodities (Common Fund, sugar, coffee, tin), aid (International Financial Institutions replenishments) which have demonstrated that the Carter Administration is responsive to the aspirations of peoples in developing countries.

But this task is only begun. We share the globe with more than 4 billion people, more than three-quarters of whom live in developing nations, most of them poor. By the end of this century, the population of developing countries will grow by about 1.7 billion people. Their prospects for jobs, food, and peace will increasingly affect our own prospects. These nations can be the fastest-growing market for our exports, as they are today, or they can become sources for new immigration and hostility toward the industrial democracies.

Thus, America's defense, energy, and economic security depend on stability and growth not only among our allies, but among our friends in the Third World. It is unacceptable that the United States ranks 13th among 17 major industrial powers in percentage of GNP devoted to development assistance.

The Democratic Administration will work with the Congress to develop and sustain policies and programs of economic cooperation with the developing nations, guided by the test of mutual interest. We will approach the global negotiations next year on economic relations between the industrial North and developing South in this positive spirit. We will contribute the United States' fair share to the capital of the multilateral development banks and agencies, and we will continue substantial and innovative U.S. programs of direct development assistance to low-income countries.

These policies will be reflected in further concentration of U.S. development assistance in countries that make good use of aid and on programs that address the basic needs of poor people, especially food, health, and voluntary family planning services. We will increase U.S. and multilateral technical and financial assistance to oil-importing nations for the development of their energy resources. The participation of U.S. private enterprises in the economic growth of developing nations will be selectively encouraged, with due regard for our own employment objectives.

We are deeply concerned about the growing problem of world hunger as reported by the President's Commission on World Hunger. We are determined to increase our resources, and to seek a similar increase on the part of other nations, with a view toward solving this problem by the end of the century.

Together with our allies, the Democratic Administration will challenge OPEC and the Communist nations to reach a new collective worldwide commitment to economic development. All sides must increase their contributions for this development, so that the world may escape the spectre of international bankruptcy from rising energy costs and rising burdens of debt. Development in the Third World is vital to international political and economic stability and therefore to our own national security.

In all of our relations with developing nations, we will actively promote the cause of human rights and express America's abhorrence of the denial of freedom.

Our security depends critically on events in the Middle East, Asia, Latin America, and Africa, events marked by either the pursuit of goals common to or conflicting with our interests. We will continue to cooperate with key friendly developing nations in security relations and in economic measures ensuring our mutual security. Great care will be exercised in our security assistance activities to avoid stimulating regional arms races or needlessly diverting resources from development to armament.

The Third World

Under the previous Republican Administration relations with the Third World were at their nadir. The United States appeared hostile and indifferent to the developing world's aspirations for greater justice, respect, and dignity. All this has changed.

Latin America and the Caribbean

In stark contrast to the policies of previous Republican Administrations, this Democratic Administration has begun to forge a new, collaborative relationship with nations of Latin America and the Caribbean; one resting on a firm commitment to human rights, democratization, increased economic and industrial development, and non-intervention.

We must now move innovatively to strengthen our ties with our neighbors in the Western Hemisphere, first to obviate any vacuum for outside intervention and second to promote bilateral approaches for social progress and economic development including energy resources.

Through systematic and structural high-level attention to the problems of the Western Hemisphere we will mobilize the resources of our government to achieve this end. One such possibility to be considered is to appoint an Under Secretary of State for the Western Hemisphere. This would encourage both economic and political freedom throughout the Hemisphere.

We have given particular attention to developing a more balanced relationship with Mexico, a country with which we share so many important interests and also problems.

The successful negotiation of the Panama Canal Treaties—after fourteen fruitless years of effort—was seen as an indication of our willingness to treat Latin America on the basis of mutual respect. With those treaties ratified, the United States in 1980 is not only identified with the cause of human rights and democracy, but also we have opened a new chapter in our relations with the nations of this Hemisphere. Moreover, through regular multilateral consultations at all levels, more balanced relationships with the nations in the region have been forged.

The United States has worked hard to encourage the expansion of democracy in Latin America, respect for human rights, and the preservation of national independence and integrity from the threat of Soviet and Cuban intervention.

For the first time, an approach has been developed and tailored to the unique needs and aspirations of the Caribbean area. The Administration has supported change within a Democratic framework; more than doubled aid programs; and worked with twenty-nine other nations and fifteen international institutions to establish the Caribbean Group for Cooperation in Economic Development, which has quadrupled external aid to the region.

Through strengthened relations with the Caribbean Community and the Andean Pact, the Administration has worked to enhance subregional cooperation as well.

President Carter has worked for peace in the region. By signing Protocol I of the Treaty of Tlatelolco, President Carter has demonstrated his support for non-proliferation objectives in the Hemisphere. We support its ratification. By supporting regional efforts at arms restraints, the United States has taken the lead in trying to reduce the possibilities for conflict in the region.

We reaffirm our commitment to the protection of universally recognized and fundamental human rights throughout the Americas by urging that the Senate ratify the American Convention on Human Rights, which was signed by President Carter in June 1977.

We will join with other like-minded states in pursuing human rights, democracy, and economic development throughout the region. We will uphold our own law and terminate all aid except for clearly humanitarian purposes to human rights violators. In our relationships with Argentina, Chile, El Salvador, Guatemala, Haiti and others throughout the Hemisphere we will press further for respect for human rights and political liberalization. In Central America especially, we will align ourselves with those who are trying to build a better future out of the aftermath of tyranny, corruption and civil war.

We will oppose a spiral of confrontation with Cuba, for its own sake, but we will not evade the real issues between that country and the United States. Under no condition will we accept a Soviet military offensive capability based in Cuba or anywhere else in the Hemisphere.

In order to permit the pursuit of normal relations between our countries, Cuba should stop its disorderly movement of those seeking to leave; it should cooperate with the international community to develop a fair and orderly emigration program; it must withdraw its armed forces from Africa; it must cease subversive activities throughout the Hemisphere; and it should follow the principles of the American Convention on Human Rights.

Asia

The establishment of normal diplomatic and economic relations with China is an historic foreign policy achievement.

Progress in U.S.–China relations was stalled in 1977, but with patience, political courage and historic vision,

the deadlock was broken by this Democratic Administration.

In the fifteen months since normalization, the benefits of normalization have already become clear: trade, travel, cultural exchange, and, most important of all, the security and stability of the Pacific region is greater now than at any time in this century.

The Democratic Party commits itself to a broadening and deepening of our relationship with China in a way that will benefit both our peoples and the peace and security of the world. We will continue to seek new areas where the United States and China can cooperate in support of common interests. We have not and will not play "China cards" or other dangerous games; nor will we allow our relationship with any other country to impede our efforts to continue the process of normalization of relations with China.

In 1976, the so-called Korea-gate affair had badly hurt our ties to Korea. A friendly and increasingly frank dialogue with the Korean government has been promoted. We will continue not only to fulfill our commitment to security, but equally to the promotion of a more democratic government. North and South Korea have renewed their dialogue and made a difficult but hopeful start down a long, uncertain road. In our relationships with the Philippines, Taiwan and others in the region, we will also press for political liberalization and human rights.

With ASEAN, the Democratic Administration has developed a coherent and supportive approach, encouraging the cohesion of those five nations just at the time when their unity was being tested by the Vietnamese aggression in Kampuchea. ASEAN now stands as one of the most viable regional organizations in the world. The Democratic Party recognizes the important role the U.S. territories and other emerging island states in the Pacific Basin play in the solidification of defense and economic ties with the ASEAN nations. The Democratic Party commits itself to humanitarian aid to the people of East Timor.

Africa

Africa will be of central importance to American foreign policy in the 1980s. By the end of the previous Republican Administration in 1977, the United States had little credibility in Black Africa, for they had made little or no attempt to see African problems from an African perspective. Our policy had no clearly defined goals. As a consequence, our attempts to bring an end to the war in Southern Africa were ineffective. We were becoming, in African eyes, irrelevant—even antagonistic—to African aspirations.

The Democratic Administration developed a long-term African policy—a policy that is viable on its own merits and does not treat Africa as an appendage to great-power competition. It recognized the need for a new approach to the Continent, an approach based on mutual respect, fundamental concern for human rights and the necessity for economic justice.

Considerable success has been achieved, perhaps most notably in Southern Africa. Our diplomatic efforts there have been instrumental in helping to bring about a peaceful settlement in Rhodesia—now Zimbabwe—while lessening Soviet/Cuban influence in the area. We will continue to assist in the reconstruction and development of an independent Zimbabwe, as a means of promoting stability in the region.

Much remains to be done. Many of the fifty African nations are politically unstable and economically weak—partially as a result of their colonial heritage, but increasingly, due to endemic drought and the economic dislocation resulting from ever-rising energy costs.

The Democratic Party pledges itself to continue efforts to improve U.S. relations with all African nations, on the basis of mutual respect and a mutual commitment to enhance economic justice and human dignity everywhere, with particular emphasis on the recurrent problem of drought and starvation. U.S. aid in the form of grain and foodstuffs must be continued but, in addition, we must seek with African governments ways of removing famine permanently from the African Continent.

The Democratic Party pledges itself to the process of economic reconstruction in Zimbabwe within the context of a coherent multi-donor development plan for all the cooperating nations of the Southern African region.

The Democratic Party pledges active support for self-determination in Namibia, and for full social and economic justice for all the peoples of Southern Africa.

The Democratic Administration will press for the withdrawal of Soviet and Cuban troops.

In Southern Africa, we will exert our influence to promote progress toward majority rule and to end the racist system of apartheid. We condemn the brutal suppression of Black Native African people in Soweto and Capetown by the South African regime and support increased political and economic pressure on this oppressive regime, through legal sanctions.

We support increased pressure through legal diplomatic sanctions on the oppressive South African regime. Initially we will divest, under legal procedures, South African holdings of all public institutions and deploy full legal economic sanctions until that government abandons its undemocratic apartheid system.

Following the removal of Cuban troops from Angola, we will seek to normalize relations with Angola. We will strengthen relations with nations committed to the objectives of economic development, respect for human rights and political liberalization. In the western Sahara we will support a negotiated settlement to the conflict.

The United Nations and International Agencies

In each of the regions of the globe, international organizations and agencies will be tested in the coming decade and will play an increasingly crucial role. The United Nations remains the only forum where rich and poor, East and West, and neutral nations can come together to air their grievances, participate in respected forums of world opinion, and find mechanisms to resolve disputes without resort to force. In particular, in recent months the UN has been a forum for expressing the world's condemnation and rejection of both the hostage-taking in Iran and the Soviet invasion of Afghanistan.

The United Nations is also vital in other ways—through its international refugee efforts, coordination of development assistance, support for agricultural research, and worldwide eradication of disease.

In the next decade, international monetary and development institutions will also be under increasing pressure. Their efforts must be expanded to meet more fully the urgent needs of the two-thirds of the world's population which suffers the damaging and depressing effects of underdevelopment.

The United Nations and these agencies perform a vital role in the search for peace. They deserve America's continuing support—and they will receive it from the Democratic Administration. We support the U.S. position on freedom of the press to be voted again in Belgrade during the 1980 UNESCO meeting.

We support the call in Section 503 of the Foreign Relations Authorization Act of 1978, for the United States to make "a major effort toward reforming and restructuring the United Nations system."

We also endorse that portion of the President's report to Congress in March, 1978 on UN reform and restructuring which calls for the Senate "to re-examine the Connally reservations" "the creation of a U.N. Peacekeeping Reserve composed of national contingents trained in peacekeeping functions," the establishment of "a new UN senior post as High Commissioner of Human Rights," and the development of autonomous sources of income for the international community.

We will work toward new structures which will enhance the UN in the fields of economic development, including international trade organizations, higher education, volunteer service, mediation and conciliation, international disarmament, implementation of the Law of the Sea Agreement, and controlling international terrorism.

Into the 1980s

As we look to the 1980s, we have a full and challenging agenda.

With our allies, we face the challenge of building greater unity of action while preserving the diversity of our democracies. Europe is increasingly united and is finding its own identity and voice. We must forge new links of consultation and revive the political process within the North Atlantic Alliance so that Europe remains America's partner in meeting the challenges to our common security and economic interests. We must find ways to include Japan in this process, broadening the mechanisms for cooperation which exist in current international forums, such as the Seven-Nation Summit.

With the Third World countries, we must continue to do our part in the realization of their aspirations for justice, respect, and freedom. We must continue to work for full political participation by all in South Africa, including independence and majority rule in Namibia. We must work to strengthen democracy in the Caribbean and Central America in the face of efforts by the Cubans to export their failed revolution. Throughout Latin America, we must continue to cooperate for the realization of greater human rights and the fulfillment of basic human needs. In Asia, we must continue to strengthen our relationships with our friends and allies as they confront the twin dangers flowing from the Soviet invasion of Afghanistan and the Soviet-backed invasion of Cambodia.

We must persevere with the Middle East peace process. There is no viable alternative. We can welcome initiatives from other countries so long as they contribute to the Camp David process that is leading toward a comprehensive peace in that region. But we will oppose efforts that undermine Camp David while offering no viable alternative. Our goal is to see the achievement of a comprehensive peace for all parties.

With our defenses, we will continue to meet the requirements of the Administration's five-year defense program, including the deployment of the MX missile,

cruise missiles, the Trident submarine, and long-range theater nuclear forces in Europe. At the same time, we intend to increase readiness and strengthen the all-volunteer force with a standby system of draft registration. We will continue with our allies to meet the commitments of the long-term NATO defense program and, as we strengthen our military capabilities and presence in Southwest Asia and the region of the Persian Gulf, we will look to our allies to assume more of the burden for the defense and security of Europe. Finally, we must recognize that development assistance represents a crucial part of our national security. As such, we may have to make a greater contribution of resources to these programs.

In the field of arms control, in addition to ratification of SALT II, we must proceed to more comprehensive and drastic reductions and qualitative limitations on strategic nuclear forces. SALT III must also include effective limitations and reductions in long-range theater nuclear forces based on the principle of equality. We must pursue to a conclusion a comprehensive test ban, effective curbs in the international traffic of conventional arms and a more rigorously effective international regime to prevent the spread of nuclear weapons and weapons technology. We must bring to at least an initial conclusion the negotiations for mutual and balanced force reductions in Europe. The decade of the 1980s is not to become the decade of violence. We must make renewed efforts to stabilize the arms competition and widen the scope of arms control arrangements.

As we look to the future, we hope the progress in arms control and the strength and determination we shall demonstrate in the face of Soviet aggression in Afghanistan will soon result in the fashioning of a stronger, more productive relationship with the Soviet Union. We favor a genuine detente—one with equivalent benefits to ourselves and the Soviets, one that is based on genuine restraint, one that benefits all mankind by harnessing the enormous potential of our two societies for cooperation rather than competition and confrontation. This will take patience, but we shall persevere, for the prize is peace.

By reaffirming America's values as the centerpiece of our foreign policy and by pursuing realistically the requirements of military strength, the Democratic Party is forging a new and broader consensus among the American people in support of our foreign policy. We are turning the tide against the paralysis of despair that came from a tragic war in Asia and political scandal at home. We are restoring America to its rightful place, not only as the strongest nation in the world, but as the nation which is the champion of human justice and freedom.

— 1984 —

PREAMBLE

A fundamental choice awaits America—a choice between two futures.

It is a choice between solving our problems, and pretending they don't exist; between the spirit of community, and the corrosion of selfishness; between justice for all, and advantage for some; between social decency and social Darwinism; between expanding opportunity and contracting horizons; between diplomacy and conflict; between arms control and an arms race; between leadership and alibis.

America stands at a crossroads.

Move in one direction, and the President who appointed James Watt will appoint the Supreme Court majority for the rest of the century. The President who proposed deep cuts in Social Security will be charged with rescuing Medicare. The President who destroyed the Environmental Protection Agency will decide whether toxic dumps get cleaned up. The President who fought the Equal Rights Amendment will decide whether women get fair pay for their work. The President who launched a covert war in Central America will determine our human rights policy. The President who abandoned the Camp David process will oversee Middle East policy. The President who opposed every nuclear arms control agreement since the bomb went off will be entrusted with the fate of the earth.

We offer a different direction.

For the economy, the Democratic Party is committed to economic growth, prosperity, and jobs. For the individual, we are committed to justice, decency, and opportunity. For the nation, we are committed to peace, strength, and freedom.

In the future we propose, young families will be able to buy and keep new homes—instead of fearing the explosion of their adjustable-rate mortgages. Workers will feel secure in their jobs—instead of fearing layoffs and lower wages. Seniors will look forward to retirement—instead of fearing it. Farmers will get a decent return on their investment—instead of fearing bankruptcy and foreclosure.

Small businesses will have the capital they need—instead of credit they can't afford. People will master technology—instead of being mastered or displaced by it. Industries will be revitalized—not abandoned.

Students will attend the best colleges and vocational schools for which they qualify—instead of trimming their expectations. Minorities will rise in the mainstream of economic life—instead of waiting on the sidelines. Children will dream of better days ahead—and not of nuclear holocaust.

Our Party is built on a profound belief in America and Americans.

We believe in the inspiration of American dreams, and the power of progressive ideals. We believe in the dignity of the individual, and the enormous potential of collective action. We believe in building, not wrecking. We believe in bridging our differences, not deepening them. We believe in a fair society for working Americans of average income; an opportunity society for enterprising Americans; a caring society for Americans in need through no fault of their own—the sick, the disabled, the hungry, the elderly, the unemployed; and a safe, decent and prosperous society for all Americans.

We are the Party of American values—the worth of every human being; the striving toward excellence; the freedom to innovate; the inviolability of law; the sharing of sacrifice; the struggle toward justice; the pursuit of happiness.

We are the Party of American progress—the calling to explore; the challenge to invent; the imperative to improve; the importance of courage; the perennial need for fresh thinking, sharp minds, and ambitious goals.

We are the Party of American strength—the security of our defenses; the power of our moral values; the necessity of diplomacy; the pursuit of peace; the imperative of survival.

We are the Party of American vision—the trustees of a better future. This platform is our road map toward that future.

CHAPTER I. ECONOMIC GROWTH, PROSPERITY AND JOBS

Introduction

Building a prosperous America in a changing world: that is the Democratic agenda for the future. To build that America, we must meet the challenge of long-term, sustainable, noninflationary economic growth. Our future depends on it.

To a child, economic growth means the promise of quality education. To a new graduate, it means landing a good first job. To a young family, growth means the opportunity to own a home or a car. To an unemployed worker, it means the chance to live in dignity again. To a farmer, growth means expanding markets, fair prices, and new customers. To an entrepreneur, it means a shot at a new business. To our nation, it means the ability to compete in a dramatically changing world economy. And to all in our society, growth—and the prosperity it brings—means security, opportunity, and hope. Democrats want an economy that works for everyone—not just the favored few.

For our party and our country, it is vital that 1984 be a year of new departures.

We have a proud legacy to build upon: the Democratic tradition of caring, and the Democratic commitment to an activist government that understands and accepts its responsibilities.

Our history has been proudest when we have taken up the challenges of our times, the challenges we accept once again in 1984—to find new ways, in times of accelerating change, to fulfill our historic commitments. We will continue to be the Party of justice. And we will foster the productivity and growth on which justice depends.

For the 1980's, the Democratic Party will emphasize two fundamental economic goals. We will restore rising living standards in our country. And we will offer every American the opportunity for secure and productive employment.

Our program will be bold and comprehensive. It will ask restraint and cooperation from all sectors of the economy. It will rely heavily on the private sector as the prime source of expanding employment. And it will treat every individual with decency and respect.

A Democratic Administration will take four key steps to secure a bright future of long-term economic growth and opportunity for every American:

- Instead of runaway deficits, a Democratic Administration will pursue overall economic policies that sharply reduce deficits, bring down interest rates, free savings for private investment, prevent another explosion of inflation and put the dollar on a competitive footing.
- In place of conflict, a Democratic Administration will pursue cooperation, backed by trade, tax and financial regulations that will serve the long-term growth of the American economy and the broad national interest.
- Instead of ignoring America's future, a Democratic Administration will make a series of long-term investments in research, infrastructure, and above all in people. Education, training and retraining will become a central focus in an economy built on change.

The Future If Reagan Is Reelected

"Since the Reagan Administration took office, my wife and I have lost half our net worth. Took us 20 years to build that up, and about three to lose it. That is hard to deal with. . . ."—David Sprague, Farmer, Colorado (Democratic Platform Committee Hearing, Springfield, Illinois, April 27, 1984)

"There's got to be something wrong with our government's policy when it's cheaper to shut a plant down than it is to operate it. . . . The Houston Works plant sits right in the middle of the energy capital of the world and 85 percent of our steel went directly into the energy-related market, yet Japan could sit their products on our docks cheaper than we can make it and roll it there."—Early Clowers, President, Steel Workers Local 2708 (Democratic Platform Committee Hearing, Houston, Texas, May 29, 1984).

A Democratic future of growth and opportunity, of mastering change rather than hiding from it, of promoting fairness instead of widening inequality, stands in stark contrast to another four years of Ronald Reagan. Staying the course with Ronald Reagan raises a series of hard questions about a bleak future.

What would be the impact of the Republican deficit if Mr. Reagan is reelected?

A second Reagan term would bring federal budget deficits larger than any in American history—indeed, any in world history. Under the Republicans' policies, the deficit will continue to mount. Interest rates, already rising sharply, will start to soar. Investments in the future will be slowed, then stopped. The Reagan deficits mortgage the future and threaten the present.

Mr. Reagan has already conceded that these problems exist. But as he said in his 1984 Economic Report to the Congress, he prefers to wait until after the election to deal with them. And then, he plans "to enact spending reductions coupled with tax simplification that will eventually eliminate our budget deficit."

What will Mr. Reagan's plan for "tax simplification" mean to average Americans if he is reelected?

Ronald Reagan's tax "reforms" were a bonanza for the very wealthy, and a disaster for poor and middle-class Americans. If reelected, Mr. Reagan will have more of the same in store. For him, tax simplification will mean a further freeing of the wealthy from their obligation to pay their fair share of taxes and an increasing burden on the average American.

How will Mr. Reagan's "spending reductions" affect average Americans if he is reelected?

If he gets a second term, Mr. Reagan will use the deficit to justify his policy of government by subtraction. The deficits he created will become his excuse for destroying programs he never supported. Medicare, Social Security, federal pensions, farm price supports and dozens of other people-oriented programs will be in danger.

If Mr. Reagan is reelected, will our students have the skills to work in a changing economy?

If we are to compete and grow, the next generation of Americans must be the best-trained, best-educated in history. While our competitors invest in educating their children. Mr. Reagan cuts the national commitment to our schools. While our competitors spend greater and greater percentages of their GNP on civilian research and development, this President has diverted increasing portions of ours into military weaponry. These policies are short-sighted and destructive.

If Mr. Reagan is reelected, will basic industries and the workers they employ be brought into the future?

The Republican Administration has turned its back on basic industries and their communities. Instead of putting forward policies to help revitalize and adjust, Mr. Reagan tells blameless, anxious, displaced workers to abandon their neighborhoods and homes and "vote with their feet."

America's economic strength was built on basic industries. Today, in a changing economy, they are no less important. Strong basic industries are vital to our economic health and essential to our national security. And as major consumers of high technology, they are catalysts for growth in newly emerging fields. We need new approaches to ensure strong American basic industries for the remainder of this century and beyond.

Can the road to the future be paved with potholes?

Adequate roads and bridges, mass transit, water supply and sewage treatment facilities, and ports and harbors are essential to economic growth. For four years, the Reagan Administration has refused to confront adequately the growing problems in our infrastructure. Another term will bring four more years of negligence and neglect.

If Mr. Reagan is reelected, how many children will join the millions already growing up at risk?

Between 1980 and 1982, more than two million younger Americans joined the ranks of the poor: the sharpest increase on record.

With the Reagan Administration's cutbacks in prenatal care and supplemental food programs have come infant mortality rates in parts of our cities rivaling those of the poorest Latin American nations. Black infants are now twice as likely as white infants to die during the first year of life.

Cuts in school lunch and child nutrition programs have left far too many children hungry and unable to focus on their lessons.

Teenage prostitution, alcohol and drug abuse, depression, and suicide have all been linked to child abuse. The Administration has abandoned most avenues to breaking the cycle of abuse. Funding to prevent and treat child physical abuse has been cut in half. And funds to help private groups set up shelters for runaway youth are being diverted elsewhere.

If Mr. Reagan is reelected, will he ensure that our children are able to enjoy a clean, healthy environment?

Protecting our natural heritage—its beauty and its richness—is not a partisan issue. For eighty years, every American President has understood the importance of protecting our air, our water, and our health. Today, a growing population puts more demands on our environment. Chemicals which are unsafe or disposed of improperly threaten neighborhoods and families. And as our knowledge expands, we learn again and again how fragile life and health—human and animal—truly are.

Ensuring the environmental heritage of future generations demands action now. But the Reagan Administration continues to develop, lease, and sell irreplaceable wilderness lands. While thousands of toxic waste sites already exist, and more and more are being created constantly, the Reagan Administration is cleaning them up at a rate of only 1.5 per year. The environmental legacy of Ronald Reagan will be long-lasting damage that can *never* truly be undone.

If Mr. Reagan is reelected, will we be able to heat our homes and run our factories?

Twice in the past, our country has endured the high costs of dependence on foreign oil. Yet the Reagan Administration is leaving us vulnerable to another embargo or an interruption in oil supply. By failing adequately to fill the Strategic Petroleum Reserve, and trusting blindly to the market to "muddle through" in a crisis, this Administration has wagered our national security on its economic ideology. One rude shock from abroad or just one "market failure," and our country could find itself plunged into another energy crisis.

The New Economic Reality: Five Reagan Myths

Underlying the Reagan approach to the economy are five key myths: myths that determine and distort the Reagan economic policy, and ensure that it is not the basis for long-term growth.

The world has changed, but Ronald Reagan does not understand.

First, and most fundamental, the Reagan Administration continues to act as if the United States were an economic island unto itself. But we have changed from a relatively isolated economy to an economy of international interdependence. In fact, the importance of international trade to the U.S. economy has roughly doubled in a decade. Exports now account for almost 10 percent of GNP—and roughly 20 percent of U.S. manufactured goods. One in six manufacturing jobs now depends on exports, and one in three acres is now planted for the overseas market. Imports have also doubled in importance.

Financial markets are also closely linked. U.S. direct investments and commercial loans overseas now amount to hundreds of billions of dollars. A debt crisis in Mexico will affect balance sheets in San Francisco. A recession in Europe will limit the profits of U.S. subsidiaries operating in the European market. Lower overseas profits will limit the flow of earnings back to the United States—one important way the U.S. has found to help pay for the rising tide of imports. Hundreds of billions of dollars in foreign short-term capital invested here are sensitive to small shifts in interest rates or the appearance of added risk. It is only partly bad loans that brought Continental Illinois to the brink of bankruptcy. Heavily dependent on short-term foreign deposits, Continental Illinois was particularly vulnerable. Rumors that were false at the time were enough to set off a run on the bank.

The strength of American steel, the competitiveness of the U.S. machine tool industry, and the long-term potential of U.S. agriculture are no longer matters decided exclusively in Washington or by the American market. America must look to Tokyo, Paris, and the money markets in Singapore and Switzerland. Policy based on the myth that America is independent of the world around us is bound to fail.

Second, this Administration has ignored the enormous changes sweeping through the American work force.

The maturing of the baby boom generation, the sharp increase in the percentage of women seeking work, and the aging of the work force all have to be taken into account.

Decade by decade, more and more women have moved into the work force. This large-scale movement is already changing the nature of professions, altering the patterns of child care and breaking down sex-based distinctions that have existed in many types of employment.

In Ronald Reagan's vision of America, there are no single parent families; women only stay at home and care for children. Reagan's families do not worry about the effects of unemployment on family stability; they do not worry about decent housing and health care; they do not need child care. But in the real world, most Americans do. Providing adequate child care for the millions of American children who need it, and for their parents, is surely not a responsibility which belongs solely to the federal government. But, like the responsibility for decent housing and health care, it is one where federal leadership and support are essential.

The work force is also aging. For the first time in this century, the average American is 31 years of age. Coupled with greater longevity and the gradual elimination of mandatory retirement rules, older workers can be expected to increase steadily their share of the total work force.

Moreover, the kinds of jobs available in our economy are changing rapidly. The combined pressures of new products, new process technology, and foreign competition are changing the face of American industry.

New technologies, shifting economics and deregulation have opened up dozens of new careers both in traditional industrial concerns and in new businesses. Many of them did not exist at all only a few years ago.

And the change is far from over. In setting national policy, a government that ignores that change is bound to fail. In setting national policy, a government that ignores the future is short-changing the American people.

Third, the Reagan program has ignored the fundamental changes that are sweeping through the structure of American industry, the diversity of the economy and the challenges various sectors face. New products and new ways of manufacturing are part of the change. High technology is creating new competitive industries, and holding out the promise of making older industries competitive once again. Foreign competition has also had a major impact. But the tide runs much deeper than that.

In the past decade, small business and new entrepreneurs have become more and more of a driving force in the American economy. Small businesses are a growing force in innovation, employment, and the long-term strength of the American economy.

Technology itself appears to be changing the optimal size of American businesses. And unlike the conglomerate mergers of the 1960's, renewed emphasis on quality and efficient production has shifted the focus back to industry-specific experience.

An administration that sets tax policy, spending priorities, and an overall growth program without understanding the new dynamics and the diversity of American industry is weakening, rather than strengthening the American economy.

Reaganomics is based on the theory that blanket tax

cuts for business and the rich would turn directly into higher productivity, that private investors and industry would use the money saved to restore our edge in innovation and competitiveness.

In practice, the theory failed because it did not take into account the diversity within our economy. The economy is composed of a set of complex public and private institutions which are intricately interrelated and increasingly influenced by the pressures of international competition. In the international economy, multinational companies and governments cooperate to win trade advantage, often at American expense.

We are coming to understand that in an expanding number of markets, industrial strategies, rather than just the energies of individual firms, influence competitive success. Indeed, success in marketing a product may depend more on the quality and productivity of the relationship between government and business than on the quality of the product. While several foreign industrial strategies have failed, foreign governments are becoming more sophisticated in the design and conduct of their industrial strategies. The Reagan Administration is not.

Fourth, the Reagan Administration has acted as if deficits do not count. The deficits are huge and are expected to get larger—and they are a major negative factor in everything from high interest rates to the Third World debt crisis.

- Because of the huge tax cuts to benefit the wealthy, and an enormous military build-up bought on credit, the federal deficit in 1983 was equivalent to 6% of our GNP. In dollars it amounted to almost 200 billion—more than three times larger than the deficit Ronald Reagan campaigned against in 1980.
- Under the budget Reagan proposed to Congress earlier this year, the annual deficit would grow to $248 billion by 1989, and unless he makes major changes in current policy, it will exceed $300 billion. Reagan doubled the national debt during his first term. Given eight years, he will have tripled it. According to the proposed budget, at the end of his second term Reagan *by himself* will have put this country *three times deeper* into debt than *all our other Presidents combined*.
- As the Reagan debt hangs over us, more and more of our tax dollars are going nowhere. By 1989, the percentage of federal revenues to be spent on deficit interest payments alone will have doubled. *These unproductive payments will claim a staggering 42¢ on every personal income tax dollar we pay.* This huge allocation will do nothing to reduce the principal of the debt; it will only finance the interest payments.

- The interest payments on Reagan's debt are grossly out of line with historical spending patterns. Since 1981, more money has been squandered on *interest payments* on the Reagan-created debt alone than has been saved by all of Reagan's cuts in domestic spending. Non-defense discretionary spending, to be productively invested in programs to benefit the poor and middle class, and to build our social capital, is being overwhelmed by the enormous sums of money wasted on interest payments. By 1989, the annual payment will account for twice the percentage of federal revenue that we have ever set aside for such discretionary programs.
- Interest payments on the debt are rising at an alarming rate. Today the annual payment has already reached $110 billion—twice what it was four years ago. During a second Reagan term, it will double *again*, reaching $207 billion by 1989.
- The consequences for the individual taxpayer are enormous. Deficit increases under Reagan so far are equivalent to $2,387 levied from every woman, man and child alive in the United States today.
- The consequences for the nation as a whole are also enormous. The massive government borrowing necessary to service the debt will amount to about three-quarters of the entire nation's net savings between 1983 and 1986.

The pressure of the deficits on interest rates has sucked in a wave of overseas investment. Some of those investments have been made in manufacturing plants or other commercial enterprises. Much of the foreign money, however, is in the form of portfolio holdings or even more liquid short-term bank deposits. It is an uncertain source of savings for a long-term investment program. To a limited degree, it puts the country in the same risky position as Continental Illinois Bank, which relied heavily on short-term foreign deposits to make long-term domestic loans.

High interest rates will eventually take their toll on domestic investment, make their own contribution to inflationary pressure (while eventually slowing growth and inflation), and increase the tensions in the domestic banking system. They will also have a potentially devastating impact on the international economy. Each percentage point rise in U.S. interest rates adds $3–5 billion to the annual debt payments of the developing world. High American interest rates have also put added pressure on interest rates in the industrial democracies, dampening their own prospects for growth, and their ability to buy our goods.

Fifth, and finally, the Reagan Administration has virtually wished away the role of government. When it comes to the economy, *its view is that the government that governs best is one that governs not at all.*

A Democratic Administration must answer this challenge by reaffirming the principle that government must both "provide for the common defense" *and* "promote the general welfare" as coequal responsibilities under the Constitution. If the Democratic Party can succeed in correcting the present imbalance, it will reverse the cycle of pain and despair, and recapture the initiative in the area of social and economic progress.

The Reagan Administration succeeded in shifting massive resources from human needs functions of the federal budget to military-related functions and created unprecedented deficits, based on the assumption that government should have a diminished responsibility for social progress, and thus, for the welfare of the needy and disadvantaged in society. The resulting Reagan-induced recession caused tremendous suffering, threw millions of people out of work, terminated or reduced benefits, and raised the national misery index.

Mr. Reagan denies government's critical role in our economy. Government cannot, and should not, dominate our free enterprise economy. But American prosperity has been most pronounced when the government played a supportive or catalytic role in the nation's economic fortunes. There are a wide variety of examples stretching back through our entire history: government investments in roads and research, in education and training: government initiatives in opening up new economic possibilities, initiatives that started with the decision to protect domestic markets shortly after the Revolution to the ongoing commercial development of space.

Agriculture is a clear example of government cooperation with a highly competitive private sector that has yielded a harvest of economic results that is the envy of the world. The government helps fund the research, helps spread it through the economy, educates the modern farmer, influences production levels, and helps develop new markets overseas. It is America's most conspicuous example of a successful industrial strategy—combining the cooperative efforts of business, government and our universities.

Reagan's Recession and a Recovery Built on Debt

The Economic Roller Coaster. Following the first oil shock in 1973, the United States embarked on a ten-year economic roller coaster. The up-and-down performance of the economy was paralleled by erratic macro-economic policy. There were wide swings from stimulative fiscal and monetary policies causing raging inflation to government-engineered recessions.

The frequency of the cycles created a climate of uncertainty that was tailor-made to discourage and distort investment. Each cycle left the economy weaker than the one before. At the end of each recession the level of inflation was higher, and at the end of each recovery the level of unemployment had risen.

Even more disturbing was the decline in the rate of growth of productivity. By the end of the 1970's, productivity growth first stopped and then fell. Productivity growth has finally resumed—but the rate of growth remains disappointing compared both to our own economic past and the performance of other industrial economies.

Reaganomics and an Election Year Recovery. Ronald Reagan swept into office on the promise of a smaller government and a bigger private sector, of higher GNP and lower inflation, and of the elimination of federal deficits.

First, he proposed huge tax cuts. Mr. Reagan went so far as to suggest that the growth caused by his tax cuts would be so rapid that total tax revenues would actually rise even while tax rates were cut.

Second, he promised a huge defense build-up.

Third, he promised stable prices. How was he going to contain prices while stimulating rapid growth? His answer was tight money.

Fourth, the supply-siders promised growth and stable prices without the intervening pain of a recession. In effect, Reagan promised tight money without tears.

Cut taxes but raise more revenues. Arm to the teeth. Growth with stable prices. Tight money and no hard times. It just did not work out that way. Worse, there was never any reason to expect that it would. Reagan's kind of tax cuts were based neither on national economic theory nor on any empirical evidence. And wishing simply did not make it so. George Bush was right when he called Reaganomics "voodoo economics."

Instead of growth, the country had plunging production and record unemployment. Instead of increased savings and investment, the country had bankruptcy and economic decline. The Reagan policies, which were supposed to break the cycle of inflation and recession, only made it worse.

Reagan cut domestic programs, but more than offset those cuts with vastly increased defense spending. The government significantly reduced the growth of the money supply and kept real interest rates high. For a recession, real interest rates reached record highs. These interest rates brought an added problem. They attracted foreign funds and helped drive up the international value of the dollar. American business was faced with a double whammy—empty order books and high interest rates. For the increasingly large part of American business that either sells overseas or competes with imports at home, the overvalued dollar abroad meant their products cost far more compared to the foreign competition.

Reagan effectively created a tax on exports and a subsidy for imports. It was a climate that forced record bankruptcies, enormous unemployment, plant closings, and major corporate reorganizations. It was the largest and most severe economic collapse since the Great Depression.

The Reagan Administration then prepared for the election year by "staying the course" in fiscal policy (pumping up demand with huge deficits) and sharply reversing the course in monetary policy.

The Federal Reserve Board rapidly expanded the supply of money and the economy ceased to decline and began to recover.

The Millions Left Behind. But millions of Americans were left behind. Over the last two years, 1.8 million men and women have became discouraged workers and more than 5.4 million have fallen into poverty. Nearly half of all minority youth are unemployed, and Black males have effectively lost 13 percent of their labor force participation in the last two decades. Unemployment on Indian reservations continues to be among the highest in the nation. The U.S.–Mexico border has been devastated by the currency devaluations and economic crisis in Mexico. Small businesses have closed: American families are suffering hunger and poor health, as unemployment exceeds depression rates. Women continue to receive less than 60 percent of the wages that men receive, with minority women receiving far less. Millions of other Americans, including the growing number of women heading poor households or those who have been hard-hit by plant closings or obsolescent skills, avidly seek training or retraining in occupations that hold real promise for sustained employment opportunities in the future.

Millions of Americans, including those in the industrial and agricultural heartland, have been severely affected by the recent recession and the transformation in American industry that accompanied it. Furthermore, the changes seem to have come very quickly, and they do not seem to be over. Many Americans worked in auto, steel, machine tool, textile, agriculture and small business and related industries. Today for many of them, the recovery is a fiction, or seems very fragile. Plant closings have hit hard and job security and loss of health and pension benefits evoke memories from the past.

Investment in jobs for all Americans constitutes the key investment for the future of the nation. For every one million workers who go back to work, our country produces an additional $60–70 billion in goods and adds $25 billion to the federal treasury. The Democratic Party will work aggressively to stimulate employment, rebuild trade and encourage labor-intensive industrialization.

Seven Threats to the Recovery

The current election year recovery is in serious jeopardy, threatened by a series of major economic problems:

- Unless corrective action is taken soon, the current $180 billion deficit will balloon even larger by the end of the decade.
- Interest rates are high and rising. The prime rate has jumped one and one half percentage points. A credit crunch is rapidly approaching in which federal borrowing for the deficit will overwhelm private demand for funds to fuel the recovery. Mortgage rates have risen to a point where home sales and housing starts are beginning to fall. The variable rate mortgage that buffers the thrift industry against high interest rates may, in the near future, put the entire industry under pressure as steadily rising rates put mortgage payments beyond the reach of the average homeowner.
- The Federal Reserve Board faces a deficit dilemma. By expanding the money supply to help finance the deficit, the Federal Reserve runs the risk of runaway inflation. But if it limits growth by restricting the money supply, high interest rates will distort growth or tip the economy back into recession.
- The Reagan Administration has done nothing to solve America's repeated problem of reconciling steady growth with stable prices, except by causing a deep recession. Continuing high levels of unemployment still exist in various communities across the country. Many jobs have disappeared. The Reagan Administration is not interested in new forms of fighting inflation—its anti-inflation program amounts to little more than unemployment, tight money and union busting. It is a highly cynical economic selective service that drafts only the poor and the middle class to fight the war against inflation. Unrestrained by the demands of another election, a second Reagan Administration will be even less concerned about the impact of deep recession on the average working American.
- Our trade deficit is a looming disaster for the national economy. An overvalued dollar, itself the product of high interest rates, helped create a nearly $70 billion trade deficit in 1983. It will be almost twice as large in 1984. Borrowing to support the

deficits and buying abroad to maintain a recovery tilted toward consumption are eroding America's position as a creditor nation.

- America is very much a part of the international economy. And the recovery overseas has been slow to catch hold. European economies are strained by the impact of high American interest rates on their own economies. For many developing countries, growth has been slowed or even reversed by the overhang of an enormous burden of commercial and official debt. If they cannot buy our products, our economy must slow.

- The sheer size of the international debt burden is itself a threat to the recovery. It is not only a question of falling exports to Latin America. The American and international financial system has been put in peril by the weakening of debtor nations' ability to repay their debt to U.S. banks as interest rates rise.

Howard Baker called Mr. Reagan's policies a "riverboat gamble." We now know the outcome. The very wealthiest in our society have been big winners—but future generations of Americans will be the losers.

The Americans coming of age today face a future less secure and less prosperous than their parents did—unless we change course. We have an obligation to our children and to their children. We Democrats have a different vision of our future.

The Democratic Alternative: A Prosperous America in a Changing World

"There's a lot of people out there only making $3.35 an hour, and that's been since '81. That's a long time to be making $3.35 an hour. . . . Costs of living have gone up considerably. The insurance has gone up, gas, lights, water. It's a whole lot different now, it's not the same as '81. I know times have changed, but why can't the $3.35 change with them? I would like to know that, if anybody can answer. I urge the Democratic Party to develop policies and protect working people."—Doris Smith, Steward, SEIU Local 706 (Democratic Platform Committee Hearing, Houston, Texas, May 29, 1984)

"We do not have a surplus as long as one member of my family is hungry. He may live next door or on the other side of the world. However, it should not be the producer's responsibility to provide cheap food at the expense of his own children."—Roberta Archer, Farmer, Springfield, Illinois (Democratic Platform Committee Hearing, Springfield, Illinois, April 27, 1984)

"In the four years prior to Mr. Reagan taking over, I was fortunate to have four good years of employment, and I was able to put money aside in savings accounts which since

have been exhausted. My unemployment benefits are exhausted too. . . . I may not qualify for any type of public assistance and the standard of living I was accustomed to for my wife and myself and my family has drastically changed. . . . But we as Democrats can join together in harmony and unison and we can decide what is the future or the fate of our people and what is good for all of us. So I am very proud to be a Democrat."—James Price, unemployed mine worker (Democratic Platform Committee Hearing, Birmingham, Alabama, April 24, 1984)

Democratic growth is not just a matter of good numbers, but of opportunities for people. Jobs and employment are at the center of Democratic thinking. It is not only a question of legislation or appropriations. Rather, it is a philosophy that views employment as the ongoing concern of the country. Work in America is not an idle concept—but a definition of self, a door to future opportunity, and the key step in securing the economic necessities of the present.

An America at work is a moral obligation as well as the most effective way to return our economy to a high growth path. Employed people stimulate the economy, their taxes pay for the expenses of government and their production adds to our national wealth. Moreover, the social and economic fabric of the nation will be strengthened as millions of Americans who presently are frozen out of productive and dignified employment become contributing citizens.

The potential for America is unlimited. It is within our means to put America back on a long-term path that will assure both growth and broad-based economic opportunity. That is what the next Democratic Administration will do. First, we will adopt overall economic policies that will bring interest rates down, free savings for private investment, prevent another explosion of inflation, and put the dollar on a competitive basis. Second, we will invest for our future—in our people, and in our infrastructure. Third, we will promote new partnerships and participation by all levels of government, by business and labor, to support growth and productivity. Finally, government will work with the private sector to assure that American businesses and American workers can compete fully and fairly in a changing world economy.

Overall Economic Policies: A Firm Ground for Growth

A Democratic Administration will pursue economic policies which provide the basis for long-term economic growth and will allow us to fulfill our commitment to jobs for all Americans who want to work. A key part of the effort will be reducing and eventually eliminating the deficits that currently form a dark cloud over the nation's future. In addition, monetary policy must be set with an eye to stability and to the strengths or weaknesses of the economy. Finally, we will pursue policies that will promote price stability and prevent inflation from breaking out again.

Reducing the Reagan Budget Deficits

After plunging the nation into a deficit crisis, President Reagan refuses to take part in efforts to solve it. He postpones hard decisions until after the Presidential election, refusing to compromise, refusing to address revenues and defense spending seriously, refusing all but a "down payment" on the deficit. The President continues to stand apart from serious, comprehensive efforts to cut the deficit. There must be statesmanship and compromise here, not ideological rigidity or election year politics.

The Democratic Party is pledged to reducing these intolerable deficits. We will reassess defense expenditures: create a tax system that is both adequate and fair: control skyrocketing health costs without sacrificing quality of care: and eliminate other unnecessary expenditures. Through efficiency and toughness, we will restore sanity to our fiscal house.

We oppose the artificial and rigid Constitutional restraint of a balanced budget amendment. Further we oppose efforts to call a federal constitutional convention for this purpose.

Rational Defense Spending. In the last three years, the Defense Department was told by this Administration that it could have anything it wanted, and at any price. As Democrats, we believe in devoting the needed resources to ensure our national security. But military might cannot be measured solely by dollars spent. American military strength must be secured at an affordable cost. We will reduce the rate of increase in defense spending. Through careful reevaluation of proposed and existing weapons, we will stop throwing away money on unworkable or unnecessary systems; through military reform we will focus expenditure on the most cost-effective military policies. We will insist that our allies contribute fairly to our collective security, and that the Department of Defense reduces its scandalous procurement waste.

And above all else, we will seek sensible arms control agreements as a means of assuring that there will be a future for our children and that we as a nation will have the resources we need to invest for the future.

Tax Reform. America needs a tax system that encourages growth and produces adequate revenues in a fair, progressive fashion. The Democratic Party is committed to a tax policy that embodies these basic values.

The present system is unfair, complex, and encourages people to use a wide range of loopholes to avoid paying their fair share of taxes. The combination of loopholes for the few and high rates for the many is both unfair and anti-growth. It distorts investment, diverting creative energies into tax avoidance. And it makes the tax code even less comprehensible to the average American.

Our tax code must produce sufficient revenue to finance our defense and allow for investment in our future, and we will ask every American to pay his or her fair share. But by broadening the tax base, simplifying the tax code, lowering rates, and eliminating unnecessary, unfair and unproductive deductions and tax expenditures, we can raise the revenues we need and promote growth without increasing the burden on average taxpayers.

Ronald Reagan's tax program gave huge breaks to wealthy individuals and to large corporations while shifting the burden to low- and moderate-income families. The Democratic Party is pledged to reverse these unsound policies. We will cap the effect of the Reagan tax cuts for wealthy Americans and enhance the progressivity of our personal income tax code, limiting the benefits of the third year of the Reagan tax cuts to the level of those with incomes of less than $60,000. We will partially defer indexation while protecting average Americans. We will close loopholes, eliminate the preferences and write-offs, exemptions, and deductions which skew the code toward the rich and toward unproductive tax shelters. Given the fact that there has been a veritable hemorrhage of capital out of the federal budget, reflected in part by the huge budget deficit, there must be a return to a fair tax on corporate income. Under the Reagan Administration, the rate of taxation on corporations has been so substantially reduced that they are not contributing their fair share to federal revenues. We believe there should be a 15% minimum corporate tax. In addition, our tax code has facilitated the transfer of capital from the United States to investment abroad, contributing to plant closing without notice in many communities and loss of millions of jobs. We will toughen compliance procedures to reduce the $100 billion annual tax evasion.

Our country must move to a simpler, more equitable, and more progressive tax system. Our tax code can let the market put our country's savings to the best use. There must be a fair balance between corporate and personal tax increases. Wealthier taxpayers will have to shoulder a greater share of the new tax burdens. Economic distortions must be eliminated.

Controlling Domestic Spending. A balanced program for reducing Republican megadeficits must also deal with the growing costs of domestic programs. But this must be done in a way that is fair to average Americans.

Social Security is one of the most important and successful initiatives in the history of our country, and it is an essential element of the social compact that binds us together as a community. There is no excuse—as the Reagan Administration has repeatedly suggested—for slashing Social Security to pay for excesses in other areas of the budget. We will steadfastly oppose such efforts, now and in the future.

It is rather in the area of health care costs that reform is urgently needed. By 1988, Medicare costs will rise to $106 billion: by the turn of the century, the debt of the trust fund may be as great as $1 trillion. In the Republican view, the problem is the level of benefits which senior citizens and the needy receive. As Democrats, we will protect the interests of health care beneficiaries. The real problem is the growing cost of health care services.

We propose to control these costs, and to demand that the health care industry become more efficient in providing care to all Americans, both young and old. We will limit what health care providers can receive as reimbursement, and spur innovation and competition in health care delivery. The growth of alternative health care delivery systems such as HMO's, PPO's and alternatives to long-term care such as home care and social HMO's should be fostered so that high-quality care will be available at a lower cost. We must learn the difference between health care and sick care. Unlike the Republicans, we recognize that investing in preventive health care saves dollars as well as lives, and we will make the needed investment. The states must be the cornerstone of our health care policies, but a Democratic Administration will provide the leadership at the federal level to assure that health care is available to all who need help at a cost we can afford. In addition, we pledge to scour the budget for other areas of wasteful or unnecessary spending.

Monetary Policy for Growth

Reducing the deficit is the first step toward lowering interest rates and establishing the basis for fair tax and budget policies. But even with a Democratic fiscal policy reining in the deficit, the task of the Federal Reserve Board will be critical. Monetary policy must work to achieve stable real interest rates, the availability of capital for long-term investments, predictable long-term policy and stable prices. We reject the rigid adherence to monetary targets that has frequently characterized the Reagan monetary policy. Whatever targeting approach the Federal Reserve Board adopts, it must be leavened with a pragmatic appraisal of what is happening in the harsh world of the real economy, particularly the impact on unemployment, interest rates, and the international value of the dollar.

An Anti-Inflation Program

We have learned that sustained economic growth is impossible in a climate of high inflation or of inflationary expectations. The Reagan Administration's only prescription for inflation is recession—deliberate high unemployment—coupled with a relentless assault on the collective bargaining power and rights of working men and women. The Democratic Party believes that these tactics are both unacceptable and ineffective.

We will develop the following five-step program to stabilize prices:

- Growth—full order books encourage investments in new plants and equipment and research and development. The productivity growth that comes in tandem with new investments will help offset—point for point—any increase in cost.
- Increased flexibility in the marketplace—will also help keep inflationary pressures under control. There is no single policy that will make the U.S. economy more adaptable. Rather, there is a series of smaller steps which will help keep prices stable. In general, competitive markets are more likely to restrain sudden surges of prices than are markets dominated by a few large firms. No Democratic Administration will forget the use of old-fashioned antitrust policy to keep markets competitive and prices down.
- Trade policy—is also an important component of any effective anti-inflation program. Expanding world markets for American goods increase the gains from large-scale production and stimulate research and development on new products and processes.
- The price–wage spiral—as part of any effective anti-inflation program, serious policies to address the price–wage spirals and other inflationary pressures we have experienced in the past must be developed.
- We believe that an attack on sectoral sources of inflation—in food, fuel, utilities, health care, and elsewhere—is essential if price stability is to be sustained without economic distortions. Our agriculture, energy, and health programs will all promote sectoral price stability while assuring fair treatment for average Americans, including working men and women and family farmers. For example, the Strategic

Petroleum Reserve is one clear response to reducing the chance of another oil shock. The very presence of reserves in the U.S., Japan, and elsewhere reduces the likelihood of panic buying to replace suddenly threatened oil supplies. In this context, a far-reaching energy policy that emphasizes conservation and the development of alternative energy supplies will also help stabilize energy prices. And lower interest rates from reduced budget deficits will reduce upward pressure on housing costs and bring housing back within the reach of millions of Americans now excluded from the market.

Investing in People

America's greatest resource is our people. As Democrats, we affirm the need for both public and private investment—in our children; in our educational institutions and our students; in jobs, training, and transitional assistance for our workers—to build America's future. If we choose wisely, these investments will be returned to our country many times over. They are essential if we are to create an America with high-quality jobs and rising opportunities for all. And they are vital if we are to safeguard our competitive position in the world economy.

Investing in Children

Simple decency demands that we make children one of our highest national priorities. But the argument for so acting goes well beyond that. Programs for children represent the most critical investment we can make in our ability to compete in future world markets and maintain a strong national defense in the decades ahead.

Above all else, the Democratic Party stands for making the proper investment in coming generations of Americans.

Preventive efforts must be at the heart of the broad range of health, child care, and support programs for children. Helping these children makes good moral sense—and sound economic sense. Measles vaccine alone has saved $1.3 billion in medical costs in just ten years. Supplemental food programs for low-income pregnant women and infants save $3 for every dollar spent.

By improving access to medical care before and after birth, we can promote a generation of healthy mothers and healthy babies. Seeing that supplemental food programs for low-income pregnant women and infants reach all those eligible will do more than save the $40,000 now spent to treat one low-birthweight infant in a neo-natal ward. It will also reduce the risk of birth defects for such infants.

We recognize that a hungry child is a child who cannot learn. Restoring school breakfasts and school lunches for millions of children will improve their alertness and concentration in school.

Child care must also be a top priority. Helping communities establish after-school care programs will remove millions of American children from the serious risks they now face of injury, abuse and alienation by staying at home alone. Encouraging employers, churches, public centers, and private groups to provide quality, affordable child care will give millions of children whose parents must work the kind of adult supervision necessary to thrive. And setting up centers for child care information and referral will assist parents wherever they reside to locate quality care for their children.

Preventing child abuse must be at the forefront of Democratic Party concern. Local, community-based child abuse prevention programs must be strengthened and expanded. A child who learns first about the risks of sexual abuse in school will be less likely to become the target of repeated victimization. Federal challenge grants could encourage states to make local prevention efforts a real priority.

Prompt intervention efforts must also be provided for children in crisis. If we are to make any headway in breaking the cycle of child abuse, both victims and offenders must have access to treatment programs.

Juvenile offenders must not be left in adult jails where the only skills they acquire are those of the career criminal. Safe shelter and assistance must be available for the hundreds of thousands of runaway children at risk of exploitation in our cities. Local, state, and federal law enforcement agencies must refine ways to locate children who have been abducted. And children in foster care must not be allowed to graduate to the streets at age 18 without ever having known a permanent home.

We must ensure that essential surveys on children's health and welfare status are reinstated. We know more about the number of matches sold than about the number of children across the country who die in fires while alone at home. Likewise, we know less about hunger and malnutrition among children than we do about the health of the nation's poultry stock.

The Democratic Party affirms its commitment to protecting the health and safety of children in the United States. Existing laws mandating the use of automobile child restraints must be enforced, and child safety seat loaner or rental programs and public education programs must be encouraged, in order to reduce significantly the leading cause of death and serious injury among children between the ages of six months and five years—motor vehicle crashes.

The crisis devastating many of our nation's youth is nowhere more dramatically evidenced than in the alarming rate of increase in teenage suicide. Over 6,000 young people took their lives in 1983, and for each actual suicide 50 to 100 other youths attempted suicide. The underlying causes of teenage suicide, as well as its full scope, are not adequately researched or understood. We must commit ourselves to seek out the causes, formulate a national policy of prevention, and provide guidance to our state and local governments in developing means to stem this devastating tide of self-destruction. We support the creation of a national panel on teenage suicide to respond to this challenge.

A Democratic Administration which establishes these priorities can reduce the risks for our young people and improve the odds. By so doing, it will serve their future . . . and ours.

Investing in Education

No public investment is more important than the one we make in the minds, skills and discipline of our people. Whether we are talking about a strong economy, a strong defense or a strong system of justice, we cannot achieve it without a strong educational system. Our very future in international economic competition depends on skilled workers and on first-rate scientists, engineers, and managers.

We Democrats are committed to equity in education. We will insist on excellence, discipline, and high standards. Quality education depends on students, teachers and parents performing at the highest levels of achievement.

Today, education in America needs help. But, the Reagan Administration offers misleading homilies about the importance of education while aggressively slashing education programs.

This is intolerable. We know that every dollar we invest in education is ultimately returned to us six-fold. We know that the education of our citizens is critical to our democracy.

There are four key goals that a Democratic program for educational excellence must address: strengthening local capacity to innovate and progress in public education and encourage parental involvement; renewing our efforts to ensure that all children, whatever their race, income, or sex have a fair and equal chance to learn; attracting the most talented young people into teaching and enabling them to remain and develop in their profession; and ensuring that all American families can send their children on to college or advanced training.

Primary and Secondary Education.   While education is the responsibility of local government, local govern-

ments already strapped for funds by this Administration cannot be expected to bear alone the burden of undertaking the efforts we need for quality education—from teacher training, to the salaries needed to attract and retain able teachers, to new labs, to new programs to motivate talented and gifted students, to new ties between businesses and schools—without leadership at the federal level.

Democrats will provide that leadership. We call for the immediate restoration of the cuts in funding of education programs by the Reagan Administration, and for a major new commitment to education. We will create a partnership for excellence among federal, state and local governments. We will provide incentives to local school districts to concentrate on science, math, communications and computer literacy; to provide access to advanced technology. In all of these fields, but particularly in computers, there is a growing danger of a two-tier education system. The more affluent districts have adequate hardware and teachers prepared to use it. Many districts are left completely behind or saddled with a modern machine but no provision for faculty training. Every American child should have the basic education that makes computer literacy possible and useful. Major attention must be given to recruiting the finest young people into teaching careers, and to providing adequate staff development programs that enable educators to increase their effectiveness in meeting the needs of all students.

Vocational education should be overhauled to bring instructional materials, equipment, and staff up to date with the technology and practices of the workplace and target assistance to areas with large numbers of disadvantaged youth. We will insist that every child be afforded an equal opportunity to fulfill his or her potential. We will pay special attention to the needs of the handicapped.

Education is an important key to the upward mobility of all citizens and especially the disadvantaged, despite the fact that racial discrimination and other prejudices have set limits to such achievement.

The Reagan Administration has singled out for extinction the proven most successful education program—compensatory education for disadvantaged children. The Democratic Party will reverse this malicious onslaught and dramatically strengthen support in order to provide educational equity for all children.

Bilingual education enables children to achieve full competence in the English language and the academic success necessary to their full participation in the life of our nation. We reject the Reagan double-talk on bilingual education and commit ourselves to expanding and increasing its effectiveness.

We will emphasize the importance of preventing

one-third of our student body nationwide from dropping out of school in the first place. And we will supplement community-based programs encouraging students who have left school due to teenage parenthood, alcohol and drug abuse, or economic difficulties at home, to complete their educations.

Recognizing that young people who are never given an opportunity for a job will be less likely to hold one in adulthood, we will also emphasize training and employment opportunities for youth. In so doing, we need to establish a genuine working partnership with the private sector.

Private schools, particularly parochial schools, are also an important part of our diverse educational system. Consistent with our tradition, the Democratic Party accepts its commitment to constitutionally acceptable methods of supporting the education of all pupils in schools which do not racially discriminate, and excluding so-called segregation academies. The Party will continue to support federal education legislation which provides for the equitable participation in federal programs of all low- and moderate-income pupils.

For its part, when added to the traditional educational institutions of family, school and church, television has enormous promise as a teacher. When children spend more time in front of the television set than they do in the classroom, we must ask how television can help children, and why commercial broadcasters do so little programming for children today despite their legal responsibility as "public trustees" of the airwaves granted to them. The National Science Board, for instance, has recommended that commercial television stations be required to air a certain amount of information/educational programming for children each week. Properly developed, television can be an enormously efficient and effective supplemental teaching tool.

Higher Education.   We will make certain that higher education does not become a luxury affordable only by the children of the rich. That is Ronald Reagan's America. In our America, no qualified student should be deprived of the ability to go on to college because of financial circumstance.

The Democratic Party reaffirms the importance of historically Black colleges. Today the survival of many of these colleges is threatened. The programs that assist them, which have been severely weakened in recent years, must be greatly strengthened with funding targeted toward Black and Hispanic institutions.

An explosion in demand for certain types of engineers, scientists and other technical specialists is creating a shortage of faculty and Ph.D. candidates. We must encourage colleges and universities to train more scientists and engineers. More than one hundred years ago the Morrill Land Grant Act provided for agricultural colleges and programs that today still help keep American agriculture the world leader. We need a similar program today to encourage the training of scientists and engineers. At the same time, we must not neglect the arts and humanities, which enrich our spirit. The private sector must also recognize its responsibility to join partnerships which strengthen our diverse public and private higher education system.

Finally, all our educational institutions must adapt to growing numbers of adults returning to school to upgrade their skills, acquire new skills, prepare themselves for entirely new occupations, and enrich their lives.

Investing in the Arts

America is truly growing and prosperous when its spirit flourishes. The arts and humanities are at the core of our national experience. Creativity and the life of the mind have defined us at our best throughout our history. As scholars or artists, the museum-goers or students, craftsmen and craftswomen or the millions who use our libraries, countless Americans have a stake in a nation that honors and rejoices in intelligence and imagination.

The Democratic Party will set a new national tone of respect for learning and artistic achievement. Not only will the federal agencies that support them be strengthened and freed from political intimidation, but the White House itself will once again be a place where American cultural and intellectual life—in all its rich diversity—is honored. Excellence must start at the top.

Finally, the Democratic Party is also committed to the survival of public television and radio stations, which allow all Americans, regardless of ability to pay, to appreciate high-quality, alternative programming. We oppose the efforts of the Reagan Administration to enact draconian cuts which would totally undermine the viability of this nation's excellent public broadcasting system, a broadcasting system which has given the country Sesame Street, 3-2-1 Contact, and other superb children's as well as cultural and public affairs programming.

Jobs, Training, and Transitional Assistance

We must have a growing economy if we are to have jobs for all Americans who seek work. But even in a growing economy, the pressures of competition and the pace of change ensure that while jobs are being created, others are being destroyed. Prosperity will not be evenly distributed among regions and communities.

We must make special efforts to help families in economic transition who are faced with loss of homes, health benefits, and pensions. And far too many of our young people, especially minorities, do not have the training and skills they need to get their first job. Democrats believe that it is a national responsibility to ensure that the burdens of change are fairly shared and that every young American can take the first step up the ladder of economic opportunity.

Of the 8.5 million Americans still out of work, 40 percent are under 25. Unemployment among teenagers stands at almost 20 percent. Less than three percent of the jobs created in the last three and a half years have gone to young people. Black and Hispanic youth have a double burden. Unemployment for Black teenagers stands at 44 percent—a 20 percent increase in the last three years. Hispanic teens face a 26 percent unemployment rate.

As disturbing as these figures are, they do not tell the whole story. The unemployment rate measures only those teenagers who were actively looking for work, not those who have given up, completely discouraged by the lack of opportunity. Again the burden falls disproportionately on minority youth.

The Reagan Administration has dismantled virtually all of the successful programs to train and employ young people. Today, we are spending less to put young people to work than we were even under the *last* Republican Administration—70 percent less, when inflation is taken into account. Youth unemployment has skyrocketed, while government efforts to combat it have dwindled to a trickle.

Unless we address this problem now, half of an entire generation may never know what it means to work. America cannot successfully compete in the world economy if a significant portion of our future work force is illiterate, unskilled, and unemployable.

The Democratic Party must give our young people new skills and new hope; we must work hand in hand with the private sector if job training is to lead to jobs. Specifically, targeted efforts are needed to address the urgent problem of unemployment among minority teenagers. We must provide job training for those who have dropped out of school, and take every step to expand educational opportunity for those still in school. We must recognize the special needs of the over–age 50 worker and the displaced homemaker. Through education, training and retraining we must reduce these dangerously high levels of unemployment.

We must provide an opportunity for workers, including those dislocated by changing technologies, to adapt to new opportunities: we must provide workers with choices as to which skills they wish to acquire.

We know that Americans want to work. We are committed to ensuring that meaningful job training is available—for our students, for housewives returning to the workplace, and for those displaced by changing patterns of technology or trade.

- The federal government will develop a major comprehensive national job skills development policy that is targeted on the chronically unemployed and underemployed. We must train and place these Americans in high-demand labor-shortage occupations, working with the private sector so that maximum employment and job creation can be achieved.
- We will overhaul the currently antiquated unemployment compensation system, and adequately fund job search listings of local employment services.
- We will also launch meaningful training programs that lead to job placement for women who receive public assistance, in order to break the cycle of dependence and to raise their standard of living. Instead of punitive reductions in AFDC and other benefits for women who seek training and employment while receiving such assistance, beneficiaries should be given a transition period during which they are permitted to earn income in a formal training program while receiving full benefits.
- We will seriously examine new approaches to training and retraining programs that could be financed directly by government, by labor and management, or by tax free contributions.
- If cancellations of specific weapons systems result in significant economic dislocations and job loss, it is a national responsibility to address the human consequences of national policy.

Investing in Infrastructure

Economic growth requires that America invest in our infrastructure as well as in our people. Investing in infrastructure means rebuilding our bridges and roads and sewers, and we are committed to doing that. But it also means investing in our cities, in decent housing and public transportation, and in regulatory systems for finance and telecommunication that will provide a sound basis for future economic growth.

Investing in Our Cities

The Democratic Party recognizes the value of prosperous local government, and within that context we recognize that a healthy city is essential to the well-being of the nation, state, county and surrounding local governments.

Our nation's economic life depends on the economic growth of our cities. Our cities are not only the treasuries from which the nation draws its wealth, they are the centers of industry, the centers of art and culture, the breeding ground for economic innovation, and home to the majority of the American people. Our cities are among this country's greatest achievements, and they can be our country's greatest engine of economic growth.

Cities can be active partners with the federal government and private enterprise for creating new growth. They can be a dynamic entrepreneurial force—by encouraging education and research, by incubating promising new industries, by steering resources toward those most in need, and by fostering new cooperative arrangements among public agencies and private business. Cities can be a leading force for rebuilding the nation's economy.

But to do this, cities need state and national leadership which values the role of city and county government. Cities need a President willing to work and consult with mayors and county executives. They need an Administration which puts the needs of urban America on the top of the national agenda—because no plan for economic strength will survive when our cities are left behind.

Today, the Reagan Administration has turned its back on the cities. By sapping our cities' strength, this Administration is sapping our country's strength. Only the intervention of the Congress has prevented further and more devastating cuts in city-oriented programs. The Democratic Party believes in making our cities' needs a federal priority once again. We want to see again cities where people have jobs and adequate housing, cities whose bridges and mass transit are being maintained, and whose neighborhoods are safe to live in. And that will take a commitment by our federal government to help our cities again.

Toward that end, the Democratic Party pledges:

- a commitment to full employment. We believe the federal government must develop a major, comprehensive national job skills development policy targeted on the chronically unemployed and underemployed. We must launch special training programs for women who receive public assistance. We need to increase government procurement opportunities for small and minority firms and to encourage deposits of federal funds in minority-owned financial institutions. And to build for the future, the Democratic Party calls for a new national commitment to education, which must include raising standards, insisting on excellence, and giving all children a chance to learn, regardless of race, income or sex.

- a commitment to rebuilding the infrastructure of America. We need to inventory facility needs, set priorities and establish policies for the repair, maintenance, and replacement of public works by all levels of government. We need to create a federal capital budget to separate operating and capital outlays. We will consult local governments in decisions affecting the design and performance standards of facilities constructed under federal programs. And we need to create a national reconstruction fund to provide affordable loans to states and localities for infrastructure projects. This will not only rebuild the infrastructure of our cities but provide badly needed employment for people who live there.

- a commitment to housing. We must restore government's positive role in helping all Americans find adequate and affordable housing. We reaffirm our commitment to public housing for the most disadvantaged members of our society. We must strengthen our commitment to the operation and rehabilitation of current government-assisted housing. We must maintain and expand the flow of mortgage capital, and bring interest rates down with sensible economic policies. We must pull together the patchwork of housing programs and cut through the red tape to make it easier for cities to receive the assistance to meet their own needs. We must upgrade and replenish housing in minority communities and create more units for poor and low-income people. And we must enforce fair housing standards to prohibit discrimination in the housing market.

Our Party must be a vehicle for realizing the hopes, the aspirations, and the dreams of the people of this country. And that includes the people who live in cities.

Physical Infrastructure

This nation's physical infrastructure—our bridges and roads, our ports, our railroads, our sewers, our public transit and water supply systems—is deteriorating faster than we can repair it. The gap between the necessary improvements and available resources grows every year. State and local governments, strapped by Reaganomics, have been forced repeatedly to defer maintenance, and to abandon plans for construction.

As Democrats, we recognize that infrastructure is the basis for efficient commerce and industry. If our older industrial cities are to grow, if our expanding regions are to continue to expand, then we must work with state and local governments to target our investment to our most important infrastructure. There is work to be done in rebuilding and maintaining our infrastructure, and there are millions of American men and women in need of work. The federal government must take the lead in putting them back to work, and in doing so, providing the basis for private sector investment and economic growth. We need to inventory facility needs, set priorities, and establish policies for the repair, maintenance and replacement of the public works by all levels of government. We need a capital budget to separate paying for these long-term investments from regular expenditures. Furthermore, we need a national reconstruction fund to provide affordable loans to states and localities for infrastructure projects.

Financial Infrastructure

At the heart of our economy is the financial infrastructure: a set of diverse interdependent institutions and markets which are the envy of the world. We must preserve their strengths. Until very recently, the United States operated with a domestic financial system that was built in response to the stock market crash of 1929, the massive series of bank failures that accompanied the Great Depression, and the speculative excesses of the stock market. There was an emphasis on placing different types of financial activities in different institutions. Commercial banks were not to float stock market issues. Investment bankers could. Neither took equity positions in individual companies. Separate savings and credit institutions were established to support housing and consumer durables. Soundness of the system, liquidity, investor and depositor protection, neutrality of credit and capital decisions, and a wide variety of financial institutions to serve the varying needs of business and consumers have been the fundamental goals.

Bit by bit, the American financial system began to change. The domestic financial market became closely tied to the international market, which in turn had become larger, more competitive, and more volatile. Inflation, technology, the growth of foreign competition, and institutional innovation all combined to create strong pressures for change. The 1980's brought a deregulation of interest rates and a wave of deregulatory decisions by financial regulators.

These changes raise serious threats to our traditional financial goals. Before leaping into a highly uncertain financial future, the country should take a careful look at the direction deregulation is taking, and what it means to our financial system and the economy.

Telecommunications

Telecommunications is the infrastructure of the information age. The last decade has seen an explosion in new technologies, expanded competition, and growing dependence on high-quality telecommunications.

Nationwide access to those networks is becoming crucial to full participation in a society and economy that are increasingly dependent upon the rapid exchange of information. Electronically delivered messages, and not the written word, are becoming the dominant form of communication. A citizen without access to telecommunications is in danger of fading into isolation. Therefore, the proper regulation of telecommunications is critical. We must encourage competition while preventing regulatory decisions which substantially increase basic telephone rates and which threaten to throw large numbers of low-income, elderly, or rural people off the telecommunications networks. We must also ensure that workers in the telecommunications industry do not find their retirement or other earned benefits jeopardized by the consequences of divestiture.

This electronic marketplace is so fundamental to our future as a democracy (as well as to our economy) that social and cultural principles must be as much a part of communications policy as a commitment to efficiency, innovation, and competition. Those principles are diversity, the availability of a wide choice of information services and sources, access, the ability of all Americans, not just a privileged few, to take advantage of this growing array of information services and sources; and opportunity, a commitment to education and diverse ownership, particularly by minorities and women, that will give every American the ability to take advantage of the computer and the telecommunications revolution. We support the Fairness Doctrine and Equal Time requirements, along with other laws and regulations on the electronic media which encourage or require responsiveness to community needs and a diversity of viewpoints.

Housing

Decent, affordable housing has been a goal of national public policy for almost half a century, since the United States Housing Act of 1937. The Democratic Party has repeatedly reaffirmed the belief that American citizens should be able to find adequate shelter at reasonable cost. And we have been unwavering in our support of the premise that government has a positive role to play in ensuring housing opportunities for less fortunate Americans, including the elderly and the handicapped, not served by the private market.

In the last four years this long-standing commitment to decent shelter has been crippled by the underfunding, insensitivity, high interest rates, and distorted priorities of the Reagan Administration.

The Democratic Party has always accorded housing

the high priority it deserves. One essential quality will characterize this commitment in the future: It must and will be comprehensive.

By advocating a comprehensive policy which addresses the totality of our housing needs, we do not mean to suggest that all concerns have an equal claim on resources or require the same level of governmental intervention. The bulk of our resources will be concentrated on those most in need, and government must take a leadership role where others cannot or will not participate.

Within a comprehensive framework for policy development and constituency building, we will establish priorities according to principles of compassion and equity. We would like to see a special effort in two areas in the first years of a new Democratic Administration.

First, we must intensify our commitment to the adequate operation, management, and rehabilitation of the current inventory of government-assisted housing. This housing stock is not one, but the only option for the least fortunate among our lower-income families and senior citizens. It is the right thing to do and it makes economic sense to preserve our own economic investment.

Second, we must maintain and expand the flow of mortgage capital. The American dream of home ownership will fall beyond the reach of this generation and future ones if government fails to help attract new sources of capital for housing.

We will draw on our historic commitment to housing, and the best insights and energies of today's Democratic Party to address the future housing needs of all the American people. The Democratic Party will develop short-range emergency responses to the problem of homelessness as well as long-range solutions to its causes. The Democratic Party will support upgrading and replenishment of the housing stock in minority communities, with more affordable units available so that poor and low-income people can buy units with low-interest loans. Also, fair housing standards need to be vigorously enforced by the federal, state and local governments in order to deal with persistent discrimination in the housing market for buyers and renters. Finally, the expansion of public housing and other publicly assisted housing programs is a necessity due to the growth in the homeless population and in the high cost of commercially available units.

Transportation

Democrats vigorously support the concept of promoting competition in transportation and the elimination of unnecessary and inefficient regulation of the rail-road industry. Democrats also insist on ensuring a fair rate for captive shippers. It was the Democratic Party which was primarily responsible for the passage of the Staggers Rail Act of 1980, which was designed to accomplish these objectives.

The Democratic Party is committed to a policy of administering the transportation laws in a manner which will encourage competition and provide protection for captive shippers.

A comprehensive maritime policy that is tailored to the realities of today's international shipping world and to the economic, political, and military needs of the United States is a necessity. Such a policy should address all facets of our maritime industry—from shipping to shipbuilding and related activities—in an integrated manner.

Postal Service

The private express statutes guarantee the protection and security of the mail for all Americans. They are essential to the maintenance of the national postal system along with retaining rural post offices to assure the delivery of mail to all Americans.

A Framework for Growth

The American economy is a complex mix, incorporating any number of different actors and entities—private businesses, professional societies, charitable institutions, labor unions, regional development councils, and local school boards. The economy is driven by millions of individual decisions on spending and saving, on investing and wages. Government is only one force among many woven into the fabric of American economic life. Just as the wrong overall economic policy can disrupt the best private decisions, the best government economic policies will not put us on a path to long-term growth unless business, labor, and other private institutions meet their responsibilities and rise to the competitive challenge of a new era.

Private Sector Responsibilities

In many cases, the private sector is already playing a major role in laying the basis for future growth and meeting broad community responsibilities. In other cases, however, short-term considerations have been allowed to predominate at the expense of the long-term needs of the national economy.

A recent wave of mergers has been particularly troubling. A number of large corporations have focused their energies on arranging the next merger or defending against the latest takeover bid.

Many of our major competitors have targeted their efforts on investments in new methods of producing cheaper, high-quality products. To respond to the growing pressure of foreign competition, America's private sector must meet several challenges:

- Investing strategically—the more U.S. companies focus on long-term strategies to improve their competitive positions, the better off the entire economy will be.
- Managing cost and quality—U.S. companies will have to place similar emphasis on controlling costs and quality to effectively meet the best of the foreign competition.
- Competing internationally—U.S. business like other institutions in the country need to pay greater attention to the international marketplace.

Partnership, Cooperation and Participation

Partnership, cooperation and participation are central to economic growth. We need new cooperative institutions, and a steady redefinition of how labor and management, universities, the private sector, and state and local governments can work together.

- National cooperation—in developing a long-term growth strategy, there are several particularly important functions that today are poorly performed or poorly coordinated by the government; coordination and policy coherence; developing and disseminating useful economic information; anticipating economic problems; and developing long-term consensus between public and private sectors. To better accomplish these tasks, it is time that a national Economic Cooperation Council was created. Its charter would be simple and basic: (1) to collect, analyze, and disseminate economic data; (2) to create a forum where the gap between business, labor, and government is bridged, where all three develop the trust, understanding, and cooperation necessary to improve productivity; and, (3) to identify national priorities, make recommendations on how best to reach those goals, and help build consensus for action.
- State involvement—Under the guise of increasing the power of state government, the Reagan Administration has actually given the states only the power to decide what programs to cut or eliminate, because of the substantially decreased funding it has made available to the states. Should it be baby clinics, child immunization against disease, day care, maternal health, or youth services? The Democratic Party believes a strong partnership of federal, state and local governments is basic to effective and efficient decision-making, problem-solving, and provision of adequate services. We must also encourage cooperation between states and the private sector.

State development agencies are already seeking closer ties to both business and universities. And universities are increasingly looking to the private sector in setting their research agendas.

- Local and community involvement—Citizen involvement in governance should be as great as possible. The responsibility for general governance, the delivery of programs and services, and the resolution of problems should be with the level of government that is closest to the citizenry and that can still discharge those responsibilities effectively and efficiently. These levels of government must assure basic civil liberties and justice for all citizens. They must not be abrogated by any local jurisdiction. The federal government should focus on the importance of local initiatives. For example, vocational education is an area where local schools and local business will increasingly be brought together. Financial stability and adequate authority are essential prerequisites to developing successful public–private partnerships and maximizing citizen involvement in governance.

Government financial and technical assistance programs should give preference to viable worker and/or community-owned or -run businesses, especially as a response to plant shutdowns.

Broadening Labor–Management Cooperation

We support greater employee participation in the workplace. Employees should have an opportunity to make a greater contribution to workplace productivity and quality through actual ownership of the company, employee representation on corporate boards, quality work circles, and greater worker participation in management decisions. The government should encourage employee participation and ownership, particularly as an alternative to plant shutdowns. It is destructive of labor–management relations when concessions extracted from labor to preserve jobs are converted, after the restoration of profitability, into management bonuses, rather than restoring the concessions that the workers made. Such practices offend our sense of fairness, as does the Reagan Administration–inspired union-busting. Essential to fairness in the workplace is the basic right of workers to organize collectively.

Consumer Protection

The Democratic Party strongly reaffirms its commitment to federal programs which are designed to enhance and protect the health and safety of all Americans. Under the Reagan Administration, the critical missions of agencies such as the Consumer

Product Safety Commission (CPSC), the National Highway Traffic Safety Administration (NHTSA), the Food and Drug Administration (FDA), the Occupational Safety and Health Administration (OSHA), the Mine Safety and Health Administration (MSHA), and the Federal Trade Commission (FTC) have been ignored and subverted.

The Reagan Administration proposed abolishing the CPSC, which has recalled over 300 million dangerous and defective products in its 10-year history. When it failed to accomplish this, the Administration attempted to submerge CPSC in the Department of Commerce. Also failing in this attempt, the Reagan Administration inflicted massive budget and personnel cuts on the Commission. The impact has been far reaching: recalls declined 66%, inspections were cut in half and over half of CPSC's regional offices have been closed. The result has been a paralysis of mission and an America more susceptible to dangerous products.

The record at the NHTSA, the agency mandated to reduce the appalling annual highway deaths of more than 50,000 Americans, is just as shameful. The President has appointed administrators with no safety background and even less commitment to the public health mission of the agency. Critical lifesaving safety standards, such as one requiring automatic crash protection in cars, have been revoked. The enforcement of defect and recall programs, designed to remove dangerous vehicles from our roads, has been cut back. Recalls are at an all-time low and only one safety standard has been proposed in four years.

At OSHA and MSHA, we have witnessed a retreat from agency mandates to provide safe and healthful working conditions for this nation's working men and women. Existing standards have been weakened or revoked and not one single new standard has been implemented. Similarly, at the FDA there has been an important shift away from removing dangerous and ineffective drugs in favor of weakening standards for products. The FTC has run roughshod over the nation's antitrust laws, allowing 9 of the 10 largest mergers in history to occur.

The dangerous trends in all these areas must be immediately reversed to allow these vital health and safety agencies to pursue their missions aggressively, to protect and enhance the health and safety of all Americans.

Individual Empowerment

The Democratic Party's commitment to full equality is as much a part of providing individual opportunity as it is part of a program of social justice. At the heart of our values as a nation is our belief in independence. Anyone who has brought home a paycheck, bought a car, or paid off a mortgage knows the pride that economic self-sufficiency brings. And anyone who has lost a job, watched one's children go hungry, or been denied a chance at success knows the terrible indignity that comes with dependence.

As Democrats, we share that belief in independence. Our goal is to allow the greatest number of people the greatest opportunity for self-sufficiency.

As a Party, we are committed to preparing people to stand on their own; that is why we insist on adequate nutrition for our children and good educations for our young people. We are committed to permitting independence; that's why we believe discrimination on any basis must come to an end. We believe that independence should be prolonged for as long as possible; to ensure it continues even after retirement, we support Social Security and Medicare. And we believe we must preserve the self-respect of those who are unable to be completely self-sufficient—the very young, the unskilled, the disabled, the very old—and to help them toward as much independence as possible. As much as it is a strategy for long-run economic growth, individual empowerment must itself be an operating philosophy. In the welfare system, in education, and in the laws affecting everyone from shareholders to the average voter, the Democratic Party will ask if the individual is being made stronger and more independent.

America in a World Economy

The reality of international competition in the 1980's requires government policies which will assure the competitiveness of American industry and American workers. Democrats will support and encourage innovation and research and development in both the private and public sector. We will seek to strengthen America's small businesses. And we will pursue trade policies and industrial strategies to ensure that our workers and our businesses can compete fully and fairly in the international arena.

Innovation

Innovation—in process and product technology—is at the heart of our ability to compete in a world economy and produce sustained economic growth at home. And research and development, critical as it is for our growing high-technology industries, is no less important for our basic industries. In the past generation, our world leadership in innovation has been increasingly jeopardized. We have not invested enough—or wisely enough—to match our major competitors.

Research and Development. Since the mid-1960's, all the other major industrial nations have increased their expenditures for research and development more rapidly than we have. Over the past decade, manufacturing productivity rose more than four times faster in Japan, more than three times faster in France, and more than twice as fast in both West Germany and the United Kingdom than in the United States. And the number of patents granted to Americans each year has plunged by 40 percent.

The United States should revise its downward trend and increase the percentage of GNP devoted to commercially related R&D as a long-term spending goal. We must be at the cutting edge, and we will not get there without cooperation between the government and the private sector. As Democrats, our goal is to increase civilian research and development in this country, to expand its commercial application, and to provide more industries with the opportunity to take advantage of it.

At the national level, this means enhanced support for undergraduate and graduate training in science, mathematics, and engineering; increased support to refurbish and modernize university research laboratories; increased support for the National Science Foundation and similar efforts; and a commitment to civilian research and development.

Centers of Excellence. In the past generation, scientists and engineers, together with educators and business leaders throughout the United States, have begun countless new, high-technology businesses such as those in Boston, Massachusetts, California's Silicon Valley, North Carolina's Research Triangle, greater Denver, Colorado, and Austin, Texas, to establish this country as a leader in the next generation of high-technology industries—biotechnology, polymer sciences, robotics, photovoltaics, marine sciences, microelectronics. The Democratic Party will encourage and support centers that provide for cooperation of academic and entrepreneurial excellence, thereby strengthening our scientific and technological resources and creating tomorrow's jobs.

Small and Minority Business

The Democratic Party recognizes that small businesses create many, if not most of the new jobs in our country, and are responsible for much of the innovation. They are thus our greatest hope for the future. Our capacity as a nation to create an environment that encourages and nurtures innovative new businesses will determine our success in providing jobs for our people. In the private sector, spurring innovation means paying special attention to the needs of small—including minority and women-owned—and rapidly growing businesses on the cutting edge of our economy.

This will require incentives for research and development and for employee education and training, including relaxing certain restrictions on pension fund investment; targeted reform that stimulates the flow of capital into new and smaller businesses; a tax code that is no longer biased against small and rapidly growing firms; vigorous enforcement of our antitrust laws, coupled with antitrust policies that permit clearly legitimate joint research and development ventures; expanded small business access to the Export–Import Bank and other agencies involved in export promotion; and targeted reform that provides for the delivery of community-based, community-supported management assistance, and innovative means of making seed capital available for companies in our large cities, as well as our rural communities.

Rules and regulations should not weigh more heavily on new firms or small businesses than they do on the large, well-established enterprise. Risk taking is a key to economic growth in a modern industrial society. If anything, rules and regulations should encourage it.

The Small Business Administration must once again be responsive to the needs of entrepreneurs, including minorities and women. In addition, the heads of the Small Business Administration, the Minority Business Development Administration and other government agencies must ensure that the needs of smaller minority businesses are met at the regional and local levels. To further meet the needs of smaller minority businesses, we favor increasing government procurement, opportunities for smaller minority firms, encouraging deposits of federal funds in minority-owned financial institutions, and vigorously implementing all set-aside provisions for minority businesses.

The Democratic Party pledges to bring about these reforms and create a new era of opportunity for the entrepreneurs who have always led the way in our economy.

Meeting the Challenge of Economic Competition

Thirty years ago, half of all goods produced in the world were made in the United States. While we have greatly expanded our output of services, our share of manufactured products is now just one-fifth of the world's total. Once dominant U.S.-industries are now hard-pressed. In April, our trade deficit reached a stunning $12.2 billion for one month. At that rate, we would lose two million or more jobs this year alone. We will not allow our workers and our industries to be displaced by either unfair import competition, or irrational fiscal and monetary policies.

Some of these difficulties we have brought on ourselves, with shortsighted strategies, inadequate investment in plants, equipment, and innovation, and fiscal and monetary policies that have impaired our international competitiveness by distorting the value of the dollar against foreign currencies. But other difficulties have been thrust upon us by foreign nations.

The reality of the 1980's is that the international economy is the arena in which we must compete. The world economy is an integrated economy; the challenge for our political leadership is to assure that the new arena is in fact a fair playing field for American businesses and consumers. We are committed to pursuing industrial strategies that effectively and imaginatively blend the genius of the free market with vital government partnership and leadership. As Democrats, we will be guided by the following principles and policies:

- We need a vigorous, open and fair trade policy that builds America's competitive strength and that allows our nation to remain an advanced, diversified economy while promoting full employment and raising living standards in the United States and other countries of the world; opens overseas markets for American products; strengthens the international economic system; assists adjustment to foreign competition; and recognizes the legitimate interests of American workers, farmers and businesses.

- We will pursue international negotiations to open markets and eliminate trade restrictions, recognizing that the growth and stability of the Third World depends on its ability to sell its products in international markets. High technology, agriculture and other industries should be brought under the General Agreement on Tariffs and Trade. Moreover, the developing world is a major market for U.S. exports, particularly capital goods. As a result, the U.S. has a major stake in international economic institutions that support growth in the developing world.

- We recognize that the growth and development of the Third World is vital both to global stability and to the continuing expansion of world trade. The U.S. presently sells more to the Third World than to the European Community and Japan combined. If we do not buy their goods, they cannot buy ours, nor can they service their debt. Consequently, it is important to be responsive to the issues of the North/South dialogue such as volatile commodity prices, inequities in the functioning of the international financial and monetary markets, and removal of barriers to the export of Third World goods.

- If trade has become big business for the country, exports have become critical to the economic health of a growing list of American industries. In the future, national economic policy will have to be set with an eye to its impact on U.S. exports. The strength of the dollar, the nature of the U.S. tax system, and the adequacy of export finance all play a role in making U.S. exports internationally competitive.

- The United States continues to struggle with trade barriers that affect its areas of international strength. Subsidized export financing on the part of Europe and Japan has also created problems for the United States, as has the use of industrial policies in Europe and Japan. In some cases, foreign governments target areas of America's competitive strength. In other cases, industrial targeting has been used to maintain industries that cannot meet international competition—often diverting exports to the American market and increasing the burden of adjustment for America's import-competing industries. We will ensure that timely and effective financing can be obtained by American businesses through the Export–Import Bank, so that they can compete effectively against subsidized competitors from abroad.

- A healthy U.S. auto industry is essential to a strong trade balance and economy. That industry generates a large number of American jobs and both develops and consumes new technology needed for economic vitality. We believe it is a sound principle of international trade for foreign auto makers which enjoy substantial sales in the United States to invest here and create jobs where their markets are. This can promote improved trade relations and a stronger American and world economy. We also believe U.S. auto makers need to maintain high-volume small car production in the U.S. With the U.S. auto companies' return to profitability (despite continued unemployment in the auto sector), we urge expanded domestic investment to supply consumers with a full range of competitive vehicles. We support efforts by management and labor to improve auto quality and productivity, and to restrain prices.

- Where foreign competition is fair, American industry should compete without government assistance. Where competition is unfair, we must respond powerfully. We will use trade law and international negotiations to aid U.S. workers, farmers, and businesses injured by unfair trade practices.

- We need industrial strategies to create a cooperative partnership of labor, capital, and management to increase productivity and to make America competitive once more. Our keystone industries must be modernized and rebuilt, through industry-wide agreements. Where necessary, through Presidential leadership, we must negotiate industrial modernization and growth agreements that commit management to new domestic investment, higher levels of employment and worker training, as well as commit labor to ease the introduction of new technologies.

- There must be a broad consensus and commitment among labor, business and financial institutions that industry should and can be assisted, and in a particular way. We believe that all parties to modernization agreements must contribute to their success and that the government must be prepared to use a range of tools—including tax, import, and regulatory relief, and appropriate financing mechanisms—to assist this revitalization. There should be a primary emphasis on private capital in any such agreements.

- The problems of individual industries, rather than industry as a whole, is another area in which an Economic Cooperation Council will be effective. In the case of a particular industry, the Council would select sub-councils to solve specific problems. Key members of the interested businesses and unions and of financial institutions, academic specialists and other concerned and knowledgeable parties would meet to hammer out proposed strategies and agreements. It is not a question of picking winners and losers. Nor is it even always a question of some industries being more important than others. Rather, it is an opportunity for government and the private sector to forge a consensus to capture new markets, to restore an industry to competitive health, or to smooth the transition of workers and firms to new opportunities.

- We want industries to modernize so as to restore competitiveness where it is flagging. If temporary trade relief is granted, the *quid pro quo* for relief will be a realistic, hardheaded modernization plan which will restore competitiveness involving commitments by all affected parties. The public is entitled to receive a fair return on its investment. Where government initiatives are necessary to save an industry like steel, auto or textiles, we must see that those initiatives meet the needs of the whole community—workers as well as executives, taxpayers and consumers as well as stockholders.

- To facilitate the efforts of workers and communities to keep plants open and operating and, in cases in which closings are unavoidable, to help workers and communities to adapt, we support a requirement that companies give advance notification of plant closings or large-scale layoffs to their employees, surrounding communities and local governments. Where plants are nonetheless closed, we will help workers and communities to adapt.

- Finally, we need a vigorous effort to redress the cur-

rency distortions that are undermining our international competitiveness. In addition to reducing our budget deficit, we will press for improved economic coordination with the major industrialized nations; work with Japan and other countries to further liberalize currency, and investment regulations; and negotiate toward agreements that will blunt speculative currency swings and restore stability and predictability to the international monetary system.

Agriculture

Agriculture—America's largest, most fundamental industry—has been plunged into its worst depression since Herbert Hoover presided over the farm economy's collapse half a century ago. During President Reagan's stewardship of our nation's agriculture economy: real prices paid to farmers for their commodities have plummeted by twenty-one percent; real interest rates paid by farmers have increased by as much as 1,200 percent; real farm income has fallen to its lowest level since 1933; debt owed by U.S. farmers and ranchers has swelled to $215 billion; and farm foreclosures and forced sales have tripled.

Ronald Reagan has hung a "for sale" sign on America's independent, family-based system of agricultural production. While these farmers have raised their production efficiency to record highs, Reagan's policies have forced down their prices, income, and financial worth.

The Reagan Administration has been unwilling to take sensible, fiscally responsible action needed to halt this accelerating downward cycle in agriculture. Because of this failure of leadership, nearly 200,000 good farmers and ranchers, including minority farmers, have gone out of business since he took office in 1981. This is a rate of more than 1,000 families pushed off their land every week, the equivalent of all the farms and ranches in California and Iowa, our two largest agricultural states. Hundreds of thousands of the remaining enterprises teeter on the brink of bankruptcy and cannot survive another four years of this Administration's agricultural mismanagement.

This collapse is happening despite the fact that Ronald Reagan has squandered taxpayers' money on his farm policies, spending $31 billion on his programs last year alone. That is *six times* more than any other President in history has spent on farm programs, and it is *$9 billion more* than was spent on farm programs in *all eight years* of President Kennedy's and President Johnson's Administrations combined.

Like 1932 and 1960, this election year represents a watershed for American agriculture. At stake is the survival of the family farm. Under President Reagan's policies of high costs and low prices, these family farmers cannot survive. They will continue to go out of business at a historic pace, to be replaced by an industrialized structure of agriculture that is dominated by conglomerates, giant farm combinations, and tax loss ventures. Already, under Reagan, 65 percent of net farm income has been concentrated in the hands of the largest 1 percent of farms, up from 42 percent just three years ago.

The Democratic Party renews its commitment to the family farm structure of American agriculture. We believe that the public need for a reliable supply of high-quality, reasonably priced food and fiber is best met by family farm enterprises whose primary business is farming or ranching. It is from hundreds of thousands of those competitive, diverse, decentralized, entrepreneurial families that the public gains superior agricultural efficiency and productivity. Accordingly, it is in these farming families that the public finds its most sensible investment. In addition, these farmers are the ones who show greatest concern for good conservation practices, quality of food, and rural values. We need more of these farmers, not fewer.

The Democratic Party pledges action. We must solve the immediate farm crisis through a combination of humanitarian aid programs abroad, aggressive promotion of farm exports, and a fair moratorium on farm debt and foreclosure by federal credit agencies to family farm borrowers being forced out of business through no fault of their own, until a long-term program addressing the farm credit crisis can be put into place. Beginning next January with the writing of a new long-term farm bill, the Democratic Party pledges to rebuild a prosperous system of family farms and ranches. We will forge a new agreement on a farm and food policy that assures a fair deal for family farmers, consumers, taxpayers, conservationists, and others with a direct stake in the organizational structure of the food economy.

Our goal is to restore the faith of family farmers that their hard work, ingenuity, efficiency, and good stewardship will be rewarded with profit, rather than debt. We seek a program that is focused specifically on the true family farm, that encourages long-term financial planning, that is tied to locally approved soil conservation programs, and that reduces federal budget costs for farm programs.

We will target federal assistance toward true family-sized and beginning farmers' operations. We will stop good, efficient farmers from being thrown off their farms, while structuring incentives so as to achieve maximum participation in farm commodity programs. We will bring farm credit interest rates down and set supports at levels that at least enable farmers to recover actual production costs. We will use the full range of programs to reduce excess production when necessary to assure fair prices to farmers. As the overall economy improves, we will gradually adjust price supports toward a firm goal of parity of income. We will give new emphasis to producer-controlled marketing arrangements. We will revitalize the farmer-owned commodity reserve system. We will put in place tax policies that are fair to farmers, while removing unproductive incentives for investors seeking to avoid taxes. We must protect family farmers from land speculators and we must protect both farmers and consumers from income losses resulting from exorbitant pricing of middlemen. We will renew our country's historic commitment to agricultural science and education, to rural services such as cooperative electrification and telephones. We oppose Reagan Administration proposals that would more than double interest rates to rural cooperatives, and sharply reduce rural electric loan levels.

The Democratic Party reaffirms its commitment to soil and water conservation. We will actively promote the production of ethanol and other biomass sources of renewable energy and encourage conversion to energy self-sufficient farming operations.

Finally, we must reverse the annual decrease in the value and volume of U.S. farm exports which has occurred in each year of Ronald Reagan's term. Our farm exports are vital to the nation's prosperity and provide a major part of total farm income. We must restore the ability of U.S. farm products to compete in world markets, and increase worldwide demand for American agricultural products. To do this, we must make major changes in Ronald Reagan's economic policies, and correct his grossly distorted currency exchange rates, which have caused American competitiveness in international trade to decline. We must also resist efforts to lower commodity price supports; such action would only lower farm income without addressing the economic policies which are the root cause of declining competitiveness of U.S. farm products in world markets.

Critical to the recovery of farm income and exports will be the pursuit of economic policies that contribute to worldwide economic recovery. Flexible export credit programs and assurances of long-term availability of U.S. farm products will also be necessary, to restore America's preeminence as an agricultural exporter and end the destruction of the family farm brought on by Ronald Reagan.

Managing Our Natural Resources

Our economy, the quality of our lives, and the kind of opportunities that we leave to our children all depend on how well we manage our wealth of natural resources. We must harvest enough timber and food, produce enough minerals, coal, oil and gas, and provide enough electric power to keep our economy growing. We must be prepared to avoid severe dislocations when conflicts in other parts of the world force energy prices to climb. At the same time that we encourage enhanced energy production, we must recognize that conserving irreplaceable resources, using energy efficiently instead of wasting it, and protecting our environment help guarantee a better life for twenty-first-century America.

Protecting Our National Security

President Reagan has reduced our ability to defend our economy from the disruptions that would come if conflicts in other countries interrupt the world's oil supply. While the percentage of our oil imports from the Middle East has dropped, U.S. oil imports from other countries have increased. If war in the Middle East cuts back oil supplies from that region, Europe and Japan will pay higher prices to get replacement oil: a bidding war among oil-importing nations means that the price of oil all over the world, including the United States, will rise dangerously.

Ronald Reagan has refused to prepare us for that day. He has refused to fill the Strategic Petroleum Reserve as quickly as authorized by law, and in case of emergency, he has made clear that his policy will be simply to allow those who can pay the most to buy whatever supplies are available.

Our Party must spell out a comprehensive program for energy security. We should accelerate the filling of the Strategic Petroleum Reserve, so that it can play its intended role as a temporary national oil supply during future energy emergencies. And in an oil crisis, a Democratic President will make every effort to ensure that essential users—schools, farmers, hospitals, local bus and rail systems—have the supplies they need at reasonable prices. The Democratic Party will ensure that the especially vulnerable—the unemployed, the elderly, the poor—will not be unfairly forced to share the burden of rising oil prices.

Developing U.S. Energy Supplies

In today's complex world, no industrial nation can be fully self-sufficient. The United States and all countries in the free world depend on each other for resources, as markets, or as economic and political allies. But the strength of our own economy and the influence we exercise in the rest of the world are sure to be increased if we are capable of supplying more, not less, of our own energy.

America is blessed with abundant coal and natural gas, substantial supplies of oil, and plentiful reserves of uranium. Although very costly to process, vast supplies of oil shales and tar sands represent future energy sources. Significant contributions to our energy supply can be made by utilizing renewable resources and indigenous energy, such as active and passive solar systems, windpower, geothermal and ocean thermal power, and the recovery of gas from agricultural wastes, coal mines, and garbage dumps. These proven energy sources, as well as more experimental energy systems, should be encouraged for the positive environmental and economic contribution they can make to our energy security.

The Democratic Party supports the aggressive promotion of coal exports, research and development into better technologies for using coal, and assurances that rates for transporting coal are fair and reasonable. To ensure that the environment and worker safety are fully protected as coal production increases to meet our national energy needs, we will vigorously implement and strictly enforce laws governing worker safety, land reclamation, air and water quality, and the protection of agriculture, fish, and wildlife.

The Democratic Party will support research and development for solar energy and other renewable energy systems, and will provide incentives for use of solar and other emerging energy systems. We will vigorously pursue our solar energy efforts and dramatically increase funding for the Solar Energy and Energy Conservation Bank and low-income weatherization, which could put hundreds of thousands of unemployed people to work weatherizing and installing solar energy systems in millions of American homes, especially the homes of low-income Americans. We oppose the Reagan Administration's efforts to fund these programs through petroleum price overcharge refunds from the oil companies.

We will support the federal research and development efforts slashed by the Reagan Administration, to promote the discovery of new energy supplies and energy use technologies.

The Democratic Party strongly opposes the Reagan Administration's policy of aggressively promoting and further subsidizing nuclear power. Today, millions of Americans are concerned about the safety of nuclear power plants and their radioactive waste. We recognize the safety and economic factors which bring into question the viability of this energy source.

We will insist on the highest possible standards of safety and protection of public health with respect to nuclear power, including siting, design, operation, evacuation plans, and waste disposal procedures. We will require nuclear power to compete fairly in the marketplace. We will reexamine and review all federal subsidies to the nuclear industry, including the Price–Anderson Act's limits on the liability of the industry which will be considered for reauthorization in the next Congress. A Democratic Administration will give the Nuclear Regulatory Commission the integrity, competence, and credibility it needs to carry out its mandate to protect the public health and safety. We will expand the role of the public in NRC procedures.

The Democratic Party believes high-level radioactive waste and other hazardous materials should be transported only when absolutely necessary. We will guarantee states full participatory rights in all decisions affecting the movement of high-level radioactive waste within their borders. We will require radioactive waste and hazardous materials emergency response plans along transportation routes, similar to those required for nuclear power plants. The Democratic Party will act swiftly to ensure states' authority to regulate routes and schedules for radioactive and other hazardous shipments.

We will ensure that no offshore oil and gas exploration will be taken up that is inconsistent with the protection of our fisheries and coastal resources. The leasing of public lands, both onshore and offshore, will be based on present demand and land use planning processes, and will be undertaken in ways that assure fair economic return to the public, protection of the environment and full participation by state and local governments. The Coastal Zone Management Act should be amended to require initial leasing decisions to be consistent with federally approved state and territorial coastal zone management plans. Interior states should be given consultation and concurrence rights with respect to onshore leases comparable to the rights afforded coastal states with respect to offshore leases.

We believe that synthetic fuels research and development support should emphasize environmental protection technologies and standards and hold out reasonable hope of long-term economic viability. The Democratic Party proposes to reevaluate the Synthetic Fuels Corporation.

Energy Conservation

The high cost of producing and using energy now constitutes a substantial share of U.S. capital spending.

Energy conservation has become essential to our economy as well as our national security.

Strict standards of energy efficiency for home appliances, for example, could save enough money in the next 15 years to avoid the need for 40 new power plants. Better-insulated houses and apartments can sharply reduce power and heating bills for families throughout America, and help utilities avoid the high cost of building more expensive power plants.

Ronald Reagan sees no role for government in conserving energy, and he has gutted promising conservation efforts. The Democratic Party supports extension of the existing tax credits for business and residential energy conservation and renewable energy use, and expansion of those tax credits to include the incorporation of passive solar designs in new housing. The Democratic Party also supports faithful implementation of existing programs for energy efficiency standards for new appliances; upgrading of fuel efficiency standards for new automobiles; establishment of comparable fuel efficiency standards for new light trucks and vans; and development of an energy efficiency rating system to be used to advise homebuyers at the time of sale of the likely future energy costs of houses.

Lifeline Utility Rates

Recognizing that the elderly and the poor suffer most from high energy costs, the Democratic Party supports special, lower electricity and natural gas rates for senior citizens and low-income Americans.

Recycling

The Democratic Party recognizes that recovering and recycling used materials can conserve energy and natural resources, create additional jobs, reduce the costs of material goods, eliminate solid waste and litter, and avoid pollution. We will increase efforts to recover and recycle useful materials from municipal waste.

Protecting Our Environment

Americans know that industrial production and economic development do not have to mean ruined land or polluted air and water. Sound resource management, careful planning, and strict pollution control enforcement will allow us to have a prosperous economy and a healthy environment. For the last four years the Reagan Administration has assumed a radical position, working to eliminate the environmental protections forged through years of bipartisan cooperation.

Ronald Reagan's first appointees to key environmental positions have already been forced to resign. But the American people are entitled to more than the absence of scandal—they demand real action to protect the health and safety of our families and communities. The Democratic Party supports revitalizing the Environmental Protection Agency by providing it with a budget increase adequate to allow it to carry out its substantially increased responsibility to protect the people and enforce the law.

Hazardous Wastes

Thousands of dump sites across America contain highly dangerous poisons that can threaten the health and safety of families who live nearby or who depend on water supplies that could be contaminated by the poisons. Although Congress has established the Superfund for emergency cleanup of these dangerous sites, President Reagan refuses to use it vigorously. The Democratic Party is committed to enforcing existing laws, to dramatically increasing Superfund resources to clean up all sites that threaten public health, and to assuring that everyone whose health or property is damaged has a fair opportunity to force the polluters to pay for the damage. This increased support should be financed at least in part through new taxes on the generation of hazardous wastes, so companies have an economic incentive to reduce the volume and toxicity of their dangerous wastes.

The Resource Conservation and Recovery Act should be expanded to include major new requirements for safer management of newly generated toxic waste. High priority must be given to establishing and implementing a program to phase out the land disposal of untreated hazardous waste, requiring instead that it be treated by chemical, biological, or thermal processes that render it harmless and safe for disposal. The Environmental Protection Agency also should adopt standards to ensure that the safest possible methods of managing particular wastes are used, and that available methods are used to reduce the volume and toxicity of waste produced by industry.

Clean Air and Water

The Democratic Party supports a reauthorized and strengthened Clean Air Act. Statutory requirements for the control of toxic air pollutants should be strengthened, with the environmental agency required to identify pollutants known or anticipated to cause cancer and other serious diseases. The Democratic Party calls for an immediate program to reduce sulfur dioxide emissions by 50% from 1980 levels within the next decade; this program shall include interim reductions within five years of its enactment. In addition, significant progress will be made to further reductions of nitrogen oxide emissions. Our effort should be designed to reduce environmental and economic damage from acid rain while assuring such efforts do not cause regional economic dislocations. Every effort should be made to mitigate any job losses associated with any national acid rain program.

The Democratic Party is committed to strengthening the Clean Water Act to curb both direct and indirect discharge of toxic pollutants into our nation's waters, and supports a strengthened Environmental Protection Agency to assure help to American cities in providing adequate supplies of drinking water free of toxic chemicals and other contaminants.

Workplace Safety

The Democratic Party believes all Americans, in their workplaces and communities, have the right to know what hazardous materials and chemicals they may have been exposed to and how they may protect their health from such exposure. The Democratic Party supports appropriate funding levels for the Occupational Safety and Health Administration, reversing the Reagan budget cuts in that agency; vigorous enforcement of occupational safety and health standards; and worker right-to-know requirements.

Pesticides and Herbicides

The Democratic Party is committed to establishing standards and deadlines requiring all pesticides and herbicides to be thoroughly tested to ensure they do not cause cancer, birth defects, or other adverse health effects. We support rigorous research and information programs to develop and assist farmers with the use of integrated pest management and non-chemical pest control methods to reduce the health risk of controlling agricultural pests, and the establishment of strict deadlines to ensure that pesticides are fully tested and in compliance with health and safety standards. The Democratic Party is committed to ensuring that our nation's food supply is free of pesticides whose danger to health has been demonstrated, and believes it is irresponsible to allow the export to other nations of herbicides and pesticides banned for use in the U.S. and will act swiftly to halt such exports.

EPA Budget

The Democratic Party opposes the Reagan Administration's budget cuts, which have severely hampered the effectiveness of our environmental programs. The Environmental Protection Agency should receive a budget that exceeds in real dollars the agency's purchasing power when President Reagan took office, since the agency's workload has almost doubled in recent years.

International Leadership

The Democratic Party strongly opposes the Reagan Administration's abandonment of the United States' historic leadership role in international efforts to control pollution, contrary to our interests and those of our allies. We will restore immediately our nation's leadership on international environmental issues, making the United States once again the best example of an industrial nation committed to protecting its land, water and air resources, as well as those of its neighbors.

Federal Compliance

The Democratic Party will require all federal activities, including those associated with the Departments of Defense and Energy, to comply fully with federal health, safety and environmental laws.

Managing Our Public Lands

The Democratic Party believes in retaining ownership and control of our public lands, and in managing those lands according to the principles of multiple use and sustained yield, with appropriate environmental standards and mitigation requirements to protect the public interest. The Democratic Party supports the substantial expansion of the National Wilderness Preservation System, with designations of all types of ecosystems, including coastal areas, deserts, and prairies as well as forest and alpine areas. Congressional decisions to designate wilderness should include evaluations of mineral resources and other potential land values. Further, the Democratic Party believes that publicly owned timber resources should be priced at levels that reflect their true market value, taking into consideration their true costs to the government. Grazing on our public lands should not impair our grassland resources.

The Democratic Party believes the process of designating rivers for inclusion in the national wild and scenic rivers system, halted by the Reagan Administration, should be preserved in their freeflowing condition for the benefit and enjoyment of present and future generations.

The Democratic Party supports adequate funding of and restoration of federal programs to protect fully national parks, wildlife refuges, and wilderness areas from external and internal threats. Development activities within national wildlife refuges which are not compatible with the purposes for which the refuges were designated should not be allowed. The letter and the spirit of the Alaska National Interest Lands Conservation Act of 1980 should be followed, with an end to unsound land exchanges and other efforts to circumvent the law.

A new Democratic Party will provide adequate appropriations for the Land and Water Conservation Fund.

Wetlands. The Democratic Party supports coherent and coordinated federal policies to protect our nation's valuable and disappearing wetlands, which are critical nurseries for commercial fisheries and vital ecological, scenic, and recreational resources. These policies will include more active efforts to acquire threatened wetland areas, consideration of new tax incentives to encourage private efforts to preserve instead of develop wetlands, and elimination of current incentives that encourage wetlands destruction.

Wildlife. Fishing, hunting, and enjoyment of America's wildlife can continue to be an important part of our natural heritage only through active programs to maintain the diversity and abundance of plants, animals, and natural habitats. The Democratic Party supports protection of endangered species, land management to maintain healthy populations of wildlife, and full United States participation to implement international wildlife treaties.

Water Policy. The Democratic Party recognizes that finite and diminishing quantities of water, and often antiquated, inadequate, or inefficient water supply systems, threaten economic growth and the quality of life in all regions of the country. We recognize that federal leadership is necessary to meet these needs, and to do so in environmentally sound ways.

The Democratic Party supports the creation of a national water resources planning board and a comprehensive review of the nation's water needs. We support major new water policy efforts addressing several national needs:

- We will help meet our nation's infrastructure needs, including the construction of new projects which are economically and environmentally sound. New water project construction starts, by the Corps of Engineers throughout the country and by the Bureau of Reclamation in the West, are critical. In all cases, we will consider innovative and nonstructural alternatives on an equal basis.
- We will examine the water quantity and water quality issues associated with providing adequate water supply.
- We will help meet navigation, flood control, and municipal water supply system needs, with new assistance to urban areas needing financial help to rebuild deteriorating water systems.
- We will give new priority attention to improving efficiency in the use of water, recognizing that more efficient water use is often the least costly and most environmentally acceptable way to meet our water

needs and achieve the fullest possible beneficial use of our water resources.

- We will carefully coordinate federal water policy efforts with affected state governments, making possible not only cooperative financing of water investments but a commensurate sharing of decision-making authority and responsibility.
- We will provide assistance to states addressing the growing problems of groundwater depletion and contamination.

CHAPTER II. JUSTICE, DIGNITY, AND OPPORTUNITY

Introduction

Fulfilling America's highest promise, equal justice for all: that is the Democratic agenda for a just future.

For many of our citizens, it is only in the last two decades that the efforts of a broad, bipartisan coalition have begun to give real meaning to the dream of freedom and equality. During that time Democrats, spurred by the Civil Rights Movement, have enacted landmark legislation in areas including voting, education, housing and employment.

A nation is only as strong as its commitment to justice and equality. Today, a corrosive unfairness eats at the underpinnings of our society. Civil rights laws and guarantees—only recently achieved after hard-fought battles, personal sacrifice and loss of life—are imperiled by an Administration that consciously seeks to turn the clock back to an era when second-class citizenship for women and minorities, disenfranchisement, and de jure and de facto segregation were very much the facts of life for well over half of America's population. Moreover, justice encompasses more than our nation's laws. The poor, the female, the minority—many of them just like boats stuck on the bottom—have come to experience an implacable and intractable foe in the Reagan Administration.

A new Democratic Administration will understand that the age-old scourge of discrimination and prejudice against many groups in American society is still rampant and very much a part of the reason for the debilitating circumstances in which disadvantaged peoples are forced to live. Although strides have been made in combatting discrimination and defamation against Americans of various ethnic groups, much remains to be done. Therefore, we pledge an end to the Reagan Administration's punitive policy toward women, minorities, and the poor and support the reaffirmation of the principle that the government is still responsible for protecting the civil rights of all citizens. Government has a special responsibility to those whom society has historically prevented from enjoying the benefits of full citizenship for reasons of race, religion, sex, age, national origin and ethnic heritage, sexual orientation, or disability.

The goal for the coming decades is not only full justice under the law, but *economic* justice as well. In the recent past, we have put our nation on the road toward achieving equal protection of all our citizens' human rights. The challenge now is to continue to press that cause, while joining a new battle—to assure justice and opportunity in the workplace, and in the economy.

Justice for all in today's America and the America of tomorrow demands not one, but two broad guarantees. First, we must guarantee that our nation will reinforce and extend its commitment to human rights and equal opportunity. And second, we must guarantee progress on the new frontier for the future: economic and social justice.

We are determined to enforce the laws guaranteeing equal opportunity, and to complete the civil rights agenda cast aside by the Reagan Administration. No President has the right to do what this Administration has done: to read selectively from the United States Code and simply ignore the laws ensuring basic rights and opportunities because they conflict with this Administration's ideology. As Democrats, we pledge to reverse the trend towards lawlessness which has characterized this Administration, and to keep our commitments to all in our community who look to the government for defense of their rights.

But we recognize that while a first step toward a just society is to guarantee the right of all workers to compete equally for a job, the next step is assuring that enough new jobs are created to give meaningful employment to all our workers for the future.

If in past decades we won the right for minorities to ride at the front of the bus, in coming years we must assure that minorities have the opportunity to own the bus company.

It will not be enough to say that our nation must offer equal access to health care—we must put comprehensive health care within the reach of all of our citizens, at a price all can afford.

It will not do simply to guarantee women a place in the work force—women deserve an equal chance at a career leading to the board of directors.

As Democrats, we believe that human rights and an economy of opportunity are two sides of the same coin of justice. No economic program can be considered just unless it advances the opportunity of all to live a better, more dignified life. No American is afforded economic justice when he or she is denied an opportunity to reap the rewards of economic growth.

Economic justice is also economic common sense. Any who doubt that should consider the toll of welfare, crime, prisons, public housing and urban squalor on our national wealth. We will pay a high price for all the disadvantaged or disenfranchised if we fail to include them in the new economic revolution.

As Democrats, therefore, we pledge to pursue a new definition of justice that meets the new demands of our time. Under a Democratic Administration, equality and fairness under the law will be matched by justice in the economy and in the workplace.

The Future If Reagan Is Reelected

"Twenty years after the Equal Pay Act should have eradicated the last vestige of economic discrimination against women, employers have made little progress in integrating their work force. It is the Republican Governor of Washington State, and the Republican County Executive of Nassau County, New York, who are committing public resources to mount a legal defense for their jurisdictions' blatant sex discrimination practices. . . . The Reagan Administration from the outset has made it abundantly clear that civil rights and economic justice are to be sacrificed on the altar of corporate greed. . . ."—Diana Rock, Director of Women's Rights, American Federation of State, County, and Municipal Employees (Democratic Platform Committee Hearing, Cleveland, Ohio, May 21, 1984)

"The Reagan Administration, upon taking office in 1981, set upon a concerted effort to roll back civil rights protections. This attack is under way in agency enforcement, court litigation, legislative initiative, and nominations of federal appointees."—Virna M. Canson, Regional Director. West Coast Region, NAACP (Democratic Platform Committee Hearing, Los Angeles, California, May 14, 1984)

The neglect of our historic human rights commitment will already be recorded as the first legacy of Ronald Reagan's years in the White House. But suppose Mr. Reagan is reelected.

What would become of America's commitment to equal justice and opportunity if Mr. Reagan is reelected?

The hard truth is that if Mr. Reagan is reelected our most vigorous defender of the rule of law—the United States Supreme Court—could be lost to the cause of equal justice for another generation. Today, five of the nine members of that Court are over 75. Our next President will likely have the opportunity to shape that Court, not just for his own term—or even for his own lifetime—but for the rest of ours, and for our children's too.

There can be little doubt that a Supreme Court chosen by Ronald Reagan would radically restrict constitutional rights and drastically reinterpret existing laws. Today, the fundamental right of a woman to reproductive freedom rests on the votes of six members of the Supreme Court—five of whom are over 75. That right could easily disappear during a second Reagan term. Already, the protections against employment discrimination have been restricted by the Court: a Reagan Court surely would reduce them further. The same is true for the right of workers to have a healthy and safe workplace, and to organize collectively in unions. Although the statute protecting voting rights has been extended through a massive bipartisan effort, opposed by the Reagan Administration, a Reagan Supreme Court could still effectively nullify it simply by erecting impossible standards of proof. Not long ago, the Court decided it should hire independent counsel to argue that tax exemptions for racially discriminatory schools were unlawful because the Justice Department refused to do so. Can anyone imagine a Reagan Court doing that? How much easier it would be for a Reagan Court simply to agree with a Reagan Department of Justice.

If Mr. Reagan is reelected, who would protect women and minorities against discrimination?

In the first year after the Reagan Administration assumed office, the number of cases involving charges of employment discrimination filed in court by the EEOC dropped by more than 70 percent. During this Administration, the EEOC has refused to process a single comparable worth case filed by a woman. Meanwhile, the Reagan Justice Department has sought to destroy effective affirmative action remedies, and even to undermine private plans to reduce discrimination in employment. The actions of the Reagan Administration serve only to delay the day when fairness is achieved and such remedial measures are, therefore, no longer needed.

It is now clear that if Mr. Reagan is reelected, women and minorities seeking protection of their rights would be forced to contend not only with their employers, but with a hostile government. Equal employment opportunity and equity would remain elusive dreams.

If Mr. Reagan is reelected, who would assure access to justice?

Since the day of its inauguration, the Reagan Administration has conducted a continuous, full-scale war against the federal Legal Services Corporation, whose only job is to ensure that the poor are fairly heard in court, and that they get equal access to our system of justice. Thirty percent of the Corporation's lawyers have been laid off, and the Administration has used every means it could find to stack its board with people hostile to the very concept of equal justice for the poor.

In the America of Ronald Reagan, you will only get as much justice as you pay for.

If Mr. Reagan is reelected, who would protect the rights of workers?

The Republican Administration has consistently viewed the dollar costs to businesses of providing a safe workplace as more important than the impact of injury and disease on working men and women. It has appointed officials to the National Labor Relations Board who openly oppose the rights of workers to organize and bargain collectively. The Department of Labor has ignored its mandate to enforce fair labor standards and has sought to reverse hard-won gains in protections for worker health and safety.

What would happen if Mr. Reagan is reelected? Will the right to bargain collectively be eviscerated through Republican-approved abuses of the bankruptcy laws? Will the National Labor Relations Act be converted into a tool that limits working men and women and empowers only their employers? Who will ensure that our next generation does not suffer the effects of toxic substances in the workplace—substances whose existence is not even revealed to the worker?

If Mr. Reagan is reelected, who would protect the rights of senior citizens?

Speaking at Philadelphia in 1980 during his campaign, Ronald Reagan vowed to a large audience of senior citizens his strong support for Social Security. He assured thousands of senior citizens on that occasion that as President he would see to it that every commitment made by the federal government to the senior citizens was faithfully kept.

Ronald Reagan violated that promise shortly after he became President. In 1981, speaking to a joint session of Congress, President Reagan said, "We will not cut Medicare." In a matter of weeks thereafter President Reagan asked the Congress of the United States to cut $88 billion in 1981 and the following four years from Social Security programs. He proposed to reduce by a third the number of people protected by the disability insurance program. He proposed to reduce by a third the benefits a senior citizen would receive if he or she retired at 62. He proposed to cut out the burial program for recipients of Social Security.

He proposed to cut millions from programs that Democratic Administrations had provided for the education of the children of the elderly covered by Social Security, slashing the list of beneficiaries of these pro-

grams by hundreds of thousands of sons and daughters of men and women covered by Social Security. And he called for the abolition of the $122-a-month minimum benefit program, which would have dropped over three million people from Social Security altogether.

The American people then revolted, and so did the Congress. The Democratic Party put a stop to the decimation of the Social Security program, but not before President Reagan had cut $19 billion from Social Security benefits in 1981 and the ensuing four years. Democrats in Congress forced the restoration of the $122-a-month minimum benefit program to those who were covered before the Reagan cuts, but never succeeded in extending coverage to the additional 7,000 people a month who would have become eligible after the Reagan cuts.

Instead of keeping his word that he would not cut Medicare, Reagan forced Congress every year beginning in 1981 to cut billions from the Medicare program. When Social Security developed financial problems due to massive unemployment in 1982, the Reagan Administration moved to "solve" them by cutting benefits further. Only the Democrats on the Social Security Commission prevented him from doing that.

If Mr. Reagan is reelected, how would we teach our children to respect the law?

We cannot teach our children to respect the law when they see the highest officials of government flaunting it at their will. Lawlessness has been a pattern in this Administration—and it is a pattern that is unlikely to be altered if Reagan and the Republicans stay in the White House.

More than forty top Republican officials have already been implicated in all kinds of wrongdoing. Murky transactions on the fringe of organized crime, accepting gifts from foreign journalists and governments, misusing government funds, lying under oath, stock manipulations, taking interest-free loans from wealthy businessmen who later receive federal jobs—all of these are part of business as usual with Ronald Reagan's appointees.

The Republicans profess to stand for "law and order." But this is the same Administration that vetoed the bipartisan anti-crime bill in 1982. And when it comes to laws they do not like—whether they concern toxic wastes, pure food and drugs, or worker health and safety—this Administration simply makes believe they do not exist. The same is true overseas: this Administration is just as willing to ignore international law as domestic law. When we finally learned of its illegal mining of Nicaragua's harbors, the Reagan

Administration hastily attempted, the night before Nicaragua sued us, to withdraw jurisdiction over the question from the World Court. But even this maneuver was carried out in an illegal fashion that the World Court later set aside.

This Republican Administration has been unprecedentedly eager to limit public debate by instituting "security agreements" that censor ex-officials, "revising" the Freedom of Information Act, refusing visas to foreign visitors who might provide another perspective on American policies overseas, and denying our war correspondents their historic position alongside our troops. This comes as no surprise: in the first term, the Reagan Administration had a lot to hide. What would happen in a second?

If Mr. Reagan is reelected, what would happen to our unfinished civil rights agenda?

The answer is clear: an Administration which refuses to enforce the laws that are on the books can hardly be expected to respect—or even recognize—the rights of those who are not already specifically protected by existing law.

Nowhere is this Administration's hostility to equal rights and equal justice more apparent than in its attitude to the Equal Rights Amendment. As soon as the Reagan faction took control of the Republican Party at its convention in 1980, it ended that Party's forty-year commitment to passage of the Equal Rights Amendment. So long as this Administration remains in office, the proponents of unamended ERA have nothing less than an enemy in the White House. And if this is true for the women of America, it is equally true for disadvantaged minorities who must depend on this government's sense of justice to secure their rights and lead independent lives.

Since assuming office, the Reagan Administration has shown more hostility—indeed, more outright and implacable aggression—toward the American ideal of equal justice for all than even its harshest critics would have predicted in 1980. Given its first-term record, even our most pessimistic forecasts for four more Republican years may well fall short of the mark. No one knows the full extent of the damage Reagan could wreak on this country in another term. But we do know one thing: we cannot afford to find out.

The Democratic Alternative: Equal Justice for All

"The Democratic Party is challenged as never before to redirect the present dangerous course of our nation and our world, and to provide meaningful work at adequate pay for all our citizens and justice for all Americans.

"The dream of a nation fully committed to peace, jobs, and justice has fast become a nightmare under this Administration. . . .

"Our choice today is to become just a new party in power in November with new faces and new pledges—or a truly great party with the courage to develop a new vision and a new direction for the sake of our nation and our world."— Coretta Scott King (Democratic Platform Committee Hearing, Washington, DC, June 11, 1984)

"The Equal Rights Amendment is the only guarantee of full equality the women of this nation can trust and count on. We have seen in the past three and one-half years an administration that has gone out of its way to prove that laws, court decisions, executive orders, and regulations are not enough—they can be changed by a new majority, overturned, swept aside, underfunded, or rescinded. Only when the legislative protections against such discrimination are grounded in the bedrock of the Constitution can we be certain that the vagaries of changing political climates or a hostile administration will not wipe out those protections."— Judy Goldsmith, President, National Organization for Women (Democratic Platform Committee Hearing, Washington, DC, June 12, 1984)

Equal justice for all, in a Democratic future, means that every individual must have a fair and equal opportunity to fulfill his or her potential, and to be an independent, working member of our society— and it is the commitment of our Party to secure that opportunity.

We are determined to build an America of self-sufficient, independent people. We will enforce the laws guaranteeing equal opportunity and human rights, and complete the unfinished civil rights agenda. We will keep our commitments to all of the members of our community who rely upon our word to stay, or to become, independent—our senior citizens, those who served in our armed forces, the handicapped and disabled, the members of our American family who are trapped in poverty, and all Americans who look to government to protect them from the pain, expense, and dislocation caused by crime. And in fulfilling these and all the duties of government, a Democratic Administration will stand as an example to all of integrity and justice.

Equal Justice under Law

Many have suffered from historical patterns of discrimination and others, because of their recent immigration in sizeable numbers, are subject to new forms of discrimination. Over the years, the Democratic Party has voiced a commitment to eradicating these injustices. In 1948, the Democratic Platform for the first time contained a plank committing this Party to the cause of civil rights. For almost forty years, we have fought proudly for that cause. In 1964, a Democratic President and a Democratic Congress enacted the landmark legislation prohibiting discrimination in employment and public accommodations. And for nearly two decades, a bipartisan commitment has existed in Congress and in the White House to expand and enforce those laws. Until Ronald Reagan.

This Administration has sought to erode the force and meaning of constitutionally-mandated and court-sanctioned remedies for long-standing patterns of discriminatory conduct. It has attempted to create new standards under each of our nation's civil rights laws by requiring a showing of intent to discriminate, and case-by-case litigation of class-wide violations. Its interpretation of two recent Supreme Court decisions attempts to sound the death knell for equal opportunity and affirmative action.

In one case, the Administration interpreted the Court's decision as requiring that equal opportunity mandates associated with the receipt of *all* federal monies apply only to the specific program receiving federal funds. In the other, the Administration is using a ruling in favor of a *bonafide* seniority system to assault all affirmative action plans.

As Democrats, we disagree. Instead, we reaffirm our long-standing commitment to civil rights for all and we pledge to enforce the laws guaranteeing equal opportunity for all Americans. The next Democratic Administration will offer unwavering support for the following:

A Strong, Independent Civil Rights Commission. The Democratic Administration will return the Commission on Civil Rights to an independent status and increase its funding. The Commission must be restored to its original mission of ensuring the enforcement of civil rights by those federal agencies charged with the task.

Strengthened Civil Rights Enforcement. We will restore a strong Equal Employment Opportunity Commission and renew the commitment of the Department of Justice and the Department of Labor to enforce civil rights laws and executive orders. A Democratic Administration will, by vigorously enforcing laws and strengthening education and training opportunities, increase minority participation in the workplace and eliminate wage inequities which leave minorities at the bottom of the pay scale.

Equal Educational Opportunity. The Democratic Party pledges to do all it can, beginning this year, to reverse the decision of the United States Supreme Court in the Grove City College case, and to restore as the law of the land the prohibition of any use of federal financial assistance to subsidize discrimination because of race, national origin, sex, age, or disability. Fulfilling this commitment means that every institution which receives government funds must guarantee equality and equal opportunity in all of its programs.

Religious Liberty and Church/State Separation. The current Administration has consistently sought to reverse in the courts or overrule by constitutional amendment a long line of Supreme Court decisions that preserve our historic commitment to religious tolerance and church/state separation. The Democratic Party affirms its support of the principles of religious liberty, religious tolerance and church/state separation and of the Supreme Court decisions forbidding violation of those principles. We pledge to resist all efforts to weaken those decisions.

Ensure Fair Housing. We will enhance the authority of the Department of Housing and Urban Development to enforce our fair housing laws. A Democratic Administration will work to provide the Department with the resources and the power to seek cease-and-desist orders to prevent housing discrimination against minorities, women and families with children.

Affirmative Action. Democratic Party firmly commits itself to protect the civil rights of every citizen and to pursue justice and equal treatment under the law for all citizens. The Party reaffirms its longstanding commitment to the eradication of discrimination in all aspects of American life through the use of affirmative action, goals, timetables, and other verifiable measurements to overturn historic patterns and historic burdens of discrimination in hiring, training, promotions, contract procurement, education, and the administration of all federal programs. A Democratic Administration will resist any efforts to undermine the progress made under previous Democratic Administrations and shall strongly enforce federal civil rights standards such as equal opportunity, affirmative action in employment, contract procurement, education, and training. The federal government must set an example and be a model for private employers, making special efforts in recruitment, training, and promotion to aid minority Americans in overcoming both the historic patterns and the historic burdens of discrimination. We will reverse the regressive trend of the Reagan Administration by making a commitment to increase recruitment, hiring, training, retraining, procurement, and promotional opportunity at the federal level to aid minority Americans and women. We call on the public and private sectors to live up to and enforce all civil rights laws and regulations, i.e., Equal Employment Opportunity Programs,

Title VI and Title VII of the Civil Rights Act, the Fair Housing Laws, and affirmative action requirements.

Eliminate Ethnic Stereotyping and Recognize Ethnic Diversity. While strides have been made in combating discrimination and defamation against Americans of various ethnic groups, ethnic stereotyping continues. We support cooperation and understanding between racial, ethnic, and cultural groups and reject those who promote division based on fear or stereotyping which have their basis in social and economic inequity. We encourage respect for America's ethnic diversity.

Equal Access to Justice. Democrats believe that all our government processes should be open to all Americans, and that no essential right should be denied based on wealth or status. We therefore strongly support a well-funded, unrestricted Legal Services Corporation to ensure that none of our citizens is denied the full benefits of our judicial system. No American should suffer illegality or abuse simply because he or she is poor. And lawyers for the poor must not be prevented from acting in accordance with the same ethical canons as apply to lawyers for the rich: to represent their clients with all the zeal, devotion, energy, and creativity that the law allows.

Equal Rights for Women. A top priority of a Democratic Administration will be ratification of the unamended Equal Rights Amendment. In a Democratic America, the Constitution will be amended to provide:

> *Section 1.* Equality of rights under the law shall not be denied or abridged by the United States or by any State on account of sex.
> *Section 2.* The Congress shall have the power to enforce, by appropriate legislation, the provisions of this article.
> *Section 3.* This article shall take effect two years after the date of ratification.

We will insist on pay equity for women. Today, white women who can find work earn, on average, only 62 cents for every dollar earned by white men. Black women earn only 58 cents for every dollar earned by white men, and Hispanic women only 56 cents. The earnings gap—and the occupational segregation of women which it reflects—extends to all women at every educational level, but is most pronounced among Black and other women of color who are confronted by historical and contemporary racial barriers which transcend sex. The Democratic Party defines nondiscrimination to encompass both equal pay for equal work *and* equal pay for work of comparable worth, and we pledge to take every step, including enforcement of current law and amending the

Constitution to include the unamended ERA, to close the wage gap.

We also support efforts to reform private and civil service pension rules to ensure equal treatment for women, prohibit discrimination in insurance practices, and improve enforcement of child-support obligations.

Our Party also recognizes that women cannot compete equally with men so long as they are expected to choose between having a job and having a family. The Democratic Party calls for universally available daycare with federal or business funding, for meaningful part-time work, and for flex-time on the job so that women—and men—can shape even full-time jobs around their family schedules.

Political Empowerment for Minorities and Women. The Democratic Party is committed to placing women as well as minorities in positions of power in government. We establish the goal of doubling the number of minorities and women in Congress by 1988. We will create and fund a talent bank of minorities and women to fill policy positions in the next Administration. We will recruit women and minorities to run for Governorships and all state and local offices. The Democratic Party (through all of its campaign committees) will commit to spending maximum resources to elect women and minority candidates and offer these candidates in-kind services, including political organizing and strategic advice. And the bulk of all voter registration funds will be spent on targeted efforts to register minorities and women.

Reproductive Freedom. The Democratic Party recognizes reproductive freedom as a fundamental human right. We therefore oppose government interference in the reproductive decisions of Americans, especially government interference which denies poor Americans their right to privacy by funding or advocating one or a limited number of reproductive choices only. We fully recognize the religious and ethical concerns which many Americans have about abortion. But we also recognize the belief of many Americans that a woman has a right to choose whether and when to have a child. The Democratic Party supports the 1973 Supreme Court decision on abortion rights as the law of the land and opposes any constitutional amendment to restrict or overturn that decision. We deplore violence and harassment against health providers and women seeking services, and will work to end such acts. We support a continuing federal interest in developing strong local family planning and family life education programs and medical research aimed at reducing the need for abortion.

The Rights of Workers. The nation established a labor policy more than a generation ago whose purpose is to encourage collective bargaining and the right of workers to organize to obtain this goal. The Democratic Party is committed to extending the benefit of this policy to all workers and to removing the barriers to its administration. To accomplish this, the Democratic Party supports: the repeal of Section 14B of the National Labor Relations Act; labor law reform legislation; a prohibition on the misuse of federal bankruptcy law to prevent the circumvention of the collective bargaining process and the destruction of labor–management contracts; and legislation to allow building trades workers the same peaceful picketing rights currently afforded industrial workers.

We support the right of public employees and agricultural workers to organize and bargain collectively, and we will act to assure that right. Inasmuch as farm workers are excluded from coverage under the National Labor Relations Act, the Democratic Party recognizes the heroic efforts of farm workers to gain contracts and their right under the law to use boycotts as an effective tool to achieve such ends. We must restore to federal workers their First Amendment rights by reforming the Hatch Act. We must also protect federal and private sector workers from invasions of their privacy by prohibiting the use of polygraphs and other "truth test" devices. In addition, the Mine Health Safety Act and the Occupational Health and Safety Act must be property administered, with the concern of the worker being the highest priority. All efforts to weaken or undermine OSHA's basic worker protection provisions, or to shirk the duty to enforce them, are unacceptable and intolerable. For the victims of occupational disease, we insist on legislation to assure just compensation and adequate health care for these workers as well as vigorous enforcement action by OSHA to eradicate the causes of occupational disease. All fair labor standards acts, such as the minimum wage and Davis–Bacon protections, must be effectively enforced. We reject the so-called "sub-minimum wage" as an appropriate tool of social or economic policy. We strongly oppose workfare which penalizes welfare recipients and undercuts the basic principle of equal pay for equal work. Workfare is not a substitute for a jobs program.

The Responsibility of Economic Institutions. The Democratic Party continues to support the struggle of all citizens to secure economic equality. Therefore, we support policies calling for increased involvement of minorities and women in job training and apprenticeship programs. The Democratic Party *encourages* all economic institutions, including business and labor, to work actively to ensure that leadership at all levels of decision-making reflects the ethnic and gender diversity of the relevant work force by expanding opportunities for training and advancement.

Enforcing the Voting Rights Act. The right to vote—and to have one's vote counted fully and fairly—is the most important civil right of every American citizen. For without it, no other social, economic, or political rights can be fully realized.

Nothing is more shameful in the record of the Reagan Administration than its willful refusal to fulfill its responsibility to guarantee the voting rights of every American. Instead of moving America forward by expanding voting rights and by eliminating barriers to voting by minority citizens, the Reagan Administration fought a year-long, rear-guard action against efforts to strengthen the Voting Rights Act.

The Democratic Party commits itself to a wholly different course than that of the Reagan Administration. For while we are proud of our record of commitment to civil rights in the past, we recognize that the test of our commitment is what a Democratic Administration will do in the future. Despite the great progress in securing voting rights for minority Americans in the past, there remain throughout our nation voting rules, practices, and procedures that have been and are used to discriminate against many citizens to discourage or deny their right to register and to vote, or dilute their vote when they do.

A Democratic President and Administration pledge to eliminate any and all discriminatory barriers to full voting rights, whether they be at-large requirements, second primaries, gerrymandering, annexation, dual registration, dual voting or other practices. Whatever law, practice, or regulation discriminates against the voting rights of minority citizens, a Democratic President and Administration will move to strike it down.

This is more than a verbal pledge, for minority citizens have waited far too long already to realize their full voting rights.

To prevent any further delay, the Democratic Party pledges to fund a serious, in-depth study of the use of second primaries and other practices throughout the nation that may discriminate against voting rights. This study shall be completed in ample time prior to the 1986 elections for the Party to act.

The Democratic Party commits to use its full resources to eliminate any second primary, gerrymandering, at-large requirements, annexation, dual registration, dual voting or other voting practices that discriminate or act to dilute votes of minority citizens.

Wherever a runoff primary or other voting practice is found to be discriminatory, the state Party shall take provable, positive steps to achieve the necessary legislative or party rules changes.

Provable positive steps shall be taken in a timely fashion and shall include the drafting of corrective legislation, public endorsement by the state Party of such legislation, efforts to educate the public on the need for such legislation, active support for the legislation by the state Party lobbying state legislators, other public officials, Party officials and Party members, and encouraging consideration of the legislation by the appropriate legislative committees and bodies.

A Democratic Administration pledges also that the Justice Department shall initiate a similar study, and use the full resources of the law to eliminate any voting practice, such as second primaries, gerrymandering, annexation, dual registration, dual voting, or any other practice that discriminates or acts to dilute votes of minority citizens.

A Democratic President and Administration will use the full resources of the Voting Rights Act of 1982, with its strengthened enforcement powers, to investigate and root out any and all discriminatory voting barriers. A Democratic President will appoint as Attorney General, as Assistant Attorney General for Civil Rights, and throughout the Justice Department individuals with a proven record of commitment to enforcing civil rights and voting rights for all our citizens. The full resources of the Justice Department shall be used to investigate fully and speedily all alleged instances of discriminatory barriers. And a Democratic Administration shall use the full resources of the law and the power of government, and shall seek new legislation, if needed, to end discrimination in voting wherever it exists.

We are committed to a massive, nationwide campaign to increase registration and voting participation by women and minorities, including Blacks, Asian Americans, native Americans, and Hispanics. Moreover, our Party must call for the creation of a new program to strengthen our democracy and remove existing obstacles to full participation in the electoral process. We should allow registration and voting on the same day (same-day plans have worked well in several states) and we should provide mail-in registration forms throughout our communities. We should consider holding our elections on weekends or holidays, instituting 24-hour voting days, staggering voting times, and closing all polling places across the country at the same time.

We call on the television networks and all other media in the case of presidential elections to refrain from projecting winners of national races, either implicitly or explicitly, while any polls are still open in the continental United States; in the case of state elections, to refrain from projecting winners within a state, either implicitly or explicitly, while any polls in that state are still open.

Voting Rights for the District of Columbia. The Democratic Party supports self-determination for the District of Columbia that guarantees local control over local affairs and full voting representation in Congress. Towards this end, the Democratic Party supports the attainment of statehood for New Columbia; ratification of the District of Columbia Voting Rights Amendment; legislative, judicial, and fiscal autonomy; and a formula-based federal payment.

Puerto Rico. We continue to support Puerto Rico's right to enjoy full self-determination and a relationship that can evolve in ways that will most benefit U.S. citizens in Puerto Rico. The Democratic Party respects and supports the desire of the people of Puerto Rico, by their own will, freely expressed in a peaceful and democratic process, to associate in permanent union with the United States either as a commonwealth or as a state or to become an independent nation. We are also committed to respecting the cultural heritage of the people of Puerto Rico and to the elimination of the discriminatory or unfair treatment of Puerto Ricans as U.S. citizens under federal programs.

A Fair and Humane Immigration Policy. Our nation's outdated immigration laws require comprehensive reform that reflects our national interests and our immigrant heritage. Our first priority must be to protect the fundamental human rights of American citizens and aliens. We will oppose any "reforms" that violate these rights or that will create new incentives for discrimination against Hispanic Americans and other minorities arising from the discriminatory use of employer sanctions. Specifically, we oppose employer sanctions designed to penalize employers who hire undocumented workers. Such sanctions inevitably will increase discrimination against minority Americans. We oppose identification procedures that threaten civil liberties, as well as any changes that subvert the basic principle of family unification. And we will put an end to this Administration's policies of barring foreign visitors from our country for political or ideological reasons. We strongly oppose "bracero" or guest-worker programs as a form of legalized exploitation. We firmly support a one-tiered legalization program with a 1982 cut-off date.

The Democratic Party will implement a balanced, fair, and non-discriminatory immigration and refugee policy consistent with the principle of affording all applications for admission equal protection under the law. It will work for improved performance by the Immigration and Naturalization Service in adjudicating petitions for permanent residence and naturalization. The Party will also advocate reform within the INS to improve the enforcement operations of the

Service consistent with civil liberties protection. The correction of past and present bias in the allocation of slots for refugee admissions will be a top priority. Additionally, it will work to ensure that the Refugee Act of 1980, which prohibits discrimination on the basis of ideology and race in adjudicating asylum claims, is complied with. The Party will provide the necessary oversight of the Department of State and the Immigration and Naturalization Service so as to ensure that the unjustifiable treatment visited upon the Haitian refugees will never again be repeated.

The Democratic Party will formulate foreign policies which alleviate, not aggravate, the root causes of poverty, war, and human rights violations and instability which compel people to flee their homelands.

We support the creation of an international body on immigration to address the economic development problems affecting Mexico and Latin American countries which contribute to unauthorized immigration to the U.S. and to respond to the backlog of approved immigrant visas.

To pursue these and other goals, the Democratic Party nominee upon election shall establish the following national advisory committees to the President and the national Democratic Party: civil rights and justice; fair housing; affirmative action; equal rights for women; rights for workers, immigration policy; and voting rights. These committees shall be representative on the basis of geography, race, sex, and ethnicity.

Dignity for All.   As Democrats, we take pride in our accomplishments of the past decades in enacting legislation to assure equality and in fighting the current efforts of this Administration to turn its back on equal opportunity. But we also recognize that so long as any Americans are subject to unfair discrimination, our agenda remains unfinished. We pledge to complete the agenda, and to afford dignity for all.

- We reaffirm the dignity of all people and the right of each individual to have equal access to and participation in the institutions and services of our society. To ensure that government is accessible to those Americans for whom English is a second language, we call for federal hiring and training initiatives to increase the number of government employees skilled in more than one language. All groups must be protected from discrimination based on race, color, sex, religion, national origin, language, age, or sexual orientation. We will support legislation to prohibit discrimination in the workplace based on sexual orientation. We will assure that sexual orientation *per se* does not serve as a bar to participation in the military. We will support an enhanced effort to learn the cause and cure of AIDS, and to provide treatment for people with AIDS. And we will ensure that foreign citizens are not excluded from this country on the basis of their sexual orientation.

- We have long failed to treat the original inhabitants of this land with the dignity they deserve. A Democratic Administration will work in partnership with Indian nations to target assistance to address the twin problems of unemployment and poverty, recognizing appropriate Native American rights to self-determination and the federal government's fiduciary responsibility to the Native American nations. We will take the lead in efforts to resolve water and other natural resources claims of Native Americans. We must also reevaluate the mission of the Bureau of Indian Affairs in light of its troubled record.

- We owe history and ourselves a formal apology and a promise of redress to Japanese Americans who suffered unjust internment during World War II. No commitment to civil liberties could be complete without a formal apology, restitution of position, status or entitlements, and reparations to those who suffered deprivation of rights and property without due process forty years ago.

- The Democratic Party strongly condemns the Ku Klux Klan, the American Nazi Party, and other hate groups. We pledge vigorous federal prosecution of actions by the Klan and American Nazi Party that violate federal law, including the enactment of such laws in jurisdictions where they do not exist. We further condemn those acts, symbols, and rituals, including cross-burnings, associated with anti–civil rights activities. We urge every state and local government to pursue vigorous prosecution of actions by the Klan and Nazi Party and other such groups that violate state or local law.

Americans Abroad.   Americans abroad play a vital role in promoting the ideals, culture, and economic well-being of the United States. They are entitled to equitable treatment by their government and greater participation in decisions which directly affect them.

The Democratic Party will work to remedy the unique problems that U.S. citizens encounter abroad. In particular, we will consider ways to: protect their rights; eliminate citizenship inequities; make it easier for them to vote; have their interests actively represented in the federal government; provide them with fair coverage in federal social programs; honor the principles of residency in taxation; and ensure the adequate education of federal dependents abroad.

Insular Areas.   The territories are in spirit full partners in the American political family; they should always be so treated. Their unique circumstances require the sensitive application of federal policy and special assistance. Their self-determination, along with that of the Trust Territory of the Pacific Islands, is an American commitment.

Democrats will work with the territories to improve their relationship with the rest of the United States and obtain equal rights for their citizens, including the right to vote for President. A Democratic President and Congress will coordinate their interests as foreign and domestic policy is made. We are committed to providing territorial America with essential assistance and equitable participation in federal programs. We will promote the growth and ensure the competitive position of territorial private sectors. It is Democratic policy that, together with the territories, the United States should strive to assist and develop closer relations with the territories' neighbors in the Caribbean and Pacific regions.

Economic Justice: Keeping Our Commitments

For some, the goal of independence requires greater support and assistance from government. We pledge to provide that support. Justice demands that we keep our commitments and display our compassion to those who most need our help—to veterans and seniors, to disadvantaged minorities, to the disabled and the poor—and we will.

A Healthy America. As Democrats we believe that quality health care is a necessity for everyone. We reaffirm our commitment to the long-term goal of comprehensive national health insurance and view effective health care cost containment as an essential step toward that goal. Health cost containment must be based on a strong commitment to quality of service delivery and care. We also pledge to return to a proper emphasis on basic scientific research and meeting the need for health professionals—areas devasted by the Reagan Administration.

Sickle Cell Anemia. Sickle cell disease is a catastrophic illness that affects thousands of persons annually. Its victims include, but are not limited to, Blacks, Hispanics, and persons of Mediterranean ancestry including Turks, Greeks, and Italians. Its morbidity rate is particularly high among infants, women and children.

Despite the compelling need for a national policy of sickle cell disease prevention and control, the present Administration has dramatically reduced the federal commitment to research and funding. The Democratic Party, on the other hand, pledges to make sickle cell a national health priority because we believe that only the federal government can adequately focus the necessary resources to combat such a major public health problem. Specifically, we pledge that a Democratic Administration will restore the National Sickle Cell Anemia Control Act to provide health parity to those individuals and families whose lives are threatened by this chronic and debilitating disorder.

Opportunities for the Elderly. There are more than 26 million Americans over the age of 65, and their numbers are growing rapidly. Most have spent a lifetime building America and raising the next generation, and when they choose to retire—and it should be their choice—they deserve to retire with dignity and security. Yet for millions of Americans, particularly women, minorities, and ethnic Americans, old age means poverty, insecurity, and desperation.

Beginning with President Franklin D. Roosevelt, the Democratic Party has been dedicated to the well-being of the senior citizens of America. President Roosevelt gave to the elderly Social Security. The following Democratic Administrations provided the elderly with Medicare, the Older Americans Act, the nutrition program, low-cost housing, elderly employment programs and many others to make lives longer, healthier and happier for senior citizens, those who have done so much to make America the great nation it is today. This Reagan Republican Administration is the first administration to stop the progress of aid to the elderly and to cut back on every helpful program which Democratic Administrations had enacted for our elders.

Now we have a crisis facing the country with respect to Medicare. Funds will be short in four years. Again, the Reagan Republican Administration, speaking recently through the Social Security Advisory Council, proposed that the way to meet this financial crisis was to make the people already paying into Medicare pay more and to cut benefits by raising the age of eligibility from 65 to 67.

Too many elderly people covered by Medicare are not able to pay the deductible now required by Medicare. We Democrats will never add more to the burdens of the people now covered by Medicare. Nor will we Democrats allow benefits to be cut under Medicare by raising the age of eligibility, for we know that Medicare, which Democratic leadership established in 1964, is the only chance that millions of senior citizens have to get the health care they need.

To date, the needs of America's ethnic elderly have not been met. Ethnic American elderly number over seven million persons, or approximately one quarter of the total population of people over 65. A close examination of data from the U.S. Census reveals that nearly one-half of this ethnic population who are 65 years of age or older do not speak English. To assure the well-being of ethnic seniors who comprise a large segment of our elderly population, we should promote programs to strengthen family life, care for the elderly, and spur neighborhood revitalization and development of "language barrier–free" social and health services.

We also know that the number of senior citizens as a percentage of the population is rapidly growing. The Democratic Party is committed to the principle of forbidding any discrimination on account of age against the elderly, either in holding a job or obtaining one. We offer to the elderly an opportunity for additional training or retraining that will enable them to do better at the jobs they have or to turn to other jobs which they would like better.

In short, the Democratic Party, which for so long has been the champion of the elderly, assures the senior citizens of America that it will maintain its longstanding good faith with them. Whatever is right and good for the senior citizen shall always be close to the heart of the Democratic Party and ever a primary dedication of our Party.

It is the cherished aim and high purpose of the Democratic Party to make the last part of the long journey of life for our senior citizens as long, as healthy, and as happy as may be.

As Democrats, we are proud of the programs we have created—Social Security and Medicare—to allow our senior citizens to live their lives independently and with dignity, and we will fight to preserve and protect those programs. We will work for decent housing and adequate nutrition for our senior citizens, and we will enforce the laws prohibiting age discrimination. We will not break faith with those who built America.

The Social Security Administration long had a reputation for administrative efficiency and high-quality public service. Problems which have emerged under the current Administration—the financing crises, a deteriorating computer system, and arbitrary terminations of benefits to hundreds of thousands of disabled Americans—threaten the agency's ability to carry out its mission. The current Administration's policies have shaken people's confidence in the entire Social Security system.

The policies and operations of the Social Security Administration must be carefully and fully investigated to reform its operations so that the elderly and disabled receive the services and treatment to which they are entitled. In particular, we should explore the recommendation that the Social Security Administration become an independent agency.

Opportunities for Disabled Americans. There are 36 million people with disabilities in the United States who look to our government for justice. As Democrats, we have long recognized that a disability need not be an obstacle to a productive, independent life and we have fought to guarantee access to facilities, and adequate training and support to meet the special needs of the disabled. This Administration has closed its eyes to those needs, and in so doing, violated a fundamental trust by seeking to condemn millions of disabled Americans to dependency. We will insist that those who receive federal funds accommodate disabled employees—a requirement this Administration sought to eliminate. We will insist that benefits be available for those who cannot work, and that training is available for those who need help to find work.

The Democratic Party will safeguard the rights of the elderly and disabled to remain free from institutionalization except where medically indicated. The rights of the disabled within institutions should be protected from violations of the integrity of their person. Also, we will promote accessible public transportation, and buildings, make voting booths accessible, and strictly enforce laws such as the entire Rehabilitation Act of 1973.

Opportunities for Veterans. This country has a proud tradition of honoring and supporting those who have defended us. Millions of Americans in the years after World War II went to college and bought their homes thanks to GI benefits. But for the latest generation of American veterans, needed support and assistance have been missing.

The nation has begun to welcome home with pride its Vietnam veterans, as reflected in the extraordinary Vietnam Veterans Memorial which was built through public contributions. The Democratic Party shares the nation's commitment to Vietnam veterans.

No President since the beginning of the Vietnam War has been so persistently hostile to Vietnam veterans programs as Ronald Reagan. He has sought to dismantle the Readjustment Counseling Centers, opposed employment and Agent Orange benefits, as well as basic due process at the Veterans Administration, including judicial review.

The Vietnam War divided our nation. Many of the rifts remain, but all agree on the respect due Vietnam veterans for their distinguished service during a troubled time. The Democratic Party pledges to reverse Ronald Reagan's Vietnam veterans policies, helping our nation come together as one people. And we believe it is especially important that we end discrimination against women and minority veterans, particularly in health and education programs.

We believe that the government has a special obligation to all of this nation's veterans, and we are committed to fulfilling it—to providing the highest-quality health care, improving education and training, and providing the assistance they need to live independent and productive lives.

Opportunities for the Poor.   For the past four years, this Administration has callously pursued policies which have further impoverished those at the bottom of the economic ladder and pushed millions of Americans, particularly women and children, below the poverty line. Thanks to the Reagan budget cuts, many of the programs upon which the poor rely have been gutted—from education to housing to child nutrition. Far from encouraging independence, the Administration has penalized those seeking to escape poverty through work, by conditioning assistance on non-participation in the workplace. The figures tell part of the story:

- Today, 15 percent of all Americans live below the poverty line;
- Over three million more children are in poverty today than there were in 1979;
- Over half of all Black children under age three live in poverty;
- More than one-third of all female-headed households are below the poverty line, and for non-white families headed by women with more than one child, the figure is 70 percent.

But the numbers tell only part of the story; numbers do not convey the frustration and suffering of women seeking a future for themselves and their children, with no support from anyone; numbers do not recount the pain of growing numbers of homeless men and women with no place to sleep, or of increasing infant mortality rates among children born to poor mothers. Numbers do not convey the human effects of unemployment on a once stable and strong family.

As Democrats, we call upon the American people to join with us in a renewed commitment to combat the feminization of poverty in our nation so that every American can be a productive, contributing member of our society. In that effort, our goal is to strengthen families and to reverse the existing incentives for their destruction. We therefore oppose laws requiring an unemployed parent to leave the family or drop out of the work force in order to qualify for assistance and health care. We recognize the special need to increase the labor force participation of minority males, and we are committed to expanding their opportunities through education and training and to enforcing the laws which

guarantee them equal opportunities. The plight of young mothers must be separately addressed as well: they too need education and training, and quality child care must be available if they are to participate in such programs. Only through a nation that cares and a government that acts can those Americans trapped in poverty move toward meaningful independence.

The Hungry and the Homeless.   In the late 1960's, the nation discovered widespread hunger and malnutrition in America, especially among poor children and the elderly. The country responded with a national effort, of which Americans should be justly proud. By the late 1970's, medical researchers found that hunger had nearly been eliminated.

Since 1980, however, hunger has returned. High unemployment coupled with deep cutbacks in food assistance and other basic support programs for poor families have led to conditions not seen in this country for years. Studies in hospitals and health departments document increases in numbers of malnourished children. Increasing numbers of homeless wander our cities' streets in search of food and shelter. Religious organizations, charities and other agencies report record numbers of persons standing in line for food at soup kitchens and emergency food pantries.

Strong action is needed to address this issue and to end the resurgence of hunger in America. The Democratic Party is committed to reversing regressive Reagan policies and to providing more adequate food aid for poor families, infants, children and elderly and handicapped persons. It is time to resume the national effort, jettisoned in 1980, to ensure that less fortunate Americans do not go without adequate food because they are too poor to secure a decent diet. As Democrats, we call upon the American people to join with us in a renewed commitment to fight hunger and homelessness so that every American can be a productive, contributing member of our society.

Hunger is an international problem as well. In many countries it threatens peace and stability. The United States should take the lead in working with our allies and other countries to help wipe hunger from the face of the earth.

A Democratic President will ensure that the needs of the world's children are given priority in all U.S. foreign assistance programs and that international assistance programs are geared toward increasing the self-reliance of local populations and self-sufficiency in food production.

Integrity in Government

As Democrats, we believe that the American people are entitled to a government that is honest, that is open, and that is fully representative of this nation and its people, and we are committed to providing it.

After four years in which the roll of dishonor in the Administration has grown weekly and monthly—from Richard Allen to Rita Lavelle, from Thomas Reed to James Watt—it is time for an end to the embarrassment of Republican cronyism and malfeasance. Our appointments will be ones of which Americans can be proud. Our selection process in staffing the government will be severe. We will not tolerate impropriety in a Democratic Administration.

We must work to end political action committee funding of federal political campaigns. To achieve that, we must enact a system of public financing of federal campaigns. At the same time, our Party should assure that a system of public financing be responsive to the problem of underrepresentation of women and minorities in elective offices.

We Democrats are not afraid to govern in public and to let the American people know and understand the basis for our decisions. We will reverse current Administration policies that permit the wide-spread overclassification of documents lacking a relationship to our national security. We will rescind Reagan Administration directives imposing undue burdens on citizens seeking information about their government through the Freedom of Information Act.

We will insist that the government, in its relations with its own employees, set a standard of fairness which is a model for the private sector. We believe, moreover, that an Administration that cannot run its own house fairly cannot serve the American people fairly. We will ensure that government's number-one priority is the performance of its mission under the law, and not the implementation of the narrow political agenda of a single Party. Sound management and fair government cannot be administered by a politicized work force. Neither can it be accomplished by a demoralized work force. A Democratic Administration will not devalue the pay, benefits, and retirement rights of federal workers guaranteed under the law. We will work to reverse personnel policies, including the contracting out of work traditionally performed by public employees, that have made it impossible for current federal employees to recommend a career in federal service to our nation's young people.

Our judicial system must be one in which excellence and access are the foundations. It is essential to recruit people of high integrity, outstanding competence, and high quality of judgment to serve in our nation's judiciary. And we oppose efforts to strip the federal courts of their historic jurisdiction to adjudicate cases involving questions of federal law and constitutional right.

Crime

No problem has worried Americans more persistently over the past 20 years than the problem of crime. Crime and the fear of crime affect us all, but the impact is greatest on poor Americans who live in our cities. Neither a permissive liberalism nor a static conservatism is the answer to reducing crime. While we must eliminate those elements—like unemployment and poverty—that foster the criminal atmosphere, we must never let them be used as an excuse.

Although the primary responsibility for law enforcement rests at the local level, Democrats believe the federal government can play an important role by encouraging local innovation and the implementation of new crime control methods as their effectiveness is shown. And when crime spills across state borders, the federal government must take the lead, and assume responsibility for enforcing the law. This Administration has done neither. It has talked "law and order" while cutting law enforcement budgets. It has decried the influence of drugs, while cutting back on customs enforcement.

As a result, drug trafficking and abuse have risen to crisis proportions in the United States. In 1983, an estimated 60 tons of cocaine, 15,000 tons of marijuana, and 10 tons of heroin entered the United States, clear evidence that we are losing the effort overseas to control the production and transshipment of these and other dangerous drugs. Domestically, the illicit trafficking in drugs is a $100-billion-per-year business; the economic and social costs to our society are far higher.

Today, in our country, there are 25 million regular abusers of marijuana, close to 12 million abusers of cocaine, and half a million heroin addicts. Since 1979, hospital emergency room incidents—including deaths—related to cocaine have soared 300 percent, incidents related to heroin have climbed 80 percent. According to the 1983 National High School Survey on Drug Abuse, 63 percent of high school seniors have tried an illicit drug, and 40 percent have tried a drug other than marijuana. Alcohol abuse is also a serious problem which must be faced.

- For this reason, the Democratic Party believes it is essential to make narcotics control a high priority on the national agenda, and a major consideration in our dealings with producer and transshipment countries, particularly if they are recipients of U.S. assistance.
- At the national level, the effort must begin by introducing a comprehensive management plan to eliminate overlap and friction between the 113 different federal agencies with responsibilities for fighting crime, particularly with respect to the control of

drug traffic. We must provide the necessary resources to federal agencies and departments with responsibility for the fight against drugs.

- To spur local law enforcement efforts, establishment of an independent criminal justice corporation should be considered. This corporation could serve as a means of encouraging community-based efforts, such as neighborhood citizen watches, alternative deployment patterns for police, and community service sentencing programs, which have proven effective.
- Violent acts of bigotry, hatred and extremism aimed at women, racial, ethnic and religious minorities and gay men and lesbians have become an alarmingly common phenomenon. A Democratic Administration will work vigorously to address, document, and end all such violence.
- We believe that victims of crime deserve a workable program of compensation. We call for sentencing reforms that routinely include monetary or other forms of restitution to victims. The federal government should ensure that victims of violent federal crime receive compensation. We need to establish a federal victim compensation fund, to be financed, in part, by fines and the proceeds from the sale of goods forfeited to the government.
- We support tough restraints on the manufacture, transportation, and sale of snubnosed handguns, which have no legitimate sporting use and are used in a high proportion of violent crimes.
- We will establish a strong federal–state partnership to push for further progress in the nationwide expansion of comprehensive, community-based anti–drunk driving programs. With the support of citizens, private-sector business and government at all levels, we will instutionalize fatality and injury reduction on the nation's highways.
- We support fundamental reform of the sentencing process so that offenders who commit similar crimes receive similar penalties. Reform should begin with the establishment of appropriately drafted sentencing guidelines, and judges deviating from such guidelines should be required to provide written reasons for doing so.
- Finally, we believe that the credibility of our criminal courts must be restored. Our courts should not be attacked for failing to eliminate the major social problem of crime—courts of justice were not designed, and were never intended, to do that. A Democratic Administration will encourage experimentation with alternative dispute-resolution mechanisms, diversion programs for first and non-violent offenders, and other devices to eliminate the congestion in our courts and restore to them an atmosphere in which they can perform their intended job: doing real individualized justice, in an orderly way.

CHAPTER III. PEACE, SECURITY, AND FREEDOM

Introduction

Building a safer future for our nation and the world: that is the Democratic agenda for our national security. Every responsibility before our nation, every task that we set, pales beside the most important challenge we face—providing new leadership that enhances our security, promotes our values, and works for peace.

The next American President will preside over a period of historic change in the international system. The relatively stable world order that has prevailed since World War II is bursting at the seams from the powerful forces of change—the proliferation of nuclear and conventional weapons, the relentless Soviet military build-up, the achievement of rough nuclear parity between the Soviet Union and the United States, the increasingly interdependent nature of the international economic order, the recovery and rise of European and Asian powers since the devastation of the Second World War, and the search for a new American political consensus in the wake of Vietnam and Lebanon and in the shadow of a regional crisis in Central America.

The greatest foreign policy imperative of the Democratic Party and of the next President is to learn from past mistakes and adapt to these changes, rather than to resist or ignore them. While not underestimating the Soviet threat, we can no longer afford simplistically to blame all of our troubles on a single "focus of evil," for the sources of international change run even deeper than the sources of superpower competition. We must see change as an opportunity as well as a challenge. In the 1980's and beyond, America must not only make the world safe for diversity; we must learn to thrive on diversity.

The Democratic Party believes that it is time to harness the full range of America's capacity to meet the challenges of a changing world. We reject the notion that America is beset by forces beyond its control. Our commitment to freedom and democracy, our willingness to listen to contrasting viewpoints, and our ingenuity at devising new ideas and arrangements have given us advantages in an increasingly diverse world that no totalitarian system can match.

The Democratic Party has a constructive and confident vision of America's ability to use all of our economic, political, and military resources to pursue our wide-ranging security and economic interests in a diverse and changing world. We believe in a responsible defense policy that will increase our national security. We believe in a foreign policy that respects our allies, builds democracy, and advances the cause of human rights. We believe that our economic future lies in our ability to rise to the challenge of international economic competition by making our own industries more competitive. Above all, we believe that our security requires the direct, personal involvement of the President of the United States to limit the Soviet military threat and to reduce the danger of nuclear war.

We have no illusions about the forces arrayed against the democratic cause in our time. In the year made famous by George Orwell, we can see the realization of many of his grimmest prophecies in the totalitarian Soviet state, which has amassed an arsenal of weapons far beyond its defensive needs. In the communist and non-communist world, we find tyrannical regimes that trample on human rights and repress their people's cry for economic justice.

The Reagan Administration points to Soviet repression—but has no answer other than to escalate the arms race. It downgrades repression in the noncommunist world, by drawing useless distinctions between "totalitarian" and "authoritarian" regimes.

The Democratic Party understands the challenge posed by the enemies of democracy. Unlike the Reagan Administration, however, we are prepared to work constructively to reduce tensions and make genuine progress toward a safer world.

The Democratic Party is confident that American ideals and American interests reinforce each other in our foreign policy: the promotion of democracy and human rights not only distinguishes us from our adversaries, but it also builds the long-term stability that comes when governments respect their people. We look forward to the 21st Century as a century of democratic solidarity where security, freedom, and peace will flourish.

Peace, freedom and security are the essence of America's dream. They are the future of our children and their children.

This is the test where failure could provide no opportunity to try once more. As President Kennedy once warned: "We have the power to make this the best generation of mankind in the history of the world—or to make it the last."

The Future If Reagan Is Reelected

"Star Wars is not the path towards a less dangerous world. A direct and safe road exists: equitable and verifiable deep cuts in strategic offensive forces. We must abandon the illusion that ever more sophisticated technology can remove the perils that science and technology have created."—Statement by Dr. Jerome B. Wiesner, Dr. Carl Sagan, Dr. Henry Kendall, and Admiral Noel Gavier (Democratic Platform Committee Hearing, Washington, D.C., June 12, 1984)

"The minister of the apartheid government recently boasted of the fruitful relationship between Pretoria and Washington since the advent of the Reagan regime. Now apartheid South Africa has acquired the military muscle to bomb, to maim, to kill men, women, and children, and to bully these states into negotiating with apartheid through the threat of increased military action. This may be hailed as a victory for apartheid and for the Reagan Administration, but in truth it can only create anger and contempt in the African people."—Professor Dennis Brutus, Northwestern University (former political prisoner in South Africa) (Democratic Platform Committee Hearing, New York, New York, April 9, 1984)

Suppose Mr. Reagan is reelected. How would he deal with the serious threats that face us and our children?

Under Mr. Reagan, the nuclear arms race would continue to spiral out of control. A new generation of destabilizing missiles will imperil all humanity. We will live in a world where the nuclear arms race has spread from Earth into space.

Under Mr. Reagan, we would continue to over-emphasize destabilizing and redundant nuclear weapons programs at the expense of our conventional forces. We will spend billions for weapons that do not work. We will continue to ignore proposals to improve defense management, to get a dollar's worth for each dollar spent, and to make our military more combat-effective and our weapons more cost-effective.

Under Mr. Reagan, regional conflicts would continue to be dangerously mismanaged. Young Americans may be sent to fight and die needlessly. The spread of nuclear materials to new nations and the spread of sophisticated conventional weapons to virtually every nation on earth will continue unabated.

Can America afford a President so out of touch with reality that he tells us, "I think the world is safer and further removed from a possible war than it was several years ago"?

Can America afford the recklessness of a President

who exposed American Marines to mortal danger and sacrificed over 260 of them in a bungled mission in Lebanon against the advice of the Joint Chiefs of Staff, and brought upon us the worst U.S. military disaster since the Vietnam War?

Can America afford the irresponsibility of a President who undermines confidence in our deterrent with misleading allegations of Soviet nuclear "superiority" and whose Administration beguiles the American public with false claims that nuclear war can be survived with enough shovels?

Can America afford the unresponsiveness of a President who thwarts the will of the majority of Americans by waging a secret war against Nicaragua?

In a second Reagan term, will our heavens become a nuclear battleground?

In 1980, candidate Ronald Reagan promised the American people a more secure world. Yet, as President:

- He has raced to deploy new weapons that will be destabilizing and difficult to verify. He has pressed for a multi-billion-dollar chemical weapons' program. He has launched his trillion dollar "Star Wars" arms race in space.
- He has relaxed controls on nuclear proliferation, thus enhancing the risk that nuclear weapons will be acquired and used by unstable governments and international terrorists.
- He has become the first President since the Cold War to preside over the complete collapse of all nuclear arms negotiations with the Soviets.
- He has rejected SALT II, threatened the ABM Treaty, and abandoned the goal of a complete ban on nuclear weapons tests that has been pursued by every President since Eisenhower. He has refused to seek negotiations to limit anti-satellite weapons that could threaten our vital early-warning and military satellites. Over 250 strategic missiles and bombers that would have been eliminated under SALT II are still in Soviet hands.

Can we afford four more years of a Pentagon spending binge?

In 1980, candidate Ronald Reagan and the Republican Party promised the American people a defense spending increase "to be applied judiciously to critically needed programs." Yet, as President:

- He has initiated the largest peacetime defense build-up in our history with no coherent plan for integrating the increased programs into an effective military posture.
- He has slighted training and readiness of our conventional forces in favor of big-ticket nuclear items,

"preparing," in the words of General Maxwell Taylor, "for the least possible threats to the neglect of the most probable."

- He has brought us the worst-managed and most wasteful Defense Department in history. Under the Pentagon's wasteful purchasing system. the American taxpayer has paid $435 for a $17 claw hammer, $1100 for a 22-cent plastic steel cap, over $2000 for a 13-cent plain round nut, and $9600 for a 12-cent Allen wrench.

Can we afford four more years of dangerous foreign policy failures?

In 1980, candidate Ronald Reagan and the Republican Party promised "to put America on a sound, secure footing in the international arena." Yet, as President:

- He has contributed to the decline of U.S.–Soviet relations to a perilous point. Instead of challenges, he has used easy and abusive anti-Soviet rhetoric as a substitute for strength, progress, and careful use of power.
- He has strained vital U.S. alliances through his bungled efforts to stop the Soviet natural gas pipeline, his inflammatory nuclear rhetoric and policies, and his failure to support the efforts of our democratic allies to achieve a negotiated political solution in Central America.
- He has had as many Middle East policies as he has had staff turnovers. First, he offered strategic cooperation to Israel as if it were a gift. Then he took it away to punish Israel as if it were not our ally. Then he pressured Israel to make one-sided concessions to Jordan. Then he demanded that Israel withdraw from Lebanon. Then he pleaded with them to stay. Then he did not accept their offer of medical help for our wounded Marines. He undercut American credibility throughout the Middle East by declaring Lebanon a vital interest of the United States and then withdrawing.
- He has failed to understand the importance for the United States of a solid relationship with the African continent—not only from the perspective of human decency, but also from enlightened concern for our own self-interest. By his lack of sensitivity and foresight, he has ignored the fate of millions of people who need our help in developing their economies and in dealing with the ravages of drought, and he has jeopardized our relations with countries that are important to U.S. security and well-being.
- He has brought us a strategy in Central America and the Caribbean that has failed. Since he took office, the region has become much more unstable; the

hemisphere is much more hostile to us, and the poverty is much deeper. Today in El Salvador, after more than a billion dollars in American aid, the guerrillas are stronger than they were three years ago, and the people are much poorer. In Nicaragua, our support for the *contras* and for the covert war has strengthened the totalitarians at the expense of the moderates. In Honduras, an emerging democracy has been transformed into a staging ground for possible regional war. And in Costa Rica our backing for rebels based there is in danger of dragging that peaceful democracy into a military confrontation with Nicaragua. In Grenada, Mr. Reagan renounced diplomacy for over two years, encouraging extremism, instability, and crisis. By his failure to avoid military intervention, he divided us from our European allies and alienated our friends throughout the Western Hemisphere. And by excluding the press, he set a chilling precedent, greatly hampering public scrutiny of his policies. After three and one-half years of Mr. Reagan's tunnel vision, extremism is stronger, our democratic friends are weaker, and we are further than ever from achieving peace and security in the region.

- He is the first President to fail to support publicly the ratification of the Genocide Convention. His Vice President has praised the Philippine dictator for his "love of democracy," his first Secretary of State announced that human rights would be replaced as a foreign policy priority, and his first nominee for Assistant Secretary of State for Human Rights was rejected by the U.S. Senate as unfit for that post. He has closely identified the United States with the apartheid regime in South Africa, and he has time and again failed to confront dictators around the globe.

This is an unprecedented record of failure. But President Reagan is content to make excuses for failure. President Reagan blames Congress and the Democratic Party. He rebukes Americans deeply and genuinely concerned about the threat of nuclear war. He rails at the Soviet Union—as if words alone, without strategy or effective policy, will make that nation change its course.

It is time for Democrats and Americans to apply a tough standard to Ronald Reagan. Let us paraphrase the question he asked in 1980: Are we safer today than we were three and a half years ago? Are we further from nuclear war? After more than a thousand days of Mr. Reagan, is the world anywhere less tense, anywhere closer to peace?

Americans throughout this land are answering with a resounding no.

President Reagan himself is responsible—responsible for four years of a failed foreign policy. America elects its President to lead. It does not elect its President to make excuses.

The Democratic Party believes that it is time to harness the full power of America's spirit and capacity to meet the challenges of a changing world.

The Democratic Party has a different and positive vision of America's future. What is at stake may be freedom and survival itself.

The Democratic Alternative: A Safer Future for Our Nation and the World

"I do not see why we think of Democracy as so weak and so vulnerable. Let us for heaven's sake have some confidence in America and not tremble, fearing that our society will fall apart at the least rattle of the door. If I were constructing this platform, I would ask that its planks be carved out of self-confidence, and planted in belief in our own system."—Historian Barbara Tuchman (Democratic Platform Committee Hearing, New York, New York, April 9, 1984)

"The Democratic Party requires a foreign policy which approaches the problems that confront us primarily in their national and regional contexts, rather than viewing them, as the Reagan Administration does, almost exclusively as a manifestation of the "evil empire's" efforts to extend its sway over the entire globe. What we need is a foreign policy which promotes the cause of human rights by opposing tyranny on the part of left- as well as right-wing governments, rather than a foreign policy, like the one we have now, which supports virtually every reactionary and repressive regime that professes to be anticommunist."—Honorable Stephen J. Solarz, U.S. Representative, New York (Democratic Platform Committee Hearing, New York, New York, April 9, 1994)

There is no higher goal for the Democratic Party than assuring the national security of the United States. This means a strong national defense, vigorous pursuit of nuclear arms control, and a foreign policy dedicated to advancing the interests of America and the forces of freedom and democracy in a period of global transformation. This will require new leadership, strong alliances, skillful diplomacy, effective economic cooperation, and a foreign policy sustained by American strength and ideals. And to hold the support of the American people, our leaders must also be careful and measured in the use of force.

The Democratic Party is committed to a strong national defense. Democrats know that a relentless Soviet military build-up—well beyond its defensive needs—directly challenges world security, our democratic values, and our free institutions. On the nature of the Soviet threat and on the essential issue of our nation's security, Americans do not divide. On the common interest in human survival, the American and Soviet peoples do not divide.

Maintaining strong and effective military forces is essential to keeping the peace and safeguarding freedom. Our allies and adversaries must never doubt our military power or our will to defend our vital interests. To that end, we pledge a strong defense built in concert with our allies, based on a coherent strategy, and supported by a sound economy.

In an age of about 50,000 nuclear weapons, however, nuclear arms control and reductions are also essential to our security. The most solemn responsibility of a President is to do all that he or she can to prevent a single nuclear weapon from ever being used. Democrats believe that mutual and verifiable controls on nuclear arms can, and must be, a serious integral part of national defense. True national security requires urgent measures to freeze and reverse the arms race, not the pursuit of the phantom of nuclear superiority or futile Star Wars schemes.

The Democratic Party believes that the purpose of nuclear weapons is to deter war, not to fight it. Democrats believe that America has the strength and tenacity to negotiate nuclear arms agreements that will reduce the risk of nuclear war and preserve our military security.

Today we stand at one of the most critical junctures in the arms race since the explosion of the first atomic bomb. Mr. Reagan wants to open the heavens for warfare.

His Star Wars proposal would create a vulnerable and provocative "shield" that would lull our nation into a false sense of security. It would lead our allies to believe that we are retreating from their defense. It would lead to the death of the ABM Treaty—the most successful arms control treaty in history—and this trillion-dollar program would provoke a dangerous offensive and defensive arms race.

If we and our allies could defend our populations effectively against a nuclear war, the Democratic Party would be the first to endorse such a scheme. Unfortunately, our best scientists agree that an effective population defense is probably impossible. Therefore, we must oppose an arms race where the sky is no longer the limit.

Arms Control and Disarmament

Ronald Reagan is the first American President in over twenty years who has not reached any significant arms control agreements with the Soviet Union, and he is the first in over fifty years who has not met face to face with Soviet leaders. The unjustified Soviet walkout from key nuclear talks does not excuse the arms control failures of the Administration.

To reopen the dialogue, a Democratic President will propose an early summit with regular, annual summits to follow with the Soviet leaders, and meetings between senior civilian and military officials, in order to reduce tensions and explore possible formal agreements. In a Democratic Administration, the superpowers will not communicate through megaphones.

A new Democratic Administration will implement a strategy for peace which makes arms control an integral part of our national security policy. We must move the world back from the brink of nuclear holocaust and set a new direction toward an enduring peace, in which lower levels of military spending will be possible. Our ultimate aim must be to abolish all nuclear weapons in a world safe for peace and freedom.

This strategy calls for immediate steps to stop the nuclear arms race, medium-term measures to reduce the dangers of war, and long-term goals to put the world on a new and peaceful course.

The first practical step is to take the initiative, on January 20, 1985, to challenge the Soviets to halt the arms race quickly. As President Kennedy successfully did in stopping nuclear explosions above ground in 1963, a Democratic President will initiate temporary, verifiable, and mutual moratoria, to be maintained for a fixed period during negotiations so long as the Soviets do the same, on the testing of underground nuclear weapons and anti-satellite weapons; on the testing and deployment of all weapons in space, on the testing and deployment of new strategic ballistic missiles now under development; and on the deployment of nuclear-armed, sea-launched cruise missiles.

These steps should lead promptly to the negotiation of a comprehensive, mutual and verifiable freeze on the testing, production, and deployment of all nuclear weapons.

Building on this initiative, the Democratic President will:

- update and resubmit the SALT II Treaty to the Senate for its advice and consent.
- pursue deep, stabilizing reductions in nuclear arsenals within the framework of SALT II, in the meantime observing the SALT II limits ourselves and insisting that the Soviets do likewise.
- propose the merging of the intermediate-range and strategic arms limitations, if the President judges that this could advance a comprehensive arms limitation agreement with the Soviet Union.

- immediately resubmit to the Senate for its advice and consent the 1974 Threshold Test Ban Treaty and the 1976 Peaceful Nuclear Explosions Treaty.
- conclude a verifiable and comprehensive Test Ban Treaty.
- reaffirm our commitment to the ABM Treaty, ensure U.S. compliance, and vigorously demand answers to questions about Soviet compliance through the Standing Consultative Commission and other appropriate channels.
- actively pursue a verifiable, anti-satellite weapons treaty and ban on weapons in space.
- seek a verifiable international ban on the production of nuclear weapons–grade fissile material, such as plutonium and highly enriched uranium.
- undertake all-out efforts to halt nuclear proliferation.
- terminate production of the MX missile and the B-1 bomber.
- prohibit the production of nerve gas and work for a verifiable treaty banning chemical weapons.
- establish U.S.–Soviet nuclear risk reduction centers and other improved communications for a crisis.
- invite the most eminent members of the scientific community to study and report on the worldwide human suffering and the long-term environmental damage which would follow in the days after a nuclear war, and take into account as fully as possible the results of such study in the formulation of our nuclear weapons and arms control policies.
- strengthen broad-based, long-term public support for arms control by working closely with leaders of grass-roots, civic, women's, labor, business, religious and professional groups, including physicians, scientists, lawyers, and educators.
- provide national leadership for economic adjustment for affected communities and industries, and retraining for any defense workers affected by the termination or cutbacks in weapons programs.
- initiate, in close consultation with our NATO allies, a strategy for peace in Europe including:
  - achieving a balance of conventional forces in order to reduce reliance on nuclear weapons and to permit the Atlantic Alliance to move toward the adoption of a "no first use" policy;
  - mutually pulling back battlefield nuclear weapons from the frontlines of Europe, in order to avoid the necessity of having to make a "use them or lose them" choice should hostilities erupt in Europe;
  - negotiating new approaches to intermediate nuclear force limits along the lines of the "walk in the woods" proposal, and then seeking to move closer to zero INF deployments by the U.S. and U.S.S.R.;
  - negotiating significant mutual and balanced reductions in conventional forces of both NATO and the Warsaw Pact, and confidence-building measures to reduce the dangers of a surprise attack.

We are under no illusion that these arms control proposals will be easy to achieve. Most will involve patience and dedication, and above all leadership in the pursuit of peace, freedom, and security. The Soviets are tough negotiators and too often seek to use arms control talks for their propaganda purposes. On this issue—preventing nuclear war—America must lead, and the Democratic Party intends to lead. Without our leadership the nations of the world will be tempted to abandon themselves, perhaps slowly at first, but then relentlessly to the quest for nuclear weapons, and our children will look back with envy upon today's already dangerous nuclear world as a time of relative safety.

Defense Policy

The Reagan Administration measures military might by dollars spent. The Democratic Party seeks prudent defense based on sound planning and a realistic assessment of threats. In the field of defense policy, the Democratic Administration will:

- Work with our NATO and other allies to ensure our collective security, especially by strengthening our conventional defenses so as to reduce our need to rely on nuclear weapons, and to achieve this at increased spending levels, with funding to continue at levels appropriate to our collective security, with the firm hope that successful steps to reduce tensions—and to obtain comprehensive and verifiable arms control agreements—will guarantee our nation both military security and budgetary relief.
- Cancel destabilizing or duplicative weapons systems, while proceeding in the absence of appropriate arms control agreements with necessary modernization of our strategic forces.
- Scale back the construction of large, expensive and vulnerable nuclear carriers.
- Modernize our conventional forces by balancing new equipment purchases with adequate resources spent on training, fuel, ammunition, maintenance, spare parts, and airlift and sealift to assure combat readiness mobility, and by providing better equipment for our Reserves and National Guard.
- Reorganize Pentagon management and strengthen the JCS system to reduce interservice rivalries, promote military leadership over bureaucratic skills, assure effective execution of policies and decisions, undertake better multi-year planning based upon realistic projections of available resources, and reduce conflicts of interest.

- Ensure open and fair competitive bidding for procurement of necessary equipment and parts, and establish a system of effective, independent testing of weapons for combat conditions.
- Implement a program of military reform. Our forces must be combat ready; our doctrines should emphasize out-thinking and out-maneuvering our adversaries; and our policies should improve military organization and unit cohesion.
- Press our European allies to increase their contributions to NATO defense to levels of effort comparable to our own—an approach that the Administration undercut by abandoning the NATO-wide agreement concluded by its Democratic predecessor—and pursue improved trans-Atlantic economic cooperation and coordination of arms procurement.
- Recognize that the heart of our military strength is people, Americans in uniform who will have the skills and the will to maintain the peace. The men and women of our armed services deserve not only proper pay and benefits, but the nation's recognition, respect and gratitude as well.
- Recognize the importance of the intelligence community and emphasize its mission as being dedicated to the timely collection and analysis of information and data. A Democratic Administration will also recognize the urgent need to de-politicize the intelligence community and to restore professional leadership to it.
- Oppose a peacetime military draft or draft registration.
- Oppose efforts to restrict the opportunities of women in the military based solely on gender. The Reagan Administration has used the combat designation as an arbitrary and inappropriate way to exclude women from work they can legitimately perform. Women nurses and technicians, for example, have long served with distinction on the front lines: women must not be excluded from jobs that they are trained and able to perform.
- Seek ways to expand programs such as VISTA, the Young Adult Conservation Corps, and the Peace Corps.

These and other qualitative improvements will ensure effective American strength at affordable cost. With this strength, we will restore the confidence of our fellow citizens and our allies; we will be able to mount an effective conventional defense; and we will present our adversaries with a credible capability to deter war.

The Democratic Party is committed to reversing the policies of the Reagan Administration in the area of military and defense procurement. Public accounts reveal a four-year record of waste, fraud, conflicts of interest, and indications of wrongdoing. Administration officials have engaged in practices that have cost the taxpayers billions of dollars. Further, the Reagan Administration has ignored legal remedies to stop the abuses, recover the funds, and punish those responsible.

A Democratic President will demand full disclosure of all information, launch a thorough investigation, and seek recovery of any tax funds illegally spent. This will be a major step towards restoring integrity to defense procurements and reducing unnecessary expenditures in the defense budget.

Foreign Policy

The purpose of foreign policy is to attain a strong and secure United States and a world of peace, freedom and justice. On a planet threatened by dictatorships on the left and right, what is at stake may be freedom itself. On a planet shadowed by the threat of a nuclear holocaust, what is at stake may be nothing less than human survival.

A Democratic Administration will comprehend that the gravest political and security dangers in the developing world flow from conditions that open opportunities for the Soviet Union and its surrogates: poverty, repression and despair. Against adversaries such as these, military force is of limited value. Such weapons as economic assistance, economic and political reform, and support for democratic values by, among other steps, funding scholarships to study at U.S. colleges and universities, must be the leading elements of our presence and the primary instruments of American influence in the developing countries.

To this end, a Democratic President will strengthen our Foreign Service, end the present practice of appointing unqualified persons as Ambassadors, strengthen our programs of educational and cultural exchange, and draw upon the best minds in our country in the quest for peace.

A Democratic Administration will initiate and establish a Peace Academy. In the interests of balancing this nation's investment in the study of making war, the Peace Academy will study the disciplines and train experts in the arts of waging peace.

The Democratic Party is committed to ensuring strong representation of women and minorities in military and foreign policy decision-making positions in our government.

In addition, a Democratic President will understand that as Commander-in-Chief, he or she directs the forces of peace as well as those of war, and will restore an emphasis on skilled, sensitive, bilateral and multilateral diplomacy as a means to avert and resolve international conflict.

A Democratic President will recognize that the United States, with broad economic, political, and security interests in the world, has an unparalleled stake in the rule of international law. Under a Democratic Administration, there will be no call for clumsy attempts to escape the jurisdiction of the International Court of Justice, such as those put forth by the Reagan Administration in connection with its mining of the harbors of Nicaragua.

A Democratic President will reverse the automatic militarization of foreign policy and look to the causes of conflict to find out whether they are internal or external, whether they are political or primarily social and economic.

In the face of the Reagan Administration's cavalier approach to the use of military force around the world, the Democratic Party affirms its commitment to the selective, judicious use of American military power in consonance with constitutional principles and reinforced by the War Powers Act.

A Democratic President will be prepared to apply military force when vital American interests are threatened, particularly in the event of an attack upon the United States or its immediate allies. But he or she will not hazard American lives or engage in unilateral military involvement:

- Where our objectives are not clear;
- Until all instruments of diplomacy and nonmilitary leverage, as appropriate, have been exhausted;
- Where our objectives threaten unacceptable costs or unreasonable levels of military force;
- Where the local forces supported are not working to resolve the causes of conflict;
- Where multilateral or allied options for the resolution of conflict are available.

Further, a Democratic Administration will take all reasonable domestic action to minimize U.S. vulnerability to international instability, such as reducing Western reliance on Persian Gulf oil and other strategic resources. To this end, a Democratic Administration will implement, with our allies, a multilateral strategy for reduction of allied dependence on critical resources from volatile regions of the world.

U.S. covert operations under a Democratic President will be strictly limited to cases where secrecy is essential to the success of an operation and where there is an unmistakable foreign policy rationale. Secrecy will not be used simply to hide from the American people policies they might be expected to oppose.

Finally, a Democratic President will recognize our democratic process as a source of strength and stability, rather than an unwelcome restraint on the control of foreign policy. He or she will respect the War Powers Resolution as a reflection of wise judgment that the sustained commitment of America's fighting forces must be made with the understanding and support of Congress and the American people. A Democratic President will understand that United States leadership among nations requires a proper respect for law and treaty obligations, and the rights of men and women everywhere.

Europe and the Atlantic Alliance. American leadership is not about standing up to our friends. It is about standing up with them, and for them. In order to have allies, we must act like one.

Maintaining a strong alliance is critically important. We remain absolutely committed to the defense of Europe, and we will work to ensure that our allies carry their fair share of the burden of the common defense. A Democratic Administration in turn will commit itself to increased consultation on security affairs. We must work to sustain and enhance Western unity.

We must persuade the next generation of Europeans that America will use its power responsibly in partnership with them. We Democrats affirm that Western security is indivisible. We have a vital interest in the security of our allies in Europe, and it must always remain clear that an attack upon them is the same as an attack upon us—by treaty and in reality.

A strong Western alliance requires frank discussions among friends about the issues that from time to time divide us. For example, we must enter into meaningful negotiations with the European Community to reduce their agricultural export subsidies which unfairly impair the competitiveness of American agricultural products in third-country markets.

A Democratic President will encourage our European friends to resolve their long-standing differences over Ireland and Cyprus.

The Democratic Party supports an active role by the United States in safeguarding human rights in Northern Ireland and achieving an enduring peaceful settlement of that conflict. We oppose the use of plastic bullets in Northern Ireland, and we urge all sides to reject the use of violence. The Democratic Party supports a ban on all commercial transactions by the U.S. government with firms in England and Ireland that practice, on an on-going basis, discrimination in Northern Ireland on the basis of race, religion, or sex. We affirm our strong commitment to Irish unity—achieved by consent and based on reconciliation of all the people of Ireland. The Democratic Party is greatly encouraged by the historic and hopeful Report of the New Ireland Forum which holds the promise of a real breakthrough. A Democratic President will promptly appoint a special envoy and urge the British as well as the political leaders in Northern Ireland to review the findings and proposals of the Forum with open hearts and open minds, and will appeal to them to join a new initiative for peace. The Congress and a Democratic President will stand ready to assist this process, and will help promote jobs and investments, on a nondiscriminatory basis, that will represent a significant contribution to the cause of peace in Ireland.

In strong contrast to President Reagan's failure to apply effective diplomacy in Cyprus and the Eastern Mediterranean, a Democratic President will act with urgency and determination to make a balanced policy in the area and a peaceful resolution of the Cyprus dispute a key foreign policy priority. A Democratic President will utilize all available U.S. foreign policy instruments and will play an active, instead of a passive, role in the efforts to secure implementation of U.N. Resolutions so as to achieve removal of Turkish troops, the return of refugees, reestablishment of the integrity of the Republic of Cyprus, and respect for all citizens' human rights on Cyprus.

United States–Soviet Relations. U.S. relations with the Soviet Union are a critical element of our security policy. All Americans recognize the threat to world peace posed by the Soviet Union. The U.S.S.R. is the only adversary with the capability of destroying the United States. Moreover, Americans are more generally concerned about the Soviet leadership's dangerous behavior internationally and the totalitarian nature of their regime. The Brezhnev Doctrine proclaims Soviet willingness to maintain communist regimes against the opposition of their own people. Thus, Soviet troops have invaded and today continue to wage war on the proud people of Afghanistan. In Poland, a military government, acting under Soviet pressure, has sought to crush the indomitable spirit of the Polish people and to destroy Solidarity, a free trade union movement of ten million members and the first such movement in a communist country. In recent years, the Soviet Union and its allies have played a more aggressive role in countries around the world. At the same time, the Soviet military arsenal, nuclear and conventional, far exceeds that needed for its defense.

Yet we also recognize that the Soviets share a mutual interest in survival. They, too, have no defense against a nuclear war. Our security and their security can only be strengthened by negotiation and cooperation.

To shape a policy that is both firm and wise, we must first stand confident and never fear the outcome of any competition between our systems. We must see the Soviet Union as it is—neither minimizing the threats that Soviet power and policies pose to U.S. interests, nor exaggerating the strength of a Soviet regime beset by economic stagnation and saddled with a bankrupt and sterile ideology. We must join with our allies and friends to maintain an effective deterrent to Soviet power. We must pursue a clear, consistent and firm policy of peaceful competition toward the Soviet Union, a steady and pragmatic approach that neither tolerates Soviet aggression and repression nor fuels Soviet paranoia.

The job of an American President is both to check Soviet challenges to our vital interests, and to meet them on the common ground of survival. The risk of nuclear war cannot be eliminated overnight. But every day it can be either increased or decreased. And one of the surest ways to increase it is to cut off communications.

The Democratic Party condemns continued Soviet persecution of dissidents and refuseniks, which may well have brought Nobel laureate Andrei Sakharov and his wife to the verge of death in internal exile in Gorki. We will not be silent when Soviet actions, such as the imprisonment of Anatoly Shcharansky and Ida Nudel and thousands of others, demonstrate the fundamentally repressive and anti-Semitic nature of the Soviet regime. A Democratic Administration will give priority to securing the freedom to emigrate for these brave men and women of conscience, including Jews and other minorities, and to assuring their fair treatment while awaiting permission to leave. These freedoms are guaranteed by the Universal Declaration of Human Rights and by the Helsinki Final Act which the Soviets have signed and with whose provisions they must be required to comply. Jewish emigration, which reached the level of fifty thousand per year during the last Democratic Administration and which has virtually ended under its Republican successor, must be renewed through firm, effective diplomacy. We also recognize that Jewish emigration reached its height at the same time there was an American Administration dedicated to pursuing arms control, expanding mutually beneficial trade, and reducing tensions with the Soviet Union—fully consistent with the interests of the United States and its allies. It is no contradiction to say that while pursuing an end to the arms race and reducing East–West tensions, we can also advance the cause of Soviet Jewish emigration.

Eastern Europe. We must respond to the aspirations and hopes of the peoples of Eastern Europe and encourage, wherever possible, the forces of change and pluralism that will increase these people's freedom from Soviet tyranny and communist dictatorship. We should encourage Eastern European countries to pursue independent foreign policies and to permit greater liberalization in domestic affairs, and we should seek independent relationships to further these objectives with them.

The Democratic Party condemns the Soviet repression by proxy in Poland and the other countries of Eastern Europe. The emergence of the free trade union Solidarity is one of the most formidable developments in post-war Europe and inspires all who love freedom. The struggle of the Polish people for a democratic society and religious freedom is eloquent testimony to their national spirit and bravery that even a brutal martial law regime cannot stamp out.

Today the Jaruzelski regime claims to have ended the harshest repressive measures. Yet it continues to hold political prisoners, it continues to mistreat them, and it continues to hunt down members of Solidarity.

The Democratic Party agrees with Lech Walesa that the underground Solidarity movement must not be deprived of union freedoms. We call for the release of all political prisoners in Poland and an end to their harassment, the recognition of the free trade union Solidarity, and the resumption of progress toward liberty and human rights in that nation. A Democratic President will continue to press for effective international sanctions against the Polish regime until it makes satisfactory progress toward these objectives.

The Middle East. The Democratic Party believes that the security of Israel and the pursuit of peace in the Middle East are fundamental priorities for American foreign policy. Israel remains more than a trusted friend, a steady ally, and a sister democracy. Israel is strategically important to the United States, and we must enter into meaningful strategic cooperation.

The Democratic Party opposes this Administration's sales of highly advanced weaponry to avowed enemies of Israel, such as AWACS aircraft and Stinger missiles to Saudi Arabia. While helping to meet the legitimate defensive needs of states aligned with our nation, we must ensure Israel's military edge over any combination of Middle East confrontation states. The Democratic Party opposes any consideration of negotiations with the PLO, unless the PLO abandons terrorism, recognizes the state of Israel, and adheres to U.N. Resolutions 242 and 338.

Jerusalem should remain forever undivided with free access to the holy places for people of all faiths. As stated in the 1976 and 1980 platforms, the Democratic Party recognizes and supports the established status of Jerusalem as the capital of Israel. As a symbol of this stand, the U.S. Embassy should be moved from Tel Aviv to Jerusalem.

The Democratic Party condemns this Administration's failure to maintain a high-level Special Negotiator for the Middle East, and believes that the Camp David peace process must be taken up again

with urgency. No nation in the Middle East can afford to wait until a new war brings even worse destruction. Once again we applaud and support the example of both Israel and Egypt in taking bold steps for peace. We believe that the United States should press for negotiations among Israel, Jordan, Saudi Arabia, and other Arab states. We reemphasize the fundamental principle that the prerequisite for a lasting peace in the Middle East remains an Israel with secure and defensible borders, strong beyond a shadow of a doubt; that the basis for peace is the unequivocal recognition of Israel's right to exist by all other states, and that there should be a resolution of the Palestinian issue.

The United States and our allies have vital interests in the Persian Gulf. We must be prepared to work with our allies in defense of those interests. We should stand by our historic support for the principle of freedom on the high seas. At the same time, we and our allies should employ active diplomacy to encourage the earliest possible end to the Iran/Iraq conflict.

The Western Hemisphere. The Western Hemisphere is in trouble. Central America is a region at war. Latin America is experiencing the most serious economic crisis in 50 years. The Inter-American system is on the verge of collapse. Concern about U.S. policies has risen sharply.

It is time to make this Hemisphere a top priority. We need to develop relations based on mutual respect and mutual benefit. Beyond essential security concerns, these relations must emphasize diplomacy, development and respect for human rights. Above all, support for democracy must be pursued. The Reagan Administration is committing the old error of supporting authoritarian military regimes against the wishes of the people they rule, but the United States was not founded, and defended for 200 years with American blood, in order to perpetuate tyranny among our neighbors.

The Hemisphere's nations must strive jointly to find acceptable solutions with judgments and actions based on equally applied criteria. We must condemn violations of human rights, aggression, and deprivation of basic freedoms wherever they occur. The United States must recognize that the economic and debt crisis of Latin America also directly affects us.

The Reagan Administration has badly misread and mishandled the conflict in Central America. The President has chosen to dwell on the strategic importance of Central America and to cast the struggle in almost exclusively East–West terms. The strategic importance of Central America is not in doubt, nor is the fact that the Soviet Union, Cuba and Nicaragua have all encouraged instability and supported revolution in the region. What the President ignores, however, are the indigenous causes of unrest. Historically, Central America has been burdened by widespread hunger and disease. And the historic pattern of concentrated wealth has done little to produce stable democratic societies.

Sadly, Mr. Reagan has opted for the all too frequent American response to the unrest that has characterized Central America—military assistance. Over the past 100 years, Panama, Nicaragua, and Honduras have all been occupied by U.S. forces in an effort to suppress indigenous revolutionary movements. In 1954, CIA-backed forces successfully toppled the government of Guatemala.

President Reagan's massive transfusions of military aid to El Salvador are no substitute for the social and economic reforms that are necessary to undermine the appeal the guerrillas hold for many Salvadorans. The changes and upheavals in El Salvador and Nicaragua are home-grown, but they are exacerbated by forces from outside of Central America. The undoubted communist influence on these revolutions cannot be nullified by the dispatch of naval and air armadas to the waters off Nicaragua and thousands of troops to the jungles of Honduras. The solution lies with a new policy that fosters social, economic and political reforms that are compatible with our legitimate vital interests while accommodating the equally legitimate forces of change.

America must find a different approach. All too often, the United States thinks in terms of what it can do *for* the nations of Latin America and the Caribbean region. Rarely does it think in terms of what it can do *with* them. Even with the best of intentions, the difference is more than rhetorical, for paternalism can never be disguised and it is always resented—whether we choose to label it a "special relationship" or to call it a "defensive shield." Acting *for* the nations of the Hemisphere rather than acting in concert with them is the surest way of repeating the mistakes of the past and casting a dark shadow over the future.

It need not be. There is an alternative, a good alternative. The great Mexican patriot Benito Juarez pointed the way and said it best: "Between men as between nations, respect for the rights of others is peace." Working with our hemispheric neighbors produces understanding and cooperation. Doing something for them produces resentment and conflict.

Democrats know there is a real difference between the two and a Democratic President will seek the advice and counsel of the authentic democratic voices within the region—voices that may be heard north and south, east and west; the voices of President Miguel de la Madrid of Mexico, President Belisario Betancur of Colombia, and President Raul Alfonsin of Argentina; the voices of President Jorge Blanco of the Dominican Republic. Prime Minister Tom Adams of Barbados, and President Alberto Monge of Costa Rica. By consulting with and listening carefully to these leaders, and to their democratic colleagues elsewhere in the region, the next Democratic President of the United States will fashion a policy toward the region which recognizes that:

- the security and well-being of the Hemisphere are more a function of economic growth and development than of military agreements and arms transfers;
- the mounting debt crisis throughout the region poses a broader threat to democratic institutions and political stability than does any insurgency or armed revolutionary movement;
- there is an urgent and genuine need for far-reaching economic, social and political reforms in much of the region and that such reforms are absolutely essential to the protection of basic human rights;
- the future belongs as much to the people of the region—the politically forgotten and the economically deprived—as it does to the rich and powerful elite;
- preservation and protection of U.S. interests in the Hemisphere requires mutual respect for national sovereignty and demilitarization of the region, prior consultation in accordance with the Rio Treaty and the OAS Charter regarding application of the Monroe Doctrine and the use of military force, and a multilateral commitment to oppose the establishment of Soviet and Cuban military bases, strategic facilities, or combat presence in Central America or elsewhere in Latin America;
- efforts to isolate Cuba only serve to make it more dependent on the Soviet Union; U.S. diplomatic skills must be employed to reduce that level of dependence and to explore the differences that divide us with a view to stabilizing our relations with Cuba. At the same time we must continue to oppose firmly Cuban intervention in the internal affairs of other nations. Progress in our relationship will depend on Cuba's willingness to end its support for violent revolution, to recognize the sovereignty and independence of other nations by respecting the principle of non-intervention, to demonstrate respect for human rights both inside and outside of Cuba, and to abide by international norms of behavior.

Mindful of these realities and determined to stop widening, militarizing, and Americanizing the conflict, a Democratic President's immediate objective will be to stop the violence and pursue a negotiated political solution in concert with our democratic allies in the Contadora group. He or she will approach Central American policy in the following terms:

- First, there must be unequivocal support for the Contadora process and for the efforts by those countries to achieve political solutions to the conflicts that plague the Central American region.
- Second, there must be a commitment on the part of the United States to reduce tensions in the region. We must terminate our support for the *contras* and other paramilitary groups fighting in Nicaragua. We must halt those U.S. military exercises in the region which are being conducted for no other real purpose than to intimidate or provoke the Nicaraguan government or which may be used as a pretext for deeper U.S. military involvement in the area. And we must evidence our firm willingness to work for a demilitarized Central America, including the mutual withdrawal of all foreign forces and military advisors from the region. A Democratic President will seek a multilateral framework to protect the security and independence of the region which will include regional agreements to bar new military bases, to restrict the numbers and sophistication of weapons being introduced into Central America, and to permit international inspection of borders. This diplomatic effort can succeed, however, only if all countries in Central America, including Nicaragua, will agree to respect the sovereignty and integrity of their neighbors, to limit their military forces, to reject foreign military bases (other than those provided for in the Panama Canal Treaties), and to deny any external force or power the use of their territories for purposes of subversion in the region. The viability of any security agreement for Central America would be enhanced by the progressive development of pluralism in Nicaragua. To this end, the elections proposed for November are important; how they are conducted will be an indication of Nicaragua's willingness to move in the direction of genuine democracy.
- Third, there must be a clear, concise signal to indicate that we are ready, willing and able to provide substantial economic resources, through the appropriate multilateral channels, to the nations of Central America, as soon as the Contadora process achieves a measure of success in restoring peace and stability in the region. In the meantime, of course, we will continue to provide humanitarian aid and refugee relief assistance. The Democratic Administration will work to help churches and universities which are providing sanctuary and assistance to Guatemalan, Haitian,

and Salvadoran refugees, and will give all assistance to such refugees as is consistent with U.S. law.
- Fourth, a Democratic President will support the newly elected President of El Salvador in his efforts to establish civilian democratic control, by channeling U.S. aid through him and by conditioning it on the elimination of government-supported death squads and on progress toward his objectives of land reform, human rights, and serious negotiations with contending forces in El Salvador, in order to achieve a peaceful democratic political settlement of the Salvadoran conflict.
- Fifth, a Democratic President will not use U.S. armed forces in or over El Salvador or Nicaragua for the purpose of engaging in combat unless:

    1) Congress has declared war or otherwise authorized the use of U.S. combat forces

    2) the use of U.S. combat forces is necessary to meet a clear and present danger of attack upon the U.S., its territories or possessions or upon U.S. embassies or citizens, consistent with the War Powers Act.

These are the key elements that evidence very real differences between the Democrats' approach to Central America and that of the Reagan Administration. And they are the key elements that will offer the American public a choice—a very significant choice—between war and peace in the Central American region.

A Democratic President would seek to work with the countries of the Caribbean to strengthen democratic institutions. He or she would not overlook human rights by refusing to condemn repression by the regimes of the right or the left in the region. A Democratic President would give high priority to democracy, freedom, and to multilateral development. A Democratic President would encourage regional cooperation and make of that important area a showplace rather than a footstool for economic development. Finally, support for democracy must be pursued in its own right, and not just as a tactic against communism.

Human rights principles were a cornerstone of President Carter's foreign policy and have always been a central concern in the Inter-American system. Regional multilateral action to protect and advance human rights is an international obligation.

A Democratic President must not overlook human rights, refusing to condemn repression by the regimes of the right or the left in the region. Insistence that governments respect their obligations to their people is a criterion that must apply equally to all. It is as important in Cuba as in El Salvador, Guatemala as in Nicaragua, in Haiti as in Paraguay and Uruguay.

A Democratic Administration would place protection of human rights in a core position in our relations with Latin America and the Caribbean. It would particularly seek multilateral support for such principles by strengthening and backing the InterAmerican Commission on Human Rights, and by encouraging the various private organizations in the Hemisphere dedicated to monitoring and protecting human rights.

Africa. The Democratic Party will advocate a set of bold new initiatives for Third World nations in general and Africa in particular. Hunger, drought, and famine have brought untold suffering to millions in Africa. This human misery—and the armies of nationless—requires a policy of substantial increases in humanitarian assistance, a major thrust in agricultural technology transfer, and cessation of the unfortunate tendency to hold such aid hostage to East–West confrontation or other geopolitical aims. The United States also must offer substantially greater economic assistance to these nations, while engaging in a North–South multilateral dialogue that addresses mutual economic development strategies, commodities pricing, and other treaties relevant to international trade. A Democratic President will join with our friends within and outside the continent in support of full respect for the sovereignty and territorial integrity of all African states. Africa is the home of one-eighth of the world's population and a continent of vast resources. Our national interest demands that we give this rich and diverse continent a much higher priority.

A Democratic President will reverse the Reagan Administration's failed policy of "constructive engagement" and strongly and unequivocally oppose the apartheid regime in South Africa. A Democratic Administration will:

- exert maximum pressure on South Africa to hasten the establishment of a democratic, unitary political system within South Africa.
- pursue scrupulous enforcement of the 1977 U.N. arms embargo against South Africa, including enforcement of restrictions on the sale of "dual use" equipment.
- impose a ban on all new loans by U.S. business interests to the South African government and on all new investments and loans to the South African private sector, until there is substantial progress toward the full participation of all the people of South Africa in the social, political, and economic life in that country and toward an end to discrimination based on race or ethnic origin.
- ban the sale or transfer of sophisticated computers

and nuclear technology to South Africa and the importation of South African gold coins.

- reimpose export controls in effect during the Carter Administration which were relaxed by the Reagan Administration.
- withdraw landing rights to South African aircraft.

The Democratic Party condemns South Africa for unjustly holding political prisoners. Soviet harassment of the Sakharovs is identical to South African house arrests of political opponents of the South African regime. Specifically, the detention of Nelson Mandela, leader of the African National Congress, and Winnie Mandela must be brought to the world's attention, and we demand their immediate release. In addition, we demand the immediate release of all other political prisoners in South Africa.

A Democratic Administration will work as well toward legitimate rights of self-determination of the peoples of Namibia by:

- demanding compliance with U.N. Security Council Resolution 435—the six-year-old blueprint for Namibian independence;
- imposing severe fines on U.S. companies that violate the United Nations decree prohibiting foreign exploitation of Namibian mineral wealth until Namibia attains independence;
- progressively increasing effective sanctions against South Africa unless and until it grants independence to Namibia and abolishes its own abhorrent apartheid system.

Asia. Our relationship with the countries of Asia and the Pacific Basin will continue to be of increasing importance. The political, cultural, economic, and strategic ties which link the United States to this region cannot be ignored.

With our Asian friends and allies, we have a common cause in preserving the security and enhancing democracy in the area.

With our Asian trading partners, we share a common interest in expanding commerce and fair trade between us, as evidenced by the 33 percent of total American trade now conducted with those countries.

And with the growing number of Asian/Pacific-Americans, we welcome the strength and vitality which increased cultural ties bring to this country.

Our relationship with Japan is a key to the maintenance of peace, security, and development in Asia and the Pacific region. Mutual respect, enhanced cooperation, and steady diplomacy must guide our dealings with Japan. At the same time, as allies and friends, we must work to resolve areas of disagreement. A Democratic President, therefore, will press for increased access to Japanese as well as other Asian markets for American firms and their products. Finally, a Democratic President will expect Japan to continue moving toward assuming its fair share of the burden of collective security—in self-defense as well as in foreign assistance and democratic development.

Our security in the Pacific region is also closely tied to the well-being of our long-time allies, Australia and New Zealand. A Democratic President will honor and strengthen our security commitment to ANZUS as well as to other Southeast Asian friends.

Our relationship with the People's Republic of China must also be nurtured and strengthened. The Democratic Party believes that our developing relations with the PRC offer a historic opportunity to bring one quarter of the world's population into the community of nations, to strengthen a counterweight to Soviet expansionism, and to enhance economic relations that offer great potential for mutual advantage. At the same time, we recognize our historic ties to the people on Taiwan and we will continue to honor our commitments to them, consistent with the Taiwan Relations Act.

Our own principles and interests demand that we work with those in Asia, as well as elsewhere, who can encourage democratic institutions and support greater respect for human rights. A Democratic President will work closely with the world's largest democracy, India, and maintain mutually beneficial ties. A Democratic President will press for the restoration of full democracy in the Philippines, further democratization and the elimination of martial law in Taiwan, the return to freedom of speech and press in South Korea, and restoration of human rights for the people of East Timor. Recognizing the strategic importance of Pakistan and the close relationship which has existed between our two countries, a Democratic President would press to restore democracy and terminate its nuclear weapons program. Finally, a Democratic President would press for the fullest possible accounting of Americans still missing in Indochina.

For the past four years, the Soviet Union has been engaged in a brutal effort to crush the resistance of the people of Afghanistan. It denies their right to independence. It is trying to stamp out their culture and to deny them the right to practice their religion, Islam. But despite appalling costs, the people of Afghanistan continue to resist—demonstrating the same qualities of human aspiration and fortitude that made our own nation great. We must continue to oppose Soviet aggression in Afghanistan. We should support the efforts of the Afghanistan freedom fighters with material assistance.

If the Soviet Union is prepared to abide by the principles of international law and human dignity, it should find the U.S. prepared to help produce a peaceful settlement.

Global Debt and Development

The Democratic Party will pursue policies for economic development, for aid and trade that meet the needs of the people of the developing world and that further our own national interest. The next Democratic President will support development policies that meet the basic needs of the poor for food, water, energy, medical care, and shelter rather than "trickle down" policies that never reach those on the bottom. The next Democratic Administration will give preference in its foreign assistance to countries with democratic institutions and respect for human rights.

A Democratic President will seek to cut back record U.S. budget deficits and interest rates not only for our own economic well-being, but to reduce the economic crisis confronting so many industrialized and developing states alike.

Mr. Reagan has perceived national security in very limited and parochial terms, and thus has failed completely to grasp the significance of the international debt which now has sky-rocketed to some $800 billion. In 1983, some thirty nations accounting for half of this total were forced to seek restructuring of their debts with public and private creditors because they were unable to meet their debt payments.

The U.S. economy is directly linked to the costs of these loans through their variable interest rates (tied to the U.S. prime rate). A rise in the U.S. prime rate by one percent added more than $4 billion to the annual interest costs associated with these external debts. The struggle to meet their external debts has slashed the purchasing power of these developing countries and forced them to curtail imports from the U.S. This accounts for one-third to one-half of the adverse turn in the U.S. trade deficit, which is projected to reach $130 billion this year.

The social and political stability of these developing countries is seriously challenged by the debt crisis. In light of the interdependence of the international economy, the crisis also threatens the very foundation of the international financial system. To answer these dangers, the Democratic Administration will:

- Call immediately for discussions on improving the functioning of the international monetary systems and on developing a comprehensive long-term approach to the international debt problem.

- Instruct the Treasury Department to work with the Federal Reserve Board, U.S. bank regulators, key private banks, and the finance ministers and central bankers of Europe and Japan to develop a short-term program for reducing the debt service obligations of less developed countries, while 1) preserving the safety and soundness of the international banking system and 2) ensuring that the costs of the program are shared equitably among all parties to existing and rescheduled debts.
- Recommend an increase in the lending capacity of the World Bank, as well as an increase in the lending capacity of the Export–Import Bank of the U.S., to ensure that debtor nations obtain adequate capital for investment in export industries.
- Review international trade barriers which limit the ability of these countries to earn foreign exchange.

Security assistance can, in appropriate circumstances, help our friends meet legitimate defense needs. But shifting the balance from economic development toward military sales, as has occurred over the past three and one-half years, sets back the cause of peace and justice, fuels regional arms races, and places sophisticated weapons in the hands of those who could one day turn them back upon us and upon our friends and allies. The Democratic Party seeks now, as in the past, effective international agreements to limit and reduce the transfer of conventional arms.

A Democratic President will seize new opportunities to make major advances at limited cost in the health and survival of the world's poorest people—thus enabling more people to contribute to and share in the world's resources, and promoting stability and popular participation in their societies.

Recognizing that unrestrained population growth constitutes a danger for economic progress and political stability, a Democratic President will restore full U.S. support for national and international population programs that are now threatened by the policies of the Reagan Administration.

A Democratic President will work to see the power and prestige of the U.S. fully committed to the reform and strengthening of the United Nations and other international agencies in the pursuit of their original purposes—peace, economic and social welfare, education, and human rights.

Because of the economic instability caused by global debts and by other problems, unprecedented migration into the United States and other parts of the world is occurring in the form of economic refugees. The Democratic Party will support economic development programs so as to aid nations in reducing migration from their countries, and thereby reduce the flow of economic refugees to the U.S. and other parts of the world.

Rather than scuttling the international Law of the Sea negotiations after over a decade of bipartisan U.S. involvement, a Democratic President will actively pursue efforts to achieve an acceptable treaty and related agreements that protect U.S. interests in all uses of ocean space.

Human Rights and Democratic Solidarity

The Democratic Party believes that we need new approaches to replace the failed Republican policies. We need sustained, personal, Presidential leadership in foreign policy and arms control. We need a President who will meet with the Soviets to challenge them to reduce the danger of nuclear war, who will become personally involved in reviving the Camp David peace process, who will give his or her full support to the Contadora negotiations, and who will press the South Africans to repeal their policies of apartheid and destabilization. We need a President who will understand that human rights and national security interests are mutually supportive. We need a President to restore our influence, enhance our security, pursue democracy and freedom, and work unremittingly for peace. With firm purpose, skill, sensitivity, and a recovery of our own pride in what we are, a Democratic President will build an international alliance of free people to promote these great causes.

A Democratic President will pursue a foreign policy that advances basic civil and political rights—freedom of speech, association, thought and religion, the right to leave, freedom of the integrity of the person, and the prohibition of torture, arbitrary detention and cruel, inhuman and degrading treatment—and that seeks as well to attain basic, economic, social, and cultural rights. A Democratic President's concern must extend from the terror of the Russian Gulag to the jails of Latin American generals. The banning of South African Blacks is no more acceptable than the silencing of Cuban poets. A Democratic President will end U.S. support for dictators throughout the world from Haiti to the Philippines. He or she will support and defend the observance of basic human rights called for in the Universal Declaration of Human Rights and the Helsinki Final Act. He or she will seek, through both quiet diplomacy and public measures, the release of political prisoners and the free immigration of prosecuted individuals and peoples around the world. He or she will seek U.S. ratification of the Genocide

Convention, the International Covenants on Human Rights, and the American Convention on Human Rights, as well as the establishment of a U.N. High Commissioner for Human Rights. He or she will fulfill the spirit as well as the letter of our legislation calling for the denial of military and economic assistance to governments that systematically violate human rights.

The Democratic Party believes that whether it is in response to totalitarianism in the Soviet Union or repression in Latin America and East Asia, to apartheid in South Africa or martial law in Poland, to terrorism in Libya or the reign of terror in Iran, or to barbaric aggression in Southeast Asia and Afghanistan, the foreign policy of the United States must be unmistakably on the side of those who love freedom.

As Democrats and as Americans, we will make support for democracy, human rights, and economic and social justice the cornerstone of our policy. These are the most revolutionary ideas on our planet. They are not to be feared. They are the hallmarks of the democratic century that lies before us.

— 1988 —

WE THE PEOPLE OF THE DEMOCRATIC PARTY OF THE UNITED STATES OF AMERICA, in order to initiate the changes necessary to keep America strong and make America better, in order to restore competence, caring and incorruptibility to the Federal Executive Branch and get it working again fairly for all Americans, and in order to secure for our children a future of liberty and opportunity,

Hereby pledge our Party, our leaders, our elected officials and our every individual effort to fulfilling the following fundamental principles for all members of the American family.

WE BELIEVE that all Americans have a fundamental right to economic justice in a stronger, surer national economy that must grow steadily without inflation, that can generate a rising standard of living for all and fulfill the desire of all to work in dignity up to their full potential in good health with good jobs at good wages, an economy that is prosperous in every region, from coast to coast, including our rural towns and our older industrial communities, our mining towns, our energy producing areas and the urban areas that have been neglected for the past seven years. We believe that, as a first-rate world power moving into the 21st century, we can have a first-rate full-employment economy, with an indexed minimum wage that can help lift and keep families out of poverty, with

training and employment programs—including child care and health care—that can help people move from welfare to work, with portable pensions and an adequate Social Security System, safeguarded against emasculation and privatization, that can help assure a comfortable and fulfilling old age, with opportunities for voluntary national public service, above and beyond current services, that can enrich our communities, and with all workers assured the protection of an effective law that guarantees their rights to organize, join the union of their choice, and bargain collectively with their employer, free from anti-union tactics.

WE BELIEVE that the time has come for America to take charge once again of its economic future, to reverse seven years of "voodoo economics," "trickle down" policies, fiscal irresponsibility, and economic violence against poor and working people that have converted this proud country into the world's largest debtor nation, mortgaged our children's future by tripling our national debt, placed home ownership out of reach for most young families, permitted the rise of poverty and homelessness on the streets of America, reduced the buying power of working men and women, and witnessed the decline of our industrial, natural resource and mining base, the unending tragedy of family farm foreclosures, an unhealthy dependence on foreign energy and foreign capital, and the increasing foreign ownership of our land and natural resources.

WE BELIEVE that it is time for America to meet the challenge to change priorities after eight years of devastating Republican policies, to reverse direction and reassert progressive values, to reinvest in its people within a strong commitment to fiscal responsibility. If we are seriously to pursue our commitments to build a secure economic future for all Americans we must provide the resources to care for our newborns, educate our children, house the homeless, heal the sick, wage total war on drugs and protect the environment. Investing in America and reducing the deficit requires that the wealthy and corporations pay their fair share and that we restrain Pentagon spending. We further believe that we must invest in new priorities, in lifelong education and training, in targeted economic development, in a healthy small business community and in retooled American industry; that it is time for the broad revitalization of home town America, involving financial institutions in the provision of crucial credit by encouraging special commitments in exchange for bailing out those that are failing, reforming and expanding community reinvestment laws, and reversing the trend of financial concentration and deregulation, all combining to reverse the insecurity that has increasingly troubled our workers and their families in this rapidly changing society that has left some communities and regions behind. There is no good reason why the nation we love, the greatest and richest nation on earth, should rank first among the industrialized nations in output per person but nearly last in infant mortality, first in the percentage of total expenditures devoted to defense but nearly last in the percentage devoted to education and housing.

WE BELIEVE that government should set the standard in recognizing that worker productivity is enhanced by the principle of pay equity for working women and no substandard wage competition for public contracts; by family leave policies that no longer force employees to choose between their jobs and their children or ailing parents; by safe and healthy work places, now jeopardized by seven callous years of lowered and unenforced occupational safety standards for American workers; and by major increases in assistance making child care more available and affordable to low- and middle-income families, helping states build a strong child care infrastructure, setting minimum standards for health, safety, and quality, and thereby enabling parents to work and their children to get an early start on their education and personal fulfillment. We believe that the strength of our families is enhanced by programs to prevent abuse and malnutrition among children, crime, dropouts and pregnancy among teenagers and violence in the family; by aggressive child support enforcement; and by emphasizing family preservation and quality foster care. We further believe that our nation faces a crisis of under-investment in our children, particularly in the early years of life. Strong, healthy babies with early opportunities that foster intellectual, emotional and physical growth begin school with an enhanced foundation for learning. There are few better investments for this country than prenatal care, infant nutrition and preschool education, and there are few more successful programs than WIC, Head Start, and prenatal care. We know what works; yet these successful programs have been starved for funds. The Democratic Party pledges to meet this urgent need by providing the funding necessary to reach those unserved children who are—and must be—our national priority.

WE BELIEVE that America needs more trade, an Administration willing to use all the tools available to better manage our trade in order to export more American goods and fewer American jobs, an Administration willing to recognize in the formulation and enforcement of our trade laws that workers' rights are important human rights abroad as well as at home,

and that advance notice of plant closings and major layoffs is not only fundamentally right but also economically sound. We believe that we can and must improve our competitiveness in the world economy, using our best minds to create the most advanced technology in the world through a greater commitment to civilian research and development and to science, engineering and mathematics training, through more public–private and business–labor cooperation and mutual respect, through more intergovernmental partnerships, and through a better balance between fiscal and monetary policy and between military and civilian research and development. We further believe in halting such irresponsible corporate conduct as unproductive takeovers, monopolistic mergers, insider trading, and golden parachutes for executives by reinvigorating our anti-trust and securities laws, reviewing large mergers, and discouraging short-term speculation taking place at the expense of long-term investment.

WE BELIEVE that the education of our citizens, from Head Start to institutions of higher learning, deserves our highest priority; and that history will judge the next Administration less by its success in building new weapons of war than by its success in improving young minds. We now spend only two cents of every federal dollar for education. We pledge to better balance our national priorities by significantly increasing federal funding for education. We believe that this nation needs to invest in children on the front side of life by expanding the availability of pre-school education for children at risk; to invest in its teachers through training and enrichment programs, including a National Teacher Corps to recruit teachers for tomorrow, especially minorities, with scholarships today; to commit itself for the first time to the principle that no one should be denied the opportunity to attend college for financial reasons; to ensure equal access to education by providing incentives and mechanisms for the equalization of financing among local school districts within each state; to reverse cuts made in compensatory reading, math and enrichment services to low-income children; and to expand support for bilingual education, historically Black and Hispanic institutions, the education of those with special needs, the arts and humanities, and an aggressive campaign to end illiteracy.

WE BELIEVE that illegal drugs pose a direct threat to the security of our nation from coast to coast, invading our neighborhoods, classrooms, homes and communities large and small; that every arm and agency of government at every federal, state and local level—including every useful diplomatic, military, educational, medical and law enforcement effort necessary—should at long last be mobilized and coordinated with private efforts under the direction of a National Drug "Czar" to halt both the international supply and the domestic demand for illegal drugs now ravaging our country; and that the legalization of illicit drugs would represent a tragic surrender in a war we intend to win. We believe that this effort should include comprehensive programs to educate our children at the earliest ages on the dangers of alcohol and drug abuse, readily available treatment and counseling for those who seek to address their dependency, the strengthening of vital interdiction agencies such at the U.S. Coast Guard and Customs, a summit of Western hemispheric nations to coordinate efforts to cut off drugs at the source, and foreign development assistance to reform drug-based economies by promoting crop substitution.

WE BELIEVE that the federal government should provide increased assistance to local criminal justice agencies, enforce a ban on "cop killer" bullets that have no purpose other than the killing and maiming of law enforcement officers, reinforce our commitment to help crime victims, and assume a leadership role in securing the safety of our neighborhoods and homes. We further believe that the repeated toleration in Washington of unethical and unlawful greed among too many of those who have been governing our nation, procuring our weapons and polluting our environment has made far more difficult the daily work of the local policemen, teachers and parents who must convey to our children respect for justice and authority.

WE BELIEVE that we honor our multicultural heritage by assuring equal access to government services, employment, housing, business enterprise and education to every citizen regardless of race, sex, national origin, religion, age, handicapping condition or sexual orientation; that these rights are without exception too precious to be jeopardized by federal judges and Justice Department officials chosen during the past years—by a political party increasingly monolithic both racially and culturally—more for their unenlightened ideological views than for their respect for the rule of law. We further believe that we must work for the adoption of the Equal Rights Amendment to the Constitution; that the fundamental right of reproductive choice should be guaranteed regardless of ability to pay; that our machinery for civil rights enforcement and legal services to the poor should be rebuilt and vigorously utilized; and that our immigration policy should be reformed to promote fairness, nondiscrimination and family reunification and to reflect our constitutional freedoms of speech, association and travel.

We further believe that the voting rights of all minorities should be protected, the recent surge in hate violence and negative stereotyping combatted, the discriminatory English-only pressure groups resisted, our treaty commitments with Native Americans enforced by culturally sensitive officials, and the lingering effects of past discrimination eliminated by affirmative action, including goals, timetables, and procurement set-asides.

WE BELIEVE that the housing crisis of the 1980s must be halted—a crisis that has left this country battered by a rising tide of homelessness unprecedented since the Great Depression, by a tightening squeeze on low- and moderate-income families that is projected to leave seven million people without affordable housing by 1993, and by a bleak outlook for young working families who cannot afford to buy their homes. We believe that steps should be taken to ensure a decent place to live for every American. We believe that homelessness—a national shame—should be ended in America; that the supply of affordable housing should be expanded in order to avoid the projected shortfall; that employer-assisted housing and development by community based nonprofit organizations should be encouraged; that the inventory of public and subsidized housing should be renovated, preserved and increased; that foreclosed government property should be restored to productive use; and that first-time homebuyers should be assisted.

WE BELIEVE that we can rebuild America, creating good jobs at good wages through a national reinvestment strategy to construct new housing, repair our sewers, rebuild our roads and replace our bridges. We believe that we must pursue needed investment through innovative partnerships and creative financing mechanisms such as a voluntary program to invest a portion of public and private pension funds as a steady source of investment capital by guaranteeing security and a fair rate of return and assuring sound project management.

WE BELIEVE that all Americans should enjoy access to affordable, comprehensive health services for both the physically and mentally ill, from prenatal care for pregnant women at risk to more adequate care for our Vietnam and other veterans, from well-baby care to childhood immunization to Medicare; that a national health program providing federal coordination and leadership is necessary to restrain health care costs while assuring quality care and advanced medical research; that quality, affordable, long-term home and health care should be available to all senior and disabled citizens, allowing them to live with dignity in the most appropriate setting; that an important first step toward comprehensive health services is to ensure that every family should have the security of basic health insurance; and that the HIV/AIDS epidemic is an unprecedented public health emergency requiring increased support for accelerated research on, and expedited FDA approval of, treatments and vaccines, comprehensive education and prevention, compassionate patient care, adoption of the public health community consensus on voluntary and confidential testing and counseling, and protection of the civil rights of those suffering from AIDS-Related Complex or testing positive for the HIV antibody.

WE BELIEVE that the last seven years have witnessed an unprecedented assault on our national interest and national security through the poisoning of our air with acid rain, the dumping of toxic wastes into our water, and the destruction of our parks and shores; that pollution must be stopped at the source by shifting to new, environmentally sound manufacturing and farming technologies; that the federal government must promote recycling as the best, least costly way to solve the trash crisis, aggressively enforce toxic waste laws and require polluters to be responsible for future clean-up costs; that this nation must redouble its efforts to provide clean waterways, sound water management and safe drinkable ground water throughout the country; that our national parks, forests, wildlife refuges, and coastal zones must be protected and used only in an environmentally sound manner; that all offshore oil drilling in environmentally sensitive areas should be opposed; and that regular world environmental summits should be convened by the United States to address the depletion of the ozone layer, the "greenhouse effect," the destruction of tropical forests and other global threats and to create a global action plan for environmental restoration.

WE BELIEVE that all Americans, producers and consumers alike, benefit when food and fiber are produced not by a few large corporations and conglomerates but by hundreds of thousands of family farmers obtaining a fair price for their product; that the disastrous farm policies of the last seven years, despite record federal spending, have forced hundreds of thousands of families from their farms while others are struggling to survive; and that a workable agricultural policy should include supply management, reasonable price supports, soil conservation and protection of rural water quality, credit and foreclosure relief, the return of federally held foreclosed lands to minority beginning and restarting farmers, the development of new uses and markets of American farm products, improved disaster relief, and the revitalization of rural America through new sources of capital for rural business and new federal support for rural health care, housing, education, water supply and infrastructure. We further believe that no person should go to bed hungry and that we must renew the fight against hunger at home and abroad, make food available to those nations who need it and want it, and convene an international conference of food producing nations.

WE BELIEVE that a balanced, coherent energy policy, based on dependable supplies at reasonable prices, is necessary to protect our national security, ensure a clean environment, and promote stable economic growth and prosperity, both nationally and in our energy producing regions; that the inevitable transition from our present, nearly total dependence on increasingly scarce and environmentally damaging non-renewable sources to renewable sources should begin now; that such a policy includes increased cooperation with our hemispheric neighbors, filling the Strategic Petroleum Reserve, promoting the use of natural gas, methanol and ethanol as alternative transportation fuels, encouraging the use of our vast natural gas and coal reserves while aggressively developing clean coal technology to combat acid rain, and providing targeted new incentives for new oil and gas drilling and development, for the development of renewable and alternative sources of energy, and for the promotion of energy conservation. We believe that with these changes the country could reduce its reliance on nuclear power while insisting that all plants are safe, environmentally sound and assured of safe waste disposal.

WE BELIEVE that this country's democratic processes must be revitalized: by securing universal, same-day and mail-in voter registration as well as registration on the premises of appropriate government agencies; by preventing the misuse of at-large elections, the abuse of election day challenges and registration roll purges, any undercounting in the national census, and any dilution of the one-person, one-vote principle; by ending discrimination against public employees who are denied the right to full political participation; by supporting statehood for the District of Columbia; by treating the offshore territories under our flag equitably and sensitively under federal policies, assisting their economic and social development and respecting their right to decide their future in their relationship with the United States; by empowering the commonwealth of Puerto Rico with greater autonomy within its relationship with the United States to achieve the economic, social and political goals of its people, and by giving it just and fair participation in federal programs; by assuring and pledging the full and equal access of women and minorities to elective office and party endorsement; and by minimizing the domination and distortion of our elections by moneyed interests.

WE BELIEVE in a stronger America ready to make the tough choices of leadership in an ever dangerous world; militarily stronger in our overall defense and anti-terrorist capabilities and in the cohesion of our military alliances; economically stronger at home and in the global marketplace: intellectually stronger in the advances of our schools, science and technology; and spiritually stronger in the principles we exemplify to the world.

WE BELIEVE in a clear-headed, tough-minded, decisive American foreign policy that will reflect the changing nature of threats to our security and respond to them in a way that reflects our values and the support of our people, a foreign policy that will respect our Constitution, our Congress and our traditional democratic principles and will in turn be respected for its quiet strength, its bipartisan goals, and its steadfast attention to the concerns and contributions of our allies and international organizations. We believe that we must reassume a role of responsible active international leadership based upon our commitment to democracy, human rights and a more secure world; that this nation, as the world power with the broadest global interests and concerns, has a greater stake than any in building a world at peace and governed by law; that we can neither police the world nor retreat from it: and that to have reliable allies we must be a reliable ally.

WE BELIEVE that our national strength has been sapped by a defense establishment wasting money on duplicative and dubious new weapons instead of investing more in readiness and mobility; that our national strength will be enhanced by more stable defense budgets and by a commitment from our allies to assume a greater share of the costs and responsibilities required to maintain peace and liberty; and that as military spending and priorities change, government should encourage the conversion of affected military facilities and the retraining of workers to facilitate the creation of new forms of communication, space development and new peacetime growth and productivity.

WE BELIEVE in an America that will promote peace and prevent war—not by trading weapons for hostages, not by sending brave Americans to undefined missions in Lebanon and Honduras, not by relaxing our vigilance on the assumption that long-range Soviet interests have permanently changed, not by toasting a tyrant like Marcos as a disciple of democracy, but by maintaining a stable nuclear deterrent sufficient to counter any Soviet threat, by standing up to any American adversaries whenever necessary and sitting down with them whenever possible, by making clear our readiness to use force when force is required to protect our essential security commitments, by testing the intentions of the new Soviet leaders about arms control, emigration, human rights and other issues, and by matching them not merely in rhetoric but in reciprocal initiatives and innovation, which takes advantage of what may be the greatest opportunity of our lifetime to establish a new, mutually beneficial relationship with the Soviet Union, in which we engage in joint efforts to combat environmental threats, explore peaceful uses of space and eradicate disease and poverty in the developing world, and in a mutual effort transform the arms race that neither side can win into a contest for people's minds, a contest we know our side will win.

WE BELIEVE in following up the INF Treaty, a commendable first step, with mutual, verifiable and enforceable agreements that will make significant reductions in strategic weapons in a way that diminishes the risk of nuclear attack by either superpower; reduce conventional forces to lower and equivalent levels in Europe, requiring deeper cuts on the Warsaw Pact side; ban chemical and space weapons in their entirety; promptly initiate a mutual moratorium on missile flight testing and halt all nuclear weapons testing while strengthening our efforts to prevent the spread of these weapons to other nations before the nightmare of nuclear terrorism engulfs us all.

WE BELIEVE in an America that recognizes not only the realities of East–West relations but the challenges and opportunities of the developing world; that will support and strengthen international law and institutions, promote human and political rights and measure them by one yardstick, and work for economic growth and development. We believe that we must provide leadership, compassion and economic assistance to those nations stunted by overwhelming debt, deprivation and austerity, and that we must work to promote active agreements between developing and industrial countries, and the major public and commercial lenders to provide debt relief and sustain economic growth and democracy in Latin America, Asia, and the poorest continent, Africa, which deserves special attention. We further believe that we must enlist the trade surplus nations to join with us in supporting new aid initiatives to fuel growth in developing countries that, though economically depressed, are rich in human and natural potential.

WE BELIEVE this country should work harder to stop the supplies of arms, from both East and West, that fuel conflict in regions such as the Persian Gulf and Angola. Deeply disturbed that the current Administration has too long abandoned the peace process in the Middle East and consistently undermined it in Central America, we believe that this country, maintaining the special relationship with Israel founded upon mutually shared values and strategic interests, should provide new leadership to deliver the promise of peace and security through negotiations that has been held out to Israel and its neighbors by the Camp David Accords. We support the sovereignty, independence, and territorial integrity of Lebanon with a central government strong enough to unite its people, maintain order and live in peace in the region. We are committed to Persian Gulf security and freedom of navigation of international waters, and to an end to the Iran–Iraq war by promoting United Nations efforts to achieve a ceasefire and a negotiated settlement, through an arms embargo on the combatants. We further believe that the United States must fully support the Arias Peace Plan, which calls for an end to the fighting, national reconciliation, guarantees of justice, freedom, human rights and democracy, an end to support for irregular forces, and a commitment by the Central American governments to prevent the use of their territory to destabilize others in the region. Instead of the current emphasis on military solutions we will use negotiations and incentives to encourage free and fair elections and security for all nations in the region. We will cease dealing with drug smugglers and seek to reconcile our differences with countries in Central America, enabling the United States and other countries to focus on the pressing social and economic needs of the people of that region. We further believe in pursuing a policy of economic cooperation instead of confrontation with Mexico and our other hemispheric friends; in helping all developing countries build their own peaceful democratic institutions free from foreign troops, subversions and domination and free from domestic dictators and aggressors; in honoring our treaty obligations; and in using all the tools at our disposal including diplomacy, trade, aid, food, ideas, to defend and enlarge the horizons of freedom on this planet.

WE BELIEVE in an America that will promote human rights, human dignity and human opportunity in every country on earth; that will fight discrimination, encourage free speech and association and decry oppression in nations friendly and unfriendly, Communist and non-Communist, that will encourage our European friends to respect human rights and resolve their long-standing differences over Northern Ireland and Cyprus; that will encourage wherever possible the forces of pluralism and democracy in Eastern Europe and that will support the struggle for human rights in Asia.

WE BELIEVE the apartheid regime in South Africa to be a uniquely repressive regime, ruthlessly deciding every aspect of public and private life by skin color, engaging in unrelenting violence against its citizens at home and promoting naked aggression against its neighbors in Africa. We believe that the time has come to end all vestiges of the failed policy of constructive engagement, to declare South Africa a terrorist state, to impose comprehensive sanctions upon its economy, to lead the international community in participation in these actions, and to determine a date certain by which United States corporations must leave South Africa. We further believe that to achieve regional security in Southern Africa, we must press forcefully for Namibia's independence by calling for the end of South Africa's illegal occupation, a cease fire and elections, must end our counterproductive policy in Angola and must offer support and further assistance to Mozambique and other frontline states.

IN SUM, WE BELIEVE it is time for America to change and move forward again in the interest of all its families—to turn away from an era in which too many of America's children have been homeless or hungry and invest in a new era of hope and progress, an era of secure families in a secure America in a secure world.

WE BELIEVE the American dream of opportunity for every citizen can be a reality for all Americans willing to meet their own responsibilities to help make it come true. We believe that governments at the national, state and local level, in partnerships between those levels and in partnerships with the private sector, exist to help us solve our problems instead of adding to them. We believe in competent, pragmatic governments, accountable to the people, led by men and women dedicated not to self-interest but to service, motivated not by ideology but by American ideals, governing not in a spirit of power and privilege but with a sense of compassion and community. For many years, in state and local capitals across this nation, Democrats have been successfully solving problems and helping people with exactly this kind of innovative government.

THEREFORE, THE DEMOCRATIC PARTY in Convention assembled and united, the Party of hope and change and fairness for all, hereby declares its readiness to end the stalemate in Washington by challenging, encouraging and inviting the American people—challenging them to do their patriotic best to meet their community responsibilities, encouraging them to protect and preserve their families, our most precious assets, and inviting them to join with us in leading the land we love to a brighter and still greater future of opportunity and justice for all.

— 1992 —
PREAMBLE

Two hundred summers ago, this Democratic Party was founded by the man whose burning pen fired the spirit of the American Revolution—who once argued we should overthrow our own government every 20 years to renew our freedom and keep pace with a changing world. In 1992, the party Thomas Jefferson founded invokes his spirit of revolution anew.

Our land reverberates with a battle cry of frustration that emanates from America's very soul—from the families in our bedrock neighborhoods, from the unsung, workaday heroes of the world's greatest democracy and economy. America is on the wrong track. The American people are hurting. The American Dream of expanding opportunity has faded. Middle class families are working hard, playing by the rules, but still falling behind. Poverty has exploded. Our people are torn by divisions.

The last 12 years have been a nightmare of Republican irresponsibility and neglect. America's leadership is indifferent at home and uncertain in the world. Republican mismanagement has disarmed government as an instrument to make our economy work and support the people's most basic values, needs and hopes. The Republicans brought America a false and fragile prosperity based on borrowing, not income, and so will leave behind a mountain of public debt and a backbreaking annual burden in interest. It is wrong to borrow to spend on ourselves, leaving our children to pay our debts.

We hear the anguish and the anger of the American people. We know it is directed not just at the Republican administrations that have had power, but at government itself.

Their anger is justified. We can no longer afford business as usual—neither the policies of the last 12 years of tax breaks for the rich, mismanagement, lack of leadership and cuts in services for the middle class and the poor, nor the adoption of new programs and new spending without new thinking. It is time to listen to the grassroots of America, time to renew the spirit of citizen activism that has always been the touchstone of a free and democratic society.

Therefore we call for a *revolution in government*—to take power away from entrenched bureaucracies and narrow interests in Washington and put it back in the hands of ordinary people. We vow to make government more decentralized, more flexible, and more accountable—to reform public institutions and replace public officials who aren't leading with ones who will.

The Revolution of 1992 is about restoring America's economic greatness. We need to rebuild America by abandoning the something-for-nothing ethic of the last decade and putting people first for a change. Only a thriving economy, a strong manufacturing base, and growth in creative new enterprise can generate the resources to meet the nation's pressing human and social needs. An expanding, entrepreneurial economy of high-skill, high-wage jobs is the most important family policy, urban policy, labor policy, minority policy and foreign policy America can have.

The Revolution of 1992 is about putting government back on the side of working men and women—to help those who work hard, pay their bills, play by the rules, don't lobby for tax breaks, do their best to give their kids a good education and to keep them away from drugs, who want a safe neighborhood for their families, the security of decent, productive jobs for themselves, and a dignified life for their parents.

The Revolution of 1992 is about a radical change in the way government operates—not the Republican proposition that government has no role, nor the old notion that there's a program for every problem, but a shift to a more efficient, flexible and results-oriented government that improves services, expands choices, and empowers citizens and communities to change our country from the bottom up. We believe in an activist government, but it must work in a different, more responsive way.

The Revolution of 1992 is about facing up to tough choices. There is no relief for America's frustration in the politics of diversion and evasion, of false choices or of no choices at all. Instead of everyone in Washington blaming one another for inaction, we will act decisively—and ask to be held accountable if we don't.

Above all the Revolution of 1992 is about restoring the basic American values that built this country and will always make it great: personal responsibility, individual liberty, tolerance, faith, family and hard work. We offer the American people not only new ideas, a new course, and a new President, but a return to the enduring principles that set our nation apart: the promise of opportunity, the strength of community, the dignity of work, and a decent life for senior citizens.

To make this revolution, we seek a *New Covenant* to repair the damaged bond between the American people and their government, that will expand *opportunity*, insist upon greater individual *responsibility* in return, restore *community*, and ensure *national security* in a profoundly new era.

We welcome the close scrutiny of the American people, including Americans who may have thought the Democratic Party had forgotten its way, as well as all who know us as the champions of those who have been denied a chance. With this platform we take our case for change to the American people.

I. OPPORTUNITY

Our Party's first priority is opportunity—broad-based, non-inflationary economic growth and the opportunity that flows from it. Democrats in 1992 hold nothing more important for America than an economy that offers growth and jobs for all.

President Bush, with no interest in domestic policy, has given America the slowest economic growth, the slowest income growth, and the slowest jobs growth since the Great Depression. And the American people know the long Bush recession reflects not just a business cycle, but a long-term slide, so that even in a fragile recovery we're sinking. The ballooning Bush deficits hijacked capital from productive investments. Savings and loan sharks enriched themselves at their country's expense. The stock market tripled, but average incomes stalled, and poverty claimed more of our children.

We reject both the do-nothing government of the last twelve years and the big government theory that says we can hamstring business and tax and spend our way to prosperity. Instead we offer a third way. Just as we have always viewed working men and women as the bedrock of our economy, we honor business as a noble endeavor, and vow to create a far better climate for firms and independent contractors of all sizes that empower their workers, revolutionize their workplaces, respect the environment, and serve their communities well.

We believe in free enterprise and the power of market forces. But economic growth will not come without a national economic strategy to invest in people. For twelve years our country has had no economic vision, leadership or strategy. It is time to put our people and our country first.

Investing in America

The only way to lay the foundation for renewed American prosperity is to spur both public and private investment. We must strive to close both the budget deficit and the investment gap. Our major competitors invest far more than we do in roads, bridges, and the information networks and technologies of the future. We will rebuild America by investing more in transportation, environmental technologies, defense conversion, and a national information network.

To begin making our economy grow, the President

and Congress should agree that savings from defense must be reinvested productively at home, including research, education and training, and other productive investments. This will sharply increase the meager nine percent of the national budget now devoted to the future. We will create a "future budget" for investments that make us richer, to be kept separate from those parts of the budget that pay for the past and present. For the private sector, instead of a sweeping capital gains windfall to the wealthy and those who speculate, we will create an investment tax credit and a capital gains reduction for patient investors in emerging technologies and new businesses.

Support for Innovation

We will take back the advantage now ceded to Japan and Germany, which invest in new technologies at higher rates than the U.S. and have the growth to show for it. We will make the R&D tax credit permanent, double basic research in the key technologies for our future, and create a civilian research agency to fast-forward their development.

The Deficit

Addressing the deficit requires fair and shared sacrifice of all Americans for the common good. In 12 Republican years a national debt that took 200 years to accumulate has been *quadrupled*. Rising interest on that debt now swallows one tax dollar in seven. In place of the Republican supply-side disaster, the Democratic investment, economic conversion and growth strategy will generate more revenues from a growing economy. We must also tackle spending, by putting everything on the table; eliminate non-productive programs; achieve defense savings; reform entitlement programs to control soaring health care costs; cut federal administrative costs by 3 percent annually for four years; limit increases in the "present budget" to the rate of growth in the average American's paycheck; apply a strict "pay as you go" rule to new non-investment spending; and make the rich pay their fair share in taxes. These choices will be made while protecting senior citizens and without further victimizing the poor. This deficit reduction effort will encourage private savings, eliminate the budget deficit over time, and permit fiscal policies that can restore America's economic health.

Defense Conversion

Our economy needs both the people and the funds released from defense at the Cold War's end. We will help the stalwarts of that struggle—the men and women who served in our armed forces and who work in our defense industries—make the most of a new era. We will provide early notice of program changes to give communities, businesses and workers enough time to plan. We will honor and support our veterans. Departing military personnel, defense workers, and defense support personnel will have access to job retraining, continuing education, placement and relocation assistance, early retirement benefits for military personnel, and incentives to enter teaching, law enforcement and other vital civilian fields. Redirected national laboratories and a new civilian research agency will put defense scientists, engineers and technicians to work in critical civilian technologies. Small business defense firms will have technical assistance and transition grants and loans to help convert to civilian markets, and defense dependent communities will have similar aid in planning and implementing conversion. We will strongly support our civilian space program, particularly environmental missions.

The Cities

Only a robust economy will revitalize our cities. It is in all Americans' interest that the cities once again be places where hard-working families can put down roots and find good jobs, quality health care, affordable housing, and decent schools. Democrats will create a new partnership to rebuild America's cities after 12 years of Republican neglect. This partnership with the mayors will include consideration of the seven economic growth initiatives set forth by our nation's mayors. We will create jobs by investing significant resources to put people back to work, beginning with a summer jobs initiative and training programs for inner city youth. We support a stronger community development program and targeted fiscal assistance to cities that need it most. A national public works investment and infrastructure program will provide jobs and strengthen our cities, suburbs, rural communities and country. We will encourage the flow of investment to inner city development and housing through targeted enterprise zones and incentives for private and public pension funds to invest in urban and rural projects. While cracking down on redlining and housing discrimination, we also support and will enforce a revitalized Community Reinvestment Act that challenges banks to lend to entrepreneurs and development projects; a national network of Community Development Banks to invest in urban and rural small businesses; and microenterprise lending for poor people seeking self-employment as an alternative to welfare.

Agriculture and the Rural Community

All Americans, producers and consumers alike, benefit when our food and fiber are produced by hundreds of thousands of family farmers receiving fair prices for their products. The abundance of our nation's food and fiber system should not be taken for granted. The revolution that lifted America to the forefront of world agriculture was achieved through a unique partnership of public and private interests. The inattention and hostility that has characterized Republican food, agricultural and rural development policies of the past twelve years have caused a crisis in rural America. The cost of Republican farm policy has been staggering and its total failure is demonstrated by the record number of rural bankruptcies.

A sufficient and sustainable agriculture economy can be achieved through fiscally responsible programs. It is time to reestablish the private/public partnership to ensure that family farmers get a fair return for their labor and investment, so that consumers receive safe and nutritious foods, and that needed investments are made in basic research, education, rural business development, market development and infrastructure to sustain rural communities.

Workers' Rights

Our workplaces must be revolutionized to make them more flexible and productive. We will reform the job safety laws to empower workers with greater rights and to hold employers accountable for dangers on the job. We will act against sexual harassment in the workplace. We will honor the work ethic—by expanding the earned income tax credit so no one with children at home who works full-time is still in poverty; by fighting on the side of family farmers to ensure they get a fair price for their hard work; by working to sustain rural communities; by making work more valuable than welfare; and by supporting the right of workers to organize actively without fear of intimidation or permanent replacement during labor disputes.

Lifelong Learning

A competitive American economy requires the global market's best-educated, best-trained, most flexible workforce. It's not enough to spend more on our schools; we must insist on results. We oppose the Bush Administration's efforts to bankrupt the public school system—the bedrock of democracy—through private school vouchers. To help children reach school ready to learn, we will expand child health and nutrition programs and extend Head Start to all eligible children, and guarantee all children access to quality, affordable child care. We deplore the savage inequalities among public schools across the land, and believe every child deserves an equal chance to get a world-class education. Reallocating resources toward this goal must be a priority. We support education reforms such as site-based decision-making and public school choice, with strong protections against discrimination. We support the goal of a 90 percent graduation rate, and programs to end dropouts. We will invest in educational technology, and establish world-class standards in math, science and other core subjects and support effective tests of progress to meet them. In areas where there are no registered apprenticeship programs, we will adopt a national apprenticeship-style program to ease the transition from school to work for non–college bound students so they can acquire skills that lead to high-wage jobs. In the new economy, opportunity will depend on lifelong learning. We will support the goal of literacy for all Americans. We will ask firms to invest in the training of all workers, not just corporate management.

A Domestic GI Bill

Over the past twelve years skyrocketing costs and declining middle class incomes have placed higher education out of reach for millions of Americans. It is time to revolutionize the way student loan programs are run. We will make college affordable to *all* students who are qualified to attend, *regardless of family income*. A Domestic GI Bill will enable all Americans to borrow money for college, so long as they are willing to pay it back as a percentage of their income over time or through national service addressing unmet community needs.

Affordable Health Care

All Americans should have universal access to quality, affordable health care—not as a privilege, but as a right. That requires tough controls on health costs, which are rising at two to three times the rate of inflation, terrorizing American families and businesses and depriving millions of the care they need. We will enact a uniquely American reform of the health care system to control costs and make health care affordable; ensure quality and choice of health care providers; cover all Americans regardless of preexisting conditions; squeeze out waste, bureaucracy and abuse; improve primary and preventive care including child immunization and prevention of diseases like tuberculosis now becoming rampant in our cities; provide expanded education on the relationship between diet

and health; expand access to mental health treatment services; provide a safety net through support of public hospitals; provide for the full range of reproductive choice—education, counseling, access to contraceptives, and the right to a safe, legal abortion; expand medical research; and provide more long-term care, including home health care. We will make ending the epidemic in breast cancer a major priority, and expand research on breast, cervical and ovarian cancer, infertility, reproductive health services and other special health needs of women. We must be united in declaring war on AIDS and HIV disease, implement the recommendations of the National Commission on AIDS and fully fund the Ryan White Care Act; provide targeted and honest prevention campaigns; combat HIV-related discrimination; make drug treatment available for all addicts who seek it; guarantee access to quality care; expand clinical trials for treatments and vaccines; and speed up the FDA drug approval process.

Fairness

Growth and equity work in tandem. People should share in society's common costs according to their ability to pay. In the last decade, mounting payroll and other taxes have fallen disproportionately on the middle class. We will relieve the tax burden on middle class Americans by forcing the rich to pay their fair share. We will provide long-overdue tax relief to families with children. To broaden opportunity, we will support fair lending practices.

Energy Efficiency and Sustainable Development

We reject the Republican myth that energy efficiency and environmental protection are enemies of economic growth. We will make our economy more efficient, by using less energy, reducing our dependence on foreign oil, and producing less solid and toxic waste. We will adopt a coordinated transportation policy, with a strong commitment to mass transit; encourage efficient alternative-fueled vehicles; increase our reliance on clean natural gas; promote clean coal technology; invest in R&D on renewable energy sources; strengthen efforts to prevent air and water pollution; support incentives for domestic oil and gas operations; and push for revenue-neutral incentives that reward conservation, prevent pollution and encourage recycling.

Civil and Equal Rights

We don't have an American to waste. Democrats will continue to lead the fight to ensure that no American suffer discrimination or deprivation of rights on the basis of race, gender, language, national origin, religion, age, disability, sexual orientation, or other characteristics irrelevant to ability. We support the ratification of the Equal Rights Amendment; affirmative action; stronger protection of voting rights for racial and ethnic minorities, including language access to voting; and continued resistance to discriminatory English-only pressure groups. We will reverse the Bush Administration's assault on civil rights enforcement, and instead work to rebuild and vigorously use machinery for civil rights enforcement; support comparable remedies for women; aggressively prosecute hate crimes; strengthen legal services for the poor; deal with other nations in such a way that Americans of any origin do not become scapegoats or victims of foreign policy disputes; provide civil rights protection for gay men and lesbians and an end to Defense Department discrimination; respect Native American culture and our treaty commitments; require the United States Government to recognize its trustee obligations to the inhabitants of Hawaii generally, and to Native Hawaiians in particular; and fully enforce the Americans with Disabilities Act to enable people with disabilities to achieve independence and function at their highest possible level.

Commonwealths and Territories

We recognize the existing status of the Commonwealth of Puerto Rico and the strong economic relationship between the people of Puerto Rico and the United States. We pledge to support the right of the people of the Commonwealth of Puerto Rico to choose freely, and in concert with the U.S. Congress, their relationship with the United States, either as an enhanced commonwealth, a state or an independent nation. We support fair participation for Puerto Rico in federal programs.

We pledge to the people of American Samoa, Guam, the Northern Mariana Islands, and the Virgin Islands just and fair treatment under federal policies, assisting their economic and social development. We respect their right and that of the people of Palau to decide freely their future relationship with the U.S. and to be consulted on issues and policies that directly affect them.

II. RESPONSIBILITY

Sixty years ago, Franklin Roosevelt gave hope to a nation mired in the Great Depression. While government should promise every American the opportunity to get ahead, it was the people's responsibility, he said, to make the most of that opportunity: "Faith in America demands that we recognize the new terms of the old social contract. In the strength of great hope we must all shoulder our common load."

For twelve years, the Republicans have expected too little of our public institutions and placed too little faith in our people. We offer a new social contract based neither on callous, do-nothing Republican neglect, nor on an outdated faith in programs as the solution to every problem. We favor a third way beyond the old approaches—to put government back on the side of citizens who play by the rules. We believe that by what it says and how it conducts its business, government must once again make responsibility an instrument of national purpose. Our future as a nation depends upon the daily assumption of personal responsibility by millions of Americans from all walks of life—for the religious faiths they follow, the ethics they practice, the values they instill, and the pride they take in their work.

Strengthening the Family

Governments don't raise children, people do. People who bring children into this world have a responsibility to care for them and give them values, motivation and discipline. Children should not have children. We need a national crackdown on deadbeat parents, an effective system of child support enforcement nationwide, and a systematic effort to establish paternity for every child. We must also make it easier for parents to build strong families through pay equity. Family and medical leave will ensure that workers don't have to choose between family and work. We support a family preservation program to reduce child and spousal abuse by providing preventive services and foster care to families in crisis. We favor ensuring quality and affordable child care opportunities for working parents, and a fair and healthy start for every child, including essential pre-natal and well baby care. We support the needs of our senior citizens for productive and healthy lives, including hunger prevention, income adequacy, transportation access and abuse prevention.

Welfare Reform

Welfare should be a second chance, not a way of life. We want to break the cycle of welfare by adhering to two simple principles: no one who is able to work can stay on welfare forever, and no one who works should live in poverty. We will continue to help those who cannot help themselves. We will offer people on welfare a new social contract. We'll invest in education and job training, and provide the child care and health care they need to go to work and achieve long-term self-sufficiency. We will give them the help they need to make the transition from welfare to work, and require people who can work to go to work within two years in available jobs either in the private sector or in community service to meet unmet needs. This will restore the covenant that welfare was meant to be a promise of temporary help for people who have fallen on hard times.

Choice

Democrats stand behind the right of every woman to choose, consistent with *Roe* v. *Wade*, regardless of ability to pay, and support a national law to protect that right. It is a fundamental constitutional liberty that individual Americans—not government—can best take responsibility for making the most difficult and intensely personal decisions regarding reproduction. The goal of our nation must be to make abortion less necessary, not more difficult or more dangerous. We pledge to support contraceptive research, family planning, comprehensive family life education, and policies that support healthy childbearing and enable parents to care most effectively for their children.

Making Schools Work

Education is a cooperative enterprise that can only succeed if everyone accepts and exercises personal responsibility. Students must stay in school and do their best; parents must get involved in their children's education; teachers must attain, maintain, and demonstrate classroom competency; school administrators must enforce discipline and high standards of educational attainment; governments must end the inequalities that create educational ghettos among school districts and provide equal educational opportunity for all; and ensure that teachers' pay measures up to their decisive role in children's lives; and the American people should recognize education as the core of our economy, democracy and society.

Labor–Management Responsibilities

The private sector is the engine of our economy and the main source of national wealth. But it is not enough for those in the private sector just to make as much money as they can. The most irresponsible people in all the 1980s were those at the top of the ladder: the inside traders, quick buck artists, and S&L kingpins who looked out for themselves and not for the country. America's corporate leaders have a responsi-

bility to invest in their country. CEOs, who pay themselves 100 times what they pay the average worker, shouldn't get big raises unrelated to performance. If a company wants to overpay its executives and underinvest in the future or transfer jobs to foreign countries, it shouldn't get special treatment and tax breaks from the Treasury. Managers must work with employees to make the workplace safer, more satisfying and more efficient.

Workers must also accept added responsibilities in the new economy. In return for an increased voice and a greater stake in the success of their enterprises, workers should be prepared to join in cooperative efforts to increase productivity, flexibility and quality. Government's neutrality between labor and management cannot mean neutrality about the collective bargaining process, which has been purposely crippled by Republican administrations. Our economic growth depends on processes, including collective bargaining, that permit labor and management to work together on their common interests, even as they work out their conflicts.

Responsibility for the Environment

For ourselves and future generations, we must protect our environment. We will protect our old-growth forests, preserve critical habitats, provide a genuine "no net loss" policy on wetlands, reduce our dependence on toxic chemicals, conserve the critical areas, and address ocean pollution by reducing oil and toxic waste spills at sea. We believe America's youth can serve its country well through a civilian conservation corps. To protect the public health, we will clean up the environmental horrors of federal facilities, insist that private polluters clean up their toxic and hazardous wastes, and vigorously prosecute environmental criminals. We will oppose Republican efforts to gut the Clean Air Act in the guise of competitiveness. We will reduce the volume of solid waste and encourage the use of recycled materials while discouraging excess packaging. To avoid the mistakes of the past, we will actively support energy efficiency, recycling, and pollution prevention strategies.

Responsible Government

Democrats in 1992 intend to lead a revolution in government, challenging it to act responsibly and be accountable, starting with the hardest and must urgent problems of the deficit and economic growth. Rather than throw money at obsolete programs, we will eliminate unnecessary layers of management, cut administrative costs, give people more choices in the service they get, and empower them to make those choices. To foster greater responsibility in government at every level, we support giving greater flexibility to our cities, counties and states in achieving federal mandates and carrying out existing programs.

Responsible Officials

All branches of government must live by the laws the rest of us obey, determine their pay in an open manner that builds public trust, and eliminate special privileges. People in public office need to be accessible to the people they represent. It's time to reform the campaign finance system, to get big money out of our politics and let the people back in. We must limit overall campaign spending and limit the disproportionate and excessive role of PACs. We need new voter registration laws that expand the electorate, such as universal same-day registration, along with full political rights and protections for public employees and new regulations to ensure that the airwaves truly help citizens make informed choices among candidates and policies. And we need fair political representation for all sectors of our country—including the District of Columbia, which deserves and must get statehood status.

III. RESTORING COMMUNITY

The success of democracy in America depends substantially on the strength of our community institutions: families and neighborhoods, public schools, religious institutions, charitable organizations, civic groups and other voluntary associations. In these social networks, the values and character of our citizens are formed, as we learn the habits and skills of self-government, and acquire an understanding of our common rights and responsibilities as citizens.

Twelve years of Republican rule have undermined the spirit of mutual dependence and obligation that binds us together. Republican leaders have urged Americans to turn inward, to pursue private interests without regard to public responsibilities. By playing racial, ethnic and gender-based politics they have divided us against each other, created an atmosphere of blame, denial and fear, and undone the hard-fought battles for equality and fairness.

Our communities form a vital "third sector" that lies between government and the marketplace. The wisdom, energy and resources required to solve our problems are not concentrated in Washington, but can be found throughout our communities, including America's non-profit sector, which has grown rapidly over the last decade. Government's best role is to enable people and communities to solve their own problems.

America's special genius has been to forge a community of shared values from people of remarkable and diverse backgrounds. As the party of inclusion, we take special pride in our country's emergence as the world's largest and most successful multiethnic, multiracial republic. We condemn antisemitism, racism, homophobia, bigotry and negative stereotyping of all kinds. We must help all Americans understand the diversity of our cultural heritage. But it is also essential that we preserve and pass on to our children the common elements that hold this mosaic together as we work to make our country a land of freedom and opportunity for all.

Both Republican neglect and traditional spending programs have proven unequal to these challenges. Democrats will pursue a new course that stresses work, family and individual responsibility, and that empowers Americans to liberate themselves from poverty and dependence. We pledge to bolster the institutions of civil society and place a new emphasis on civic enterprises that seek solutions to our nation's problems. Through common, cooperative efforts we can rebuild our communities and transform our nation.

Combatting Crime and Drugs

Crime is a relentless danger to our communities. Over the last decade, crime has swept through our country at an alarming rate. During the 1980s, more than 200,000 Americans were murdered, four times the number who died in Vietnam. Violent crimes rose by more than 16 percent since 1988 and nearly doubled since 1975. In our country today, a murder is committed every 25 minutes, a rape every six minutes, a burglary every 10 seconds. The pervasive fear of crime disfigures our public life and diminishes our freedom.

None suffer more than the poor: an explosive mixture of blighted prospects, drugs and exotic weaponry has turned many of our inner city communities into combat zones. As a result, crime is not only a symptom but also a major cause of the worsening poverty and demoralization that afflicts inner city communities.

To empower America's communities, Democrats pledge to restore government as the upholder of basic law and order for crime-ravaged communities. The simplest and most direct way to restore order in our cities is to put more police on the streets. America's police are locked in an unequal struggle with crime: since 1951 the ratio of police officers to reported crimes has reversed, from three-to-one to one-to-three. We will create a Police Corps, in which participants would receive college aid in return for several years of service after graduation in a state or local police department. As we shift people and resources from defense to the civilian economy, we will create new jobs in law enforcement for those leaving the military.

We will expand drug counselling and treatment for those who need it, intensify efforts to educate our children at the earliest ages to the dangers of drug and alcohol abuse, and curb demand from the street corner to the penthouse suite, so that the U.S., with five percent of the world's population, no longer consumes 50 percent of the world's illegal drugs.

Community Policing

Neighborhoods and police should be partners in the war on crime. Democrats support more community policing, which uses foot patrols and storefront offices to make police officers visible fixtures in urban neighborhoods. We will combat street violence and emphasize building trust and solving the problems that breed crime.

Firearms

It is time to shut down the weapons bazaars. We support a reasonable waiting period to permit background checks for purchases of handguns, as well as assault weapons controls to ban the possession, sale, importation and manufacture of the most deadly assault weapons. We do not support efforts to restrict weapons used for legitimate hunting and sporting purposes. We will work for swift and certain punishment of all people who violate the country's gun laws and for stronger sentences for criminals who use guns. We will also seek to shut down the black market for guns and impose severe penalties on people who sell guns to children.

Pursuing ALL Crime Aggressively

In contrast to the Republican policy of leniency toward white collar crime—which breeds cynicism in poor communities about the impartiality of our justice system—Democrats will redouble efforts to ferret out and punish those who betray the public trust, rig financial markets, misuse their depositors' money or swindle their customers.

Further Initiatives

Democrats also favor innovative sentencing and punishment options, including community service and boot camps for first-time offenders; tougher penalties for rapists; victim-impact statements and restitution to ensure that crime victims will not be lost in the complexities of the criminal justice system; and initiatives to make our schools safe, including alternative schools for disruptive children.

Empowering the Poor and Expanding the Middle Class

We must further the new direction set in the Family Support Act of 1988, away from subsistence and dependence and toward work, family and personal initiative and responsibility. We advocate slower phasing out of Medicaid and other benefits to encourage work; special savings accounts to help low-income families build assets; fair lending; an indexed minimum wage; an expanded Job Corps; and an end to welfare rules that encourage family breakup and penalize individual initiative, such as the $1,000 limit on personal savings.

Immigration

Our nation of immigrants has been invigorated repeatedly as new people, ideas and ways of life have become part of the American tapestry. Democrats support immigration policies that promote fairness, nondiscrimination and family reunification, and that reflect our constitutional freedoms of speech, association and travel.

Housing

Safe, secure housing is essential to the institutions of community and family. We support homeownership for working families and will honor that commitment through policies that encourage affordable mortgage credit. We must also confront homelessness by renovating, preserving and expanding the stock of affordable low-income housing. We support tenant management and ownership, so public housing residents can manage their own affairs and acquire property worth protecting. Operating assistance would be continued for as long as necessary.

National Service

We will create new opportunities for citizens to serve each other, their communities and their country. By mobilizing hundreds of thousands of volunteers, national service will enhance the role of ordinary citizens in solving unresolved community problems.

The Arts

We believe in public support for the arts, including a National Endowment for the Arts that is free from political manipulation and firmly rooted in the First Amendment's freedom of expression guarantee.

IV. PRESERVING
OUR NATIONAL SECURITY

During the past four years, we have seen the corrosive effect of foreign policies that are rooted in the past, divorced from our values, fearful of change and unable to meet its challenges. Under President Bush, crises have been managed, rather than prevented; dictators like Saddam Hussein have been wooed, rather than deterred; aggression by the Serbian regime against its neighbors in what was Yugoslavia has been met by American timidity rather than toughness; human rights abusers have been rewarded, not challenged; the environment has been neglected, not protected; and America's competitive edge in the global economy has been dulled, not honed. It is time for new American leadership that can meet the challenges of a changing world.

At the end of World War II, American strength had defeated tyranny and American ingenuity had overcome the Depression. Under President Truman, the United States led the world into a new era, redefining global security with bold approaches to tough challenges: containing communism with the NATO alliance and in Korea; building the peace through organizations such as the United Nations; and advancing global economic security through new multilateral institutions.

Nearly a half century later, we stand at another pivotal point in history. The collapse of communism does not mean the end of danger or threats to our interests. But it does pose an unprecedented opportunity to make our future more secure and prosperous. Once again, we must define a compelling vision for global leadership at the dawn of a new era.

Restructuring Our Military Forces

We have not seen the end of violence, aggression and the conflicts that can threaten American interests and our hopes for a more peaceful world. What the United States needs is not the Bush Administration's Cold War thinking on a smaller scale, but a comprehensive restructuring of the American military enterprise to meet the threats that remain.

Military Strength

America is the world's strongest military power and we must remain so. A post–Cold War restructuring of American forces will produce substantial savings beyond those promised by the Bush Administration, but that restructuring must be achieved without undermining our ability to meet future threats to our security. A military structure for the 1990s and beyond must be built on four pillars: *First*, a survivable nuclear force to deter any conceivable threat, as we reduce our nuclear arsenals through arms control negotiations and other reciprocal action. *Second*, conventional forces shifted toward projecting power wherever our vital national interests are threatened. This means reducing the size of our forces in Europe, while meeting our obligations to NATO, and strengthening our rapid deployment capabilities to deal with new threats to our security posed by renegade dictators, terrorists, international drug traffickers, and the local armed conflicts that can threaten the peace of entire regions. *Third*, maintenance of the two qualities that make America's military the best in the world—the superiority of our military personnel and of our technology. These qualities are vital to shortening any conflict and saving American lives. *Fourth*, intelligence capabilities redirected to develop far more sophisticated, timely and accurate analyses of the economic and political conditions that can fuel new conflicts.

Use of Force

The United States must be prepared to use military force decisively when necessary to defend our vital interests. The burdens of collective security in a new era must be shared fairly, and we should encourage multilateral peacekeeping through the United Nations and other international efforts.

Preventing and Containing Conflict

American policy must be focused on averting military threats as well as meeting them. To halt the spread of nuclear and other weapons of mass destruction, we must lead a renewed international effort to get tough with companies that peddle nuclear and chemical warfare technologies, strengthen the International Atomic Energy Agency, and enforce strong sanctions against governments that violate international restraints. A Comprehensive Test Ban would strengthen our ability to stop the spread of nuclear weapons to other countries, which may be our greatest future security threat. We must press for strong international limits on the dangerous and wasteful flow of conventional arms to troubled regions. A U.S. troop presence should be maintained in South Korea as long as North Korea presents a threat to South Korea.

Restoring America's Economic Leadership

The United States cannot be strong abroad if it is weak at home. Restoring America's global economic leadership must become a central element of our national security policies. The strength of nations, once defined in military terms, now is measured also by the skills of their workers, the imagination of their managers and the power of their technologies.

Either we develop and pursue a national plan for restoring our economy through a partnership of government, labor and business, or we slip behind the nations that are competing with us and growing. At stake are American jobs, our standard of living and the quality of life for ourselves and our children.

Economic strength—indeed our national security—is grounded on a healthy domestic economy. But we cannot be strong at home unless we are part of a vibrant and expanding global economy that recognizes human rights and seeks to improve the living standards of all the world's people. This is vital to achieving good-quality, high paying jobs for Americans.

Trade

Our government must work to expand trade, while insisting that the conduct of world trade is fair. It must fight to uphold American interests—promoting exports, expanding trade in agricultural and other products, opening markets in major product and service sectors with our principal competitors, and achieving reciprocal access. This should include renewed authority to use America's trading leverage against the most serious problems. The U.S. government also must firmly enforce U.S. laws against unfair trade.

Trade Agreements

Multilateral trade agreements can advance our economic interests by expanding the global economy. Whether negotiating the North American Free Trade Agreement (NAFTA) or completing the GATT negotiations, our government must assure that our legitimate concerns about environmental, health and safety, and labor standards are included. Those American workers whose jobs are affected must have the benefit of effective adjustment assistance.

Promoting Democracy

Brave men and women—like the hero who stood in front of a tank in Beijing and the leader who stood on a tank in Moscow—are putting their lives on the line for democracy around the world. But as the tide of democracy rose in the former Soviet Union and in China, in the Baltics and South Africa, only reluctantly did this Administration abandon the status quo and embrace the fight for freedom.

Support for democracy serves our ideals and our interests. A more democratic world is a world that is more peaceful and more stable. An American foreign policy of engagement for democracy must effectively address:

Emerging Democracies

Helping to lead an international effort to assist the emerging—and still fragile—democracies in Eastern Europe and the former Soviet Union build democratic institutions in free market settings, demilitarize their societies and integrate their economies into the world trading system. Unlike the Bush Administration, which waited too long to recognize the new democratic governments in the Baltic countries and the nations of the former Soviet Union, we must act decisively with our European allies to support freedom, diminish ethnic tensions, and oppose aggression in the former communist countries, such as Bosnia-Herzegovina, which are struggling to make the transition from communism to democracy. As change sweeps through the Balkans, the United States must be sensitive to the concerns of Greece regarding the use of the name Macedonia. And in the post–Cold War era, our foreign assistance programs in Africa, the Caribbean, Latin America and elsewhere should be targeted at helping democracies rather than tyrants.

Democracy Corps

Promoting democratic institutions by creating a Democracy Corps to send American volunteers to countries that seek legal, financial and political expertise to build democratic institutions, and support groups like the National Endowment for Democracy, the Asia Foundation, and others.

China Trade Terms

Conditioning of favorable trade terms for China on respect for human rights in China and Tibet, greater market access for U.S. goods, and responsible conduct on weapons proliferation.

South Africa

We call for maintenance of state and local sanctions against South Africa, support of an investment code of conduct, and diplomatic pressure until there is an irreversible, full and fair accommodation with the black majority to create a democratic government with full rights for all its citizens. We deplore the continuing violence, especially in Boipatong Township, and are concerned about the collapse of the negotiations. The U.S. Government should consider reimposing federal sanctions. The Democratic Party supports the creation of a South African/American Enterprise Fund that will provide a new interim government with public and private funds to assist in the development of democracy in South Africa.

Middle East Peace

Support for the peace process now under way in the Middle East, rooted in the tradition of the Camp David Accords. Direct negotiations between Israel, her Arab neighbors and Palestinians, with no imposed solutions, are the only way to achieve enduring security for Israel and full peace for all parties in the region. The end of the Cold War does not alter America's deep interest in our longstanding special relationship with Israel, based on shared values, a mutual commitment to democracy, and a strategic alliance that benefits both nations. The United States must act effectively as an honest broker in the peace process. It must not, as has been the case with this Administration, encourage one side to believe that it will deliver unilateral concessions from the other. Jerusalem is the capital of the state of Israel and should remain an undivided city accessible to people of all faiths.

Human Rights

Standing everywhere for the rights of individuals and respect for ethnic minorities against the repressive acts of governments—against torture, political imprisonment, and all attacks on civilized standards of human freedom. This is a proud tradition of the Democratic Party, which has stood for freedom in South Africa and continues to resist oppression in Cuba. Our nation should once again promote the principle of sanctuary for politically oppressed people everywhere, be they Haitian refugees, Soviet Jews seeking U.S. help in their successful absorption into Israeli society, or Vietnamese fleeing communism. Forcible return of anyone fleeing political repression is a betrayal of American values.

Human Needs

Support for the struggle against poverty and disease in the developing world, including the heartbreaking famine in Africa. We must not replace the East–West conflict with one between North and South, a growing divide between the industrialized and developing world. Our development programs must be reexamined and restructured to assure that their benefits truly help those most in need to help themselves. At stake are the lives of millions of human beings who live in hunger, uprooted from their homes, too often without hope. The United States should work to establish a specific plan and timetable for the elimination of world hunger.

Cyprus

A renewed commitment to achieve a Cyprus settlement pursuant to the United Nations resolutions. This goal must now be restored to the diplomatic agenda of the United States.

Northern Ireland

In light of America's historic ties to the people of Great Britain and Ireland, and consistent with our country's commitment to peace, democracy and human rights around the world, a more active United States role in promoting peace and political dialogue to bring an end to the violence and achieve a negotiated solution in Northern Ireland.

Preserving the Global Environment

As the threat of nuclear holocaust recedes, the future of the earth is challenged by gathering environmental crises. As governments around the world have sought the path to concerted action, the Bush Administration—despite its alleged foreign policy expertise—has been more of an obstacle to progress than a leader for change, practicing isolationism on an issue that affects us all. Democrats know we must act now to save the health of the earth, and the health of our children, for generations to come.

Addressing Global Warming

The United States must become a leader, not an impediment, in the fight against global warming. We should join our European allies in agreeing to limit carbon dioxide emissions to 1990 levels by the year 2000.

Ozone Depletion

The United States must be a world leader in finding replacements for CFCs and other ozone depleting substances.

Biodiversity

We must work actively to protect the planet's biodiversity and preserve its forests. At the Rio Earth Summit, the Bush Administration's failure to negotiate a biodiversity treaty it could sign was an abdication of international leadership.

Developing Nations

We must fashion imaginative ways of engaging governments and business in the effort to encourage developing nations to preserve their environmental heritage.

Population Growth

Explosive population growth must be controlled by working closely with other industrialized and developing nations and private organizations to fund greater family planning efforts.

As a nation and as a people, we have entered into a new era. The Republican President and his advisors are rooted in Cold War precepts and cannot think or act anew. Through almost a half century of sacrifice, constancy and strength, the American people advanced democracy's triumph in the Cold War. Only new leadership that restores our nation's greatness at home can successfully draw upon these same strengths of the American people to lead the world into a new era of peace and freedom.

In recent years we have seen brave people abroad face down tanks, defy coups, and risk exodus by boat on the high seas for a chance at freedom and the kind of opportunities we call the American Dream. It is time for Americans to fight against the decline of those same opportunities here at home.

Americans know that, in the end, we will all rise or fall together. To make our society one again, Democrats will restore America's founding values of family, community and common purpose.

We believe in the American people. We will challenge all Americans to give something back to their country. And they will be enriched in return, for when individuals assume responsibility, they acquire dignity. When people go to work, they rediscover a pride that was lost. When absent parents pay child support, they restore a connection they and their children need. When students work harder, they discover they can learn as well as any on earth. When corporate managers put their workers and long-term success ahead of short-term gain, their companies do well and so do they. When the leaders we elect assume responsibility for America's problems, we will do what is right to move America forward together. This is our new covenant with the American people.

ELECTIONS

— 1828 —

Andrew Jackson won the 1828 contest against John Quincy Adams in a landslide election in which Jackson took 178 electoral votes to Adams's 83. Jackson won the South, the Midwest, and the mid-Atlantic states, while Adams's strength was in New England. In terms of popular vote, Jackson secured more than 640,000 votes, or roughly 56%, while Adams gained over 500,000 votes, or 44%. Jackson was helped by the new voting rules that expanded the suffrage to many who previously had not qualified. In addition, he had a strong organization and campaign manager in Martin Van Buren of New York. Van Buren's group raised approximately $1 million and successfully used the press and post to solidify Jackson's organization.

In the election, Jackson criticized the Adams administration's policies of public works and energetic government. In addition, Jackson reminded voters that he had received a plurality of both the popular and electoral vote in 1824. He was prevented from winning that race because of what he termed a corrupt deal between Adams and Henry Clay.

— 1832 —

Incumbent Democratic President Andrew Jackson had little difficulty defeating perenniel Whig candidate Henry Clay of Kentucky. Jackson won the popular vote by a majority of more than 225,000 votes (54.2% to 37.4%). The results in the electoral college were equally lopsided; Jackson took 219 votes to Clay's 49. William Wirt, the Anti-Mason Party candidate, received 7 votes, while the independent Democrat Floyd of South Carolina won his state's 11 votes.

Jackson's campaign focused on his accomplishments as president as well as the threat that the Bank of the United States posed to the nation. He portrayed himself as "the direct representative of the people."

— 1836 —

The Democratic Party nominated Vice President Martin Van Buren to face a trio of regional Whig candidates (William Henry Harrison was selected to run in most of New England and the Midwest, Hugh White of Tennessee ran in the South, and Daniel Webster ran in Massachusetts). The Whig strategy of defeating Van Buren wth regional candidates who would combine votes in the electoral college failed when Van Buren was able to win a majority of votes. Van Buren garnered 764,176 of the popular votes, or 50.8%, to 737,124, or 49.0% of the vote, for the three Whigs. In the electoral college, Van Buren won with 170 votes to Harrison's 73, White's 26, and Webster's 14. Independent Democrat Mangum of South Carolina took his home state and its 11 electoral votes.

During the campaign, Van Buren supported Jackson's opposition to the rechartering of the Bank of the United States. On the increasingly important issue of

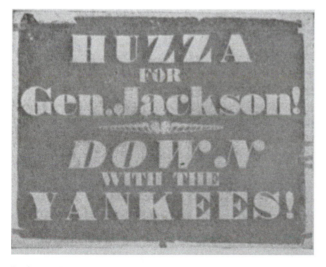

Jackson Campaign Poster. *Source:* Library of Congress.

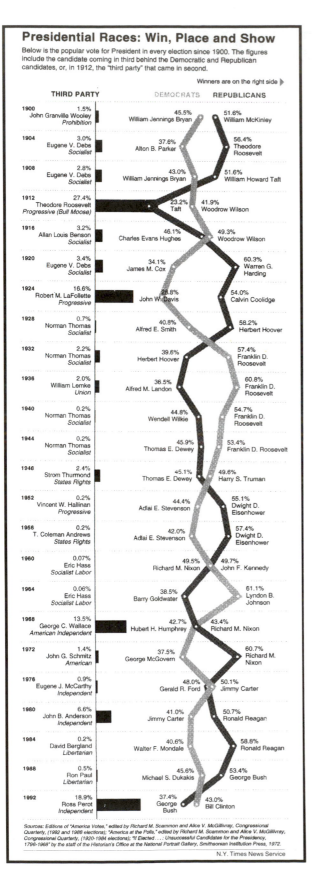

Presidential Races: Win, Place and Show

Below is the popular vote for President in every election since 1900. The figures include the candidate coming in third behind the Democratic and Republican candidates, or, in 1912, the "third party" that came in second.

Winners are on the right side ▶

THIRD PARTY	DEMOCRATS	REPUBLICANS
1900 1.5% John Granville Wooley *Prohibition*	45.5% William Jennings Bryan	51.6% William McKinley
1904 3.0% Eugene V. Debs *Socialist*	37.6% Alton B. Parker	56.4% Theodore Roosevelt
1908 2.8% Eugene V. Debs *Socialist*	43.0% William Jennings Bryan	51.6% William Howard Taft
1912 27.4% Theodore Roosevelt *Progressive (Bull Moose)*	23.2% Taft / 41.9% Woodrow Wilson	
1916 3.2% Allan Louis Benson *Socialist*	46.1% Charles Evans Hughes	49.3% Woodrow Wilson
1920 3.4% Eugene V. Debs *Socialist*	34.1% James M. Cox	60.3% Warren G. Harding
1924 16.6% Robert M. LaFollette *Progressive*	28.8% John W. Davis	54.0% Calvin Coolidge
1928 0.7% Norman Thomas *Socialist*	40.8% Alfred E. Smith	58.2% Herbert Hoover
1932 2.2% Norman Thomas *Socialist*	39.6% Herbert Hoover	57.4% Franklin D. Roosevelt
1936 2.0% William Lemke *Union*	36.5% Alfred M. Landon	60.8% Franklin D. Roosevelt
1940 0.2% Norman Thomas *Socialist*	44.8% Wendell Wilkie	54.7% Franklin D. Roosevelt
1944 0.2% Norman Thomas *Socialist*	45.9% Thomas E. Dewey	53.4% Franklin D. Roosevelt
1948 2.4% Strom Thurmond *States Rights*	45.1% Thomas E. Dewey	49.6% Harry S. Truman
1952 0.2% Vincent W. Hallinan *Progressive*	44.4% Adlai E. Stevenson	55.1% Dwight D. Eisenhower
1956 0.2% T. Coleman Andrews *States Rights*	42.0% Adlai E. Stevenson	57.4% Dwight D. Eisenhower
1960 0.07% Eric Hass *Socialist Labor*	49.5% Richard M. Nixon	49.7% John F. Kennedy
1964 0.06% Eric Hass *Socialist Labor*	38.5% Barry Goldwater	61.1% Lyndon B. Johnson
1968 13.5% George C. Wallace *American Independent*	42.7% Hubert H. Humphrey	43.4% Richard M. Nixon
1972 1.4% John G. Schmitz *American*	37.5% George McGovern	60.7% Richard M. Nixon
1976 0.9% Eugene J. McCarthy *Independent*	48.0% Gerald R. Ford	50.1% Jimmy Carter
1980 6.6% John B. Anderson *Independent*	41.0% Jimmy Carter	50.7% Ronald Reagan
1984 0.2% David Bergland *Libertarian*	40.6% Walter F. Mondale	58.8% Ronald Reagan
1988 0.5% Ron Paul *Libertarian*	45.6% Michael S. Dukakis	53.4% George Bush
1992 18.9% Ross Perot *Independent*	37.4% George Bush	43.0% Bill Clinton

Sources: Editions of "America Votes," edited by Richard M. Scammon and Alice V. McGillivray, Congressional Quarterly, (1992 and 1988 elections); "America at the Polls," edited by Richard M. Scammon and Alice V. McGillivray, Congressional Quarterly, (1920-1984 elections); "If Elected . . . : Unsuccessful Candidates for the Presidency, 1796-1968" by the staff of the Historian's Office at the National Portrait Gallery, Smithsonian Institution Press, 1972.

N.Y. Times News Service

slavery, he continued to defend it where it already existed in the Union.

— 1840 —

Incumbent Democratic President Martin Van Buren lost the election of 1840 to Whig candidate William Henry Harrison by 150,000 votes (52.9% to 46.8%). In the electoral college, however, the defeat was more stunning, with Van Buren winning only 60 electoral votes from the states of New Hampshire, Virginia, South Carolina, Alabama, Arkansas, Missouri, and Illinois (Harrison's home state) to Harrison's 19 states and 234 electoral votes.

Despite the superior party apparatus that Van Buren had developed over the years, his campaign was unable to separate the president from the economic depression that gripped the country.

— 1844 —

In the election of 1844, the Democratic presidential candidate, James K. Polk, won a narrow victory over the Whig candidate, Henry Clay. In the electoral college the vote was 107 to 105. Polk's strength was in the Deep South and western states, while Clay did well in border states, including winning Polk's home state of Tennessee—albeit by only 113 votes—and in the Atlantic states. Fewer than 40,000 votes separated the two men in the popular vote totals. Polk garnered 49.5% of the vote, and Clay had 48%.

In the campaign, the major election issue was expansion of the Union. While Clay struggled to define his position on the issue, Polk strongly endorsed the reoccupation of Oregon and the annexation of Texas. In fact, Polk was chosen as the Democratic candidate because Martin Van Buren had agreed with Clay not to make a campaign issue out of expansion. This agreement cost Van Buren the party's nomination and Clay the election.

— 1848 —

With the Democratic Party bypassing President James K. Polk, who had committed himself to a single term, the party selected Polk's vice president, Lewis Cass of Michigan. Cass was known as the developer of the idea of squatter sovereignty, later known as popular sovereignty, whereby the settlers of a region would determine if they were to enter the Union as a slave or free state. Cass faced two opponents in the election.

Democratic Candidates for President and Vice President, 1848: Cass and Butler. *Source:* Library of Congress.

The Whig Party nominated a political neophyte, General Zachary "Old Rough and Ready" Taylor, a hero of the Mexican War, who refused to comment on current affairs. A group of discontented Democrats, Whigs, and Liberty Party members offered former President Martin Van Buren on the Free Soil Party ticket; their slogan, "free soil, free speech, free labor, and free men," became a major foundation for the Republican Party. In the three-person race, Cass was defeated 163 electoral votes to 127. Although Van Buren had not won any electoral votes, he took over 290,000 votes in an election lost by Cass by fewer than 140,000 votes.

— 1852 —

The Democrats, having nominated a "dough-face" (a northerner with southern sympathies), former senator

and Mexican War veteran Franklin Pierce of New Hampshire, believed they had a candidate who above all else could offend no one. In the election, Pierce faced the last Whig Party nominee, General Winfield "Old Fuss and Feathers" Scott, who had outdistanced both President Millard Fillmore and Daniel Webster for the party's nod on the 53rd ballot. Pierce's close popular vote victory of 51% to 44% was amplified into an electoral college landslide of 254 votes for Pierce and 42 for Scott. Pierce won every state except Kentucky, Tennessee, Vermont, and Massachusetts.

The campaign was largely devoid of debate on issues because both major parties wanted to avoid opening the tenuous political peace of the Compromise of 1850. Instead, the campaign was marked by mudslinging on both sides. Pierce was attacked as a drunk and a coward, while Scott was mocked for his arrogance.

— 1856 —

In the election of 1856, the Democrats nominated a southern-sympathizing northerner, James Buchanan of Pennsylvania. Buchanan faced the first Republican Party candidate, John C. Frémont, and Whig-American Party candidate Millard Fillmore. In a close contest, Buchanan was able to win a plurality of the popular vote of 1.8 million, or 45.3%, to Frémont's 1.3 million votes, or 33.1%, and Fillmore's 870,000, or 21.5%. The electoral college was equally tight, with Buchanan winning 174 votes to Frémont's 114. Fillmore was only able to win Maryland and its eight electoral votes. Buchanan's strength was in the South and West; he also picked up his home state of Pennsylvania and neighboring New Jersey and Delaware.

Buchanan did little active campaigning. He did, however, address the major campaign issue by releasing statements denouncing the abolitionist movement and congressional interference in the westward expansion of slavery into the territories.

— 1860 —

The election of 1860 was the most critical election in American history. The outcome of this contest led to the secession of the southern states and a long bloody Civil War. The Democratic Party was in disarray leading up to the election. Two candidates were offered. Senator Stephen A. Douglas of Illinois had been nominated by the party regulars, and southern Democrats who had bolted the convention after Douglas was

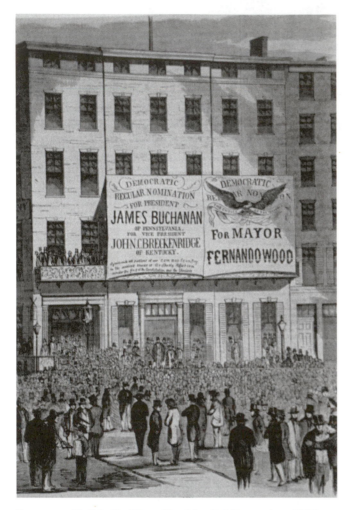

Tammany Hall in Its Glory. Presidential Campaign, 1856.
Source: Library of Congress.

nominated offered their own candidate, former Buchanan Vice President, John Breckinridge of Kentucky. The embryotic Republican Party nominated Representative Abraham Lincoln of Illinois. The split in the Democratic Party cost them the election, which went to Lincoln in a plurality vote. Lincoln garnered more than 1.8 million votes, or 39.8% of the popular vote, to Douglas's nearly 1.4 million, or 29.5%, and Breckinridge's 800,000, or 18.1%. In the electoral college, Democratic candidate Douglas was able to garner only 12 votes, having won Missouri and part of New Jersey. Lincoln won the election with 180 electoral votes, while Breckinridge secured 72 votes and the Constitutional Union Party candidate, John Bell, garnered 39 votes.

The campaign focused exclusively on the issue of slavery and continuance of the Union if Lincoln were elected. The Democrats lost the election and the debate over slavery because they were unable to remain a united political party.

— 1864 —

With the 11 Confederate states not voting, the election of 1864 pitted incumbent Republican President Abraham Lincoln against a former Union general and copperhead, George B. McClellan, for the Democrats. McClellan was able to win 1.8 million votes (45%), but it was not enough to beat Lincoln's 2.2 million (55%). In the electoral college, McClellan was able to win the votes of only three states—Kentucky, New Jersey, and Delaware—and their 21 votes; Lincoln was successful in securing 212 electoral votes.

McClellan's campaign had little going for it. Without the 11 southern and traditionally Democratic states participating, he had little chance of winning. But McClellan and fellow Democrats attempted to capitalize on the protracted nature of the war and Lincoln's abuse of martial law. During the campaign, McClellan stressed that if he were elected, an immediate end to the hostilities and a negotiated peace would ensue.

— 1868 —

With three states—Virginia, Texas and Mississippi— still not voting because of Reconstruction, the Democratic presidential nominee, former New York Governor Horatio Seymour, faced the Republican Civil War general, Ulysses S. Grant. The election of 1868 marked the first occasion where blacks were enfranchised. Nearly 500,000 southern blacks voted in the election, which Grant won by only 306,000 votes. There were wide claims of fraud, and the southern states' ballots were counted by Congress. The electoral count was a rout, with Grant taking 214 votes to Seymour's 80. Seymour won eight states including New York and Georgia, where voting fraud probably carried the day for the Democratic nominee.

The campaign focused mostly on rhetoric, with Republicans waving the "bloody shirt" to remind voters that it was their party that had saved the Union and brought peace to the land. In addition, the activities of the Ku Klux Klan were used by Republicans to show the true nature of southerners. For a short time, the Democratic Party considered dropping Seymour as their candidate as the party had not fared well in October elections in Ohio, Indiana, and Pennsylvania. The party decided against this move as Grant's victory was apparent.

— 1872 —

After receiving the nomination of both the Liberal Republican Party and the Democratic Party, publisher

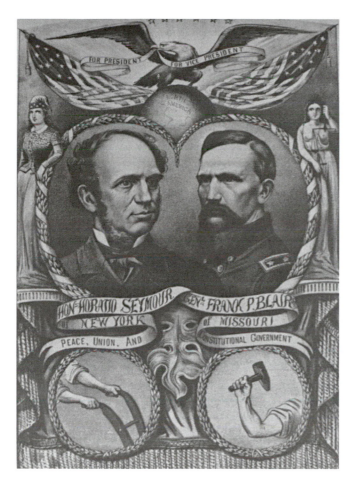

Seymour–Blair Campaign Poster, 1868. *Source:* Library of Congress.

Horace Greeley was thoroughly trounced in the general election by incumbent President Ulysses S. Grant. Grant won the popular vote by nearly 700,000 votes (56% to 44%). Before the electoral votes could be cast, however, Greeley died. His 63 votes were splintered among four candidates. Grant handily won the electoral college, taking 286 ballots. In the election, Congress chose not to count the votes of Arkansas and Louisiana because of widespread voter fraud.

While new political issues such as tariffs, monetary policy, civil service reform, foreign policy, and territorial expansion faced the nation, the campaign focused on personalities. Greeley was no match for Grant, the savior of the Union.

— 1876 —

The election of 1876 was the most controversial election in the history of the Republic. The Democratic nominee, Governor Samuel J. Tilden of New York, had won a majority of the popular vote. He outpaced his

Republican opponent, Rutherford B. Hayes, by 4,288,546 (51%) to 4,034,311 (48%). But in a much-disputed count of the electoral votes, Hayes was declared the winner by 185 electoral votes to 184. The electoral votes of Oregon, Florida, Louisiana, and South Carolina were determined by a special commission established in 1877 to resolve the conflict over who had won the votes. By consistent votes of 8 to 7, the commission of five senators, five representatives and five Supreme Court justices decided the votes belonged to Hayes. Tilden, a practical politician, made a deal with Hayes that in return for quietly accepting the results, U.S. troops would be removed from the South, ending Reconstruction.

During the campaign, Republicans used the rhetoric of the "bloody shirt" to stir an emotion-based support for their candidate. Tilden, in contrast, emphasized the need for political reform, a topic he was eminently qualified to discuss, as he had against Tammany Hall's "Boss" Tweed.

Democratic Candidates for President and Vice President, 1872: Greeley and Brown. *Source:* Library of Congress.

Democratic Candidates for President and Vice President, 1876: Tilden and Hendricks. *Source:* Library of Congress.

— 1880 —

Taking a page out of the Republican Party's nomination strategies, the Democrats nominated a Civil War general, Winfield Scott, as their candidate in 1880. The Republicans nominated Representative James A. Garfield of Ohio after a protracted convention in which they rejected a third term for President Ulysses S. Grant and James G. Blaine of Maine. In a popular vote of more than 9.2 million votes cast, Scott lost by fewer than 2,000 votes. The results in the electoral college were not as close; Scott won 155 electoral votes to Garfield's 214. Scott's strength was in the solidly Democratic South and the western states of California and Nevada.

In their campaign the Democrats continued to call for basic reforms of the civil service and a lowering of tariffs. The results of the election of 1876 gave the Democrats additional proof of Republican corruption.

— 1884 —

The election of 1884 pitted against each other two men of extraordinary political accomplishments. The Democrats nominated Governor Grover Cleveland of New York, while the Republicans gave the nod to Speaker of the House James G. Blaine of Maine. In a close race where Cleveland's home state of New York would decide the election, Cleveland pulled out a narrow victory after the Blaine campaign had mishandled New York. Cleveland won a popular vote plurality over Blaine of less than 30,000 votes. In the electoral college the margin of victory was also narrow, 219 to 182. With his victory, Cleveland became the first Democrat elected president since James Buchanan in 1856.

Cleveland's personal life was a major campaign issue. A bachelor, he had fathered a child out of wedlock who he supported financially. Republicans emphasized this moral fault by chanting, "Ma, ma, where's my pa? Gone to the White House, Ha, ha, ha." Democrats could also make use of scandal against Blaine, who had benefited financially from his dealing with railroads. In the end, the election turned on the economic hard times that gripped the nation. Voters sought a change from the Republican leadership in the White House that had been steady for more than two decades.

— 1888 —

In the election of 1888 the Democrats renominated President Grover Cleveland. Cleveland lost the election to Benjamin Harrison, a Civil War veteran and grandson of President William Henry Harrison. In a close election, Cleveland's strength was in the southern and border states. But in the two key states of Indiana, Harrison's home, and New York, Cleveland's home, Cleveland lost both of them. Despite the fact that Cleveland won a plurality of the popular vote, 5,234,488 (48.6%) to Harrison's 5,443,892 (47.8%), the result in the electoral college was for Harrison, 233 to 168.

Much of the campaign turned on Cleveland's strong call for tariff reform. Cleveland was forced to play down the issue when his own party did not support the drastic overhaul he proposed. Additionally, his position was portrayed as dangerous to the livelihoods of both business owners and workers.

— 1892 —

The election of 1892 was a rematch of the 1888 election. Former President Grover Cleveland was easily renomi-

Democratic Candidates for President and Vice President, 1880: Hancock and English. *Source:* Library of Congress.

Democratic Candidates for President and Vice President, 1884: Cleveland and Hendricks. *Source:* Library of Congress.

Cleveland Campaign Banner, 1892. *Source:* Library of Congress.

nated by the conservative element of his party after he reiterated his opposition to the silver standard. New York City capitalist William C. Whitney provided two important services to the Democrats and Cleveland's election. First, he was effective in raising campaign funds. In fact, he raised more money for Cleveland than the GOP could garner for Harrison. Second, he brokered a cease-fire between Cleveland and the Tammany Hall machine. Cleveland won the election by nearly 380,000 votes and the electoral college 277 to 145.

Little separated the two candidates in terms of issues. Cleveland's reconciliation with Tammany and the political ties with western populists gave the Democratic nominee a second term. Nevertheless, the party suffered defeats in the House of Representatives, losing 17 seats despite winning the White House.

— 1896 —

For the election of 1896, Democrats nominated William Jennings Bryan, who at 36 was the youngest man ever nominated. Bryan represented the populist element of the party. His "Cross of Gold" speech denouncing the gold standard as crucifying the average man cata-

pulted him into the spotlight. Party members such as Cleveland, who supported the gold standard, found themselves out of the majority. The Republicans nominated Governor William McKinley of Ohio, whose campaign was headed by Cleveland businessman Mark Hanna. Bryan lost the election in close balloting, 51% to 47%. If 21,000 votes in six states had been cast differently, Bryan would have won the electoral college. Instead, he lost in that body 271 to 176.

Bryan was an active campaigner who traveled throughout the country making more than 600 speeches. A grand orator, he argued that only by replacing the gold standard with the free unlimited minting of silver at a ratio of 16 to 1 could economic prosperity be brought to all Americans.

— 1900 —

The election of 1900 was a rematch of the 1896 election, which pitted populist Democrat William Jennings

Bryan Campaign Poster. *Source:* Library of Congress.

Democratic Candidates for President and Vice President, 1904: Parker and Davis. *Source:* Library of Congress.

Bryan of Nebraska against incumbent Republican President William McKinley. Bryan's share of both the popular vote and the electoral college declined in the four intervening years. Bryan garnered 6.4 million votes, or 45.5% of the popular vote, to McKinley's 7.2 million, or 51.7%. The Democrat's strength was in the South and in a few western "free silver" states. In the electoral college, McKinley easily won by a margin of 292 to 155.

During the campaign, Bryan continued to show his talent as an orator and active campaigner. He stressed the need to convert to the unlimited coinage of silver as a way of expanding economic prosperity. Additionally, he criticized the McKinley administration's policies that had led to international expansion and American imperialism.

matched against a fellow New Yorker, incumbent Republican President Theodore Roosevelt, who had assumed the office after McKinley's assassination in 1901. Parker was thoroughly beaten by Roosevelt, polling only 5.1 million votes, or 37.6% of the popular vote, to Roosevelt's 7.6 million votes, or 56.4%. In the electoral college, Parker was only able to garner the votes of the southern states and their 140 electoral votes. Roosevelt, however, won big with 336 votes.

Silver was not an issue in the election of 1904 because Parker supported the gold standard. Instead, he emphasized the themes of anti-imperialism and anti-monopoly in his campaign. Only the former offered any real distinction between the two candidates, and most Americans took pride in their newfound role in the world.

— 1904 —

In the election of 1904, the Democratic Party turned away from its 1896 and 1900 standard-bearer, William Jennings Bryan, in favor of a New York court of appeals chief justice, Alton C. Parker. Parker was

— 1908 —

For the third and final time, the Democratic Party nominated William Jennings Bryan. The Republicans countered with the hand-picked successor of Theodore Roosevelt, William Howard Taft of Ohio.

Wilson Campaign Button. *Source:* Three Lions.

The results of the election were not even close, as Taft outpolled Bryan by more than a million votes and orchestrated an electoral college landslide of 321 to 162.

The campaign saw both major candidates on the stump. Bryan focused on the question "Shall the people rule?" He advocated the reduction of the tariff and strict antitrust enforcement. He argued that the government and the Republican Party were controlled by big business. But when Democratic National Committee treasurer C.N. Haskill was implicated in a bribery scandal involving Standard Oil, the moral high ground could not be claimed by the party.

— 1912 —

With the election of the Democratic nominee, Woodrow Wilson, the party gained control of the White House for only the third time since the Civil War. Aiding Wilson in his victory was the deep split in the Republican Party caused by the third-party run of Theodore Roosevelt. While Roosevelt and the Republican standard-bearer President William Howard Taft split votes, Wilson was able to capture a plurality of the popular vote in 29 states while winning a majority in 11 southern states. The vote in the electoral college was not even close: Wilson won 435 votes to Roosevelt's 88 and Taft's 8.

The campaign was dominated by a strong progressive force that was taking control of the country. While little separated Wilson from Roosevelt, the differences between Wilson and Taft were more marked. In the end, the Wilson administration adopted many of the proposed reforms of Roosevelt's third party.

— 1916 —

The Democratic Party entered the election of 1916 solidly behind their candidate, incumbent President Woodrow Wilson. Wilson faced Republican Supreme Court Justice Charles Evans Hughes. In a close election, Wilson won the popular vote with 9.1 million votes, or 49.2%, to Hughes's 8.5 million votes, or 45.1%. In the all-important electoral college, however, Wilson was able to eke out a victory of 277 votes to 254. Wilson won 30 states including the South and West, but Hughes made the race close by winning the more populated eastern and midwestern states.

During the campaign, Wilson stressed that he had been able to keep America out of the growing hostilities in Europe. The party called for continuity in leadership in this time of peril. Additionally, the administration ran on its record of achievement, committing itself to the continued implementation of progressive reforms.

— 1920 —

The election of 1920 found the Democratic Party in disarray. After a protracted convention in which Ohio

Cox and Roosevelt Campaign Poster. *Source:* Library of Congress.

Governor James M. Cox was nominated over treasury secretary and son-in-law of Woodrow Wilson, William Gibbs McAdoo, the party squared off against the Republicans and their nominee, Senator Warren G. Harding of Ohio. Harding soundly defeated his fellow Ohioan by nearly 7 million popular votes and a 404-to-127 electoral college trouncing.

The campaign focused largely on the Democratic Party's commitment to the Treaty of Versailles and the League of Nations. In addition, the ticket had all the baggage of the Wilson administration, the popularity of which was plummeting.

— 1924 —

A highly divided Democratic convention nominated on the 103rd ballot John W. Davis of New York as its standard-bearer for the election of 1924. In the contest, Davis faced incumbent Republican President Calvin "Silent Cal" Coolidge. Davis was soundly defeated in a three-man race that included Progressive candidate Robert La Follette of Wisconsin. Davis could muster only 8.4 million popular votes, or 28.9%, to Coolidge's 15.7 million votes, or 54.1%. La Follette garnered 4.8 million votes, or 16.6% of the popular returns. In the electoral college, the defeat was equally humiliating for the Democratic nominee. Davis earned only 136 votes—all from the South—to Coolidge's 382. La Follette won the 13 electoral votes of his home state of Wisconsin.

Politically conservative, the Democratic candidate was little different from his Republican rival. With Davis unable to inspire the electorate, the American voter chose a Republican over a Democrat with Republican ideas.

— 1928 —

For the first time in history, the election of 1928 saw a major party candidate who was a Roman Catholic. The Democratic Party nominated New York Governor Alfred E. Smith as their candidate. Smith's opponent was wartime food administrator and secretary of commerce under President Calvin Coolidge, Herbert Hoover. Smith was crushed in the election by Hoover, who beat the New Yorker by more than 6 million votes (58.2% to 40.8%). Smith won only 8 states and 87 electoral votes to Hoover's 40 states and 444 votes.

Smith was an active campaigner, drawing large crowds in southern New England. But Smith's religion and his position against Prohibition were major handicaps even within his own party.

"The Sidewalks of New York," the Official Campaign Song of Al Smith. *Source:* Library of Congress.

— 1932 —

The election of 1932 saw an end to the Republican Party stranglehold on the White House that had existed since the Civil War. The Democratic nominee, Franklin Delano Roosevelt, parlayed dissatisfaction with the Republican Party and its candidate, President Herbert Hoover, into a landslide victory. Roosevelt capitalized on the repudiation of Hoover by beating him by more than 7 million votes. In the electoral college, Roosevelt whipped Hoover 472 to 59. Hoover carried only the three northern New England states of Vermont, New Hampshire, and Maine, plus Pennsylvania and a split of Connecticut.

Roosevelt campaigned as a progressive who sought to use the immense power of the federal government to attack economic ills and alleviate human suffering. While he often received conflicting advice from his "brain trust" of advisers, Roosevelt used the full force of the Democratic National Committee to secure his victory.

— 1936 —

The election of 1936 reinforced the electoral victory that President Franklin D. Roosevelt had secured in 1932. With his defeat of the Republican candidate, Governor Alfred M. Landon of Kansas, Roosevelt saw the ascendance of his party to the status of the majority party for the first time in two generations. Roosevelt beat Landon by more than 10 million votes. Landon was able to carry only two states, Vermont and Maine. Roosevelt's electoral college victory was 523 to 8.

Roosevelt campaigned on his program of the New Deal. He stressed that only through active government intervention could America recover from the worldwide depression. Active in the campaign, he crossed the nation giving whistle-stop speeches to thousands of supporters.

— 1940 —

The election of 1940 saw the unprecedented election of a president for a third term. While President Franklin D. Roosevelt had not actively sought renomination by his party, when the Democrats assembled in Chicago renominated him, he accepted. Roosevelt's opponent in the general election was utilities millionaire Wendell L. Willkie, a lifelong Democrat who broke with the party over many aspects of the New Deal. The election results in 1940 were not as overwhelming as those of 1936. Roosevelt beat Willkie by 5 million votes and carried the electoral college 449 to 82.

With his reelection never in doubt, Roosevelt campaigned on his New Deal record. He actively supported candidates for Congress including some Republicans whom he believed were more supportive of his measures than conservative Democrats.

— 1944 —

Democrats had little difficulty in selecting a candidate for the election of 1944. Unlike in 1940, incumbent Democratic President Franklin D. Roosevelt let his party know he wanted a fourth term. The Republicans nominated New York Governor Thomas Dewey. While the margin of victory was not as large as those of 1936 or 1940, Roosevelt handily and decisively defeated Dewey by more than 3.5 million votes, with 53.4% of the popular vote for Roosevelt and 45.9% for Dewey. The electoral college tally was 432 for Roosevelt and 99 for Dewey.

With the country involved in World War II in both Europe and the Pacific, Roosevelt's campaign stressed the need for continuity of leadership in world affairs. The American voter was convinced that a change of horses in midstream was unadvisable because it could be seen as a weakness in the country's resolve.

— 1948 —

The Democratic Party failed to find an alternative candidate to incumbent President Harry S. Truman, who had assumed the office upon FDR's death in 1945. Truman surprised many by his electoral victory over Republican Thomas Dewey. By a plurality vote, Truman won the popular totals with slightly more than 24 million votes to Dewey's nearly 22 million votes. In the electoral college, Truman garnered 303 votes to Dewey's 189. States' rights Democratic candidate Strom Thurmond won 39 electoral votes.

During the campaign, Truman did not veer from his liberal agenda. He continued to frustrate Republican legislators by vetoing measures including the Taft–Hartley Act. In an aggressive move, Truman campaigned in the old whistle-stop fashion, giving over 250 speeches and traveling over 20,000 miles after Labor Day. Sticking to the tradition of FDR, Truman emphasized the prosperity that the New Deal had

"Dewey Defeats Truman." A Beaming Truman Holds Up a Premature *Chicago Tribune* Headline, 1948. *Source:* Library of Congress.

brought the country and urged voters to continue with their support of the liberal agenda.

— 1952 —

The election of 1952 pitted a reluctant Democratic candidate, Governor Adlai E. Stevenson, against a Republican war hero, Dwight D. Eisenhower. The resulting election was a landslide victory for Eisenhower, who garnered 442 electoral votes to Stevenson's 89. Stevenson was able to win only nine states, all from the South. In terms of the popular vote, Eisenhower captured 6 million more votes than Stevenson.

During the campaign, Stevenson showed himself to be an eloquent speaker; however, his campaigned suffered from inefficiency and a growing tension between him and Truman. Stevenson learned the tough political rule of never running against a war hero.

— 1956 —

In a rematch of the 1952 election, Democratic nominee Adlai E. Stevenson was once again trounced by Republican Dwight D. Eisenhower. Stevenson's performance in 1956 was worse than that of 1952. He carried only seven states (North Carolina, South Carolina, Georgia, Alabama, Mississippi, Arkansas, and Missouri) and their 73 electoral votes to Ike's 41 states and 457 electoral votes. In terms of popular votes, Stevenson garnered 26 million votes, or 42% of the vote, to the president's 35.6 million, or 57.4%.

Little had changed in campaign strategies from 1952 to 1956. Stevenson offered the voter a more liberal alternative to the moderate Eisenhower. The campaign did try to link Ike to the more conservative and distasteful elements of the Republican Party, such as Senator Joseph McCarthy of Wisconsin. Still, voters had little reason to opt for the eloquent Stevenson.

— 1960 —

The election contest of 1960 between Democratic Senator John F. Kennedy of Massachusetts and Republican Vice President Richard M. Nixon was one of the closest in American history. Kennedy narrowly defeated Nixon in the popular vote, by a mere 115,000 votes (49.7% to 49.6%). The votes in the electoral college did not reflect this closeness, as Kennedy was able to win elector-rich Illinois and Texas. The final count gave Kennedy 303 votes to Nixon's 219.

Kennedy's campaign was careful not to criticize

JFK Campaign Buttons. *Source:* National Archives.

Eisenhower, the most popular politician of the period, but Kennedy did speak in terms that painted the Eisenhower years as a time of drift. His campaign theme was "It's time to get the country moving again." In a series of televised debates—the first in American history—Kennedy was a more appealing candidate to the voter. In addition, Kennedy addressed the issue of his religion head-on by stating that there was a wall of separation between his personal religious beliefs (Roman Catholicism) and his public duties.

— 1964 —

In the election of 1964, President Lyndon B. Johnson, who had taken office after Kennedy's assassination in 1963, faced a Republican opponent, Senator Barry Goldwater of Arizona, who had been nominated by the conservative wing, a small but strong portion of the Republican Party. The final outcome of the election was a landslide victory for Johnson, who won 61% of the popular vote and 486 of the 538 electoral votes.

Johnson ran a quiet campaign, preferring to play the role of president. The Goldwater campaign hardly posed a threat to the incumbent president.

— 1968 —

The Democratic nominee, Vice President Hubert Humphrey, emerged from the violence-scarred convention to face former Vice President Richard M. Nixon in the 1968 election. Humphrey lost the popular vote by a mere 500,000 votes. But the electoral college totals overwhelmingly supported Nixon's victory, 301 to 191. Governor George Wallace, who had run as an independent, pulled 46 electoral votes and nearly 10 million votes in the South.

Humphrey had the difficult task of unifying the divided Democratic Party in time for the November election. To aid his campaign, he employed a professional ad agency to handle the making of television commercials, a decision also made by Nixon. In the end, the division of the 1968 convention was too great a chasm for Humphrey to bridge.

— 1972 —

The Democratic nominee, Senator George McGovern of South Dakota, was crushed by incumbent President Richard M. Nixon in the election of 1972. Nixon garnered nearly 61% of the popular vote and 520 electoral votes. McGovern, a committed liberal, was able to win only Massachusetts and the District of Columbia for 17 electoral votes.

McGovern had no end of problems during his campaign. His initial choice for vice presidential running mate, Senator Thomas Eagleton of Missouri, had to be dropped from the ticket because of the revelation that he had undergone electroshock therapy for depres-

sion. McGovern offered the American voter a clear choice of a committed liberal versus the conservative-leaning incumbent president. In the end, the American voter was unwilling to take the liberal risk.

— 1976 —

The 1976 presidential election offered the Democratic Party a chance to redeem itself after the humiliating McGovern run of 1972. The Democrats nominated a political outsider, former Governor James E. "Jimmy" Carter, for president. The Republican standard-bearer

Campaign Buttons For and Against McGovern. *Source:* National Archives.

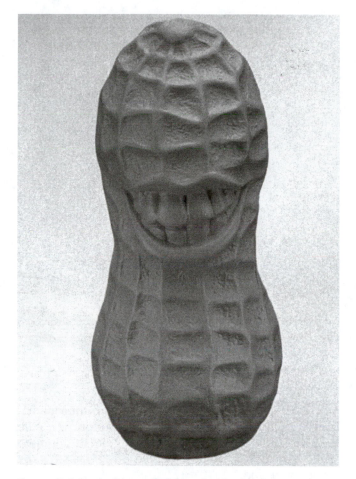

Carter Coinbank. *Source:* Smithsonian Institution.

was President Gerald R. Ford, who had assumed the office after Nixon resigned. Ford was the first person to hold the office of president who had not been elected (Ford had been appointed after Nixon Vice President Spiro Agnew resigned on charges of tax fraud). Carter ran well in the South and among blacks, who turned out in large numbers. In the end, the political unknown captured a majority (50.1%) of the popular vote and dominated the electoral college 297 to 240.

Carter was able to bring together the old Roosevelt coalition of voters during the campaign. Running as a political outsider, Carter made the political scandal of Watergate a central issue in the campaign. Arguing that the government belonged to honest men like himself, he urged voters to turn out the man who had pardoned Nixon.

— 1980 —

The election of 1980 marked the first occasion since 1932 when voters ousted a sitting president. Incumbent James E. "Jimmy" Carter lost a lopsided election to the Republican nominee, former Governor Ronald Reagan of California. Reagan garnered 8 million more votes than Carter as well as 489 electoral votes to Carter's 49. In the end, Carter was able to win only six states (Minnesota, Maryland, West Virginia, Georgia, Hawaii, and part of Rhode Island) plus the District of Columbia.

The campaign focused on the many failures of the Carter administration, both domestically, where inflation and unemployment were high, and in foreign affairs, when Americans were being held hostage in Iran. Carter had a difficult time shifting attention from these issues to any that were more favorable.

— 1984 —

The election of 1984 was an exercise in futility for the Democrats and their nominee, former Carter Vice President Walter Mondale. Despite the historic step of choosing a female running mate, Representative Geraldine Ferraro of New York, the ticket generated little enthusiasm with the American voter. In the end, incumbent Republican President Ronald Reagan won the biggest landslide in American history. Mondale lost the popular election by nearly 17 million votes and the electoral college 525 to 13. Mondale was able to win only his home state of Minnesota and the Democratic bastion of the District of Columbia.

Mondale's campaign faced an uphill fight as the economy was growing nicely and Americans had regained pride in their role in the world. Mondale's campaign asked voters to think of the possible consequences of a continued Reagan administration. Most of them liked the prospect. Even the advantage that Mondale had with women because of the nomination of Ferraro was lost as concerns over her husband's finances were raised.

— 1988 —

Even though Republican President Ronald Reagan was ineligible to run again, the 1988 election was still a referendum on him. The Democrats nominated a political outsider, Governor Michael Dukakis of Massachusetts, to run against Reagan Vice President George Bush. Bush won the election handily by more than 7 million popular votes and a 426-to-112 vote in the electoral college. Dukakis won only nine states plus the District of Columbia. Nevertheless, his defeat had not been as severe as those of Carter and Mondale against the more popular Reagan.

The Dukakis campaign focused on the issue of competency, rather than ideology. Dukakis painted himself as an able technocrat who could manage the affairs of the United States. He often seemed uncomfortable with a debate that centered on issues and, more important, values. In a televised debate, for example, he badly responded to a question of whether he would support the death penalty for someone who had raped his wife, Kitty.

— 1992 —

At the beginning of 1992, the prospects for a Democratic takeover of the White House in November looked bleak. An incumbent Republican president, George Bush, was at his height of popularity. The Democrats nominated the little-known governor of Arkansas, William J. "Bill" Clinton. By election time, Clinton had cut into Bush's popularity and scored an electoral victory few would have predicted months earlier. In a three-way race that included independent candidate H. Ross Perot, Clinton garnered a plurality of nearly 45 million (43%) of the popular vote, outdistancing Bush's 39 million (37.5%) and Perot's nearly 20 million (18.9%). In the electoral college, Clinton won 370 votes to Bush's 168.

Clinton, a gifted campaigner, was able to shape the scope of the election campaign. He was able to deflect criticism of his marital infidelity, Vietnam draft record,

Clinton–Gore Campaign Button. *Source:* Buscemi.

and accusations that he had smoked marijuana. Instead, Clinton focused on the economy as the biggest issue of the campaign. His retort to the more senior and foreign policy oriented Bush was, "It's the economy, stupid."

APPENDIXES

APPENDIX 1

The Charter and the Bylaws
of the Democratic Party of the United States
As Amended by the Democratic National Committee
on January 21, 1995

Democratic National Committee
430 South Capitol St., SE, Washington, D.C. 20003

CONTENTS

Charter of the Democratic Party
of the United States

CHARTER OF THE DEMOCRATIC
PARTY OF THE UNITED STATES

Preamble

We, the Democrats of the United States of America,
united in common purpose, hereby rededicate ourselves to the principles which have historically sustained our Party. Recognizing that the vitality of the
Nation's political institutions has been the foundation
of its enduring strength, we acknowledge that a political party which wishes to lead must listen to those it
would lead, a party which asks for the people's trust
must prove that it trusts the people and a party which
hopes to call forth the best the Nation can achieve must
embody the best of the Nation's heritage and traditions.

What we seek for our Nation, we hope for all people:
individual freedom in the framework of a just society,
political freedom in the framework of meaningful participation by all citizens. Bound by the United States
Constitution, aware that a party must be responsive to
be worthy of responsibility, we pledge ourselves to
open, honest endeavor and to the conduct of public affairs in a manner worthy of a society of free people.

Under God, and for these ends and upon these principles, we do establish and adopt this Charter of the
Democratic Party of the United States of America.

Article One

**The Democratic Party of the United States
of America**

The Democratic Party of the United States of America
shall:

Section 1.   Nominate and assist in the election of
Democratic candidates for the offices of President and
Vice President of the United States;

Section 2.   Adopt and promote statements of policy;

Section 3.   Assist state and local Democratic Party organizations in the election of their candidates and the
education of their voters;

Section 4.   Establish standards and rules of procedure to afford all members of the Democratic Party

full, timely and equal opportunities to participate in decisions concerning the selection of candidates, the formulation of policy, and the conduct of other Party affairs, without prejudice on the basis of sex, race, age (if of voting age), color, creed, national origin, religion, economic status, sexual orientation, ethnic identity or physical disability, and further, to promote fair campaign practices and the fair adjudication of disputes. Accordingly, the scheduling of Democratic Party affairs at all levels shall consider the presence of any religious minorities of significant numbers of concentration whose level of participation would be affected;

Section 5. Raise and disburse monies needed for the successful operation of the Democratic Party;

Section 6. Work with Democratic public officials at all levels to achieve the objectives of the Democratic Party; and

Section 7. Encourage and support codes of political ethics that embody substantive rules of ethical guidance for public officials and employees in federal, state and local governments, to assure that public officials shall at all times conduct themselves in a manner that reflects creditably upon the office they serve, shall not use their office to gain special privileges and benefits and shall refrain from acting in their official capacities when their independence of judgement would be adversely affected by personal interest or duties.

Article Two

National Convention

Section 1. The Democratic Party shall assemble in National Convention in each year in which an election for the office of President of the United States is held.

Section 2. The National Convention shall be the highest authority of the Democratic Party, subject to the provisions of this Charter. The National Convention shall recognize the state and other Parties entitled to participate in the conduct of the national affairs of the Democratic Party, including its conventions, conferences and committees. State Party rules or state laws relating to the election of delegates to the National Convention shall be observed unless in conflict with this Charter and other provisions adopted pursuant to authority of the Charter, including the resolutions or other actions of the National Convention. In the event of such conflict with state laws, state Parties shall be required to take provable positive steps to bring such laws into conformity and to carry out such other measures as may be required by the National Convention or the Democratic National Committee.

Section 3. The National Convention shall nominate a candidate for the office of President of the United States, nominate a candidate for the office of Vice President of the United States, adopt a platform and act upon such other matters as it deems appropriate.

Section 4. The National Convention shall be composed of delegates equally divided between men and women. The delegates shall be chosen through processes which:

(a) assure all Democratic voters full, timely and equal opportunity to participate and include affirmative action programs toward that end,

(b) assure that delegations fairly reflect the division of preferences expressed by those who participate in the Presidential nominating process,

(c) exclude the use of the unit rule at any level,

(d) do not deny participation for failure to pay a cost, fee or poll tax,

(e) restrict participation to Democrats only, and

(f) except with respect to persons referred to in Section 5(b) of this Article, begin within the calendar year of the Convention, provided, however, that fairly apportioned and openly selected state Party Committees, elected no earlier than January 1 of the preceding mid-term Congressional election year, from states not having state conventions authorized to elect delegates shall not be precluded from selecting such portion of their respective state delegations, according to the standards provided in this Charter and the Bylaws, as may be specifically authorized by the Democratic National Committee in the Call to the Convention,

(g) prohibit unpledged and uncommitted delegates, except delegates or alternates expressing an uncommitted preference shall be permitted to be elected at the district level, in which event, if such preference meets the applicable threshold and qualifies for at-large or similar delegates or alternates, such at-large or similar delegates or alternates shall be allocated to that uncommitted preference as if it were a presidential candidate,

(h) notwithstanding any provision to the contrary in this Section:

(i) provide for all of the members of the Democratic National Committee to serve as unpledged delegates,

(ii) provide for each state, territory or commonwealth to select a number of unpledged delegates equal to one (1) such delegate for every four (4) votes on the Democratic National Committee from that state, territory or commonwealth, pursuant to Article Three, Section 2(a) and 2(b) of the Charter, and

(iii) permit unpledged delegates consisting of:
1) the President and Vice President of the United States, if Democrats,
2) the Democratic members of the United States Senate and the Democratic members of the House of Representatives,
3) the Democratic Governors,
4) former Democratic Presidents and Vice Presidents of the United States,
5) former Democratic Majority Leaders of the United States Senate,
6) former Democratic Speakers of the United States House of Representatives,
7) former Chairs of the Democratic National Committee,
8) such delegates shall not be permitted to have alternates and such delegates shall constitute an exception to Subsection (b) of this Section 4.

Section 5.   The delegate vote allocable to each state shall be determined as provided in the Bylaws, consistent with the formula:

(a) giving equal weight to population, which may be measured by electoral vote, and to the Democratic vote in elections for office of the President; and
(b) which shall also provide additional delegate positions to members of the Democratic National Committee; and
(c) which may also provide additional delegate positions to Democratic elected public officials specifically designated by the Democratic National Committee in the Call to the Convention, subject to the provisions of Section 4.

Article Three

Democratic National Committee

Section 1.   The Democratic National Committee shall have general responsibility for the affairs of the Democratic Party between National Conventions, subject to the provisions of this Charter and to the resolutions or other actions of the National Convention. This responsibility shall include:

(a) issuing the Call to the National Convention;
(b) conducting the Party's Presidential campaign;
(c) filling vacancies in the nominations for the office of President and Vice President;
(d) formulating and disseminating statements of Party policy;
(e) providing for the election or appointment of a Chairperson, five Vice Chairpersons, three of whom shall be of the opposite sex of the Chairperson, one of whom shall be the President of the Association of State Democratic Chairs and one of whom shall be the Vice Chairperson for Voter Registration and Participation, a Treasurer, a Secretary, a National Finance Chair and other appropriate officers of the National Committee and for the filling of vacancies; and
(f) all other actions necessary or appropriate in order to carry out the provisions of this Charter and the objectives of the Democratic Party.

Section 2.   The Democratic National Committee shall be composed of:

(a) the Chairperson and the highest ranking officer of the opposite sex of each recognized state Democratic Party;
(b) two hundred additional members apportioned to the states on the basis set forth in Article Two, Section 5(a) of the Charter, consistent with the full participation goals of Sections 3 and 4 of Article Eight of the Charter; provided that each state shall have at least two such additional members;
(c) the Chairperson of the Democratic Governors' Association and two additional governors, of whom, to the extent possible, at least one shall be of the opposite sex of the Chairperson, as selected by the Association;
(d) the Democratic Leader in the United States Senate and the Democratic Leader in the United States House of Representatives and one additional member of each body, who, to the extent possible, shall be of the opposite sex of, and appointed by, the respective leaders;
(e) the Chairperson, the five Vice Chairpersons, the National Finance Chair, the Treasurer, and the Secretary of the DNC;
(f) the Chairperson of the National Conference of Democratic Mayors and two additional mayors, at least one of whom shall be of the opposite sex of the Chairperson, as selected by the Conference;
(g) the President of the Young Democrats of America and two additional members, at least one of whom shall be of the opposite sex of the President, as selected by the organization biennially in convention assembled;
(h) the Chairperson of the Democratic County Officials and two additional county officials, at least one of whom shall be of the opposite sex of the Chairperson, as selected by the organization;
(i) the Chairperson of the Democratic State Legislative Leaders Association and two additional state legislators, at least one of whom shall be of the opposite sex of the Chairperson, as selected by the Association;

(j) the Chairperson of the National Democratic Municipal Officials Conference and two additional municipal officials, at least one of whom shall be of the opposite sex of the Chairperson, as selected by the Conference;

(k) the President of the National Federation of Democratic Women and two additional members selected by the Federation;

(l) the President of the College Democrats of America and the Vice President, who shall be of the opposite sex, as elected by the organization annually;

(m) the Chairperson of the National Association of Democratic State Treasurers and the Vice Chair, who shall be of the opposite sex, as selected by the Association;

(n) the Chairperson of the National Association of Democratic Lieutenant Governors and the Vice Chair, who shall be of the opposite sex, as selected by the Association;

(o) the Chairperson of the Democratic Association of Secretaries of State and the Vice Chair, who shall be of the opposite sex, as selected by the Association;

(p) additional members as provided in Article Nine of this Charter. No more than sixty-five additional members of the Democratic National Committee may be added by the foregoing members.

Section 3. Members of the Democratic National Committee apportioned to the states and those provided for in Article Eleven who are not otherwise members by virtue of Party office, shall be selected by each state Democratic Party in accordance with standards as to participation established in the Bylaws of the Democratic Party for terms commencing on the day the National Convention adjourns and terminating on the day the next Convention adjourns. Such members shall be selected during the calendar year in which a National Convention is held, through processes which assure full, timely and equal opportunity to participate. Vacancies shall be filled by the state Party as provided in the Bylaws. The members of the National Committee from each state shall be divided as equally as practicable between committeemen and committeewomen. Members of the Democratic National Committee who serve by virtue of holding public or Party office shall serve on the Committee only during their terms in such office. Members of the Democratic National Committee added by the other members shall serve a term that runs coterminously with the Chairperson of the Democratic National Committee, through the election of the new Chairper-

son, and until their successors are chosen; members in this category shall have the right to vote for the new Chairperson. Members of the Democratic National Committee who serve by virtue of holding state Party office shall be selected by such Parties in accordance with standards as to participation established in the Bylaws.

Section 4. The Bylaws may provide for removal of members of the Democratic National Committee for cause by a two-thirds vote of the National Committee and may also require continued residence in the jurisdiction represented by the member and affirmative support for the Democratic Presidential and Vice Presidential nominees as a condition of continued membership thereon.

Section 5. The Democratic National Committee shall meet at least once each year. Meetings shall be called by the Chairperson, by the Executive Committee of the Democratic National Committee, or by written request of no fewer than one-fourth of the members of the Democratic National Committee.

Article Four

Executive Committee

Section 1. There shall be an Executive Committee of the Democratic National Committee, which shall be responsible for the conduct of the affairs of the Democratic Party subject to this Charter, the National Convention and the Democratic National Committee.

Section 2. The Executive Committee shall be elected by and serve at the pleasure of the members of the Democratic National Committee. The size, composition and term of office shall be determined by the Democratic National Committee, provided that the number of members elected by the regional caucuses of members of the Democratic National Committee shall be no fewer than fourteen less than the number selected by other means.

Section 3. The Executive Committee shall meet at least four times each year. Meetings shall be called by the Chairperson or by written request of no fewer than one-fourth of its members. The Executive Committee shall keep a record of its proceedings which shall be available to the public.

Article Five

National Chairperson

Section 1. The National Chairperson of the Democratic Party shall carry out the programs and policies of the National Convention and the Democratic National Committee.

Section 2.   The National Chairperson, the five Vice Chairpersons, the National Finance Chair, the Treasurer, and the Secretary, shall be elected:

(a) at a meeting of the Democratic National Committee held after the succeeding presidential election and prior to March 1 next, and,

(b) whenever a vacancy occurs. The National Chairperson shall be elected and may be removed by a majority vote of the Democratic National Committee, and each term shall expire upon the election for the following term.

Section 3.   The National Chairperson shall preside over meetings of the Democratic National Committee and of the Executive Committee. In the event of a vacancy in the office of the National Chairperson, the designated Vice Chair as provided for in Article Two, Section 12(b) of the Bylaws, or the next-highest-ranking officer of the National Committee present at the meeting shall preside.

Section 4.   The National Chairperson shall serve full time and shall receive such compensation as may be determined by agreement between the Chairperson and the Democratic National Committee. In the conduct and management of the affairs and procedures of the Democratic National Committee, particularly as they apply to the preparation and conduct of the Presidential nomination process, the Chairperson shall exercise impartiality and even-handedness as between the Presidential candidates and campaigns. The Chairperson shall be responsible for ensuring that the national officers and staff of the Democratic National Committee maintain impartiality and even-handedness during the Democratic Party Presidential nominating process.

Article Six

Party Conference

The Democratic Party may hold a National Party Conference between National Conventions. The nature, agenda, composition, time and place of the Party Conference shall be determined by the Democratic National Committee.

Article Seven

National Finance Organizations

Section 1.   The Democratic National Committee shall establish National Finance Organizations which shall have general responsibility for the finances of the Democratic Party. These National Finance Organizations shall raise funds to support the Democratic Party and shall advise and assist state Democratic Parties and candidates in securing funds for their purposes.

Section 2.   The National Finance Chair shall be elected or approved by the Democratic National Committee.

Article Eight

Full Participation

Section 1.   The Democratic Party of the United States shall be open to all who desire to support the Party and who wish to be known as Democrats.

Section 2.   Discrimination in the conduct of Democratic Party affairs on the basis of sex, race, age (if of voting age), color, creed, national origin, religion, economic status, sexual orientation, ethnic identity or physical disability is prohibited, to the end that the Democratic Party at all levels be an open party.

Section 3.   To encourage full participation by all Democrats, with particular concern for minority groups, Blacks, Native Americans, Asian/Pacific Americans, Hispanics, women and youth in the delegate selection process and in all Party affairs, as defined in the Bylaws, the National and State Democratic Parties shall adopt and implement an affirmative action program which provides for representation as nearly as practicable of the aforementioned groups, as indicated by their presence in the Democratic electorate. This program shall include specific goals and timetables to achieve this purpose.

Section 4.   This goal shall not be accomplished either directly or indirectly by the national or state Democratic Parties' imposition of mandatory quotas at any level of the delegate selection process or in any other Party affairs, as defined in the Bylaws; however, representation as nearly as practicable of minority groups, Blacks, Native Americans, Asian/Pacific Americans, Hispanics, women and youth, as indicated by their presence in the Democratic electorate, as provided in this Article, shall not be deemed a quota.

Section 5.   Performance under an approved affirmative action program and composition of the Convention delegation shall be considered relevant evidence in the challenge of any state delegation. If a state Party has adopted and implemented an approved and monitored affirmative action program, the Party shall not be subject to challenge based solely on delegate composition or solely on primary results.

Section 6.   Notwithstanding Section 5 above, equal division at any level of delegate or committee positions between delegate men and delegate women or committeemen and committeewomen shall not constitute a violation of any provision thereof.

Article Nine

General Provisions

Section 1. Democratic Party means the Democratic Party of the United States of America.

Section 2. The Bylaws shall provide for states in which the Democratic nominee for President or electors committed to the nominee did not appear on the ballot in elections used for apportionment formulae.

Section 3. For the purposes of this Charter, the District of Columbia shall be treated as a state containing the appropriate number of Congressional Districts.

Section 4. For the purposes of this Charter, Puerto Rico shall be treated as a state containing the appropriate number of Congressional Districts.

Section 5. Recognized Democratic Party organizations in areas not entitled to vote in Presidential elections may elect such voting delegates to National Conventions as the Democratic National Committee provides in the Call to the Convention.

Section 6. Guam, the Virgin Islands, and American Samoa shall each have one vote on the Democratic National Committee, which vote shall be shared by the Chairperson, the highest ranking officer of the opposite sex, the National Committeeman and the National Committeewoman, except as may otherwise be provided by the Bylaws. Democrats Abroad shall have two votes on the Democratic National Committee, which votes shall be shared by the Chairperson, the highest ranking officer of the opposite sex, three National Committeemen and three National Committeewomen except as may otherwise be provided by the Bylaws.

Section 7. The Bylaws shall provide for regional organizations of the Party.

Section 8. To assure that the Democratic nominee for the office of President of the United States is selected by a fair and equitable process, the Democratic National Committee may adopt such statements of policy as it deems appropriate with respect to the timing of Presidential nominating processes and shall work with state Parties to accomplish the objectives of such statements.

Section 9. The Democratic National Committee shall maintain and publish a code of fair campaign practices, which shall be recommended for observance by all candidates campaigning as Democrats.

Section 10. The Democratic Party shall not require a delegate to a Party convention or caucus to cast a vote contrary to his or her expressed preference.

Section 11. Voting by proxy shall not be permitted at the National Convention. Voting by proxy shall otherwise be permitted in Democratic Party affairs only as provided in the Bylaws of the Democratic Party.

Section 12. All meetings of the Democratic National Committee, the Executive Committee, and all other official Party committees, commissions and bodies shall be open to the public, and votes shall not be taken by secret ballot.

Section 13. The Democratic National Committee shall prepare and make available to the public an annual report concerning the financial affairs of the Democratic Party.

Section 14. In the absence of other provisions, Robert's Rules of Order (as most recently revised) shall govern the conduct of all Democratic Party meetings.

Section 15. The text of the Charter and the Bylaws, or portions thereof, shall be made available in other languages as needed upon reasonable request.

Section 16. The membership of the Democratic National Committee, the Executive Committee, Democratic state central committees, and all national official Party Conventions, committees, commissions, and like bodies shall be equally divided between men and women. State Parties shall take provable positive steps to achieve legislative changes to bring the law into compliance with this provision wherever this provision conflicts with state statutes.

Section 17. *Democratic Party Credo.* We Democrats are the oldest political party in America and the youngest in spirit. We will remain so, because we enjoy the challenge of government. Time and again, for almost two centuries, the Democratic Party has made government work—to build and defend a nation, to encourage commerce, to educate our children, to promote equal opportunity, to advance science and industry, to support the arts and humanities, to restore the land, to develop and conserve our human and natural resources, to preserve and enhance our built environment, to relieve poverty, to explore space. We have reached difficult and vital goals.

We recognize that the capacity of government is limited but we regard democratic government as a force for good and a source of hope.

At the heart of our party lies a fundamental conviction, that Americans must not only be free, but they must live in a fair society.

We believe it is the responsibility of government to help us achieve this fair society:

- a society where the elderly and the disabled can lead lives of dignity and where Social Security remains an unshakable commitment;
- a society where all people can find jobs in a growing full-employment economy;
- a society where all workers are guaranteed without question the legal right to join unions of their own choosing and to bargain collectively for decent wages and conditions of employment;
- a society where taxes are clearly based on ability to pay;
- a society where the equal rights of women are guaranteed in the Constitution;
- a society where the civil rights of minorities are fully secured and where no one is denied the opportunity for a better life;
- a society where both public and private discrimination based upon race, sex, age, color, creed, national origin, religion, ethnic identity, sexual orientation, economic status, philosophical persuasion or physical disability are condemned and where our government moves aggressively to end such discrimination through lawful means;
- a society where we recognize that the strengthening of the family and the protection of children are essential to the health of the nation;
- a society where a sound education, proper nutrition, quality medical care, affordable housing, safe streets and a healthy environment are possible for every citizen;
- a society where the livelihoods of our family farmers are as stable as the values they instill in the American character;
- a society where a strong national defense is a common effort, where promoting human rights is a basic value of our foreign policy, and where we ensure that future by ending the nuclear arms race.

This is our purpose and our promise.

Article Ten

Amendments, Bylaws, and Rules

Section 1. This Charter may be amended by a vote of a majority of all of the delegates to the National Convention, provided that no such amendment shall be effective unless and until it is subsequently ratified by a vote of the majority of the entire membership of the Democratic National Committee. This Charter may also be amended by a vote of two-thirds of the entire membership of the Democratic National Committee. At least thirty days written notice shall be given of any National Committee meeting at which action will be taken pursuant to this Section; and any proposed amendment shall be given to all members of the National Committee and shall be released to the national news media. This Charter may also be amended by a vote of two-thirds of the entire membership of any Democratic Party Conference called under the authority of this Charter for such purpose.

Section 2. Bylaws of the Democratic Party shall be adopted to provide for the governance of the affairs of the Democratic Party in matters not provided for in this Charter. Bylaws may be adopted or amended by a majority vote of:

(a) the National Convention; or
(b) the Democratic National Committee provided that thirty days written notice of any proposed Bylaw or amendment has been given to all members of the National Committee.

Unless adopted in the form of an amendment to this Charter or otherwise designated, any resolution adopted by the National Convention relating to the governance of the Party shall be considered a Bylaw.

Section 3. Each official body of the Democratic Party created under the authority of this Charter shall adopt and conduct its affairs in accordance with written rules, which rules shall be consistent with this Charter, the Bylaws and other provisions adopted pursuant to authority of the Charter, including resolutions or other actions of the National Convention. The Democratic National Committee shall maintain copies of all such rules and shall make them available upon request.

Section 4. Each recognized state Democratic Party shall adopt and conduct its affairs in accordance with written rules. Copies of such rules and of any changes or amendments thereto shall be filed with the Democratic National Committee within thirty days following adoption.

Resolution of Adoption

Section 1. The Democratic Party of the United States of America, assembled in a Conference on Democratic Party Organization and Policy pursuant to resolution adopted by the 1972 Democratic National Convention and the Call to the Conference hereby adopts for the governance of the Party the Charter attached hereto.

BYLAWS

Adopted Pursuant to the Charter
of the Democratic Party of the United States

Article One

Democratic National Convention

Section 1. The National Convention is the highest authority of the Democratic Party, subject to the provisions of the Charter.

Section 2. The National Convention shall adopt permanent rules governing the conduct of its business at the beginning of each Convention, and until the adoption of such permanent rules, the Convention and the activities attendant thereto shall be governed by temporary rules set forth in the Call to the National Convention.

Section 3. Delegates to the National Convention shall be allocated in the Call to the Convention consistent with the Charter.

Article Two

Democratic National Committee

Section 1. *Duties and Powers.* The Democratic National Committee shall have general responsibility for the affairs of the Democratic Party between National Conventions, subject to the provisions of the Charter and to the resolutions or other official actions of the National Convention. This responsibility shall include, but not be limited to:

(a) Issuing the Call to the National Convention;

(b) Conducting the Party's Presidential Campaign;

(c) Filling vacancies in the nominations for the office of the President and Vice President;

(d) Assisting state and local Democratic Party organizations in the election of their candidates and the education of their voters;

(e) Formulating and disseminating statements of Party policy, promoting programs for the systematic study of public policy issues, through participation of members of the Democratic National Committee and through specific projects administered under the authority of the Chairperson of the Democratic National Committee;

(f) Providing for the election or appointment of a Chairperson, five Vice Chairpersons, three of whom shall be of the opposite sex of the Chairperson, one of whom shall be the President of the Association of State Democratic Chairs and one of whom shall be Vice Chairperson for Voter Registration and Participation, a Treasurer, a National Finance Chair, a Secretary and other appropriate officers of the National Committee as shall be determined by the Committee, and for the filling of vacancies;

(g) Establishing and maintaining National Headquarters of the Party;

(h) Promoting and encouraging Party activities at every level, including but not limited to the following:
   (i) promoting and encouraging implementation of all Party mandates;
   (ii) the fulfillment by the Party of its platform pledge and other commitments;
   (iii) establishment and support of an adequate system of political research;
   (iv) the preparation, distribution and communication of Party information to its members and the general public;
   (v) the development and maintenance of a program of public relations for the Party; and
   (vi) development of a program for the coordination of Party committees, organizations, groups, public officials and members.

(i) Devising and executing ways and means of financing activities of the Party;

(j) Taking such other action as may be necessary and proper to carry out the provisions of the Charter, these Bylaws, the resolutions and other official actions to achieve the objectives of the Party and the Convention; and

(k) Approval of the budget of the Democratic National Committee.

Section 2. *Membership.* The Democratic National Committee shall be composed of:

(a) The Chairperson and the highest ranking officer of the opposite sex of each recognized state Democratic Party as defined by Article Nine of the Charter;

(b) Two hundred additional members apportioned to the states on the basis set forth in Article Two, Section 5(a) of the Charter, provided that each state shall have at least two additional members;

(c) The Chairperson of the Democratic Governors' Association and two additional governors, of whom, to the extent possible, at least one shall be of the opposite sex of the Chairperson, as selected by the Association;

(d) The Democratic Leader in the United States Senate and the Democratic Leader in the United States House of Representatives and one additional member of each body, who, to the extent possible, shall be of the opposite sex of, and appointed by the respective leaders;

(e) The Chairperson, five Vice Chairpersons, the

National Finance Chair, the Treasurer and the Secretary of the Democratic National Committee;

(f) The Chairperson of the National Conference of Democratic Mayors and two additional mayors, at least one of whom shall be of the opposite sex of the Chairperson, as selected by the Conference;

(g) The President of the Young Democrats of America and two additional members, at least one of whom shall be of the opposite sex of the President, as selected by the organization biennially in convention assembled;

(h) The President of the National Federation of Democratic Women and two additional members selected by the Federation;

(i) The Chairperson of the Democratic County Officials and two additional members, at least one of whom shall be of the opposite sex of the Chairperson, as selected by the organization;

(j) The Chairperson of the Democratic State Legislative Leaders Association and two additional state legislators, at least one of whom shall be of the opposite sex of the Chairperson, as selected by the Association;

(k) The Chairperson of the National Democratic Municipal Officials Conference and two additional municipal officials, of whom, to the extent possible, at least one shall be of the opposite sex of the Chairperson, as selected by the Conference;

(l) Additional members as provided in Article Nine of the Charter;

(m) The President of the College Democrats of America and the Vice President, who shall be of the opposite sex, as elected by the organization annually;

(n) The Chairperson of the National Association of Democratic State Treasurers and the Vice Chair, who shall be of the opposite sex, as selected by the Association;

(o) The Chairperson of the National Association of Democratic Lieutenant Governors and the Vice Chair, who shall be of the opposite sex, as selected by the Association;

(p) The Chairperson of the Democratic Association of Secretaries of State and the Vice Chair, who shall be of the opposite sex, as selected by the Association;

(q) No more than sixty-five additional members of the Democratic National Committee may be added by the foregoing members.

Section 3.   *Selection of Members.*

(a) Members of the Democratic National Committee apportioned to the states pursuant to the provisions of Section 2(b) of this Article and those apportioned pursuant to the provisions of Article Nine of the

Charter who are not otherwise members by virtue of Party office shall be selected by each state or territorial Democratic Party in accordance with standards as to participation established under Section 11 of this Article through processes which assure full, timely and equal opportunity to participate. The method of selection for such members shall be described in detail in each state or territory's Party rules and shall be by one of the following methods or any combination thereof:

(i) by a meeting of the National Convention delegation from the state or territory authorized to elect National Committee members, at an open meeting called within the calendar year of the Convention after effective public notice of the agenda;

(ii) by state or territorial Primary within the calendar year of the National Convention;

(iii) by state or territorial Party committees in an open meeting within the calendar year of the National Convention called after effective public notice of the agenda;

(iv) by a state or territorial convention authorized to select national committee members in an open meeting within the calendar year of the National Convention called after effective public notice of the agenda; and

(v) by such other method as may be adopted by a state or territorial Party and approved by the Democratic National Committee.

(b) Selection by any of the above methods shall be held to meet the requirements of full, timely and equal opportunity to participate if the selecting body has been established according to law and the Charter and the rules of such body have been approved by the Democratic National Committee.

(c) Members of the Democratic National Committee who serve by virtue of holding Party office shall be selected by each state Party in accordance with standards as to participation appearing in Section 11 of this Article.

(d) When the number of members apportioned to a state or territory pursuant to Section 2(b) of this Article or Article Nine of the Charter is even, there shall be equal division of members between men and women. In such cases where the number is odd, the variance between men and women may not be greater than one.

Section 4.   *Certification and Eligibility of Members.*

(a) Members of the Democratic National Committee provided for in Section 2 of this Article shall be certified to the National Committee as follows:

(i)   those authorized under subsections (a) and (b) of Section 2 shall be certified by the proper Party authority of the state or territory;

(ii) those authorized under subsection (c) of Section 2 shall be certified by the Chairperson of the Democratic Governors' Association;

(iii) those authorized under subsection (d) of Section 2 shall be certified by the Democratic Leader in the United States Senate for the members from that body and by the Democratic Leader in the United States House of Representatives for the members from that body;

(iv) those authorized under subsection (f) of Section 2 shall be certified by the Chairperson of the Conference of Democratic Mayors;

(v)   those authorized under subsection (g) of Section 2 shall be certified by the President of the Young Democrats of America;

(vi) those authorized under subsection (h) of Section 2 shall be certified by the President of the National Federation of Democratic Women;

(vii) those authorized under subsection (i) of Section 2 shall be certified by the Chairperson of the Democratic County Officials Conference;

(viii) those authorized under subsection (j) of Section 2 shall be certified by the Chairperson of the Democratic State Legislative Leaders Association;

(ix) those authorized under subsection (k) of Section 2 shall be certified by the Chairperson of the National Democratic Municipal Officials Conference;

(x)   those authorized under subsection (m) of Section 2 shall be certified by the President of the College Democrats of America;

(xi) those authorized under subsection (n) of Section 2 shall be certified by the Chairperson of the National Association of Democratic State Treasurers;

(xii) those authorized under subsection (o) of Section 2 shall be certified by the Chairperson of the National Association of Democratic Lieutenant Governors:

(xiii) those authorized under subsection (p) of Section 2 shall be certified by the Chairperson of the Democratic Association of Secretaries of State;

(xiv) those otherwise authorized under Section 2 shall be certified by the Chairperson of the Democratic National Committee.

(b) No person who is not or who does not continue to be a resident for voting purposes of the jurisdiction which he or she represents shall be eligible to hold such office.

(c) No person shall be entitled to vote on a challenge to his or her credentials.

(d) Contests involving membership or challenges to credentials of members shall be heard and adjudicated by the National Committee as determined or provided in Article Two, Section 10(b) of these Bylaws.

Section 5. *Resignation or Removal of Members.*

(a) A member of the Democratic National Committee may resign by written notice to the Chairperson of the National Committee, and such resignation shall be effective immediately.

(b) After notice and opportunity for public hearing and upon grounds found by the National Committee to constitute good and sufficient cause, the National Committee may remove a member by two-thirds vote of the National Committee.

(c) Failure of any member of the National Committee to declare affirmatively his or her support for the Democratic Presidential and Vice Presidential nominees within thirty (30) days after the adjournment of the National Convention shall constitute good and sufficient cause for removal.

Section 6. *Vacancies.* Vacancies created by resignation or removal of any member of the National Committee shall be filled as follows:

(a) Vacancies in membership apportioned to the states and territories pursuant to Section 2(b) of this Article and Article Nine of the Charter shall be filled by a state or territorial Party in open meeting called after effective public notice of the agenda.

(b) Vacancies created by the removal or resignation of a state Chairperson or highest ranking officer of the opposite sex shall be filled only by their successors in accordance with Section 3(b) of this Article.

(c) Vacancies in the at-large membership of the National Committee shall be filled by the National Committee.

(d) Vacancies in positions filled by the Democratic Governors' Association, the Democratic Mayors Conference, the House and Senate Leadership, the Young Democrats of America, the Democratic County Officials Conference, the State Legislative Leaders Association, the National Federation of

Democratic Women, the National Democratic Municipal Officials Conference, and the College Democrats of America shall be filled by the selecting authority, and in the case where the selecting authority is not in session nor will be in session for a year subsequent to the vacancy, by the body charged with fulfilling the responsibilities of operating the organization between meetings of the full group.

Section 7. *Meetings.*

(a) The National Committee shall meet as soon as possible after the adjournment of the National Convention on the call of the Chairperson. The Committee is authorized to organize with those members already selected, including any person seated temporarily as provided in Section 10(b)(iv) and entitled to serve as of the first meeting of the Committee. They shall select those members of the Executive Committee who are selected by the Regional Caucuses, who shall serve with those who serve by reason of office until the next regular meeting of the Democratic National Committee.

(b) At least two meetings of the National Committee shall be held each year upon call of the Chairperson and after notice to members, unless any such meeting is dispensed with by prior vote of a majority of the full membership of the National Committee.

(c) Special meetings of the National Committee may be held upon the call of the Chairperson with the approval of the Executive Committee with reasonable notice to the members, and no action may be taken at such a special meeting unless such proposed action was included in the notice of the special meeting. The foregoing notwithstanding, a special meeting to fill a vacancy on the National ticket shall be held on the call of the Chairperson, who shall set the date for such meeting in accordance with the procedural rules provided for in Article Two, Section 8(d) of these Bylaws.

(d) No later than thirty (30) days before each regularly scheduled meeting, and as soon as possible before a special meeting of the Democratic National Committee, the Secretary of the Democratic National Committee shall send written notice of the date, time and place of such meeting, and the tentative agenda to all members of the Democratic National Committee.

(e) Upon the written request of twenty-five percent (25%) or more of the members of the National Committee, filed with the Chairperson within a period of thirty (30) days, it shall be the duty of the Chairperson within fifteen (15) days from receipt of such request to issue a call for a meeting of the National Committee. The date of such meeting shall be fixed by the Chairperson not later than thirty (30) days nor earlier than fifteen (15) days from the date of the call.

Section 8. *Quorum and Voting.*

(a) A majority of the full membership of the Democratic National Committee present in person or by proxy shall constitute a quorum, provided that no less than forty percent (40%) of the full membership be present in person for the purpose of establishing a quorum; provided, however, that for purposes of voting to fill a vacancy on the National ticket, a quorum shall be a majority of the full membership present in person.

(b) Except as otherwise provided in the Charter or in these Bylaws, all questions before the Democratic National Committee shall be determined by majority vote of those members present and voting in person or by proxy.

  (i) Up to sixty-five additional members at-large of the Democratic National Committee added by the remaining members pursuant to Article Three, Section 2 of the Charter and ten members at-large of the Executive Committee selected by the Democratic National Committee pursuant to Article Three, Section 2 of the Bylaws may be elected by plurality vote of the members voting in person or by proxy; and

  (ii) A roll call may be requested by a vote of twenty-five percent (25%) of those Democratic National Committee members present and voting.

(c) Each member of the National Committee shall be entitled to one vote on each issue before it, except that Guam, the Virgin Islands, and American Samoa shall each be entitled to a total of only one vote. This vote shall be shared among the Chairperson, the highest ranking officer of the opposite sex, the National Committeeman and the National Committeewoman who are present and voting. Democrats Abroad shall have two votes on the Democratic National Committee, which votes shall be shared by the Chairperson, the highest ranking officer of the opposite sex, three National Committeemen and three National Committeewomen.

(d) Voting to fill a vacancy on the National ticket shall be in accord with procedural rules adopted by the Rules and Bylaws Committee and approved by the Democratic National Committee.

(e) Proxy voting shall be permitted. Proxies may be either general or limited and either instructed or uninstructed. All proxies shall be in writing and transferable if so specified. No DNC member may at any one time hold or exercise proxies for more than one other DNC member; provided, however, that proxy voting shall not be permitted in voting to fill a vacancy on the National ticket.

(f) The Chairperson of the National Committee may refer matters to the members of the National Committee for consideration and vote by mail, provided, however, that if members aggregating more than twenty percent (20%) of the full membership shall so request, the matter shall be presented to the next meeting of the National Committee.

Section 9. *Regional Caucuses.* There shall be four Regional Caucuses of the members of a Democratic National Committee, comprised as follows:

Eastern

  Connecticut
  Delaware
  District of Columbia
  Maine
  Maryland
  Massachusetts
  New Hampshire
  New Jersey
  New York
  Pennsylvania
  Puerto Rico
  Rhode Island
  Vermont
  Virgin Islands
  Democrats Abroad ($\frac{1}{2}$ vote)

Southern

  Alabama
  Arkansas
  Florida
  Georgia
  Kentucky
  Louisiana
  Mississippi
  North Carolina
  South Carolina
  Tennessee
  Texas
  Virginia
  West Virginia
  Democrats Abroad ($\frac{1}{2}$ vote)

Midwestern

  Illinois
  Indiana
  Iowa
  Kansas
  Michigan
  Minnesota
  Missouri
  North Dakota
  Ohio
  Oklahoma
  South Dakota
  Wisconsin
  Democrats Abroad ($\frac{1}{2}$ vote)

Western

  Alaska
  American Samoa
  Arizona
  California
  Colorado
  Guam
  Hawaii
  Idaho
  Montana
  Nevada
  New Mexico
  Oregon
  Utah
  Washington
  Wyoming
  Democrats Abroad ($\frac{1}{2}$ vote)

Section 10. *Committees.*

(a) In addition to the Committees otherwise provided for in the Charter there shall be the following standing committees of the Democratic National Committee:
   (i) Credentials Committee;
   (ii) Resolutions Committee;
   (iii) Rules and Bylaws Committee.

(b) (i) The Credentials Committee shall receive and consider all challenges to the credentials of Democratic National Committee members.
   (ii) Any challenge to the credentials of a member of the Democratic National Committee may be made by any Democrat from the state or territory of the member challenged or any member of the Democratic National Committee and shall be filed by Registered Mail (return receipt requested) within

thirty (30) days of the selection of such member.

(iii) The Credentials Committee shall determine the validity of the credentials of those elected to the National Committee, and decide all challenges to the seating of such members. The Credentials Committee shall provide each party to a dispute a reasonable opportunity to be heard, and may give an opportunity for submission of briefs and oral argument and shall render a written report on the issues to the National Committee.

(iv) The National Committee shall proceed to a determination of such contest or contests as its first order of business, if feasible, including the temporary seating of challenged members, in order that the members may participate in other business before the National Committee.

(c) (i) The Resolutions Committee shall receive and consider all resolutions proposed by a member of the Democratic National Committee on matters of policy proposed for adoption by the Democratic National Committee, and shall report in writing. Said report shall contain the text of each resolution recommended by the Committee for adoption, and shall identify resolutions considered but not recommended for adoption; and

(ii) Resolutions shall be submitted to the Secretary of the Democratic National Committee at least twenty-one (21) days prior to the meeting of the National Committee, and copies of all such resolutions shall be sent to each member no less than fourteen (14) days prior to the National Committee meeting, provided that the Executive Committee may vote to submit urgent timely resolutions to the National Committee even though not submitted within these time periods.

(d) (i) The Rules and Bylaws Committee shall receive and consider allrecommendations for adoption and amendments to the Rules and Bylaws of the National Committee and to the Charter of the Democratic Party of the United States;

(ii) recommendations for amendment to the Charter of the Democratic Party of the United States shall be received by the Rules and Bylaws Committee no less than sixty (60) days prior to a regular meeting of the Democratic National Committee, provided that the Executive Committee may approve direct submission of a recommended amendment to the Charter if the requirements of timeliness of the Charter are otherwise met;

(iii) recommendations for amendment to the Bylaws or adoption of Rules for the Democratic National Committee shall be submitted to the Rules Committee no less than thirty (30) days prior to a meeting of the National Committee, and the Secretary of the National Committee shall mail such proposed recommendations to the members no less than thirty (30) days prior to the National Committee. It shall be the responsibility of the member of the National Committee submitting a Bylaws Amendment to distribute a copy to all members of the Committee within the time required by these Bylaws for consideration, or submit the request to the Secretary with ample time to make such distribution;

(iv) The Executive Committee may refer to the Rules and Bylaws Committee for preliminary consideration the temporary Rules of the National Convention to be included in the Call to the Convention, and the Executive Committee may adopt the recommendations of the Rules and Bylaws Committee as such temporary Convention rules;

(v) the Rules and Bylaws Committee shall conduct a continuing study of the Bylaws, Rules and Charter and make periodic recommendations for amendment, extension or other action, provided that any such recommendations by the Rules and Bylaws Committee be submitted to the members of the National Committee at the time the agenda is presented; and

(vi) the report of the Rules and Bylaws Committee shall be in writing and shall contain the full text of action recommended and shall identify recommendations not approved by the Committee for adoption.

(e) The National Committee may from time to time create such other standing or *ad hoc* committees as it shall deem appropriate.

(f) Except as otherwise provided in the Charter or in these Bylaws, the members of all committees of the National Committee shall be appointed by the Chairperson of the Democratic National Committee, in consultation with the Executive Committee, subject to ratification by the Democratic National Committee, and shall be appointed to serve for the tenure of the Chairperson.

(g) The provisions of Section 8(e) of this Article shall apply to committees of the National Committee.

(h) All matters referred to any council, special committee, standing committee, conference or any other sub-group must be acted upon and said action reported to the body which originated the reference.

Section 11.   *Participation in All Party Affairs.*

(a) The Democratic Party of the United States shall be open to all who desire to support the Party and who wish to be known as Democrats. Participation in the affairs of the Democratic Party shall be open pursuant to the standards of non-discrimination and affirmative action incorporated into the Charter of the Democratic Party of the United States.

(b) (i) The National, state, and local Democratic Party organizations shall undertake affirmative action programs designed to encourage the fullest participation of all Democrats in all Party Affairs. All Party Affairs shall mean all activities of each official Party organization commencing at the lowest level and continuing up through the National Democratic Party. Such activities shall include but need not be limited to the processes in which delegates are selected to the National Democratic Convention; Party officials are nominated or selected; Party policy, platforms, and rules are formulated; and regular programs of voter registration, public education and public relations. Such programs may be developed and sponsored in cooperation with the Democratic National Committee.

(ii) National and state Democratic Parties shall carry out programs to facilitate and increase the participation of low- and moderate-income persons. These programs shall include provisions and resources for outreach and recruitment to achieve representation and equitably minimize economic factors which act to bar full participation by such persons.

(iii) State and National Parties shall act affirmatively to develop and implement appropriate education, training, fund-raising and outreach programs directed at low- and moderate-income Democrats and shall implement rules and regulations of the Party in their most constructive interpretation to effect increased participation and representation by people of low and moderate income. Non-discrimination as it relates to this Section 11(b) and as provided in Article Eight, Section 2 of the Charter shall be strictly enforced.

(c) (i) Each state or territorial Party shall require each unit of the Party which holds such meetings to publicize effectively and in a timely fashion the dates, times, and places of all such meetings, and the name or names of the person responsible for such meetings.

(ii) Notice of meetings shall be published as required in this Section prior to the meeting. Such notice may appear as legal notice, paid advertisement, news item, direct mail, radio or television announcement, or in such other form as may reasonably be designed to notify Democrats of the meeting provided no state, territorial, or county Party is required to purchase paid advertising; and

(iii) If challenged, a state or territorial Party shall be deemed to be in compliance with this Section upon proof of effective notice from the reporting unit of the Party.

(d) If a county or any local unit of the state or territorial Party fails to comply with the foregoing provisions of this Section, the state or territorial Party may assume responsibility for setting dates, times and places for local meetings and for giving notice of the same as provided in this Section.

(e) Each state or territorial Party may establish such procedures and structures as are necessary to ensure compliance with this Section, including procedures for review of complaints of non-compliance with this Section by any unit of the political process, including the state.

(f) If a state or territorial Party is alleged to have failed to comply with this Section, the alleged non-compliance shall be referred to the Democratic National Committee for review provided that any person alleging non-compliance at any level shall be a resident of the affected jurisdiction and provided that any person alleging non-compliance of a state or territorial Party with this Section shall have exhausted all remedies provided by the state or territorial Party.

Section 12.   *Duties and Responsibilities of the Chairperson.*

(a) The Chairperson shall be the chief executive officer of the Democratic National Committee and shall exercise authority delegated to him or her by the Democratic National Committee and the Democratic National Committee's Executive Committee in carrying out the day-to-day activities of the Committee.

(b) By the time of the next DNC meeting following his or her election, the Chairperson shall designate a Vice Chair who will have authority to act as

Chairperson should a vacancy occur or should the Chairperson become incapacitated. In the event of such succession, the designated Vice Chair will serve in the capacity of the Chairperson until a new Chairperson is elected at the next regularly scheduled meeting of the full Democratic National Committee.

Article Three

Executive Committee

Section 1. Powers and Duties. The Executive Committee of the Democratic National Committee shall be responsible for the conduct of the affairs of the Democratic Party in the interim between the meetings of the full Committee. This responsibility shall include, but not be limited to:

(a) Authority for the Democratic National Committee between meetings thereof;

(b) Recommending approval of the budget of the Democratic National Committee, electing the members of the National Education and Training Council, approving the budget and overseeing the operations of such Council; and

(c) Reporting all of its proceedings to the Democratic National Committee.

Section 2. Membership. The Executive Committee shall be composed of:

(a) The Chairpersons of the Regional Caucuses of the Democratic National Committee who must be members of the Democratic National Committee;

(b) Four members elected by each of the Regional Caucuses of the Democratic National Committee, who shall be equally divided between men and women and all of whom shall be members of the Democratic National Committee;

(c) The Chairperson, the five Vice Chairpersons, the Treasurer, and the Secretary of the Democratic National Committee;

(d) The National Finance Chair;

(e) The Chairperson of the Democratic Governors' Association or his or her designee from that Association, who must be a member of the Democratic National Committee;

(f) The Democratic Leader of the United States Senate or his or her designee, who must be a member of the Democratic National Committee, and the Democratic Leader from the United States House of Representatives or his or her designee, who must be a member of the Democratic National Committee;

(g) The Chairperson of the National Conference of Democratic Mayors or his or her designee, who must be a member of the Democratic National Committee;

(h) The Chairperson of the Democratic State Legislative Leaders Association or his or her designee from that Association, who must be a member of the Democratic National Committee;

(i) The Chairperson of the National Democratic County Officials or his or her designee, who must be a member of the Democratic National Committee;

(j) The Chairperson of the National Democratic Municipal Officials Conference or his or her designee, who must be a member of the Democratic National Committee;

(k) The President of the Young Democrats of America or his or her designee, who must be a member of the Democratic National Committee;

(l) Three additional members of the Association of State Democratic Chairs to be selected by the Association;

(m) The President of the National Federation of Democratic Women or her designee, who must be a member of the Democratic National Committee;

(n) The Chairs of the Hispanic and Black Caucuses of the Democratic National Committee;

(o) The Chair of the Women's Caucus of the Democratic National Committee or her designee, who must be a member of the Democratic National Committee;

(p) Ten members at-large, elected by the Democratic National Committee, who shall be equally divided between men and women, all of whom must be members of the Democratic National Committee.

(q) Any designee as provided for in this Section may not otherwise be a member of the Executive Committee and must be a member of the organization or constituency he or she is designated to represent.

Section 3. Election of Members.

(a) Elected members of the Executive Committee shall be elected:
   (i) at the first meeting of the Democratic National Committee held after the National Convention;
   (ii) at a meeting of the Democratic National Committee held after the succeeding presidential election and prior to March 1 next; and
   (iii) whenever a vacancy occurs.

(b) Members of the Executive Committee shall serve until the election of their successors. Upon the resignation of a member, a successor shall be selected by the original official authority to serve the unexpired portion of the term.

Section 4. *Meetings.* The Executive Committee shall meet at least four times each year. Meetings shall be called by the Chairperson or by written request of no fewer than one-fourth of its members. The Executive Committee shall keep a record of its proceedings which shall be available to the public.

Section 5. *Quorum and Voting.* The provisions of Section 8 of Article Two of these Bylaws shall apply to the Executive Committee.

Article Four

National Finance Organizations

Section 1. *Duties and Powers.* The National Finance Organizations of the Democratic Party shall have general responsibility for the finances of the Democratic Party for raising funds to support the Democratic Party and the Democratic National Committee to advise and assist state Democratic Parties and candidates in securing funds for their purposes. The National Finance Chair and the Treasurer will advise the National Chairperson of the Democratic Party and the Executive Committee of the Democratic National Committee with respect to the finances of the Democratic Party.

Article Five

Amendments

Bylaws may be adopted or amended by majority vote of:

(a) the National Convention; or
(b) the Democratic National Committee provided that thirty (30) days written notice of any proposed Bylaw or amendment has been given to all members of the National Committee. Unless adopted in the form of an amendment to the Charter or otherwise designated, any resolution adopted by the National Convention relating to the governance of the Party shall be considered a Bylaw.

APPENDIX 2

Democratic Leaders and Whips of the House of Representatives

Congress	Majority/Minority	Leader	Whip
56th	Minority	James D. Richardson	Oscar W. Underwood
57th	Minority	James D. Richardson	James T. Lloyd
58th	Minority	John Sharp Williams	James T. Lloyd
59th	Minority	John Sharp Williams	James T. Lloyd
60th	Minority	Williams/Champ Clark	James T. Lloyd
61st	Minority	Champ Clark	None
62nd	Majority	Oscar W. Underwood	None
63rd	Majority	Oscar W. Underwood	Thomas M. Bell
64th	Majority	Claude Kitchin	None
65th	Majority	Claude Kitchin	None
66th	Minority	Champ Clark	None
67th	Minority	Claude Kitchin	William A. Oldfield
68th	Minority	Finis J. Garrett	William A. Oldfield
69th	Minority	Finis J. Garrett	William A. Oldfield
70th	Minority	Finis J. Garrett	Oldfield/John McDuffie
71st	Minority	John N. Garner	John McDuffie
72nd	Majority	Henry T. Rainey	John McDuffie
73rd	Majority	Joseph H. Byrnes	Arthur H. Greenwood

Congress	Majority/Minority	Leader	Whip
74th	Majority	William B. Bankhead	Patrick J. Boland
75th	Majority	Sam Rayburn	Patrick J. Boland
76th	Majority	Rayburn/John W. McCormack	Patrick J. Boland
77th	Majority	John W. McCormack	Boland/Robert Ramspeck
78th	Majority	John W. McCormack	Robert Ramspeck
79th	Majority	John W. McCormack	Ramspeck/John J. Sparkman
80th	Minority	Sam Rayburn	John W. McCormack
81st	Majority	John W. McCormack	J. Percy Priest
82nd	Majority	John W. McCormack	J. Percy Priest
83rd	Minority	Sam Rayburn	John W. McCormack
84th	Majority	John W. McCormack	Carl Albert
85th	Majority	John W. McCormack	Carl Albert
86th	Majority	John W. McCormack	Carl Albert
87th	Majority	McCormack/Carl Albert	Albert/Hale Boggs
88th	Majority	Carl Albert	Hale Boggs
89th	Majority	Carl Albert	Hale Boggs
90th	Majority	Carl Albert	Hale Boggs
91st	Majority	Carl Albert	Hale Boggs
92nd	Majority	Hale Boggs	Thomas P. O'Neill Jr.
93rd	Majority	Thomas P. O'Neill Jr.	John J. McFall
94th	Majority	Thomas P. O'Neill Jr.	John J. McFall
95th	Majority	James C. Wright Jr.	John Brademas
96th	Majority	James C. Wright Jr.	John Brademas
97th	Majority	James C. Wright Jr.	Thomas S. Foley
98th	Majority	James C. Wright Jr.	Thomas S. Foley
99th	Majority	James C. Wright Jr.	Thomas S. Foley
100th	Majority	Thomas S. Foley	Tony Coelho
101st	Majority	Thomas S. Foley	Tony Coelho
102nd	Majority	Richard S. Gephardt	William H. Gray III
103rd	Majority	Richard S. Gephardt	David E. Bonior
104th	Minority	Richard S. Gephardt	David E. Bonior

APPENDIX 3

Democratic Leaders in the Senate

Congress	Majority/Minority	Leader	Whip
62nd	Minority	Thomas S. Martin	None
63rd	Majority	John W. Kern	J. Hamilton Lewis
64th	Majority	John W. Kern	J. Hamilton Lewis
65th	Majority	Thomas S. Martin	J. Hamilton Lewis
66th	Minority	Martin/Oscar W. Underwood	Peter G. Gerry
67th	Minority	Oscar W. Underwood	Peter G. Gerry
68th	Minority	Joseph T. Robinson	Peter G. Gerry
69th	Minority	Joseph T. Robinson	Peter G. Gerry
70th	Minority	Joseph T. Robinson	Peter G. Gerry
71st	Minority	Joseph T. Robinson	Morris Sheppard
72nd	Minority	Joseph T. Robinson	Morris Sheppard

Congress	Majority/Minority	Leader	Whip
73rd	Majority	Joseph T. Robinson	J. Hamilton Lewis
74th	Majority	Joseph T. Robinson	J. Hamilton Lewis
75th	Majority	Robinson/Alben W. Barkley	J. Hamilton Lewis
76th	Majority	Alben W. Barkley	Sherman Minton
77th	Majority	Alben W. Barkley	Lister Hill
78th	Majority	Alben W. Barkley	Lister Hill
79th	Majority	Alben W. Barkley	Lister Hill
80th	Minority	Alben W. Barkley	Scott W. Lucas
81st	Majority	Scott W. Lucas	Francis Myers
82nd	Majority	Ernest W. McFarland	Lyndon Baines Johnson
83rd	Minority	Lyndon Baines Johnson	Earle Clements
84th	Majority	Lyndon Baines Johnson	Earle Clements
85th	Majority	Lyndon Baines Johnson	Mike Mansfield
86th	Majority	Lyndon Baines Johnson	Mike Mansfield
87th	Majority	Mike Mansfield	Hubert H. Humphrey
88th	Majority	Mike Mansfield	Hubert H. Humphrey
89th	Majority	Mike Mansfield	Russell Long
90th	Majority	Mike Mansfield	Russell Long
91st	Majority	Mike Mansfield	Edward M. Kennedy
92nd	Majority	Mike Mansfield	Robert C. Byrd
93rd	Majority	Mike Mansfield	Robert C. Byrd
94th	Majority	Mike Mansfield	Robert C. Byrd
95th	Majority	Robert C. Byrd	Alan Cranston
96th	Majority	Robert C. Byrd	Alan Cranston
97th	Minority	Robert C. Byrd	Alan Cranston
98th	Minority	Robert C. Byrd	Alan Cranston
99th	Minority	Robert C. Byrd	Alan Cranston
100th	Majority	Robert C. Byrd	Alan Cranston
101st	Majority	George J. Mitchell	Alan Cranston
102nd	Majority	George J. Mitchell	Wendell H. Ford
103rd	Majority	George J. Mitchell	Wendell H. Ford
104th	Minority	Tom Daschle	Wendell H. Ford

APPENDIX 4

Party Defections in Congress

Name	State	Year	House/Senate	Direction
Wayne Morse	OR	1952	Senate	R → I → D
Strom Thurmond	SC	1964	Senate	D → R
Albert W. Watson	SC	1965	House	D → R
Harry F. Byrd Jr.	VA	1970	Senate	D → I
Ogden R. Reid	NY	1972	House	R → D
Donald W. Reigle	MI	1973	House	R → D
John Jarman	OK	1975	House	D → R

Name	State	Year	House/Senate	Direction
Peter A. Peyser	NY	1976	House	R → D
Eugene A. Atkinson	PA	1981	House	D →R
Bob Stump	AZ	1981	House	D → R
Phil Gramm	TX	1983	House	D → R
Andy Ireland	FL	1984	House	D →R
Bill Grant	FL	1989	House	D → R
Tommy Robinson	OK	1989	House	D → R
Richard Shelby	AL	1994	Senate	D → R
Ben Nighthorse Campbell	CO	1995	Senate	D → R
Greg Laughlin	TX	1995	House	D → R
Berry Tauzin	LA	1995	House	D → R
Mike Parker	MS	1995	House	D → R
Jimmy Hayes	LA	1995	House	D → R

APPENDIX 5

Democratic Party Convention Sites and Dates

1822
The Atheneum
Baltimore, MD
May 21–23

1836
Fourth Presbyterian Church
Baltimore, MD
May 20–22, 1835

1840
Hall of Musical Association
Baltimore, MD
May 5–6

1844
Old Fellows' Hall
Baltimore, MD
May 27–29

1848
Universalist Church
Baltimore, MD
May 22–25

1852
Maryland Institute Hall
Baltimore, MD
June 1–5

1856
Smith and Nixon's Hall
Cincinnati, OH
June 2–6

1860
Hall of South Carolina Institute
Charleston, SC
April 23–28, May 1–3
Northern Wing Convention
Front Street Theater
Baltimore, MD
June 18–23

1864
The Amphitheater
Chicago, IL
August 29–31

1868
Tammany Hall
New York, NY
July 4–9

1872
Ford's Opera House
Baltimore, MD
July 9–10, 1871

1876
Merchants' Exchange
St. Louis, MO
June 27–29

1880
Music Hall
Cincinnati, OH
June 22–24

1884
Exposition Hall
Chicago, IL
July 8–11

1888
Exposition Building
St. Louis, MO
June 5–7

1892
Specially Constructed Building
Chicago, IL
June 21–23

1896
The Coliseum
Chicago, IL
July 7–11

1900
Convention Hall
Kansas City, MO
July 4–6

1904
The Coliseum
St. Louis, MO
July 6–9

1908
Civic Auditorium
Denver, CO
July 7–10

1912
Fifth Maryland Regiment Armory
Baltimore, MD
June 25–29, July 1–2

1916
The Coliseum
St. Louis, MO
June 14–16

1920
Civic Auditorium
San Francisco, CA
June 28–30, July 1–3, 5–6

1924
Madison Square Garden
New York, NY
June 24–July 9

1928
Sam Houston Hall
Houston, TX
June 26–29

1932
Chicago Stadium
Chicago, IL
June 27–30, July 1–2

1936
Convention Hall
Philadelphia, PA
June 23–27

1940
Chicago Stadium
Chicago, IL
July 15–18

1944
Chicago Stadium
Chicago, IL
July 19–21

1948
Convention Hall
Philadelphia, PA
July 12–14

1952
International Amphitheater
Chicago, IL
July 21–26

1956
International Amphitheater
Chicago, IL
August 13–17

1960
Los Angeles Memorial Sports Arena and Coliseum
Los Angeles, CA
July 11–15

1964
Convention Center
Atlantic City, NJ
August 24–27

1968
International Amphitheater
Chicago, IL
August 26–29

1972
Convention Hall
Miami Beach, FL
July 10–13

1984
Moscone Center
San Francisco, CA
July 16–19

1992
Madison Square Garden
New York, NY
July 13–16

1976
Madison Square Garden
New York, NY
July 12–15

1988
The Omni
Atlanta, GA
July 18–21

1996
United Center
Chicago, IL
August 26–29

1980
Madison Square Garden
New York, NY
August 11–14

APPENDIX 6

Chairs of the Democratic National Committees

1848–52	Benjamin F. Hallett	1943–44	Frank C. Walker
1852–56	Robert M. McLane	1944–47	Robert E. Hannegan
1856–60	David A. Smalley	1947–49	J. Howard McGrath
1860–72	August Belmont	1949–51	William M. Boyle Jr.
1872–76	Augustus Schell	1951–52	Frank E. McKinney
1876–77	Abram Stevens Hewitt	1952–55	Stephen A. Mitchell
1887–89	Willam H. Barnum	1955–60	Paul M. Butler
1889–92	Calvin Stewart Brice	1960–61	Henry M. Jackson
1892–96	William F. Harrity	1961–68	John M. Bailey
1896–1904	James K. Jones	1968–69	Laurence O'Brien
1904–8	Thomas Taggart	1969–70	Fred R. Harris
1908–12	Norman E. Mack	1970–72	Laurence O'Brien
1912–16	William F. McCombs	1972	Jean Westwood
1916–19	Vance C. McCormick	1972–77	Robert Strauss
1919–20	Homer S. Cummings	1977	Kenneth Curtis
1920–21	George H. White	1977–81	John C. White
1921–24	Cordell Hull	1981–85	Charles A. Manatt
1924–28	Clement L. Shaver	1985–89	Paul G. Kirk Jr.
1928–32	John J. Raskob	1989–93	Ronald H. Brown
1932–40	James A. Farley	1993–	Donald Fowler
1940–43	Edward J. Flynn		

APPENDIX 7

Democratic State Committee Headquarters

Alabama
4120 Third Avenue South
Birmingham, AL 35222
(205) 595-9090

Alaska
P.O. Box 10-4199
Anchorage, AK 99510
(907) 258-3050

Arizona
P. O. Box 1944
Phoenix, AZ 85001
(602) 257-9136

Arkansas
1300 West Capitol
Little Rock, AR 72201
(501) 374-2361

California
329 Bryant Street, Suite 3
San Francisco, CA 94107
(415) 896-5503

Colorado
1600 Downing Street, Sixth Floor
Denver, CO 80218
(303) 830-8989

Connecticut
634 Asylum Avenue
Hartford, CT 06105
(203) 278-6080

Delaware
P. O. Box 2065
Wilmington, DE 19899
(302) 632-3051

District of Columbia
1012 14th Street N.W., Suite 803
Washington, DC 20005
(202) 347-2489

Florida
P. O. Box 1758
Tallahassee, FL 32302
(904) 222-3411

Georgia
1100 Spring Street, Suite 250
Atlanta, GA 30367
(404) 872-1992

Hawaii
661 Auahi Street, #206
Honolulu, HI 96813
(808) 536-2258

Idaho
Box 445
Boise, ID 83701
(208) 336-1815

Illinois
218 North Jefferson Street
Chicago, IL 60606
(312) 930-5855

Indiana
P. O. Box 3366
Indianapolis, IN 46206
(317) 237-3366

Iowa
2116 Grand Avenue
Des Moines, IA 50312
(515) 244-7292

Kansas
P. O. Box 1914
Topeka, KS 66601
(913) 234-0425

Kentucky
P. O. Box 694
Frankfort, KY 40602
(502) 695-4828

Louisiana
340 St. Joseph Street
Baton Rouge, LA 70802
(504) 336-4155

Maine
P. O. Box 5258
Augusta, ME 04330
(207) 622-6233

Maryland
224 Main Street
Annapolis, MD 21401
(301) 280-2300

Massachusetts
45 Bromfield Street, 7th Fl.
Boston, MA 02108
(617) 426-4760

Michigan
606 Townsend
Lansing, MI 48933
(517) 371 5410

Minnesota
525 Park Street, Suite 100
St. Paul, MN 55103
(612) 293-1200

Mississippi
P. O. Box 1583
Jackson, MS 39205
(601) 969-2913

Missouri
P. O. Box 719
Jefferson City, MO 65102
(314) 636-5241

Montana
P. O. Box 802
Helena, MT 59624
(406) 442-9520

Nebraska
7156 South 14th Street
Lincoln, NE 68508
(402) 475-4584

Nevada
1155 East Sahara Avenue, Suite 17
Las Vegas, NV 89104
(702) 732-3366

New Hampshire
922 Elm Street, Suite 210
Manchester, NH 03101
(603) 622-9606

New Jersey
48 West Lafayette Street
Trenton, NJ 08608
(609) 392-3367

New Mexico
315 8th Street S.W.
Albuquerque, NM 87102
(505) 842-8208

New York
60 East 42nd Street, Suite 1801
New York, NY 10165
(212) 986-2955

North Carolina
P. O. Box 12196
Raleigh, NC 27605
(919) 821-2777

North Dakota
1902 East Divide Avenue
Bismarck, ND 58501
(701) 255-0460

Ohio
88 East Broad Street, Suite 1920
Columbus, OH 43215
(614) 221-6563

Oklahoma
116 East Sheridan Street, Suite G100
Oklahoma City, OK 73104
(405) 239-2700

Oregon
P. O. Box 15057
Salem, OR 97309
(503) 370-8200

Pennsylvania
510 North Third Street
Harrisburg, PA 17101
(717) 238-9381

Rhode Island
1991 Smith Street
North Providence, RI 02911
(401) 232-3800

South Carolina
P. O. Box 5965
Columbia, SC 29250
(803) 799-7798

South Dakota
P. O. Box 737
Sioux Falls, SD 57101
(606) 335-7337

Tennessee
42 Rutledge Street
Nashville, TN 37210
(615) 244-1336

Texas
815 Brazos Street, Suite 200
Austin, TX 78701
(512) 478-8746

Utah
833 East 400 South, Suite 101
Salt Lake City, UT 84102
(801) 328-0239

Vermont
P. O. Box 336, 100 State Street
Montpelier, VT 05602
(802) 229-5986

Virginia
1001 East Broad Street, Suite 1125
Richmond, VA 23219
(804) 644-1966

Washington
P. O. Box 4027
Seattle, WA 98104
(206) 583-0664

West Virginia
405 Capitol Street, Suite 804
Charleston, WV 25301
(304) 342-8121

Wisconsin
126 South Franklin Street
Madison, WI 53703-3494
(608) 255-5172

Wyoming
P. O. Box 1964
Casper, WY 82602
(307) 234-8862

APPENDIX 8

House Election Victories by Party, 1860–1996

Between 1860 and 1996, 27,025 House elections were held in the United States. Of these, 13,976 were won by the Democrats and 12,400 by the Republicans. The remaining 649 elections were won by independents and third parties (ITPs). Interestingly, the growing duopoly of the electoral system is proved by the fact that over the years, the number of electoral victories by ITPs has dwindled to a trickle. Between 1860 and 1895 the ITPs won 509 seats. The relative number was 100 between 1895 and 1931, 38 between 1932 and 1965, and only 2 since 1966.

While the two major parties have maintained some measure of parity in most states, there are a number of exceptions, particularly in the South and in the Midwest and Northeast. Thus, Vermont has returned only one Democrat to the House since 1860, while on the other end of the spectrum Texas has sent 1,067 Democrats but only 104 Republicans. Right in the middle is New York, which has elected exactly 1,290 Republicans and 1,290 Democrats in the 136-year period.

State	Democrat	Republican	State	Democrat	Republican
Alabama	476	64	Nebraska	65	181
Alaska	6	14	Nevada	36	30
Arizona	59	70	New Hampshire	24	120
Arkansas	327	24	New Jersey	333	440
California	676	672	New Mexico	50	28
Colorado	105	108	New York	1290	1290
Connecticut	157	192	North Carolina	537	106
Delaware	34	35	North Dakota	11	98
Florida	341	117	Ohio	566	885
Georgia	614	39	Oklahoma	247	366
Hawaii	34	2	Oregon	77	119
Idaho	31	84	Pennsylvania	693	1281
Illinois	658	907	Rhode Island	74	76
Indiana	366	421	South Carolina	325	64
Iowa	97	484	South Dakota	28	91
Kansas	55	320	Tennessee	420	180
Kentucky	469	140	Texas	1067	104
Louisiana	432	52	Utah	44	57
Maine	27	206	Vermont	1	106
Maryland	304	132	Virginia	470	127
Massachusetts	332	546	Washington	142	157
Michigan	313	638	West Virginia	202	109
Minnesota	132	339	Wisconsin	177	442
Mississippi	381	35	Wyoming	9	44
Missouri	608	217			
Montana	54	41	Total	13,976	12,400

APPENDIX 9

Party Affiliations in Congress, 1860–1996

In the 136 years from 1860 to 1996, the Democrats controlled the House of Representatives for 80 years and the Republicans for 56 years. In contrast, the Republicans controlled the Senate for 72 years and the Democrats for 62 years; Republicans and Democrats were equally divided in the Senate of the 47th Congress (1881 to 1883), with 37 members each. To provide a framework for comparison, the Republicans have held the White House for 84 years and the Democrats for 52 years.

Both parties have had their sojourns in the political wilderness for extended periods of time. The Democrats, crippled by the Civil War, never really tasted power until the New Deal. (The Wilson era was in fact a gift from Theodore Roosevelt to the Democratic Party.) But having gained power in 1932, the Democrats have held on to it with rare tenacity. For a period of 62 years between 1932 and 1994 (with the exception of the 80th and 83rd Congresses), the Democrats have reigned on the Hill and dominated the legislative agendas. This is a record of longevity unmatched in the annals of political parties.

Year	Congress	House		Senate	
		Democrat	Republican	Democrat	Republican
1861–63	37th	43	105	10	31
1863–65	38th	75	102	9	36
1865–67	39th	42	149	10	42
1867–69	40th	49	143	11	42
1869–71	41st	63	149	11	56
1871–73	42nd	104	134	17	52
1873–75	43rd	92	194	19	49
1875–77	44th	169	109	29	45
1877–79	45th	153	140	36	39
1879–81	46th	149	130	42	33
1881–83	47th	135	147	37	37
1883–85	48th	197	118	36	38
1885–87	49th	183	140	34	43
1887–89	50th	169	152	37	39
1889–91	51st	159	166	37	39
1891–93	52nd	235	88	39	47
1893–95	53rd	218	127	44	38
1895–97	54th	105	244	39	43
1897–99	55th	113	204	34	47
1899–1901	56th	163	185	26	53
1901–03	57th	151	197	31	55
1903–05	58th	178	208	33	57
1905–07	59th	136	250	33	57
1907–09	60th	164	222	31	61
1909–11	61st	172	219	32	61
1911–13	62nd	228	161	41	51
1913–15	63rd	291	127	51	44
1915–17	64th	230	196	56	40
1917–19	65th	216	210	53	42
1919–21	66th	190	240	47	49
1921–23	67th	301	131	37	59
1923–25	68th	205	225	43	51

Year	Congress	House		Senate	
		Democrat	Republican	Democrat	Republican
1925–27	69th	183	247	39	56
1927–29	70th	195	237	46	49
1929–31	71st	167	267	39	56
1931–33	72nd	220	214	47	48
1933–35	73rd	310	117	60	35
1935–37	74th	319	103	69	25
1937–39	75th	331	89	76	16
1939–41	76th	261	164	69	23
1941–43	77th	268	162	66	28
1943–45	78th	218	208	58	37
1945–47	79th	242	190	56	38
1947–49	80th	188	245	45	51
1949–51	81st	263	171	54	42
1951–53	82nd	234	199	49	47
1953–55	83rd	211	221	47	48
1955–57	84th	232	203	48	47
1957–59	85th	233	200	49	47
1959–61	86th	283	153	64	34
1961–63	87th	263	174	65	35
1963–65	88th	258	177	67	33
1965–67	89th	295	140	68	32
1967–69	90th	247	187	64	36
1969–71	91st	243	192	57	43
1971–73	92nd	254	180	54	44
1973–75	93rd	239	192	56	42
1975–77	94th	291	144	60	37
1977–79	95th	292	143	61	38
1979–81	96th	276	157	58	41
1981–83	97th	243	192	53	46
1983–85	98th	269	165	54	46
1985–87	99th	252	182	53	47
1987–89	100th	258	177	55	45
1989–91	101st	259	174	55	45
1991–93	102nd	267	167	56	44
1993–95	103rd	258	176	57	43
1995–97	104th	199	233	46	53

GENERAL INDEX

A

Abolitionists, **3**:203, 223
Abortion, **3**:63, 67–69, 197–200; antiabortion Democrats, **3**:69; Ferraro and, **3**:276; 1980 platform on, **4**:729; 1984 platform on, **4**:802; Reagan and, **3**:69
Abridgment of the Debates of Congress (Benton), **3**:268
Abzug, Bella, **3**:198
Act for Relief of Sick and Disabled Seamen, **3**:130
Adair County, Iowa, H.A. Wallace's birthplace, **3**:245
Adams, Charles Francis, **3**:29
Adams, John, **3**:2–4, 96, 142
Adams, John Quincy, **3**:5, 25, 211, 212; on Polk, **3**:12; switching to the Democratic Party, **3**:22; John W. Taylor and, **3**:266; Van Buren and, **3**:230
Adamson Act of 1916, **3**:233
Adarand Contractors, **3**:71
Adarand v. Pena, **3**:70–71
Addams, Jane, **3**:197
Advisory Committee on Education, **3**:119
"The Advocates," **3**:249–50
Affirmative action, **3**:69–72, 163; 1984 platform on, **4**:801–2
Afghanistan, **3**:204, 206, 243
AFL-CIO, **3**:140, 141
Africa, **3**:243; 1972 platform on, **4**:686; 1976 platform on, **4**:718–19; 1980 platform on, **4**:767–68; 1984 platform on, **4**:882
African Americans, **3**:72–76; affirmative action, **3**:69–72; alliance with the Democratic Party, **3**:72, 74, 75, 154–55, 165, 168; Carter administration and, **3**:75; citizenship for, **3**:73; Civil Rights Act of 1866, **3**:73; Civil Rights Act of 1964, **3**:69, 214; Clinton administration and, **3**:76; Davis and, **3**:45; *Dred Scott* decision, **3**:16; elected to Congress, **3**:73, 74; end of segregation in the armed forces, **3**:54; equal rights for, **3**:182; first African American mayor of a major American city, **3**:291; first African American Democrat to be elected to the Ohio legislature, **3**:291; full

African Americans (*continued*)
integration in public places, **3**:57–58, 294; integration in the major leagues, **3**:272; integration of Little Rock Central High School, **3**:275–76; Jesse Jackson and, **3**:280; Million Man March, **3**:1; National Association for the Advancement of Colored People (NAACP), **3**:288; 1980 platform on appointments of, **3**:745; Republican party and, **3**:73, 75; Richard Russell and, **3**:289; segregation during the Roosevelt administration, **3**:50; segregation during the Wilson administration, **3**:41; segregation during World War I, **3**:268; Stennis and, **3**:291; student college test scores, **3**:70; Truman and, **3**:74; vote for George Wallace, **3**:294; voting after the Civil War, **3**:22, 182; voting patterns, **3**:61, 74, 75, 294; Voting Rights Act of 1965, **3**:75, 152, 214; voting rights for, **3**:57–58, 73, 74, 75, 197, 271, 277
Agnew, Spiro, **3**:60, 144, **4**:856
Agricultural Adjustment Act of 1933, **3**:226
Agriculture, 1920 platform on, **3**:508–9; 1924 platform on, **4**:517; 1928 platform on, **4**:525–26; 1936 platform on, **4**:534; 1952 platform on, **4**:555–57; 1956 platform on, **4**:573–74; 1976 platform on, **4**:709–10
Aid to Families with Dependent Children (AFDC), **3**:195–96
AIDS, **4**:805, 828
Alabama, **3**:14, 290, 293; base of the Confederate States of America, **3**:19; Democratic state committee headquarters, **4**:880; governors of, **3**:401–2; 1968 convention and, **4**:448
Alabama Democratic Party, **3**:257
Alabama Independent Democratic Party, **4**:448
Alaska, blanket primary in, **3**:166; Democratic state committee headquarters, **4**:880; governors of :402; oil pipeline in, **3**:206; purchase of **3**:124, 202; statehood for, **3**:228, 290
Albany Law School, **3**:253
Albany Regency, **3**:229, 230
Albany, New York, **3**:273

Albert, Carl B., **3**:106, 256–57, **4**:448
Algiers, Louisiana, **3**:267
Alien Registration Act, **3**:127
Alien and Sedition Acts, **3**:4, 138, 142, 181
Allende, Salvador, **3**:243
Amelia County, Virginia, **3**:261
Amendments, constitutional. *See individual amendments by number*
"America First" rallies, **3**:51
American Association for Social Security (AASS), **3**:178
American Association of Retired Persons (AARP), **3**:178
American Bar Association, **3**:53
American Civil Liberties Union (ACLU), **3**:129, 174, 250
The American Conflict (Greeley), **3**:251
American Federation of Labor (AFL), **3**:138, 140
American Labor Party in New York, **3**:186
American Railway Union, **3**:208
American Republican Party, **3**:173
American system, **3**:181
American University, **3**:17
American Woman Suffrage Association, **3**:197
The American Voter (Campbell et al.), **3**:170, 192, 193
American Youth Congress, **3**:289
Americans for Democratic Action, **3**:288
Americas, 1976 platform on the, **4**:718
Americorp program, **3**:22
Amherst, New Hampshire, Greeley's birthplace, **3**:250
Amnesty, **3**:137
Anaconda Copper Mining Company, **3**:294
Anderson, Clinton P., **3**:131–32
Anderson, John, **3**:206
Anderson, South Carolina, **3**:263
Annapolis, U.S. Naval Academy at, **3**:204
Angola, **3**:243
Anthony, Susan B., **3**:197
Anti-ballistic missile (ABM) system, **3**:77–78
Anti-ballistic missile treaty of 1972, **3**:77, 113
Antidiscrimination policy, **3**:198–99
Anti–Drug Abuse Act of 1986, **3**:111
Anti–Drug Abuse Act of 1988, **3**:110, 117

Numbers in bold indicate volume; page numbers in italic indicate illustration.

Numbers in bold indicate volume; page numbers in italic indicate illustration.

Numbers in bold indicate volume; page numbers in italic indicate illustration.

Chavez, Cesar, **4**:662
Cheatham, Henry P., **3**:290
Chemical Weapons Convention, **3**:78
Cherokee Indians, **3**:181
Chesterfield County, Virginia, **3**:261
Cheves, Langdon, **3**:258
Chicago, Illinois, **3**:283; 1864 convention in, **4**:430; 1884 convention in, **4**:434; 1892 convention in, **4**:435; 1896 convention in, **4**:435, *436*, 437; 1932 convention in, **4**:441; 1940 convention in, **4**:442–43; 1944 convention in, **4**:443; 1952 convention in, **4**:443; 1956 convention in, **4**:444–45; 1968 convention in, **4**:447–48; hog market, futures speculations, **3**:292; rail strike and, **3**:208; rail transportation and, **3**:15, 19
Chicago Sun, **3**:51
Chicago Tribune, **3**:51, 54, 294
Chicago Federation of Labor, **3**:128
Child Labor Act of 1919, **3**:23
Children, **3**:36, 144, 145; Aid to Families with Dependent Children (AFDC), **3**:195–96; rights of, **4**:663–64
Chile, **3**:243
China, **3**:216, 260, 284; 1972 platform on, **3**:686. *See also* People's Republic of China
Chinese Americans, **3**:152–53
Chinese Exclusion Act of 1882, **3**:136, 153
Choctaw Club, **3**:268
Christian Coalition, **3**:63, 176
Christian County, Kentucky, Adlai Ewing Stevenson's birthplace, **3**:244
Christmas, federal and state holiday, **3**:173
Church, Frank, **3**:143, 205, 242
Churchill, Winston S., **3**:54, 226, 228
Cincinnati, Ohio, 1856 convention in, **4**:429; 1880 convention in, **4**:429
Cincinnati Enquirer, **3**:247
Cincinnati Law School, **3**:259
Circleville, Ohio, *Watchman*, **3**:20
Civil rights, **3**:179, 192, 217–18, 269; Harry Byrd and, **3**:271; Democratic Party and, **3**:155, 168; Paul Douglas and, **3**:274; Dukakis and, **3**:250; Humphrey and, **3**:239–40; immigration and, **3**:136; Jesse Jackson and, **3**:280; 1949 platform on, **4**:549; 1952 platform on, **4**:563–64; 1956 platform on, **4**:582; 1960 platform on, **4**:604–5; 1980 platform on, **4**:743–44; 1984 platform on, **4**:797–810; Richard Russell and, **3**:289; Stennis and, **3**:291; Truman and, **3**:229
Civil Rights Act of 1866, **3**:73
Civil Rights Act of 1875, **3**:73
Civil Rights Act of 1964, **3**:75; affirmative action and, **3**:69–71; Robert C. Byrd and, **3**:271; education and, **3**:121; L.B. Johnson and, **3**:214; states' rights and, **3**:183; women and, **3**:198
Civil service reform: Arthur and, **3**:28; Cleveland and, **3**:30; 1872 convention and issue of, **4**:432; 1872 platform on, **4**:464; 1876 platform on, **4**:466–67

Civil War, U.S., **3**:20–21, 252; 1864 platform on, **4**:462; veterans' old-age and disability pensions, **3**:27, 176
Civilian Conservation Corps (CCC), **3**:49, 226
Claiborne, Charles F., **3**:268
Clark, James B. "Champ," **3**:39, 258–59, **4**:438
Clarke, James P., **3**:272
Clarksburg, West Virginia, J.W. Davis's birthplace, **3**:248
Clay, Henry, **3**:90, 212, 222; Whig Party and, **3**:10–11; slavery issue and, **3**:13–14
Claybrook, Joan, **3**:188
Clayton Antitrust Act of 1914, **3**:40–41, 233
Clements, Earle C., **3**:272–73
Cleveland, Ohio, **3**:19, 291
Cleveland, Ann, **3**:206
Cleveland, Richard, **3**:206
Cleveland, Steven Grover, **3**:28–*29*, *30*–35, *184*, 206–7, 208; 1884 convention and, **4**:434; 1888 convention and, **4**:435; 1888 platform on, **4**:471; 1892 convention and, **4**:435; 1884 election and, **3**:29–31, *91*; foreign policy, **3**:124; Gorman and, **3**:277; David B. Hill and, **3**:279; marriage to Frances Folsom, **3**:32, 91; railroad strike and, **3**:34; "retrenchment" and, **3**:79; Stevenson and, **3**:244; tariff issue and, **3**:31, 32, 190; vetoes, **3**:31, 208
Cleveland NOW, **3**:291
Clinton, George, **3**:42
Clinton, Hillary Rodham, **3**:63; health care reform, **3**:134, 210
Clinton, William Jefferson "Bill," **3**:62–63, 209–*10*, 244; abortion and, **3**:69; affirmative action and, **3**:71; African Americans and, **3**:76; L. Aspin and, **3**:267; L. Bentsen and, **3**:268–69; R. Brown and, **3**:270; campaign slogans, **3**:95; campaign symbols, **3**:95; Catholic vote for, **3**:151; Cold War and, **3**:101; crime policy, **3**:108, 111; defense, **3**:112–13; drug policy, **3**:111, 117; the economy and 1992 campaign, **4**:858; education policy, **3**:122; foreign policy, **3**:27; gun control and, **3**:129; health care reform and, **3**:134, 180; Hispanic vote for, **3**:52; labor and, **3**:140; media and, **3**:145; minimum wage and, **3**:146; "new Democrat" philosophy, **3**:114, 169; 1988 convention and, **4**:451; 1992 convention and, **4**:452; presidency, **3**:209–10; "reinventing government" policies, **3**:81; school prayer and, **3**:176; Social Security and, **3**:210; term limits and, **3**:185; tort reform and, **3**:188; trade policy and, **3**:189, 191; welfare reform and, **3**:196; women's rights and, **3**:198
Coates, Daniel R., **3**:128
Cobb, Howell, **3**:259
Cockrell, Francis M., **3**:437
Coelho, Anthony L., **3**:273
Cohelan, Jeffery, **3**:274

Cold War, **3**:54–57, 62, 76–78, 99–101; Democratic Party and, **3**:168; Kennedy and, **3**:216; media restriction during, **3**:143; refugees during, **3**:136
Coleman, Ann, **3**:201
Colfax, Schuyler, **3**:23
College Democrats, **3**:116
College of William and Mary, **3**:257
Collie, Melissa, **3**:104–5
Colombia, **4**:820
Colorado, **3**:12; Democratic state committee headquarters, **4**:880; governors of, **3**:404–5; term limits and, **3**:184
Columbia Law School, **3**:224
Columbia River, **3**:223
Columbia University, **3**:286; Bureau of Applied Statistics voting behavior study, **3**:191–92
Columbus, New Mexico, **3**:234
Commerce, Texas, **3**:265
Commission on Civil Rights, **3**:229
Commission on Party Structure and Delegate Selection, **3**:252, **4**:448
Commission on Rules, **4**:448
Committee on Indian Affairs, **3**:263
Committee to Re-elect the President (Nixon), **3**:84
Common Cause, **3**:84, 87
The Commoner, **3**:246
Communications Act of 1934, **3**:128, 144
Communism: immigration and, **3**:136; in government, **3**:284
Communist party: doctrinal party, **3**:186; Smith Act of 1939 and, **3**:27
Comprehensive Drug Abuse and Control Act, **3**:110, 117
Compromise of 1850, **3**:13–14, 219, 220; 1852 platform on, **4**:429, 458
Comstock, Anthony, **3**:143
Comstock Laws, **3**:143
Concord Cabal, **3**:219
Confederate States of America, **3**:19, 203, 236, 259, 261
Confederate veterans, **3**:27
Congregationalists, New England, **3**:173
Congress, U.S.: African Americans elected to, **3**:73, 74; congressional elections, **3**:101–3; Democratic members of, **4**:295–401; "do-nothing" 80th Congress, **3**:54, **4**:443; party affiliations in Congress, 1860–1996, **4**:883–84; party defectors in, **4**:876–77; party organization in, **3**:157–59; Senate leaders, **4**:875–76; term limits, **3**:8, 183–85
Congress of Industrial Organizations (CIO), **3**:82, 140
Congressional Campaign Committee, **3**:159
Congressional caucus system, nominating a presidential candidate, **3**:4, 5
Congressional elections, **3**:101–2
Congressional party leadership: House Democrats, **3**:106; House leaders, **3**:105–6; House leaders and whips,

Numbers in bold indicate volume; page numbers in italic indicate illustration.

Numbers in bold indicate volume; page numbers in italic indicate illustration.

Numbers in bold indicate volume; page numbers in italic indicate illustration.

N

Numbers in bold indicate volume; page numbers in italic indicate illustration.

S

Numbers in bold indicate volume; page numbers in italic indicate illustration.

Numbers in bold indicate volume; page numbers in italic indicate illustration.

Numbers in bold indicate volume; page numbers in italic indicate illustration.

Weicker, Lowell P., **3**:187

Weiss, Dr. Carl A., **3**:283

Welfare, **3**:194–96; defined, **3**:194; Democratic Party approach to, **3**:195–96; 1940 platform on improving the people's, **4**:541–42; right's organizations, **4**:665

Welfare, social, **3**:176–77, 179; O'Neill and, **3**:263

Welfare reform, **3**:196, **4**:700; 1956 platform on, **4**:574–78; 1992 platform on, **4**:835–36

Welfare systems, **3**:179, 194–95

Wells, David A., **3**:190

Wellstone, Paul, **3**:134

Wesleyan University, **3**:232

West Berlin, occupation of, **3**:217

West Point, U.S. Military Academy at, **3**:251

West Virginia, **3**:22, 274; Democratic state committee headquarters, **4**:882; governors of, **3**:425

Westchester County, New York, **3**:270

Western Hemisphere, 1984 platform on, **4**:819–22

Wheeler, Burton K., **3**:294

Whig Party, **3**:6, 8–10, 189, 230; Greeley and, **3**:250; Protestantism and, **3**:173

Whig-Republican Party, **3**:150

White, Byron R., **3**:68–69, 200

White, George, **3**:73

White, Hugh, **3**:9, 843

White citizens councils, **3**:55

White minority groups, **3**:150–51

White Slave-Trade Act, **3**:108

White supremacy, **3**:165, 232, 286, 290

Whitewater, **3**:268–69

Whitney, William C., **4**:850

Why England Slept (Kennedy), **3**:215

Why I Was Wrong (Wallace), **3**:245

Why Not the Best (Carter), **3**:204

Wiggins, Hank, **3**:260

Wilderness areas, **3**:214

Wilfred Funk, Incorporated, **3**:215

Wilkinson, Charles "Bud," **3**:278

William and Mary College, **3**:261

Williams, Edward Bennet, **4**:450

Williams, John Sharp, **3**:278

Willkie, Wendell, **3**:51, *183*

Wilmington Ten, **3**:279

Wilmot, David, **3**:12, 223

Wilmot Proviso, **3**:261

Wilson, Edith Bolling Galt, **3**:233

Wilson, Ellen Louise Axson, **3**:232, 233

Wilson, Peter B. "Pete," **3**:71

Wilson, Thomas Woodrow, **3**:39–40, 41–44, *232–35*; Bryan and, **3**:246; campaign slogans, **3**:92, *93*; campaign strategy, **3**:97; J.B. Clark and, **3**:258; J.W. Davis and, **3**:248; foreign policy, **3**:125, 233; 14 Points speech, **3**:42, 234; freedom of speech and, **3**:127; Garner and, **3**:237; labor and, **3**:139; T. Marshall and, **3**:241; media control during World War I and, **3**:142–43; "New Freedom Programs," **3**:182; 1912 convention and, **4**:438–39; 1916 convention and, **4**:439; 1916 platform on, **4**:499; 1920 convention and, **4**:439; 1920 platform on, **4**:505–6; nomination of, **3**:39; presidency, **3**:40–44; progressive reform and, **3**:79; H.T. Rainey and, **3**:264; Rayburn and, **3**:265; F.D. Roosevelt and, **3**:225; T. Roosevelt and, **3**:234; Vardaman and, **3**:293; women's suffrage and, **3**:41, 185, 198; World War I and, **3**:41–43

Wilson–Gorman Tariff Act of 1894, **3**:190, 280

Winchester, Illinois, **3**:248

Winchester, Jonas, **3**:250

Windsor Locks, Connecticut, **3**:277

Winograd Commission, **3**:149

Wisconsin, **3**:13, 15, 288; Democratic state committee headquarters, **4**:882; governors of, **3**:425; primary, **3**:165, 166; Progressive Party of, **3**:186

Wolf, George, **3**:236

Wolfinger, Raymond E., **3**:193

Women, **3**:36, 44, 196–200; abortion, **3**:63, 67–69, 198, 199–200, 276, **4**:802; affirmative action, **3**:69–70; antidiscrimination policy, **3**:198–99; creation of Prohibition Party, **3**:185; and Democratic Party, **3**:141, 149, 252; first woman elected governor without having succeeded her husband, **3**:277; first woman elected to the Senate, **3**:272; National Organization for Women (NOW), **3**:198, 199; National Woman Suffrage Association, **3**:197; National Woman's Party (NWP), **3**:185, 199; 1980 platform on women in business, **4**:725–26; 1980 platform on appointments of, **4**:745; 1984 platform on equal rights for women, **4**:802; 1984 platform on political empowerment for minorities and women, **4**:802; representation at party conventions, **3**:149, 166, **4**:450; United Nations Convention on the Elimination of All Forms of

Women (*continued*) Discrimination Against Women, **3**:199; United Nations, International Women's Year, **3**:198; welfare recipients, **3**:196; Women's Division of Democratic Party, **4**:450; women's rights, **4**:664

Women's suffrage, **3**:197–98; 1916 platform on, **4**:439; Wilson and, **3**:41

Women and Economics (Gilman), **3**:198

Women's Bureau, Department of Labor, **4**:509

Women's Health and Equity Act, **3**:133

Work and Responsibility Act of 1994, **3**:196

WORK slots, **3**:196

Workers' compensation, **3**:233

Working conditions, **3**:36

Workingman's Party, **3**:6–7

World Trade Organization (WTO), **3**:191

World War I, **3**:41–43; government control during, **3**:182; 1920 platform on disabled veterans of, **4**:510; Wilson's foreign policies and, **3**:41–43, 234–35, 506

World War II, **3**:51–53, 224, 226; media restrictions during, **3**:143

Wright, James Claude, Jr., **3**:107, 158, 266–67

Wright, Silas, **4**:428

Wyoming, **3**:12, 197; Democratic state committee headquarters, **4**:882; governors of, **3**:425

Wyoming, USS, **3**:204

Y

Yale University, **3**:255, 273

Yalta Conference, **3**:226, 271

Yancy, William Lowndes, **3**:19

Yarborough, Ralph W., **3**:268

"Yellow journalism," **3**:142

Young, Andrew, **3**:75

Young Citizens for Johnson, **3**:267

Young Democrats, **3**:116

Youth's rights, **4**:664–65

Z

Zapple Doctrine, **3**:144

Zimmerman note (Alfred Zimmerman), **3**:42, 234

BIOGRAPHICAL INDEX

Numbers in bold indicate volume; page numbers in italic indicate illustration.

Numbers in bold indicate volume; page numbers in italic indicate illustration.

Numbers in bold indicate volume; page numbers in italic indicate illustration.

Numbers in bold indicate volume; page numbers in italic indicate illustration.

GEOGRAPHICAL INDEX

Numbers in bold indicate volume; page numbers in italic indicate illustration.

Numbers in bold indicate volume; page numbers in italic indicate illustration.

Numbers in bold indicate volume; page numbers in italic indicate illustration.

INDEX OF MINORITIES AND WOMEN

Numbers in bold indicate volume; page numbers in italic indicate illustration.

Numbers in bold indicate volume; page numbers in italic indicate illustration.